Lecture Notes in Computer Science   3237

Commenced Publication in 1973
Founding and Former Series Editors:
Gerhard Goos, Juris Hartmanis, and Jan van Leeuwen

Carol Peters   Julio Gonzalo
Martin Braschler   Michael Kluck (Eds.)

Comparative Evaluation of Multilingual Information Access Systems

4th Workshop of the
Cross-Language Evaluation Forum, CLEF 2003
Trondheim, Norway, August 21-22, 2003
Revised Papers

 Springer

Volume Editors

Carol Peters
Istituto di Scienza e Tecnologie dell'Informazione
Consiglio Nazionale delle Ricerche (ISTI-CNR)
Via G. Moruzzi 1, 56124 Pisa, Italy
E-mail: carol.peters@isti.cnr.it

Julio Gonzalo
Universidad Nacional de Educación a Distancia (UNED)
Departamento de Lenguajes y Sistemas Informáticos
c/ Juan del Rosal, 16, 28040 Madrid, Spain
E-mail: julio@lsi.uned.es

Martin Braschler
Eurospider Information Technology AG
Schaffhauser Str. 18, 8006 Zürich, Switzerland
E-mail: martin.braschler@eurospider.com

Michael Kluck
Informationszentrum Sozialwissenschaften der
Arbeitsgemeinschaft Sozialwissenschaftlicher Institute e.V. (IZ)
Lennéstr. 30, 53113 Bonn, Germany
E-mail: kluck@bonn.iz-soz.de

Library of Congress Control Number: 2004115726

CR Subject Classification (1998): H.3, I.2, H.4

ISSN 0302-9743
ISBN 3-540-24017-9 Springer Berlin Heidelberg New York

Springer is a part of Springer Science+Business Media

springeronline.com

© Springer-Verlag Berlin Heidelberg 2004
Printed in Germany

Typesetting: Camera-ready by author, data conversion by Scientific Publishing Services, Chennai, India
Printed on acid-free paper   SPIN: 11342052   06/3142   5 4 3 2 1 0

Preface

The fourth campaign of the Cross-language Evaluation Forum (CLEF) for European languages was held from January to August 2003. Participation in this campaign showed a slight rise in the number of participants from the previous year, with 42 groups submitting results for one or more of the different tracks (compared with 37 in 2002), but a steep rise in the number of experiments attempted. A distinctive feature of CLEF 2003 was the number of new tracks and tasks that were offered as pilot experiments. The aim was to try out new ideas and to encourage the development of new evaluation methodologies, suited to the emerging requirements of both system developers and users with respect to today's digital collections and to encourage work on many European languages rather than just those most widely used. CLEF is thus gradually pushing its participants towards the ultimate goal: the development of truly multilingual systems capable of processing collections in diverse media.

The campaign culminated in a two-day workshop held in Trondheim, Norway, 21–22 August, immediately following the 7th European Conference on Digital Libraries (ECDL 2003), and attended by more than 70 researchers and system developers. The objective of the workshop was to bring together the groups that had participated in the CLEF 2003 campaign so that they could report on the results of their experiments. Attendance at the workshop was thus limited to participants in the campaign plus several invited guests with recognized expertise in the multilingual information access field. This volume contains thoroughly revised and expanded versions of the preliminary papers presented at the workshop accompanied by detailed analyses of the results in the various track overview papers and thus provides an exhaustive record of the CLEF 2003 campaign.

CLEF 2003 was conducted within the framework of a project of the Information Society Technologies programme of the European Commission (IST-2000-31002). The campaign was organized in collaboration with the US National Institute of Standards and Technology (NIST) and with the support of the DELOS Network of Excellence for Digital Libraries. The support of NIST and DELOS in the running of the evaluation campaign is gratefully acknowledged. We would also like to thank the other members of the Workshop Steering Committee for their assistance in the coordination of this event.

June 2004

Carol Peters
Julio Gonzalo
Martin Braschler
Michael Kluck

CLEF 2003 Workshop Steering Committee

Martin Braschler, Eurospider Information Technology, Switzerland
Khalid Choukri, Evaluations and Language Resources Distribution Agency,
  Paris, France
Marcello Federico, Centro per la Ricerca Scientifica e Tecnologica, Istituto
  Trentino di Cultura, Italy
Julio Gonzalo Arroyo, Departamento de Lenguajes y Sistemas Informáticos,
Universidad Nacional de Educación a Distancia, Madrid, Spain
Donna Harman, National Institute of Standards and Technology, USA
Gareth Jones, University of Exeter, UK
Noriko Kando, National Institute of Informatics, Japan
Michael Kluck, IZ Sozialwissenschaften, Bonn, Germany
Bernardo Magnini, Centro per la Ricerca Scientifica e Tecnologica, Istituto
  Trentino di Cultura, Italy
Douglas W. Oard, University of Maryland, USA
Carol Peters, ISTI-CNR, Pisa, Italy
Mark Sanderson, University of Sheffield, UK
Peter Schäuble, Eurospider Information Technology, Switzerland
Ellen Voorhees, National Institute of Standards and Technology, USA

Table of Contents

Part I. Ad-hoc Text Retrieval Tracks

Mainly Cross-Language Experiments

Monolingual Experiments

Part II. Domain-Specific Document Retrieval

Part III. Interactive Cross-Language Retrieval

Part IV. Cross-Language Question Answering

Part V. Cross-Language Image Retrieval

Part VI. Cross-Language Spoken Document Retrieval

Introduction

Julio Gonzalo[1] and Carol Peters[2]

[1] UNED, c/Juan del Rosal, 16, 28040 Madrid, Spain
julio@lsi.uned.es
[2] ISTI-CNR, Area di Ricerca, 56124 Pisa, Italy
carol.peters@isti.cnr.it

This volume reports the results of the fourth campaign of the Cross Language Evaluation Forum (CLEF). This campaign consisted of a number of comparative evaluations for multilingual systems (and system components) performing document retrieval (on open-domain or domain-specific collections, and involving both batch and interactive systems), and for cross-language question answering, image and spoken document retrieval.

42 research groups from industry and academia, from 14 different countries around the globe, participated in this comparative research initiative. As in previous years, the participating groups consisted of a nice mix of new-comers (14) and veteran groups (28) coming back for a second, third or even fourth time. Another important trend that was again noticeable was the progression of many of the returning groups to a more complex task, from monolingual to bilingual, from bilingual to multilingual, from pure text retrieval tasks to tasks that involve searching collections in multimedia.

The results of the experiments of the CLEF 2003 campaign were first presented at the Workshop, held in Trondheim, Norway, 21-22 August. These proceedings contain thoroughly revised and expanded versions of the preliminary system reports published in the CLEF 2003 Working Notes and distributed at the Workshop. Many of the papers also include descriptions of additional experiments and results as groups often further optimize their systems or try out new ideas as a consequence of the discussions during the workshop.

From Cross-Language Text Retrieval to Multilingual Information Access

From its initial campaign in 2000, the Cross Language Evaluation Forum (CLEF) has fostered the creation of a research and development community around the Cross Language Information Retrieval (CLIR) domain, broadly understood as that sector of multidisciplinary research interested in the challenge of retrieving information across language boundaries. Up until 2003, the main focus of CLEF was the study of the multilingual text retrieval problem, defined as a fully automatic process in which a query (a statement of user needs) in one language is used to retrieve a single ranked set of documents from a text collection in a number of languages. Over the years, CLEF has considered and evaluated variants and components of this challenge: bilingual information retrieval (where a query

C. Peters et al. (Eds.): CLEF 2003, LNCS 3237, pp. 1–6, 2004.

in one language searches in a document collection in a different language) and monolingual information retrieval (in European languages other than English). The strategy adopted has been to offer a series of progressively more complex tasks on an increasingly large and varied multilingual corpus, in order to stimulate the development of fully multilingual retrieval systems capable of handling many languages at the same time and of easily adapting to meet the demands of new languages.

However, from the very beginnings, it was clear to the organisers of CLEF that retrieving documents across language boundaries is only a component of usable multilingual search applications, albeit a core one. The real challenge is broader: helping users to search, browse, recognize and use information (rather than documents) from (possibly interlinked) sets of multilingual, multimedia information objects. Relevant topics include not only multilingual document retrieval, but also image retrieval (with image captions in different languages), cross-language speech retrieval, multilingual information extraction and question answering systems, the interactive aspects of multilingual retrieval, etc. Researchers often refer to this broader problem as "Multilingual Information Access (MLIA)". We thus decided that a goal of CLEF should be to stimulate system research and development in this wider direction.

CLEF 2003 has thus made an initial - and promising - move into the evaluation of multilingual information access systems with the introduction of a number of pilot experiments aimed at investigating different aspects of the CLIR/MLIA paradigm. The paper by Braschler and Peters, this volume, gives an overview of the organisation of CLEF 2003 with brief descriptions of all the different tracks offered and the test collections provided. Here below we attempt to summarise the range of Multilingual Information Access problems addressed in the 2003 campaign:

Ad hoc Open-Domain and Domain-Specific Text Retrieval: The so-called ad hoc tracks (testing monolingual, bilingual and multilingual text retrieval systems) and the domain-specific retrieval track remained the core CLEF tracks in the 2003 campaign. The goal is to offer participants the chance to test and tune systems handling many different languages and searching across languages, to investigate the problems involved, and to experiment with new approaches. As in previous editions, a lot of work was done on different kinds of text indexing, on experimenting with various types of translation resources and combinations of them and, in the multilingual tasks, on the best methods for merging the documents found in collections in different languages into a single result set. The overview paper by Braschler, this volume, discusses the trends observed in these tracks in 2003 in much more detail.

Multilingual Question Answering (QA@CLEF): An exploratory track introduced in CLEF 2003 aimed at testing question answering systems finding exact answers to open-domain questions in target collections in languages other than English (the monolingual QA task) or in languages other than that of the question (the cross-language QA task). The participation in the track was limited to just eight groups as this was the very first time that cross-language QA system evaluation had been offered to the community and research in this area was only in its initial stages. However, the track attracted a lot of attention, and is already helping to boost research in the topic. Evidence of this is the fact that eighteen groups have registered for this track in CLEF 2004. The results of this initial QA track have shown that the cross-language QA problem is significantly harder than its monolingual counterpart, and perhaps more difficult to solve accurately than cross-language document retrieval, because the "bag of translations" approach is far too crude to locate specific pieces of information within a text.

Cross-Language Spoken Document Retrieval (CL-SDR): A second CLEF 2003 pilot experiment regarded cross-language spoken document retrieval. This track explored the problem of retrieving voice recordings, via automatic transcriptions, in languages different from the query language. Again, this problem introduces new challenges in the multilingual context, because some state-of-the-art translation techniques cannot be directly applied on error-prone speech transcriptions. Although this track is currently still concerned with a particular type of text retrieval - written queries in one language are matched somehow against automatically transcribed spoken documents - it represents a first step towards the development of truly multi-media cross-language retrieval systems.

Cross-Language Retrieval in Image Collections (ImageCLEF): Another step in the multimedia direction was the introduction of a cross-language track on an image collection. Cross-language retrieval using image captions in a different language from the query is perhaps the only cross-language information access problem which is directly helpful for users, without further translation aids. Images are generally interpretable whatever the native language of the user. At the same time, this is a particularly challenging task from the point of view of cross-language text retrieval, because image captions are significantly smaller and less redundant than documents. It is thus to be expected that different retrieval strategies could be needed. This pilot track had considerable success, and has lead to a continuation and considerable expansion both of the tasks offered and of the scope in CLEF 2004, which includes content-based retrieval and interactive image retrieval. An idea of the interest aroused by this track is shown by the fact that while just four groups participated in the 2003 experiment, twenty-one different groups have registered for 2004.

Interactive Cross-Language Information Retrieval (iCLEF): From a user point of view, a system that accepts a query in his/her native language and returns a list of foreign-language documents is only one component in cross-language search assistance. For instance, how will the user recognize relevant information in an unfamiliar language? And how can the user best formulate, translate and refine queries? The interactive track addresses these problems. iCLEF has been part of CLEF since its second campaign in 2001. Unlike interactive monolingual retrieval (where it has been traditionally difficult to measure quantitative differences between alternative approaches), different interactive strategies have been shown to produce quite different results (in terms of precision and recall) in this evaluation framework.

Altogether, the CLEF 2003 tracks constitute the largest comparative evaluation of multilingual information access components and applications ever attempted and the success of the pilot tracks has lead to their confirmation and expansion in CLEF 2004.

Reporting the CLEF 2003 Experiments

This volume is organized into separate sections for each of the main evaluation tasks discussed above. However, it begins with three introductory papers discussing different aspects of the organisation of information retrieval evaluation campaigns. The first two papers focus on the organisation of CLEF: Martin Braschler and Carol Peters describe the overall organization of the CLEF 2003 evaluation campaign, with a particular focus on the cross-language ad hoc and domain-specific retrieval tracks and Thomas Mandl and Christa Womser-Hacker analyse the reliability of the CLEF multilingual topic set for the cross-language document retrieval tasks. Finally, Noriko Kando presents the evaluation experience of the NTCIR workshop, which is the main forum for the evaluation of Information Access technologies in Asian languages.

The rest of the volume is structured as follows. Part I is dedicated to the ad-hoc retrieval tracks and has two sub-sections. The first reports on cross-language work - both multilingual and bilingual - while the second contains those papers describing the specifically monolingual-only experiments. The thirty one papers included cover most of the state-of-the-art approaches to cross-language and monolingual retrieval problems in the multiple language context and also present many new and interesting ideas. This section begins with an overview of the trends observed and the results obtained in these tracks by Martin Braschler. Part II presents the experiments in domain-specific document retrieval on the GIRT collection of structured social science documents. It starts with an overview by Michael Kluck and includes three papers describing monolingual and cross-language experiments on structured document retrieval. Part III describes the user-inclusive experiments in the iCLEF track, starting with an overview by the track organizers (Doug Oard and Julio Gonzalo) and reporting six experiments on query reformulation and/or document selection issues.

The rest of the volume is devoted to other kinds of information access tasks: Part IV consists of ten pioneering papers on multilingual question answering. It begins with two papers providing a track overview and a detailed description of the test corpus that has been constructed by this track from the international group that coordinated these experiments, headed by Bernardo Magnini. Part V includes five papers on cross-language image retrieval, beginning with a track overview by Paul Clough and Mark Sanderson. Finally, Part VI describes in detail the pilot evaluation of cross-language spoken document retrieval systems at CLEF, and includes an overview by the track coordinators, Marcello Federico and Gareth Jones, followed by four other papers giving detailed descriptions of the experiments.

The volume ends with an Appendix listing the results of all runs submitted to the ad-hoc retrieval tasks. For reasons of space, only the most significant figures for each run are included. An exhaustive listing of the results can be found on the main CLEF website in the Working Notes for CLEF2003.

For more information on the activities of CLEF and the agenda for CLEF 2004, visit the CLEF websites:

CLEF main site	www.clef-campaign.org
Interactive retrieval (iCLEF)	nlp.uned.es/iCLEF
Question Answering (QA@CLEF)	clef-qa.itc.it
Image Retrieval (ImageCLEF)	ir.shef.ac.uk/imageclef2004
Spoken Document Retrieval (CL-SDR)	hermes.itc.it/clef-sdr04.html

Acknowledgments

We have numerous people and organisations to thank for their help in the running of CLEF 2003. First of all, we should like to thank the other members of the CLEF Consortium and, in particular, Martin Braschler, Eurospider, Khalid Choukri, ELRA/ELDA, Donna Harman, NIST, and Michael Kluck, IZ-Bonn, for all their efforts at making both the campaign and the workshop a great success. We also express our immense gratitude to Francesca Borri, ISTI-CNR, who has been responsible for the administrative management of the CLEF project and has worked very hard to ensure a smooth day-by-day organisation. However, it would be impossible to run CLEF without considerable assistance from many other groups, working mainly on a voluntary basis. Here below we list some of them:

Associated Members of the CLEF Consortium

- Department of Information Studies, University of Tampere, Finland - responsible for work on the Finnish collection
- Human Computer Interaction and Language Engineering Laboratory, SICS, Kista, Sweden - responsible for work on the Swedish collection
- University of Twente, Centre for Telematics and Information Technology, The Netherlands - responsible for work on the Dutch collection
- Universität Hildesheim, Institut für Angewandte Sprachwissenschaft - Informationswissenschaft, Germany - responsible for checking and revision of the multilingual topic set
- College of Information Studies and Institute for Advanced Computer Studies, University of Maryland, College Park, MD, USA - co-organisers of iCLEF
- Centro per la Ricerca Scientifica e Tecnologica, Istituto Trentino di Cultura, Italy, main coordinators of the multilingual question answering track and co-organisers of the cross-language spoken document retrieval track
- University of Exeter, co-organisers of the cross-language spoken document retrieval track
- University of Sheffield, coordinators of the cross-language image retrieval track

Furthermore, we should like to thank colleagues from the Natural Language Processing Lab, Department of Computer Science and Information Engineering, National Taiwan University, for preparing topics in Chinese, the National Institute of Informatics, Tokyo, for the post-campaign Japanese topics, and the Moscow State University, Russia, for their assistance in obtaining the Russian collection.

We also gratefully acknowledge the support of all the data providers and copyright holders, and in particular:

- The Los Angeles Times, for the American English data collection;
- Le Monde S.A. and ELDA: Evaluations and Language resources Distribution Agency, for the French data;
- Frankfurter Rundschau, Druck und Verlagshaus Frankfurt am Main; Der Spiegel, Spiegel Verlag, Hamburg, for the German newspaper collections;
- InformationsZentrum Sozialwissenschaften, Bonn, for the GIRT database;
- Hypersystems Srl, Torino and La Stampa, for the Italian newspaper data;
- Agencia EFE S.A. for the Spanish newswire data;
- NRC Handelsblad, Algemeen Dagblad and PCM Landelijke dagbladen/Het Parool for the Dutch newspaper data;
- Aamulehti Oyj for the Finnish newspaper documents;
- Tidningarnas Telegrambyrå for the Swedish newspapers;
- The Herald 1995, SMG Newspapers, for the British English newspaper data;
- Schweizerische Depeschenagentur, Switzerland, for the French, German and Italian Swiss news agency data;
- Russika-Izvestia for the Russian collection;
- St Andrews University Library for the image collection;
- NIST for access to the TREC-8 and TREC-9 SDR transcripts.

Without their help, this evaluation activity would be impossible.

CLEF 2003 Methodology and Metrics

Martin Braschler[1] and Carol Peters[2]

[1] Eurospider Information Technology AG,
Schaffhauserstr. 18, 8006 Zürich, Switzerland
[1]Université de Neuchâtel, Institut interfacultaire d'informatique,
Pierre-à-Mazel 7, CH-2001 Neuchâtel, Switzerland
martin.braschler@eurospider.com
[2] ISTI-CNR, Area di Ricerca, 56124 Pisa, Italy
carol.peters@isti.cnr.it

Abstract. We describe the overall organization of the CLEF 2003 evaluation campaign, with a particular focus on the cross-language ad hoc and domain-specific retrieval tracks. The paper discusses the evaluation approach adopted, describes the tracks and tasks offered and the test collections used, and provides an outline of the guidelines given to the participants. It concludes with an overview of the techniques employed for results calculation and analysis for the monolingual, bilingual and multilingual and GIRT tasks.

1 Introduction

The Cross-Language Evaluation Forum (CLEF) uses a comparative evaluation approach. Comparative evaluation consists of deciding on a control task - which may correspond either to the function of a complete information retrieval system or to that of a single component, of defining the protocol and metrics to be used, of identifying system or component developers interested in participating, and of organizing an evaluation campaign - which includes the acquisition and distribution of appropriate data for training and testing the systems. In the case of CLEF, performance measures are calculated on the basis of a test collection of documents, sample queries and relevance assessments for these queries with respect to documents in the collection.

CLEF mainly adopts a corpus-based, automatic scoring method for the assessment of system performance, based on ideas first introduced in the Cranfield experiments [1] in the late 1960s. This methodology is widely employed and accepted in the information retrieval community and is the approach used by the popular series of TREC conferences [2], which are the "gold standard" for this form of evaluation campaign. The implications of adopting the Cranfield paradigm are discussed in detail in [3]. In CLEF, we have adapted this methodology to suit the needs of multilingual system evaluation.

As described in the Introduction to this volume, CLEF 2003 has represented a turning point in the CLEF series of evaluation campaigns by extending considerably the scope of investigation to include not only cross-language text retrieval problems

C. Peters et al. (Eds.): CLEF 2003, LNCS 3237, pp. 7–20, 2004.
© Springer-Verlag Berlin Heidelberg 2004

and automatic document processing but also to consider other important aspects of the CLIR paradigm. Our goal for future campaigns is to offer a comprehensive set of tasks covering all major aspects of multilingual, multimedia system performance with particular attention to the needs of the end-user.

In this paper, we describe the organization of the CLEF 2003 campaign, with a particular focus on the so-called ad hoc and domain-specific retrieval tracks. The aim is to give an exhaustive record of the technical setup for these tracks in order to provide readers, who have never participated in CLEF or similar evaluation campaigns, with the necessary background information in order to understand the details of the experiments described in Part I of this volume and to be able to interpret the result pages in the Appendix. The paper is thus a revised and updated version of similar papers included in previous CLEF Proceedings and is considered essential reading for newcomers to the CLEF campaigns or for those intending to replicate CLEF experiments. More detailed information on the organization of the other tracks in CLEF 2003 can be found in the Track Overviews in the other sections of this volume.

The rest of the paper is organized as follows. In Section 2 we first briefly describe all the tracks, tasks and the data collections provided for CLEF 2003 and then outline the instructions given to the participants in the ad hoc and GIRT tracks. Section 3 describes the techniques and measures used for results calculation and analysis for the these tracks, and Section 4 explains how the results are presented in the Appendix.

2   Agenda for CLEF 2003

CLEF campaigns are organized according to a predefined schedule, with a series of strict deadlines. The dates are determined in order to be as compatible as possible with those of two other major Information Retrieval system evaluation activities: the Text Retrieval Conference TREC sponsored by the National Institute of Standards and Technology [4], and the NACSIS Test Collection for Information Retrieval (NTCIR) initiative sponsored by the National Institute for Informatics of Tokyo [5]. The dates vary slightly from year to year, mainly in order to respect the tradition of holding the annual workshop in conjunction with the European Digital Library Conference (ECDL).

The main dates for 2003 were:

- First release of Call for Participation - November 2002
- Data Collection Release – 30 January 2003
- Topic Release - from 15 March 2003
- Receipt of runs from participants – 18 May 2003
- Release of relevance assessments and individual results – 1 July 2003
- Submission of paper for Working Notes – 20 July 2003
- Workshop – 21-22 August 2003, Trondheim, Norway, following ECDL2003.

2.1   Evaluation Tracks

Over the years, the range of activities offered to participants in the initial cross-language information retrieval (CLIR) track at TREC and subsequent CLEF campaigns has expanded and been modified in order to meet the needs of the research community. Consequently, the campaign is now structured into several distinct tracks[1] (see also [6]). Some of these tracks are in turn structured into multiple tasks. Here below we describe all the tracks and tasks offered by CLEF 2003.

Multilingual Information Retrieval. This has been the main track in CLEF and we have made it progressively more difficult over the years as our aim has been to stimulate the development of truly multilingual retrieval systems. It requires searching a collection of documents in a number of different languages for relevant items using a selected query language, ordering the results according to relevance and listing them in a single ranked list. In CLEF 2002, the document collection for this track contained English, German, French, Italian and Spanish texts. For CLEF 2003, two distinct multilingual tasks were offered: multilingual-4 and multilingual-8. The collection for multilingual-4 contained English, French, German and Spanish documents. Multilingual-8 also included documents in: Dutch, Finnish, Italian and Swedish. A common set of topics (i.e. structured statements of information needs from which queries are extracted) was prepared in ten languages: Dutch, English, Finnish, French, German, Italian, Spanish, Swedish, Russian, and Chinese. Japanese was added to the CLEF 2003 topic set post-campaign.

Bilingual Information Retrieval. Many newcomers to CLIR system evaluation prefer to begin with the simpler bilingual track before moving on to tackle the more complex issues involved in multilingual retrieval. CLEF 2000 offered the possibility for a bilingual search on an English target collection, using any other language for the queries. CLEF 2001 offered two distinct bilingual tracks with either English or Dutch target collections. In CLEF 2002 the choice was extended to all of the target document collections, with the single limitation that only newcomers to a CLEF cross-language evaluation task could use the English target document collection. This decision had the advantage of encouraging experienced groups to experiment with "different" target collections, rather than concentrating on English, but it had the strong disadvantage that the results were harder to assess in a comparative evaluation framework. There were simply too many topic-target language combinations, only receiving a few experiments each. Consequently, for CLEF 2003, we offered a very different choice. The main objective in the 2003 bilingual track was to encourage the tuning of systems running on challenging language pairs that do not include English, but also to ensure comparability of results. For this reason, runs were only accepted for one or more of the following source -> target languages pairs: Italian -> Spanish,

---

[1] While the cross-language activities in earlier TREC campaigns were organized as a single track (the CLIR track at TREC), the larger CLEF campaigns are themselves structured into multiple tracks.

German -> Italian, French -> Dutch and Finnish -> German. Again newcomers were allowed to choose to search the English document collection using a European topic language. At the last moment, we acquired a Russian collection and thus also included Russian as a target collection in the bilingual task, permitting any language to be used for the queries.

Monolingual (non-English) IR. Many of the issues involved in IR are language dependent. CLEF provides the opportunity for monolingual system testing and tuning, and for building test suites in European languages other than English[2] In CLEF 2003, we provided the opportunity for monolingual system testing and tuning in Dutch, Finnish, French, German, Italian, Russian, Spanish and Swedish.

The monolingual, bilingual and multilingual tracks are collectively also known as the CLEF ad hoc tracks.

Domain-Specific Mono- and Cross-Language Information Retrieval. The rationale for this task is to study CLIR on other types of collections, serving a different kind of information need. The information that is provided by domain-specific scientific documents is far more targeted than news stories and contains much terminology. It is claimed that the users of this type of collection are typically interested in the completeness of results. This means that they are generally not satisfied with finding just some relevant documents in a collection that may contain many more. Developers of domain-specific cross-language retrieval systems need to be able to tune their systems to meet this requirement. See [7] for a discussion of this point. In CLEF 2003, this track was based on the GIRT-4 database of structured social science documents, with an associated controlled vocabulary in English, German and Russian (see Kluck, this volume for more information). The GIRT collection could be queried either monolingually or cross-language. Topics were prepared in English, German and Russian.

Interactive CLIR (iCLEF). The aim of the tracks listed so far is to measure system performance mainly in terms of its effectiveness in document ranking. However, this is not the only issue that interests the user. User satisfaction with an IR system is based on a number of factors, depending on the functionality of the particular system. Examples include the ways in which a system can help the user when formulating a query or the ways in which the results of a search are presented. These questions are of great importance in CLIR systems where it is common to have users retrieving documents in languages with which they are not familiar. An interactive track that has focused on both user-assisted query formulation and document selection has been implemented with success since CLEF 2001 and was offered again in 2003. See the track overview by Oard and Gonzalo, this volume, for more information.

Multilingual Question Answering (QA@CLEF). This was a completely new track introduced for the first time, as a pilot experiment, at CLEF 2003. It consisted of

---

[2] Already well catered for by TREC.

several tasks and offered the possibility to test monolingual question answering systems running on Spanish, Dutch and Italian texts, and cross-language systems using questions in Dutch, French, German, Italian and Spanish to search an English document collection. The aim was both to stimulate monolingual work in the question answering area on languages other than English and to encourage the development of the first experimental systems for cross-language QA. The track was an important innovation for CLEF and encouraged the participation of groups with a strong background in natural language processing in addition to expertise in information retrieval. More details can be found in the track overview by Magnini et al., this volume.

Cross-Language Spoken Document Retrieval (CL-SDR). The current growth of multilingual digital material in a combination of different media (e.g. image, speech, video) means that there is an increasing interest in systems capable of automatically accessing the information available in these archives. For this reason, the DELOS Network of Excellence for Digital Libraries[3] supported a preliminary investigation aimed at evaluating systems for cross-language spoken document retrieval in 2002. The aim was to establish baseline performance levels and to identify those areas where future research was needed. The results of this pilot investigation were first presented at the CLEF 2002 Workshop and are reported in Jones and Federico [8]. As a result of this first investigation, a cross-language spoken document retrieval track was offered in CLEF 2003. See the track overview by Federico and Jones, this volume.

Cross-Language Retrieval in Image Collections (Image CLEF). This track was offered for the first time in CLEF 2003 as a pilot experiment. The aim is to test the effectiveness of systems to retrieve as many relevant images as possible on the basis of an information need expressed in a language different from that of the document collection. Queries were made available in five languages (Dutch, French, German, Italian and Spanish) to search a British-English image collection. Searches could make use of the image content, the text captions or both. The background to the track is described in more detail in the overview by Clough and Sanderson, this volume.

These last two tracks show the effort that is now being made by CLEF to progress from text retrieval tasks to tasks that embrace multimedia.

2.2 The Test Collections

The main CLEF test collection is formed of sets of documents in different European languages but with common features (same genre and time period, comparable content); a single set of topics rendered in a number of languages; relevance judgments determining the set of relevant documents for each topic. A separate test collection has been created for systems tuned for domain-specific tasks.

---

[3] More information on DELOS can be found at http://www.delos.info/

Document Collections for CLEF 2003. The main document collection in CLEF 2003 consisted of well over 1.5 million documents in nine languages – Dutch, English, Finnish, French, German, Italian, Russian, Spanish and Swedish. This collection has been expanded gradually over the years. The 2000 collection consisted of newspaper, news magazine and news agency articles mainly from 1994 in four languages: English, French, German and Italian. Two languages were added in 2001: Spanish and Dutch. Swedish and Finnish were introduced for the first time in CLEF 2002. Russian was an important addition in 2003 as it is the first collection in the CLEF corpus that does not use the Latin-1 (ISO-8859-1) encoding system. Parts of this collection were used for the mono-, bi- and multilingual tracks and for the question answering and interactive tracks.

The domain-specific collection consists of the GIRT database of German social science documents, with controlled vocabularies for English-German and German-Russian. The GIRT texts were first used in the TREC CLIR tracks and have been expanded for CLEF. In 2003 a third, even more extensive version of the GIRT database was introduced, consisting of more than 150,000 documents in an English-German parallel corpus. The image track used a collection of historical photographs made available by St. Andrews University in Scotland. The cross-language spoken document retrieval track used the TREC-8 and TREC-9 spoken document collections.

Table 1 gives further details with respect to the source and dimensions of the main multilingual document collection used in CLEF 2003. It gives the overall size of each subcollection, number of documents contained, and three key figures indicating some typical characteristics of the individual documents: the median length in bytes, tokens and features. Tokens are "word" occurrences, extracted by removing all formatting, tagging and punctuation, and the length in terms of features is defined as the number of distinct tokens occurring in a document. Table 2 shows which parts of the multilingual collection were used in the various CLEF 2003 multilingual, bilingual and monolingual tasks.

Topics. The groups participating in the multilingual, bilingual and monolingual tracks derive their queries in their preferred language from a set of topics created to simulate user information needs. Following the TREC philosophy, each topic consists of three parts: a brief title statement; a one-sentence description; a more complex narrative specifying the relevance assessment criteria. The title contains the main keywords, the description is a "natural language" expression of the concept conveyed by the keywords, and the narrative adds extra syntax and semantics, stipulating the conditions for relevance assessment. Queries can be constructed from one or more fields. Here below we give the English version of a typical topic from CLEF 2003.

```
<top>
<num> C148 </num>
<EN-title> Damages in Ozone Layer </EN-title>
<EN-desc> What holes in the ozone layer are not an effect of pollution? </EN-desc>
<EN-narr> Not all damage to the ozone layer is caused by pollution. Relevant documents will
give information on other causes for holes in the ozone layer. </EN-narr>
</top>
```

Table 1. Sources and dimensions of the main CLEF 2003 document collection

Collection	Added in	Size (MB)	No. of docs	Median size of docs. (Bytes)	Mediansize of docs. (Tokens)	Median size of docs. (Features)
Dutch: Algemeen Dagblad 94/95	2001	241	106483	1282	166	112
Dutch: NRC Handelsblad 94/95	2001	299	84121	2153	354	203
English: LA Times 94	2000	425	113005	2204	421	246
English: Glasgow Herald 95	2003	154	56472	2219	343	202
Finnish: Aamulehti 94/95	2002	137	55344	1712	217	150
French: Le Monde 94	2000	158	44013	1994	361	213
French: ATS 94	2001	86	43178	1683	227	137
French: ATS 95	2003	88	42615	1715	234	140
German: Frankfurter Rundschau 94	2000	320	139715	1598	225	161
German: Der Spiegel 94/95	2000	63	13979	1324	213	160
German: SDA 94	2001	144	71677	1672	186	131
German: SDA 95	2003	144	69438	1693	188	132
Italian: La Stampa 94	2000	193	58051	1915	435	268
Italian: AGZ 94	2001	86	50527	1454	187	129
Italian: AGZ 95	2003	85	48980	1474	192	132
Russian: Izvestia 95	2003	68	16761			
Spanish: EFE 94	2001	511	215738	2172	290	171
Spanish: EFE 95	2003	577	238307	2221	299	175
Swedish: TT 94/95	2002	352	142819	2171	183	121

SDA/ATS/AGZ = Schweizerische Depeschenagentur (Swiss News Agency)
EFE = Agencia EFE S.A (Spanish News Agency)
TT = Tidningarnas Telegrambyrå (Swedish newspaper)

The motivation behind using structured topics is to simulate query "input" for a range of different IR applications, ranging from very short to elaborate query formulations, and representing keyword-style input as well as natural language formulations. The latter potentially allows sophisticated systems to make use of morphological analysis, parsing, query expansion and similar features. In the cross-language context, the transfer component must also be considered, whether dictionary or corpus-based, a fully-fledged MT system or other. Different query structures may be more appropriate for testing one or the other approach.

The number of tokens per document can vary slightly across systems, depending on the definition of what constitutes a token. Consequently, the number of tokens and features given in this table are approximations and may differ from actual implemented systems.

Table 2. Document collections used in CLEF 2003

TASK	DE	EN	ES	FI	FR	IT	NL	RU	SW	GIRT-4 St And.	TREC SDR
Multi-4	X	X	X		X						
Multi-8	X	X	X	X	X	X	X		X		
Bilingual (depending on task)	X	X*	X			X	X	X			
Monolingual (depending on task)	X		X	X	X	X	X	X	X		
GIRT										X	
iCLEF CLEF2002 data only		X	X						X		
QA@CLEF CLEF2002 data only	X	X				X	X				
ImageCLEF										X	
CL-SDR											X

* only for newcomers

CLEF topics for the ad hoc and GIRT tracks are developed on the basis of the contents of the multilingual document collection. For each language, native speakers propose a set of topics covering events of local, European and general importance. The topics are then compared over the different sites to ensure that a high percentage of them will find some relevant documents in all collections, although the ratio can vary considerably. The fact that the same topics are used for the mono-, bi-, and multilingual tracks is a significant constraint. While in the multilingual task, it is of little importance if a given topic does not find relevant documents in all of the collections; in both the bilingual and monolingual tracks, where there is a single target collection, a significant number of the queries must retrieve relevant documents. Once the topics have been selected, they are prepared in all the collection languages by skilled translators translating into their native language. They can then be translated into additional languages, depending on the demand from the participating systems.

For CLEF 2003, 60 such topics were developed on the basis of the contents of the multilingual collection and topic sets were produced in all nine document languages. Additional topic sets in Chinese and Japanese were also prepared. Separate sets of 25 topics were developed for the GIRT task in German, English and Russian. The CLEF topic generation process and the issues involved are described in detail in [9,10].

Relevance Judgments. The relevance assessments for the ad hoc and GIRT tracks are produced in the same distributed setting and by the same groups that work on the topic creation. CLEF uses methods adapted from TREC to ensure a high degree of consistency in the relevance judgments. All assessors follow the same criteria when judging the documents. An accurate assessment of relevance of retrieved documents for a given topic implies a good understanding of the topic. This is much harder to achieve in the distributed scenario of CLEF where understanding is influenced by language and cultural factors. A continual exchange of e-mail for discussion and verification between the assessors at each site is thus necessary during the relevance assessment stage to ensure, as far as possible, that the decisions taken as to relevance are consistent over sites, and over languages.

The practice of assessing the results on the basis of the "Narrative" means that only using the "Title" and/or "Description" parts of the topic implicitly assumes a particular interpretation of the user's information need that is not (explicitly) contained in the actual query that is run in the experiment. The fact that the information contained in the title and description fields could have additional possible interpretations has influence only on the absolute values of the evaluation measures, which in general are inherently difficult to interpret. However, comparative results across systems are usually stable when considering different interpretations. These considerations are important when using the topics to construct very short queries to evaluate a system in a web-style scenario.

The number of documents in large test collections such as CLEF makes it impractical to judge every document for relevance. Instead, approximate recall figures are calculated by using pooling techniques. The results submitted by the participating groups are used to form a "pool" of documents for each topic and for each language by collecting the highly ranked documents from all the submissions. The pooling procedure is discussed later in this paper.

2.3 Instructions to Participants

Guidelines for the ad hoc and GIRT tracks were made available to CLEF 2003 participants shortly after the data release date[4]. These guidelines provide a definition of the system data structures and stipulate the conditions under which they can be used.

System Data Structures. To carry out the retrieval tasks of the CLEF campaign, systems have to build supporting data structures. Allowable data structures can consist of the original documents, or any new structures built automatically (such as inverted files, thesauri, conceptual networks, etc.) or manually (such as thesauri, synonym lists, knowledge bases, rules, etc.) from the documents. They may not be modified in response to the topics. For example, participants are not allowed to add topic words that are not already in the dictionaries used by their systems in order to

---

[4] The other tracks provided their own guidelines for participants.

extend coverage. The CLEF tasks are intended to represent the real-world problem of an ordinary user posing a question to a system. For cross-language tasks, the question is posed in one language and relevant documents must be retrieved in whatever language they have been written. If an ordinary user could not make the change to the system, the participating groups must not make it after receiving the topics.

There are several parts of the CLEF data collections that contain manually assigned, controlled or uncontrolled index terms. These fields are delimited by specific SGML tags. Since the primary focus of CLEF is on retrieval of naturally occurring text over language boundaries, these manually indexed terms must not be indiscriminately used as if they are a normal part of the text. If a group decides to use these terms, they should be part of a specific experiment that utilizes manual indexing terms, and these runs should be declared as manual runs. However, learning from (e.g. building translation sources from) such fields is permissible.

Constructing the Queries. There are many possible methods for converting the topics into queries that a system can execute. The ad hoc tracks in CLEF define two broad categories, "automatic" and "manual", based on whether any manual intervention is used. When more than one set of results are submitted, the different sets may correspond to different query construction methods or, if desired, can be variants within the same method. The manual query construction method includes both runs in which the queries are constructed manually and then executed without looking at the results and runs in which the results are used to alter the queries through some manual operation. Manual runs should be appropriately motivated in a CLIR context, e.g. a run using manual translations of the topic into the document language(s) is not what most people consider cross-language retrieval. Allowing different kinds of manual intervention in the manual query construction method makes it harder to do comparisons between experiments. CLEF strongly encourages groups to determine what constitutes a base run for their experiments and to include these runs (officially or unofficially) to allow useful interpretations of the results. Unofficial runs are those not submitted to CLEF but evaluated using the trec_eval package available from Cornell University [11].

Submission of Results. At CLEF 2003, as a consequence of limited evaluation resources, we accepted a maximum of 5 runs for each multilingual task and a maximum of 10 runs overall for the bilingual tasks, including all language combinations. We also accepted a maximum of 16 runs for the monolingual tasks (there were eight languages to choose from). As an additional side constraint – and in order to encourage diversity, we did not allow more than 4 runs for any language combination. A final restriction was that participants were allowed to submit a maximum of 30 runs in total for the multilingual, bilingual and monolingual tasks. We also accepted a maximum of 5 runs for the GIRT monolingual task and a maximum of 10 runs for the GIRT cross-language task.

In all, a participating group doing all tasks could submit at most 45 runs by sending the maximum number of runs for each of the individual tasks and their respective language combinations. Typically, the maximum number was lower, due to the choice of tasks by each group. In order to facilitate comparison between results, there was a mandatory run: Title + Description (per experiment, per topic language).

3   Result Calculation

3.1   Measures

The effectiveness of IR systems can be objectively evaluated by an analysis of a set of representative sample search results. To this end, as mentioned, test queries are used to retrieve the best matching documents. Effectiveness measures are then calculated based on the relevance assessments. Popular measures usually adopted for exercises of this type are Recall and Precision.

$$\text{Recall and Precision } \pi_r(q) := \frac{\left| D_r^{rel}(q) \right|}{\left| D_r(q) \right|},$$

where $D_r(q) := \{d_1, ..., d_r\}$ is the answer set to query q containing the first r documents. The choice of a specific value for r is necessary because recall and precision are set-based measures, and evaluate the quality of an unordered set of retrieved documents. Choosing a low value for r implies that the user is interested in few, high-precision documents, whereas a high value for r means that the user conducts an exhaustive search. $D^{rel}(q)$ is the set of all relevant documents, and $D_r^{rel}(q) := D^{rel}(q) \cap D_r(q)$ is the set of relevant documents contained in the answer set [12]. When precision and recall are determined for every possible size of the answer set, a plot of the corresponding values results in a saw tooth curve (see Table 3). In the next step, typically a replacement curve is defined by assigning for every recall value $\rho \in [0,1]$ a precision value as follows:

$$\Pi_q(\rho) := \max\{\pi_r(q) | \rho_r(q) \geq \rho\}$$

Using this "interpolation step", we obtain a monotonically decreasing curve where each recall value corresponds to a unique precision value (see Figure 1). This "ceiling operation" can be interpreted as looking only at the theoretically optimal answer sets for which recall and precision cannot be improved simultaneously by inspecting further documents.

When evaluating a system with a set of queries (60 in CLEF 2003), an averaging step is introduced that produces the final recall/precision curve:

$$\Pi(\rho) := \frac{1}{|Q|} \sum_{q \in Q} \Pi_q(\rho)$$

where $|Q|$ denotes the number of queries.

Often people prefer single value measures to a more complex performance indicator, such as a recall/precision curve. The advantage of such single value measures lies in easy comparison, their danger in too much abstraction: if relying exclusively on a single value, the ability to judge a system's effectiveness for different user preferences, such as exhaustive search or high-precision results, is lost.

Table 3. Precision/recall figures for sample query and corresponding relevance assessments

rank r	relevant to q.	$\rho_r(q)$	$\pi_r(q)$
1	+	0.20	1.00
2	-	0.20	0.50
3	-	0.20	0.33
4	+	0.40	0.50
5	-	0.40	0.40
6	-	0.40	0.33
7	+	0.60	0.43
8	+	0.80	0.50
9	-	0.80	0.44
10	+	1.00	0.50

The most popular single value measure for assessing the effectiveness of information retrieval systems is average precision. To calculate the average precision value, the precision after each relevant document found in the result list is determined as outlined above. The list of precision values that is obtained is then used to calculate an average. No interpolation is used to calculate the final average.

3.2 Pooling

All evaluations in the CLEF campaigns are based on the use of relevance assessments, i.e. judgments made by human "assessors" with respect to the usefulness of a certain document to answer a user's information need. As discussed earlier, CLEF uses a set of topics as a sample of possible information needs that could be formulated by real users. Theoretically, for each of these topics, all documents in the test collection would have to be judged for relevance. Since this judging ("assessment") involves a human assessor reading the complete document, this is a laborious process. With the size of today's test collections, which contain hundreds of thousands or even millions of documents (the CLEF multilingual track used over 1.5 million documents for 2003), this becomes impractical.

Therefore, evaluation campaigns such as CLEF often use an alternative strategy, only assessing a fraction of the document collection for any given topic. This implies – for every query – eliminating all those documents from consideration that were not retrieved by any participant with a high rank in their lists of results. The reasoning behind this strategy is discussed in detail in [6]. The remaining documents, which share the property of having been retrieved as a highly ranked document by at least one participant, form a "document pool" that is then judged for relevance. The number of result sets per participant that are used for pooling, and the establishing of the separation between "highly ranked" and other documents (the so-called "pool depth") are dictated to some extent by practical needs (i.e. available resources for assessment).

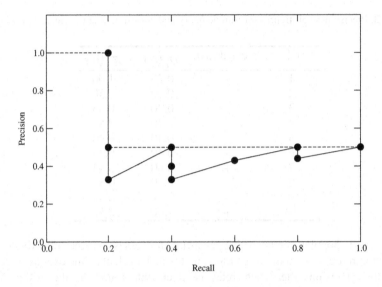

Fig. 1. Interpolation of recall/precision values

In the CLEF 2003 campaign, only selected results sets (slightly more than half of all results sets) were included in the pool. From these sets, the top 60 documents were used for pool formation. In [6] we discuss the implications of using a document pool vs. judging all documents in a collection.

4   Results Presentation

In the Appendix we give a listing of all runs and their characteristics and compare the top entries for the ad hoc and GIRT tasks. We show the recall/precision curves for at most five groups. The best entries by the respective groups have been chosen with the topic fields fixed to title+description (mandatory for every participant) and only automatic experiments used. For the multilingual, bilingual to English, bilingual to Russian and GIRT experiments, the top entries regardless of topic language are presented.

The individual results and statistics for all the ad hoc and GIRT official experiments in CLEF 2003 can be found on the CLEF website (http://www. clef-campaign.org/) in the CLEF 2003 Working Notes, posted in the Publications area.

Acknowledgments

As mentioned, CLEF began its life as a track for cross-language information retrieval systems within TREC. When setting up a larger, independent initiative, the CLEF organizers have benefited considerably from the experiences gained at TREC. Much of the methodology employed in the CLEF campaigns is based on TREC, and the authors would like to express their gratitude in particular to Donna Harman and Ellen Voorhees.

Section 3.1 of this paper is based on a description contained in [12]. We thank Peter Schäuble for his contribution.

References

1. Cleverdon, C.: The Cranfield Tests on Index Language Devices. In Sparck-Jones, K., Willett, P. (eds.): Readings in Information Retrieval, Morgan Kaufmann (1997) 47--59.
2. Harman, D.: The TREC Conferences. In Kuhlen, R., Rittberger, M. (eds.): Hypertext - Information Retrieval - Multimedia: Synergieeffekte Elektronischer Informationssysteme, Proceedings of HIM '95, Universitätsverlag Konstanz, 9--28
3. Voorhees, E.: The Philosophy of Information Retrieval Evaluation. In Peters, C., Braschler, M., Gonzalo, J., and Kluck, M. (eds.): Evaluation of Cross-Language Information Retrieval Systems. Lecture Notes in Computer Science, Vol.2069, Springer Verlag (2002) 355--370
4. Text REtrieval Conference (TREC) Series: http://trec.nist.gov/
5. NTCIR (NII-NACSIS Test Collection for IR Systems): http://research.nii.ac.jp/ntcir/
6. Braschler, M. CLEF 2003 - Overview of Results: This volume.
7. Gey, F.C., Kluck, M.: The Domain-Specific Task of CLEF – Specific Evaluation Strategies in Cross-Language Information Retrieval. In C. Peters (Ed.). Cross-Language Information Retrieval and Evaluation. Lecture Notes in Computer Science 2069, Springer Verlag, pp 48-56
8. Jones, G. J. F., Federico, M.: Cross-Language Spoken Document Retrieval Pilot Track Report. In Peters, C., Braschler, M., Gonzalo, J., Kluck, M.(eds.): Advances in Cross-Language Information Retrieval: Results of the CLEF 2002 Evaluation Campaign, Lecture Notes in Computer Science, Vol. 2785, Spinger Verlag, pp 446-457.
9. Womser-Hacker, C.: Multilingual Topic Generation within the CLEF 2001 Experiments. In Peters, C., Braschler, M., Gonzalo, J., and Kluck, M. (eds.): Evaluation of Cross-Language Information Retrieval Systems. Lecture Notes in Computer Science, Vol.2069, Springer Verlag (2002) 389--393
10. Mandl, T., Womser-Hacker, C.: Linguistic and Statistical Analysis of the CLEF Topics. This volume.
11. ftp://ftp.cs.cornell.edu/pub/smart/
12. Schäuble, P.: Content-Based Information Retrieval from Large Text and Audio Databases. Section 1.6 Evaluation Issues, Pages 22-29, Kluwer Academic Publishers, 1997.

Analysis of the Reliability of the Multilingual Topic Set for the Cross Language Evaluation Forum

Thomas Mandl and Christa Womser-Hacker

University of Hildesheim, Information Science, Marienburger Platz 22,
D-31141 Hildesheim, Germany
{mandl, womser}@uni-hildesheim.de

Abstract. The reliability of the topics within the Cross Language Evaluation Forum (CLEF) needs to be validated constantly to justify the efforts for experiments within CLEF and to demonstrate the reliability of the results as far as possible. The analysis presented in this paper is concerned with several aspects. Continuing and expanding a study from 2002, we investigate the difficulty of topics and the correlation between the retrieval quality for topics and the occurrence of proper names.

1 Introduction

Topics are an essential aspect of experiments for information retrieval evaluation [1]. The topic creation for a multilingual environment requires especial care in order to avoid cultural or linguistic bias to influence the semantics of a topic formulation [2]. A thorough translation check of all translated topics in CLEF assures that the translations all include the same semantics [3].

The question remains whether linguistic aspects of the topics have any influence on the retrieval performance. In this study, we focused on the impact of proper names in topics and found significant a correlation to the average precision.

2 Analysis of Information Retrieval Evaluation Results

The validity of large-scale information retrieval experiments has been the subject of a considerable amount of research. Zobel concluded that the TREC (Text REtrieval Conference[1]) experiments are reliable as far as the ranking of the systems are concerned [4]. Voorhees & Buckley have analyzed the reliability of experiments as a function of the size of the topic set [5]. They concluded that the typical size of the topics set in TREC is sufficient for a satisfactory level of reliability.

Further research is dedicated toward the question whether the expensive human relevance judgements are necessary or whether the constructed document pool of the highest ranked documents from all runs may serve as an reliable approximation of the

---

[1] http://trec.nist.gov

C. Peters et al. (Eds.): CLEF 2003, LNCS 3237, pp. 21–28, 2004.

human judgements. According to a study by Soboroff et al., the ranking of the systems in TREC correlates positively to a ranking based on the document pool without further human judgement [6]. However, there are considerable differences in the ranking which are especially significant in the highest ranks. The human judgements are therefore necessary to achieve the highest reliability of the system ranking. The assessment by different jurors also results in different sets of relevant documents. However, the assignment to different jurors does not result in a different system ranking [7].

3 Difficulty of Topics

The notion of the difficulty of topics has been of great interest in the IR community. The question, what makes a topic a difficult one, remains unsolved.

Voorhees & Harman measured the difficulty of TREC topics from two perspectives [8]. One was the estimation of experts and the second was the actual outcome of the systems measured as the average precision which systems achieved for that topic. They found no correlation between the two measures. This result was confirmed in a study of the topics of the Asian languages retrieval evaluation NTCIR[2] [9]. Furthermore, Eguchi et al. tried to find whether the system ranking changes when different difficulty levels of topics were considered. They conclude, that changes in the system ranking occur, however, the Kendall correlation coefficient between the overall rankings does not drop below 0.69. For that analysis, the actual difficulty measured by the precision of the runs was used. The overall rankings remain stable, however, top ranks could be affected. When considering this result, we need to be aware, that the number of topics in the sub sets with different difficulties is lower than in the overall set [9]. According to the results from another study which analyzed the reliability of experiments as a function of the size of the topic set, such a small set does not lead to completely reliable results [5].

We conducted a study for the CLEF topics of the year 2003 to investigate the correlation between perceived topic difficulty and actual performance of the systems. We call the average precision of the best run for a topic the system difficulty. Accordingly, the human estimation of difficulty is called the intellectual difficulty of a topic.

The intellectual difficulty was surveyed during the CLEF topic creation meeting. The organizers and topic creators present were asked to judge whether a topic would be difficult for systems and whether it would be difficult for the human jurors to assess the relevance of the documents.

The system difficulty was extracted from the output of the trec_eval program which was mailed to all participants as part of the result.

Surprisingly, only a weak correlation of 0.14 could be found between the system and the intellectual difficulty. However, the judgments about the difficulty of the assessment yielded a stronger positive correlation (0.30) to the topic system difficulty. The CLEF campaign also provides the number of relevant documents for each topic.

---

[2] http://research.nii.ac.jp/ntcir/

The judgments about the difficulty of the assessment show a negative correlation (−0.27) to the number of relevant documents found. These two correlation measures are statistically significant.

Obviously, it is very difficult even for experts to judge the outcome of the complex of topic and systems in the context of a large collection.

4 Proper Names and Retrieval Performance

Much of the work in information retrieval needs to be dedicated to natural language processing. Phenomena like different word forms or compound words face challenges for information retrieval systems. Therefore, the occurrence of linguistic phenomena may favor some systems especially suited for these phenomena. In this context, it may be interesting to look at systems which perform well and demonstrate weaknesses for topics which are generally solved with good quality (or vice versa).

A study has been carried out for the CLEF campaign 2001 [10]. It revealed no strong correlation between any single linguistic phenomenon and the system difficulty of a topic. Not even the length of a topic showed any substantial effect. However, when calculating the sum of all phenomena assessed, we found a positive correlation. The more linguistic phenomena available, the better systems solved a topic on average. The availability of more variations of a word seems to provide stemming algorithms with more evidence for the extraction of the stem, for example. Consequently, the stem may be recognized with higher accuracy. This study will be extended to the topics and results quality of all available CLEF runs.

Intellectual analysis of the results and the properties of the results had identified proper names as a potential indicator for retrieval performance. Because of that, proper names in the CLEF topic set were analyzed in more detail. The analysis included all topics from the campaigns in the years 2001 and 2002. The number of proper names in the topics were assessed intellectually. In addition, the retrieval performance of the runs for the topics was extracted from the CLEF proceedings.

Overall, we found a significant positive relation between the number of proper names present. The more proper names a topic contains, the better the retrieval results are. There is a high deviation, however, the trend is statistically significant.

In detail, the following relations were investigated: For the CLEF topics number 41 to 200, the average precision of the best run was available. For the topics 41 throughout 140, the average of all runs for that topic was available. It was calculated as the average of all average precision values. Thus, one best and one average result for each topic was identified. The topics were ordered according to the number of proper names they contained. Each subset of topics and their performance values were assigned to the number of proper names. For these sets, the basic statistics are shown in Table 1 and 2.

Table 1. Best run for each topic in relation to the number of proper names in the topic (topic 41 to 200)

Number of proper names	0	1	2	3	4	5	6
Number of Topics	42	43	40	20	9	4	2
Average of Best System per Topic	0.62	0.67	0.76	0.83	0.79	0.73	0.81
Minimum of Best System per Topic	0.090	0.12	0.036	0.28	0.48	0.40	0.63
Standard Deviation of Best System per Topic	0.24	0.24	0.24	0.18	0.19	0.29	0.26

Table 2. Average precision of runs for topic in relation to the number of proper names in the topic (topic 41 to 140)

Number of proper names	0	1	2	3	4	5
Number of Topics	33	22	20	13	8	3
Maximum of Average Performance per Topic	0.49	0.52	0.74	0.69	0.58	0.60
Average of Average Performance per Topic	0.21	0.29	0.39	0.39	0.32	0.46
Minimum of Average Performance per Topic	0.02	0.10	0.14	0.12	0.17	0.28
Standard Deviation of Average Performance	0.13	0.13	0.16	0.17	0.15	0.17

The graphic representation of the values of table 1 and 2 in figure 1 and 2 respectively suggests a positive correlation. This impression can be confirmed by a statistical analysis. The average performance correlates with a value of 0.43 to the number of proper names and the best performance with a value of 0.26. Disregarding the topics from the campaign in 2003 leads to a correlation coefficient of 0.35. All relations are statistically significant. The assumption of independence of the two parameters can be rejected with a probability of over 95%.

This study suggests that the presence of proper names in queries enhances the chances of retrieval systems to find relevant documents. As a consequence, the presence of proper names in the CLEF topic set should be carefully monitored. The system rankings for topics with and without proper names should be evaluated.

This analysis of proper names could be extended to consider the number of tokens, to include the number of individual words present in the proper names as well as abbreviations of proper names.

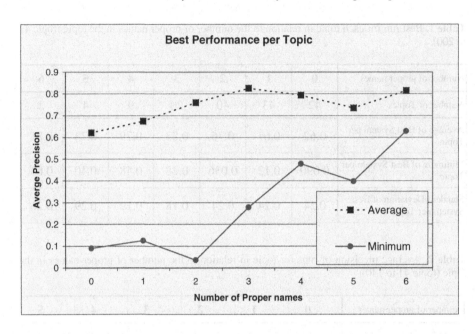

Fig. 1. Relationship between number of proper names and retrieval performance for the best runs

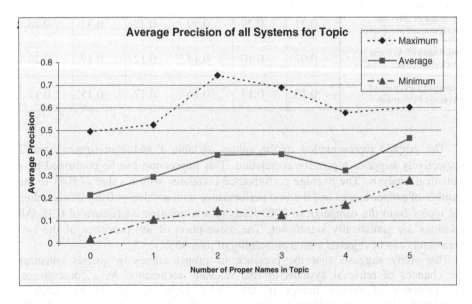

Fig. 2. Relationship between number of proper names and retrieval performance for the best runs

5 Proper Names in the Multilingual Topic Set

An objection against the reliability of the CLEF experiments could arise from the multilingual aspects of the topic set. Are the topics in one language easier for the systems than in another? Does this lead to a bias in the multilingual track where different languages are used as starting point? For example, due to the stylistic modifications in a language, more occurrences of proper names or more hetero-geneous word forms may be introduced in the topic formulation. Because proper names were identified as an important aspect, we analyzed the stability of the distribution of proper names over the topic set. The results are shown in table 3.

Table 3. Number of proper names per language in the CLEF topics 41 to 140

Topic Language	Tokens of Proper Names
DE	246
EN	205
SV	171
ES	122
FR	167
IT	169

The number of proper names seems to differ quite substantially over the languages. Probably, the stylistic and grammatical necessities lead to different numbers of names. Because the number of proper names seems to have influence on the retrieval quality, as shown in chapter 4, this fact needs to be considered. The performance of systems utilizing different topic languages needs to be analyzed. Further detailed analysis on this aspect is necessary.

6 Outlook

The investigations reported in this article has shown a significant correlation between the number of proper names in topics and the average precision of systems for the CLEF campaigns. In additional experiments with the CLEF data, we intend to test whether the exploitation of this knowledge can be exploited for system improvement. Topics could be forwarded to different sub-systems according to the number of proper names they contain. These sub-systems can be specialized in dealing with topics with or without proper names.

Overall, our study has found no bias in the topics of the CLEF campaign. As a result, no reservations toward the validity of the results arise from this research. This work needs to continue throughout the campaign and has to be extended to further aspects in the future. More detailed analysis of the performance of systems on different topics is necessary to explain the success or failure of systems for certain tasks. Such research could ultimately lead to better retrieval systems.

For users of information retrieval systems, this finding is valuable for the creation of better queries. For real world retrieval systems another important aspect needs to be considered. The popularity or frequency of topics differs greatly [11]. The average user satisfaction will be higher, when systems work well for highly frequent queries on popular topics.

Acknowledgements

We would like to thank Martin Braschler for providing the crucial data for our study. We also acknowledge the participation of the CLEF organization team during the topic creation meeting. Furthermore, we acknowledge the work of several students from the University of Hildesheim who contributed to this analysis as part of their course work.

References

1. Sparck Jones, K.: Reflections on TREC. In: Information Processing & Management 31(3) (1995) 291-314
2. Kluck, M., Womser-Hacker, C.: Inside the Evaluation Process of the Cross-Language Evaluation Forum (CLEF): Issues of Multilingual Topic Creation and Multilingual Relevance Assessment. In: Rodríguez, M. G., Araujo, C. P. S. (eds.): Proceedings of the Third International Conference on Language Resources and Evaluation, LREC 2002, Las Palmas de Gran Canaria, 29-31 May 2002, ELRA, Paris (2002) 573-576
3. Womser-Hacker, C.: Multilingual Topic Generation within the CLEF 2001 Experiments. In: Peters, C., Braschler, M., Gonzalo, J., Kluck, M. (eds.): Evaluation of Cross-Language Information Retrieval Systems: Second Workshop of the Cross-Language Evaluation Forum, CLEF 2001, Darmstadt, Germany, September 3-4, 2001. Revised Papers. Lecture Notes in Computer Science, Vol. 2406. Springer-Verlag, Berlin Heidelberg New York (2002) 389-393
4. Zobel, J.: How Reliable are the Results of Large-Scale Information Retrieval Experiments? In: Proceedings of the Annual International ACM Conference on Research and Development in Information Retrieval (SIGIR '98). Melbourne (1998) 307-314
5. Voorhees, E., Buckley, C.: The Effect of Topic Set Size on Retrieval Experiment Error. In: Proceedings of the Annual International ACM Conference on Research and Development in Information Retrieval (SIGIR '02). Tampere, Finland (2002) 316-323
6. Soboroff, I., Nicholas, C., Cahan, P.: Ranking Retrieval Systems without Relevance Judgments. In: Proceedings of the Annual International ACM Conference on Research and Development in Information Retrieval (SIGIR '01). New Orleans (2001) 66-73
7. Voorhees, E.: Variations in relevance judgments and the measurement of retrieval effectiveness. In: Proceedings of the 21st Annual International ACM SIGIR Conference on Research and Development in Information Retrieval (SIGIR '98). Melbourne. (1998) 315-223
8. Voorhees, E., Harman, D.: Overview of the Sixth Text REtrieval Conference. In: Voorhees, Ellen, Harman, Donna (eds.): The Sixth Text REtrieval Conference (TREC-6). NIST Special Publication. National Institute of Standards and Technology. Gaithersburg, Maryland. http://trec.nist.gov/pubs/ (1997)

9. Eguchi, K., Kuriyama, K., Kando, N.: Sensitivity of IR Systems Evaluation to Topic Difficulty. In: Rodríguez, M. G., Araujo, C. P. S. (eds.): Proceedings of the Third International Conference on Language Resources and Evaluation, LREC 2002, Las Palmas de Gran Canaria, 29-31 May 2002, ELRA, Paris (2002) 585-589

10. Mandl, T., Womser-Hacker, C.: Linguistic and Statistical Analysis of the CLEF Topics. In: Peters, C., Braschler, M., Gonzalo, J., Kluck, M. (eds.): Advances in Cross- Language Information Retrieval: Third Workshop of the Cross-Language Evaluation Forum, CLEF 2002, Rome, Italy, September 19 - 20, 2002 ; revised papers. Lecture Notes in Computer Science; Vol. 2785. Springer-Verlag, Berlin Heidelberg New York (2003) 505-511

11. Lempel, R., Moran, S.: Predictive Caching and Prefetching of Query Results in Search Engines. In: Proceedings of the Twelfth International World Wide Web Conference (WWW 2003). Budapest. ACM Press (2003) 19-28

Evaluation of Information Access Technologies
at the NTCIR Workshop

Noriko Kando

National Institute of Informatics (NII), Tokyo 101-8430, Japan
kando@nii.ac.jp
http://research.nii.ac.jp/~kando/

Abstract. This paper introduces the *NTCIR Workshop*, a series of evaluation
workshops that are designed to enhance research in information access
technologies, such as information retrieval, cross-lingual information retrieval,
text summarization, question answering and text mining, by providing
infrastructure for large-scale evaluations. A brief history, the test collections,
and recent progress after the previous *CLEF* Workshop are described,
highlighting the differences from *CLEF*. To conclude, some thoughts on future
directions are suggested.

1 Introduction

The *NTCIR Workshop* [1][1] is a series of evaluation workshops designed to enhance
research in information access (IA) technologies including information retrieval (IR),
cross-lingual information retrieval (CLIR), automatic text summarization, question
answering and text mining.

The aims of the *NTCIR* project are:

1. to encourage research in information access technologies by providing large-
   scale test collections that are reusable for experiments;
2. to provide a forum for research groups interested in cross-system comparisons
   and exchanging research ideas in an informal atmosphere; and
3. to investigate methodologies and metrics for evaluation of information access
   technologies and methods for constructing large-scale reusable test collections.

Essentially, the main goal of the *NTCIR* project is to provide infrastructure for large-
scale evaluations. The importance of such infrastructure in IA research has been widely
recognized. Fundamental text processing procedures for IA, such as stemming and
indexing include language-dependent procedures. In particular, processing texts written

---

[1] *NTCIR-3* and *-4* were sponsored by the National Institute of Informatics (NII) and *Japanese
MEXT Grant-in-Aid for Scientific Research on Informatics (#13224087)* in and after
FY2001. The patent task was organized in collaboration with the Japan Intellectual Property
Rights Association and NII, and the *CLIR* Task was organized in collaboration with the
National Taiwan University and the Korean Institute for Scientific and Technological
Information (KISTI).

C. Peters et al. (Eds.): CLEF 2003, LNCS 3237, pp. 29–43, 2004.

in Japanese or other East Asian languages such as Chinese is quite different from processing English, French or other European languages, because there are no explicit boundaries (i.e., no spaces) between words in a sentence. The *NTCIR* project therefore started in late 1997 with emphasis on, but not limited to, Japanese or other East Asian languages, and its series of workshops has attracted international participation.

1.1 Information Access

The term "information access" (IA) includes the whole process from when a user realizes his/her information needs, through the activity of searching for and finding relevant documents, and then utilizing information extracted from them. A traditional IR system returns a ranked list of retrieved documents that are likely to contain information relevant to the user's needs. This is one of the most fundamental core processes of IA. It is, however, not the end of the story for the users. After obtaining a ranked list of retrieved documents, the user skims the documents, performs relevance judgments, locates the relevant information, reads, analyses, compares the contents with other documents, integrates, summarizes and performs information-based work such as decision making, problem solving or writing, based on the information obtained from the retrieved documents. We have looked at IA technologies to help users utilize the information in large-scale document collections. IR, summarization and question answering are part of a "family", aiming at the same target, although each of them has been investigated by rather different communities[2].

1.2 Focus of *NTCIR*

As shown in Figure 1, we have looked at both traditional laboratory-type IR system testing and the evaluation of challenging technologies. For the laboratory-type testing, we placed emphasis on IR and CLIR with Japanese or other Asian languages and testing on various document genres. For the challenging issues, the target is to shift from document retrieval to technologies that utilize "information" in documents, and investigation of methodologies and metrics for more realistic and reliable evaluation. For the latter, we have paid attention to users' information-seeking tasks in the experiment design. These two directions have been supported by a forum of researchers and by their discussions.

From the beginning, CLIR has been one of the central interests of *NTCIR*, because CLIR between English and own-languages is critical for international information transfer in Asian countries, and it is challenging to perform CLIR between languages with completely different structures and origins such as English and Chinese or English and Japanese.

In the rest of this paper, the following section provides a brief history of *NTCIR*. Section 3 describes the *NTCIR Test Collections,* Section 4 reports recent progress

---

[2] In addition, the problem of "how to define a user's search question" is also included in the scope of IA although this has not been explicitly investigated in NTCIR so far.

after our reports at the previous CLEF workshops [2–4], and Section 5 outlines the features of the coming NTCIR Workshop, *NTCIR-4*. Section 6 provides a summary.

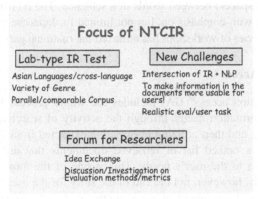

Fig. 1. Focus of *NTCIR*

2 NTCIR

2.1 History of *NTCIR*

In *NTCIR*, a workshop is held about once every one and a half years, *i.e.*, with intervals of about 18 months. Because we respect the interaction between participants, we consider the whole process from initial document release to the final meeting to be the "workshop". Each workshop selects several research areas called "Tasks", or a "Challenges" for the more challenging tasks. Each task has been organized by the researchers of the domain and a task may consist of more than one subtask. Figure 2 shows the evolution of the tasks in the *NTCIR Workshops* and Table 1 is a list of subtasks and test collections used in the tasks [5–7].

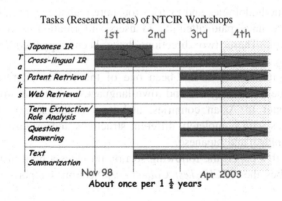

Fig. 2. Tasks of *NTCIR Workshops*

As shown in Table 1, the fourth *NTCIR Workshop* will host five tasks: *CLIR*, the Patent Retrieval Task *(PATENT)*, the Question Answering Challenge *(QAC)*, the Text Summarization Challenge *(TSC)*, and the WEB Task *(WEB)* and their sub-tasks.

Table 1. History of *NTCIR Workshops*

	Period	Tasks	Subtasks	Test collections
1	Nov.1998-Sept.1999	Ad Hoc IR	J-JE	NTCIR-1
		CLIR	J-E	
		Term Extraction	Term Extraction/ Role Analysis	
2	June 2000-March 2001	Chinese Text Retrieval	Chinese IR: C-C	CIRB010
			CLIR: E-C	
		Japanese&English IR	Monolingual IR: J-J, E-E	NTCIR-1, -2
			CLIR: J-E, E-J, J-JE, E-JE	
		Text Summarization	Intrinsic - Extraction/Free generated	NTCIR-2Summ
			Extrinsic - IR task-based	
3	Oct. 2001-Oct. 2002	CLIR	Single Language IR:C-C,K-K,J-J	NTCIR-3CLIR
			Bilingual CLIR:x-J,x-C, x-K	
			Multilingual CLIR:x-CJE	
		Patent	Cross Genre w/ or w/o CLIR CCKE-J	NTCIR-3 PATENT
			[Optional] Alianment, RST Analysis of Claims	
		Question Answering	Subtask-1: Five Possible Answers	NTCIR-3QA
			Subtask-2: One Set of All the Answers	
			Subtask-3: Series of Questions	
		Text Summarization	Single Document Summarization	NTCIR-3 SUMM
			Multi-document Summarization	
		Web Retrieval	Survey Retrieval	NTCIR-3 WEB
			Target Retrieval	
			[Optional] Speech-Driven	
4	Apr. 2003 - June 2004	CLIR	Single Language IR:C-C,K-K,J-J	NTCIR-4CLIR
			Bilingual CLIR:x-J,x-C, x-K	
			Pivoted Bilingual CLIR	
			Multilingual CLIR:x-CKJE	
		Patent	"Invalidity Search"= Search Patents by a Patent	NTCIR-4 PATENT
			[Feasibility] Automatic Patent Map Creation	
		Question Answering	Subtask-1: Five Possible Answers	NTCIR-4 QA
			Subtask-2: One Set of All the Answers	
			Subtask-3: Series of Questions	
		Text Summarization	Multi-document Summarization	NTCIR-4 SUMM
		Web Retrieval	Informational Retrieval	NTCIR-4 WEB
			Navigational Retrieval	
			[Pilot] Geographical Information	
			[Pilot] (Search Results) Topical Classification	

n-m: n=query language, m=document language(s), J:Japanese, E:English, C:Chinese, K:Korean, x:any of CJKE

2.2 Participants

As shown in Figures 3 and 4, the number of participants has gradually increased. Different tasks attracted different research groups although many participate in more than one task, or change the tasks they participate in over workshops. Many international participants have enrolled in CLIR. The Patent Retrieval task attracted many participants from company research laboratories and "veteran" *NTCIR* participants. The *WEB* task has participants from various research communities such as machine learning and DBMS. The number of collaborating teams across different organizations has increased in recent *NTCIR*s.

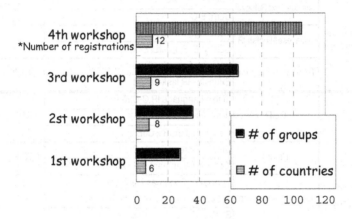

Fig. 3. Number of Participating Groups

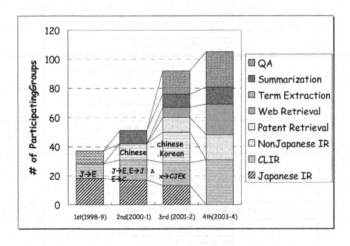

Fig. 4. Participating Groups per Task

Table 2. Test collections constructed by *NTCIR*

NTCIR Test Collections; IR and QA

collection	task	documents						Task data		
		genre	filename	lang	year	# of doc	size	topic/ question lang	#	relevance judge
NTCIR-1	IR	sci. abstract	ntc1-je	JE	1988-1997	339,483	577MB	J	83	3 grades
			ntc1-j	J		332,918	312MB			
			ntc1-e	E		187,080	218MB		60	
	TE*5		ntc1-tmrc	J		2,000	-	-	-	-
CIRB010	IR	news	CIRB010	C_t	1998-1999	132,173	132MB	C_tE	50	4 grades
NTCIR-2	IR	sci. abstract	ntc2-j	J	1986-1999**	400,248	600MB	JE	49	4 grades
			ntc2-e	E		134,978	200MB			
NTCIR-3 CLIR	IR	news	KEIB010	K	1994	66,146	74MB	C_tKJE	30	4 grades
			CIRB011	C_t		132,173				
			CIRB020			249,508				
			Mainichi	J	1998-1999	220,078	870MB	C_tKJE	50	4 grades
			EIRB010			10,204				
			Mainichi Daily	E		12,723				
NTCIR-3 PATENT	IR	patent full	kkh *3	J	1998-1999	697,262	18GB	C_tC_sKJE	31	3 grades
		abstract	jsh *3	J	1995-1999	1,706,154	1,883MB			
		abstract	paj *3	E	1995-1999	1,701,339	2,711MB			
NTCIR-3 QA	QA	news	Mainichi	J	1998-1999	220,078	282MB	J*	1200	exact answer
NTCIR-3 WEB	IR	Web (html/text)	NW100G-01	multi ple*4	crawled in 2001	11,038,720	100GB	J*	47	4grades + relative
			NW10G-01			1,445,466	10GB			
NTCIR-4 CLIR	IR	news	CIRB011	Ct		132,173				
			CIRB020			249,203				
			Hankookilbo +	K		149,921				
			Chosenilbo +			104,517				
			Mainichi	J	1998-1999	220,078	ca.3GB	CtKJE	60	4 grades
			Yomiuri +			373,558				
			EIRB010			10,204				
			Mainichi Daily	E		12,723				
			Korea Times +			19,599				
			Hong Kong			96,683				
			Xinhua +			208,167				
NTCIR-4 PATENT	IR	patent full	Publication of unexamined patent application	J	1993-2002	ca. 3,500,000	ca.45GB	CtCsKJE		
		abstract	Patnet Abstracts of Japan (PAJ) +	E	1993-2002	ca. 3,500,000	ca.10GB			
NTCIR-4 QA	QA	news	Mainichi	J	1998-1999	220,078	ca.776MB	J*		
			Yomiuri +			373,558				
NTCIR-4 WEB	IR	Web (html/text)	NW100G-01	multi ple*4	crawled in 2001	11,038,720	100GB	J*		

J:Japanese, E:English, C:Chinese (C_t:Traditional Chinese, C_s: Simplified Chinese), K:Korean;
"+" indicates the document collection newly added for NTCIR-4
* English translation is ava ** gakkai subfiles: 1997-1999, kaken subfiles: 1986-1997
*3: kkh : Publication of unexamined patent application, jsh: Japanese abstract, paj: English translation c
*4: almost Japanese or English (some in other languages)
*5: Term extraction/ role analysis

NTCIR Text Summarization

collection	task	documents					summaries		
		genre	filename	lang	year	# of doc	types	analysts	total#
NTCIR-2 SUMM	single doc	news	Mainichi	J	1994.1995 .1998	180 doc	7	3	3780
NTCIR-2 TAO	single doc	news	Mainichi	J	1998	1000 doc	2	1	2000
NTCIR-3 SUMM	single doc	news	Mainichi	J	1998-	60 docs	7	3	1260
	multi doc		Mainichi	J	1999	50 sets	2	3	300
NTCIR-4 SUMM	multi doc	news	Mainichi	J	1998-				
			Yomiuri		1999				

3   Test Collections

The test collections constructed for the *NTCIR Workshops* are listed in Table 2. In the *NTCIR* project the term "test collection" is used for any kind of data set usable for system testing and experiments although it often means IR test collections used in search experiments. One of our interests is to prepare realistic evaluation infrastructures, and efforts include scaling up the document collection, document genres, languages, topic structure and relevance judgments.

3.1   Documents

Documents have been collected from various domains or genres. Formats of the documents are basically the same as in the TREC or CLEF collections, plain text with SGML-like tags. Each of the specialized document genre collections contained characteristic fields for the genre: the Web collection contains items such as HTML tags, hyperlinks and the URL of the document; the patent collection has tags indicating the document structure of the patent; and both patent and scientific document collections have parallel corpora of English and Japanese abstracts. The task (experiment) design and relevance judgment criteria were set according to the nature of the document collection and of the user community who use this type of document in their everyday tasks.

3.2   Topics

A sample topic record is shown in Figure 5. Topics are defined as statements of "user's requests" rather than "queries", which are the strings actually submitted to the system, because we wish to allow both manual and automatic query construction from the topics. Emphasis has been shifted towards the topic structure to allow more realistic experiments as well as to see the effect of background information on the topic. The characteristics are summarized in the following.

Topic Structure: Topic structure has changed slightly in each *NTCIR*. A topic basically consists of a <TITLE>, a description <DESC>, and a detailed narrative

<NARR> of the search request, similar to those used in CLEF and TREC. It may contain additional fields as shown in Table 3. Most *NTCIR* collections contain a list of concepts <CONC>, but they are not heavily used by participants.

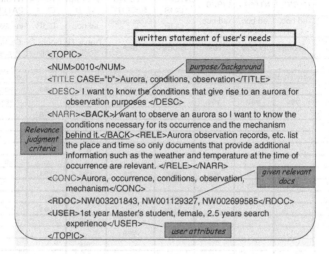

Fig. 5. Sample topic (*NTCIR-3 WEB*)

<TITLE> as Query: A title was originally defined as a very short description, or "nickname" of the topic, but since *NTCIR-3 WEB*[3] it has changed its status to a "query", a string put into a search engine by users and defined as a comma-separated list of up to three terms.

Structured <NARR>: Originally, a narrative <NARR> was defined to the topic authors as containing background knowledge, purpose of the search, detailed explanation of the topic, criteria for relevance judgment, term definitions, and so on. Since *NTCIR-3 WEB*, such information categories in <NARR> are explicitly marked by tags like <BACK> and <RELE>, as shown in Figure 5. The purpose of this change is to examine explicitly the effect of additional information on the search effectiveness.

Mandatory Runs: Any combination of topic fields can be used in experiments for research purposes. In the Workshop, *Mandatory Runs* are defined for each task, and every participant must submit at least one mandatory run using the specified topic field only. The purpose of this is to enhance cross-system comparisons by basing them on common conditions and to see the effectiveness of the additional information. Mandatory runs were originally "<DESC> only", but have gradually shifted to "<TITLE> only" as well as "<DESC> only".

---

[3] Topic authors are instructed to sort the terms in <TITLE> in descending order of importance to express the search request in the same way as users input the terms as queries. The relation between the terms is specified as an attribute of the <TITLE> in the WEB Task.

Table 3. Topic fields

Topic Structure of NTCIR IR Test Collections

	NTCIR-1	NTCIR-2	CIRB010	NTCIR-3 CLIR	NTCIR-3 PATENT	NTCIR-3 WEB	NTCIR-4 CLIR	NTCIR-4 PATENT	NTCIR-4 WEB
Task	ad hoc, CLIR	ad hoc, CLIR	ad hoc, CLIR	CLIR	Cross-genre, CLIR	ad hoc	CLIR	invalidity	ad hoc, other
Mandatory Run *	D-only	D-only	N/A	D-only	S+A	T-only, D-only	T-only, D-only	CLAIM-only	T-only, D-only
Topic Field									
TITLE **	very short	very short	very short	very short	very short	query	query	very short	query
DESC	yes	yes	yes	yes	yes	yes	yes	yes	yes
NARR (unstructured)	yes	yes	yes	yes	yes			yes	
NARR (structured)						yes	yes		yes
NARR. BACK *10						yes	yes		yes
NARR. RELE *10						yes	yes		yes
NARR. TERM *10						yes	yes		yes
PURPOSE *7								yes	
CONC	yes	yes	yes	yes	yes	yes	yes		
FIELDS	yes	yes							
TLANG / LANG *3				yes			yes		
SLANG *3				yes			yes		
RDOC *4						yes			
PI *4					yes				
USER *5						yes			yes
ARTICLE *6					yes				
DOC *9								yes	
SUPPLEMENT *6					yes				
CLAIM *8								yes	
COMP *8								yes	
COMP. CNUM *8								yes	

*: D-only=DESC only, T-only=TITLE only, A+S= run using ARTICLE and SUPPLEMENT only

**: "very short"=very short description of search request; "qeury"=comma separated term list

*3: TLANG/LANG=target language, the language of the topic; SLANG=source language, the language the topic originally constructed.

*4: RDOC=known relevant documents; PI=the patent for the invention mentioned in the news articles.

*5: USER=users' attribute

*6: ARTICLE=a news article reporting an invention; SUPPLEMENT=memorandam to focus the issues in the article relevant to the user's needs; if a human knowledgeable searcher reads ARTICLE and SUPPLEMENT, he/she understand the user's search request as specif

*7: Purpose of search (only "invalidity search" for NTCIR-4 PATENT)

*8: CLAIM=Target claim in the query patent. It was used as qeury of the search and may consists of multiple components; COMP=Component of a claim; CNUM=Claim component ID

*9: Query patent fulltext (fulltext of a patent that is used as a query of the search)

*10: BACK=Background knowledge/purpose of search; RELE=relevance judgment criteria; TERM=term definitions

3.3 Relevance Judgments

Relevance judgments are done by pooling, and the format and methods used are basically the same as other evaluation projects including CLEF and TREC. The differences may be summarized as follows:

1. Pooling strategies are slightly different according to the task.

    - Additional interactive recall-oriented searches are performed to improve the exhaustivity (*NTCIR-1, -2*) [8]

- Additional interactive recall-oriented searches are performed by professional patent intermediaries *(PATENT)* [9]
- A "One-click distance model", in which hyperlinked documents can be seen in *WEB* [10]
- Cross-lingual pooling for parallel or quasi-parallel documents (*NTCIR-1, -2*)[8]
- Graded-depth pooling: pool creation using top10, 11–20, 21–30, 31–41, (PATENT) [9]

2. Multi-grade and relative relevance judgments

- Highly Relevant, Relevant, Partially Relevant [5–7], Irrelevant; Best Relevant, Second Best, Third Best, and so on. [10]

3. Judgments include the extracted passages to show the reason why the assessors assessed the documents as "relevant"
4. Pooled document lists to be judged are sorted in descending order of likelihood of being relevant (not the order of the document IDs)
5. Relevance judgment files may be prepared for each of the target language document sub-collections in CLIR

Item 4, sorting pooled documents, helps assessors judge consistently over a long list of pooled documents to be judged (typically 2000–3000 documents). Relevance judgments may change over assessors and over time. If relevant documents appear frequently in the first part of the list, it is easier for the non-professional assessors to set and confirm their criteria for relevance judgments, and then they can always refer to those documents to re-confirm their own relevance judgment criteria when they go to lower ranked documents. We understand there may be a "order effect" which may skew the judgments, but we have used this strategy intentionally as the practical and most effective one in *our* environment, based on the comparative tests and interviews with assessors.

For item 5, a topic in multilingual *CLIR* cannot always obtain a sufficient number of relevant documents on every language's document sub-collection, and this is the natural situation in multi-lingual CLIR. As a result, some topics cannot be used in experiments on specific language documents. We have not found a way to manage this issue and the only strategy we could take in *NTCIR-4 CLIR* is to increase the number of topics, so that a larger number of topics can be used across the document sub-collections to improve the stability of the evaluation.

Assessors are users of the document genre, judgments are done by the topic author except for CLIR in *NTCIR-3* and *-4* because topics are created in cooperation by multiple countries, and then translated into each language and tested for usability on each language's document sub-collection. Judging other users' topics is sometimes hard for users and takes more time.

In the first two *NTCIRs*, we used two assessors per topic then tested inter-assessors consistency and found that the inconsistency among multiple assessors on a topic does not affect the stability of the evaluation when tested on a sufficient number of topics. Based on this, a single assessor per topic is used in and after *NTCIR-3*.

3.4 Evaluation

For evaluation, the trec-eval program [11] is used by setting two thresholds of the levels of relevance judgments, i.e., *"Rigid Relevance"* regards "Relevant" and "Highly Relevant" as "Relevant", *"Relaxed Relevance"* regards "Partially Relevant" or higher as "Relevant". As additional metrics, several metrics for multi-grade relevance judgments have been proposed including *weighted mean average precision* (wMAP), *weighted reciprocal rank* (WRR, for *WEB* task) [15], and *discounted cumulative gain* (DCG) [12–13].

For Question Answering, *mean reciprocal rank* (MRR) is used for subtask 1, returning five possible answers with no penalty for wrong answers, and F-measure is used for subtask 2, returning one set of all the answers with penalties given for wrong answers. For subtask 3, a series of questions are used. For Text Summarization, in *NTCIR-3*, content-based and readability-based intrinsic evaluation was used for both single document and multi-document summarization, and a new evaluation methodology based on revision (edit distance) of system summaries by the professional analysts who created the model summaries was proposed.

4 Further Analysis of *NTCIR-3*

Following our reports at previous CLEFs [2–4] and the overview papers in the Proceedings of *NTCIR-3* [7], several additional analyses were done on the *NTCIR-3* results and collection.

For the *PATENT* retrieval task, although a new strategy for cross-genre retrieval called "term distillation" was proposed by the Ricoh group [16] and worked well on the collection, many research questions regarding patent retrieval remained unsolved in *NTCIR-3*. For example:

1. Is there any particular IR model (or weighting scheme) specifically effective for patents?
2. The influence of the wide variation of document length (from 100 words to 30,000 word tokens in a document!)
3. Indexing (Character bi-grams *vs.* Word-based)
4. Target document collections: Full text *vs.* abstract (many commercialized systems use abstracts only)

For question 1, it was reported at the *SIGIR 2000 Workshop on Patent Retrieval* that *tf* was not effective on patents, but we could not find concrete answers to the question from the *NTCIR-3* work.

To answer these questions, the *NTCIR-3* Patent Task organizers conducted additional experiments on the patent collection and newspaper collection, and tested eight different weighting schemes including both vector space as well as probabilistic models, on six different document subcollections in *NTCIR-3 PATENT*, using four different indexing strategies (character bi-grams, words, compound terms and a hybrid of character bi-grams and words), and three different topic lengths in the system [14].

For *WEB*, one participating group was a collaboration of research groups with strong backgrounds in content-based text retrieval and web-link analysis, and this worked well for *NTCIR-3 WEB*. Further analysis on the effect of links in the *WEB* collection showed that link-based approaches generally worked well, especially on short queries like using TITLE only, or more specifically the first term of the TITLE, i.e., the most important terms for the users (topic authors) [15].

5   Challenges at *NTCIR-4*

As shown in Table 1, the Fourth NTCIR Workshop is hosting five tasks, *CLIR, PATENT, QAC, TSC*, and *WEB* and their sub-tasks. The evaluation *schedule* varies according to task:

April 2003: Document Release
June–September 2003: Dry Run
October–December 2003: Formal Run
20 February 2004: Evaluation Results Release
2–5 June 2004: Workshop Meeting at NII, Tokyo Japan

For further information, please consult the NTCIR Web site at http://research.nii.ac.jp/ntcir and http://research.nii.ac.jp/ntcir/ntc-ws4, or contact the author.

5.1   NTCIR-4 CLIR

As this is the second multilingual *CLIR* at *NTCIR*, the task design will be a continuation of the previous one. Only minor revisions were made to solve the major problems raised in the assessment on the *NTCIR-3*, as follows:

- Enlarge the English and Korean document collections to be comparable to the Chinese and Japanese ones, about 3 GB in total.
- A new sub-task of Pivot Language Bilingual CLIR
- Restrict the pairings of topic and document languages, so that comparisons will be more fruitful
- Make a T-only run mandatory as well as a D-only run
- Question-type topics were categorized according to the nature and types of the answers to obtain a good balance of topic sets

The new sub-task, pivot CLIR, uses English as a pivot language, then tests the effectiveness of the transitive CLIR. It is a practical approach to Multilingual CLIR in environments with less availability of direct translation resources but rich in those between each of the languages and English.

5.2   *NTCIR-4* Question Answering (*QAC*) and Text Summarization (*TSC*)

QAC plans three subtasks as at *NTCIR-3*. Of the three, subtasks 1 and 2 will be done without major change. The only exceptions are the use of different question sets for subtasks 1 and 2, and an increase in the number of topics containing multiple answers. It was decided to avoid overestimates of the groups by ignoring the possibility of multiple answers and returning only the first priority answer to every question in subtask 2.

QAC subtask 3, answering a series of questions, is one of the major focuses of the *NTCIR-4 QAC*. The number of sequences was increased from the previous *QAC*, and the task design aimed at tackling the problems resembling the real-world "Report Writing" on a topic. For the first, each of the topic authors set a topic for the report, and then set a series of specific questions relating to the topic. Each of the questions asks a particular aspect of the topic.

This task design is also related to the *TSC*, in which a topic and a set of documents on the topic were provided to automatic summarizers that were requested to produce a summary based on the given document set. For the evaluation, the content of the system produced summaries were assessed by assessors using a set of questions relating to the topic -- whether the summary contained sufficient content to answer each of the questions or not.

It can be said that those sets of questions used in *QAC* and *TSC* represent the attributes or aspects of the given topic. The "topic - subtopics" relationship was also looked at in CLIR, where the types of the topics were investigated.

5.3 Specialized Genre Related Tasks at *NTCIR-4*: Patent and WEB

Both *PATENT* and *WEB* tasks plan Main task(s) and Feasibility or Pilot studies for more challenging tasks as follows:

PATENT – Main: Invalidity Task: To search patents to invalidate the query patents. The claims of the query patents are used as queries and they are segmented into components relating to the inventions or technologies comprising the investigation, then related patents are searched. A patent may be invalidated by one patent or by a combination of multiple patents. The search returns document IDs as well as relevant passages.

PATENT – Feasibility: Long term research plan over NTCIR-4 and -5: Automatic Patent Map Creation, a kind of text mining – detect sets of technologies used in a set of patents, extract them, and make a table showing the relationship between technologies and patents, and evolution or trends among them.

WEB – Main: Informational Search and Navigation-Oriented Search, to find the most informative and reliable page.

WEB – Pilot: Geographically oriented and Topical classifications of the Search results.

For details, please visit the Web site of each task, which are linked to the NTCIR's main Web site.

6 Summary

A brief history of *NTCIR* and recent progress after *NTCIR-3* are reported in this paper. One of the characteristic features of the *NTCIR workshops* is the targeting of "information access" technologies, covering the whole process of users obtaining and utilizing the information in the documents that they are interested in. This approach should demonstrate the intersection between all the related technologies including IR, Summarization, QA and Text Mining, and treat them as a "family". We are also interested in understanding the users' information tasks behind the laboratory-type testing. We are in the process of the fourth iteration in a series. Evaluation must change according to the technologies' evolution and the changes in social needs. We have been and are struggling towards this goal. Collaboration and any suggestions or advice are always more than welcome.

References

1. NTCIR Project: http://research.nii.ac.jp/ntcir/
2. Kando, N.: NTCIR Workshop: Japanese- and Chinese-English cross-lingual information retrieval and evaluation. multi-grade relevance judgments. In: Peters, C. (ed.): Cross-Language Information Retrieval and Evaluation: Workshop of the Cross-Language Evaluation Forum, CLEF2000. Lecture Notes in Computer Science, Vol. 2069, Springer-Verlag, Berlin (2001) 24–33
3. Kando, N.: CLIR system evaluation at the second NTCIR workshop. In: Peters, C., Braschler, M., Gonzalo, J., Kluck, M. (eds): Evaluation of Cross-Language Information Retrieval System: Second Workshop of the Cross-Language Evaluation Forum, CLEF 2001. Lecture Notes in Computer Science, Vol. 2406, Springer-Verlag, Berlin (2002) 371–388
4. Kando, N.: CLIR at NTCIR Workshop 3; Cross-language and cross-genre retrieval. In: Peters, C., Braschler, M., Gonzalo, J., Kluck, M. (eds): Advances in Cross-Language Information Retrieval: Third Workshop of the Cross-Language Evaluation Forum, CLEF 2002. Lecture Notes in Computer Science, Vol. 2785 (2003) 485-504
5. Kando, N., Nozue, T. (eds): NTCIR Workshop 1: Proceedings of the First NTCIR Workshop on Research in Japanese Text Retrieval and Term Recognition. Tokyo Japan, Aug. 30–Sept. 1, 1999. NII, Tokyo (1999) ISBN 4-924600-77-6. (http://research.nii.ac.jp/ntcir/ workshop/OnlineProceedings/)
6. Eguchi, K., Kando, N., Adachi, J. (eds): NTCIR Workshop 2: Proceedings of the Second NTCIR Workshop on Research in Chinese and Japanese Text Retrieval and Text Summarization. Tokyo Japan, June 2000–March 2001. NII, Tokyo, (2001) ISBN 4-924600-96-2, (http://research.nii.ac.jp/ntcir/workshop/OnlineProceedings2/)
7. Oyama, K., Ishida, E., Kando, N. (eds): NTCIR Workshop 3: Proceedings of the Third NTCIR Workshop on Research in Information Retrieval, Question Answering and Summarization, Tokyo Japan, Oct. 2001–Oct. 2002. ISBN-4-86049-016-9, NII, Tokyo (2003) (http://research.nii.ac.jp/ntcir/ workshop/OnlineProceedings3/)
8. Kuriyama, K., Yoshioka, M., Kando, N.: Construction of a large scale test collection NTCIR-2: The effect of additional interactive search and cross-lingual pooling. IPSJ Transactions on Databases, Vol. 43, No. SIG2 (TOD13) (March 2002) 48–59 (in Japanese)
9. Iwayama, M., Fujii, A., Kando, N., Takano, A.: Overview of the patent retrieval task at NTCIR-3. In: NTCIR Workshop 3: Proceedings of the Third NTCIR Workshop on Research in Information Retrieval, Question Answering and Summarization, Tokyo Japan, Oct. 2001–Oct. 2002, NII, Tokyo, (2003) (http://research.nii.ac.jp/ntcir/workshop/OnlineProceedings3/NTCIR3-OV-PATENT-IwayamaM.pdf)

10. Eguchi, K., Oyama, K., Ishida, E., Kando, N., Kuriyama, K.: Overview of web retrieval task at the Third NTCIR Workshop. In: NTCIR Workshop 3: Proceedings of the Third NTCIR Workshop on Research in Information Retrieval, Question Answering and Summarization, Tokyo Japan, Oct. 2001–Oct. 2002, NII, Tokyo (2003) (http://research.nii.ac.jp/ntcir/workshop/OnlineProceedings3/NTCIR3-OV-WEB-EguchiK.pdf)
11. Buckley, C.: trec_eval IR evaluation package. Available from ftp://ftp.cs.cornell.edu/pub/smart/
12. Jarvelin, K., Kekalainen, J.: IR evaluation methods for retrieving highly relevant documents. In: Proceedings of the 23rd Annual International ACM-SIGIR Conference on Research and Development in Information Retrieval. Athens Greece, July 2000. ACM Press, New York (2000) 41–48
13. Voorhees, E.M.: Evaluation by highly relevant documents. In: Proceedings of the 24th Annual International ACM SIGIR Conference on Research and Development in Information Retrieval (SIGIR 2001), New Orleans, Sept. 2001. ACM Press, New York (2001) 74–82
14. Iwayama, M., Fujii, A., Kando, N., Marukawa, K.: Empirical study on retrieval models for different document genres: Patents and newspaper articles. In: Proceedings of the 26th Annual International ACM SIGIR Conference on Research and Development in Information Retrieval (SIGIR 2003), Toronto, Canada, July 2003. ACM Press, New York (2003) 251-258
15. Eguchi, K., Oyama, K., Ishida, E., Kando, N., and Kuriyama K.: Evaluation methods for web retrieval tasks considering hyperlink structure, IEICE Transaction on Information and Systems. Vol. E86-D, No. 9 (2003) 1804-1813
16. Itoh, H., Mano, H., Ogawa, Y.: Term distillation for cross-DB retrieval. In: NTCIR Workshop 3: Proceedings of the Third NTCIR Workshop on Research in Information Retrieval, Question Answering and Summarization, Tokyo Japan, Oct. 2001–Oct. 2002, NII, Tokyo (2003) (http://research.nii.ac.jp/ntcir/workshop/OnlineProceedings3/NTCIR3-PATENT-ItohH.pdf)

CLEF 2003 – Overview of Results

Martin Braschler

Eurospider Information Technology AG,
Schaffhauserstr. 18, 8006 Zürich, Switzerland
martin.braschler@eurospider.com
Université de Neuchâtel, Institut interfacultaire d'informatique,
Pierre-à-Mazel 7, CH-2001 Neuchâtel, Switzerland

Abstract. The fourth CLEF campaign, CLEF 2003, was marked by a large increase in the number of experiments submitted by participants. More complex tasks (multilingual retrieval on documents written in eight different languages), new document sources, and a new, ninth document language, Russian, led to a wide variety of work being conducted in this campaign. This paper discusses the tracks that have been offered since the beginnings of CLEF, and that still have the highest participation, i.e. the ad-hoc and domain-specific tracks. Collectively, these tracks attracted 33 participating groups who submitted more than 400 experiments. This overview gives a brief description of the tracks and tasks, and summarizes the principal research results. A discussion of the validity of the results, in terms of the completeness of the relevance assessments used in the test collection and of the statistical significance of some of the results, is also given.

1 Introduction

The fourth CLEF campaign was held in 2003. Overviews of earlier CLEF campaigns have been published elsewhere (see [2] for CLEF 2000, [3] for CLEF 2001, and [4] for CLEF 2002). CLEF, a successor to the TREC-6 to TREC-8 cross-language information retrieval (CLIR) tracks [9], has over the years grown into an evaluation forum with more than 40 participating groups. While the number of participants has increased most explosively in the first two years of CLEF campaigns, lately the main area of growth has been in the number of distinct experiments submitted for evaluation. Since this growth in number is coupled with added complexity of the experiments, the 2003 campaign has produced a very "rich" set of results. This paper attempts to provide an overview of the activities in the tracks[1] that have been offered since the beginning of the CLEF campaign, sometimes referred to as the "main" tracks: the "multilingual track" (multilingual information retrieval on news documents), the "bilingual track" (cross-language information retrieval on news documents for certain language pairs), the "monolingual track" (monolingual

---

[1] The campaign is structured into several tracks, which explore different research questions.

C. Peters et al. (Eds.): CLEF 2003, LNCS 3237, pp. 44–63, 2004.
© Springer-Verlag Berlin Heidelberg 2004

information retrieval on news documents)[2] and the "domain-specific track" (monolingual and bilingual domain-specific information retrieval).

In addition to these "main" tracks, CLEF 2003 featured an "interactive track" (first introduced in 2001), a "multi-language question answering track" (new for 2003), a "cross-language speech retrieval track" (first pilot experiments in 2002), and a cross-language image retrieval track (new for 2003). These tracks, and the experiments conducted for them, become increasingly important to CLEF as research into cross-language information retrieval (CLIR) expands into new areas. The results of these tracks are discussed elsewhere ([13], [12], [8], [6]).

Apart from briefly discussing the setup of the tracks, the participants, and how the experiments are distributed (Section 2), the paper mainly attempts to investigate the principal research trends that can be observed (Section 3), summarize the results obtained from the participants' experiments (Sections 4) and explore the statistical significance of these results (Section 5). It also analyzes the validity of the test collection that was produced for the campaign (Section 6). The paper closes with a summary and conclusions (Section 7).

2 Tracks and Tasks

The tracks and tasks covered in this paper were defined as follows:

- *Multilingual Track*: In a change from 2002, two different multilingual tasks were offered: the Multilingual-8 task, which consisted of searching a document collection containing documents written in eight languages, and the Multilingual-4 task, which restricted the document collection to four core languages. A grand total of nearly 1.6 million documents in the languages Dutch, English, Finnish, French, German, Italian, Spanish and Swedish made up the multilingual collection. English, French, German and Spanish were designated as the core languages for the smaller Multilingual-4 task. The multilingual track was the "main" activity of the campaign. Participants had a free choice of 10 topic languages[3] (document languages plus Chinese and Russian).
- *Bilingual Track*: A few handpicked pairs of languages were offered as bilingual tasks. The pairs were selected to represent different (research) challenges:
  - o *Finnish to German*, as a pair covering the Uralic and Germanic languages, with both languages rich in compound words,
  - o *Italian to Spanish*, as a pair of closely related Romance languages, potentially opening the possibility for language-independent approaches,
  - o *German to Italian*, as a pair of widely used languages covering both the Germanic and Romance groups, and
  - o *French to Dutch*, to cater for a traditionally strong community of Dutch groups participating in the CLEF campaign.

---

[2] The multilingual, bilingual and monolingual tracks are sometimes referred to collectively as "ad-hoc" tracks.

[3] A eleventh language, Japanese, was added post-campaign.

- o In addition, bilingual retrieval from any topic language to English was offered specifically for newcomers; plus bilingual retrieval to Russian from any language was offered as Russian was a new collection in the 2003 campaign.
- *Monolingual Track:* Participants had a choice of 8 topic languages (DE, ES, FI, FR, IT, NL, RU, SV)4. For this track, the query language was identical to the document language.
- *Domain-specific Track (GIRT):* The track studied domain-specific retrieval, with a choice of three topic languages (DE, EN, RU). Retrieval took place on German and English abstracts and documents from the domain of social sciences. An accompanying thesaurus was available.

Participants sent their results ("runs") in the form of ranked lists containing those documents that best match a given query. For reasons of tractability by the campaign organizers, the maximum number of runs for each task was limited.

In total, 42 groups from 14 different countries participated in one or more of the tracks and tasks that were offered for CLEF 2003 (see Table 1). Of these, 33 groups submitted at least one experiment for the ad-hoc tracks. Table 2 compares the number of participants and experiments to those of earlier TREC CLIR tracks [9] and earlier CLEF campaigns. While the first two CLEF campaigns in 2000 [2] and 2001 [3] were clearly a breakthrough in promoting larger participation, especially from European groups, the growth in the number of participants has slowed somewhat since. The growth has now shifted to the number of experiments submitted by the participants. CLEF has a high retention rate of participants as evidenced in Table 1.

A total of 415 experiments were submitted, an increase of more than 45% compared to last year, and more than double the total of the 2001 campaign. A breakdown into the individual tasks can be found in Table 3.

Nine different query languages were used for experiments (DE, EN, ES, FI, FR, IT, NL, RU, SV). English, French, German, Italian and Spanish were the most popular query languages. The most popular query language was English, with many people using it for multilingual experiments. Table 4 shows a summary of the query languages and their use.

Queries were provided to participants in the form of "topics", which are textual formulations of statements of information need by hypothetical users. CLEF topics are structured into multiple fields (title, description and narrative), which provide increasingly more detailed representations of a search request. The title typically contains one to three words, whereas the description is usually one sentence long. The narrative, the longest representation, contains an elaborate formulation of the information need, which is several sentences long. Participants constructed queries for their systems either automatically or manually out of these topic statements, using any combination of the fields.

---

[4] The paper uses ISO 639 language codes to abbreviate names of languages in some of the lists.

Table 1. List of CLEF 2003 participants. The stars (*,**,***) denote the number of previous campaigns that a participant has taken part in

BBN/UMD (US)	OCE Tech. BV (NL) **
CEA/LIC2M (FR)	Ricoh (JP)
CLIPS/IMAG (FR)	SICS (SV) **
CMU (US) *	SINAI/U Jaen (ES) **
Clairvoyance Corp. (US) *	Tagmatica (FR) *
COLE Group/U La Coruna (ES) *	U Alicante (ES) **
Daedalus (ES)	U Buffalo (US)
DFKI (DE)	U Amsterdam (NL) **
DLTG U Limerick (IE)	U Exeter (UK) **
ENEA/La Sapienza (IT)	U Oviedo/AIC (ES)
Fernuni Hagen (DE)	U Hildesheim (DE) *
Fondazione Ugo Bordoni (IT) *	U Maryland (US) ***
Hummingbird (CA) **	U Montreal/RALI (CA) ***
IMS U Padova (IT) *	U Neuchâtel (CH) **
ISI U Southern Cal (US)	U Sheffield (UK) ***
ITC-irst (IT) ***	U Sunderland (UK)
JHU-APL (US) ***	U Surrey (UK)
Kermit (FR/UK)	U Tampere (FI) ***
Medialab (NL) **	U Twente (NL) ***
NII (JP)	UC Berkeley (US) ***
National Taiwan U (TW) **	UNED (ES) **

Table 2. Growth in the number of participants and experiments

Year	# Participants	# Experiments
TREC-6 (1997)	13	$(95)^5$
TREC-7 (1998)	9	27
TREC-8 (1999)	12	45
CLEF 2000	20	95
CLEF 2001	31+3	198
CLEF 2002	34+3	282
CLEF 2003	33+9	415

A large majority of runs (374 out of 415 runs) used only the title and description fields of the topics for query construction, ignoring the narrative part. Participants were required to submit at least one title+description ("TD") run per task tackled in order to increase comparability. Without doubt, this has contributed to the large

---

[5] In TREC6, only bilingual retrieval was offered, which resulted in a large number of runs combining different pairs of languages [9]. Starting with TREC7, multilingual runs were introduced, which usually consist of multiple runs for the individual languages that are merged. The number of experiments for TREC6 is therefore not directly comparable to later years.

number of runs using this combination of topic fields. Furthermore, there may have been a perception by the participants that shorter queries were more "realistic" for many operational settings. Even so, using all topic fields ("TDN", longest possible queries) was the second most popular choice (21 runs). 12 runs used only the title field ("T", resulting in very short queries). The remaining runs used more "exotic" combinations.

Table 3. Experiments listed by track/task

Task	# Participants	# Runs
Multilingual-8	7	33
Multilingual-4	14	53
Bilingual FI->DE	2	3
Bilingual X->EN	3	15
Bilingual IT->ES	9	25
Bilingual DE->IT	8	21
Bilingual FR->NL	3	6
Bilingual X->RU	2	9
Monolingual DE	13	30
(Monolingual EN)	(5)	11
Monolingual ES	16	38
Monolingual FI	7	13
Monolingual FR	16	36
Monolingual IT	13	27
Monolingual NL	11	32
Monolingual RU	5	23
Monolingual SV	8	18
Domain-Specific GIRT->DE	4	16
Domain-Specific GIRT->EN	2	6

Table 4. Experiments listed by query/topic language

Language	# Runs
DE German	69
EN English	97
ES Spanish	54
FI Finnish	16
FR French	49
IT Italian	54
NL Dutch	32
RU Russian	26
SV Swedish	18

All tracks covered in this paper used a distinction between "automatic" and "manual" runs, based on the methodology employed for query construction. The overwhelming majority of experiments were conducted using automatic query construction. Manual experiments are useful in establishing baselines and in improving the overall quality of relevance assessment pools. Therefore, an increase in the number of these experiments would be welcome; especially since they also tend to focus on interesting aspects of the retrieval process that are not usually covered by batch evaluations. However, since manual experiments tend to be a resource-intensive undertaking, it seems likely that most of the participants interested in this form of work concentrated their efforts on experiments for the interactive track.

3 Characteristics of the Experiments

Table 5 gives some key figures for the CLEF 2003 multilingual document collection. The collection was extended over the 2002 version by adding new documents in English, French, German, Italian, Spanish and Russian. This new data contains news stories from the year 1995, thereby expanding the coverage of the CLEF collection, which to date had mainly covered 1994. The new English collection, from the Glasgow Herald, for the first time introduced British English text to the campaign (as opposed to the texts from the Los Angeles Times that had been used exclusively as source for English documents in previous campaigns). Russian was added as a new language in 2003, which is of special interest due to its use of a different character set from the other languages used in CLEF (Cyrillic versus Latin character set). As can be seen from Table 5, the 2003 collection compares well to the widely used TREC-7 and TREC-8 ad-hoc retrieval test collections, both in terms of size and with regard to the amount of topics and relevance assessments. Experiments ("runs") for the multilingual, bilingual and monolingual tasks were conducted by retrieving documents from all or part of this collection.

With CLEF building on earlier campaigns organized either by the same organizers or under different umbrellas (TREC in North America, NTCIR in East Asia), there are participants that have worked on this type of evaluation for several years. Open discussion at the workshop and public availability of the proceedings result in CLEF acting as a "trendsetter", and methods that work well one year are adapted eagerly by other participants in following campaigns. This, and the bringing together of a community of interested researchers, are clearly key contributions that CLEF (and TREC and NTCIR) plays in distributing successful ideas for cross-language retrieval.

Table 5. Characteristics of the CLEF 2003 multilingual document collection

Collection	# Partici- pants.	# Lang.	# Docs.	Size in MB	# Docs. Assessed	# Topic.	# Assessed/ Topic
CLEF 2003	33+9	9	1,611,178	4124	188,475	60	~3100
CLEF 2002	34+3	8	1,138,650	3011	140,043	50	~2900
CLEF 2001	31+3	6	940,487	2522	97,398	50	1948
CLEF 2000	20	4	368,763	1158	43,566	40	1089
TREC-8 CLIR	12	4	698,773	1620	23,156	28	827
TREC-8 AdHoc	41	1	528,155	1904	86,830	50	1736
TREC-7 AdHoc	42+4	1	528,155	1904	~80,000	50	~1600

We have tried to highlight some of the trends that we can discern from the experiments conducted for the 2003 campaign:

- Participants spent a lot of effort on detailed fine-tuning per language, per weighting scheme, and per translation resource type
- Groups thought about (generic) ways to "scale" up to new languages
- Merging of different (intermediate) retrieval results continued to be a hot issue; however, no merging approach besides well-known simple ones has been widely adopted yet. Newer methods that have been adopted by groups include collection size-based merging and 2-step merging.
- A few resources were very popular, among them the "Snowball" stemmers, stopword lists by Université de Neuchâtel, some machine translation systems, dictionaries by "Freelang", and others.
- Query translation is still the favorite choice to cross the language barrier.
- Stemming and decompounding are still actively debated; and a slightly increase in the use of linguistics can be discerned.
- Monolingual tracks were "hotly contested", and for some (especially the most frequently used) languages, very similar performance was obtained by the top groups.
- The new definition of the bilingual tasks forced people to think about "inconvenient" language pairs, stimulating some of the most original work.
- Returning participants usually improve performance. There seems to be an advantage for "veteran groups". This is especially true for the large Multilingual-8 task, where such veteran groups dominated. It seems that scaling up to this many languages takes its time. The Multilingual-4 task was very competitive.
- Some blueprints to "successful CLIR" seem now to be in place, and some of the "older" systems resemble each other. There is a trend towards systems combining different types of translation resources. The question arises as to whether we are headed towards a monoculture of CLIR systems.

For a detailed discussion of these and other features of the 2003 experiments, please refer to the individual participants' papers in this volume.

4 Results

The individual results of the participants are reported in detail in this volume and in the appendix to the Working Notes [7], which were distributed to the participants at the CLEF 2003 workshop and are also available on the CLEF website. The focus of this paper and the number of experiments submitted make it impossible to provide exhaustive lists of all individual results. In the following, we summarize the results for the multilingual, bilingual, monolingual and domain-specific track briefly, emphasizing on comparisons between different groups.

4.1 Multilingual Track

The multilingual track is the hardest track to complete in CLEF and is therefore the main focus of the activities. In CLEF 2003, the track was divided into two tasks, the Multilingual-8 and Multilingual-4 task. Seven groups submitted 33 runs to the Multilingual-8 task, a very encouraging number considering the difficulties in handling so many languages simultaneously. Figure 1 shows the best entries of the five top performing groups in terms of average precision figures. Only entries using the title+description topic field combination were used for this comparison. Multilingual-4, the smaller task, had double the number of participants, namely fourteen. These groups submitted a grand total of 53 runs for the task (Figure 2).

As can be seen, there is a greater difference in the top performances for the Multilingual-8 track than for Multilingual-4. Clearly, long-time participants had an advantage in the larger task. The results for Multilingual-4 are very close, showing that groups have a good understanding of how to tune their systems well to the most popular languages. The top entries for the large multilingual task used elaborate combination approaches that help them handle the difficulties of the languages (see e.g. [5], [15], [11]).

4.2 Bilingual Track

The 2003 campaign offered a newly defined bilingual track that was structured into four subtasks related to specific language pairs, an additional subtask for newcomers only (bilingual retrieval to English) and a last subtask for bilingual

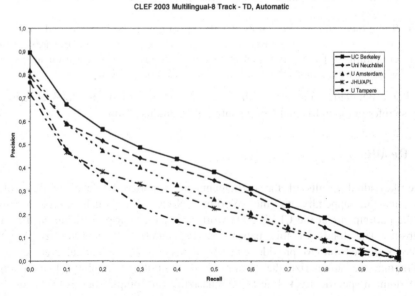

Fig. 1. Best performing entries of the top five participants for the large Multilingual-8 task. The precision/recall curve, giving precision values at varying levels of recall, is shown. Only experiments using the title+description topic fields are included

retrieval to Russian. This was a departure from 2002, where the CLEF consortium responded to numerous requests from participants and opened the bilingual track to all eight target languages (DE, ES, FI, FR, IT, NL, SV; and EN for newcomers or under special conditions only). While allowing for added flexibility in testing the systems on the participants' part, this decision made comparing different bilingual experiments somewhat harder, since experiments on different target languages use different document sets. It was therefore necessary to investigate eight different result sets, one for each target language.

The introduction of specific language pairs led to a larger number of participants per pair, while allowing to concentrate on specific research issues associated with the choice of the languages. Table 6 shows the best entries by the top five performing participants for each target language, including only runs using the mandatory title+description topic field combination.

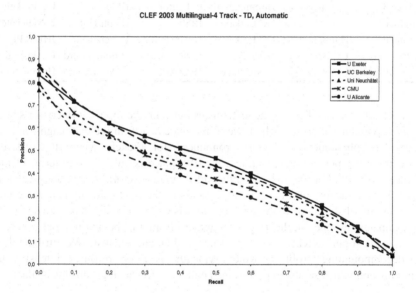

Fig. 2. Best performing entries of the top five participants for the Multilingual-4 task. The precision/recall curve, giving precision values at varying levels of recall, is shown. Only experiments using the title+description topic fields are included

Table 6. Best entries for the bilingual track. At most the top five participants for each target language (title+description topic fields only) are shown

Target Lang.	1st	2nd	3rd	4th	5th
Biling FI->DE	UC Berkeley	JHU/APL			
Biling X->EN	Daedalus	IMS/U Padua			
Biling IT->ES	U Alicante	UC Berkeley	CMU	IRST	JHU/APL
Biling DE->IT	JHU/APL	U Exeter	CMU	UC Berkeley	U Amsterdam
Biling FR->NL	JHU/APL	U Amsterdam	UC Berkeley		
Biling X->RU	UC Berkeley	U Amsterdam			
Biling FI->DE	UC Berkeley	JHU/APL			

4.3 Monolingual Track

The CLEF 2003 campaign offered monolingual retrieval for all target languages besides English. Again, Table 7 summarizes the best entries of the top five performing groups for the title+description topic field combination.

Table 7. Best entries for the monolingual track. The top five participants for each target language (title+description topic fields only) are shown

Target Lang.	1st	2nd	3rd	4th	5th
DE German	Hummingbird	UC Berkeley	U Exeter	U Neuchâtel	U Amsterdam
ES Spanish	F. U. Bordoni	U Neuchâtel	IRST	Hummingbird	Ricoh/USL
FI Finnish	Hummingbird	UC Berkeley	JHU/APL	U Neuchâtel	U Amsterdam
FR French	U Neuchâtel	Hummingbird	F. U. Bordoni	IRST	UC Berkeley
IT Italian	F. U. Bordoni	UC Berkeley	IRST	Ricoh/USL	U Neuchâtel
NL Dutch	Hummingbird	UC Berkeley	U Amsterdam	U Neuchâtel	JHU/APL
RU Russian	UC Berkeley	JHU/APL	U Neuchâtel	Hummingbird	U Amsterdam
SV Swedish	UC Berkeley	U Neuchâtel	JHU/APL	U Amsterdam	Hummingbird

As clearly seen in Table 8 the differences between the top performers for some of the most popular languages, which were introduced early in the campaigns, are quite small. This phenomenon is most pronounced for French, where the difference between the top performing group and the fifth place is only 2.4% in terms of mean average precision. For the more recently added languages, differences are greater, and thus the potential for substantial improvements in the next campaigns may be more. An exception of some sort to these conclusions is German, which has been adopted by the campaign as one of the target languages from the beginning, but where the difference is slightly greater than for French, Italian and Spanish. We attribute this to the decompounding problem, which typically is more resource intensive than stemming and which seems to pose some challenges to which groups must adapt.

Table 8. Percentual difference between the best performing experiment of the top placed group and the best performing experiment of the fifth placed group in terms of mean average precision

Task	Diff. To 5th Place
Monolingual DE	+12.3%
Monolingual ES	+7.3%
Monolingual FI	+17.2%
Monolingual FR	+2.4%
Monolingual IT	+9.1%
Monolingual NL	+10.4%
Monolingual RU	+28.0%
Monolingual SV	+25.3%

4.4 Domain-Specific Retrieval Track

The domain-specific track attracted fewer participants and had fewer entries than the other tracks discussed in this paper. We again give a summary of the best entries of the top performing groups for the title+description topic field combination (Table 9).

Table 9. Best entries for the domain-specific track. The top five participants for each target language (title+description topic fields only) are shown

Target Lang.	1st	2nd	3rd	4th	5th
GIRT->DE	UC Berkeley	U Amsterdam	FU Hagen	ENEA	
GIRT->EN	UC Berkeley	ENEA			

The smaller number of participants makes it difficult to draw overall conclusions. Indeed, the performance obtained by the groups was very dissimilar, probably due to a mixture of monolingual and bilingual experiments and due to the different degree of tuning for the characteristics of the domain-specific data. A detailed description of the different experiments for the domain-specific track can be found in the respective papers contained in this volume.

5 Statistical Significance Testing

The CLEF campaigns use, for reasons of practicality, a limited number of queries (60 in 2003; up from an initial 40 in 2000 and 50 in 2001 and 2002), which are intended to represent a more or less appropriate sample of all possible queries that users would want to ask from the collection. When the goal is to validate how well results can be expected to hold beyond this particular set of queries, statistical testing can help to determine what differences between runs appear to be real as opposed to differences that are due to sampling issues. We aim to identify runs with results that are significantly different from the results of other runs. "Significantly different" in this context means that the difference among the performance scores for the runs in question appear greater than what might be expected by pure chance. As with all statistical testing, conclusions will be qualified by an error probability, which was chosen to be 0.05 in the following. We have designed our analysis to follow closely the methodology used by a similar analysis carried out for TREC [17].

Using the IR-STAT-PAK tool [1], a statistical analysis of the results for the multilingual track was carried out for the first time after the 2001 campaign. We have repeated this analysis in 2002, and expanded it for 2003. The tool provides an Analysis of Variance (ANOVA), which is the parametric test of choice in such situations but requires that some assumptions concerning the data be checked. Hull [10] provides details of these; in particular, the scores in question should be approximately normally distributed and their variance has to be approximately the same for all runs. IR-STAT-PAK uses the Hartley test to verify the equality of variances. In the case of the CLEF multilingual collection, it indicates that the assumption is violated. For such cases, the program offers an arcsine transformation,

$$f(x) = \arcsin(\sqrt{x})$$

which Tague-Sutcliffe [16] recommends for use with Precision/Recall measures, and which we have therefore applied.

The ANOVA test proper only determines if there is at least one pair of runs that exhibit a statistical difference. Following a significant ANOVA, various comparison procedures can be employed to investigate significant differences. IR-STAT-PAK uses the Tukey T test for grouping the runs.

One way to present the overall results is in tabular form, which we chose for the following presentation of the analysis of the Multilingual-8 and Multilingual-4 tasks.

Looking at the result (Table 10 and Table 11), all runs that are included in the same group (denoted by "X") do not have a significantly different performance. All runs scoring below a certain group perform significantly worse than at least the top entry of that group. Likewise, all runs scoring above a certain group perform significantly better than at least the bottom entry in that group. To determine all runs that perform significantly worse than a certain run, determine the rightmost group that includes the run. All runs scoring below the bottom entry of that group are significantly worse. Conversely, to determine all runs that perform significantly better than a given run, determine the leftmost group that includes the run. All runs that score better than the top entry of that group perform significantly better.

It is well-known that it is fairly difficult to detect statistically significant differences between retrieval runs based on 60 queries [17], [18]. While 60 queries remains a good choice based on practicality for doing relevance assessments, statistical testing would be one of the areas to benefit most from having additional topics. This fact is addressed by the measures taken to ensure stability of at least part of the document collection across different campaigns, which allows participants to run their system on aggregate sets of queries for post-hoc experiments.

For the 2003 campaign, we conducted statistical analysis of the "pools of experiments" for all target collections of the multilingual, bilingual and monolingual tasks: the eight language multilingual collection (Table 10), the four language multilingual collection (Table 11), and the eight non-English monolingual collections (Table 12). We do not report numbers for the English monolingual and domain-specific collections, as there were too few experiments to produce a consistent picture.

For the 2003 campaign, the picture is somewhat less clear than in 2002, where we observed a fairly clear division of runs into performance groups for the multilingual track.

For the Multilingual-8 task, there is some division between the entries by the top performing groups UC Berkeley, Université de Neuchâtel and University of Amsterdam compared to the rest of the groups. This division is slightly less clear between U Amsterdam and JHU/APL as the third and fourth group, respectively, but fairly pronounced between UC Berkeley, U Neuchâtel and the other groups from U Tampere downwards. As mentioned before, veteran groups have submitted the best performing experiments.

Table 10. Results of statistical analysis (ANOVA) on the experiments submitted for the large Multilingual-8 track. All experiments, regardless of topic language or topic fields, are included. Results are therefore only valid for comparison of individual pairs of runs, and not in terms of absolute performance

Arcsine-transformed average precision values, Run IDs										
0.63941	UniNEml	X								
0.63699	bkmul8en3	X								
0.59807	bkmul8en2	X	X							
0.58374	bkmul8en1	X	X	X						
0.57940	UniNEml4	X	X	X						
0.57933	UniNEml1	X	X	X						
0.54374	UniNEml2	X	X	X	X					
0.54219	UniNEml3	X	X	X	X					
0.53290	UAmsC03EnM8SS4G	X	X	X	X					
0.53080	UAmsC03EnM84GiSb	X	X	X	X					
0.51692	UAmsC03EnM8SS4G6		X	X	X	X				
0.47626	UAmsC03EnM84Gr			X	X	X	X			
0.47082	UAmsC03EnM84Gr6			X	X	X	X			
0.46960	aplmuen8b			X	X	X	X			
0.46030	aplmuen8a				X	X	X			
0.41480	UTAmul1					X	X	X		
0.41167	UTAmul4					X	X	X		
0.41052	UTAmul5					X	X	X		
0.41036	UTAmul2					X	X	X		
0.40982	UTAmul3					X	X	X		
0.39399	uja03LargeRRPrf					X	X			
0.37298	uja03LargeRSV2m						X	X	X	
0.37126	uja03LargeRR						X	X	X	
0.33118	UBENmultirf3							X	X	
0.33014	uja03LargeRSV2							X	X	
0.32183	UBENmultirf1							X	X	
0.30814	UBENmultirf2							X	X	
0.26865	UBESmultirf3								X	
0.26865	UBESmultishort2								X	
0.26667	UBESmultirf1								X	
0.26417	UBESmultirf2								X	
0.14714	UBENmultishort3									X
0.14631	UBENmultishort2									X

Table 11. Results of statistical analysis (ANOVA) on the experiments submitted for the Multilingual-4 track. All experiments, regardless of topic language or topic fields, are included. Results are therefore only valid for comparison of individual pairs of runs

Arcsine-transformed avg. precision values, Run IDs															
0.70441	exemulttc	X													
0.69861	bkmul4en3	X													
0.69533	UniNEms	X													
0.67936	bkmul4en2	X	X												
0.65612	UniNEms4	X	X	X											
0.64085	cmuM4lowfbre	X	X	X	X										
0.63730	bkmul4en1	X	X	X	X										
0.63625	UniNEms1	X	X	X	X										
0.63352	cmuM4fbre	X	X	X	X										
0.63250	UniNEms2	X	X	X	X										
0.63069	UniNEms3	X	X	X	X										
0.60997	exemult4s	X	X	X	X	X									
0.60953	exemult4p	X	X	X	X	X									
0.60488	exemult4u	X	X	X	X	X									
0.59983	IRn-m-exp-sp	X	X	X	X	X									
0.59953	IRn-mi-exp-sp	X	X	X	X	X	X								
0.59253	cmuM4lowfb	X	X	X	X	X	X	X							
0.58839	IRn-m-exp-nsp	X	X	X	X	X	X	X							
0.58441	UAmsC03EnM44GiSb	X	X	X	X	X	X	X							
0.58138	exemult4d	X	X	X	X	X	X	X							
0.57950	UAmsC03EnM4SS4G	X	X	X	X	X	X	X							
0.55475	IRSTen2xx_1		X	X	X	X	X	X	X						
0.55253	IRn-m-nexp-sp		X	X	X	X	X	X	X						
0.54866	IRSTen2xx_2		X	X	X	X	X	X	X						
0.54757	IRSTen2xx_3			X	X	X	X	X	X						
0.54495	IRn-m-nexp-nsp			X	X	X	X	X	X						
0.54285	IRSTen2xx_4			X	X	X	X	X	X						
0.53832	UHImlt4R2			X	X	X	X	X	X						
0.53664	UAmsC03EnM44Gr			X	X	X	X	X	X						
0.53051	cmuM4fb			X	X	X	X	X	X						
0.52895	spxxQTordirect			X	X	X	X	X	X						
0.52671	aplmuen4a		X	X	X	X	X	X	X						
0.51804	UHImlt4R1			X	X	X	X	X	X						
0.51127	aplmuen4b			X	X	X	X	X	X						
0.48759	spxxQTor3				X	X	X	X	X	X					
0.46800	uja03ShortRRPrf				X	X	X	X	X	X					
0.46458	spxxQTdoc					X	X	X	X	X	X				
0.44014	uja03ShortRR						X	X	X	X	X	X			
0.42893	uja03ShortRSV2m						X	X	X	X	X	X			
0.42679	spxxQTorall						X	X	X	X	X	X			
0.39626	xrce_ML4_run2							X	X	X	X	X			
0.36998	uja03ShortRSV2								X	X	X	X	X		
0.34886	NTUm4TopnTpCw									X	X	X	X		
0.33893	NTUm4TopnLinear									X	X	X	X	X	
0.33333	NTUm4TopnTp										X	X	X	X	
0.33148	NTUm4Topn											X	X	X	
0.31548	lic2mes1											X	X	X	
0.26438	lic2mde1												X	X	
0.25501	spxxQTorallr												X	X	
0.24534	lic2mfr2												X	X	
0.24140	lic2mfr1												X	X	
0.21585	lic2men1													X	
0.00017	kcca300														X

Table 12. Results of statistical analysis (ANOVA) on the experiments submitted for the individual monolingual subcollections. The table shows the ratio of groups that submitted at least one experiment with a performance difference that is not statistically significant compared to the top performance against the total number of groups submitting experiments for that target collection

Target collection	Number of groups in the "top group" of the statistical analysis/ total number of groups
"DE" German	10/13
"ES" Spanish	15/18
"FI" Finnish	6/7
"FR" French	15/16
"IT" Italian	13/16
"NL" Dutch	9/11
"RU" Russian	5/5
"SV" Swedish	4/8

Multilingual-4 was very competitive, with many groups obviously already having a good understanding of the languages involved. This leads to a fairly continuous field of performances, with no clear drop-offs between groups. The top six groups submitted at least one experiment with a performance difference that is not statistically significant with regard to the top performing entry (by University of Exeter).

In addition to the two multilingual tasks, we have also examined non-English monolingual target collections. These analyses include both the respective monolingual runs, but also the bilingual runs to that target language, i.e. the German analysis contains both German monolingual and Finnish->German bilingual experiments. The fact that the monolingual tasks were so competitive this year, and that many groups submitted experiments with very similar performance, is also reflected in this analysis, with practically all groups submitting at least one experiment with a performance difference from the top performing experiment that is not statistically significant (Table 12). Note, however, that experiments of very different character are mixed in this analysis.

6 Coverage of Relevance Assessments

The results reported in the CLEF campaigns rely heavily on the concept of judging the relevance of documents with respect to the topics. The relevance of a document is judged by human assessors, making this a costly undertaking. These relevance assessments are then used for the calculation of the recall/precision figures that underlie the graphs and figures presented to the participants.

Their central importance for the calculation of many popular evaluation measures means that relevance assessments are not without critics. Generally, concerns mentioned focus mostly on two aspects: the "quality" and the "coverage" ("completeness") of the assessments.

The first concern stems from the subjective nature of relevance, which can lead to disagreements between different assessors or even when the same assessor judges a document twice. Such disagreements can emerge from, among other things, personal bias of the judge, or a lack of understanding of the topics and documents. There is no "solution" for obtaining universal relevance judgments. Rather, researchers that rely upon the results from an evaluation campaign such as CLEF have to be aware of this issue and its implications. Numerous studies have analyzed the impact of disagreement in judging on the validity of evaluation results. These studies generally conclude that as long as sufficient consistency is maintained during judging, the ranking and comparison of systems is stable even if the absolute performance values calculated on the basis of the assessments change. The quality and consistency of the assessments in CLEF is ensured by following a well-proven methodology based on TREC experience. More details of relevance assessment processes can be found in [14].

The problem of coverage arises from practical considerations in the production of the relevance assessments. While it is comparatively easy to judge a substantial part of the top-ranked results submitted by participants, it is much harder to judge the documents that were not part of any of the submitted result sets, since the number of such documents is usually far greater than that of the documents retrieved in result sets. This is especially the case with today's large test collections, such as used in CLEF. Judging the non-retrieved documents is necessary to calculate some evaluation measures such as recall.

In order to keep costs manageable, only documents included and highly ranked in at least one result set are judged for relevance (with the union of all judged result sets forming a "document pool" for assessment). This implies that some relevant documents potentially go undetected if they are not retrieved by any of the participating systems. The assertion is that a sufficient number of diverse systems will turn up most relevant documents this way. Figures calculated based on these "limited" assessments are then a good approximation of theoretical figures based on complete assessments. A potential problem is the usability of the resulting test collection for the evaluation of a system that did not contribute to this "pool of judged documents". If such a system retrieves a substantial number of unjudged documents that are relevant, but went undetected, it is unfairly penalized when calculating the evaluation measures. An investigation into whether the assessments for the CLEF multilingual collection provide sufficient coverage follows below.

One way to analyze the coverage of the relevance judgments is by focusing on the "unique relevant documents" [20]. For this purpose, a unique relevant document is defined as a document that was judged relevant with respect to a specific topic, but that would not have been part of the pool of judged documents had a certain group not participated in the evaluation, i.e., only one group retrieved the document with a score high enough to have it included in the judgment pool. This addresses the concern that systems not directly participating in the evaluation are unfairly penalized. Subtracting relevant documents only found by a certain group, and then reevaluating the results for this group, simulates the scenario that this group was a non-participant. The smaller the change in performance that is observed, the higher is the probability that the relevance assessments are sufficiently complete.

This kind of analysis has been run by the CLEF consortium since the 2000 campaign for the multilingual track. In 2002, we expanded the analysis to include an investigation of the subcollections formed by the individual target languages. A total of $n+1$ sets of relevance assessments are used: the original set, and n sets that are built by taking away the relevant documents uniquely found by one specific participant. The results for every experiment are then recomputed using the set without the group-specific relevant documents. We chose the same analysis for 2003. The key figures obtained after rerunning the evaluations can be found in Table 13.

Table 13. Key values of the pool quality analysis: mean and maximum change in average precision when removing the pool contribution of one participant, and associated standard deviation

Track		Mean difference	Max difference	StdDev difference
Multilingual-8	Absolute	0.0005	0.0014	0.0009
	Percentage	0.24%	0.77%	0.51%
Multilingual-4[6]	Absolute	0.0007	0.0025	0.0016
	Percentage	0.33%	2.06%	0.77%
DE German	Absolute	0.0013	0.0038	0.0026
	Percentage	0.29%	1.04%	0.64%
EN English	Absolute	0.0021	0.0052	0.0033
	Percentage	0.73%	2.09%	1.35%
ES Spanish[7]	Absolute	0.0022	0.0109	0.0050
	Percentage	0.52%	3.11%	1.21%
FI Finnish	Absolute	0.0004	0.0011	0.0008
	Percentage	0.09%	0.31%	0.19%
FR French	Absolute	0.0009	0.0070	0.0020
	Percentage	0.19%	1.58%	0.43%
IT Italian	Absolute	0.0010	0.0096	0.0025
	Percentage	0.34%	3.03%	0.79%
NL Dutch	Absolute	0.0016	0.0082	0.0033
	Percentage	0.38%	2.03%	0.80%
RU Russian	Absolute	0.0040	0.0139	0.0053
	Percentage	1.36%	5.92%	1.94%
SV Swedish	Absolute	0.0023	0.0073	0.0053
	Percentage	0.59%	2.02%	1.35%

[6] One experiment that was an extreme outlier in terms of performance was removed before calculation of the Multilingual-4 figures to avoid a non-representative skew in the numbers.

[7] Two experiments that were extreme outliers in terms of performance were removed before calculation of the Spanish figures to avoid a non-representative skew in the numbers.

The quality of a document pool can therefore be judged by the mean performance difference in terms of average precision that is obtained if the pool had been missing the contribution of a specific group. This difference should be as small as possible, indicating that the pool is "sufficiently exhaustive" and that adding more documents to the pool, such as documents found by an additional participant, probably will not substantially influence results and/or rankings. As we also found for all previous campaigns, the pool used for the multilingual tasks is very stable. The maximum change in performance scores is 0.77% for the Multilingual-8, and 2.06% for the Multilingual-4 task. These small differences influence only direct comparisons between systems that have practically identical performance, and where the original performance differences cannot be considered statistically significant in any case. The value of the multilingual pool for reuse in post-hoc experiments should therefore be assured, and the validity of the results reported by CLEF should be given within the inherent limits of interpretation (restricted set of queries, characteristics of evaluation measure and others).

The pools for individual target languages are smaller, since they are restricted to the document set of that language. Only runs for that language, and therefore a smaller number than for the multilingual pool, contributed. As a consequence, it is not surprising that differences found for the individual languages tend to be somewhat higher than for the multilingual pool. We feel, however, that they are still comfortably within acceptable limits, and they do indeed compare favorably with numbers reported for comparable collections in the past [19]. Not surprisingly, the pool for Russian is the least stable, owing to being introduced late in the campaign and having fewer contributions than other languages. There were, as noted in the table, some issues with a few outliers that obfuscate the measures somewhat, but we believe that all pools should be of comparable quality across the other languages.

7 Conclusions

We have reported on the results obtained for the 2003 campaign in the ad-hoc and domain-specific tracks and their interpretation. CLEF 2003 experienced substantial growth in the number of experiments submitted. The paper summarizes the main characteristics of the 415 experiments submitted for the campaign, and discusses trends observed and the principal results. Analysis of statistical significance of performance differences has been conducted for all subcollections formed by the individual languages, as well as for the multilingual tasks, where we provide corresponding tabulated results. Lastly, we investigate the validity of the results by analyzing the completeness of the relevance assessment pools, which is critical for calculating the performance measures used by CLEF.

In summary, we can conclude that, much as for 2002, people adopt each other's ideas and methods across campaigns, and that those returning groups that have the experience to build complex combination systems have performed well in the multilingual tasks. More than ever, for the monolingual track we observe that good performance in a wide variety of target languages requires careful fine tuning for all these languages. The monolingual tasks were extremely competitive this year, with many groups obtaining good performance results.

The ad-hoc tracks, which have been offered since the beginning of the CLEF campaigns, seem to have matured considerably. A challenge will be to determine how to adapt them in the future to continue stimulating new research challenges for the CLIR field.

Statistical analysis allows to qualify and better interpret the results as published by CLEF. As evidenced by an analysis of the experiments that we present, fairly large performance differences are needed to reach a level of statistical significance. This is especially true for the monolingual tasks. For this kind of testing, having a maximum number of queries available is of great benefit. The CLEF consortium strives for stability in the test collections to allow post-hoc experiments with combined resources from several campaigns for this reason.

Finally, the results published by CLEF are only as good as the data they build on. We judge the quality of the relevance assessments by investigating their completeness through pool quality evaluation. We find that the CLEF relevance assessments appear very stable, making them suitable for reuse in post-hoc experiments, and further validating the results published during the campaigns.

Acknowledgments

Thanks go to Carol Peters for corrections to the draft version of this paper.

References

1. Blustein, J.: IR STAT PAK. URL: http://www.csd.uwo.ca/~jamie/IRSP-overview.html
2. Braschler, M.: CLEF 2000 – Overview of Results. In: Cross-Language Information Retrieval and Evaluation. CLEF 2000, LNCS 2069, Springer Verlag (2001) 89-101.
3. Braschler, M.: CLEF 2001 – Overview of Results. In: Evaluation of Cross-Language Information Retrieval Systems. CLEF 2001, LNCS 2406, Springer Verlag (2002) 9-26.
4. Braschler, M.: CLEF 2002 – Overview of Results. In: Advances in Cross-Language Information Retrieval, CLEF 2002, LNCS 2785, Springer Verlag (2003) 9-27.
5. Chen, A., Gey, F. C.: Combining Query Translation and Document Translation in Cross-Language Retrieval. In this volume.
6. Clough, P., Sanderson, M.: The CLEF 2003 Cross Language Image Retrieval Track. In this volume.
7. Cross-Language Evaluation Forum: Results of the CLEF 2003 Cross-Language System Evaluation Campaign. Working Notes for the CLEF 2003 Workshop. Volume II: Appendices. Electronic version available at www.clef-campaign.org.
8. Federico, M., Jones, G. J. F.: The CLEF 2003 Cross-Language Spoken Document Retrieval Track. In this volume.
9. Harman, D., Braschler, M., Hess, M., Kluck, M., Peters, C., Schäuble, P., Sheridan P.: CLIR Evaluation at TREC. In: Cross-Language Information Retrieval and Evaluation. CLEF 2000, LNCS 2069, Springer Verlag (2001) 7-23.

10. Hull, D. A: Using Statistical Testing in the Evaluation of Retrieval Experiments. In: Proceedings of the 16th Annual International ACM SIGIR Conference on Research and Development in Information Retrieval, Pittsburg, USA (1993) 329-338.
11. Kamps, J., Monz, C., de Rijke, M., Sigurbjörnsson, B.: Language-dependent and Language-independent Approaches to Cross-Language Text Retrieval. In this volume.
12. Magnini, B., Romagnoli, S., Vallin, A., Herrera, J., Peñas, A., Peinado, V., Verdejo, F., de Rijke, M.: The Multiple Language Question Answering Track at CLEF 2003. In this volume.
13. Oard, D. W., Gonzalo, J.: The CLEF 2003 Interactive Track. In this volume.
14. Peters, C., Braschler, M.: European Research Letter: Cross-language System Evaluation: The CLEF campaigns, In: Journal of the American Society for Information Science and Technology, 52(12) (2001) 1067-1072.
15. Savoy, J.: Report on CLEF-2003 Multilingual Tracks. In this volume.
16. Tague-Sutcliffe, J.: The Pragmatics of Information Retrieval Experimentation, Revisited. In: Readings in Information Retrieval, Morgan Kaufmann Publishers, San Francisco, CA, USA (1997) 205-216.
17. Tague-Sutcliffe, J., Blustein, J.: A Statistical Analysis of the TREC-3 Data. In: Proc. TREC-3, NIST Special Publication 500-226. Page 385ff, 1994.
18. Voorhees, E., Buckley, C.: The Effect of Topic Set Size on Retrieval Experiment Error. In: Proceedings of the 25th Annual International ACM SIGIR Conference on Research and Development in Information Retrieval (2002) 316-323.
19. Vorhees, E., Harman, D.: Overview of the Eighth Text REtrieval Conference (TREC-8). In: Proc. TREC-8, NIST Special Publication 500-246, (1999) 1-24.
20. Zobel, J.: How reliable are the results of large-scale information retrieval experiments? In: Proceedings of the 21st Annual International ACM SIGIR Conference on Research and Development in Information Retrieval, Pages 307-314, 1998.

Report on CLEF-2003 Multilingual Tracks

Jacques Savoy

Institut interfacultaire d'informatique, Université de Neuchâtel,
Pierre-à-Mazel 7, 2001 Neuchâtel, Switzerland
Jacques.Savoy@unine.ch
http://www.unine.ch/info/clef/

Abstract. For our third participation in the CLEF evaluation campaign, our objective for both multilingual tracks is to propose a new
merging strategy that does not require a training sample to access the
multilingual collection. As a second objective, we want to verify whether
our combined query translation approach would work well with new requests.

1 Introduction

Based on our experiments of last year [1], we are participating in both the small
and large multilingual tracks. In the former, we retrieve documents written in
the English, French, Spanish, and German languages based on a request written
in one given language. Within the large multilingual track, we also had to consider documents written in Italian, Dutch, Swedish, and Finnish. As explained in
Section 2, and for both multilingual tracks, we adopt a combined query translation strategy that is able to produce queries in seven European languages based
on an original request written in English. After this translation phase, we search
in the corresponding document collection using our retrieval scheme (bilingual
retrieval) [1], [2]. In Section 3, we carry out a multilingual information retrieval,
investigating various merging strategies based on the results obtained during our
bilingual searches.

2 Bilingual Information Retrieval

In our experiments, we have chosen the English as the query language from which
requests are to be automatically translated into seven different languages, using
five different machine translation (MT) systems and one bilingual dictionary.
The following freely available translation tools were used:

1. SYSTRAN™   babel.altavista.com/translate.dyn,
2. GOOGLE™   www.google.com/language_tools,
3. FREETRANSLATION™ www.freetranslation.com,
4. INTERTRAN™   www.tranexp.com:2000/InterTran,
5. REVERSO ONLINE™ translation2.paralink.com,
6. BABYLON™   www.babylon.com.

When translating an English request word-by-word using the Babylon bilingual dictionary, we decided to pick only the first translation available (labeled

C. Peters et al. (Eds.): CLEF 2003, LNCS 3237, pp. 64–73, 2004.
© Springer-Verlag Berlin Heidelberg 2004

"Babylon 1"), the rst two terms (labeled "Babylon 2") or the rst three available translations (labeled "Babylon 3"). Table 1 shows the resulting mean average precision using translation tools, using the Okapi probabilistic model and based on word-based indexing scheme. Of course, not all tools can be used for each language, and thus as shown in Table 1 various entries are missing (indicated with the label "N/A"). From this data, we see that usually the Reverso or the FreeTranslation system produce interesting retrieval performance. We found only two translation tools for the Swedish and the Finnish languages but unfortunately their overall performance levels were not very good.

Table 1. Mean average precision of various single translation devices (TD queries, word-based indexing, Okapi model)

Language	Mean average precision						
	French 52 que.	German 56 que.	Spanish 57 que.	Italian 51 que.	Dutch 56 que.	Swedish 54 que.	Finnish 45 que.
Manual	51.64	44.54	48.85	48.80	46.86	40.54	46.54
Systran	40.55	32.86	36.88	35.43	N/A	N/A	N/A
Google	40.67	30.05	36.78	35.42	N/A	N/A	N/A
FreeTrans	**42.70**	31.65	39.37	**37.77**	**29.59**	N/A	N/A
InterTran	33.65	24.51	28.36	33.84	22.04	23.08	9.72
Reverso	42.55	**35.01**	**41.79**	N/A	N/A	N/A	N/A
Babylon 1	41.99	31.62	33.35	33.72	28.81	**26.89**	**9.74**
Babylon 2	39.88	31.67	31.20	27.59	27.19	20.66	N/A
Babylon 3	36.66	30.19	29.98	26.32	24.93	21.67	N/A

A particular translation tool may however produce acceptable translations for a given set of requests, but may perform poorly for other queries. This is a known phenomenon [3], even for manual translations. When studying various (manual) translations of the Bible, D. Knuth noted:

"Well, my rst surprise was that there is a tremendous variability between the di erent translations. I was expecting the translations do di er here and there, but I thought that the essential meaning and syntax of the original language would come through rather directly into English. On the contrary, I almost never found a close match between one translation and another. ... The other thing that I noticed, almost immediately when I had only looked at a few of the 3:16s, was that no translation was consistently the best. Each translation I looked at seemed to have its good moments and its bad moments." [4]

To date we have not been able to detect when a given translation will produce satisfactory retrieval performance and when it will fail. Thus before carrying out the retrieval, we have chosen to generate a translated query by concatenating two or more translations. Table 2 shows the retrieval e ectiveness for such combinations, using the Okapi probabilistic model (word-based indexing). The top

part of the table indicates the exact query translation combination used while
the bottom part shows the mean average precision achieved by our combined
query translation approach. The resulting retrieval performance is better than
the best single translation scheme indicated in the row labeled "Best" (except
for the strategy "Comb 1" in Spanish).

Table 2. Mean average precision of various combined translation devices (TD queries,
word-based indexing, Okapi model)

	Mean average precision						
Language	French 52 que.	German 56 que.	Spanish 57 que.	Italian 51 que.	Dutch 56 que.	Swedish 54 que.	Finnish 45 que.
Comb 1	Rev+Bal	Rev+Bal	Rev+Bal	Fre+Bal	Int+Bal	Int+Bal	Int+Bal
Comb 2	Rev+Sy +Bal	Rev+Sy +Bal	Rev+Sy +Bal	Fre+Go +Bal	Fre+Bal	Int+Ba2	
Comb 2b	Rev+Go +Bal	Rev+Go +Bal	Rev+Go +Bal	Fre+Int +Bal	Fre+Ba2		
Comb 3	Rev+Go+ Fre+Bal	Rev+Sys +Int+Bal	Rev+Go+ Fre+Bal	Fre+Go+ Int+Bal	Fre+Int +Bal		
Comb 3b	Rev+Go+ Int+Bal	Rev+Go+ Int+Bal	Go+Fre+ Sys+Ba2	Fre+Go+ Sys+Bal	Fre+Int +Ba2		
Comb 3c		Rev+Sys +Fre+Bal	Rev+Fre +Bal				
Best	42.70	35.01	41.79	37.77	29.59	26.89	9.74
Comb 1	45.68	37.91	40.77	41.28	31.97	**28.85**	**13.32**
Comb 2	45.20	39.98	42.75	41.10	33.73	26.25	
Comb 2b	45.22	39.74	42.71	41.21	31.19		
Comb 3	**46.33**	39.25	**43.15**	**42.09**	**35.58**		
Comb 3b	45.65	39.02	42.15	40.43	34.45		
Comb 3c		**40.66**	42.72				

As described in [2], for each language, we used a data fusion search strategy
using both the Okapi and Prosit probabilistic models (word-based for French,
Spanish and Italian; word-based, decompounding, and n-grams for German,
Dutch, Swedish and Finnish). The data shown in Table 3 indicates that our
data fusion approaches usually show better retrieval e ectiveness (except for the
Spanish and Italian language) than do the best single IR models used in these
combined approaches (row labeled "Single IR"). Of course, before combining the
result lists, we could also automatically expand the translated queries using a
pseudo-relevance feedback method (Rocchio's approach in the present case). The
resulting mean average precision (as shown in Table 4) results in relatively good
retrieval performance, usually better than the mean average precision depicted
in Table 3, except for the Finnish language.

Table 3. Mean average precision of automatically translated queries using various data fusion approaches (Okapi & Prosit models)

Language	Mean average precision						
	French	German	Spanish	Italian	Dutch	Swedish	Finnish
	52 que.	56 que.	57 que.	51 que.	56 que.	54 que.	45 que.
data fusion on	2 IR	3 IR	2 IR	2 IR	6 IR	6 IR	3 IR
Q combination	Comb 3b	Comb 3b	Comb 2	Comb 3	Comb 3b	Comb 1	Comb 1
Single IR	45.65	39.02	42.75	42.09	34.45	28.85	13.32
combSUM	46.37	43.02	42.09	41.18	**34.84**	**34.96**	**20.95**
combRSV%	46.29	42.68	41.96	40.50	35.51	32.04	17.74
NormN, Eq. 1	**46.30**	**43.06**	41.94	40.52	35.48	32.56	17.93
round-robin	45.94	40.41	42.18	41.42	31.89	29.88	19.35

Table 4. Mean average precision using various data fusion approaches and blind query expansion (Okapi & Prosit models)

Language	Mean average precision						
	French	German	Spanish	Italian	Dutch	Swedish	Finnish
	52 que.	56 que.	57 que.	51 que.	56 que.	54 que.	45 que.
data fusion on	2 IR	3 IR	2 IR	2 IR	6 IR	6 IR	3 IR
Q combination	Comb 3b	Comb 3b	Comb 2	Comb 3	Comb 3b	Comb 1	Comb 1
Single IR	45.65	39.02	42.75	42.09	34.45	28.85	13.32
combSUM	47.82	51.33	47.14	48.58	**43.00**	**42.93**	**19.19**
combRSV%	49.05	51.50	48.43	48.57	41.19	40.73	17.07
NormN, Eq. 1	**49.13**	**51.83**	**48.68**	**48.62**	41.32	41.53	17.21
round-robin	48.94	46.98	48.14	48.62	36.64	37.18	16.97

3 Multilingual Information Retrieval

Using the original and the translated queries, we then search for pertinent items within each of the four and eight corpora respectively. From each of these result lists and using a merging strategy, we need to produce a unique ranked result list showing the retrieved items. As a rst approach, we considered the round-robin (RR) approach whereby we took one document in turn from all individual lists [5].

To account for the document score computed for each retrieved item (denoted RSV_k for document D_k), we might formulate the hypothesis that each collection is searched by the same or a very similar search engine and that the similarity values are therefore directly comparable [6]. Such a strategy is called raw-score merging and produces a nal list sorted by the document score computed by each collection.

Unfortunately the document scores cannot be directly compared, thus as a third merging strategy we normalized the document scores within each collection by dividing them by the maximum score (i.e. the document score of the retrieved record in the rst position) and denoted them "Norm Max". As a variant of this normalized score merging scheme (denoted "NormN"), we may normalize the document RSV_k scores within the ith result list, according to the following formula:

$$NormN\ RSV_k = \frac{RSV_k - MinRSV^i}{MaxRSV^i - MinRSV^i} \tag{1}$$

As a fth merging strategy, we might use the logistic regression [7] to predict the probability of a binary outcome variable, according to a set of explanatory variables [8]. In our current case, we predict the probability of relevance of document D_k given both the logarithm of its rank (indicated by $ln(rank_k)$) and the original document score RSV_k as indicated in Equation 2. Based on these estimated relevance probabilities (computed independently for each language using the S+ software [9]), we sort the records retrieved from separate collections in order to obtain a single ranked list. However, in order to estimate the underlying parameters, this approach requires that a training set be developed. To do so in our evaluations we used the CLEF-2002 topics and their relevance assessments.

$$Prob\ [D_k\ is\ rel\ |\ rank_k, RSV_k] = \frac{e^{\alpha+\beta_1 \cdot ln(rank_k)+\beta_2 \cdot RSV_k}}{1 + e^{\alpha+\beta_1 \cdot ln(rank_k)+\beta_2 \cdot RSV_k}} \tag{2}$$

As a new merging strategy, we suggest merging the retrieved documents according to the Z-score, taken from their document scores. Within this scheme, we need to compute, for the ith result list, the average of the RSV_k (denoted $MeanRSV^i$) and the standard deviation (denoted $StdevRSV^i$). Based on these values, we may normalize the retrieval status value of each document D_k provided by the ith result list, by computing the following formula:

$$NormZ\ RSV_k = \alpha_i \cdot \left[\frac{RSV_k - MeanRSV^i}{StdevRSV^i} + \delta_i\right] \tag{3}$$

$$with\ \delta_i = \frac{MeanRSV^i - MinRSV^i}{StdevRSV^i}$$

within which the value of δ_i is used to generate only positive values, and α_i (usually xed at 1) is used to reflect the retrieval performance of the underlying retrieval model.

The justi cation for such a scheme is as follows. If the RSV_k distribution is linear, as shown in Table 5 and in Figure 1, there is no great di erence between a merging approach based on Equation 1 or the proposed Z-score merging strategy. It is our point of view (and this point must still be veri ed), that such a distribution may appear when the retrieval scheme cannot detect any relevant items. However, after viewing di erent result lists provided from various queries and corpora, it seems that the top-ranked retrieved items usually provide a much greater RSV values than do the others (see Table 6 and Figure 2). Thus, our underlying idea is to emphasis this di erence between these rst retrieved documents and the rest of the retrieved items, by assigning a greater normalized RSV value to these top-ranked documents.

Table 5. Result list #1

Rank	RSV	NormZ	NormN
1	4	3.13049517	1.0
2	3.75	2.90688837	0.92857143
3	3.5	2.68328157	0.85714286
4	3.25	2.45967478	0.78571429
5	3	2.23606798	0.71428571
6	2.75	2.01246118	0.64285714
7	2.5	1.78885438	0.57142857
8	2.25	1.56524758	0.5
9	2	1.34164079	0.42857143
10	1.75	1.11803399	0.35714286
11	1.5	0.89442719	0.28571429
12	1.25	0.67082039	0.21428571
13	1	0.4472136	0.14285714
14	0.75	0.2236068	0.07142857
15	0.5	0	0

Table 7 depicts the mean average precision achieved by each single collection (or language) whether the queries used are manually translated (row labeled "Manual") or translated using our automatic translation scheme (row labeled "Auto.").

Table 8 depicts the retrieval e ectiveness of various merging strategies. This data illustrates that the round-robin (RR) scheme presents an interesting performance and this strategy will be used as a baseline. On the other hand, the raw-score merging strategy results in very poor mean average precision. The normalized score merging based on Equation 1 (NormN) shows degradation over the simple round-robin approach (34.92 vs. 36.71, -4.9% in the small, automatic experiment, and 26.52 vs. 29.81, -11% in the large automatic experiment). Using our logistic model with both the rank and the document score as explanatory variables (row labeled "Logistic"), the resulting mean average precision is better than the round-robin merging strategy.

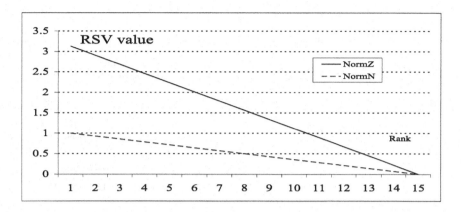

Fig. 1. Graph of normalized RSV (Result list #1)

Table 6. Result list #2

Rank	RSV	NormZ	NormN
1	10	2.57352157	1.0
2	9.9	2.54726114	0.98979592
3	9.8	2.52100072	0.97959184
4	9	2.31091733	0.89795918
5	8.2	2.10083393	0.81632653
6	7	1.78570884	0.69387755
7	6.2	1.57562545	0.6122449
8	4.5	1.12919824	0.43877551
9	3	0.73529188	0.28571429
10	2.1	0.49894806	0.19387755
11	1.4	0.31512509	0.12244898
12	1.2	0.26260424	0.10204082
13	1	0.21008339	0.08163265
14	0.5	0.07878127	0.03061224
15	0.2	0	0

Table 7. Mean average precision of each individual result lists used in our multilingual search

Lang.	Mean average precision							
	English 54 que.	French 52 que.	German 56 que.	Spanish 57 que.	Italian 51 que.	Dutch 56 que.	Swedish 54 que.	Finnish 45 que.
Manual	53.25	52.61	56.03	53.69	51.56	50.24	48.77	54.51
Auto.	53.60	49.13	51.33	48.14	48.58	43.00	42.93	19.19

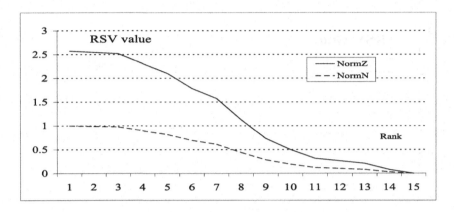

Fig. 2. Graph of normalized RSV (Result list #2)

Table 8. Mean average precision of various merging strategies

	Mean average precision (% change)			
Task	Multi-4		Multi-8	
	EN, FR, DE, SP Small, manual 60 queries	EN, FR, DE, SP Small, auto. 60 queries	+IT, NL, SV, FI Large, manual 60 queries	+IT, NL, SV, FI Large, auto. 60 queries
Merging				
RR, baseline	38.80	36.71	34.18	29.81
Raw-score	6.48 (-83.3%)	16.48 (-55.1%)	11.69 (-65.8%)	13.65 (-54.2%)
Norm Max	16.82 (-56.6%)	33.91 (-7.6%)	16.11 (-52.9%)	25.62 (-14.1%)
NormN (Eq. 1)	16.90 (-56.4%)	34.92 (-4.9%)	15.96 (-53.3%)	26.52 (-11.0%)
Logistic		37.58 (+2.4%)		**32.85** (+10.2%)
Biased RR	42.28 (+9.0%)	**39.20** (+6.8%)	37.24 (+9.0%)	32.26 (+8.2%)
NormZ (Eq 3)	39.44 (+1.6%)	35.07 (-4.5%)	33.40 (-2.3%)	27.43 (-8.0%)
NormZ $\alpha_i = 1.25$	41.94 (+8.1%)	37.46 (+2.0%)	36.80 (+7.7%)	29.72 (-0.3%)
NormZ $\alpha_i = 1.5$	**42.35** (+9.1%)	37.67 (+2.6%)	**37.67** (+10.2%)	29.94 (+0.4%)
NormZ coll-d	41.28 (+6.4%)	37.24 (+1.4%)	36.25 (+6.1%)	29.62 (-0.6%)

Table 9. Mean average precision of various data fusion operators on two or three merging strategies

	Mean average precision (% change)			
Task	Multi-4		Multi-8	
	EN, FR, DE, SP Small, manual bRR, Z-1.5	EN, FR, DE, SP Small, auto. bRR, log., Z-1.5	+IT, NL, SV, FI Large, manual bRR, Z-1.5	+IT, NL, SV, FI Large, auto. bRR, log., Z.15
Data fusion				
combSUM	42.86	38.52	37.47	31.37
combRSV%	**43.49**	38.71	**38.37**	32.65
NormN	43.45	38.68	38.36	32.55
round-robin	43.35	**40.32**	38.36	**33.68**

Table 10. Description and mean average precision (MAP) of our official runs (small multilingual runs in the top part, and large multilingual in the bottom)

Run name	Query Lang.	Form	Type	Merging	Parameters	MAP
UniNEms	English	TD	manual	biased RR		42.28
UniNEms1	English	TD	automatic	Logistic		37.58
UniNEms2	English	TD	automatic	NormZ	α_i = 1.25	37.46
UniNEms3	English	TD	automatic	NormZ	coll-d	37.24
UniNEms4	English	TD	automatic	biased RR		**39.20**
UniNEml	English	TD	manual	biased RR		37.24
UniNEml1	English	TD	automatic	Logistic		**32.85**
UniNEml2	English	TD	automatic	NormZ	α_i = 1.25	29.72
UniNEml3	English	TD	automatic	NormZ	coll-d	29.62
UniNEml4	English	TD	automatic	biased RR		32.26

As a simple alternative, we also suggest a biased round-robin ("Biased RR" or "bRR") approach which extracts not one document per collection per round but one document for the French, English, Italian, Swedish and Finnish corpus and two from the German, Spanish and Dutch collection (representing larger corpora). This merging strategy results in interesting retrieval performance. Finally, the new Z-score merging approach seems to provide generally satisfactory performance. Moreover, we may multiply the normalized Z-score by an α value (performance under the label "NormZ α_i = 1.25" or "NormZ α_i = 1.5"). Under the label "NormZ coll-d", the α values are collection-dependant and are xed as follows: EN: 1, FR: 0.9, DE: 1.2, SP: 1.25, IT: 0.9, NL: 1.15, SV: 0.95, and FI: 0.9.

Of course, we may combine the two or three best merging strategies (performance depicted in Table 8, namely the "biased round-robin" (denoted "bRR"), "logistic regression" (or "log.") and the "NormZ α_i = 1.5" (or "Z-1.5")). Using various data fusion operators, the retrieval e ectiveness of these data fusion approaches are shown in Table 9. Finally, the descriptions of our o cial runs for the small and large multilingual tracks are shown in Table 10.

4   Conclusion

In this fourth CLEF evaluation campaign, we have evaluated various query translation tools, together with a combined translation strategy, resulting in a retrieval performance that is worth considering. However, while a bilingual search can be viewed as easier for some pairs of languages (e.g., from an English query into a French document collection), this task is clearly more complex for other languages pairs (e.g., English to Finnish). On the other hand, the multilingual, and more precisely the large multilingual task, shows how searching documents written in eight di erent languages can represent a challenge. In this case, we have proposed a new simple merging strategy based on the Z-score computed from the document scores, a merging scheme that seems to result in interesting performance.

Acknowledgments. The author would like to thank C. Buckley from SabIR for giving us the opportunity to use the SMART system. This research was supported in part by the Swiss National Science Foundation (grant #21-66 742.01).

References

1. Savoy, J.: Report on CLEF-2002 Experiments: Combining Multiple Sources of Evidence. In: Peters, C., Braschler, M., Gonzalo, J., Kluck, M. (Eds.): Advances in Cross-Language Information Retrieval. Lecture Notes in Computer Science: Vol. 2785. Springer-Verlag, Berlin Heidelberg New York (2003), 66–90
2. Savoy, J.: Report on CLEF-2003 Monolingual Tracks: Fusion of Probabilistic models for Effective Monolingual Retrieval. In *this volume*
3. Savoy, J.: Combining Multiple Strategies for Effective Cross-Language Retrieval. IR Journal, (2004) to appear
4. Knuth, D. E.: Things a Computer Scientist Rarely Talks About. CSLI Publications, Stanford (2001)
5. Voorhees, E. M., Gupta, N. K., Johnson-Laird, B.: The Collection Fusion Problem. In Proceedings of TREC'3, NIST, Publication #500-225, Gaithersburg (1995) 95–104
6. Kwok, K. L., Grunfeld, L., Lewis, D. D.: TREC-3 Ad-hoc, Routing Retrieval and Thresholding Experiments using PIRCS. In Proceedings of TREC'3, NIST Publication #500-225, Gaithersburg (1995) 247–255
7. Hosmer, D.W., Lemeshow, S.: Applied Logistic Regression. 2nd edn. John Wiley, New York (2000)
8. Le Calvé, A., Savoy, J.: Database Merging Strategy based on Logistic Regression. Information Processing & Management, **36** (2000) 341–359
9. Venables, W.N., Ripley, B.D.: Modern Applied Statistics with S-PLUS. Springer, New York (1999)

The Impact of Word Normalization Methods and Merging Strategies on Multilingual IR

Eija Airio, Heikki Keskustalo, Turid Hedlund, and Ari Pirkola

Department of Information Studies,
University of Tampere, Finland
{eija.airio, heikki.keskustalo}@uta.fi,
turid.hedlund@shh.fi, pirkola@tukki.jyu.fi

Abstract. This article deals with both multilingual and bilingual IR. The source language is English, and the target languages are English, German, Finnish, Swedish, Dutch, French, Italian and Spanish. The approach of separate indexes is followed, and four different merging strategies are tested. Two of the merging methods are classical basic methods: the Raw Score method and the Round Robin method. Two simple new merging methods were created: the Dataset Size Based method and the Score Difference Based method. Two kinds of indexing methods are tested: morphological analysis and stemming. Morphologically analyzed indexes perform a slightly better than stemmed indexes. The merging method based on the dataset size performs best.

1 Introduction

Word inflection is a well known source of problems in information retrieval. In the case words are indexed in their inflected forms, the most common word forms should be added into the query or truncation should be applied. Another basic approach to solve the inflection problem is to normalize index words, and respectively, to normalize query words.

The two basic approaches to index a multilingual document collection are to build a separate index for each document language, and to build a common multilingual index. If the first approach is followed, retrieval must be performed seperately from each index. Subsequently, the result lists have to be merged.

The impact of two different word normalizing approaches (with respect to individual indexes) and of four result merging strategies on the retrieval result are investigated in this article. Our approach utilizes separate indexes.

The UTACLIR query translation system is applied in the tests. UTACLIR is developed at University of Tampere (UTA) [1]. It was originally designed for the CLEF 2000 and 2001 campaigns. The system has been developed from separate programs for every language pair towards a unified system for multiple language pairs.

C. Peters et al. (Eds.): CLEF 2003, LNCS 3237, pp. 74–84, 2004.

2 Word Normalization Methods

The area of linguistics concerned with the internal structure of words is called morphology. Inflectional morphology studies word forms and grammatical relations between words, for example plural of nouns, or tempus of verbs. Derivational morphology goes beyond the syntax: it may affect word meaning as well. The impact of morphology on information retrieval is language dependent. English, for example, has quite weak morphology, and word inflection does not have a great impact on IR. On the other hand, there are languages with strong morphology (e.g. Hungarian, Hebrew and Finnish), which may have hundreds or thousands of word form variants. The impact of word inflection on IR is considerable in these cases [2].

The two main approaches to handle inflection are: (a) to normalize index words, or (b) to leave index words inflected and let users handle the problem. The latter approach puts the responsibility for using the right search technique on the user, exemplified by the search engines of the Internet. This is understandable because of the huge amounts and large diversity of data. Users of Internet search engines are guided either to use truncation (for example Alta Vista, http://www.altavista.com/) or to supply all requested word forms (for example Google, http://www.google.com/).

There are two kinds of word normalization methods: stemming and morphological analysis. The purpose of stemming is to reduce morphological variance of words. There are several stemming techniques. The simplest stemming algorithms only remove plural endings, while more developed ones handle a variety of suffixes in several steps [2]. Stemming is a normalization approach compatible with languages with weak morphology, because their inflection rules are easy to apply in a stemming algorithm. Stemming may not be the best normalizing method for languages with strong morphology, because it is not possible to create simple rules for them. Morphological analyzers are more sophisticated normalizing tools. Their basis is a two-level model consisting of two major components: a lexicon system and two-level rules. Those interdependent components are based on a common alphabet, and together they form the complete description of word inflection [3].

3 Merging Methods

There are many ways to merge result lists. One of the simplest is *the Round Robin method*, which bases on the idea that document scores are not comparable across collections. Because one is ignorant about the distribution of relevant documents in the retrieved lists, an equal number of documents is taken from the beginning of each result list [4].

The Raw Score method is based on the assumption that document scores are comparable across collections [4]. The lists are sorted directly according to document scores. The raw score approach has turned out to be one of the best basic methods ([5], [6], [7]).

Also different methods for normalizing the scores have been developed. A typical *Normalized Score method* is to divide the score by the maximum score of the retrieval result in each collection. Some other balancing factors can be utilized as well.

Several more sophisticated approaches have been developed, but there have not been any breakthroughs.

4 The UTACLIR Process

In the UTACLIR process, the user gives the source and the target language codes and the search request as input. The system uses external resources (bilingual dictionaries, morphological analyzers, stemmers, n-gramming functions and stop lists) according to the language codes [8].

UTACLIR processes source words as follows:

1) a word is normalized utilizing a morphological analyzer (if possible)
2) source language stop words are removed
3) the normalized word is translated (if possible)
4) if the word is translatable, the resulting translations are normalized (by a morphological analyzer or a stemmer, depending on the target language code)
5) target language stop words are removed (in the case that a morphological analyzer was applied in phase 4)
6) if the word is untranslatable in phase 4, the two most highly ranked words obtained by n-gram-matching from the target index are selected as query words.

5 Runs and Results

In this section, we first describe the language resources used, then the collections, and the merging strategies adopted in our runs. Finally, we report the results of the runs we have performed.

5.1 Language Resources

We used the following language resources in the tests:

- Motcom GlobalDix multilingual translation dictionary) by Kielikone plc. Finland (18 languages, total number of words 665,000, 25,000 English - Dutch, 26,000 English - Finnish, 30,000 English – French, 29,000 English – German, 32,000 English – Italian, 35,000 English – Spanish and 36,000 English – Swedish entries)
- Morphological analyzers FINTWOL (Finnish) GERTWOL (German), SWETWOL (Swedish) and ENGTWOL (English) by Lingsoft plc. Finland
- Stemmers for Spanish and French, by ZPrise
- A stemmer for Italian, by the University of Neuchatel
- A stemmer for Dutch, by the University of Utrecht
- SNOWBALL Stemmers for English, German, Finnish and Swedish, by Dr Martin Porter

- English stop word list, created on the basis of InQuery's default stop list for English
- Finnish stop word list, created on the basis of the English stop list
- Swedish stop word list, created at the University of Tampere
- German stop word list, created on the basis of the English stop list

5.2 Test Collections and Indexes

The test collections of the "large multilingual" (Multilingual-8) track of CLEF 2003 were used for the tests.

Twelve indexes were built for the tests. For English, Finnish, German and Swedish we built two indexes: one utilizing a stemmer, and one utilizing a morphological analyzer. For Dutch, French, Italian and Spanish we built one stemmed index each.

The *InQuery* system, provided by the Center for Intelligent Information Retrieval at the University of Massachusetts, was utilized in indexing the databases and as a test retrieval system.

5.3 Merging Methods Applied

The *Raw Score* merging method was selected for the baseline run, because the raw score method is one of the best basic methods. The *Round Robin* method was included in the tests because of its simplicity. In addition we created two novel simple merging methods: the *Dataset Size Based method* and the *Score Difference Based* method.

The *Dataset Size Based* method is based on the assumption that it is likely that more relevant documents are found in a large dataset than in a small dataset. The number of document items taken from single result sets was calculated as follows: T * n / N, where T is the number of document items per topic in the single result list (in CLEF 2003 it was 1000), n is the dataset size and N is the total number of documents (the sum of documents in all the collections). 185 German, 81 French, 99 Italian, 106 English, 285 Spanish, 120 Dutch, 35 Finnish and 89 Swedish documents were selected for every topic in these test runs.

In *Score Difference Based* method every score is compared with the best score for the topic. Only documents with the difference of scores under the predefined value are taken to the final list. This is based on the assumption that documents whose scores are much lower than the score of the top document, may not be relevant.

5.4 Monolingual and Bilingual Runs

Two monolingual runs and ten bilingual runs were made for the multilingual track (see Table 1). The monolingual runs are in English, and the retrieval was performed in both a morphologically normalized and stemmed index, respectively. Two English – Finnish, English – German and English – Swedish runs were performed (also in morphologically normalized and stemmed indexes). English – Dutch, English –

French, English – Italian and English – Spanish runs were performed solely with a stemmed index.

The average precision of these runs varied from 17.4 % (English – Dutch) to 46.3 % (monolingual English with the stemmed index). The morphologically normalized English – Finnish run achieved the best result (34.0 %) among the bilingual runs.

The monolingual and bilingual runs give the possibility to compare the performance of the morphological analyzer with the performance of the stemmer. The results of the two monolingual English runs do not differ prominently from each other: the run with the stemmed index performed 1.5 % better than the run with the morphologically normalized index. The results of bilingual English – Finnish, English – German and English – Swedish runs are different. The stemmed indexes give much worse results than morphologically normalized indexes. The difference is -29.9 % in English – Swedish runs, -17.1 in English – German runs and –44.1 % in English – Finnish runs, when the results given by the stemmers are compared with the results obtained in morphologically analyzed indexes.

Table 1. Average precision (%) of monolingual and bilingual runs (source language English)

Type of run	Index type	Average precision %	Change (%)
monolingual English	morph.anal.	45.6	
	stemmed	46.3	+1.5
English-Finnish	morph.anal.	34.0	
	stemmed	19.0	-44.1
English-Swedish	morph.anal.	27.1	
	stemmed	19.0	-29.9
English-German	morph.anal.	31.0	
	stemmed	25.7	-17.1
English-Dutch	stemmed	17.4	
English-French	stemmed	32.1	
English-Italian	stemmed	30.6	
English-Spanish	stemmed	28.3	

Next, individual queries of English – Finnish, English – Swedish and English – German runs are analyzed more closely. We pay attention particularly to those queries where the morphological analyzer produced much better results than the stemmer. Two query types, where the morphological analyzer was superior to the stemmer, were found.

Phrases – Compounds (Phrases Written Together). A closer analysis of individual queries of the two English – Finnish runs shows that the greatest performance differences can be detected in the queries containing phrases. Source query number 187 includes a phrase "nuclear transport". The parts of this phrase are translated independently. In Finnish compounds are used instead of phrases. The corresponding word in Finnish is "ydinjätekuljetus". When *stemming* is applied during indexing, compounds are not split, so we have only the compound "ydinjätekuljetus" in stemmed form in the index. No matches are found during retrieval, because the query includes only the individual parts of the phrase, not the full compound. When indexing is performed utilizing the *morphological analyzer*, compounds are split, and the full compound as well as parts in basic form are indexed. In retrieval, parts of the phrases now match parts of the compound. See Examples 1 and 2 in the Appendix.

The same phenomenon can be seen in Query 141 in English – Swedish runs. The phrase in the source query is "letter bomb", and the translated query includes Swedish variants for those words. The stemmed index includes only the compound "brevbomb" (letter bomb) in its stemmed form. The morphologically analyzed index includes the compound as well as its parts in basic form. See Examples 3 and 4 in the Appendix.

The English Query 184 includes the phrase "maternity leave". In the English – German run the parts of this phrase are translated independently into the German word "Mutterschaft" and the words "Erlaubnis verlassen zuräklassen Urlaub lassen überlassen hinterlassen", respectively. Again, the stemmed index includes only the compound "Mutterschaftsurlaub" in its stemmed form, but the morphologically analyzed index includes the parts of the compound as well. See Examples 5 and 6 in the Appendix.

Strong Morphology. When analysing the performance of individual queries of the stemmed English – Finnish and English – Swedish runs, another basic reason for bad results can be found: strong morphology, and the inability of stemmers to cope with it. The source query 183 includes the word "remains", which is translated into Finnish as "tähteet maalliset jäännökset". The word "tähteet" is further stemmed into the string "täht". The problem is in the fact that also the word "tähti" (star) has the same stem, which causes noise in retrieval. See Example 7 in the Appendix.

A similar phenomenon can be found in the English - Swedish run in Query 148. The word "layer" is translated into the Swedish word "lager", which is further stemmed to a string "lag". In Swedish there is a word "lag" (law), which has the same stem "lag". See Example 8 in the Appendix.

5.5 Multilingual Runs

There are two variables in our multilingual runs: the index type and the merging approach. The index types are (a) morphologically analyzed / stemmed, where English, Finnish, German and Swedish indexes are morphologically analyzed, while Dutch, French, Italian and Spanish indexes are stemmed, and (b) solely stemmed, where all the indexes are stemmed. The merging approaches are the Raw Score method, the Dataset Size Based method, the Score Difference Based method (with difference value 0.08) and the Round Robin method. We tested two index types and four merging approaches, thus we have eight different runs.

The differences between the results of the multilingual runs are quite minor (see Table 2). The runs with morphologically analyzed / stemmed indexes seem to perform better than the runs with solely stemmed indexes. The best result, 20.2% average precision, was achieved by the run performed in the morphologically normalized / stemmed indexes, applying the dataset size based method. The raw score method performed worst among both index types. Even the simple round robin approach produced better results than the raw score method. However, all results are within a range of 1.7%.

Table 2. Average precision (%) of multilingual runs

Index type	Merging strategy	Average precision %	Difference %	Change (%)
morphologically analyzed/ stemmed (baseline)	raw score	19.8		
morphologically analyzed/ stemmed	dataset size based	20.2	+0.4	+2.0
morphologically analyzed/ stemmed	score diff. per topic	19.9	+0.1	+0.5
morphologically analyzed/ stemmed	round robin	20.1	+0.3	+1.6
solely stemmed	raw score	18.5	-1.3	-6.6
solely stemmed	dataset size based	18.7	-1.1	-5.6
solely stemmed	score diff. per topic	18.7	-1.1	-5.6
solely stemmed	round robin	18.6	-1.2	-6.1

6 Discussion and Conclusion

The combined impact of different normalizing methods, stemming and morphological analysis, on the IR performance has not been investigated widely. The reason for that is presumably the fact that English is the traditional document language in IR tests. English is a language with simple morphology, which implies that stemming is an adequate word form normalization method. Our monolingual English tests with CLEF 2003 data support this: the result with the stemmed English index is a little better than the result with the morphologically normalized index. The bilingual test we made with Finnish, German and Swedish indexes show opposite results. The results with stemmed indexes in these languages are much worse than the results with the index built utilizing a morphological analyzer. This is in line with earlier research: Braschler and Ripplinger discovered that stemming improves the results in retrieving German documents, but morphological analysis with compound splitting produces the best result [9]. When high precision is demanded, stemming is not an adequate normalizing method with languages with strong morphology, especially in compound rich languages.

Two main reasons for the success of the morphological analyzers compared with stemmers were found. First, when phrases are used in the source language while the target language uses compounds instead, stemmers do not handle properly queries including phrases. When indexing is performed utilizing a stemmer, compounds are not split, and only the full compound is indexed in stemmed form. The target query includes only the parts of the phrase translated and stemmed, and no matches are found in retrieval. However, when the morphological analyzer is utilized during indexing and the compounds are split, components of compounds are also indexed, and matches are found. Second, if the target language is morphologically rich, and the stemmer is unable to handle the morphological variation, loss of precision is presumable. The problems caused by phrases vs. compounds were found in English – Finnish, English – Swedish and English – German runs, while the problems caused by rich inflection were found only in English – Finnish and English – Swedish runs.

We had two index variables in our multilingual tests: (a) morphologically analyzed (English, Finnish, German and Swedish) / stemmed (Dutch, French, Italian and Spanish) indexes and (b) stemmed indexes. Our tests showed that runs with indexes of type (a) outperform those of (b). We cannot show that morphologically analyzed indexes always perform better in multilingual (and bilingual) runs, because we are lacking Dutch, French, Italian and Spanish morphological tools. It is possible, that as for English, also in other morphologically weak languages, stemmers are more suitable normalizing tools than morphological analyzers.

On the other hand, the most used IR systems in real life are the search engines of the Internet. They use inflected indexes, which means that the users have to handle inflection. Truncation is possible with some search engines, while others guide their users to supply all the possible forms of their search words. Loss of recall is liable, but recall may not be important in WWW searching. In many cases, precision is more important, which may be good even if the user has not perfect language skills.

In most multilingual experiments, separate indexes are created for different languages, and various result merging strategies are tested. The results of experiments with the merged index are not very promising ([10], [11]). In real life, the situation of separate indexes and result merging occurs quite rarely, however. This would be a reason to direct research towards the strategies of the merged index approach.

Acknowledgements

The *InQuery* search engine was provided by the Center for Intelligent Information Retrieval at the University of Massachusetts.

ENGTWOL (Morphological Transducer Lexicon Description of English): Copyright (c) 1989-1992 Atro Voutilainen and Juha Heikkilä.

FINTWOL (Morphological Description of Finnish): Copyright (c) Kimmo Koskenniemi and Lingsoft plc. 1983-1993.

GERTWOL (Morphological Transducer Lexicon Description of German): Copyright (c) 1997 Kimmo Koskenniemi and Lingsoft plc.

TWOL-R (Run-time Two-Level Program): Copyright (c) Kimmo Koskenniemi and Lingsoft plc. 1983-1992.

GlobalDix Dictionary Software was used for automatic word-by-word translations. Copyright (c) 1998 Kielikone plc, Finland.

MOT Dictionary Software was used for automatic word-by-word translations. Copyright (c) 1998 Kielikone plc, Finland.

This work was partly financed by CLARITY (Information Society Technologies Programme, IST-2000-25310).

References

1. Hedlund, T., Keskustalo, H., Pirkola, A., Airio, E., Järvelin, K.: Utaclir @ CLEF 2001 – Effects of Compound Splitting and N-gram Techniques. Evaluation of Cross-language Information Retrieval Systems. Lecture Notes in Computer Science; Vol. 2406. Springer-Verlag, Germany (2002) 118-136
2. Krovetz, R.: Viewing Morphology as an Inference Process. Proceedings of the 16th Annual International ACM SIGIR Conference on Research and Development in Information Retrieval (1993) 191–202
3. Koskenniemi, K.: Two-level Morphology: A General Computational Model for Word-Form Recognition and Production. University of Helsinki, Finland. Publications No. 11 (1983)
4. Hiemstra, D., Kraaij, W., Pohlmann, R., Westerveld, T.: Translation Resources, Merging Strategies, and Relevance Feedback for Cross-Language Information Retrieval. Cross-Language Information Retrieval and Evaluation. Lectures in Computer Science, Vol. 2069. Springer-Verlag, Germany (2001) 102-115
5. Chen, A.: Cross-language Retrieval Experiments at CLEF 2002. Working Notes for the CLEF 2002 Workshop, Italy (2002) 5-20
6. Moulinier, I., Molina-Salgado, H.: Thomson Legal and Regulatory Experiments for CLEF 2002. Working Notes for the CLEF 2002 Workshop, Italy (2002) 91-96
7. Savoy, J., Rasolofo, Y.: Report on the TREC-9 Experiment: Link-Based Retrieval and Distributed Collections. Proceedings of the Ninth Text Retrieval Conference, NIST Special Publication 500-249, Department of Commerce, National Institute of Standards and Technology (2001) 579–588
8. Airio, E., Keskustalo, H., Hedlund, T., Pirkola, A. UTACLIR @ CLEF2002 – Bilingual and Multilingual Runs with a Unified Process. Advances in Cross-Language Information Retrieval. Results of the Cross-Language Evaluation Forum - CLEF 2002. Lecture Notes in Computer Science, Vol. 2785, Springer-Verlag, Germany (2003)
9. Braschler, M., Ripplinger, B. (2003). Stemming and Decompounding for German Text Retrieval. Advances in Information Retrieval. Lecture Notes in Computer Science, Vol. 2633. Springer-Verlag, Germany (2003) 177-192
10. Chen, A.: Multilingual Information Retrieval Using English and Chinese Queries. Evaluation of Cross-Language Information Retrieval Systems. Lecture Notes in Computer Science; Vol. 2406. Springer-Verlag, Germany (2002) 44-58
11. Nie, J.: Towards a unified approach to CLIR and multilingual IR. SIGIR 2002 Workshop I, Cross-language information retrieval: a research map. University of Tampere, Finland (2002) 8–14

Appendix

Example 1.
English – Finnish query no. 187 with the morphologically analyzed index
Average precision 100 %
#sum(#syn(ydin) #syn(kuljetus matkanaikana rahtimaksu kulkuneuvo pika kuljettaa) #syn(saksa) #syn(pitää jonakin löytää huomata löytö) #syn(todistus huhu   pamaus   ilmoittaa   ilmoittautua)   #syn(esittää vastalause   vastalause paheksunta mielenosoitus rähinä vetoomus vastustaa kyseenalaistaminen) #syn(kuljetus) #syn(radioaktiivinen) #syn(tuhlata jäte haaskaus erämaa) #syn(pyörä majava majavannahka) #syn(astia kontti) #syn(saksa));

Example 2.
English – Finnish query no. 187 with the stemmed index
Average precision 16.7 %
#sum(#syn(yd) #syn(kuljetus matkan aik rahtimaksu kulkuneuvo pika kuljet) #syn(saks) #syn(löytä huoma pitää j löytö) #syn(todistus huhu pamaus ilmoit ilmoittautu) #syn(vastalaus paheksun mielenosoitus räh vetoomus vastust esittää vastalaus kyseenalaistamin) #syn(kuljetus) #syn(radioaktiivin) #syn(tuhl jäte haaskaus eräm) #syn(pyörä majav majavannahk) #syn(ast kont) #syn(saks));

Example 3.
English – Swedish query no. 141 with the morphologically analyzed index
Average precision 100.0 %
#sum(#syn(bokstav brev typ) #syn(bomb bomba) #syn(bluesbasera @bauer) #syn(komma på anse fynd) #syn(information) #syn(explosion utbrott spricka) #syn(bokstav brev typ) #syn(bomb bomba) #syn(studio) #syn(television tv tv-apparat tv) #syn(ränna segelränna kanal kanalisera) #syn(pro far förbivid proffs) #syn(7) #syn(lägga fram sätta upp höra upp presentera hallåa framlägga framföra) #syn(kabellag @arabella) #syn(bluesbasera @bauer));

Example 4.
English – Swedish query no. 141 with the stemmed index
Average precision 14.3 %
#sum(#syn(bokstav brev typ) #syn(bomb) #syn(bauer griesbaum)#syn(finn komma på ans fynd) #syn(information) #syn(explosion utbrot sprick) #syn(bokstav brev typ) #syn(bomb) #syn(studio) #syn(television tv tv-appar tv) #syn(ränn segelrän kanal kanaliser) #syn(pro far förbi, vid proff) #syn(7) #syn(presenter hallå framlägg lägga fram sätta upp höra upp) #syn(rabell larabell) #syn(bauer griesbaum));

Example 5.
English – German query no. 184 with the morphologically analyzed index
Average precision 67.5 %
#sum(#syn(mutterschaft) #syn(erlaubnis verlassen zurüklassen urlaub lassen berlassen hinterlassen) #syn(europa) #syn(finden feststellen fund)   #syn(geben anrufen nachgeben nachgiebigkeit) #syn(information) #syn(versorgung

vergtüng vorkehrung vorrat bestimmung) #syn(betreffen beunruhigen
beschäftigen angelegenheit sorge unternehmen) #syn(länge stük) #syn(
mutterschaft) #syn(erlaubnis verlassen zurüklassen urlaub lassen ßerlassen
hinterlassen) #syn(europa));

Example 6.
English – German query no. 184 with the stemmed index
Average precision 2.7 %
#sum(#syn(mutterschaft) #syn(erlaubnis verlass zurucklass urlaublass uberlass
hinterlass) #syn(europ) #syn(find feststell fund) #syn(geb anruf nachgeb
nachgieb) #syn(information) #syn(versorg vergut vorkehr vorrat bestimm)
#syn(betreff beunruh beschaft angeleg sorg unternehm) #syn(stuck) #syn(
mutterschaft) #syn(erlaubnis verlass zurucklass urlaub lass uberlass hinterlass)
#syn(europ));

Example 7.
English – Finnish query no. 183 with the stemmed index
Average precision 0.0 %
#sum(#syn(aasialain) #syn(dinosaurus) #syn(täht maalliset jäännöks) #syn(jäädä
jäädä ed) #syn(ran lohko puolue osuus ranniko hiekkaran äyräs rooli lävits ero)
#syn(as tehtäv) #syn(dinosaurus) #syn(täht maalliset jäännöks) #syn(jäädä
jäädä ed) #syn(perust perustu löytä huoma pitää j) #syn(löytä huoma pitää j
löytö));

Example 8.
English – Swedish query no. 148 with the stemmed index
Average precision 4.7 %
#sum(#syn(skad skadestånd) #syn(frisk hav luft ozon störtskur) #syn(lag
värphön) #syn(hål slå hål träffa hålet) #syn(frisk hav luft ozon störtskur) #syn(
lag värphön) #syn(effek verkan åstadkomm) #syn (förorening)).

JHU/APL Experiments in Tokenization
and Non-word Translation

Paul McNamee and James Mayfield

The Johns Hopkins University Applied Physics Laboratory,
11100 Johns Hopkins Road,
Laurel, MD 20723-6099, USA
{mcnamee, mayfield}@jhuapl.edu

Abstract. In the past we have conducted experiments that investigate the benefits and peculiarities attendant to alternative methods for tokenization, particularly overlapping character n-grams. This year we continued this line of work and report new findings reaffirming that the judicious use of n-grams can lead to performance surpassing that of word-based tokenization. In particular we examined: the relative performance of n-grams and a popular suffix stemmer; a novel form of n-gram indexing that approximates stemming and achieves fast run-time performance; various lengths of n-grams; and the use of n-grams for robust translation of queries using an aligned parallel text. For the CLEF 2003 evaluation we submitted monolingual and bilingual runs for all languages and language pairs and multilingual runs using English as a source language. Our key findings are that shorter n-grams ($n=4$ and $n=5$) outperform a popular stemmer in non-Romance languages, that direct translation of n-grams is feasible using an aligned corpus, that translated 5-grams yield superior performance to words, stems, or 4-grams, and that a combination of indexing methods is best of all.

1   Introduction

In the past we have examined a number of issues pertaining to how documents and queries are represented. This has been a particular interest in our work with the HAIRCUT retrieval system due to the consistent success we have observed with the use of overlapping character n-grams. Simple measures that can be uniformly applied to text processing, regardless of language, reduce developer effort and appear to be at least as effective as approaches that rely on language-specific processing, and perhaps more so. They are increasingly used when linguistic resources are unavailable (see [1][2][3]), but in general have not been widely adopted. We believe that this may be due in part to a belief that n-grams are not as effective as competing approaches (an idea that we attempt to refute here), and also due to a fear of increased index-time and run-time costs. We do not focus on the second concern here; few studies addressing the performance implications of n-gram processing have been undertaken (but see [4]), and we hope this gap is soon filled.

Over this past year we investigated several issues in tokenization. Using the CLEF 2002 and 2003 test suites as an experimental framework, we attempt to answer the following questions:

C. Peters et al. (Eds.): CLEF 2003, LNCS 3237, pp. 85–97, 2004.
© Springer-Verlag Berlin Heidelberg 2004

- Should diacritical marks be retained?
- What length of character n-grams results in the best performance?
- Does the optimal length vary by language?
- Are n-grams as effective as stemmed words?
- Can n-gram processing be sped up?
- What peculiarities arise when n-grams are used for bilingual retrieval?

We submitted official runs for the monolingual, bilingual, and multilingual tracks and participated in the first cross-language spoken document benchmark [5]. For all of our runs we used the HAIRCUT system and a statistical language model similarity calculation. Many of our official runs were based on n-gram processing though we found that by using a combination of n-grams and stemmed words better performance can usually be obtained. For our bilingual runs we relied on pre-translation query expansion. We also developed a new method of translating queries, using n-grams rather than words as the elements to be translated. This method does not suffer from several key obstacles in dictionary-based translation, such as word lemmatization, matching of multiple word expressions, and out-of-vocabulary words such as common surnames [6].

2   Methods

HAIRCUT supports a variety of indexing terms and represents documents using a bag-of-terms model. Our general method is to process the text for each document, reducing all terms to lower-case. Generally words were deemed to be white-space delimited tokens in the text; however, we preserve only the first 4 digits of a number and we truncate any particularly long tokens (those greater than 35 characters in length).   Once words are identified we optionally perform transformations on the words to create indexing terms (*e.g.*, stemming). So-called stopwords are retained in our index and the dictionary is created from all words present in the corpus.

We have wondered whether diacritical marks have much effect upon retrieval performance - for a long time we have been retaining diacritical marks as part of our ordinary lexical processing, in keeping with a keep-it-simple approach. One principled argument for retaining inflectional marks is that they possess a deconflationary effect when content words that differ only in diacritics have different meanings. For example, the English words resume (to continue) and résumé (a summary of one's professional life) can be distinguished by differences in diacritics. On the other hand, such marks are not always uniformly applied, and furthermore, if retained, might distinguish two semantically related words. Stephen Tomlinson investigated preservation of diacritics using the CLEF 2002 collection and reported that it was helpful in some cases (Finnish) and harmful in others (Italian and French) [7]. We found similar results (see Table 1), though the effect is seen only for words, not n-grams. As there is practically no effect, we opted to remove such accents routinely. Intuitively we thought that removing the distinction might improve corpus statistics when n-grams are used. Whenever stemming was used, words were first stemmed, and then any remaining marks were removed; this enabled the stemmer to take advantage of marks when present. N-grams were produced from the same sequence of words; however, we attempt to detect sentence boundaries to prevent generating n-grams across sentence boundaries.

Table 1. Absolute difference in mean average precision when accented marks were removed

language	DE	EN	ES	FI	FR	IT	NL	SV
words	-0.0002	0.0028	0.0146	-0.0363	0.0139	0.0076	-0.0005	0.0045
4-grams	-0.0028	-0.0093	0.0019	0.0075	0.0077	-0.0090	0.0009	-0.0056

HAIRCUT uses gamma compression to reduce the size of the inverted file. Within-document positional information is not retained, but both document-id and term frequencies are compressed. We also produce a 'dual file' that is a document-indexed collection of term-ids and counts. Construction of this data structure doubles our on-disk space requirements, but confers advantages such as being able to quickly examine individual document representations. This is particularly useful for automated (local) query expansion. Our lexicon is stored as a B-tree but nodes are compressed in memory to maximize the number of in-memory terms subject to physical memory limitations. For the indexes created for CLEF 2003 memory was not an issue as only $O(10^6)$ distinct terms were found in each collection.

We use a statistical language model for retrieval akin to those presented by Miller *et al.* [8] and Hiemstra [9] with Jelinek-Mercer smoothing [10]. In this model, relevance is defined as

$$P(D \mid Q) = \prod_{q \in Q} [\alpha P(q \mid D) + (1 - \alpha)P(q \mid C)],$$

where Q is a query, D is a document, C is the collection as a whole, and α is a smoothing parameter. The probabilities on the right side of the equation are replaced by their maximum likelihood estimates when scoring a document. The language model has the advantage that term weights are mediated by the corpus. Our experience has been that this type of probabilistic model outperforms a vector-based cosine model or a binary independence model with Okapi BM25 weighting.

For the monolingual, bilingual, and multilingual tasks, all of our submitted runs were based on a combination of several base runs. Our method for combination was to normalize scores by probability mass and to then merge documents by score. All of our runs were automatic runs and used only the title and description topic fields.

3   Monolingual Experiments

For our monolingual work we created several indexes for each language using the permissible document fields appropriate to each collection. Our four basic methods for tokenization were unnormalized words, stemmed words obtained through the use of the Snowball stemmer, 4-grams, and 5-grams. Information about each index is shown in Table 2.

Table 2. Summary information about the test collection and index data structures

Lang	#docs	%docs	#rel	%rel	index size (MB) / unique terms (1000s)			
					words	stems	4-grams	5-grams
DE	294805	18.3	1825	18.2	265 / 1188	219 / 860	705 / 219	1109 / 1230
EN	166754	10.3	1006	10.0	143 / 302	123 / 235	504 / 166	827 / 917
ES	454041	28.2	2368	23.6	303 / 525	251 / 347	990 / 217	1538 / 1144
FI	55344	3.4	483	4.8	89 / 977	60 / 520	136 / 138	229 / 709
FR	129804	8.1	946	9.4	91 / 262	76 / 178	277 / 144	440 / 724
IT	157558	9.7	809	8.0	115 / 374	92 / 224	329 / 144	529 / 721
NL	190605	11.8	1577	15.7	161 / 683	147 / 575	469 / 191	759 / 1061
RU	16715	1.0	151	1.5	25 / 253	25 / 253	44 / 136	86 / 569
SV	142819	8.9	889	8.8	94 / 505	80 / 361	258 / 162	404 / 863
total	1608445		10054		1286 MB	1073 MB	3712 MB	5921 MB

From the table above it can be seen that the percentage of relevant documents for each subcollection is closely related to its contribution to the overall number of documents. This would suggest that collection size might be a useful factor for multilingual merging. We also note that n-gram indexing results in increased disk storage costs. This cost is driven by the increased number of postings in the inverted file when n-gram indexing is performed.

Our use of 4-grams and 5-grams as indexing terms represents a departure from previous work using 6-grams [11]. We conducted tests using various lengths of n-grams for all eight CLEF 2002 languages and found that choices of $n=4$ or $n=5$ performed best. Figure 1 charts performance for six term indexing strategies; a value of $\alpha=0.5$ was used throughout and no relevance feedback was attempted.

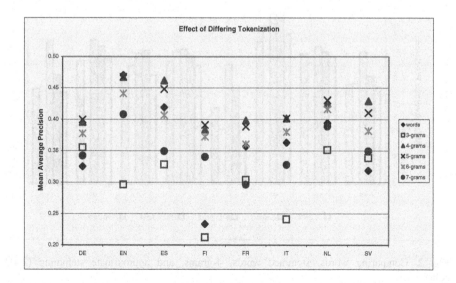

Fig. 1. Relative efficacy of different tokenization methods using the CLEF 2002 test set. Note that blind relevance feedback was not used for these runs

We determined that use of $n=4$ or $n=5$ is best in all eight languages though it is hard to distinguish between the two. 6-grams are not as effective in these languages. There are differences in performance depending on the value of smoothing constant, α, that is used, though we have yet to test whether these differences are significant or merely represent overtraining on the 2002 test set. The effect of smoothing parameter selection in language model-based retrieval was investigated by Zhai and Lafferty [12]. We report on our results investigating the effect of n-gram length, with additional detail and further experiments in a forthcoming manuscript [13].

In addition to determining good values for n, we also wanted to see if n-grams remained an attractive technique in comparison to stemmed words. Having no substantive experience with stemming, we were pleased to discover that the Snowball stemmer [14], a derivative of the Porter stemmer extended to many languages by Porter, provides a set of rules for all of the CLEF 2003 languages. Furthermore, the software contains Java bindings so it fit seamlessly with the HAIRCUT system. We decided to make a comparison between raw words, stems, 4-grams, 5-grams, and a surrogate technique based on n-grams that might approximate stems. Our n-gram approximation to stemming was based on picking the word-internal n-gram for each word with lowest document frequency (*i.e.,* we picked the least common n-gram for each word). As an example, consider the words 'juggle', 'juggles', and 'juggler'. The least common 5-gram for the first two is 'juggl', however the least common 5-gram for 'juggler' is 'ggler'[1]. The least common 4-gram for all three words is 'jugg'. We hypothesize that high IDF n-gram affixes will span portions of words that exhibit little morphological variation.

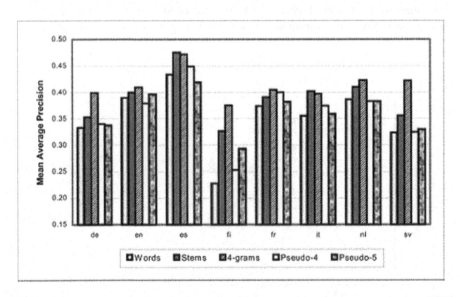

Fig. 2. Comparing words, stemmed words, 4-grams, and approximate stemming (2002 collection)

---

[1] The Snowball stemmer also fails to transform juggler to a canonical form.

This method has the advantage of providing some morphological normalization, but it does not increase the number of postings in an inverted file. This can be viewed either as a way to approximate stems or a way of lowering the computational cost of using n-grams. We found that n-grams did outperform stems, and that our pseudo stems based on n-grams were better than raw words, but not as effective as a rule-based stemmer (see Figure 2). Details about this work can be found in Mayfield and McNamee [15].

On the 2003 test collection we produced base runs for words, stems (using the Snowball stemmer), 4-grams, and 5-grams. Performance (based on average precision) for each is reported in Table 3. All of these runs used blind relevance feedback and used an α value of 0.3 with words and stems, or 0.8 with n-grams. None of these runs were submitted as official runs; instead, we created hybrid runs using multiple methods. In the past we have found that combination from multiple runs can confer a nearly 10% improvement in performance. Savoy has also reported improvements from multiple term types [3].

Table 3. Mean average precision for CLEF 2003 base runs with maximal values highlighted

	DE	EN	ES	FI	FR	IT	NL	RU	SV
words	0.4175	0.4988	0.4773	0.3355	0.4590	0.4856	0.4615	0.2550	0.3189
stems	0.4604	0.4679	0.5277	0.4357	0.4780	0.5053	0.4594	0.2550	0.3698
4-grams	0.5056	0.4692	0.5011	0.5396	0.5244	0.4313	0.4974	0.3276	0.4163
5-grams	0.4869	0.4610	0.4695	0.5468	0.4895	0.4568	0.4618	0.3271	0.4137

To produce our official monolingual runs we decided to combine runs based on the Snowball stemmer with runs using n-grams as indexing terms. Runs named *aplmoxxa* used 4-grams and stems while runs named *aplmoxxb* used 5-grams and stems. However, due to a mistake while creating the scripts used to produce all of our runs, we inadvertently failed to perform blind relevance feedback for our monolingual submissions. Routinely we expand queries to 60 terms using additional terms ranked after examining the top 20 and bottom 75 (of 1000) documents. Failing to use blind relevance feedback had a detrimental effect on our official runs. Our official monolingual runs are described in Table 4 and corrected scores are presented on the far right.

It appears that several of our runs would have increased substantially in performance if we had correctly used blind relevance feedback. Relative improvements of more than 5% were seen in German, Russian, and Spanish, although performance would have dropped slightly in Swedish. The German and Spanish document collections are the two largest in the entire test suite. We wonder if relevance feedback may be more beneficial when larger collections are available, a conjecture partially explored by Kwok and Chan [16].

4   Bilingual Experiments

This year the Bilingual task focused on retrieval involving four language pairs, which notably did not contain   English as a source or target language. This is only signifi-

Table 4. Official results for monolingual task. The shaded row contains results for a comparable, unofficial English run. The two columns at the far right report a corrected value for mean average precision when blind relevance feedback is applied, and the relative difference compared to the corresponding official run

run id	MAP	=Best	>=Median	Rel. Found	Relevant	# topics	MAP'	% change
aplmodea	0.4852	2	31	1721	1825	56	0.5210	7.39%
aplmodeb	0.4834	2	27	1732			0.5050	4.46%
aplmoena	0.4943			977	1006	54	0.5040	1.96%
aplmoenb	0.5127			980			0.5074	-1.03%
aplmoesa	0.4679	3	32	2226	2368	57	0.5311	13.50%
aplmoesb	0.4538	3	32	2215			0.5165	13.82%
aplmofia	0.5514	12	31	475	483	45	0.5571	1.03%
aplmofib	0.5459	9	31	475			0.5649	3.49%
aplmofra	0.5228	9	35	924	946	52	0.5415	3.58%
aplmofrb	0.5148	9	37	920			0.5168	0.39%
aplmoita	0.4620	7	21	776	809	51	0.4784	3.54%
aplmoitb	0.4744	8	22	771			0.4982	5.02%
aplmonla	0.4817	3	42	1485	1577	56	0.5088	5.63%
aplmonlb	0.4709	2	40	1487			0.4841	2.86%
aplmorua	0.3389	2	17	115	151	28	0.3728	10.00%
aplmorub	0.3282	4	16	113			0.3610	10.00%
aplmosva	0.4515	7	36	840	889	53	0.4358	-3.47%
aplmosvb	0.4498	6	38	838			0.4310	-4.18%

cant because of the difficulty in locating direct translation resources for some language pairs and the fact that many translation resources are available when English is one of the languages involved. The four language pairs are German to Italian, Finnish to German, French to Dutch, and Italian to Spanish.

For the 2002 campaign we relied on a single translation resource: bilingual wordlists extracted from parallel corpora. We built a large alignable collection from a single source, the Official Journal of the EU [17], and we again used this resource as our only source of translations for 2003. The parallel corpus grew by about 50% this year, so a somewhat larger resource was available. First we describe the construction of the parallel corpus and the extraction of our bilingual wordlists, then we discuss our overall strategy for bilingual retrieval, and finally we report on our official results.

Our collection was obtained through a nightly crawl of the Europa web site where we targeted the Official Journal of the European Union [17]. The Journal is available in each of the E.U. languages and consists mainly of governmental topics, for example, trade and foreign relations. We had data available from December 2000 through May 2003. Though focused on European topics, the time span is 5 to 8 years after the CLEF-2002 document collection. The Journal is published electronically in PDF format and we wanted to create an aligned collection. We started with 33.4 GB of PDF documents and converted them to plain text using the publicly available *pdftotext* software (version 1.0). Once converted to text, documents were split into pieces using conservative rules for page breaks and paragraph breaks. Many of the documents are written in outline form, or contain large tables, so this pre-alignment processing is not easy. We ended up with about 300MB of text, per language, that could be aligned.   Alignment was carried out using the *char_align* program [18]. In this way we created an aligned collection of approximately 1.2 million passages; these 'documents' were each about 2 or 3 sentences in length.

We performed pairwise alignments between languages pairs, for example, between German and Italian. Once aligned, we indexed each pairwise-aligned collection using the technique described for the CLEF-2003 document collections. Again, we created four indexes per sub-collection, per language – one each of words, stems, 4-grams and 5-grams. Our goal was to support query term translation, so for each source language term occurring in at least 4 documents, we attempted to determine a translation of the same token type in the target language. At this point we should mention that the 'proper' translation of an n-gram is decidedly slippery – clearly there can be no single correct answer.   Nonetheless, we simply relied on the large volume of n-grams to smooth topic translation.   For example, the central 5-grams of the English phrase 'prime minister' include 'ime_m', 'me_mi', and 'e_min'. The derived 'translations' of these English 5-grams into French are 'er_mi', '_mini', and 'er_mi', respectively.   This seems to work as expected for the French phrase 'premier ministre', although the method is not foolproof. Consider n-gram translations from the phrase 'communist party' (parti communiste): '_commu' (mmuna), 'commu' (munau), 'ommun' (munau), 'mmuni' (munau), 'munis' (munis), 'unist' (unist), 'nist_' (unist), 'ist_p' (ist_p), 'st_pa' (1_re_), 't_par' (rtie_), '_part' (_part), 'party' (rtie_), and 'arty_' (rtie_). The lexical coverage of translation resources is a critical factor for good CLIR performance, so the fact that almost any n-gram has a 'translation' should improve performance. The direct translation of n-grams may offer a solution to several key obstacles in dictionary-based translation. Word normalization is not essential since sub-word strings will be compared. Translation of multiword expressions can be approximated by translation of word-spanning n-grams. Out-of-vocabulary words, particularly proper nouns, can be be partially translated by common n-gram fragments or left untranslated in close languages.

We extracted candidate translations as follows. First, we would take a candidate term as input and identify documents containing this term in the source language subset of the aligned collection. Up to 5000 documents were considered; we bounded the number for reasons of efficiency and because we felt that performance was not enhanced appreciably when a greater number of documents was used. If no document contained this term, then it was left untranslated. Second, we would identify the corresponding documents in the target language. Third, using a statistic that is similar to mutual information, we would extract a single potential translation. Our statistic is a function of the frequency of occurrence in the whole collection and the frequency in the subset of aligned documents. In this way we extracted the single-best target language term for each source language term in our lexicon (not just the query terms in the CLEF topics). When 5-grams were used this process took several days.

Table 5 lists examples of translating within the designated language pairs using each type of tokenization. Mistakes are evident; however, especially when pre-translation expansion is used the overall effectiveness is quite high. We believe the redundancy afforded by translating multiple n-grams for each query word also reduces loss due to erroneous translations. Finally, incorrect translations may still prove helpful if they are a collocation rather than an actual translation.

Table 5. Examples of term-to-term translation

	Desired Mapping	DEIT		FIDE		FRNL		ITES	
		DE	IT	FI	DE	FR	NL	IT	ES
words	Milk	milch	latte	maidon	milch	lait	melk	latte	leche
	Olympic	olympische	olimpico	olympialaisiin	olympischen	olympique	olympisch	olimpico	olimpico
stems	Milk	milch	latt	maido	Milch	lait	melk	latt	lech
	Olympic	olymp	olimp	olymp	Olymp	olymp	olympisch	olimp	olimp
4-grams	first 4-gram (milk)	milc	latt	maid	Land	lait	melk	latt	lech
	last 4-gram (milk)	ilch	latt	idon	milc	lait	melk	atte	acte
	first 4-gram (olympic)	olym	olim	olym	olym	olym	olym	olim	olim
	last 4-gram (olympic)	sche	rope	siin	n_au	ique	isch	pico	pico
5-grams	first 5-gram (milk)	milch	_latt	maido	milch	_lait	_melk	latte	leche
	last 5-gram (milk)	milch	_latt	aidon	milch	lait_	_melk	latte	leche
	first 5-gram (olympic)	olymp	olimp	olymp	olymp	olymp	_olym	olimp	olimp
	last 5-gram (olympic)	ische	urope	isiin	ichen	pique	pisch	mpico	_olim

We remain convinced that pre-translation query expansion is a tremendously effective method to improve bilingual performance [19]. Therefore we used each CLEF 2003 document collection as an expansion collection for the source language queries. Queries were expanded to a list of 60 terms, and then we attempted to translate each using our corpus-derived resource. In the past we have been interested in using n-grams as terms, however, we have worked with bilingual wordlists for translation. This year we decided to create translingual mappings using the same tokenization in both the source and target languages. Thus for each of the four language pairs, we created four different lists (for a total of 16): one list per type of indexing term (*i.e.,* word, stem, 4-gram, or 5-gram). Again using experiments on the CLEF 2002 collection, we determined that mappings between n-grams were more efficacious than use of word-to-word or stem-to-stem mappings. Thus different tokenization can be used for initial search, pre-translation expansion, query translation, and target language retrieval. In testing we found the best results using both n-grams and stems for an initial source-language search, then we extracted ordinary words as 'expansion' terms, and finally we translated each n-gram contained in the expanded source language word list into n-grams in the target language (or stems into stems, as appropriate). The process is depicted in Figure 3:

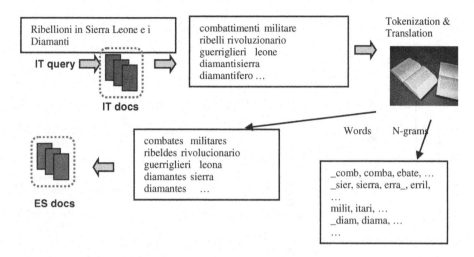

Fig. 3. Illustration of bilingual processing. The initial input to translation is an expanded list of plain words extracted from a set of documents obtained by retrieval in the source language collection. These words are optionally tokenized (e.g., to stems or n-grams), and the constituent query terms are then translated using the mappings derived from the parallel texts. Multiple base runs are combined to create a final ranked list

Table 6. Official results for bilingual task

run id	MAP	% mono	=Best	>=Median	Rel. Found	Relevant	# topics
aplbideita	0.4264	89.88	11	38	789	809	51
aplbideitb	0.4603	97.03	12	45	780		
aplbifidea	0.3454	71.19	16	39	1554	1825	56
aplbifideb	0.3430	70.69	16	42	1504		
aplbifrnla	0.4045	83.97	15	33	1493	1577	56
aplbifrnlb	0.4365	90.62	13	33	1442		
aplbiitesa	0.4242	90.66	5	32	2174	2368	57
aplbiitesb	0.4261	91.07	4	38	2189		

The performance of APL's official bilingual runs are described in Table 6.

Our runs named *aplbixxyya* are bilingual runs that were translated directly from the source language to the target language; each run was a combination of four base runs that either used words, stems, 4-grams, or 5-grams, with (post-translation) relevance feedback. The runs named *aplbixxyyb* were combined in the same way, however the four constituent base runs did not make use of post-translation feedback. When words or stems were used a value of 0.3 was used for alpha; when n-grams were used the value was 0.5. The base runs are compared in Figure 4.

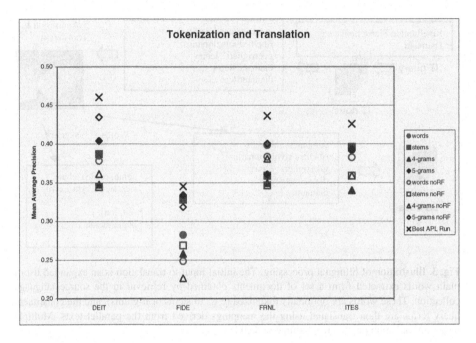

Fig. 4. Analysis of the base-runs used for bilingual retrieval. The best APL run was achieved in each instance through run combination

From observing the data in Table 6 and Figure 4, it would appear that the use of post-translation feedback did not enhance performance when multiple runs were combined. The two types of runs seemed to perform similarly in two language pairs (Finnish to German and Italian to Spanish); however, the merged runs without relevance feedback did better for the German to Italian and French to Dutch runs.

Combination of methods resulted in between a 3 and 10% gain depending on language pair. We have not yet had the opportunity to retrospectively analyze the contribution to our overall performance of pre-translation expansion.

5   Multilingual Experiments

We initially thought to create runs for the multilingual task in the exact same way as for the bilingual task. However, we decided to use English as our source language and we had to create translation lists for seven languages using four tokenization types (a total of 28 mappings). Construction of the 5-gram lists took longer than expected and so we had to modify our plans for our official submission. We decided to submit a hybrid run based on words, stems, and 4-grams; merging was again accomplished using normalized scores. As with the bilingual task, runs ending in 'a' denote the use of post-translation relevance feedback, while runs ending in 'b' did not use feedback (see Table 7).

Table 7. APL results for multilingual task

run id	Task	MAP	=Best	>=Median	Rel. Found	Relevant	# topics
aplmuen4a	4	0.2926	3	33	4377	6145	60
aplmuen4b	4	0.2747	0	34	4419		
aplmuen8a	8	0.2377	4	28	5939	9902	60
aplmuen8b	8	0.2406	1	41	5820		

6 Conclusions

For the first time we were able to directly compare words, various lengths of character n-grams, a suffix stemmer, and an n-gram alternative to stemming, all using the same retrieval engine. We found that n-grams of shorter lengths ($n=4$ or $n=5$) were preferable across the CLEF 2003 languages and that n-grams generally outperformed use of the Snowball stemmer: 4-grams had a 8% mean relative advantage across the 9 languages compared to stems; however stemming was better in Italian and Spanish (by 17% and 5% respectively). We found best performance can be obtained using a combination of methods. If emphasis is placed on accuracy over storage requirements or response time, this approach is reasonable. For bilingual retrieval we identified a method for direct translation of n-grams instead of word-based translation. Without the use of relevance feedback, 5-grams outperformed stems by an average of 17% over the four bilingual pairs though 4-grams appeared to lose much of their monolingual superiority. When feedback was used, the gap narrowed substantially.

This work should not be taken as an argument against language resources, but rather as further evidence that knowledge-light methods can be quite effective, when optimized. We are particularly excited about the use of non-word translation (*i.e.,* using direct n-gram translation) as this appears to have the potential to avoid several pitfalls that plague dictionary-based translation of words.

References

1. Monz, C., Kamps, J., de Rijke, M.: The University of Amsterdam at CLEF 2002. Working Notes of the CLEF 2002 Workshop. (2002) 73-84
2. Reidsma, D., Hiemstra, D., de Jong, F., Kraaij, W.: Cross-language Retrieval at Twente and TNO. Working Notes of the CLEF 2002 Workshop. (2002) 111-114
3. Savoy, J.: Cross-language information retrieval: experiments based on CLEF 2000 corpora. Information Processing and Management, Vol. 39(1). (2003) 75-115
4. Miller, E., Shen, D., Liu, J., Nicholas, C.: Performance and Scalability of a Large-Scale N-gram Based Information Retrieval System. In the Journal of Digital Information, Vol. 1(5). (2000)
5. McNamee P., Mayfield, J.: N-grams for Translation and Retrieval in CL-SDR. In this volume.
6. Pirkola, A., Hedlund, T., Keskusalo, H., Järvelin, K.: Dictionary-Based Cross-Language Information Retrieval: Problems, Methods, and Research Findings. In Information Retrieval, Vol. 4. (2001) 209-230

7. Tomlinson, S.: Experiments in 8 European Languages with Hummingbird SearchServer at CLEF 2002. Working Notes of the CLEF 2002 Workshop. (2002) 203-214

8. Miller, D., Leek, T., Schwartz, R.: A hidden Markov model information retrieval system. In Proceedings of the 22nd Annual International ACM SIGIR Conference on Research and Development in Information Retrieval. (1999) 214-221

9. Hiemstra, D.: Using Language Models for Information Retrieval. Ph. D. Thesis. Center for Telematics and Information Technology, The Netherlands, (2000)

10. Jelinek F., Mercer, R.: Interpolated Estimation of Markov Source Parameters from Sparse Data. In Gelsema, E. and Kanal, L. (eds.): Pattern Recognition in Practice. North Holland, (1980) 381-402

11. McNamee, P., Mayfield, J.: Scalable Multilingual Information Access. In C. Peters, M. Braschler, J. Gonzalo and M. Kluck (eds): Advances in Cross-Language Information Retrieval. CLEF 2002 workshop, revised papers. LNCS 2785 Springer (2003).

12. Zhai C., Lafferty, J.: A Study of Smoothing Methods for Language Models Applied to Ad Hoc Information Retrieval. In Proceedings of the 24th Annual International ACM SIGIR Conference on Research and Development in Information Retrieval. (2001) 334-342

13. McNamee, P., Mayfield, J.: Character N-gram Tokenization for European Language Text Retrieval. Information Retrieval 7 (1-2): 73-97 (2004).

14. Porter, M.: Snowball: A Language for Stemming Algorithms. Available online at http://snowball.tartarus.org/texts/introduction.html, (visited 13 March 2003).

15. Mayfield J., McNamee, P.: Single N-gram Stemming. In the Proceedings of the 26th Annual International ACM SIGIR Conference on Research and Development in Information Retrieval. (2003) 415-416

16. Kwok, K., Chan, M.: Improving Two-Stage Ad-Hoc Retrieval for Short Queries. In the Proceedings of the 21st International ACM SIGIR Conference on Research and Development in Information Retrieval. (1998) 250-256

17. http://europa.eu.int/

18. Church, K.: Char_align: A program for aligning parallel texts at the character level. In: Proceedings of the 31st Annual Meeting of the Association for Computational Linguistics. (1993) 1-8

19. McNamee, P., Mayfield, J.: Comparing Cross-Language Query Expansion Techniques by Degrading Translation Resources. In: Proceedings of the 25th Annual International Conference on Research and Development in Information Retrieval. (2002) 159-166

Report on CLEF-2003 Experiments: Two Ways of Extracting Multilingual Resources from Corpora

[F]Nicola Cancedda, [F]Hervé Déjean, [F]Éric Gaussier,
[F]Jean-Michel Renders, and [*]Alexei Vinokourov

[F]Xerox Research Centre Europe,
[*]Royal Holloway University of London
[F]Firstname.Lastname@xrce.xerox.com
[*]alexei@cs.rhul.ac.uk

Abstract. We present two main approaches to cross-language information retrieval based on the exploitation of multilingual corpora to derive cross-lingual
term-term correspondences. These two approaches are evaluated in the framework
of the multilingual-4 (ML4) task.

1 Introduction

Most approaches to Cross-Language Information Retrieval (CLIR) rely on query translation based on existing machine-readable dictionaries and/or translation systems ([1–5],
to name but a few), and face the problem of the adequacy of existing bilingual resources
to the collection that is searched. However, when this collection is multilingual, one
may benefit from automatically extracted bilingual lexicons, which can display a better
coverage and allow for more accurate translations of queries. This perspective is mentioned in [3], even though the authors failed to derive accurate bilingual lexicons from
their collection. It is indirectly exploited in [6] where the authors derive a probabilistic
translation lexicon, based on IBM translation models 1 and 2 ([7]), from a corpus of
parallel texts different from the searched collection.

We want to experiment here with two methods to exploit parallel corpora for CLIR
purposes. The first one relies on the inference of a bilingual semantic representation via
cross-language canonical correlation analysis, whereas the second one, more traditional,
relies on the extraction of bilingual lexicons from parallel corpora.

However, the CLEF-2003 multilingual collection is not parallel, but comparable, that
is to say that rather than being translations of one another, documents cover the same
topics, in the same domains. Nevertheless, up to now, extraction methods developed
on comparable corpora, unlike methods for parallel corpora, have not provided results
good enough to be directly used in CLIR, as is argued in [8]. This indicates that a
compromise between the use of parallel and comparable corpora has to be found, so as
to derive query translation modules that display both accuracy and coverage properties.
In addition to the above-mentioned methods, we will thus report on experiments aimed
at combining bilingual lexicons extracted from parallel and comparable corpora. In
our case, the parallel corpus retained is the JOC[1], whereas the comparable one is the

---

[1] Used in the Arcade evaluation task, www.lpl.univ-aix.fr/projects/arcade

C. Peters et al. (Eds.): CLEF 2003, LNCS 3237, pp. 98–107, 2004.
© Springer-Verlag Berlin Heidelberg 2004

collection itself. The implicit goal behind these experiments is to develop state-of-the-art query translation modules, fully adapted to the collection to be searched.

2   Linguistic Preprocessing

As a preprocessing step, we tag and lemmatize corpora, queries and bilingual resources. Only lexical words (nouns, verbs, adverbs, adjectives) are indexed and only single word entries in our resources are used. Our (lexicon-based) lemmatizer provides a partial segmentation for the German compounds. Additionally, we segment German words which were not decomposed by the lemmatizer using the following patterns:

Pattern	Segmentation
A([^aeuioy])sB	A([^aeuioy]) B
A-B	A B

German spelling (umlaut and eszett) is also normalized.

3   Canonical Correlation Analysis for Cross-Lingual Retrieval

In this work we automatically model a semantic correspondence between terms of different languages, in the spirit of cross-lingual latent semantic indexing (CL-LSI) [9]. In CL-LSI, using a parallel corpus, after merging each pair into a single 'document', the frequent co-occurrence of two terms in the same document can be interpreted as an indication of cross-language correlation. In this framework, a common vector-space, including words from both languages, is created and then the training set is analysed in this space using SVD. This problem can be regarded either as an unsupervised problem with paired documents, or as a supervised monolingual problem with very complex labels (i.e. the label of an English document could be its French counterpart). In either way, the data can be readily obtained without an explicit labeling effort, and furthermore there is no loss of information in compressing the meaning of a document into a discrete label. As an alternative to CL-LSI, we employ Canonical Correlation Analysis (CCA) [10] [11] to learn a representation of text that captures aspects of its meaning. Given a paired bilingual corpus, this method defines two embedding spaces for the documents of the corpus, one for each language, and an obvious one-to-one correspondence between points in the two spaces. CCA then finds projections in the two embedding spaces for which the resulting projected values are highly correlated. In other words, it looks for particular combinations of words that appear to have the same co-occurrence patterns in the two languages. Our hypothesis is that finding such correlations across a paired bilingual corpus will locate the underlying semantics, since we assume that the two languages are 'conditionally independent', or that the only thing they have in common is their meaning. The directions would carry information about the *concepts* that stood behind the process of generation of the text and, although expressed differently in different languages, are, nevertheless, semantically equivalent. This representation is then used for the retrieval task, providing a better performance than LSI on some tested corpora

[12]. Such directions are then used to calculate the coordinates of the documents in a 'language independent' way. Of course, particular statistical care is needed for excluding 'spurious' correlations. We have shown that the correlations we find are not the effect of chance, and that the resulting representation significantly improves performance of retrieval systems [12]. Indeed, the correlation between English and French documents can be explained by means of relations between the generative processes of the two versions of the documents, that we assume to be conditionally independent given the *topic* or *content*. Under such assumptions, hence, these correlations detect similarities in content between the two documents, and can be exploited to derive a semantic representation of the text. The CCA machinery is briefly given below.

3.1   Canonical Correlation Analysis

For us, the multivariate random variables to which CCA is applied correspond to document-vectors (in the bag of words representation) in English and French, and there is a one-to-one relation between them corresponding to documents that are translations of each other. We will now consider sets of words that are correlated between the two languages (sets of words in the two languages that have a correlated pattern of appearance in the corpus). We will assume that such sets approximate the notion of 'concepts' in each language, and that such concepts are the translation of each other. Rather than considering plain sets, we will consider terms to have a degree of membership in a given set. In other words, the term t_i will be assigned a weight α_i for each concept we consider, and every concept will correspond to a vector $\alpha_x \in \Re^n$ in English, and a vector $\alpha_y \in \Re^m$ in French. We will use that weight α_i to form linear combinations of terms, so that they can define a direction in the term space.

Suppose as for CL-LSI we are given *aligned* texts in, for simplicity, two languages, i.e. every text in one language $x_i \in \Re^n$ is a translation of text $y_i \in \Re^m$ in another language. In practice, each text can correspond to a complete document, a paragraph, or a sentence. The finer the textual units, the more accurate the correlation statistics. Our hypothesis is that having aligned texts $S_x = (x_1, ..., x_\ell) \subseteq \Re^n$ and $S_y = (y_1, ..., y_\ell) \subseteq \Re^m$ we can learn (semantic) directions $\hat{w}_x$ and $\hat{w}_y$ where we use the notation $\hat{w} = \frac{w}{||w||}$ so that the projections $\hat{w}'_x x$ and $\hat{w}'_y y$ of input data images from the different languages would be maximally correlated. These new random variables are univariate, and linear combinations of the previous ones. We consider optimizing this quantity with respect to the choice of $\hat{w}_1 \in \Re^n$ and $\hat{w}_2 \in \Re^m$. This leads to the following objective functions and optimization problems:

$$\rho = \max_{w_x, w_y} \mathrm{corr}(\hat{w}'_x x, \hat{w}'_y y)$$

This optimization problem can be transformed into a generalized eigenvalue problem as follows. We are looking for the maximum correlation directions:

$$\text{maximize } \rho = \frac{\mathrm{cov}(x,z)}{\mathrm{var}x \cdot \mathrm{var}z} = \frac{E[xz]}{\sqrt{E[xx]E[zz]}} = \frac{E[\mathbf{w}'_x \mathbf{C}'_{xz}\mathbf{w}_z]}{\sqrt{E[\mathbf{w}'_x \mathbf{C}'_{xx}\mathbf{w}_x]E[\mathbf{w}'_z \mathbf{C}_{zz}\mathbf{w}_z]}}$$
$$\text{subject to } ||\mathbf{w}_x|| = ||\mathbf{w}_z|| = 1$$

where we are using the covariance matrix:

$$C = \begin{pmatrix} C_{xx} & C_{xz} \\ C_{zx} & C_{zz} \end{pmatrix} = E\left(\begin{pmatrix} \mathbf{x} \\ \mathbf{z} \end{pmatrix} \begin{pmatrix} \mathbf{x} \\ \mathbf{z} \end{pmatrix}' \right)$$

The solutions of this problem can be obtained by solving a related generalized eigen-problem

$$A\mathbf{w} = \lambda B\mathbf{w} \qquad (1)$$

and the solution $\mathbf{w}$ directly provides the directions $\mathbf{w}_x$ and $\mathbf{w}_z$ of maximum correlation:

$$A = \begin{pmatrix} 0 & C_{xz} \\ C_{zx} & 0 \end{pmatrix}$$

$$B = \begin{pmatrix} C_{xx} & 0 \\ 0 & C_{zz} \end{pmatrix}$$

$$\mathbf{w} = \begin{pmatrix} \mu_x \mathbf{w}_x \\ \mu_z \mathbf{w}_z \end{pmatrix}$$

Note that if λ is an eigenvalue, so is $-\lambda$ thus the spectrum is $\{\lambda_1, -\lambda_1, ..., \lambda_N, -\lambda_N\}$.

3.2   Application of CCA to the Cross-Lingual Retrieval Task

The kernel CCA procedure identifies a set of projections from both languages into a common semantic space. This provides a natural framework for performing cross-language information retrieval. We first select a number d of semantic dimensions, $1 \leq d \leq N$, with largest correlation values ρ. To process an incoming query q we expand q into the vector representation for its language $\widetilde{q}$ and project it onto the d canonical $\mathcal{F}$-correlation components: $[q] = A^T Z^T \widetilde{q}$ using the appropriate vector for that language, where A is an $N \times d$ matrix whose columns are the first solutions of (1) for the given language sorted by eigenvalue in descending order. Notice that in this case we use the standard dot product to perform the projection, but non-linear projections can also be obtained by replacing the dot product with a non-linear kernel.

3.3   Learning on Paired Data

The whole training collection consists of 1.3 million pairs of aligned text chunks (sentences or smaller fragments) from the 36th Canadian Parliament proceedings. We used only the first 1000 documents. The raw text was split into sentences with Adwait Ratna-parkhi's MXTERMINATOR and the sentences were aligned with I. Dan Melamed's GSA tool (for details on the collection and also for the source see [13]).

The text was split into 'paragraphs' based on '***' delimiters and these 'paragraphs' were treated as separate documents. After removing stop-words in both French and English parts and rare words (i.e. appearing less than three times) we obtained 5159×1000 term-by-document 'English' matrix and 5611×1000 'French' matrix (we also removed a few documents that appeared to be problematic when split into paragraphs).

Table 1. Upper bound of the coverage of lexicons extracted from different sources

Elra	Oxford-Hachette	Hansard	JOC	ML4
0.78	0.78	0.80	0.90	0.98

3.4   Experimental Results

The test corpus and queries were processed by Xerox Research Centre Europe as explained in Section 2. The results were unimpressive due to the fact that we restricted ourselves only to the French part - Le Monde - due to the lack of time. Possibly there were also bugs in software and we are working to reveal them, renewed results may appear in the final version.

4   Query Translation

We want to assess in this section the usefulness of bilingual lexicons extracted from collections. In order to illustrate the potential gain this approach could yield, we conducted the following simple experiment. We first collected all the English terms from the queries associated to the CLEF multilingual task, from years 2000 to 2003. We then tried to evaluate whether or not we were able to translate those terms with manually built, existing dictionaries, and whether or not we were able to translate them with bilingual lexicons automatically derived from multilingual collections. To this end, we retained two multilingual dictionaries, the ELRA dictionary[2], and the Oxford-Hachette[3]. For corpora, we retained a part of the Hansard[4], the JOC corpus (already mentioned in footnote 1, comprising ca. 3.5 millions English tokens), and the CLEF ML4 collection itself. For each term present in the set of English queries, we checked whether it was present in the lexicons associated with the above resources. The percentage of English terms found in the lexicons is summarized in Table 1.

As may have been noticed, the figures we obtained are only upper bounds on the actual coverage of each resource, since the presence of a term in a dictionary does not imply that the proposed translation(s) are appropriate for the collection at hand. Furthermore, there is an important qualitative difference between manually built and automatically extracted lexicons, a difference that may well balance the advantage for corpus-based methods displayed ina ble 1. However, were we able to accurately extract bilingual lexicons from corpora, Table 1 shows that we would have an important gain over using existing, general purpose dictionaries. Table 2 supports this fact and shows how the average precision evolves, on a sub-part of ML4, according to the lexicon used to translate queries.

The column (JOC+ML4) combines the lexicons extracted from the JOC and ML4 corpora, as detailed in Section 4.3. The bilingual runs correspond to English queries

---

[2] Multilingual dictionary, available from ELRA, www.elra.info, comprising ca. 45000 English entries.

[3] Bilingual English-French dictionary, comprising ca. 45000 English entries.

[4] In fact a sub-part of it, comprising ca. 20 millions English tokens.

Table 2. Performance of different lexicons for query translation

Average precision	Elra	JOC	ML4	JOC+ML4
Bilingual	0.29	0.365	0.228	0.388
Multilingual (merge)	0.192	0.289	0.165	0.302
French (bilingual)	0.271	0.362	0.188	0.389
German (bilingual)	0.276	0.361	0.203	0.380
Spanish (bilingual)	0.304	0.411	0.221	0.431

translated in the corresponding target language (all these experiments, as well as the following ones, are based on the vector-space model). As can be noted, the use of automatically derived bilingual lexicons significantly outperforms the use of existing dictionaries on this collection.

We are now going to review the methods we used for extracting bilingual lexicons from parallel and comparable corpora.

4.1 Bilingual Lexicon Extraction from Parallel Corpora

Recent research has demonstrated that statistical alignment models can be highly successful at extracting word correspondences from parallel corpora ([7, 14–17]) among others. All these studies are based on the assumption that, once documents have been aligned at the sentence level, the more two words from different languages co-occur in aligned sentences, the more likely that they are translations of each other. In the present paper, we rely on the word-to-word translation lexicon obtained from parallel corpora, following the method described in [19], which can be summarized as follows.

We first represent co-occurrences between words across translations by a matrix, the rows of which represent the source language words, the columns the target language words, and the elements of the matrix the expected alignment frequencies (EAFs) for the words appearing in the corresponding row and column. Empty words are added in both languages in order to deal with words with no equivalent in the other language.

The estimation of the expected alignment frequency is based on the Iterative Proportional Fitting Procedure (IPFP) presented in [20]. This iterative procedure updates the current estimate $n_{ij}^{(k)}$ of the EAF of source word i with target word j, using the following two-stage equations:

$$n_{ij}^{(k,1)} = \sum_{s,(i,j)\in s} n_{ij}^{(k-1,2)} \times \frac{s_i}{n_{i.}^{(k-1,2)}}$$

$$n_{ij}^{(k,2)} = \sum_{s,(i,j)\in s} n_{ij}^{(k,1)} \times \frac{s_j}{n_{.j}^{(k,1)}}$$

where $n_{i.}$ and $n_{.j}$ are the current estimates of the row and column marginals, s is a pair of aligned sentences containing words i and j, and s_i and s_j are the observed frequencies of words i and j in s. The initial estimates $n_{ij}^{(0,2)}$ are the observed frequencies of co-occurrences, obtained by considering each pair of aligned sentences and by incrementing the alignment frequencies accordingly. The sequence of updates will eventually converge and the EAFs are then normalized (by dividing each element n_{ij} by the row marginal $n_{i.}$), so as to yield probabilistic translation lexicons, in which each source word is associated with a target word through a score. In the remainder of the paper, we will use $P_1(t|s)$ to denote the probability of selecting target word t as translation for source word s, as given by this method.

4.2   Bilingual Lexicon Extraction from Comparable Corpora

Bilingual lexicon extraction from non-parallel but comparable corpora has been studied by a number of researchers, [8, 21–24] among others. Their work relies on the assumption that if two words are mutual translations, then their more frequent collocates (taken here in a very broad sense) are likely to be mutual translations as well. Based on this assumption, a standard approach consists in building context vectors, for each source and target word, which aim at capturing the most significant collocates. The target context vectors are then translated using a general bilingual dictionary, and compared with the source context vectors.

Our implementation of this strategy relies on the following steps:

1. For each word w, build a context vector by considering all the words occurring in a window centered on w, run through the corpus. Each word i in the context vector of w is then weighted with a measure of its association with w. However, in order to ensure we make adequate use of the prior knowledge provided by the general dictionary, we include w in its context vector. Lastly, we have used here a window of 5 words before and after w, and retained the mutual information as the measure of association.
2. The context vectors of the target words are then translated with our general bilingual dictionary, leaving the weights unchanged (when several translations are proposed by the dictionary, we consider all of them with the same weight)
3. The similarity of each source word s, for each target word t, is computed on the basis of the cosine measure
4. The similarities are then normalized to yield a probabilistic translation lexicon, $P_2(t|s)$.

4.3   Model Combination

Because they contain different information, the comparable and parallel corpora yield different translations that need be combined in order to obtain a complete translated query. Such a combination should account for the fact that for some source words the information provided by the comparable corpus is more reliable than that provided by the parallel one (as is the case when the source word is not present in the parallel corpus), whereas for some other source words the situation is reversed. However, because of time constraints, we were not able to adopt this strategy, and had to resort to a simpler linear combination, in which the final vector representing the query in target language is given by:

$$\vec{q_t} = (\alpha \times P_1 + (1 - \alpha) \times P_2) \times \vec{q_s} \qquad (2)$$

α is a scalar representing the weight associated with the translation provided by the parallel corpus. We optimized the value of α on the queries corresponding to years 2000 to 2002.

4.4   Multilingual Merging

Our strategy to merge results from different languages relies on the fact that if we use "similar" translation matrices, and if the scoring method is identical for each language, then the results from different languages can be merged directly. Using similar translation matrices means that the length (as measured by the norm) of target queries should be identical (since they all issue from the same English query). In order to ensure this, we normalise each target query by its length ($\vec{q_t} \rightarrow \frac{\vec{q_t}}{\| \vec{q_t} \|}$). Furthermore, to get an equivalent, on the English collection, of the translation step used in the other languages, we consider the English sub-collection to constitue a comparable corpus on its own, from which we build a term-term co-occurrence matrix in exactly the same way as we built a translation matrix in Section 4.2 (the source and target languages being identical here). This matrix is then used to expand English queries with most similar terms.

4.5   Weighting Schemes

Table 3 shows the results we obtained with two different weighting schemes on the ML4 collection, for the 2003 queries. Note that queries are weighted prior to translation.

Table 3. Influence of weighting schemes

Weighting scheme	Average precision
Lnu/ntn	0.2118
Ltc/ntn	0.1860

The results displayed in Table 3 are obtained by translating queries with the combination of the lexicons derived from JOC and ML4 as explained above. Despite the important difference the two weighting schemes have on the monolingual collections (cf. e.g. [5]), we see here that the bilingual retrieval, followed by the multilingual merge, flattens the difference to only ca. 2.5 points.

5   Conclusion

We have tested two main approaches to cross-language information retrieval based on the exploitation of multilingual corpora to derive cross-lingual term-term correspondences. The first approach makes use of parallel corpora to derive an interlingual semantic representation of documents, using canonical correlation analysis. The second approach aims at directly extracting bilingual lexicons, both from parallel and comparable corpora, to be used for query translation. Our experiments show that the second approach outperforms a standard approach using existing bilingual dictionaries for query translation. We plan in the future to pursue the promising road of bilingual lexicon extraction from comparable corpora.

Acknowledgements

This research was partially supported by the European Commission under the KerMIT Project No. IST-2001-25431.

References

1. Hull, D., Grefenstette, G.: Querying across Languages: a Dictionary-Based Approach to Multilingual Information Retrieval. In Proceedings of the 19th Annual International ACM SIGIR Conference on Research and Development in Information Retrieval (1996).
2. Ballesteros, L., Croft, B.W.: Phrasal Translation and Query Expansion Techniques for Cross-Language Information Retrieval. In Proceedings of the 20th Annual International ACM SIGIR Conference on Research and Development in Information Retrieval (1997).
3. Davis, M.W. and Ogden, W.C.: QUILT: Implementing a Large-Scale Cross-Language Text Retrieval System. In Proceedings of the 20th Annual International ACM SIGIR Conference on Research and Development in Information Retrieval (1997).
4. Gey, F.C., Jiang, H., Petras, V., Chen, A.: Cross-Language Retrieval for the CLEF Collections - Comparing Multiple Methods of Retrieval. In Proceedings of the Cross-Language Evaluation Forum, CLEF 2000. LNCS 2069. Springer (2001) 116–128.
5. Savoy, J.: Report on CLEF-2002 Experiments: Combining Multiple Sources of Evidence. In Proceedings of CLEF 2002. LNCS 2785 (2003) 66–90.
6. Nie, J.-Y., Simard, M., Isabelle P., Durand R.: Cross-language information retrieval based on parallel texts and automatic mining of parallel texts from the Web. In Proceedings of the 22nd Annual International ACM SIGIR Conference on Research and Development in Information Retrieval (1999).
7. Brown, P., Della Pietra, S., Della Pietra, V., Mercer, R.L.: The Mathematics of Statistical Machine Learning Translation: Parameter Estimation. Computational Linguistics 19(2) (1993) 263–311
8. Peters, C., Picchi, E.: Capturing the Comparable: A System for Querying Comparable Text Corpora. In Bolasco, S., Lebart, L., Salem, A. (eds.). JADT'95 - 3rd International Conference on Statistical Analysis of Textual Data (1995) 255–262.
9. Littman, M.L., Dumais, S.T., Landauer, T.K.: Automatic cross-language information retrieval using latent semantic indexing. In Grefenstette, G. (ed.). Cross language information retrieval. Kluwer (1998).
10. Bach, F.R., Jordan, M.I.: Kernel indepedendent component analysis. Journal of Machine Learning Research 3 (2002)1–48.
11. Lai, P.L., Fyfe, C.: Kernel and nonlinear canonical correlation analysis. International Journal of Neural Systems 10(5) (2000) 365-377.
12. Vinokourov, A., Shawe-Taylor, J., Cristianini, N.: Inferring a Semantic Representation of Text via Cross-Language Correlation Analysis. In Advances of Neural Information Processing Systems 15 (2002).
13. Germann, U.: Aligned Hansards of the 36th Parliament of Canada. http://www.isi.edu/natural-language/download/hansard/ (2001). Release 2001-1a.
14. Dagan, I., Itai, I.: Word Sense Disambiguation using a Second Language Monolingual Corpus. Computational Linguistics 2(4) (1994).
15. Gale, W.A., Church, K.W.: A Program for Aligning Sentences in Bilingual Corpora. In Meeting of the Association for Computational Linguistics (1991) 177–184.

16. Gaussier, E.: Flow Network Models for Word ALignment and Terminology Extraction from Bilingual Corpora. In Proceedings of the joint 17th International Conference on Computational Linguistics and 26th Annual Meeting of the Association for Computational Linguistics (1998) 444-450.
17. Hiemstra, D.: Using Statistical Methods to create a Bilingual Dictionary. Masters Thesis. Universiteit Twente (1996).
18. Hull, D.: Automating the constuction of bilingual terminology lexicons. Terminlogy 5(2) (1997).
19. Gaussier, E., Hull, D., Ait-Mokhtar, S.: Term Alignment in Use: Machine-Aided Human Translation. In J. Véronis (ed.) Parallel Text Processing Alignment and Use of Translation Corpora. Kluwer Academic Publishers (2000).
20. Bishop, Y., Fienberg, S., Holland, P.: Discrete Multivariate Analysis. MIT Press (1975).
21. Tanaka, K., Iwasaki, H.: Extraction of Lexical Translations from Non-Aligned Corpora. In International Conference on Computational Linguistics, COLING'96 (1996).
22. Shahzad, I., Ohtake, K., Masuyama, S., Yamamoto, K.: Identifying Translations of Compound Nouns Using Non-aligned Corpora. In Proceedings of the Workshop MAL'99 (1999) 108–113.
23. Rapp, R.: Automatic Identification of Word Translations from Unrelated English and German Corpora. In Proceedings of the European Association for Computational Linguistics (1999).
24. Fung, P.: A Statistical View on Bilingual Lexicon Extraction: From parallel corpora to non-parallel corpora. In Jean Véronis (ed.) Parallel Text Processing. Alignment and Use of Translation Corpora. Kluwer Academic Publishers (2000).

Combining Query Translation and Document Translation in Cross-Language Retrieval

Aitao Chen[1] and Fredric C. Gey[2]

[1] School of Information Management and Systems,
University of California at Berkeley, CA 94720-4600, USA
aitao@sims.berkeley.edu
[2] UC Data Archive & Technical Assistance (UC DATA),
University of California at Berkeley, CA 94720-5100, USA
gey@ucdata.berkeley.edu

Abstract. This paper describes monolingual, bilingual, and multilingual retrieval experiments using the CLEF 2003 test collection. The paper compares query translation-based multilingual retrieval with document translation-based multilingual retrieval where the documents are translated into the query language by translating the document words individually using machine translation systems or statistical translation lexicons derived from parallel texts. The multilingual retrieval results show that document translation-based retrieval is slightly better than the query translation-based retrieval on the CLEF 2003 test collection. Furthermore, combining query translation and document translation in multilingual retrieval achieves even better performance.

1 Introduction

One focus of this paper is on the use of parallel texts for creating statistical translation lexicons to support cross-language retrieval (bilingual or multilingual) and for creating stemmers to support both monolingual and cross-language retrieval. Another focus is on evaluating the effectiveness of translating documents by translating document words individually using translation lexicons created from machine translation (MT) systems or from parallel texts, and the effectiveness of combining query translation and document translation in cross-language retrieval. At CLEF 2003, we participated in the *monolingual, bilingual, multilingual-4,* and *multilingual-8* retrieval tasks. The retrieval system we used at CLEF 2003 is described in detail in our CLEF 2002 paper [5].

2 New Resources

This section describes the new resources that we developed and were used in our CLEF 2003 runs.

C. Peters et al. (Eds.): CLEF 2003, LNCS 3237, pp. 108–121, 2004.

2.1   Stoplists

We gleaned 436 Swedish stopwords from a Swedish grammar book written in English [10], and created a stoplist of 567 Finnish stopwords gathered from two Finnish textbooks written in English [1, 2]. A foreign language textbook written in English usually gives the English translations of the foreign words mentioned in the textbook. We included in a stoplist those foreign words whose English translations are English stopwords. The stoplist used in indexing Finnish topics includes additional stopwords found in the previous CLEF Finnish topics. The stoplist used in indexing Swedish topics also includes additional stopwords found in the previous CLEF Swedish topics. The CLEF 2003 topics were not used for constructing stoplists.

2.2   Base Lexicons

We developed a Finnish and a Swedish base lexicons for splitting Finnish and Swedish compounds. The base lexicons were largely automatically generated. A base lexicon should include all and only the words and their variants that are not compounds. Our approach to creating a base lexicon is to start with a wordlist and then remove compounds in the wordlist. The remaining words make up the base lexicon. We first combined the Finnish words in the Finnish document collection and the Finnish words found in the Finnish version of the ispell spelling checker. We removed the words of 10 or more characters that can be decomposed into two or more component words of at least 5 characters. The decompounding procedure used was described in [5]. To decompose the long words in the initial Finnish wordlist using the decompounding procedure, we need a base lexicon. The base lexicon for splitting compounds in the initial Finnish wordlist consists of the words that are at least 7-character long, the 6-character words that occur at least 50 times in the Finnish collection, and the 5-character words that occur at least 100 times in the Finnish collection. This base lexicon was used to split compounds in the initial wordlist, and the words that can be decomposed were removed from the initial wordlist. We also removed from the initial wordlist all the words that are one to four characters long. Lastly we manually removed some of the remaining long words that look like compounds to us who do not know Finnish or Swedish. Our Finnish base lexicon consists of the remaining words on the wordlist. The Swedish base lexicon was created in the same way. Both the wordlist for the Finnish spelling checker and the wordlist for the Swedish spelling checker were downloaded from http://packages.debian.org/unstable/text/ispell.html.

2.3   Statistical Translation Lexicons

We downloaded the Official Journal of the European Union [8] for 1998, 1999, the first four months of 2000, and 2002 minus July and August. The documents are in PDF format and available in 11 languages, including all 8 languages involved in the multilingual-8 retrieval task. The year 2002 version of the *ps2ascii* conversion program on a Linux machine was used to convert the source PDF files into text files. The converted texts are noisy in that many words were strung together. For instance, sometimes the English articles (i.e, a, an, the), pronouns, and prepositions are combined with the preceding or the following word. Sometimes two content words are concatenated, resulting in many compounds in all eight languages. In an one-page English document, in the converted texts, we found words like *culturalmix*, *andthe*, *xenophobiaand*, *inproclaiming*, *allhelped*, and more.

The original texts in PDF format are presented in two-column format. When a word is broken into two parts, a dash character is appended to the first part at the end of a line, and the second part starts on a new line. After the PDF files are converted into texts, there are many words with a dash inserted in the middle. For instance, the German word *Be-ämpfung* (the first part *Be-* appears at the end of a line, while the second part *ämpfung* starts on the following line) was converted into *Be- a"mpfung*. We did not, but should have, removed the dash and the additional space after the dash character.

Later we found another PDF to texts conversion program named *pdftotext*, also available on a Linux machine. The texts converted from PDF files using *pdftotext* look much cleaner. The same word *Be-ämpfung* was converted into *Bekämpfung* using *pdftotext*. Not only the diacritic mark was retained in its original form, but also the dash character inserted into the word was taken out by *pdftotext*.

After the diacritic marks were restored in the converted texts, the text files were aligned at the line level (a line may contain a long paragraph), then at the sentence level, after splitting a line into sentences, using a length-based alignment program [9]. Because many words in the converted texts were joined together after conversion, we used our decompounding procedure to split compounds (including the ones created by joining two or more consecutive words in the conversion process) into their component words. About 316,000 unique compounds in the English texts were split into their component words. Our decompounding procedure does not split compounds into words that are three or fewer characters long, so we had to write special programs to split compounds that contain short words like the English article *an* or preposition *of*.

From the sentence-aligned parallel texts, we created six statistical translation lexicons using the GIZA++ toolkit [13]: 1) English to Dutch; 2) English to Finnish; 3) English to Swedish; 4) Dutch to English; 5) Finnish to English; and 6) Swedish to English. We were unable to use the toolkit to create statistical translation lexicons between Italian and Spanish, German and Italian, French and Dutch, and Finish and German because of the large vocabulary sizes in these languages and limited memory on our machine. To support bilingual retrieval, we created three translation dictionaries from the sentence-aligned parallel texts based on statistical association, the maximum likelihood ratio test statistic [7]. The three dictionaries are the Italian to Spanish, German to Italian, and Finnish to German translation lexicons. We did not have adequate time to create a French to Dutch dictionary from the French/Dutch parallel texts before the results were due. The procedure for creating translation lexicons from sentence-aligned parallel texts using statistical association measures is described in detail in [4].

2.4   Stemmers

In [6] we present an algorithm for automatically generating an Arabic stemmer from an Arabic to English machine translation system and an English stemmer. The words in the Arabic documents are translated individually into English, then the English translations are conflated using an English stemmer. All the Arabic words whose English translations share the same English stem are grouped together to form one cluster. In stemming, all the Arabic words in the same cluster are conflated to the same word. The words in a cluster are generally either morphologically or semantically related.

We developed one Finnish stemmer and one Swedish stemmer from the English/Finnish and English/Swedish parallel texts based on the same idea. As mentioned in Section 2.3, we generated one Finnish to English and one Swedish to English translation lexicons from the parallel texts. For a Finnish word, we chose the English translation of the highest translation probability, i.e., the most likely English translation, as its translation. So every Finnish word in the parallel texts has just one English translation. The Finnish words in the parallel texts that have the same English translation were grouped together to form a cluster. The English texts were stemmed using an English morphological analyzer [11] before the Finnish/English texts were fed into GIZA++ for creating statistical translation lexicon. The English morphological stemmer maps plural nouns into the singular form, verbs into the infinitive form, and adjectives in comparative or superlative into the positive form. The Finnish words in the same cluster were conflated into the same stem in stemming. The Swedish stemmer was generated in the same way. For example, the Swedish words *diamanten, diamanterna, diamanteroch, diamanthande, diamantrika, diamantsek, diamanter* and *diamant* were grouped into the same cluster, which also includes some other words, since the most likely English translations of these words have the same English stem *diamond* according to the Swedish to English statistical translation lexicon automatically generated from the Swedish/English parallel texts. In stemming, these Swedish words were conflated into the same stem. The cluster of Finnish words whose most likely English translations, according to the Finnish to English statistical translation lexicon created from the Finnish/English parallel texts, share the same English stem *diamond* includes *timantit, timanteista, timanttialan, timanttien, timantteja, timantti, timanttierä, timantin, timanttialanyritysten, timanttiteol, veritimanteistä*, and more. All these words were conflated to the same Finnish stem in stemming.

2.5   English Spelling Normalizer

The CLEF 2003 English collection contains newspaper articles published in the U.S. and Britain. The British English spellings were changed into the American English spellings in indexing the English documents and English topics. We used extract the words that have both spellings in the collection and built a table that maps the British spellings to the American spellings. The table has about 2,700 entries, each one mapping one British English word into the corresponding American English word. For example, the word *watercolour* is changed into *watercolor*, *finalised* into *finalized*, *paediatrician* into *pediatrician*, and *offences* into *offenses*.

3   Fast Document Translation

To translate a large collection of documents from a source language to a target language using a machine translation system can be computationally intensive and may take a long time. In this section we present an approximate but fast approach to translating source documents into a target language using bilingual lexicons derived from machine translation systems or parallel texts. We first collect all the unique words in the source documents, then translate the source words individually into the target language using a machine translation system. Once we have the translations of all the source words, we can translate a source document into the target language by replacing the words in the source document with their translations in the target language. The translation is only approximate, but very fast. It is approximate since the same source word is always translated into the same target word. When a source word has multiple meanings under different contexts in the source documents, the translations of the source word may not be the same in the target language. For example, in translating English into French, the English word *race* is translated into the French word *race*. However, the English word *race* is polysemous, it could mean *human race* or *race in sports*. When it means *race* in sports, the appropriate French translation is not *race*, but *course*. For multilingual retrieval, one can translate the document collections into the topic language using this method if one can find a MT system capable of translating documents into the topic language. When MT systems are not available but parallel texts are, one can derive a bilingual lexicon from the parallel texts, and then use the bilingual lexicon to translate the source documents into the target language by translating the documents words individually. If neither MT systems nor parallel texts are available, one can still translate documents word-by-word using bilingual dictionaries as was done in [12]. When a multilingual document collection is translated into the topic language, one can index the translated documents together and search the queries directly against the translated document collection. This approach to multilingual retrieval does not require any merging of individual ranked lists of retrieved documents as noted in [3].

4   Test Collection

The document collection for the multilingual-8 IR task consists of 190,604 Dutch, 169,477 English, 55,344 Finnish, 129,806 French, 294,809 German, 157,558 Italian, 454,045 Spanish, and 142,819 Swedish newswire and newspaper articles published in 1994 and 1995. There are 60 test topics available in many languages. The multilingual-4 IR task uses the English, French, German, and Spanish documents. See Peters and Braschler (in this volume) for details on the test collection, the tasks, and evaluation of CLEF 2003.

5   Experimental Results

All retrieval runs reported in this paper used only the *title* and *description* fields in the topics. The IDs and average precision values of the official runs are presented in bold face, other runs are unofficial ones.

5.1   Monolingual Retrieval Experiments

This section presents the results of our monolingual retrieval runs on eight languages. Stopwords were removed from both documents and topics, the remaining words were stemmed using either the Snowball stemmers [14] developed by Martin Porter or the automatically generated stemmers from parallel texts. For Dutch, Finnish, German and Swedish monolingual runs, the compounds were split, whenever possible, into their component words before stemming, and only their component words were retained in document and topic indexes. A compound is split into its component words only when all the component words are present in the base lexicon, otherwise it is not split and is retained as a compound in the indexes. The same decompounding procedure was applied in all four languages, using language-specific base lexicons. For automatic query expansion, 10 terms from the top-ranked 10 documents after the initial search were combined with the original query. All the monolingual runs included automatic query expansion via blind relevance feedback. Table 1 presents the monolingual retrieval results for eight languages. Column 3 gives the number of topics for each language that have at least one relevant document. The average precision values presented in the table were computed with respect to only the topics having at least one relevant document. For all monolingual runs, only the *title* and *desc* fields in the topics were used as shown in column 4. Columns 5 and 7 present the overall recall values without and with query expansion, respectively; and columns 6 and 8 present the average precision values without and with query expansion, respectively. The last column labeled *change* shows the improvement of average precision with query expansion over without it. As Table 1 shows, query expansion increased the average precision of the monolingual runs for all eight languages, the improvement ranging from 6.76% for French to 16.76% for Italian. The Finnish monolingual run **bkmonofi2** used the Finnish statistical stemmer generated from the English-Finnish parallel texts, and the Swedish monolingual run **bkmonosv2** used the Swedish statistical stemmer generated from the English-Swedish parallel texts. All other runs presented in Table 1 used the Snowball stemmers, including the Muscat stemmers.

Table 2 presents the performances of Dutch, Finnish, German, and Swedish monolingual retrieval with different indexing features, which are *decompounding*, *stemming*, and *query expansion*. The column labeled *stoplist* gives the average

Table 1. Monolingual IR performance

run id	language	number topics	topic fields	without expansion recall	precision	with expansion recall	precision	change
bkmonoen1	English	54	TD	980/1006	0.5011	992/1006	0.5496	9.68%
bkmononl1	Dutch	56	TD	1484/1577	0.4955	1519/1577	**0.5304**	7.04%
bkmonofi1	Finnish	45	TD	462/483	0.4972	476/483	**0.5633**	13.29%
bkmonofi2	Finnish	45	TD	457/483	0.4626	472/483	**0.4962**	7.26%
bkmonofr1	French	52	TD	917/946	0.4986	923/946	**0.5323**	6.76%
bkmonode1	German	56	TD	1712/1825	0.5111	1767/1825	**0.5678**	11.09%
bkmonoit1	Italian	51	TD	770/809	0.4809	801/809	**0.5615**	16.76%
bkmonoes1	Spanish	57	TD	2214/2368	0.4556	2301/2368	**0.5091**	11.74%
bkmonosv1	Swedish	54	TD	959/1006	0.4727	987/1006	**0.5465**	15.61%
bkmonosv2	Swedish	54	TD	894/1006	0.4404	953/1006	**0.4982**	13.12%

precision values of the monolingual runs when only the stopwords were removed. The last seven columns present the average precision values of the monolingual retrieval with additional indexing features. Stopwords were removed in all monolingual runs presented in Table 2. Without stemming and query expansion, decompounding alone improved the average precision from 7.10% for Finnish to 30.59% for German in comparison to the average precision when only stopwords were removed. With decompounding, stemming, and query expansion, the average precision increased from 22.16% for Dutch to 52.35% for German. Note that decompounding substantially increased the German monolingual retrieval performance, so did stemming to Finnish monolingual retrieval performance. The Snowball stemmers were used, when stemming was applied, in the monolingual runs presented in Table 2. Without decompounding and query expansion, the statistical Finnish stemmer increased the average precision of the Finnish monolingual retrieval from 0.3801 to 0.4304, an 13.21% increase; and the statistical Swedish stemmer increased the Swedish monolingual retrieval average precision from 0.3630 to 0.3844, an 5.90% increase. Both statistical stemmers were not as effective as the manually constructed Snowball stemmers. The precision of the German topic 174 with the title "Bayerischer Kruzifixstreit" (Bavarian Crucifix Quarrel) increased from 0.0937 without decompounding to 0.7553 with decompounding. The compound *kruzifixstreit* does not occur in the German document collection, while its component words, *kruzifix* and *streit*, occur 147 and 7,768 times, respectively, in the German document collection.

The Swedish topic 177 with the title "Mjölkkonsumtion i Europa" (Milk Consumption in Europe) has 9 relevant documents, but none was retrieved when compounds were not split. The precision for this topic increased from 0.0 to 0.2396 when compounds were decomposed. The compound *mjölkkonsumtion* occurs only once in the Swedish document collection. Another example is the Swedish topic 199 with the title "Ebolaepidemi i Zaire" (Ebola Epidemic in Zaire) that has 38 relevant documents in total, but the compound *ebolaepidemi* occurs only 4 times in total, once in four Swedish documents. The precision for this topic was increased from 0.2360 before decompounding to 0.6437 af-

Table 2. Evaluation of decompounding, stemming, and query expansion

language	topic fields	stoplist	additional features						
			decomp	stem	expan	decomp stem	decomp expan	stem expan	decomp stem expan
Dutch	TD	0.4342	0.4673	0.4480	0.4744	0.4955	0.5126	0.4962	**0.5304**
			7.62%	3.18%	9.26%	14.12%	18.06%	14.28%	22.16%
German	TD	0.3727	0.4867	0.4220	0.4294	0.5111	0.5473	0.4804	**0.5678**
			30.59%	13.23%	15.21%	37.13%	46.85%	28.90%	52.35%
Finnish	TD	0.3801	0.4071	0.4974	0.4204	0.4972	0.4469	0.5541	**0.5633**
			7.10%	30.86%	10.60%	30.81%	17.57%	45.78%	48.20%
Swedish	TD	0.3630	0.4224	0.4121	0.4331	0.4727	0.4880	0.4838	**0.5465**
			16.36%	13.53%	19.31%	30.22%	34.44%	33.28%	50.55%

ter decompounding. The compound *mjölkkonsumtion* was split into *mjölk* and *konsumtion*, and *ebolaepidemi* into *ebola* and *epidemi* after decompounding.

The precision for Dutch topic 171 with the title "Ijshockeyfinale in Lillehammer" (Lillehammer Ice Hockey Finals) increased from 0.0215 before decompounding to 0.3982 after decompounding. This topic has 18 relevant documents in the Dutch collection, but the compound *ijshockeyfinale* occurs only twice in total, once in two documents. After decompounding, the Dutch compound *ijshockeyfinale* was split into *ijshockey* and *finale*.

The Finnish topic 159 with the title of "Pohjanmeri, öljy ja ympäristö" (North Sea Oil Environment) has 6 relevant documents. After splitting the compound *ympristnsuojelun* into *ympristn* and *suojelun*, and the compound *Pohjanmerell* into *Pohjan* and *merell*, the precision increased from 0.0698 without decompounding to 0.4660 with decompounding. Both of the decomposed compounds occur in the *desc* field. Note that the English translations of the Dutch, Finnish, German and Swedish titles in the examples presented above are the English titles in the corresponding CLEF 2003 English topics.

5.2   Bilingual Retrieval Experiments

We submitted 1 Finnish to German, 1 French to Dutch, 2 German to Italian, and 2 Italian to Spanish bilingual runs. The average precision values for the six official bilingual runs (in bold face) with additional bilingual runs are presented in Table 3. For **bkbideit1**, **bkbifide1** and **bkbiites1** runs, the query words in the *title* and *desc* fields, after removing stopwords, were translated into the document language using bilingual translation lexicons created from the Official Journal parallel texts. The bilingual translation lexicons used in these three runs were developed using the maximum likelihood ratio test statistic as the association measure. Only the top-ranked translation was retained for each query word. For the **bkbideit2** run, the German topics were translated into English, then into Italian using the L&H MT system, For the **bkbiites2** run, the Italian topics were translated into English, then into Spanish also using the L&H MT

system. By the time when the results were due, we still did not have a French
to Dutch translation lexicon, so we translated the French topics into English
using the L&H MT system, then translated the English topic words into Dutch
using the English to Dutch statistical translation lexicon built from the English-
Dutch parallel texts. The version of L&H MT system that we used does not
translate English to Dutch. The English query words translated from French were
individually translated into Dutch, and only the top-ranked Dutch translation
for each translated English word was retained.

Table 3. Performance of bilingual retrieval runs

run id	topic fields	topic language	document language	translation resources	average precision
bkbifide1	TD	Finnish	German	parallel texts	**0.3814**
bkbifrnl1	TD	French	Dutch	L&H; parallel texts	**0.3446**
bkbideit1	TD	German	Italian	parallel texts	**0.3579**
bkbideit2	TD	German	Italian	L&H	**0.3859**
bkbiites1	TD	Italian	Spanish	parallel texts	**0.4340**
bkbiites2	TD	Italian	Spanish	L&H	**0.4003**
bkbiennl1	TD	English	Dutch	parallel texts	0.4045
bkbienfi1	TD	English	Finnish	parallel texts	0.3011
bkbienfr1	TD	English	French	L&H	0.4156
bkbiende1	TD	English	German	L&H	0.4694
bkbienit1	TD	English	Italian	L&H	0.4175
bkbienes1	TD	English	Spanish	L&H	0.4303
bkbiensv1	TD	English	Swedish	parallel texts	0.3568

The last seven bilingual runs using English topics were used in our multilingual retrieval runs. For the English to French, German, Italian and Spanish
bilingual runs, the English topics were translated into French, German, Italian
and Spanish using the L&H MT system, while for the English to Dutch, Finnish
and Swedish bilingual runs, the English topic words were translated into Dutch,
Finnish and Swedish using the statistical translation lexicons built from the
parallel texts. Again, only the top-ranked translation in a target language was
retained for each English query word. The version 7.0 of L&H Power translator supports bi-directional translation between English and French, English and
German, English and Italian, and English and Spanish. Our copy of the L&H
Power translator does not support translation from English to Dutch, Finnish or
Swedish, or vice versa. All the bilingual runs applied blind relevance feedback.
The top-ranked 10 terms from the top-ranked 10 documents after the initial
search were combined with the initial query.

Overall, the performances of our bilingual runs are much lower than those of
monolingual runs. The English to Finnish bilingual performance is only 53.45%
of our best Finnish monolingual performance. French topic 192 has 19 relevant
documents, all in the ATS French collection. The French title of topic 192 is
"Assassinat d'un directeur de la télévision russe", its English equivalents being

"Russian TV Director Murder" in the corresponding English topic 192. When the English title was translated into French using the L&H MT system, its French translation became "télé russe Directeur Murder". The word *télévision* occurs 39 times, and *télévisions* once in the 19 relevant documents in the TI, LD, TX, or ST fields, but the translated French word *télé* does not occur in the relevant documents. The word *assassinat* occurs 40 times, and *assassinats* once in the relevant documents, but the word *murder* does not occur in the relevant documents. The precision of the English to French bilingual run for this topic is 0.0162, while the French monolingual run precision of the same topic is 0.8844. Another example is the English topic 186 where the English to French bilingual performance is far below the French monolingual performance for the same topic. The English title of topic 186 is "Dutch Coalition Government" and its equivalent French title is "Gouvernement de coalition néerlandais". The English title word *Dutch* was translated into *hollandais* and the word *Netherlands* in the description into *Hollande*. Neither *Hollande* nor *hollandais* occurs in the 13 relevant French documents for this topic. The English to French bilingual performance for this topic is 0.0162, while the French monolingual performance of the same topic is 0.6490.

5.3   Multilingual Retrieval Experiments

Multilingual-4 Experiments. In this section, we describe our multilingual retrieval experiments using the English topics. As mentioned in section 5.2, the English topics were translated into Dutch, Finnish, French, German, Italian, Spanish and Swedish using either the L&H MT system or the statistical translation lexicons built from the parallel texts.   Table 4 presents the results of

Table 4. Multilingual-4 retrieval performances

run id	topic language	topic fields	merging strategy	recall	precision
bkmul4en1	English	TD	raw score	4668/6145	**0.3783**
bkmul4en2	English	TD	none	4605/6145	**0.4082**
bkmul4en3	English	TD	sum of raw scores	5017/6145	**0.4260**

three multilingual runs using English topics to search against the collection of documents in English, French, German and Spanish. The **bkmul4en1** run was produced by combining the English monolingual run *bkmonoen1* and three bilingual runs, *bkbienfr1*, *bkbiende1* and *bkbienes1*. The performances of the individual bilingual runs were presented in Table 3. When the results of the four individual runs were combined, the raw scores were not normalized before merging.

The **bkmul4en2** run was produced by searching the English queries against the combined collection consisting of the English documents in the English collection and the English documents translated from French, German and Spanish collections. The French, German and Spanish documents were translated into English in three steps. First, we collected all the words in the French, German and Spanish documents. Second, we translated the French, German and Spanish document words individually into English using the L&H MT system. Finally, we translated the French, German and Spanish documents into English by replacing the French, German and Spanish document words with their English translations produced in the previous step. The English documents and the translated English documents from French, German and Spanish were indexed together. This run included query expansion for which 10 terms were selected from the top-ranked 10 documents after the initial search. Note that this approach does not need to merge individual results.

The **bkmul4en3** run was produced by combining the query translation-based run **bkmul4en1** and the document translation-based run **bkmul4en2**. The relevance scores were not normalized, but summed when the same document was on both ranked lists of documents.

The run **bkmul4en2** performed better than the run **bkmul4en1** on 36 topics, but worse on 23 topics. For most of topics, the precision difference on the same topic between these two different approaches are less than 0.20. However, there are 5 topics for which the precision difference is over 0.30. The precision of topic 161 is 0.0003 in the query translation-based run **bkmul4en1**, but 0.6750 in the document translation-based run **bkmul4en2**. Topic 161 with the English title of "Diets for Celiacs" has 6 relevant documents in total in the multilingual-4 document collection, 5 being Spanish documents and 1 German document. The title word *Celiacs*, which also occurs once in the description field, was not translated into Spanish by the L&H MT system, neither into German. The precision for topic 161 is only 0.0008 using the Spanish topic translated from the English topic to search the Spanish collection. The failure of retrieving the relevant documents in the English to Spanish bilingual run ultimately led to the poor performance of the multilingual run **bkmul4en1** on topic 161. Although the English topic word *celiacs* was left untranslated by the L&H MT system, its Spanish equivalent *celíacos* in the documents was correctly translated into the English word *celiac*. This is the reason why the document translation-based run substantially outperformed the query translation-based run on this topic.

As mentioned above, the L&H MT system translated the English words *Dutch* into *hollandais* and *Netherlands* into *Hollande* in topic 186, neither actually occurring in the French documents. However, the L&H MT system translated correctly the word *néerlandais* in the French documents into the English word *Dutch*. The precision for topic 186 is 0.2213 in the **bkmul4en1** run, but 0.6167 in the **bkmul4en2** run.

Table 5. Multilingual-8 retrieval performances

run id	topic language	topic fields	merging strategy	recall	precision
bkmul8en1	English	TD	raw score	6342/10020	**0.3317**
bkmul8en2	English	TD	none	5864/10020	**0.3401**
bkmul8en3	English	TD	sum of raw scores	6677/10020	**0.3733**

Multilingual-8 Experiments. Table 5 presents the performances of three multilingual retrieval runs involving eight languages. The English topics were used in all three runs.

The **bkmul8en1** run was produced by combining the English monolingual run *bkmonoen1* and seven bilingual runs from English to the other seven document languages. The seven bilingual runs are *bkbiennl1, bkbienfi1, bkbienfr1, bkbiende1, bkbienit1, bkbienes1* and *bkbiensv1*, whose performances were presented in Table 3. The raw scores of the individual runs were not normalized before merging.

The **bkmul8en2** run was produced by searching the English queries against the combined collection consisting of the English documents in the English collection and the English documents translated from the other seven document languages. The translation of French, German and Spanish documents into English was described in section 5.3. The Italian documents were translated into English in the same way as were the French, German and Spanish documents. The Dutch, Finnish and Swedish documents were translated, word-by-word, into English using the statistical translation lexicons built from the parallel texts. For instance, a Finnish document was translated into English by replacing each Finnish word in the document with its most probably English translation found in the statistical Finnish to English lexicon developed from the Finnish-English parallel texts. The English documents and the translated English documents from the other seven document languages were indexed together. For query expansion, 10 terms were selected from the top-ranked 10 documents after the initial search.

The **bkmul8en3** run was the result of merging the query translation-based run **bkmul8en1** and the document translation-based run **bkmul8en2**. The relevance scores were not normalized but summed when the two runs were merged. The **bkmul8en2** run performed better than the **bkmul8en1** run on 34 topics, but worse on 25 topics.

The documents in our multilingual retrieval runs were translated out-of-context, since the words were individually translated into English from other document languages. We conjecture that using documents translated in-context would produce better results. For lack of computational resources, we did not translate the multilingual-4 document collection into English using MT systems and perform retrieval from the translated documents.

6   Conclusions

Decompounding, stemming, and query expansion have been shown effective in both monolingual and cross-language retrieval. The automatically generated statistical stemmers improve retrieval performances; they are, however, not as effective as the manually created stemmers. The document translation-based multilingual retrieval is slightly better than query translation-based multilingual retrieval. Combining document translation and query translation in multilingual retrieval achieves even better performance. In the document translation-based multilingual retrieval, the documents are translated into the topic language by translating the document words individually using either MT systems or translation lexicons derived from parallel texts.

Acknowledgments

This research was supported in part by DARPA under contract N66001-00-1-8911 as part of the DARPA Translingual Information Detection, Extraction, and Summarization Program (TIDES).

References

1. Aaltio, M.: Finnish for foreigners (3rd.). Otava, Helsingissa (1967).
2. Atkinson, J.: Finnish grammar (3rd). The Finnish Literature Society, [Helsinki] (1969).
3. Braschler, M., Ripplinger, B., Schäuble, P.: Experiments with the Eurospider Retrieval System for CLEF 2001. In: Peters C., Braschler, M., Gonzalo, J., Kluck, M. (eds) Evaluation of Cross-Language Information Retrieval Systems: Second Workshop of the Cross-Language Evaluation Forum, CLEF 2001, Darmstadt, Germany, September 2001. Revised Papers (2002): 102–110.
4. Chen, A., Jiang, H., Gey, F.C.: Berkeley at NTCIR-2: Chinese, Japanese, and English IR Experiments. In: Kando, N. et el. (eds.) Proceedings of the Second NTCIR Workshop Meeting on Evaluation of Chinese & Japanese Text Retrieval and Text Summarization. National Institute of Informatics, Tokyo, Japan (2001) 5:32–40.
5. Chen, A.: Cross-language Retrieval Experiments at CLEF 2002. In: Peters, C. (ed.): Working Notes for the Cross-Language Evaluation Forum (CLEF) 2002 Workshop 19-20 September, Rome, Italy (2002) 5–20.
6. Chen, A., Gey., F.C.: Building an Arabic Stemmer for Information Retrieval. In: Voorhees, E.M., Buckland, L.P. (eds.) The Eleventh Text Retrieval Conference (TREC 2002). National Institute of Standards and Technology (2002) 631–639.
7. Dunning, T.: Accurate Methods for the Statistics of Surprise and Coincidence. Computational linguistics. **19** (1993) 61–74.
8. http://europa.eu.int/
9. Gale, W.A., Church, K.W.: A Program for Aligning Sentences in Bilingual Corpora. Computational linguistics. **19** (1993) 75–102.
10. Holmes, P., Hinchliffe, I.: Swedish : A Comprehensive Grammar. Routledge, London (1994).
11. Karp, D., Schabes, Y., Zaidel, M., Egedi, D.: A Freely Available Wide Coverage Morphological Analyzer for English. Proceedings of COLING (1992).
12. Oard, D.W., Levow, G., Gabezas, G.I.: CLEF Experiments at the University of Maryland: Statistical Sstemming and backoff translation strategies", In: Peters, C. (ed.) Cross-Language Information Retrieval and Evaluation: Workshop of Cross-Language Evaluation Forum, CLEF 2000, Lisbon, Portugal, September 21-22, 2000, Revised Papers (2001): 176–187.

13. Och, F.J., Ney, H.: Improved Statistical Alignment Models. In: Proceedings of the 38th Annual Meeting of the Association for Computational Linguistics (2000) 440–447.
14. Porter, M.: Snowball: A language for stemming algorithms. Available at http://snowball.tartarus.org/texts/introduction.html (2001).

Cross-Language Experiments
with the IR-n System

Fernando Llopis and Rafael Muñoz

Grupo de investigación en Procesamiento del Lenguaje y Sistemas de Información
Departamento de Lenguajes y Sistemas Informáticos,
University of Alicante, Spain
{llopis,rafael}@dlsi.ua.es

Abstract. This paper describes the third participation of the IR-n system (U. Alicante) in CLEF 2003. Two previous participations were focused on the Spanish monolingual task. This year, we participated in three different tracks: the multilingual track (four languages), the bilingual track (Italian-Spanish) and the monolingual track (Spanish, German, French, Italian). This paper describes the experiments carried out as training procedures in order to set up the main system features. The paper also shows the scores obtained using the test data. These results show that the IR-n system obtains good scores in the three tracks, above the average of the CLEF 2003 systems.

1 Introduction

Information Retrieval (IR) systems have to find the relevant documents for a user's query from a document collection. We can find different kinds of IR systems in the literature: if the document collection and the user's question are written in the same language then the IR system is a monolingual system; if the document collection and the user's question are written in different languages then the IR system is a bilingual (two different languages) or multilingual (more than two languages) system. Obviously, the document collection for a multilingual system is in at least two different languages.

This paper presents the adaptation of the IR-n system [8] to participate in CLEF 2003. Our system participated in the following tasks:

- monolingual tasks:
  - Spanish
  - French
  - German
  - Italian
- bilingual tasks:
  - Italian-Spanish
- multilingual tasks:
  - Spanish-German-French-English

C. Peters et al. (Eds.): CLEF 2003, LNCS 3237, pp. 122–132, 2004.

The IR-n system is a passage-based IR system rather than a traditional full document system. Every passage is made up of a fragment or piece of text [1, 6]. Such systems calculate a document's relevance by studying the relevance of its passages. The IR-n system calculates the similarity between the user's query and documents on the basis of sets of passages.

This approach includes the following advantages:

- the proximity of occurrence of query terms in a document are considered.
- a new information transmission unit, more adequate for the user's needs, is defined.
- document normalization problems are avoided.

This section describes the conceptual modelling of IR-n. The following main features are presented in the following subsections:

1. The passage concept.
2. The similarity measure between the user's question and the document collection
3. The similarity measure between the user's question and the document collection on a passage basis.
4. The use of query expansion in the IR-n system

1.1   The Passage Concept

The first Passage Retrieval systems (PR) used the paragraph as the passage size. The use of the paragraph as the passage unit caused a heterogeneous collection of passages to be built due to the varying size of paragraphs. Moreover, this segmentation did not allow for situations where more than one paragraph is related to a subject. For this reason, further proposals for PR systems used more than one paragraph as the passage unit.

A different approach proposed the use of a given number of words as the passage unit [6, 1]. Such proposals solve the problem of heterogenous size of previous PR systems. Moreover, this kind of system can easily adapt the number of words to the document collection and the user's query. This flexibility is very important to increase the performance of systems [6]. However, these systems lose the syntactic structure of the document. For example, a passage made up of 100 words can include one or two incomplete sentences.

There is a unit with structure that lies between the word and the paragraph: the sentence. The main feature of the sentence is that its meaning is self-contained. This aspect is very important in Information Retrieval because an answer by the system in sentence units can be more easily understood by the user. Obviously a single sentence does not have sufficient content to determine whether a document that contains it is relevant in relation to certain topic. However, it establishes some limits and provides important evidence when several terms of the user's query appear in the same sentence. Since the sentence on its own is not sufficiently complete to define a passage, we define passages as sets of consecutive sentences. The IR-n system thus uses the sentence as the basic information unit to define passages. The size of the passage is measured in numbers of sentences and can be adapted to improve the efficiency of the IR-n system. The use of the sentence to define passages presents advantages against the use of the paragraph or the word.

The use of the paragraph as a unit to define the passage has two main problems:

- Documents in the collection may not contain explicit information about paragraphs breaks.
- Paragraphs can be used in a document for visual rather than structural reasons.

The use of a number of words as units to define the passage presents two problems:

- The number of words to be considered as a passage depends on the writing style used. The same event is reported using less words in a news agency document than in a newspaper. If the same event is also described in a novel the number of words will be probably be larger.
- If the system uses words to define the passage, the lack of structure of the text fragment considered can mean that the text retrieved cannot be understood. This is due to the fact that the passage can start and end in any part of document.

Finally, the use of sentences to define the passage presents the following advantages:

- A sentence usually expresses an idea in the document.
- Normally documents use punctuation marks to separate ideas. There are algorithms to identify each sentence in a document using their superficial structure with a precision of 100% [10].
- Sentences are full units allowing interpretable information to be shown to the user, or to be input to a system (for example a Question Answering system). For this reason, the use of sentences is preferable to approaches that define the passages using a given number of words.
- The use of sentences as the basic passage unit makes it possible to work with a heterogeneous document collection, written by different authors with different literary styles. Moreover, the size of the passage can be determined by the size of the texts in the collection, the size of the user's query, or the intended use of the retrieved passages. In this case, it is similar to the window model, where the width of the window can be adapted depending on the document collection.

At the beginning, the IR-n system used the traditional cosine measure [11]. However, further experiments carried out using other similarity measures obtained better results. The similarity measures used by the IR-n system differ from traditional IR systems in that IR-n does not use normalization factors related to the passage or document size. This is due to the fact that passage size is the same for all documents. So, the IR-n system calculates the similarity between a passage P and the user's query q in the following way:

$$sim(Q, P) = \sum_{t \in Q \wedge P} (w_{Q,t} \cdot w_{P,t}) \tag{1}$$

where:

$$w_{Q,t} = freq_{q,t} \cdot \log_e \left(\frac{N - freq_t}{freq_t} \right) \tag{2}$$

$$w_{P,t} = 1 + \log_e (1 + \log_e (freq_{p,t} + 1)) \tag{3}$$

and $freq_{Y,t}$ is the number of appearances or the frequency of term t in the passage or in the question Y. N is the total number of documents in the collection and $freq_t$ is the number of different documents that contain term t.

1.2 Similarity Measure of Documents Based on Similarity Passages

All PR systems calculate the similarity measure of the document in function of the similarity measure of their passages using the sum of similarity measures for each passage or using the best passage similarity measures for each document. The experiments carried out in [5] have been re-run by the IR-n system, obtaining better results when using the best passage similarity measures as the similarity measure of the document.

Our approach is based on the fact that if a passage is relevant then the document is also relevant. In fact, if a PR system uses the sum of every passage similarity measure then the system has the same behavior as a document-based IR system adding concepts of proximity.

Moreover, the use of the best passage similarity measure makes it possible to retrieve the best passage, thus further improving the search process.

The IR-n system calculates the similarity measure of the document based on the best passage similarity measure in the following way:

$$sim(Q, D) = \max_{\forall i: P_i \in D} sim(Q, P_i) \tag{4}$$

1.3 Query Expansion

The use of query expansion techniques make it possible to locate relevant documents that do not contain the exact words of the user's query.

Two different experiments have been carried out in order to add these techniques to the IR-n system. In CLEF 2001 [7], the system added the synonyms of the terms in the user's question. This experiment achieved lower results than using the system without question expansion. In CLEF 2002 [9], a Relevance Feedback model was proposed achieving slightly better results.

This year, the pattern proposed in [3] has been adapted for use with our passage retrieval approach. This algorithm increases the relevance of each added term according to how closely they are related to the remaining query terms in the document.

2   Training Procedure

This section describes the experiments carried out in order to obtain and optimize certain features with the aim of improving system performance. The training corpus used in these experiments was the CLEF 2002 document collection. All experiments were carried out using short questions, that is the system only used the title and description from the query. The following subsections describe the experiments carried out specific to each CLEF task.

2.1   Monolingual Experiments

The first experiments were focused on establishing the appropriate number of sentences (N) to make up the passage for each language (Spanish, Italian, German, French and English). The performance of the system was measured using the standard average interpolated precision (AvgP). For each language, the stemmers and the stop-word lists used were provided by the University of Neuchâtel and made accessible via the CLEF web site.

Table 1 shows the scores achieved for each language without query expansion. The German scores are obtained without splitting the compound nouns. The best results are shown for German, French and English using 14 sentences, for Spanish using 9 sentences and for Italian using 8 sentences. The larger size for German, English and French is due to the kind of document collections used for each language. These three collections are made up of documents with a larger number of sentences than the Spanish and Italian collections. Moreover, the lowest scores achieved for German language (0.3364) show the influence of not splitting the compound nouns. The lack of an algorithm to split compound nouns led us to use a list of the most frequent compound nouns made up of 200000 terms. The scores obtained for German using the compound list were better, as shown in Table 2.

Once, the passage size was determined for each language, the following experiment was carried out in order to study the influence of query expansion. The IR-n system uses a feedback technique to apply query expansion. It adds

Table 1. AvgP without query expansion

Size	\multicolumn{11}{c}{Passage size using number of sentences}										
	5	6	7	8	9	10	11	12	13	14	15
Spanish	0,4839	0,4974	0,5015	0,5004	**0,5042**	0,5001	0,4982	0.4978	0.4973	0.4973	0.4983
Italian	0,4073	0,4165	0,4171	**0,4207**	0,4146	0,4190	0,4188	0,4193	0,4195	0,4166	0,4158
German	0,3236	0,3278	0,3268	0,3267	0,3287	0,3293	0,3315	0,3327	0,3350	**0,3364**	0,3363
French	0,4260	0,4347	0,4442	0,4519	0,4529	0,4625	0,4655	0,4685	0,4716	**0,4731**	0,4725
English	0,4675	0,4697	0,4800	0,4883	0,4882	0,4957	0,4923	0,4945	0,4979	**0,5057**	0,5038

Table 2. German monolingual task: AvgP without query expansion using compound nouns

	Passage size using number of sentences										
Size	5	6	7	8	9	10	11	12	13	14	15
No Split	0,3236	0,3278	0,3268	0,3267	0,3287	0,3293	0,3315	0,3327	0,3350	**0,3364**	0,3363
Split	0,3843	0,3894	0,3936	0,3933	0,3972	0,3982	0,3984	0,3981	0,4003	**0,4027**	0,4021

the T most important terms from the P most relevant passages to the query according to [2]. Table 3 shows the scores achieved by the IR-n system using the 5 most frequent terms from the five and ten most relevant passages, and using the 10 most frequent terms from the five and ten most relevant passages. The best results were obtained using the 10 most relevant passages, and the 10 most frequent terms for Spanish, Italian and English, and the 5 most frequent terms for German and French. This experiment shows that query expansion increases the scores obtained for all languages.

Table 3. AvgP using question expansion

T		5		10	
P	No expansion	5	10	5	10
Spanish	0,5042	0.5176	0,5122	0,5327	**0,5441**
Italian	0,4207	0,4428	0,4583	0,4491	**0,4679**
German	0,4027	0,4379	**0,4499**	0,4148	0,4438
French	0,4731	0,4991	**0,5286**	0,4980	0,5114
English	0,5057	0,5108	0,5034	0,5066	**0,5139**

2.2   Bilingual and Multilingual Tasks

We used three different machine translations systems in order to obtain an automatic query translation. The three systems used were PowerTranslator, FreeTranslator (www. freetranslation.com) and BabelFish (www.babelfish.com); queries written in English were translated to French, Spanish and German. Once we had translated the queries, four different experiments were carried out in order to choose the best translation. The first three only used one translation while the fourth used the merge of all translations as the query. Table 3 shows the scores achieved in the four experiments, using every document collection in the same way as in the monolingual tasks. The best scores were obtained using the merge of translations. The IR-n system was run obtained three different rank document collections in multilingual task. According to [2], there are a few simple ways to merge ranked lists of documents from different collections. We used two different methods: M1 - the first method is to normalize the relevance score for each topic, dividing all relevance scores by the relevance score of the top most ranked document for the same topic; M2 - the second method uses the following formula to normalize the document.

$$rsv'_j = (rsv_j - rsv_{min})/(rsv_{max} - rsv_{min}) \qquad (5)$$

in which rsv_j is the original retrieval status value, and rsv_{min} and rsv_{max} are the minimum and maximum document scores values that a collection could achieve for the current request. Table 5 shows the scores achieved using both merging methods. These scores show that the best results are obtained using the M2 merging method.

Table 4. Translation used as monolingual task

Translation		Free	Power	Babel	Power+Free+Babel
Spanish	0,5042	0.4235	0.4336	0.4217	**0.4371**
Italian	0,4207	0.3367	0.3490	0.3480	**0.3663**
German	0,4027	0.3037	0.3092	0.3024	**0.3245**
French	0,4731	0.3835	0.4281	0.4077	**0.4291**

Table 5. Scores achieved by IR-n system with document merging

		Precision at N documents					
	Cob.	5	10	20	30	200	AvgP
M1	61.97	0.6760	0.6360	0.5860	0.5367	0.2755	0.3108
M2	72.42	0.6760	0.6480	0.6030	0.5653	0.3152	0.3621

In the bilingual task, an additional problem was found. We do not have a direct Italian-Spanish and Spanish-Italian translator. We had to translate Italian to English and then English to Spanish. This process comports more errors than a direct translation. Table 6 shows the scores achieved in the bilingual task. In the same way as for the multilingual task, the best score was obtained using the merge of translations.

Table 6. Bilingual scores using question expansion

Translation		Free	Power	Babel	Power+Free+Babel
Italian-Spanish	0,4207	0.3367	0.3490	0.3480	**0.3663**

3   Evaluation at CLEF 2003

The IR-n system used in CLEF 2003 was the best IR-n configuration obtained from the training process using the CLEF 2002 collection.

The following subsections describe the runs carried out and the scores achieved in the monolingual, bilingual and multilingual tracks.

3.1   Monolingual Track

Two different runs were submitted for each Spanish, French and Italian mono-lingual tasks. The first run did not use query expansion and the second one did (IRn-xx-noexp and IRn-xx-exp, where xx are the language $-es$, fr or $it-$). Four different runs were submitted for German. The first and second runs follow the same strategies as previous languages but without splitting the compound nouns (IRn-al-noexp-nsp and IRn-al-exp-nsp). The third and fourth experiments used the splitting of compound nouns with and without expansion (IRn-al-noexp-sp and IRn-al-exp-sp).

Table 7 shows the scores achieved for each run in the monolingual task. The IR-n system using query expansion obtained better results than the average scores of CLEF 2003 systems for Spanish, French and German and lower scores for Italian.

Table 7. CLEF 2003 official results: Monolingual tasks

Language	Run	AvgP	Dif.
Spanish	CLEF Average	0.4649	
	IRn-es-exp	0.5056	**+8.75%**
	IRn-es-noexp	0.4582	-1.44%
French	CLEF Average	0.4843	
	IRn-fr-exp	0.5128	**+5.88%**
	IRn-fr-noexp	0.4853	0%
Italian	CLEF Average	0.4903	
	IRn-it-exp	0.4802	-2.06%
	IRn-it-noexp	0.4547	-7.26%
German	CLEF Average	0.4759	
	IRn-al-nexp-nsp	0.4267	-10.34%
	IRn-al-exp-nsp.	0.4687	-1.51%
	IRn-al-nexp-sp	0.4670	-1.87%
	IRn-al-exp-sp.	0.5115	**+7.48%**

3.2   Bilingual Track

Two different runs were submitted for the Italian-Spanish bilingual task. The first run did not use query expansion and the second one did (IRn-$ites$-noexp and IRn-$ites$-exp). English was used as an intermediate language due to the lack of a direct Italian to Spanish translation system. Table 8 shows that the IR-n system using query expansion in the bilingual task achieved an increase of around 26% of the average scores of CLEF 2003 bilingual systems for this task.

3.3   Multilingual Track

Five runs were submitted for the multilingual-4 task. The results are shown in Table 9. The first run (IRn-m-noexp-nsp) shows the scores achieved by the IR-n

Table 8. CLEF 2003 official results. Italian-Spanish bilingual task

	AvgP	Dif.
CLEF Average	0.3665	
IRn-ites-noexp	0.3662	0%
IRn-ites-exp	0.4610	**+25.78%**

system without query expansion and without splitting the German compound nouns. The second one (IRn-m-exp-nsp) presents the performance of the system using query expansion and without compound noun splitting. The third and fourth runs (IRn-m-noexp-sp and IRn-m-exp-sp, respectively) are the same experiments but splitting German compound nouns. Finally, an additional experiment (IRn-mi-exp-sp) was carried out using the same passage size for all languages (10 sentences), and using query expansion and compound noun splitting. This passage size was determined experimentally in the training process.

Table 9 shows that the IR-n system improves the average scores of CLEF 2003 around 23% using the AvgP measure. Moreover, IR-n also obtains around 23% improvement using the same passage size for all collections.

Table 9. CLEF 2003 official results: Multilingual task

	AvgP	Dif.
CLEF Average	0.2752	
IRn-m-noexp-nsp	0.3024	+9.88%
IRn-m-exp-nsp.	0.3281	+19.22%
IRn-m-noexp-sp	0.3074	+11.7%
IRn-m-exp-sp.	0.3377	**+22.71%**
IRn-mi-exp-sp.	0.3373	+22.56%

4   Conclusions

Our general conclusions are positive. On the one hand, the IR-n system has obtained better than average results for CLEF 2003, with the exception of the Italian monolingual task. Moreover, we remark that all the runs submitted only used short queries (title and description) and the average provided by the CLEF organization consists of all system results (systems using both short or long queries). The improvement we achieved using a list of the most frequent compound nouns in German has led us to develop an algorithm to split compound nouns which we hope will be used in our next participation.

We also want to emphasize the good performance of the IR-n system in our first participation in the bilingual and multilingual tracks. This performance is shown using the official ranking for CLEF 2003 (Tables 10 and 11, these tables only present the 5 best systems of all participants). We had planned to use a

Table 10. CLEF 2003 official ranking: Multilingual-4 task

System	Score
U. Exeter	0.4376
UC. Berkeley	0.4260
U. Neuchâtel	0.3920
CMU	0.3773
U. Alicante	0.3377

Table 11. CLEF 2003 official ranking: Bilingual IT task

System	Score
U. Alicante	0.4610
UC. Berkeley	0.4340
CMU	0.4269
IRST	0.4262
JHU/APL	0.4261

new method but time constraints prevented us from submitting a new run. We hope to participate with the new method in the next campaign.

We should like to underline the good scores achieved using the same passage size for all languages. Our final observation is that, on the basis of the scores obtained in our participation in CLEF 2003, the IR-n system is a language-independent passage-based information retrieval system.

Acknowledgments

This work has been partially supported by the Spanish Government (CICYT) with grant TIC2003-07158-C04-01 and (PROFIT) with grant FIT-150500-2002-416.

References

1. Callan, J. P.: Passage-Level Evidence in Document Retrieval. In Proceedings of the 17th Annual International Conference on Research and Development in Information Retrieval, London, UK. Springer Verlag (1994) 302–310,
2. Chen, A.: Cross-Language Retrieval Experiments at CLEF-2002. In Peters et al. [4], 5–20.
3. Chen, J., Diekema, A., Taffet, M., McCracken, N., Ozgencil, N., Yilmazel, O., Liddy, E.: Question Answering: CNLP at the TREC-10 Question Answering Track. In Tenth Text REtrieval Conference (Notebook), Vol. 500-250 of NIST Special Publication, Gaithersburg, USA, Nov 2001.
4. Peters, C., Braschler, M., Gonzalo, J., Kluck, M. (eds.): Proceedings of the Cross-Language Evaluation Forum (CLEF 2002)., Lecture Notes in Computer Science, LNCS 2785. Springer-Verlag 2003.

5. Hearst, M., Plaunt, C.: Subtopic structuring for full-length document access. In Sixteenth International ACM SIGIR Conference on Research and Development in Information Retrieval, Pittsburgh, PA, June 1993, 59–68.
6. Kaszkiel, M., Zobel, J.: Effective Ranking with Arbitrary Passages. Journal of the American Society for Information Science and Technology (JASIST), 52(4)(2001) 344–364.
7. Llopis, F., Vicedo, J.L.: IR-n system at CLEF 2002. In Peters et al. [4], 169–176.
8. Llopis, F.: IR-n un sistema de Recuperación de Información basado en pasajes. PhD thesis. Universidad de Alicante (1998).
9. Llopis, F. and Vicedo, J.L.: IR-n system, a passage retrieval system at CLEF 2001. In Proceedings of the Cross-Language Evaluation Forum (CLEF 2001). LNCS 2406. Springer-Verlag (2002) 244–252.
10. Muñoz, R. and Palomar, M.: Sentence Boundary and Named Entity Recognition in EXIT System: Information Extraction System of Notarial Texts. In Emerging Technologies in Accounting and Finance (1999) 129–142.
11. Salton, G., Buckley, C.: Term-weighting Approaches in Automatic Text Retrieval. Information Processing and Management 24(5) (1988) 513–123.

Multilingual Information Retrieval Using Open, Transparent Resources in CLEF 2003

Monica Rogati and Yiming Yang

Computer Science Department, Carnegie Mellon University, Pittsburgh, PA 15213
{mrogati, yiming}@cs.cmu.edu

Abstract. Corpus-based approaches to cross-lingual information retrieval (CLIR) have been studied and applied for many years. However, using general-purpose commercial MT systems for CLEF has been considered easier and better performing, which is to be expected given the non-domain specific nature of newspaper articles we are using in CLEF. Corpus based approaches are easier to adapt to new domains and languages; however, it is possible that their performance would be lower on a general test collection such as CLEF. Our results show that the performance drop is not large enough to justify the loss of control, transparency and flexibility. We have participated in two bilingual runs and the small multilingual run using software and data that are free to obtain, transparent and modifiable.

1 Introduction

Over the past years, a necessary condition for a good cross- or multi-lingual performance in CLEF appeared to be the use of commercial MT systems, be it purchased or freely available online (Systran etc.)[1,3,11]. Since CLEF documents are articles written in large circulation newspapers, which implies their vocabulary is general as opposed to highly technical, general-purpose MT systems perform very well. While using black boxes to cross the language barrier allowed researchers to concentrate on important issues such as stemming, query pre- and post-processing, combining black boxes outputs, and multilingual merging, [1,3,11] we believe that query translation does play an essential role in CLIR, and that understanding, control, transparency and flexibility are crucial in a research system. Online MT systems can be upgraded, lose their free status, or change parameters at will. Commercial MT systems cannot easily be adapted to a domain using highly technical vocabulary. Our goal is to attempt to move away from basing the core of our CLIR research system on a module that cannot be fully understood and modified, to which future access might not be guaranteed, and in which external changes are allowed and sometimes not even detected. The main challenge, however, is to do so while sacrificing as little performance as possible.

Our initial attempt to reach this goal (CLEF 2001) was disappointing in this respect, mainly because we disallowed using translation resources entirely and relied on the temporal correspondence between CLEF documents to produce a "parallel" corpus. In CLEF 2003 we relaxed the independence requirement to using transparent

C. Peters et al. (Eds.): CLEF 2003, LNCS 3237, pp. 133–139, 2004.
© Springer-Verlag Berlin Heidelberg 2004

data and code, freely available or available for a modest one-time fee, which we can store locally, easily modify, recompile and process, and which cannot change in uncontrollable or undetectable ways. We participated in two bilingual tasks (DE->IT, IT->ES), and the small multilingual task, which involved four languages.

Our general approach was to rely on parallel corpora and GIZA++ [8] for query translation, and on Lemur [9] for retrieval. All these resources (as well as the stemmers we used where applicable) fulfill the criteria outlined above. Moreover, with the exception of LDC data, which we did not use in the official runs but did use in preliminary experiments, all these resources are free of charge and publicly available.

In the next section we discuss the parallel data and preprocessing (stemming, stopping etc.). In the third section we discuss our approach to bilingual retrieval in general as well as approaches for situations where a parallel corpus between the two languages does not exist.

2 Data Description

We have used the European Parliament proceedings 1996-2001 [6]. It includes versions in 11 European languages: Romance (French, Italian, Spanish, Portuguese), Germanic (English, Dutch, German, Danish, Swedish), Greek and Finnish. Sentence aligned parallel corpora (English-X) have been prepared by the author of [6]. We have also prepared German-Italian and Italian-Spanish versions for the two bilingual CLEF tasks we participated in, by detecting almost identical English sentences and aligning the corresponding non-English sentences. Table 1 shows the size of the relevant parallel corpora post-processing, after stopping and stemming. Some sentence pairs have been eliminated after becoming empty post-processing. Note that our quick intersection of X-EN to Y-EN parallel corpora by taking only sentences where the English versions were close resulted in losing about ¾ of the corpus. A much better approach would have been to follow [6]'s procedure, most likely resulting in a corpus of comparable size with the English versions.

Table 1. Size of the parallel corpora (in sentences)

DE-IT	IT-ES	DE-EN	FR-EN	IT-EN	ES-EN
128505	150910	659773	674770	687890	738772

We have also experimented with several other corpora, including Hansard set A for French (available from the Linguistic Data Consortium). Although the sentence-aligned version was much larger (2.7M sentences), preliminary experiments on CLEF '01 and '02 datasets showed a consistent performance drop (usually around 10%). As a result, Hansard has not been used for CLEF 2003 experiments.

We preprocessed the parallel corpora and CLEF documents by eliminating punctuation, stopwords, and document sections disallowed in the task description. We have used the Porter stemmer for English and the rule-based stemmers and stopword lists kindly provided by J. Savoy [10]. After stemming, we have used 5-grams as a substitute for German word decompounding.

3 Bilingual Retrieval

Our main focus in bilingual retrieval has been query translation without the use of commercial MT systems, including Systran. In this section we will discuss our bilingual retrieval system using a parallel corpus, as well as the challenge of handling language pairs for which parallel corpora do not exist.

Conceptually, our approach consists of several steps:

1. Parallel corpora and test documents preprocessing
2. Dictionary generation from parallel corpora
3. Pseudo-Relevance Feedback in the source language
4. Query translation
5. Pseudo-Relevance Feedback in the target language
6. Retrieval

3.1 Dictionary Generation and Query Translation

We have used GIZA++ [8] as an implementation of IBM Model 1 [2]. GIZA++ takes a parallel corpus and generates a translation probability matrix. The number of training iterations was 10. Although GIZA++ implements the more sophisticated translation models discussed in [2], we have not used them for efficiency reasons, and because word order is not a factor during retrieval.

Query translation was done on a word-by-word basis. A significant difference from MT or online dictionary based approaches is that instead of using a rank-based cutoff (i.e. the first or first two variants for each word) we are using all translations weighted by their translation probability:

$$q_t = q_s \bullet M_{st} \qquad (1)$$

where q_t is the query in the target language, q_s is the query in the source language, and M_{st} is the translation matrix.

Our approach is similar to IBM and BBN CLIR approaches [4,5] except the translation is not integrated in the retrieval model; only the query is translated. This approach has the welcome side effect of a very focused query expansion.

3.2 Pseudo-Relevance Feedback and Retrieval

We have used the Lemur toolkit [9] to implement weighted query expansion, and we modified the retrieval interface to accept weighted queries as input. After query expansion is done in Lemur, the resulting query vector (q_s, words + weights) is extracted for future translation. After translation, q_t is loaded into Lemur for a new round of query expansion in the target language, followed by retrieval.

PRF and retrieval parameters we tuned include the number of documents to be considered relevant, the number of new query words added, the relative weight of added queries (usually 0.5) and the term weighting method. There is one such parameter set for each pre- and post- translation query expansion, and for each language pair. However, experiments on CLEF 2001 and 2002 indicated that post-translation query expansion hurts performance by diluting the query in some languages, so the second set of parameters were set to 0 for the bilingual runs.

3.3 Handling Language Pairs with No Available Parallel Corpora

The bilingual task this year was more challenging, in that we were aware of no Italian-Spanish or German-Italian parallel corpora. However, since most parallel corpora have English as one of the languages we had the option of using English as a pivot language in two ways:

1. to create a new parallel corpus if there is significant overlap (as described in Section 2). This is the least likely situation, but it does happen in the case where there is an underlying text translated in multiple languages, as it happened with the European Parliament corpus.
2. to translate first *to* English, then *from* English. This is where keeping and using translation probabilities is very useful. In traditional MT approaches, where the query is translated as a sentence twice, the (binary) mistakes accumulate, making the original meaning difficult to preserve. We believe the original meaning is easier to preserve when the entire query vector is translated, taking into account the translation probabilities:

$$q_t = q_s \bullet M_{s2EN} \bullet M_{EN2t} \qquad (2)$$

where q_t is the query in the target language, q_s is the query in the source language, and M_{X2Y} is the translation matrix for language X to language Y.

3.4 Official Runs (German-Italian and Italian-Spanish)

All our official runs use the Title and Description fields. Relevant parameters are pre-translation feedback documents/terms, and whether a new parallel corpus was created or if English was used as a pivot language during translation. In general, source-to-source feedback was helpful or did not hurt. However, we found target language feedback harmful on the 2003 data as well. Note that one of our runs was broken and has been corrected after the CLEF campaign.

Using the extracted parallel corpus directly worked better for the DE->IT task, but made no difference for IT->ES. We suspect the reason for this discrepancy is the German segmentation using 5-grams, which means the degree of fan-out for each English word is greater. The pivot language thus dilutes the query with translations of ambiguous 5-grams.

Table 2. Official Bilingual Runs

Run Name	Task	Feedback docs/terms	Parallel/Pivot	Avg. Precision
cmuG2Icombfb	G2I	10/150	Pivot	0.3439
cmuG2Icomb	G2I	0/0	Pivot	0.3124
cmuG2Iparafb	G2I	10/150	Parallel	**0.4117**
cmuG2Ipara	G2I	0/0	Parallel	0.3669
cmuI2Scombfb	I2S	15/80	Pivot	**0.4269**
cmuI2Scomb	I2S	0/0	Pivot	0.4114
cmuI2Sparafb	I2S	15/80	Parallel	0.2921 (corrected : 0.4172)
cmuI2Spara	I2S	0/0	Parallel	0.4154

4 Multilingual Retrieval

By using English as the query language we have leveraged the parallel corpora that had English as one of the languages. We have experimented with several parallel corpora, but chose the European Parliament proceedings as the corpus for our CLEF submission. We performed bilingual retrieval as described in Section 3, and we used Lemur for English monolingual retrieval. We then merged the results using the two methods described in Section 4.1. The number of feedback documents and words were tuned for each language.

4.1 Merging Strategies

We examined two simple merging strategies: normalizing the individual scores and two step RSV [7].

The first strategy consists of normalizing the first N document scores to fit in the [0,1] interval, then using the normalized scores to produce the final ranked document list. This strategy is easy, requires no training but it has been proved inferior to regression-based models or two-step RSV.

Two-step RSV is a reindexing-based method: top ranked documents from each collection are translated to the topic language, then reindexed. Note that this is fundamentally different from translating the test collection, which we would like to avoid. Only top documents are translated, instead of a large test collection. However, the disadvantage of this method is that translation and reindexing need to be done online. Document caching can somewhat alleviate this problem when there are many queries.

Translation is done on a word-by-word basis, using the translation matrix built from the parallel corpus. We use only the first two translations for efficiency; however, we allocate S slots to each untranslated word and distribute the translated words proportionally to their normalized translation probabilities. Due to lack of running time, official runs had S=3.

4.2 Official Runs (Small Multilingual)

All our official runs use the Title and Description fields.

Table 3. Official Multilingual Runs

Run Name	Feedback docs/terms pre- and post translation	Norm/2step merging	Avg. Pr.
cmuM4fb	EN: 5/30, FR:10/20-5/20, ES:5/20-10/20, DE:15/20-10/30	Norm	0.2921
cmuM4fbre	EN: 5/30, FR:10/20-5/20, ES:5/20-10/20, DE:15/20-10/30	2step	**0.3710**
cmuM4lowfb	EN: 5/30, FR:0/0-5/20, ES:0/0-10/20, DE:5/20-10/30	Norm	0.3398
cmuM4lowfbre	EN: 5/30, FR:0/0-5/20, ES:0/0-10/20, DE:5/20-10/30	2step	**0.3773**

Note that in this case the feedback made little difference among the best runs. The merging strategy had a significant impact, with the two-step RSV being better as expected.

5   Conclusion and Future Work

Our main goal in participating in this year's CLEF was to prove that freedom from opaque, uncontrollable commercial systems does not have to mean poor CLIR performance, even for general purpose collections towards which such systems are targeted. Many conceptual or implementation-related improvements can be made. They include better solutions for using a pivot language, especially when the domains do not match; better morphological processing, pseudo-relevant regression for merging etc.

References

1. Braschler, M., Gohring, A. and Shauble, P:. Eurospider at CLEF 2002. In C. Peters et al. (Eds.), Advances in Cross-Language Information Retrieval: Results of the Cross-Language Evaluation Forum - CLEF 2002, LNCS 2785, Springer (2003).
2. Brown, P.F, Pietra, D., Pietra, D, Mercer, R.L. The Mathematics of Statistical Machine Translation: Parameter Estimation. Computational Linguistics, 19 (1993) 263-312

3. Chen, A.: Cross-language Retrieval Experiments at CLEF-2002. In C. Peters et al. (Eds.), Advances in Cross-Language Information Retrieval: Results of the Cross-Language Evaluation Forum - CLEF 2002, LNCS 2785, Springer (2003).
4. Franz, M. and McCarley, J.S.:   Arabic Information Retrieval at IBM.TREC 2002 proceedings
5. Fraser, A., Xu, J., Weischedel, R.: 2002. TREC 2002 Cross-lingual Retrieval at BBN. TREC 2002 proceedings
6. Koehn, P. Europarl: A Multilingual Corpus for Evaluation of Machine Translation. Draft, Unpublished.
7. Martinez-Santiago, Martin M. and Urena, A.: SINAI on CLEF 2002: Experiments with merging strategies. In C. Peters et al. (Eds.), Advances in Cross-Language Information Retrieval: Results of the Cross-Language Evaluation Forum - CLEF 2002, LNCS 2785, Springer (2003).
8. Och, F. J. and Hermann N.: Improved Statistical Alignment Models. In Proc. of the 38th Annual Meeting of the Association for Computational Linguistics, (2000) pp. 440-447
9. Ogilvie, P and Callan, J.: Experiments using the Lemur toolkit. In Proceedings of the Tenth Text Retrieval Conference (TREC-10). (2001)
10. Savoy, J.: A stemming procedure and stopword list for general French corpora. Journal of the American Society for Information Science, 50(10) (1999) 944-952.
11. Savoy, J.: Report on CLEF-2002 Experiments: Combining multiple sources of evidence. In C. Peters et al. (Eds.), Advances in Cross-Language Information Retrieval: Results of the Cross-Language Evaluation Forum - CLEF 2002, LNCS 2785, Springer (2003).

ITC-irst at CLEF 2003: Monolingual, Bilingual, and Multilingual Information Retrieval

Nicola Bertoldi and Marcello Federico

ITC-irst - Centro per la Ricerca Scientifica e Tecnologica,
I-38050 Povo, Trento, Italy
{bertoldi,federico}@itc.it

Abstract. This paper reports on the participation of ITC-irst in the 2003 campaign of the Cross Language Evaluation Forum for the monolingual, bilingual, and small multilingual tasks. The languages considered were English, French, German, Italian, and Spanish. With respect to the ITC-irst system presented at CLEF 2002, the statistical models for bilingual document retrieval have been improved, more languages have been considered, and a novel multilingual information retrieval system has been developed, which combines several bilingual retrieval models into a statistical framework. As in the last CLEF, bilingual models integrate retrieval and translation scores over the set of N-best translations of the source query.

1 Introduction

This paper reports on the participation of ITC-irst in the Cross Language Evaluation Forum (CLEF) 2003. We participated in several tracks: monolingual document retrieval in French, German, Italian, and Spanish; bilingual document retrieval from German to Italian and from Italian to Spanish; and small multilingual document retrieval from English to English, German, French, and Spanish. The statistical cross-language information retrieval (CLIR) model presented in the CLEF 2002 evaluation [1, 2] was extended in order to cope with a multilingual target collection. Moreover, better query-translation probabilities were obtained by exploiting bilingual dictionaries and statistics from monolingual corpora. Basically, the ITC-irst system presented in the CLEF 2002 evaluation was expanded with a module for merging document rankings of different document collections generated by different bilingual systems.

Each bilingual system features a statistical model, which generates a list of the N-best query translations, and a basic IR engine, which integrates scores, computed by a standard Okapi model and a statistical language model, over multiple translations. The training of each system requires a bilingual dictionary, the target document collection, and a document collection in the source language. This paper is organized as follows. Section 2 introduces the statistical approach to multilingual IR. Section 3 briefly summarizes the main features of he ITC-irst

C. Peters et al. (Eds.): CLEF 2003, LNCS 3237, pp. 140–151, 2004.

system, and describes the retrieval procedure. Section 4 presents experimental results for each of the tracks in which we participated. Section 5 discusses preliminary work on German word decompounding and Section 6 draws some conclusions.

2 Statistical Multilingual Information Retrieval

Multilingual information retrieval can be defined as the task of searching and ranking documents relevant to a given topic, within a collection of texts in several languages. Because we presume to know the language of each document, we consider the multilingual target collection as the union of distinct monolingual collections.

2.1 Multilingual Retrieval Model

Let a multilingual collection $\mathcal{D}$ contain documents in $\mathcal{L}$ different languages, where $\mathcal{D}$ results from the union of $\mathcal{L}$ monolingual sub-collections $\mathcal{D}_1, \ldots, \mathcal{D}_\mathcal{L}$. Let $\mathbf{f}$ be a query in a given source language, eventually different from any of the $\mathcal{L}$ languages. One would like to rank documents d within the multilingual collection $\mathcal{D}$, according to the posterior probability:

$$\Pr(d \mid \mathbf{f}) \propto \Pr(\mathbf{f}, d) \tag{1}$$

where the right term of formula (1) follows from the constancy of $\Pr(\mathbf{f})$, with respect to the ranking of documents.

A hidden variable l is introduced, which represents the language of either a sub-collection or a document.

$$\Pr(\mathbf{f}, d) = \sum_l \Pr(l, \mathbf{f}, d)$$
$$= \sum_l \Pr(l) \Pr(\mathbf{f}, d \mid l) \tag{2}$$

where $\Pr(l)$ is an a-priori distribution over languages, which can be estimated or assumed uniform[1]. Formula (2) shows a weighted mixture of bilingual IR models depending on the sub-collection. However, given that we know the language of each document, we can assume that the probability $\Pr(\mathbf{f}, d \mid l)$ is defined only if d belongs to the sub-collection $\mathcal{D}_l$.

Next, a hidden variable $\mathbf{e}$ is introduced, which represents a (term-by-term) translation of $\mathbf{f}$ into language l. Hence, we derive the following decomposition:

$$\Pr(\mathbf{f}, d \mid l) = \sum_{\mathbf{e}} \Pr(\mathbf{f}, \mathbf{e}, d \mid l)$$
$$\approx \sum_{\mathbf{e}} \Pr(\mathbf{f}, \mathbf{e} \mid l) \Pr(d \mid \mathbf{e}, l) \tag{3}$$

---

[1] Uniform distribution over languages is considered in the CLEF 2003 campaign.

In deriving formula (3), we make the assumption (or approximation) that the probability of document d given query $\mathbf{f}$, translation $\mathbf{e}$ and language l, does not depend on $\mathbf{f}$. Formula (3) puts in evidence a language-dependent query-translation model, $\Pr(\mathbf{f}, \mathbf{e} \mid l)$, and a collection-dependent query-document model, $\Pr(d \mid \mathbf{e}, l)$.

The language-dependent query-translation model is defined as follows:

$$
\Pr(\mathbf{f}, \mathbf{e} \mid l) = \Pr(\mathbf{f} \mid l)\Pr_l(\mathbf{e} \mid \mathbf{f})
$$
$$
\propto \begin{cases} \dfrac{\Pr_l(\mathbf{f}, \mathbf{e})}{\displaystyle\sum_{\mathbf{e}' \in \mathcal{T}_l(\mathbf{f})} \Pr_l(\mathbf{f}, \mathbf{e}')} & \text{if } \mathbf{e} \in \mathcal{T}_l(\mathbf{f}) \\[4ex] 0 & \text{otherwise} \end{cases} \tag{4}
$$

where $\mathcal{T}_l(\mathbf{f})$ is the set of all translations of $\mathbf{f}$ into language l. For practical reasons, this set is approximated with the set of the N most probable translations computed by the basic query-translation model $\Pr_l(\mathbf{f}, \mathbf{e})$. The term $\Pr(\mathbf{f} \mid l)$ can be considered independent of l and hence be discarded. The normalization introduced in formula (4) is needed in order to obtain scores which are comparable across different languages.

The collection-dependent query-document model is derived from a basic query-document model $\Pr_l(d \mid \mathbf{e})$ as follows:

$$
\Pr(d \mid \mathbf{e}, l) = \begin{cases} \dfrac{\Pr_l(d, \mathbf{e})}{\displaystyle\sum_{d' \in \mathcal{I}(\mathbf{e}, l)} \Pr_l(d', \mathbf{e})} & \text{if } \mathbf{d} \in \mathcal{I}(\mathbf{e}, l) \\[4ex] 0 & \text{otherwise} \end{cases} \tag{5}
$$

where $\mathcal{I}(\mathbf{e}, l)$ is the set of documents in $\mathcal{D}_l$ containing at least a word of $\mathbf{e}$.

The basic query document and query translation models are now briefly described; more details can be found in [1, 2, 3]. The symbol l, which refers to the specific language or collection on which the models are estimated, will be omitted without loss of generality.

2.2   Basic Query-Document Model

The query-document model computes the joint probability of a query $\mathbf{e}$ and a document d, written in the same language. The query-document model considered in the experiments results from the combination of two different models: a language model and an Okapi based scoring function.

Language Model. The joint probability can be factored out as follows:

$$
\Pr(\mathbf{e}, d) = \Pr(\mathbf{e} \mid d)\Pr(d) \tag{6}
$$

where the a-priori probability of d, $\Pr(d)$, is assumed to be uniform, and a bag-of-words model is assumed for the probability of $\mathbf{e}$ given d:

$$\Pr(\mathbf{e} = e_1, \ldots, e_n \mid d) = \prod_{k=1}^{n} p(e_k \mid d) \tag{7}$$

Okapi. A joint probability can be in general obtained by normalizing the outcomes of a generic scoring function $s(\mathbf{e}, d)$, i.e.:

$$\Pr(\mathbf{e}, d) = \frac{s(\mathbf{e}, d)}{\sum_{e', d'} s(\mathbf{e}', d')} \tag{8}$$

The denominator, which is considered only for the sake of normalization, can be disregarded in the computation of equation (5).

The following scoring function, derived from the standard Okapi formula, is used

$$s(\mathbf{e} = e_1, \ldots, e_n, d) = \prod_{k=1}^{n} idf(e_k)^{W_d(e_k)} \tag{9}$$

where $idf(e)$ is the inverse document frequency of term e, and $W_d(e)$ is the frequency of e in document d.

Combination. Previous work [4] showed that the above two models rank documents almost independently. Hence, information about the relevant documents can be gained by integrating the scores of both methods. The two models are combined by just taking the sum of scores, after a suitable normalization.

2.3   Basic Query-Translation Model

The query-translation model computes the probability of any query-translation pair. This probability is modeled by an hidden Markov model [5] in which the observable variable is the query $\mathbf{f}$ in the source language, and the hidden variable is its translation $\mathbf{e}$ in the target language. According to this model, the joint probability of a pair $(\mathbf{f}, \mathbf{e})$ is decomposed as follows:

$$\Pr(\mathbf{f} = f_1, \ldots, f_n, \mathbf{e} = e_1, \ldots, e_n) = p(e_1) \prod_{k=2}^{n} p(e_k \mid e_{k-1}) \prod_{k=1}^{n} p(f_k \mid e_k) \tag{10}$$

The term translation probabilities $p(f \mid e)$ are estimated from a bilingual dictionary as follows:

$$\Pr(f \mid e) = \frac{\delta(f, e)}{\sum_{f'} \delta(f', e)} \tag{11}$$

where $\delta(f, e) = 1$ if the term e is one of the translations of term f and $\delta(f, e) = 0$ otherwise. This flat distribution can be refined through the EM algorithm [6] by exploiting a large corpus in the source language.

The target language model probabilities $p(e \mid e')$, are estimated on the target document collection, through an order-free bigram model, which tries to compensate for different word positions induced by the source and target languages. Let

$$p(e \mid e') = \frac{p(e, e')}{\sum_{e''} p(e'', e')} \tag{12}$$

where $p(e, e')$ is the probability of e co-occurring with e', regardless of the order, within a text window of fixed size. Smoothing of this probability is performed through absolute discounting and interpolation.

3   System Architecture

As shown in Section 2, the ITC-irst multilingual IR system features several independent bilingual retrieval systems, which return collection-dependent rankings, and a module for merging these results into a global ranking with respect to the whole multilingual collection. Moreover, language-dependent text preprocessing modules have been implemented to process documents and queries. Figure 1 shows the architecture of the system.

The monolingual version of the ITC-irst system simply follows by omitting the query-translation model, while the bilingual version is obtained by limiting the collection to one language and by omitting the merging module.

3.1   Preprocessing

In order to homogenize the preparation of data and to reduce the workload, a standard procedure was defined. More specifically, the following preprocessing steps were applied both to documents and queries in every language:

- *Tokenization* was performed to separate words from punctuation marks, to recognize abbreviations and acronyms, correct possible word splits across lines, and discriminate between accents and quotation marks.
- *Stemming* was performed by using a language-dependent Porter-like algorithm [7], freely available on the Internet[2].
- *Stop-terms removal* was applied on the documents by removing terms included in a language-dependent list made publicly available by the University of Neuchâtel[3].
- *Proper names and numbers* in queries were recognized in order to improve coverage of the dictionary.
- *Out-of-dictionary terms* which have not been recognized as proper names or numbers were removed.

---

[2] http://snowball.tartarus.org
[3] http://www.unine.ch/info/clef

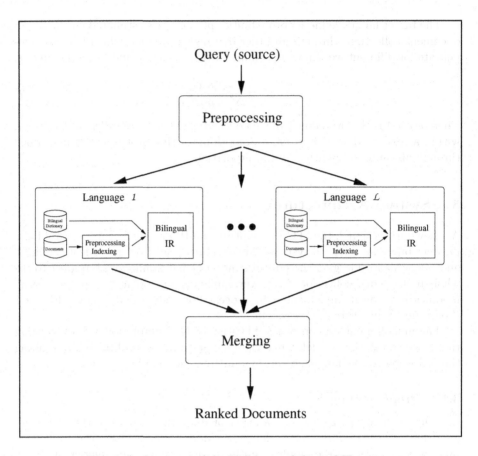

Fig. 1. Architecture of the ITC-irst multilingual IR system

3.2   Blind Relevance Feedback

After document ranking, the following Blind Relevance Feedback (BRF) technique was applied. First, the documents matching the source query **e** were ranked, then the B best ranked documents were taken and the R most relevant terms were added to the query; the retrieval phase was then repeated. In the CLIR framework, R terms are added to each single translation of the N-best list and the retrieval algorithm is repeated again. 15 new search terms were selected from the top 5 documents according to the method proposed in [8].

3.3   Merging

Given the collection-dependent rankings provided by each bilingual retrieval system, documents of the whole collection are merged into one ranking. Two merging criteria were developed.

The first, known as the `stat` method, implements the statistical model introduced in Section 2: for each language, language-dependent relevance scores of documents computed by the bilingual IR systems are normalized according to formula (4) and a global ranking is created.

The second criterion, known as the `rank` method, exploits the document rank positions only: all collection dependent rank lists are joined and documents are globally re-scored and ranked according to the inverse of their original rank position.

4   Experimental Evaluation

ITC-irst participated in three text retrieval tracks. In particular, ITC-irst submitted 4 monolingual runs in French, German, Italian, and Spanish, 4 Italian-Spanish and 2 German-Italian bilingual runs, and 4 small multilingual runs using queries in English to search documents in English, French, German, and Spanish. Some unofficial experiments were also performed for the sake of comparison. A detailed description of the tracks and the evaluation measures is given in [9].

4.1   Data

In Table 1, statistics about the target collections for the five considered languages and about the topics are reported. For each topic set (queries) we give the number of relevant documents in each collection (topics with no relevant document are not counted). Bilingual dictionaries from English to the other languages were ac-

Table 1. Statistics about target collections and queries

Language	#docs	#words	#queries	#rel.docs
English	167K	101M	54	1006
French	130K	52M	52	946
German	295K	99M	56	1825
Italian	153K	54M	51	809
Spanish	454K	172M	57	2368
Multi-4	1045K	425M	60	6145

quired from publicly available resources, mainly on the Internet. Unfortunately, German-Italian and Italian-Spanish dictionaries were not available. Hence, the missing dictionaries were automatically built from other available dictionaries using English as a pivot language. For example, the Italian-Spanish dictionary was derived by exploiting the Spanish-English and Italian-English dictionaries as follows: the translation alternatives of an Italian term are all the Spanish translations of all the English translations of that term. Table 2 reports some statistics for the bilingual dictionaries. It is worth noting that for the dictionaries generated the average number of translation alternatives is about twice as alrge as that of the original dictionaries. This would suggest that the blind dictionary

Table 2. Statistics about dictionaries

Dictionary	#entries	avg. # translations
English-French	45K	1.97
English-German	131K	1.88
English-Italian	44K	1.95
English-Spanish	47K	1.83
Italian-Spanish	66K	3.94
German-Italian	104K	3.91

generation proposed here introduces two wrong translations per entry, on the average.

Moreover, all term translation probabilities, except the German-Italian ones, were also estimated with the EM algorithm and using the corresponding document collections, i.e. those in the source languages.

4.2   Monolingual Results

Table 3 reports mAvPr scores for each official monolingual run, namely French, German, Italian, and Spanish. The performance of the English run for the multilingual track is also given. Official runs submitted to the CLEF 2003 campaign are typed in boldface.

The ITC-irst monolingual retrieval system achieved good results for all languages. As shown in the Table, more than 70% of queries have an mAvPr greater than or equal to the median values. It is also worth noticing that mAvPrs are pretty much the same for all languages.

4.3   Bilingual Results

Table 4 reports main settings and mAvPr scores for each official bilingual run. In particular, the number of N-best translations (1 vs. 10) and the type of term translation probabilities (flat vs. estimated through the EM algorithm) are indicated. Source and target languages are indicated in the run name.

Italian-Spanish results show that the estimation of translation probabilities through the EM algorithm is quite effective, especially in combination with the 10-best translations. Instead, German-Italian experiments achieve very low mAvPrs; the lack of EM estimation of the term probabilities cannot completely explain this negative performance.

The quality of the ITC-irst query translation approach is investigated by comparing monolingual and bilingual retrieval performance. In Table 5 mAvPrs for monolingual and bilingual runs for every language are shown; the 10-best translations were obtained with EM estimated translation probabilities. A relative degradation between 15% and 22% is always observed. This means that the translation process causes almost equal losses in performance for each language pair.

Table 3. Official monolingual results for French, German, Italian and Spanish. Monolingual English performance is reported, too. Comparison against the median and best values

Official Run	mAvPr	<mdn	=mdn	>mdn	bst
IRSTfr_1	.5339	15	10	27	11
IRSTde_1	.5173	16	5	35	6
IRSTit_1	.5397	11	8	32	10
IRSTes_1	.5375	17	3	37	5
IRSTen	.5458				

Table 4. Main settings and results of the bilingual official runs

Official Run	Setting	mAvPr				
IRSTit2es_1	10-best, EM	.4262	31	1	25	2
IRSTit2es_2	10-best, flat	.4006	36	1	20	2
IRSTit2es_3	1-best, EM	.4053	33	1	23	2
IRSTit2es_4	1-best, flat	.4009	35	1	21	2
IRSTde2it_1	10-best, flat	.2291	38	0	18	0
IRSTde2it_2	1-best, flat	.2437	36	0	20	0

Interestingly, for the Italian-Spanish run the performance achieved with the coupled dictionaries is comparable to that we obtained starting from English queries and using a real English-Spanish dictionary. With respect to German-Italian retrieval, a large gap was observed when using the coupled dictionary.

Differently from the Italian-Spanish task, some problems may have arisen from the creation of the bilingual dictionary. Indeed, the ratio between the intersection and the union of English words contained in the English-German and English-Italian dictionaries, is about half that for Italian-Spanish. A possible reason could be the data sparseness due to the large amount of compound names in German; a preliminary investigation of decompounding is reported in Section 5.

4.4   Multilingual Results

Table 6 reports main settings and mAvPr scores for each official multilingual run. Again source and target languages, the type of term translation probabilities (flat vs. estimated through EM algorithm), and the merging policy (looking at the rank vs. the stat) are indicated. The 10-best approach was applied for all multilingual runs.

About 60% of the queries have an mAvPr greater than or equal to the median values. The merging method based on the rank is a little more effective, but differences are very low. Again, the EM estimation of term probabilities slightly improves performance.

In order to obtain an upper bound for the multilingual retrieval system, the merging criteria were also applied to the monolingual runs. The achieved mAvPrs for this virtual experiment were .3754 and .3667 for the rank and stat

Table 5. Comparison of monolingual and bilingual performance

Language	monolingual	bilingual from English
French	.5339	.4297
German	.5173	.4378
Italian	.5397	.4184
Spanish	.5375	.4298

Table 6. Main settings and results of the official runs. Comparison against the median and best values

Official Run	Setting	mAvPr	<mdn	=mdn	>mdn	bst
IRSTen2xx_1	10-best, EM, rank	.3147	23	1	36	0
IRSTen2xx_2	10-best, EM, stat	.3089	22	2	36	1
IRSTen2xx_3	10-best, flat, rank	.3084	25	2	33	0
IRSTen2xx_4	10-best, flat, stat	.3036	25	1	34	1

criteria, respectively. The relative degradation is very similar to that observed for bilingual experiments.

Multilingual performance should be expected to be an average of the bilingual results. But this is not precisely true, because the metrics for the evaluation of retrieval performance does not take into account those topics having no relevant documents in the target collection; they are simply discarded. Retrieval systems that give a document ranking for those topics, are not penalized at all, instead of receiving a zero precision score.

In the case of the multilingual collection, i.e. the union of several language-dependent sub-collections, it can happen that there are no relevant documents for a specific topic in a given language. Unfortunately, the ITC-irst merging criteria did not take this fact into account, and generated a general ranking including documents from "non-relevant" sub-collections. A virtual experiment was made in an attempt to measure this effect. For each sub-collection and for each topic without relevant documents, ranking was removed. The system with 10-best translations, EM-estimated dictionary, and the rank merging method achieved .3318 mAvPr score, about 5% relative more than the corresponding real experiment. Hence, in general, a merging method should also be confident about the relevance of a document in a sub-collection.

5 Enhancement: German Word Decompounding

Our usual preprocessing was slightly improved in order to cope better with languages, like German, having a large amount of compound nouns, which usually represent several concepts. As retrieval is substantially based on content words, it is important to catch each basic concept expressed by compounds. Moreover, compound nouns would sensibly increase the size of the bilingual dictionary needed for query translation, and also the data sparseness. Hence, an effective decompounding procedure is required. An algorithm based on dynamic programming, which exploits a statistical word-decomposition model, was implemented. Comparative experiments were conducted in the monolingual, English-German bilingual, and multilingual tasks. Table 7 compares the mAvPr achieved by the ITC-irst system applied to German texts without and with decompounding. The 10-best translations obtained with flat translation probabilities were considered in this comparison. The figures show a consistent improvement over all runs; in the multilingual track the score increases less because German decompounding influences only one fourth of the performance, on the average.

Table 7. Comparison of retrieval performance with respect to decompounding.

Language	Setting	no decompounding	decompounding
German		.5173	.5289
English-German	10-best, flat	.4342	.4649
Multi-4	10-best, flat, stat	.3036	.3076
Multi-4	10-best, flat, rank	.3084	.3136

6   Conclusion

This paper presented a multilingual IR system developed at ITC-irst. A complete statistical model was defined which combines several bilingual retrieval models. The system was evaluated in the CLEF 2003 campaign in the monolingual, bilingual, and multilingual tracks. Our basic monolingual IR model resulted very competitive for all languages tested. The bilingual IR system seems to be strongly influenced by the bilingual translation. Better estimations of translation probabilities were obtained by applying the EM algorithm on the target collection. The multilingual IR system also achieves higher performance than the median; however, new merging criteria should be defined, which take into account those sub-collections that do not include relevant documents for a given topic. Furthermore, decompounding of German compound nouns was shown to consistently increase retrieval performance for each track: monolingual, bilingual and multilingual.

Acknowledgements

This work was carried out under the project WebFAQ, funded under the FDR-PAT program of the Province of Trento, and under the EU project PF-STAR.

References

1. Bertoldi, N., Federico, M.: ITC-irst at CLEF 2002: Using N-best query translations for CLIR. In Peters, C., Braschler, M., Gonzalo, J., Kluck, M., eds.: Advances in Cross-Language Information Retrieval. Lecture Notes in Computer Science, Vol. 2785, Springer Verlag (2003) 49–58

2. Federico, M., Bertoldi, N.: Statistical cross-language information retrieval using n-best query translations. In: Proceedings of the 25th Annual International ACM SIGIR Conference on Research and Development in Information Retrieval, Tampere, Finland (2002) 167–174

3. Bertoldi, N., Federico, M.: ITC-irst at CLEF 2001: Monolingual and bilingual tracks. In Peters, C., Braschler, M., Gonzalo, J., Kluck, M., eds.: Cross-Language Information Retrieval and Evaluation. Lecture Notes in Computer Science, Vol. 2406, Springer Verlag (2002) 94–101

4. Bertoldi, N., Federico, M.: ITC-irst at CLEF 2000: Italian monolingual track. In Peters, C., ed.: Evaluation of Cross-Language Information Retrieval Systems. Lecture Notes in Computer Science, Vol. 2069, Springer Verlag (2001) 261–272

5. Rabiner, L.R.: A tutorial on hidden Markov models and selected applications in speech recognition. In Weibel, A., Lee, K., eds.: Readings in Speech Recognition. Morgan Kaufmann (1990) 267–296

6. Dempster, A.P., Laird, N.M., Rubin, D.B.: Maximum-likelihood from incomplete data via the EM algorithm. Journal of the Royal Statistical Society, B 39 (1977) 1–38

7. Frakes, W.B., Baeza-Yates, R., eds.: Information Retrieval: Data Structures and Algorithms. Prentice Hall, Englewood Cliffs, NJ (1992)

8. Johnson, S., Jourlin, P., Jones, K.S., Woodland, P.: Spoken document retrieval for TREC-8 at Cambridge University. In: Proceedings of the 8th Text REtrieval Conference, Gaithersburg, MD (1999)

9. Braschler, M., Peters, C.: CLEF 2003: Methodology and Metrics. In this volume.

Language-Dependent and Language-Independent Approaches to Cross-Lingual Text Retrieval

Jaap Kamps, Christof Monz, Maarten de Rijke, and Börkur Sigurbjörnsson

Language & Inference Technology Group, University of Amsterdam,
Nieuwe Achtergracht 166, 1018 WV Amsterdam,
The Netherlands
{kamps, christof, mdr, borkur}@science.uva.nl

Abstract. We investigate the effectiveness of *language-dependent* approaches to document retrieval, such as stemming and decompounding, and constrast them with *language-independent* approaches, such as character n-gramming. In order to reap the benefits of more than one type of approach, we also consider the effectiveness of the combination of both types of approaches. We focus on document retrieval in nine European languages: Dutch, English, Finnish, French, German, Italian, Russian, Spanish and Swedish. We look at four different information retrieval tasks: monolingual, bilingual, multilingual, and domain-specific retrieval. The experimental evidence is obtained using the 2003 test suite of the cross-language evaluation forum (CLEF).

1 Introduction

Researchers in Information Retrieval (IR) have experimented with a great variety of approaches to document retrieval for European languages. Differences between these approaches range from the text representation used (e.g. whether to apply morphological normalization or not, or which type of query formulation to use), to the choice of search strategy (e.g., which weighting scheme to use, or whether to use blind feedback). We focus on approaches using different document representations, but using the same retrieval settings and weighting scheme. In particular, we focus on different approaches to morphological normalization or tokenization. We conducted experiments on nine European languages (Dutch, English, Finnish, French, German, Italian, Russian, Spanish, and Swedish). There are notable differences between these languages, such as the complexity of inflectional and derivational morphology [1].

A recent overview of monolingual document retrieval can be found in [2]. The options considered in [2] include word-based runs (indexing the tokens as they occur in the documents), stemming (using stemmers from the Snowball family of stemming algorithms), lemmatizing (using the lemmatizer built into the TreeTagger part-of-speech tagger), and compound splitting (for compound forming languages such as Dutch, Finnish, German, and Swedish). Additionally, there are experiments with adding character n-grams (of length 4 and 5). The

C. Peters et al. (Eds.): CLEF 2003, LNCS 3237, pp. 152–165, 2004.
© Springer-Verlag Berlin Heidelberg 2004

main lessons learned in [2] were two fold. First, there is no language for which the best performing run significantly improves over the "compound split and stem" run (treating splitting as a no-op for non-compound forming languages). Second, the hypothesis that adding 4-gramming is the best strategy is refuted for Spanish only. Notice that these comparisons did not involve combinations of runs, but only runs based on a single index.

The aim of this paper is to redo some of the experiments of [2], to investigate the combination of approaches, and to extend these experiments to a number of cross-lingual retrieval tasks (we give details below). In particular, we will investigate the effectiveness of *language-dependent* approaches to document retrieval, i.e. approaches that require detailed knowledge of the particular language at hand. The best known example of a language-dependent approach is the use of stemming algorithms. The effectiveness of stemming in English is a recurring issue in a number of studies [3, 4]. Here we consider the effectiveness of stemming for nine European languages. Another example of a language-dependent approach is the use of decompounding strategies for compound-rich European languages, such as Dutch and German [5]. Compounds formed by the concatenation of words are rare in English, although exceptions like *database* exist. We will also investigate the effectiveness of *language-independent* approaches to document retrieval, i.e., approaches that do not depend on knowledge of the language at hand. The best known example of language-independent approaches is the use of character n-gramming techniques. Finally, we will investigate whether both approaches to document retrieval can be fruitfully combined [6]. Hoping to establish the robustness and effectiveness of these approaches for a whole range of cross-lingual retrieval tasks, we supplement the monolingual retrieval experiments with bilingual retrieval experiments, with multilingual experiments, and with domain-specific experiments. Experimental evaluation is done on the test suite of the Cross-Language Evaluation Forum [7].

The paper is organized as follows. In Section 2 we describe the FlexIR system as well as the approaches used for all of the crosslingual retrieval tasks. In Section 3 we discuss our experiments for monolingual retrieval (in Section 3.1), bilingual retrieval (in Section 3.2), multilingual retrieval (in Section 3.3), and domain-specific retrieval (in Section 3.4). Finally, in Section 4 we offer some conclusions drawn from our experiments.

2   System Description

2.1   Retrieval Approach

All retrieval runs used FlexIR, an information retrieval system developed at the University of Amsterdam [5]. The main goal underlying FlexIR's design is to facilitate flexible experimentation with a wide variety of retrieval components and techniques. FlexIR is implemented in Perl and supports many types of preprocessing, scoring, indexing, and retrieval tools.

Retrieval Model. FlexIR supports several retrieval models, including the standard vector space model, language models, and probabilistic models. All runs reported in the paper use the vector space model with the Lnu.ltc weighting scheme [8] to compute the similarity between a query and a document. For all the experiments, we fixed *slope* at 0.2; the pivot was set to the average number of unique words per document.

Morphological Normalization. We apply a range of language-dependent and language-independent approaches to morphological normalization or tokenization.

Words — We consider as a baseline the straightforward indexing of the words as encountered in the collection. We do some limited sanitizing: diacritics are mapped to the unmarked character, and all characters are put in lower-case. Thus a string like 'Information Retrieval' is indexed as 'information retrieval' and a string like the German 'Raststätte' (English: motorway restaurant) is indexed as 'raststatte.'

Stemming — The stemming or lemmatization of words is the most popular language-dependent approach to document retrieval. We use the set of stemmers implemented in the Snowball language [9]. Thus a string like 'Information Retrieval' is indexed as the stems 'inform retriev.'

An overview of stemming algorithms can be found in [10]. The string processing language Snowball is specifically designed for creating stemming algorithms for use in Information Retrieval. It is partly based on the familiar Porter stemmer for English [11] and provides stemming algorithms for all the nine European languages that we consider in this paper. We perform the same sanitizing operations as for the word-based run.

Decompounding — For the compound rich languages, Dutch, German, Finnish, and Swedish, we apply a decompounding algorithm. We treat all words occurring in the CLEF corpus as potential base words for decompounding, and also use their associated collection frequencies. We ignore words of length less than four characters as potential compound parts, thus a compound must consist of at least eight characters. As a safeguard against oversplitting, we only regard compound parts that have a higher collection frequency than the compound itself. We consider linking elements -*s*-, -*e*-, and -*en*- for Dutch; -*s*-, -*n*-, -*e*-, and -*en*- for German; -*s*-, -*e*-, -*u*-, and -*o*- for Swedish; and none for Finnish. We prefer a split with no linking element over a split with a linking element, and a split with a single character linker over a two character linker.

Each document in the collection is analyzed and if a compound is identified, the compound is kept in the document and all of its parts are added to the document. Thus a string like the Dutch 'boekenkast' (English: bookshelf) is indexed as 'boekenkast boek kast.' Compounds occurring in a query are analyzed in a similar way: the parts are simply added to the query. Since we expand both the documents and the queries with compound parts, there is no need for compound formation [12].

n-Gramming — Character n-gramming is the most popular language-independent approach to document retrieval. Our n-grams were not allowed to cross word boundaries. This means that the string 'Information Retrieval' is indexed as the fourteen 4-gram tokens 'info nfor form orma rmat mati atio tion retr etri trie riev ieva eval'. We experimented with two n-gram approaches. First, we replaced the words with their n-grams. Second, we added the n-grams to the documents but kept the original words as well.

Character n-grams are an old technique for improving retrieval effectiveness. An excellent overview of n-gramming techniques for cross-lingual information retrieval is given in [13]. Again, we perform the same sanitizing operations as for the word-based run.

Character Encodings. Until CLEF 2003, the languages of the CLEF collections all used the Latin alphabet. The addition of Russian as a new CLEF language is challenging because of the use of a non-Latin alphabet. The Cyrillic characters used in Russian can appear in a variety of font encodings. The collection and topics are encoded using the UTF-8 or Unicode character encoding. We converted the UTF-8 encoding into a 1-byte per character encoding KOI8 or KOI8-R (for *Kod Obmena Informatsii* or Code of Information Exchange).[1] We did all our processing, such as lower-casing, stopping, stemming, and n-gramming, on documents and queries in this KOI8 encoding. Finally, to ensure the proper indexing of the documents using our standard architecture, we converted the resulting documents into the Latin alphabet using the Volapuk transliteration. We processed the Russian queries similar to the documents.

Stopwords. Both topics and documents were processed using the stopword lists from the Snowball stemming tool [9], for Finnish we used the Neuchâtel-stoplist [14]. Additionally, we removed topic-specific phrases such as 'Find documents that discuss ...' from the queries. We did not use a stop stem or n-gram list, but we first used a stop *word* list, and then stemmed/n-grammed the topics and documents.

Blind Feedback. Blind feedback was applied to expand the original query with related terms. Term weights were recomputed by using the standard Rocchio method [15], where we considered the top 10 documents to be relevant and the bottom 500 documents to be non-relevant. We allowed at most 20 terms to be added to the original query.

Combination Methods. For each of the CLEF 2003 languages we created base runs using a variety of indexing methods (see below). We then combined these base runs using one of two methods, either a weighted or an unweighted combination. An extensive overview of combination methods for cross-lingual information retrieval is given in [16].

---

[1] We used the excellent Perl package `Convert::Cyrillic` for conversion between character encodings and for lower-casing Cyrillic characters.

The weighted combination was produced as follows. First, we normalized the retrieval status values (RSVs), since different runs may have radically different RSVs. For each run we reranked these values in $[0, 1]$ using:

$$RSV_i' = \frac{RSV_i - min_i}{max_i - min_i};$$

this is the Min_Max_Norm considered in [17]. Next, we assigned new weights to the documents using a linear interpolation factor λ representing the relative weight of a run:

$$RSV_{new} = \lambda \cdot RSV_1 + (1 - \lambda) \cdot RSV_2.$$

For $\lambda = 0.5$ this is similar to the simple (but effective) combSUM function used by Fox and Shaw [18]. The interpolation factors λ were obtained from experiments on the CLEF 2002 data sets (whenever available). When we combine more than two runs, we give all runs the same relative weight, resulting effectively in the familiar combSUM method.

Statistical Significance. Finally, to determine whether the observed differences between two retrieval approaches are statistically significant, we used the bootstrap method, a non-parametric inference test [19, 20]. We take 100,000 resamples, and look for significant improvements (one-tailed) at significance levels of 0.95 (*); 0.99 (**); and 0.999 (***).

3   Experiments

In this section, we describe our experiments for the monolingual task, the bilingual task, the multilingual task and the domain-specific task.

3.1   Monolingual Retrieval

For the monolingual task, we conducted experiments with a number of language-dependent and language-independent approaches to document retrieval. All our monolingual runs used the title and description fields of the topics.

Baseline. Our baseline run consists of a straightforward indexing of words as encountered in the collection (with case-folding and mapping marked characters to the unmarked symbol). The mean-average-precision (MAP) scores are shown in Table 1. The baseline run is fairly high performing run for most languages. In particular, Dutch with a MAP of 0.4800 performs relatively well.

Stemming. For all eight languages, we use a stemming algorithm from the Snowball family [9] (see Section 2). The results are shown in Table 2. The results are mixed. On the one hand, we see a decrease in retrieval effectiveness for Dutch, English and Russian. On the other hand, we see an increase in retrieval effectiveness for Finnish, French, German, Italian, Spanish and Swedish. The improvements for Finnish, German and Spanish are statistically significant.

Table 1. Word-based run

	Dutch	English	Finnish	French	German	Italian	Russian	Spanish	Swedish
Words	0.4800	0.4483	0.3175	0.4313	0.3785	0.4631	0.2551	0.4405	0.3485

Table 2. Snowball stemming algorithm

	Dutch	English	Finnish	French	German	Italian	Russian	Spanish	Swedish
Words	0.4800	0.4483	0.3175	0.4313	0.3785	0.4631	0.2551	0.4405	0.3485
Stems	0.4652	0.4273	0.3998	0.4511	0.4504	0.4726	0.2536	0.4678	0.3707
%Ch.	-3.1	-4.7	+25.9	+4.6	+19.0	+2.1	-0.6	+6.2	+6.4
Stat.	-	-	*	-	***	-	-	*	-

Decompounding. Compounds are split using the method described in Section 2. We decompound documents and queries for the four compound-rich languages: Dutch, Finnish, German, and Swedish. After decompounding, we apply the same stemming procedure as above. The results are shown in Table 3. The

Table 3. Decompounding

	Dutch	Finnish	German	Swedish
Words	0.4800	0.3175	0.3785	0.3485
Split+Stem	0.4984	0.4453	0.4840	0.3957
%Ch.	+3.8	+40.3	+27.9	+13.5
Stat.	-	***	***	-

results for decompounding are positive overall. We now see an improvement for Dutch, and further improvement for Finnish, German, and Swedish.

Our results indicate that for all four compound forming languages, Dutch, Finnish, German, and Swedish, we should decompound before stemming. We treat the resulting (compound-split and) stem runs as a single language-dependent approach, where we only decompound the four compound-rich languages. The results are shown in Table 4. These resulting (compound-split and) stem runs improve for all languages, except for English and the low-performing Russian.

n-Gramming. Both topic and document words are n-grammed, using the settings discussed in Section 2. For all languages we use 4-grams, that is, character n-grams of length 4. The results for replacing the words with n-grams are shown in Table 5. We see a decrease in performance for four languages: Dutch, English, French and Italian, and an improvement for the other five languages: Finnish, German, Russian, Spanish and Swedish. The increase in retrieval effectiveness is statistically significant for Finnish and German, the decrease in performance is significant for English and Italian. The results are mixed, and the technique of character n-gramming is far from being a panacea.

Table 4. (Compound splitting and) stemming algorithms

	Dutch	English	Finnish	French	German	Italian	Russian	Spanish	Swedish
Words	0.4800	0.4483	0.3175	0.4313	0.3785	0.4631	0.2551	0.4405	0.3485
Split+Stem	0.4984	0.4273	0.4453	0.4511	0.4840	0.4726	0.2536	0.4678	0.3957
%Ch.	+3.8	-4.7	+40.3	+4.6	+27.9	+2.1	-0.6	+6.2	+13.5
Stat.	-	-	***	-	***	-	-	*	-

Table 5. 4-Gramming

	Dutch	English	Finnish	French	German	Italian	Russian	Spanish	Swedish
Words	0.4800	0.4483	0.3175	0.4313	0.3785	0.4631	0.2551	0.4405	0.3485
4-Grams	0.4488	0.3731	0.4676	0.4142	0.4639	0.3883	0.2871	0.4545	0.3751
%Ch.	-6.5	-16.8	+47.3	-4.0	+22.6	-16.2	+12.5	+3.2	+7.6
Stat.	-	**	**	-	**	**	-	-	-

Table 6. 4-Gramming while retaining words

	Dutch	English	Finnish	French	German	Italian	Russian	Spanish	Swedish
Words	0.4800	0.4483	0.3175	0.4313	0.3785	0.4631	0.2551	0.4405	0.3485
Word+4-Gr.	0.4996	0.4119	0.4905	0.4616	0.5005	0.4227	0.3030	0.4733	0.4187
%Ch.	+4.1	-8.1	+54.5	+7.0	+32.2	-8.7	+18.8	+7.4	+20.1
Stat.	-	*	***	-	***	-	*	*	*

We explore a second language-independent approach, by adding the n-grams to the free-text of the documents, rather than replacing the free-text with n-grams. The results of adding n-grams are shown in Table 6. The runs improve over pure n-grams for all the nine languages. With respect to the words baseline, we see a decrease in performance for English and Italian, and an improvement for the other seven languages: Dutch, Finnish, French, German, Russian, Spanish and Swedish. The deviating behavior for Italian may be due to the different ways of encoding marked characters in the Italian sub-collections [7]. Improvements are significant for five of the languages, namely Finnish, German, Russian, Spanish and Swedish. However, the decrease in performance for English remains significant too.

Combining. It is clear from the results above that there is no equivocal best strategy for monolingual document retrieval. For English, our baseline run scores best. For Italian, the stemmed run scores best. For the other seven languages, Word+4-Gramming scores best. Here, we consider the combination of language-dependent and language-independent approaches to document retrieval. We apply a weighted combination method, also referred to as linear fusion. From the experiments above we select the approaches that exhibit the best overall performance:

Best language-dependent approach is to decompound for Dutch, Finnish, German, and Swedish, and then apply a stemming algorithm.

Best language-independent approach is to add n-grams while retaining the original words.

In particular, we combine the (compound split and) stem run of Table 3 with the Word+4-Gram run of Table 6. The used interpolation factors are based on experiments using the CLEF 2002 test suite (whenever available). We used the following relative weights of the n-gram run: 0.25 (Dutch), 0.4 (English), 0.51 (Finnish), 0.66 (French), 0.36 (German), 0.405 (Italian), 0.60 (Russian), 0.35 (Spanish), and 0.585 (Swedish).

Table 7. Combination of (Compound-splitting and) Stemming and adding 4-Grams

	Dutch	English	Finnish	French	German	Italian	Russian	Spanish	Swedish
Words	0.4800	0.4483	0.3175	0.4313	0.3785	0.4631	0.2551	0.4405	0.3485
Combination	0.5072	0.4575	0.5236	0.4888	0.5091	0.4781	0.2988	0.4841	0.4371
%Ch.	+5.7	+2.1	+64.9	+13.3	+34.5	+3.2	+17.1	+9.9	+25.4
Stat.	-	-	***	**	***		*	***	**

The results are shown in Table 7. We find only positive results: all languages improve over the baseline, even English! Even though both English runs scored lower than the baseline (one of them even significantly lower), the combination improves over the baseline. The improvements for six of the languages, Finnish, French, German, Russian, Spanish, and Swedish, are significant. All languages except Russian improve over the best run using a single index.

3.2 Bilingual Retrieval

We restrict our attention here to bilingual runs using the English topic set. All our bilingual runs used the title and description fields of the topics. We experimented with the WorldLingo machine translation [21] for translations into Dutch, French, German, Italian and Spanish. For translation into Russian we used the PROMT-Reverso machine translation [22]. For translations into Swedish, we used the the first mentioned translation in the Babylon on-line dictionary [23]. Since we use the English topic set, the results for English are the monolingual runs discussed above in Section 3.1. We also ignore English to Finnish retrieval for lack of an acceptable automatic translation method. Thus, we focus on seven European languages.

We created the exact same set of runs as for the monolingual retrieval task described above: a word-based baseline run; a stemmed run with decompounding for Dutch, German, and Swedish; a words+4-gram run; and a weighted combination of words+4-gram and (split and) stem runs. We use the following relative weights of the words+4-gram run: 0.6 (Dutch), 0.7 (French), 0.5 (German), 0.6 (Italian), 0.6 (Russian), 0.5 (Spanish), and 0.8 (Swedish).

Table 8 shows our MAP scores for the English to Dutch, French, German, Italian, Russian, Spanish, and Swedish, bilingual runs. For our official runs for

Table 8. Bilingual runs using EN topic set. Best scores are in boldface. We compare the best scoring run with the word-based baseline run

	Dutch	French	German	Italian	Russian	Spanish	Swedish
Words	0.3554	0.3547	0.3378	0.3810	0.1379	0.3246	0.1187
(Split+)Stem	**0.4043**	0.3567	0.3968	0.3860	**0.2270**	0.3588	0.1898
Word+4-Grams	0.3690	0.3762	0.4228	0.3801	0.1983	0.3775	0.2371
Combination	0.3971	**0.3951**	**0.4479**	**0.3927**	0.2195	**0.3888**	**0.2478**
%Change	+13.8	+11.4	+32.6	+3.1	+64.6	+19.8	+108.8
Stat.Sign.	*	-	***	-	**	**	***

Table 9. Decrease in effectiveness for bilingual runs

	Dutch	French	German	Italian	Russian	Spanish	Swedish
Best monolingual	0.5072	0.4888	0.5091	0.4781	0.3030	0.4841	0.4371
Best bilingual	0.4043	0.3951	0.4479	0.3927	0.2270	0.3888	0.2478
%Change	−20.3	−19.2	−12.0	−17.9	−25.1	−19.7	−43.3
Stat.Sign.	*	-	***	-	**	**	***

the 2003 bilingual task, we refer the reader to [24]. Adding 4-grams improves retrieval effectiveness over the word-based baseline for all languages except Italian (which exhibits a marginal drop in performance). The stemmed, and decompounded for Dutch, German, and Swedish, runs do improve for all seven languages. The Dutch stemmed and decompounded run and the Russian stemmed run turn out to be particularly effective, and outperform the respective n-gram and combination runs. A conclusion on the effectiveness of the Russian stemmer, based on only the monolingual evidence earlier, would prove to be premature. Although the stemmer failed to improve retrieval effectiveness for the monolingual Russian task, it is effective for the bilingual Russian task. For the other five languages (French, German, Italian, Spanish, and Swedish) the combination of stemming and n-gramming results in the best bilingual performance. The best performing run does significantly improve over the word-based baseline for five of the seven languages: Dutch, German, Russian, Spanish, and Swedish.

The results on the English topic set are, as expected, somewhat lower than the monolingual runs. Table 9 shows the decrease in effectiveness of the best bilingual run compared to the best monolingual run for the respective target language. The difference ranges from a 12% decrease (German) to a 43% decrease (Swedish) in MAP score. The big gap in performance for Swedish is most likely a result of the use of a translation dictionary, rather than a proper machine translation. The results for the other languages seem quite acceptable, considering that we used a simple, straightforward machine translation for the bilingual tasks [21]. The bilingual results do, in general, confirm the results obtained for the monolingual task. This increases our confidence in the effectiveness and robustness of the language-dependent and language-independent approaches employed for building the indexes.

3.3   Multilingual Retrieval

We used the English topic set for our multilingual runs, using only the title and description fields of the topics. We use the English monolingual run (see Section 3.1) and the English to Dutch, French, German, Italian, Spanish, and Swedish bilingual runs (see Section 3.2) to construct our multilingual runs. There are two different multilingual tasks. The small multilingual task uses four languages: English, French, German, and Spanish. The large multilingual task extends this set with four additional languages: Dutch, Finnish, Italian, and Swedish. Recall from our bilingual experiments in Section 3.2 that we do not have an English to Finnish bilingual run, and that our English to Swedish bilingual runs perform somewhat lower due to the use of a translation dictionary.

This prompted the following three sets of experiments:

1. on the four languages of the small multilingual task (English, French, German, and Spanish),
2. on the six languages for which we have an acceptable machine translation (also including Dutch and Italian), and
3. on the seven languages (also including Swedish, but no Finnish documents) for which we have, at least, an acceptable bilingual dictionary.

For each of these experiments, we build a number of combined runs, where we use the unweighted combSUM rule introduced by [18]. First, we combine a single, uniform run per language, in all cases the bilingual words+4-gram run (see Section 3.1 and 3.2). Second, we again use a single run per language, the weighted combination of the words+4-gram and (Split+)Stem run (see Section 3.1 and 3.2). Third, we form a big pool of runs, two per language: the Word+4-Grams runs and the (Split+)Stem runs.

Table 10 shows our multilingual MAP scores for the small multilingual task (covering four languages) and for the large multilingual task (covering eight languages). For all multilingual experiments, first making a weighted combination per language outperforms the unweighted combination of all Word+4-Grams run and all (Split+)Stem runs. However, as we add languages, we see that the unweighted combination of all Word+4-Grams runs and all (Split+)Stem runs performs almost as well as the weighted combinations.

Our results show that multilingual retrieval on a subpart of the collection (leaving out one or two languages) can still be an effective strategy. However, the results also indicate that the inclusion of further languages does consistently improve MAP scores.

Table 10. Overview of MAP scores for multilingual runs

	Multi-4	Multi-8	
		(without FI/SV)	(without FI)
Word+4-Gram	0.2953	0.2425	0.2475
Combined Word+4-Gram/(Split+)Stem	0.3341	0.2806	0.2860
Both Word+n-Gram and (Split+)Stem	0.3292	0.2764	0.2843

3.4   Domain-Specific Retrieval

For our domain-specific retrieval experiments, we used the *German Information Retrieval Test-database* (GIRT). We focus on monolingual experiments using the German topics and the German collection. We used the title and description fields of the topics, and used the title and abstract fields of the collection. We experimented with a reranking strategy based on the keywords assigned to the documents, the resulting rerank runs also use the controlled-vocabulary fields in the collection.

We make three different indexes mimicking the settings used for our monolingual German experiments discussed in Section 3.1. First, we make an word-based index as used in our baseline runs. Second, we make a stemmed index in which we did not use a decompounding strategy. Third, we build a Word+4-Grams index.

Table 11 contains our MAP scores for the GIRT monolingual task. The results for the GIRT tasks show the effectiveness of stemming and n-gramming approaches over a plain word index. Notice also that the performance of German domain-specific retrieval are somewhat lower than those of German monolingual retrieval.

Table 11. Overview of MAP scores for GIRT runs

	GIRT	%Change	Stat.sign.
Words (baseline)	0.2360		
Stems	0.2832	+20.0	***
Word+4-Grams	0.3449	+46.1	***

The main aim of our domain-specific experiments is to find ways to exploit the manually assigned keywords in the collection. These keywords are based on the controlled-vocabulary thesaurus maintained by GESIS [25]. In particular, we experiment with an improved version of the keyword-based reranking strategy introduced in [6]. We calculate vectors for the keywords based on their (co-)occurrences in the collection. The main innovation is in the use of higher dimensional vectors for the keywords, for which we use the best reduction onto a 100-dimensional Euclidean space. The reranking strategy is as follows. We calculate vectors for all initially retrieved documents, by simply taking the mean of the vectors of keywords assigned to the documents. We calculate a vector for a topic by taking the relevance-weighted mean of the top 10 retrieved documents. We now have a vector for each of the topics, and for each of the retrieved documents. Thus, ignoring the RSV of the retrieved documents, we can simply rerank all documents by the euclidean distance between the document and topic vectors. Next, we combine the original text-based similarity scores with the keyword-based distances using the unweighted combSUM rule of [18].

The results of the reranking strategy are shown in the rest of Table 12. For all the three index approaches, the results are positive. There is a significant improvement of retrieval effectiveness due to the keyword-based reranking method.

Table 12. Overview of MAP scores for GIRT runs. We compare the rerank runs with the respective orginal runs

	GIRT baseline	Rerank	%Change	Stat.sign.
Words	0.2360	0.2863	+21.31%	***
Stems	0.2832	0.3361	+18.68%	***
Word+4-Grams	0.3449	0.3993	+15.77%	***

The obtained improvement is additional to the improvement due to blind feedback, and consistent even for high performing base runs.

4   Conclusions

This paper investigates the effectiveness of language-dependent and language-independent approaches to cross-lingual text retrieval. The experiments described in this paper indicate the following. First, morphological normalization does improve retrieval effectiveness, especially for languages that have a more complex morphology than English. We also showed that n-gram-based can be a viable option in the absence of linguistic resources to support deep morphological normalization. Although no panacea, the combination of runs provides a method that may help improve base runs, even high quality base runs. The interpolation factors required for the best gain in performance seem to be fairly robust across topic sets. Moreover, the effectiveness of the unweighted combination of runs is usually close to the weighted combination, and the difference seems to diminish with the number of runs being combined. Our bilingual experiments showed that a simple machine translation strategy can be effective for bilingual retrieval. The combination of bilingual runs, in turn, leads to an effective strategy for multilingual retrieval. Finally, our results for domain-specific retrieval show the effectiveness of stemming and n-gramming even for specialized collection. Moreover, manually assigned classification information in such scientific collections can be fruitfully exploited for improving retrieval effectiveness.

Our future research is to extend the described experiments to other retrieval models. In particular, we are considering the Okapi weighting scheme [26], and a language model [27]. We have started conducting initial experiments using these alternative retrieval models. In [24], we reported on Okapi and language model runs using the (decompounded and) stemmed indexes for Dutch, German, Spanish, and Swedish. In fact, these combinations of different retrieval models resulted in our best scoring official runs [24]. Our initial conclusion is that varying the retrieval model leads to improvement, and especially the combination of different retrieval models hold the promise of making retrieval more effective.

Acknowledgments

We thank Valentin Jijkoun for his help with the Russian collection. Jaap Kamps was supported by the Netherlands Organization for Scientific Research (NWO) under project numbers 400-20-036 and 612.066.032. Christof Monz was supported by NWO under project numbers 612-13-001 and 220-80-001. Maarten de Rijke was supported by NWO under project numbers 612-13-001, 365-20-005, 612.069.006, 612.000.106, 220-80-001, 612.000.207, and 612.066.032.

References

1. Matthews, P.H.: Morphology. Cambridge University Press (1991)
2. Hollink, V., Kamps, J., Monz, C., de Rijke, M.: Monolingual document retrieval for European languages. Information Retrieval **6** (2003)
3. Harman, D.: How effective is suffixing? Journal of the American Society for Information Science **42** (1991) 7–15
4. Hull, D.: Stemming algorithms – a case study for detailed evaluation. Journal of the American Society for Information Science **47** (1996) 70–84
5. Monz, C., de Rijke, M.: Shallow morphological analysis in monolingual information retrieval for Dutch, German and Italian. In Peters, C., Braschler, M., Gonzalo, J., Kluck, M., eds.: Evaluation of Cross-Language Information Retrieval Systems, CLEF 2001. Volume 2406 of Lecture Notes in Computer Science., Springer (2002) 262–277
6. Kamps, J., Monz, C., de Rijke, M.: Combining evidence for cross-language information retrieval. In Peters, C., Braschler, M., Gonzalo, J., Kluck, M., eds.: Evaluation of Cross-Language Information Retrieval Systems, CLEF 2002. Lecture Notes in Computer Science, Springer (2003)
7. CLEF: Cross language evaluation forum (2003) http://www.clef-campaign.org/.
8. Buckley, C., Singhal, A., Mitra, M.: New retrieval approaches using SMART: TREC 4. In Harman, D., ed.: The Fourth Text REtrieval Conference (TREC-4), National Institute for Standards and Technology. NIST Special Publication 500-236 (1996) 25–48
9. Snowball: Stemming algorithms for use in information retrieval (2003) http://www.snowball.tartarus.org/.
10. Frakes, W.: Stemming algorithms. In Frakes, W., Baeza-Yates, R., eds.: Information Retrieval: Data Structures & Algorithms. Prentice Hall (1992) 131–160
11. Porter, M.: An algorithm for suffix stripping. Program **14** (1980) 130–137
12. Pohlmann, R., Kraaij, W.: Improving the precision of a text retrieval system with compound analysis. In Landsbergen, J., Odijk, J., van Deemter, K., Veldhuijzen van Zanten, G., eds.: Proceedings of the 7th Computational Linguistics in the Netherlands Meeting (CLIN 1996). (1996) 115–129
13. McNamee, P., Mayfield, J.: Character n-gram tokenization for European language text retrieval. Information Retrieval **6** (2003)
14. CLEF-Neuchâtel: CLEF resources at the University of Neuchâtel (2003) http://www.unine.ch/info/clef.
15. Rocchio, Jr., J.: Relevance feedback in information retrieval. In Salton, G., ed.: The SMART Retrieval System: Experiments in Automatic Document Processing. Prentice-Hall Series in Automatic Computation. Prentice-Hall, Englewood Cliffs NJ (1971) 313–323

16. Savoy, J.: Combining multiple strategies for effective monolingual and cross-language retrieval. Information Retrieval **6** (2003)
17. Lee, J.: Combining multiple evidence from different properties of weighting schemes. In Fox, E., Ingwersen, P., Fidel, R., eds.: Proceedings of the 18th Annual International ACM SIGIR Conference on Research and Development in Information Retrieval, ACM Press, New York NY, USA (1995) 180–188
18. Fox, E., Shaw, J.: Combination of multiple searches. In Harman, D., ed.: The Second Text REtrieval Conference (TREC-2), National Institute for Standards and Technology. NIST Special Publication 500-215 (1994) 243–252
19. Efron, B.: Bootstrap methods: Another look at the jackknife. Annals of Statistics **7** (1979) 1–26
20. Efron, B., Tibshirani, R.J.: An Introduction to the Bootstrap. Chapman and Hall, New York (1993)
21. Worldlingo: Online translator (2003) `http://www.worldlingo.com/`.
22. PROMT-Reverso: Online translator (2003) `http://translation2.paralink.com/`.
23. Babylon: Online dictionary (2003) `http://www.babylon.com/`.
24. Kamps, J., Monz, C., de Rijke, M., Sigurbjörnsson, B.: The University of Amsterdam at CLEF-2003. In Peters, C., ed.: Results of the CLEF 2003 Cross-Language System Evaluation Campaign. (2003) 71–78
25. Schott, H., ed.: Thesaurus Sozialwissenschaften. Informationszentrum Sozialwissenschaften, Bonn (2002) 2 Bände: Alphabetischer und systematischer Teil.
26. Robertson, S., Walker, S., Beaulieu, M.: Experimentation as a way of life: Okapi at TREC. Information Processing & Management **36** (2000) 95–108
27. Hiemstra, D.: Using Language Models for Information Retrieval. PhD thesis, Center for Telematics and Information Technology, University of Twente (2001)

Multilingual Retrieval Experiments with MIMOR at the University of Hildesheim

René Hackl, Ralph Kölle, Thomas Mandl, Alexandra Ploedt,
Jan-Hendrik Scheufen, and Christa Womser-Hacker

University of Hildesheim, Information Science, Marienburger Platz 22,
D-31141 Hildesheim, Germany
mandl@uni-hildesheim.de

Abstract. Fusion and optimization based relevance judgements have proven to be successful strategies in information retrieval. In this year's CLEF campaign we applied these strategies to multilingual retrieval with four languages. Our fusion experiments were carried out using freely available software. We used the snowball stemmers, internet translation services and the text retrieval tools in Lucene and the new MySQL.

1 Introduction

For the CLEF 2002 campaign, we tested an adaptive fusion system based on the MIMOR model within the GIRT track [1]. For CLEF 2003, we applied the same model to multilingual retrieval with four languages. We chose English as our source language because most of the web based translation services offer translations to and/or from English. Our experiments were executed fully automatically.

2 Fusion in Information Retrieval

Fusion in information retrieval delegates a ranking task to different algorithms and considers all the results returned. The individual result lists are combined into one final result. Fusion is motivated by the observation that many retrieval systems reach comparable effectiveness, however, the overlap between their ranked lists is sometimes low [2]. The retrieval status values (RSV) are combined statically by taking the sum, the minimum or the maximum of the results from the individual systems. Linear combinations assign a weight to each method, which determines its influence on the final result. These weights may be improved for example by heuristic optimization or learning methods [3].

There has been a considerable interest in fusion algorithms in several areas of information retrieval. In web information retrieval, for example, link analysis assigns an overall quality value to all pages based mainly on the number of links that point to that page [4]. This quality measure needs to be fused with the retrieval ranking based on the document's content (e.g. [5]). Fusion is also investigated in image retrieval for

C. Peters et al. (Eds.): CLEF 2003, LNCS 3237, pp. 166–173, 2004.
© Springer-Verlag Berlin Heidelberg 2004

the combination of evidences that stem from different representations like color, texture, and forms. In XML retrieval fusion is necessary to combine the ranks assigned to a document by the structural analysis and the content analysis [6].

3 MIMOR as Fusion Framework

MIMOR (Multiple Indexing and Method-Object Relations) represents a learning approach to the fusion task, which is based on results of information retrieval research that show that the overlap between different systems is often small [2, 7]. Furthermore, relevance feedback is considered a very promising strategy for improving retrieval quality. As a consequence, the linear combination of different results is optimized through learning from relevance feedback. MIMOR represents an information retrieval system managing poly-representation of queries and documents by selecting appropriate methods for indexing and matching [7]. By learning from user feedback on the relevance of documents, the model adapts itself by assigning weights to the different basic retrieval engines. MIMOR can also be individualized; however, such personalization in information retrieval is difficult to evaluate within evaluation initiatives. MIMOR could learn an individual or group based optimization of the fusion. However, in evaluation studies, a standardized notion of relevance exists.

4 CLEF Retrieval Experiments with MIMOR

The tools we employed this year include Lucene 1.3[1], MySQL 4.0.12[2] and JavaTM-based snowball[3] analyzers. Most of the data preprocessing was carried out by Perl-scripts. This includes cleaning the collections from unnecessary and malformed tags. Especially non-SGML-conform elements, e.g. '&' in some collections instead of '&' caused problems.

In a first step after preprocessing, customized snowball stemmers were used to stem the collections and to eliminate stopwords. Stopword lists were downloaded from the University of Neuchâtel[4] and some words were added manually. Then, the collections were indexed by Lucene and MySQL. Lucene managed the job of indexing 1321 MB in less than half the time that MySQL needed.

A second step involved the translation of the English topics into French, German and Spanish. For this task we used FreeTranslation, Reverso and Linguatec[5].

Before deciding to apply these tools, a few alternative translation tools also freely available on the Internet were tested, in which case the queries of the year 2001 were

---

[1] Lucene: http://jakarta.apache.org/lucene/docs/index.html
[2] MySQL: http://www.mysql.com/
[3] Snowball: http://jakarta.apache.org/lucene/docs/lucene-sandbox/snowball/
[4] http://www.unine.ch/Info/clef/
[5] Linguatec Personal Translator: http://www.linguatec.net/online/ptwebtext/index.shtml
  Reverso: http://www.reverso.net/, Free Translation: http://www.freetranslation.com/

helpful to gather comparable data. Examining the various translations, it became apparent that the quality of machine translation was not quite satisfying, but that, at the same time, the individual translation systems did not show the same weaknesses nor made the same mistakes. Due to this fact, we decided to use more than one translation system and merge the results afterwards. It was important, therefore, to choose tools that performed best, but at the same time possessed different characteristics.

Before merging, the topics were also stemmed with snowball and stopwords were removed, according to the respective language. The translated and analyzed queries of each language were then merged by simply throwing the three translations together while eliminating duplicates. We did not try to identify any phrases.

Table 1. Results of the test runs

	Number of multilingual documents retrieved	*Average precision*	*Average document precision*
Data from 2001			
Lucene	5167 / 6892	0.288	0.325
MySQL	2873	0.103	0.136
1:1 merged	3975	0.185	0.221
4:1 merged	4984	0.267	0.309
9:1 merged	5101	0.283	0.325
17:3 merged	5056	0.276	0.319
Data from 2002			
Lucene	4454 / 6996	0.287	0.277
MySQL	2446	0.091	0.095
9:1 merged	4543	0.285	0.276
17:3 merged	4533	0.278	0.271
7:1 merged	**4553**	0.282	0.274
33:7 merged	4511	0.274	0.267

Before tackling the official run, both retrieval systems were tested. Using the data (collections and relevance assessments) from 2001 we carried out several runs. Despite their dissimilar stand-alone performances, the systems were granted equal weights for the fusion process at first (1:1). After four runs, the weights strongly favoured Lucene and we went on experimenting with the 2002 data. The peak performance of the fusion was reached at a ratio of 7:1 (= 0.875:0.125) favouring Lucene's results. This suggests that some of MySQL's best relevant results helped the overall precision. (cf. Table 1). Despite the low retrieval quality of MySQL, it still contributed to the fusion. Note, however, that we did not include the Italian collections and that we used the "perfect", that is, monolingual, queries in our tests, so there may be some bias. Italian was part of the 2001 and 2002 campaign, but it is not part of the multilingual-4 track in CLEF 2003.

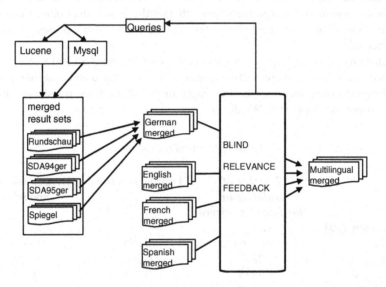

Fig. 1. Experimental setup

To further improve retrieval quality, blind relevance feedback (BRF) was implemented. We selected expansion terms with either the Robertson selection value (RSV) or the Kullback-Leibler (KL) divergence measure [8]. Exemplary results can be seen in Table 2. The precision could be improved and the number of retrieved documents was boosted (+14.8% compared to the best merged run for KL, +17.1% compared to Lucene).

Table 2. Query expansion

	Documents retrieved	*Average precision*	*Average document precision*
Lucene BRF RSV 5 10	5059	0.302	0.311
Lucene BRF KL 5 10	5216	0.314	0.328
7:1 BRF RSV 5 10	5157	0.305	0.317
7:1 BRF KL 5 10	5227	0.313	0.326

Due to time constraints, we could not determine the best parameters for BRF. A sample run without BRF took 4+ hours on our dual Pentium III 800 MHz, 1GB RAM,

SCSI 160 HDD machine. A run with BRF taking the top five documents and adding ten terms commonly took more than twelve hours. Unfortunately, some instabilities in MySQL-DB caused further delay for our experiments.

All our submitted runs use BRF KL 5 20.For the multilingual task, R1 uses the 7:1 merging scheme, whereas R2 is a Lucene-only run. Both monolingual runs are rather a by-product obtained in the course of our main (multilingual) task. The processing sequence chosen allowed for an efficient extraction of the monolingual data.

In our test runs, we were able to show that fusion helped raise at least the recall, although the results for 2003 could not confirm this finding. The Lucene-based runs generally outperform the fusion runs, except for a marginally better recall in the merged monolingual run (Table 3).

Table 3. Results 2003

	Documents retrieved	*Average precision*
UHImlt4R1	3944 / 6145	0.285
UHImlt4R2	4137 / 6145	0.306
UHImnenR1	951 / 1006	0.363
UHImnenR2	945 / 1006	0.380

5 Additional Runs

After submitting our runs for the CLEF 2003 campaign, we conducted a number of additional experimental runs to examine the performance of the retrieval systems with different setups.

MySQL, for example, automatically filters the content of the table column(s) when building a full text index, i.e. it also removes stopwords (built-in English stopword list) and words with a length of three or less characters. This signifies that the indices of the English collections might have been altered slightly compared to the indices of other collections. The removal of very small words might have had an even bigger impact on all collections. Because stemming was carried out separately before injecting the data into the database, approximately 15 % of the document terms were ignored due to this setting (Table 4).

The following runs were carried out using the CLEF 2003 data and automatically translated topics to examine the stand-alone retrieval performance of Lucene and MySQL using different strategies and configurations:

– MySQL_solo1:   A MySQL default installation, i.e. words with less than 4 characters were ignored for fulltext indexes and a built-in English stopword list was applied.
– MySQL_solo2:   Min. word length set to 1. Built-in stopword list.
– MySQL_solo3:   Min. word length set to 1. No stopword list.

Table 4. MySQL performance with varying configuration settings

	Average Precision	*Average document precision*	*Average index size per collection*
MySQL_solo1:	0.149	0.189	104.945 KB
MySQL_solo2:	0.156	0.193	123.884 KB
MySQL_solo3:	0.156	0.194	124.945 KB

The average size of the indexes per collection in the above table shows the effect of the individual configuration settings on the collections' indexes. Although the built-in English stopword list had the smallest influence, it seems interesting to mention that the indexes of all collections were similarly affected by this feature and not only the English collections.

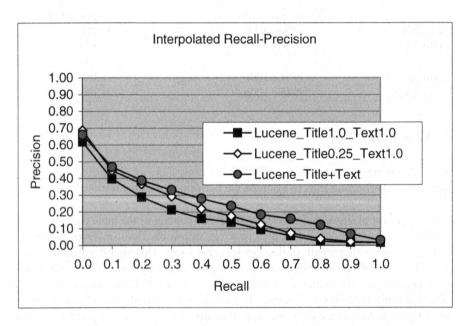

Fig. 2. Lucene performance with varying indexing and merging strategies

We also conducted two more runs with the Lucene search engine to see if the solo performance could be improved. For this task, the title and text elements of the documents were indexed separately and the resulting ranked lists were merged with varying weights. In our submitted runs the title and text elements were concatenated and indexed in a single index. The following table shows the average precision over all topics for these runs.

Table 5. Average precision for Lucene runs with varying indexing and merging strategies

	Title 1.0 / Text 1.0	*Title 0.25 / Text 1.0*	*Title + Text*
Lucene	0.205	0.255	0.282

The precision-recall graphs in Figure 2 indicate that there is room for optimization when indexing separately and applying merging weights. But the strategy we used in the submitted runs (single index) shows a much better performance over all recall levels. Although the merging weights can probably be optimized further, the cost for calculating these weights seems unreasonably high if indexing title and text together shows such good initial results.

Additional runs with the 2003 data were conducted to confirm the results of the test runs. Runs with BRF generally outperformed those without BRF. But using the original (perfect) translations of the CLEF queries instead of the automatically translated ones for all four languages, BRF as well as the fusion runs with MySQL had a negative influence on the overall performance. The average precision figures in table 6 illustrate these findings.

Table 6. Effect of BRF, fusion and translation quality on average precision

Run Name	*Average Precision*	
	No BRF	*BRF_KL_5_20*
Lucene_ perfectly_translated _queries	0.348	0.289
Lucene_ autom_translated _queries	0.249	0.306
Fusion7to1_perfectly_translated_queries	0.322	0.280
Fusion7to1_ autom_translated _queries	0.245	0.285

Examining runs that used blind relevance feedback we noticed three-letter words and numbers in the Spanish queries we could not identify at first. The documents of the Spanish collections contain strings like "01/19/00-11/94" and "gta/tg/sm", which probably are dates and abbreviations of authors. These terms, though occurring very rarely, were judged as good descriptors by the BRF algorithm, but might have produced more noise in the retrieved documents. This assumption could not yet be verified.

6 Outlook

As in 2002, we included stand-alone retrieval systems in our MIMOR fusion approach. Again, one system performed much worse than the other. Next year, we would like to participate again in a multilingual track and continue to work on merging schemes, query expansion and term weighting.

Acknowledgements

We would like to thank the Jakarta and Apache projects' teams for sharing Lucene with a wide community as well as the providers of MySQL and Snowball. Furthermore, we acknowledge the work of several students from the University of Hildesheim who implemented MIMOR as part of their course work.

References

1. Hackl, R.; Kölle, R.; Mandl, T.; Womser-Hacker, C.: Domain Specific Retrieval Experiments at the University of Hildesheim with the MIMOR System. In: Peters, C.; Braschler, M.; Gonzalo, J.; Kluck, M. (eds.): Evaluation of Cross-Language Information Retrieval Systems. Proceedings of the CLEF 2002 Workshop. Springer [LNCS] (2002)
2. Womser-Hacker, C.: Das MIMOR-Modell. Mehrfachindexierung zur dynamischen Methoden-Objekt-Relationierung im Information Retrieval. Habilitationsschrift. Universität Regensburg, Informationswissenschaft (1997)
3. Vogt, C.; Cottrell, G.: Predicting the Performance of Linearly Combined IR Systems. 21st Annual Intl. ACM SIGIR Conf. on Research and Development in Information Retrieval. Melbourne, Australia (1998) 190-196
4. Henzinger, M.: Link Analysis in Web Information Retrieval. In: IEEE Data Engineering Bulletin, 23(3) (2000) 3-8
5. Plachouras, V.; Ounis, I.: Query-Based Combination of Evidence on the Web. In: Workshop on Mathematical/Formal Methods in Information Retrieval, ACM SIGIR Conference, Tampere, Finland (2002)
6. Fuhr, N.; Großjohann, K.: XIRQL: A Query Language for Information Retrieval in XML Documents. In: 24th Annual Intl Conf on Research and Development in Information Retrieval 2001 (2001) 172-180
7. Mandl, T.; Womser-Hacker, C.: Probability Based Clustering for Document and User Properties. In: Ojala, T. (ed.): Infotech Oulo International Workshop on Information Retrieval (IR 2001). Oulo, Finnland. Sept 19-21 2001 (2001) 100-107
8. Carpineto, C.; de Mori, R.; Romano, G.; Bigi, B.: An Information-Theoretic Approach to Automatic Query Expansion. In: ACM Transactions on Information Systems. 19(1) (2001) 1-27

Concept-Based Searching and Merging for Multilingual Information Retrieval: First Experiments at CLEF 2003

Romaric Besançon, Gaël de Chalendar, Olivier Ferret, Christian Fluhr, Olivier Mesnard, and Hubert Naets

CEA-LIST,
LIC2M (Multilingual Multimedia Knowledge Engineering Laboratory),
B.P.6 - F92265 Fontenay-aux-Roses Cedex, France
{Romaric.Besancon, Gael.de-Chalendar, Olivier.Ferret, Christian.Fluhr,
Olivier.Mesnard, Hubert.Naets}@cea.fr

Abstract. This article presents the LIC2M's crosslingual retrieval system which participated in the Small Multilingual Track of CLEF 2003. This system is based on a deep linguistic analysis of documents and queries that aims at categorizing them in terms of concepts and implements an original search algorithm inherited from the SPIRIT (EMIR) system that takes into account this categorization.

1   Introduction

The system that LIC2M used for participating in the Small Multilingual Track of CLEF 2003 is based on the principles implemented by the EMIR [1] and SPIRIT [2] systems. These principles follow two main guidelines:

- to design a system that fits industrial constraints. This choice implies discarding some interesting solutions that, however, imply dealing with too large indexes or developing a system whose indexing or response times are too long;
- to design a system to retrieve information and not just documents, i.e. moving towards information extraction and question answering viewpoints.

As a consequence of these two choices, although the LIC2M system has a rather classical architecture as a crosslingual retrieval system (see Section 2), it focuses on categorizing both documents and queries by high level entities such as named entities and complex terms, which can be likened to concepts (see Section 3), and on using these entities in the retrieval process (see Section 6). More precisely, this perspective has a specific influence on the reformulation of queries (see Section 5.2) and on the strategy for merging and sorting the results obtained for each language of the document collection (see Section 6.2): a query is characterized by a set of concepts that have a linguistic instantiation for each language considered. As the link between a concept and its linguistic instantiation is stored, documents can be compared in terms of the concepts they share without taking into account their language.

C. Peters et al. (Eds.): CLEF 2003, LNCS 3237, pp. 174–184, 2004.

2   General Architecture of the System

The system is composed of four elements :

- a linguistic analyzer, which is used to process both documents and queries: the output of this analysis is a list of pairs associating a *term*, which is a normalized form of either a simple word (its lemma), a compound noun or a named entity, with its morphosyntactic category;
- an indexing module, that builds the inverted files of the documents, on the basis of their linguistic analysis: one index is built for each language of the document collection;
- a query processing module that reformulates queries, on the basis of their linguistic analysis, to suit the search (monolingual and multilingual reformulations): one query is built for each language of the document collection;
- a search engine that retrieves the most relevant documents from the indexes according to the corresponding reformulated query, and then merges the results obtained for each language, taking into account the original terms of the query (before reformulation) and their weights in order to score the documents.

3   Linguistic Processing

The linguistic processing module is a fundamental part of this system: the information search is based on a deep linguistic analysis designed to extract precise information from both documents and queries. The linguistic processing is performed separately for each language, on the basis of the language indicated by the corpus (actually, some documents are not in the corpus language – some LATimes texts are in Spanish – but we have decided to ignore this point). All documents are first converted to Unicode.

The linguistic processing is composed of a set of consecutive modules:

Morphological Analysis. All words of the documents are associated with their possible morphosyntactic categories, on the basis of a general full-form dictionary. The set of categories used in this system is larger than that of most systems: the categories contain more precise information and in particular, positional information, which permits a more efficient disambiguation. Default categories are proposed for unknown words on the basis of typographical properties (for instance, a token beginning with an uppercase letter can be considered as a proper noun);

Detection of Idiomatic Expressions. Idiomatic expressions are phrases or compound nouns that are listed in a specific dictionary (the expressions can be non-contiguous, such as phrasal verbs: *"switch ... on"*). The detection of idiomatic expressions is performed by applying a set of rules that are triggered on specific words and tested on left and right contexts of the trigger (note that the same technology is used for identifying named entities and compounds);

Part-Of-Speech Tagging. The part-of-speech tagger disambiguates the possible morphosyntactic categories proposed by the morphological analysis, on the basis of a statistical model of trigrams of categories.

Selection of Indexing Terms. A selection of content-bearing words is performed: only common nouns, proper nouns, verbs and adjectives are kept. Stoplists are also used to complete this selection by removing some remaining functional words or too frequent words;

Named Entities Recognition. Specific named entities such as persons, locations, organizations, products, events, dates and numbers are extracted on the basis of language-specific sets of rules. This module has been evaluated independently on French and English (5,000 documents for each) with a 80% precision and a 60% recall depending on the language and the entity type. A small test on 50 documents in Spanish has shown similar results.

Compound Nouns Extraction. Compound nouns are extracted on the basis of a set of syntactic patterns defined in specific rules (e.g. *Noun Preposition Noun*).

4   Indexing

The search engine described in Section 6 relies on basic functions which provide access to raw information on the collection. Efficient implementation of these basic functions allows an easy use of the global system. We built inverted files (containing, for each term found in the collection of documents, a list of all documents in which this term occurs) using the Lemur toolkit (V2.01) [3, 4]. Within this context, our design choices consist in:

1. using as indexing terms the (lemma, category) pairs resulting from the linguistic analysis. The use of lemmas allows us to limit the number of entries in the indexes (compared to the inflected forms) and to take into account a richer representation of terms in the indexing which leads to more simple reformulation in the query processing module. Adding the grammatical category should lead to more discriminating entries but we did not have the opportunity to evaluate the exact impact of this distinction;
2. indexing all content-bearing terms, without any frequency filtering, using only stoplists. In the current version, the stoplists represent approximately 60% of the text;
3. building separate indexes for each language: English, French, Spanish and German. In the CLEF document collection, the language is identified for each text and we consider that documents are monolingual (only one language per document). This leads to more manageable indexes.

The statistics of the indexing results are given for each corpus in Table 1.

Table 1. Statistics of the indexing process

	corpus size (Mo)	nb docs	nb terms	nb distinct uniterms	nb distinct compounds	index size (Mo)	memory size (Mo)
fre	326	129.806	30.756.020	297.084	2.281.349	476	185
eng	576	169.477	48.387.519	512.196	1.571.058	593	136
ger	632	287.670	55.605.358	1.076.714	179.357	603	89
spa	1.084	454.045	112.603.093	747.755	3.012.136	1.325	261

5   Query Processing

5.1   Preprocessing of the Queries

Each query is first processed through the linguistic analyzer corresponding to the query language, as described in Section 3. In order to get as much information as possible, the three fields of the query (title, description, narrative) are kept for this analysis.

The result is a query composed of a list of elements that can be a lemma associated with its part-of-speech (limited to nouns, proper nouns, verbs and adjectives), a named entity associated with its type or a compound, in a normalized form, associated with its part-of-speech[1].

The query is then filtered using a specific stoplist containing meta-words (words used in the narrative to describe what are relevant documents, such as : "document", "relevant" etc.). These meta-word stoplists have been built on the basis of CLEF 2002 topics, from a first selection using frequency information, and revised manually.

No deep semantic analysis was performed on the narrative parts to take into account, for instance, the negative descriptions of the topics (*"documents that contain ... are not relevant"*). Hence, some negative descriptive elements are kept in the final queries, which can bring some noise.

After this preprocessing, the query is a list of indexing elements in the original language of the topic. These elements are called the *concepts* of the query.

5.2   Query Reformulation

The list of query concepts is augmented with additional knowledge, using external resources for reformulation (such as monolingual and bilingual reformulation dictionaries) and using the corpus as a reference for filtering out words inferred by the reformulation.

---

[1] As the system was still under development, the compounds were not properly taken into account, especially in query expansion and translation, and were just used for monolingual search.

The reformulated query is then a list of the original query terms, called *query concepts*, and a list of inferred terms, called *search terms*. Each search term is linked to a query concept, and a weight is associated with the link. An example of query reformulation is presented in Figure 1.

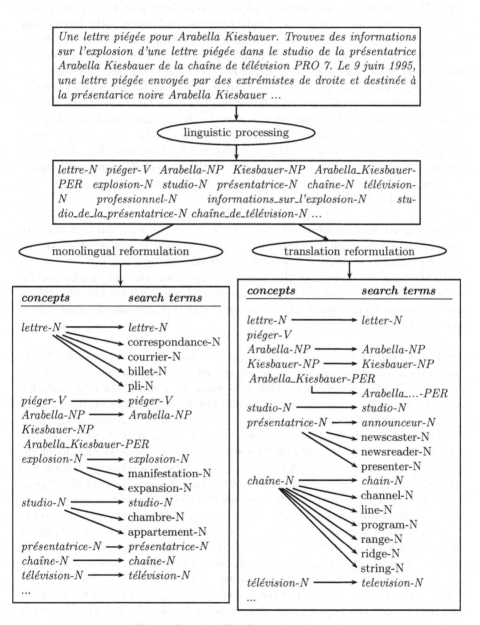

Fig. 1. An example of query construction

Translation. In order to query a corpus in a language different from the original query language, the query terms are translated using bilingual dictionaries. Each term of the query is translated into several terms in the target language. The translated words form the search terms of the reformulated query. The links between the search terms and the query concepts can also be weighted by a confidence value (between 0 and 1) indicating the confidence in the translation. In this version of the system, all translations were assigned the same weight.

In the CLEF 2003 Small Multilingual Task, we submitted runs for four different topic languages (DE, EN, ES, FR). The only language pair for which we did not have a bilingual dictionary was the Spanish/German pair. For this pair, we performed a two-step translation, using a pivot language: terms are first translated from topic language to the pivot language, and then from the pivot language to the target language. In this case, the confidence in the translation is the product of the confidences of the two successive translations. For the submitted runs, we used only one pivot language for the Spanish/German pair (chosen language was French), but a concurrent use of different pivot languages could also be used for this translation.

Monolingual Reformulation. A semantic expansion was also performed to increase the lexical variety of the query concepts, using monolingual reformulation dictionaries (containing mostly synonym information).

In the runs we submitted, this semantic expansion was only performed for monolingual query expansion. In a more general approach for crosslingual retrieval, several combinations of multi-step translation and monolingual expansion could be tested.

Topical Expansion. [5] shows that expansion based on synonyms reliably improves results if the terms of the queries are semantically disambiguated. As we did not perform such a disambiguation, we chose to reinforce the representation of each query with words that are topically linked to the query words.

The selection of such words is based on a network of lexical cooccurrences. For French, the only language for which we tested this kind of expansion, this network was built from a 39 million word corpus built from 24 months of the *Le Monde* newspaper (see [6] for more details). After a filtering procedure was applied [7] to select the cooccurrences that are likely to be supported by a topical relation, we got a network of 7,200 lemmas and 183,000 cooccurrences.

This network is used in a three-stage process that relies on a kind of bootstrapping. First, a set of words that are strongly linked to the considered query are selected from the network. The strength of this link is set according to the number of words of the query to which the word from the network is linked (3 words in our experiments). Most of these words, which are called expansion words, are topically close to the query but some of them also represent noise. The next stage aims at discarding this noise. It consists in selecting the words of the query that are the most representative of its topic. This selection is based on the words resulting from the first stage: we assume that a query word is significant if it has contributed to the selection of a minimal number of expansion words (2 words in our experiments). The final stage is identical to the first one, except that the expansion is done from the selected words of the query and not from all of its words. Moreover, the number of expansion words is arbitrarily set to 10 to avoid swamping the initial words of the query.

This topical expansion was applied to the 60 French topics of CLEF 2003. A set of expansion words was produced for 42 of them. This set was empty for the other ones, which means that it was not possible in these cases to build a significant representation of the topic of the query from the network of cooccurrences. As an example, the result of the topical expansion of the topic C164, *Les condamnations pour trafic de drogue en Europe (European Drug Sentences)*, is the following list of words: {*amende, infraction, prison, délit, procès, pénal, crime, juge, cocaïne, sursis*}.

6   Search and Merging

The original topic is transformed, during the query processing, into four different queries, one for each language. The search is performed independently for each of these queries on the index of the corresponding language. 1,000 documents are retrieved for each language. The 4,000 retrieved documents from the four corpora are then merged and sorted by their relevance to the topic. Only the first 1,000 are kept. In the following sections, we present the search technique and the merging strategy.

6.1   Search

For each expanded query, the search is performed by retrieving from the index of the corresponding language the documents containing the search terms. A term profile is then associated with each document: this profile consists in a binary vector in which each component indicates the presence or absence of a search term in the document. In this version of the system, the frequency of the term in the document is not used: to suit the purpose of building an information extraction system, we consider that a document is relevant to a topic if it contains any relevant information with respect to the topic, even if it contains also other material that is not relevant to the topic (a visualization step can then select the relevant parts and show them to the user).

Since, in the expanded query, we kept the links between the search terms and the query concepts, we can associate a concept profile with each document, indicating the presence/absence of each query concept in the documents.

The retrieved documents are then classified, grouping in the same cluster the documents that share the same concept profile. This classification is motivated by at least two reasons: it makes it easy to merge the results from different languages (see following section) and the visualization of the results is clearer: the clustering of the results, and the association of a concept profile to a cluster makes it easier for the user to search through the results (a cluster corresponding to a non-relevant subset of query concepts can simply be ignored).

6.2   Merge and Sort

Given that a concept profile is associated with each class, the merging strategy is quite straightforward: since the concepts are in the original query language, the concept profiles associated with the classes are comparable and the classes having the same profile are simply merged.

The classes are then sorted by their relevance to the query. For this purpose, we use the *idf* (inverse document frequency) weights of the terms, defined for a term t by the formula $idf(t) = \log \frac{N}{df(t)}$, where $df(t)$ is the document frequency of the term (*i.e.* the number of documents containing the term) and N is the total number of documents in the corpus.

Our first idea was to use the *idf* weights of the terms in each language, to compute the weight of a concept by some combination of the weights of the terms derived from the concept and then to associate a weight with a concept profile derived by the concepts it contains. However, in this case, the weights computed for the different languages are not comparable (*idf* weights of the terms depend on the corpora).

We thus decided to compute a crosslingual pseudo-*idf* weight of the concepts, using only the corpus composed of the 4000 documents kept as the result of the search. The *idf* weight of the concepts is computed on this corpus, using only information contained in the concept profiles of the classes and the size of the classes. A weight can then be associated with each concept profile by computing the sum of the weights of the concepts present in the profile.

The classes are then sorted by their weights: all documents in a class are given the weight of the class (the documents are not sorted inside the classes). The list of the first 1000 documents from the best classes is then built and used for the evaluation.

We used this simple weighting procedure, but a lot of other procedures can be imagined. We plan to test several more sophisticated weighting schemes, using in particular the document frequency of the search terms and the confidence weight in the expansion associations.

7   Results

Figure 2 shows the precision-recall curves of the five runs we submitted: one for each query language (French, English, Spanish and German), and an additional one in French, using topical expansion. There are few differences between them except for the Spanish run which is slightly better than the others. One probable reason for that is that the number of relevant documents for Spanish (2,368) is far greater than in the other languages (1,825 in German, 1,006 in English and 946 in French).

Table 2 gives details on the numbers and percentages of relevant documents found in each language for each run. The percentages are the percentages of relevant documents found among all the relevant documents for a given language.

Our system exhibits its best results for monolingual retrieval, which shows more work is needed on the reformulation process and its resources. With respect

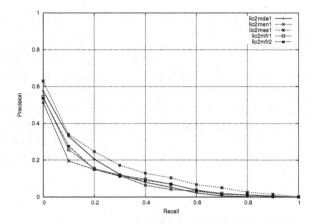

Fig. 2. Precision/recall graphs for the 5 runs submitted by LIC2M at the Small Multilingual Task of CLEF 2003

Table 2. Percentages of relevant documents of each language found depending on the interrogation language

interro. lang.	number (%) of relevant found			
	fre	eng	spa	ger
fre (run 1)	409 (43)	310 (31)	204 (9)	620 (34)
fre (run 2)	631 (67)	154 (15)	201 (8.5)	565 (31)
eng	354 (37)	546 (54)	252 (23)	274 (15)
spa	257 (27)	303 (30)	948 (40)	265 (15)
ger	333 (37)	139 (14)	115 (5)	1,060 (58)

to the resources, we see that the French-Spanish dictionary, used to reformulate between French and Spanish but also as a pivot language for Spanish to German and German to Spanish, needs particular attention as the number of relevant documents retrieved when using it is very low.

Regarding monolingual reformulation, we submitted two runs for French topics: one with only semantic expansion of queries (Run 1) and the other one with semantic and topical expansion of queries (Run 2). The results for these two runs are globally very similar: in the first case, 1543 relevant documents were returned with an R-precision of 0.1425 while in the second case, 1551 relevant documents were returned with an R-precision of 0.1438. However, the two sets of relevant documents are not identical since their intersection only contains 1305 documents. Topical expansion brings new relevant documents but also discards relevant documents brought by semantic expansion in the same proportion. More precisely, Table 2 shows that this type of expansion favors monolingual retrieval while it has a negative impact on crosslingual retrieval.

In consideration of this observation, we tested to see whether a combination of the two runs could improve the results. We adopted a basic strategy: the two lists of documents were interleaved in decreasing order of their score; only one occurrence of each document was kept and the resulting list was cut at 1000 documents. 1730 relevant documents were returned with an R-precision of 0.1443. From the viewpoint of the number of relevant documents, the benefit is low (+179 documents, *i.e.* an increase of 11.6%) but not insignificant. Moreover, most of the relevant documents that could be caught by our combination of runs were actually caught. However, from the viewpoint of R-precision, the benefit is not significant, which probably means that the rank of most of the new relevant documents is high.

8   Conclusion and Future Work

Despite the numerically modest results of our system, our participation in CLEF 2003 was encouraging since the system tested in this campaign is still under development and requires more work on both algorithms and resources.

Further developments of the system will include a more advanced linguistic analysis that will use an improved version of the Part-Of-Speech tagger and a syntactic analysis for the extraction of nominal and verbal chunks and dependencies between words inside the chunks and between the chunks. This syntactic analysis will make it possible to find compound nouns with better precision than the current method based on syntactic patterns. Compound nouns are a fundamental part of our search algorithm and their lack of identification probably accounts for a large part of our poor results. The processing of complex terms such as compound nouns and named entities in a multilingual environment should also benefit from the addition of specific translation resources. Results should also be improved by the introduction of monolingual and crosslingual relevance feedback.

References

1. Fluhr, C., Mordini, P., Moulin, A., Stegentritt, E.: EMIR Final Report. Technical Report ESPRIT project 5312, DG III, Commission of the European Union, CEA (1994)
2. Fluhr, C., Schmit, D., Ortet, P., Elkateb, F., Gurtner, K.: SPIRIT-W3, a Distributed Crosslingual Indexing and Retrieval Engine. In: INET'97. (1997)
3. Ogilvie, P., Callan, J.: Experiments using the Lemur Toolkit. In: Proceedings of TREC-2001, The Tenth Text REtrieval Conference. (2001) 103–108
4. The Lemur Project: The Lemur Toolkit for language modeling and information retrieval. (http://www-2.cs.cmu.edu/~lemur/)

5. Voorhees, E.M.: Query expansion using lexical-semantic relations. In: Proceedings of SIGIR-94, 17th ACM International Conference on Research and Development in Information Retrieval, Dublin, IE (1994) 61–69
6. Ferret, O., Grau, B.: A bootstrapping approach for robust topic analysis. Natural Language Engineering (8) (2002) 209–233
7. Ferret, O.: Filtrage thématique d'un réseau de collocations. In: TALN 2003. (2003) 347–352

CLEF 2003 Experiments at UB: Automatically Generated Phrases and Relevance Feedback for Improving CLIR

Miguel E. Ruiz

State University of New York at Buffalo,
School of Informatics, Department of Library and Information Studies,
534 Baldy Hall, Buffalo, NY 14260-1020, USA
meruiz@buffalo.edu
http://www.informatics.buffalo.edu/faculty/ruiz

Abstract. This paper presents the results obtained by the University at Buffalo (UB) in CLEF 2003. Our efforts concentrated in the monolingual retrieval and large multilingual retrieval tasks. We used a modified version of the SMART system, a heuristic method based on bigrams to generate phrases that works across multiple languages, and pseudo relevance feedback. Query translation was performed using publicly available machine translation software. Our results show small but consistent improvements in performance due to the use of bigrams. We also found that pseudo relevance feedback benefits from using these bigrams for expanding queries in all the 8 languages that we tested.

1 Introduction

This paper describes the experiments and results for the CLEF 2003 participation of the University at Buffalo. This is the first time that we participate in CLEF and most of our efforts concentrated on developing the system and resources necessary for participation. For this effort we use a modified version of the SMART system [4] as the retrieval engine. This system was modified to add ISO-Latin 1 encoding as proposed by Douglas Oard [1]. We also incorporated Porter's stemmers [2] for 11 languages, which are publicly available from snowball.tartarus.org.

Our research goal for this year is to test whether a general method for identifying phrases can be used to improve retrieval performance across several European languages. We also want to explore the effect of these terms on pseudo-relevance feedback. We participated in the large multilingual retrieval tasks EN⟶X and ES⟶X and in monolingual retrieval for 8 languages Dutch, English, Finnish, French, German, Italian, Spanish and Swedish.

Section 2 describes the document processing and representation used in our system. Section 3 presents the approach used in our monolingual runs, section 4 describes the approach used for our multilingual runs. Section 5 presents our results and analysis. Conclusions and future work is presented in section 6.

C. Peters et al. (Eds.): CLEF 2003, LNCS 3237, pp. 185–191, 2004.

2   Document Processing and Representation

We followed a standard processing method that consists in removing stopwords, and stemming the remaining words with Porter's stemmer. Additionally we used a heuristic method to try to capture phrases and proper nouns. For this purpose we preprocessed the documents to identify fragments delimited by punctuation symbols and extract bigrams (groups of two consecutive words) that don't include stopwords. The heuristic process takes into account exceptions that allow a limited number of stop words to be part of the bigram term, i.e. "Corea del Norte". A short list of exceptions was defined for all 8 languages and consists of 18 exceptions that are presented in Table 1. An example of a query with the added bigrams is presented in Table 2.

Table 1. List of stopwords allowed to be part of bigrams

Language	Stopwords
English	"of", "for"
Dutch	"voor", "van"
French	"pour","de","d'"
Spanish	"de", "para","por","del"
German	"als", "über", "von"
Italian	"di", "il"
Finnish	"ajaksi"
Nowegian and Swedish	"av", "för", "te"

Documents and queries are represented with two ctype vectors (one for original words and one for bigrams). Similarity is computed as the linear combination of the vector similarities of each ctype as follows:

$$Sim(\mathbf{d}, \mathbf{q}) = \lambda \times Sim_{Terms}(\mathbf{d}, \mathbf{q}) + \eta \times Sim_{bigrams}(\mathbf{d}, \mathbf{q}) \qquad (1)$$

where λ and η are coefficients that weight the contribution of each vocabulary, $\mathbf{d}$ is the document vector and $\mathbf{q}$ is the query vector.

We used the pivoted length normalization (Lnu.ltu) weighting scheme proposed by Singhal et al. [6]. For our runs the *slope* was fixed to 0.25 and the *pivot* was set to the average length of the documents in the collection.

3   Monolingual Retrieval

Monolingual retrieval is crucial for any successful cross-language retrieval. For this reason we decided to explore methods that could be applied across all the supported languages. For our monolingual retrieval we use several publicly available stop word lists and review some of them for several languages (English, Spanish, French, and Italian). We also used the public versions of Porter's stemmer, which are available for 11 languages at snowball.tartarus.org, adding them

Table 2. Examples of bigrams generated for a query

<top>
<num> C196 </num>
<EN-title> Merger of Japanese Banks </EN-title>
<EN-desc> Find reports on the merger of the Japanese banks Mitsubishi and
Bank of Tokyo into the largest bank in the world. </EN-desc>
<bigrams>
Merger_of_Japanese Japanese_Banks Find_reports Japanese_banks banks_Mitsubishi
Bank_of_Tokyo largest_bank
</bigrams>
</top>

<top>
<num> C196 </num>
<ES-title> Fusión de bancos japoneses </ES-title>
<ES-desc> Encontrar documentos sobre la fusión del banco japonés Mitsubishi y
el Banco de Tokyo para formar el mayor banco del mundo. </ES-desc>
<bigrams> Fusión_de_bancos bancos_japoneses Encontrar_documentos
fusión_del_banco banco_japonés japonés_Mitsubishi Banco_de_Tokyo
Tokyo_para_formar banco_del_mundo
</bigrams>
</top>

---

to the SMART system. We tested the performance of the system on each of the
8 languages of interest in the multilingual-8 task using the CLEF2002 collection.
Results of the baselines for CLEF2002 data are presented in Table 3.

For pseudo relevance feedback we assumed that the top 5 documents were
relevant and the bottom 100 documents from the 1000 retrieved were assumed
to be non-relevant. We expanded the query with 30 terms of each vocabulary
(Terms and Bigrams) using Rocchio's formula to rank the expansion term ($\alpha = 8$,
$\beta = 64$, $\gamma = 16$, relative weight of Terms and Phrases was 5:1). These settings
were determined empirically (using CLEF2002 data) across all monolingual collections.

We observed that performance was significantly improved in English by adding
Bigrams. We also noticed that pseudo relevance feedback for short and medium
queries works better when we use bigrams. For most languages (except for
Finnish) the use of bigrams improved performance in retrieval without relevance
feedback. Pseudo relevance feedback using bigrams and single terms consistently
improves performance across all languages.

Although long queries that use all fields (TDN) have a significantly higher
performance than the medium-size (TD) and short (T) queries (i.e for English
our TDN performance with bigrams was 0.5341), we decided no to include them
in this study. We are more interested in addressing whether our methods work
well for short queries.

Table 3. Monolingual performance on CLEF2002 data

Performance of Short queries (T)				
Language	Terms		Terms & bigrams	
	Baseline	Ret. Feedback	Baseline	Ret. Feedback
Dutch	0.3659	0.3788	0.3683	0.3885
English	0.3675	0.3766	0.3802	0.4035
Finnish	0.2750	0.2948	0.2725	0.3095
French	0.2963	0.3085	0.2919	0.3156
German	0.3124	0.3293	0.3178	0.3536
Italian	0.2873	0.3043	0.2800	0.3155
Spanish	0.3841	0.4105	0.3833	0.4235
Performance of Medium-size queries (TD)				
Language	Terms		Terms & bigrams	
	Baseline	Ret. Feedback	Baseline	Ret. Feedback
Dutch	0.4253	0.4352	0.4229	0.4338
English	0.4710	0.4875	0.4917	0.5142
Finnish	0.2938	0.3022	0.2903	0.3116
French	0.3937	0.4214	0.3931	0.4245
German	0.3637	0.3904	0.3706	0.4211
Italian	0.3674	0.3915	0.3589	0.4054
Spanish	0.4766	0.5031	0.4799	0.5175

4   Cross-Language Retrieval

We concentrated on exploring cross-language retrieval using as base languages English and Spanish. We used a publicly available site (www.intertran.com) to translate the queries from English or Spanish to each of the other 7 languages. These queries were then preprocessed to add bigrams and the expanded query was indexed in each of the corresponding languages. For each query, the results were re-scored using the following normalized score function [3, 5]:

$$rsv'_j = \frac{rsv_j - rsv_{min}}{rsv_{max} - rsv_{min}} \qquad (2)$$

where rsv_j is the original retrieval score, and rsv_{max} and rsv_{min} are the maximum and minimum document score of the documents retrieved for the current query. The merging program combined all 8 files, ranked the documents by the scaled scores and selected the top 1000 ranked documents for each query.

5   Results

The results that were submitted in all monolingual tasks include bigrams and pseudo-relevance feedback. Runs that end in rf1 use 30 terms to expand each query. We also tried with a more aggressive expansion strategy that uses 300 terms (runs ending in rf2).

Table 4. Monolingual performance on CLEF2003 data

Official Monolingual Runs (TD)					
Run Name	# of Queries	Avg-P	Best	≥Mean	<Mean	Worst
UBmonoNLrf1	56	0.4180	3	26	26	1
UBmonoNLrf2	56	0.4225	3	22	27	4
UBmonoENrf1	54	0.4746	12	23	19	0
UBmonoENrf2	54	0.4488	9	21	22	2
UBmonoFIrf1	45	0.4901	5	17	21	2
UBmonoFIrf2	45	0.4790	3	17	21	4
UBmonoFRrf1	52	0.4645	7	23	22	0
UBmonoFRrf2	52	0.4638	9	22	21	0
UBmonoDErf1	56	0.4425	1	24	30	1
UBmonoDErf2	56	0.4470	1	27	27	1
UBmonoITrf1	51	0.4857	6	25	20	0
UBmonoITrf2	51	0.4965	8	23	20	0
UBmonoSVrf1	54	0.3906	3	21	29	1
UBmonoSVrf2	54	0.3910	4	18	30	2
UBmonoESrf1	57	0.1231	1	2	44	10
UBmonoESrf2	57	0.1267	1	3	43	10
Unofficial Monolingual Runs					
UBmonoESrf1 (corr.)	57	0.4852	2	35	20	0
UBmonoESrf2 (corr.)	57	0.4943	2	35	20	0
UBESmono.T.rf1	57	0.3903	3	16	38	0
UBESmono.T.rf2	57	0.3965	2	21	34	0

Our official results are presented in Table 4 and Table 5. We discovered a bug in our Spanish runs that significantly affected the Spanish monolingual runs as well as all our multilingual runs (document ids from "efe95" were mapped incorrectly). The Unofficial results show the performance of the corrected runs.

In general, our monolingual performance is acceptable for all languages. The best monolingual performance was obtained for English, French and Italian. The corrected Spanish runs also show good monolingual performance. We also have included in this table two monolingual runs with short queries (using only the title). As expected they don't perform as well as the queries based on Title and Description. The results of using the more aggressive expansion strategy are mixed. In Dutch, German, Spanish and Italian this gives small improvements in average precision but in English, Finnish and Swedish performance decreases.

In terms of multilingual performance, the corrected unofficial runs show that EN⟶X and ES⟶X have about the same average precision (0.19). Short queries, as expected, perform significantly below our standard queries (TD). This seems to be a consequence of translation problems caused by lack of context. These multilingual runs also show a third type of queries that combines the results from rf1 and rf2 results (with 30 and 300 expansion terms respectively).

Table 5. Multilingual-8 performance on CLEF2003 data

Official Multilingual Runs						
English $\longrightarrow$ X						
Run Name	# of Queries	Avg-P	Best	$\geq$Mean	<Mean	Worst
UBENmultirf1	60	0.1390	1	10	48	1
UBENmultirf2	60	0.1309	1	7	52	0
UBENmultirf3	60	0.1440	1	10	49	0
UBENmultishort2	60	0.0413	0	1	37	22
UBENmultishort3	60	0.0417	0	2	38	20
Spanish $\longrightarrow$ X						
UBESmultirf2	60	0.1160	0	10	36	14
UBESmultishort2	60	0.1155	0	8	44	8
Unofficial Multilingual Runs						
English $\longrightarrow$ X						
UBENmulti.TD.rf1	60	0.1930	1	22	37	0
UBENmulti.TD.rf2	60	0.1857	1	18	41	0
UBENmulti.TD.rf3	60	0.1792	1	20	38	1
UBENmulti.T.rf1	60	0.0766	0	4	50	6
UBENmulti.T.rf2	60	0.0773	0	4	52	4
UBENmulti.T.rf3	60	0.0741	0	6	44	10
Spanish $\longrightarrow$X						
UBESmulti.TD.rf1	60	0.1913	0	29	31	0
UBESmulti.TD.rf2	60	0.1936	1	27	32	0
UBESmulti.TD.rf3	60	0.2011	2	28	30	0
UBESmulti.T.rf1	60	0.0810	0	11	44	5
UBESmulti.T.rf2	60	0.0788	0	9	45	6
UBESmulti.T.rf3	60	0.0860	0	11	43	6

The results of this strategy are mixed since it improved results for ES$\longrightarrow$X but reduced performance of EN$\longrightarrow$X queries.

6   Conclusions and Future Work

Since this was our first time participating in CLEF, we believe that we have learned many lessons from our experiments. Our experiments show that the use of our heuristic method to generate phrases combined with pseudo relevance feedback consistently improves results for all monolingual runs. In terms of multilingual retrieval we still have to work on a better way to combine results from different runs. For our next participation we plan to research the use of different alternatives for translation (instead of relying on a single MT system) since this seems to play an important role in multilingual retrieval.

References

1. Oard, D.: Adaptive Vector Space Text Filtering for Monolingual and Cross-Language Applications. PhD thesis, University of Maryland, (1996).
2. Porter, M. F.: An algorithm for suffix stripping. Program, 14, (1980), 130–137.
3. Powel, A. T., French, J. C., Callan, J., Connell, M. and Viles, C. L.: The impact of database selection on distributed searching. In: N. Belkin, P. Ingwersen, and M. Leong, (eds.): Proceedings of the 23rd Annual International ACM SIGIR Conference on Research and Development in Information Retrieval, ACM Press, New York, NY, (2000), 232–239.
4. Salton, G. (ed.): The SMART Retrieval System: Experiments in Automatic Document Processing. Prentice-Hall, Englewood Cliffs, NJ, (1983).
5. Savoy, J.: Report on CLEF-2002 experiments: Combining multiple sources of evidence. In: C. Peters (ed.), Results of the CLEF 2002 Cross-Language System Evaluation Campaign: Working Notes for the CLEF 2002 Workshop, (2002).
6. Singhal, A., Buckley, C. and Mitra, M.: Pivoted document length normalization. In: Proceedings of the 19th Annual International ACM SIGIR Conference on Research and Development in Information Retrieval. ACM Press, New York, NY, (1996), 21-29.

SINAI at CLEF 2003:
Decompounding and Merging

Fernando Martínez-Santiago[1], Arturo Montejo-Ráez[2],
Luis Alfonso Ureña-López[1], and M. Carlos Díaz-Galiano[1]

[1] Dpto. Computer Science. University of Jaén. Avda. Madrid 35. 23071 Jaén, Spain
{dofer,laurena,mcdiaz}@ujaen.es
[2] Scientific Information Service, European Organization for Nuclear Research,
Geneva, Switzerland
{Arturo.Montejo}@cern.ch

Abstract. This paper describes the application of the *two-step RSV*
and *mixed two-step RSV* merging methods in the multilingual-4 and
multilingual-8 tasks at CLEF 2003. We study the performance of these
methods compared to previous studies and approaches. A new strategy
for dealing with compound words which uses predefined vocabularies for
automatic decomposition is also presented and evaluated.

1   Introduction

The aim for CLIR (Cross-Language Information Retrieval) systems is to retrieve
a set of documents written in different languages in answer to a query in a given
language. Several approaches exist for this task, such as translating the whole
document collection into an intermediate language or translating the quesry into
every language found in the collection.

Two architectures are known for query translation: centralized and distributed
architectures [1]. A centralized architecture handles the document collections in
different languages as a single collection, replacing the original query by the sum
of translations in all possible languages found in the collection. In a distributed
architecture, documents in different languages are indexed and retrieved separately. All ranked lists are then merged into a single multilingual ranked list.

We use a distributed architecture, focusing on a solution for the merging
problem. Our merging strategy consists in calculating a new RSV (Retrieval
Status Value) for each document in the ranked lists for each monolingual collection. The new RSV, called the two-step RSV, is calculated by re-indexing the
retrieved documents according to a vocabulary generated from query translations, where words are aligned by meaning, i.e. each word is aligned with its
translations [2].

The rest of the paper has been organized into three main sections: a brief review of merging strategies and the 2-step RSV approach, a description of the proposed decompounding algorithm and a description of our experiments. Finally,
Section 5 provides some conclusions, and also outlines future research lines.

C. Peters et al. (Eds.): CLEF 2003, LNCS 3237, pp. 192–201, 2004.
© Springer-Verlag Berlin Heidelberg 2004

2   Merging Strategies and the 2-Step RSV Approach

Distributed IR architectures require result merging in order to integrate the ranked lists returned by each database/language into a single, coherent ranked list. This task can be difficult because document rankings and scores produced by each language are based on different corpus statistics such as inverse document frequencies, and possibly also different representations and/or retrieval algorithms that usually cannot be compared directly.

2.1   Traditional Merging Strategies

There are various approaches to the merging of monolingual collections. In all cases, a large decrease in precision is generated in the process (depending on the collection, between 20% and 40%) [3]. Perhaps for this reason, CLIR systems based on document translation tend to obtain results noticeably better than system driven by query translation. Most popular approaches to merging using query translation are round-robin algorithms and computing normalized scores. Other approach is depicted in [4]: a single and multilingual index is obtained for the whole set of documents in every language, without any translation. Then, the user query is translated for each language present in the multilingual collection. A query for each translation is not generated but all the translations are concatenated making up a composite query. Finally, this composite query is used to search across the entire multilingual term index. The idea is coherent, but current results with this method are disappointing [5, 6].

Finally, learning-based algorithms are very interesting, but they require training data (relevance judgments) and this is not always available. Thus, Le Calvé and Savoy [7, 8] propose a merging approach based on logistic regression and Martínez-Santiago et al. [9] improve slightly regression logistic results by using LVQ neural networks.

2.2   2-Step RSV and Mixed 2-Step RSV

Last year we obtained good results at CLEF 2002 by using a new approach called 2-step RSV [2]. This method is based on the hypothesis that: given two documents, the score of both documents will be comparable whenever the document frequency is the same for each meaningful query term and its translations. By grouping together the document frequency for each term and its translations, we ensure the compliancy of the hypothesis.

The basic idea underlying 2-step RSV is straightforward: given a query term and its translations to the other languages in the document collection, the document frequencies are grouped together [2]. In this way, the method requires recalculating the document score by changing the document frequency for each query term. Given a query term, the new document frequency will be calculated by means of the sum of the monolingual document frequency of the term and its translations. Since re-indexing the whole multilingual collection could be computationally expensive, given a query only the documents retrieved for each monolingual collection are re-indexed. These two steps are as follows:

1. The document pre-selection phase consists in translating and searching the query on each monolingual collection, in the usual way for CLIR systems based on query translation. This phase produces two results:

   - The translation of each term from the original query to the other languages as a result of the translation process. In this way, we have *queries aligned at term level*.
   - A single multilingual collection of preselected documents as result of the union of typically the first 1000 retrieved documents for each language.

2. The re-indexing phase consists of re-indexing the retrieved multilingual collection, but considering solely the query vocabulary, by grouping together their document frequencies. The query is then executed against the new index. Thus for example, if we have two languages, Spanish and English, and the term "casa" is part of the original query and it is translated to "house" and "home", both terms represent exactly the same index token. Given a document, the term frequency will be calculated as usual, but the document frequency will be the sum of the document frequency of "casa", "house" and "home"[1].

Perhaps the strongest constraint for this method is that every query term must be aligned with its translations. But this information is not always available whether using machine translation (which produces translations at phrase level) or automatic query expansion techniques such as pseudo-relevance feedback.

As a way of dealing with partially aligned queries (i.e. queries with some terms not aligned), we propose three approaches which mix evidence from aligned and not aligned terms [10, 11]:

- Raw mixed 2-step RSV method: An straightforward and effective way to partially solve this problem is by taking non-aligned words into account locally, only as terms of a given monolingual collection. Thus, given a document, the weight of a non-aligned term is the initial weight calculated in the first step of the method.

  Thus, the score for a given document d_i will be calculated in a mixed way by means of the weight of local terms and global concepts present in the query:

$$RSV_i' = \alpha \cdot RSV_i^{align} + (1 - \alpha) \cdot RSV_i^{nonalign} \qquad (1)$$

  where RSV_i^{align} is the score calculated by means of aligned terms, such as the original 2-step RSV method proposes, while $RSV_i^{nonalign}$ is calculated locally. Finally, α is a constant (usually fixed to $\alpha = 0.75$).

- Normalized mixed 2-step RSV method: Since the weights of the aligned and non-aligned words are not comparable, the proposal of a raw mixed 2-step RSV seems counterintuitive. AIn an attempt to make RSV_{align} and $RSV_{nonalign}$ comparable, we normalize those values:

---

[1] Actually, we subtract the number of documents where both "house" and "home" terms appear. Thus, given a document which contains both terms, we avoid counting the same document twice.

$$RSV_i' = \alpha \cdot \frac{RSV_i^{align} - \min(RSV^{align})}{\max(RSV^{align}) - \min(RSV^{align})}$$

$$+(1-\alpha) \cdot \frac{RSV_i^{nonalign} - \min(RSV^{nonalign})}{\max(RSV^{nonalign}) - \min(RSV^{nonalign})} \qquad (2)$$

– Mixed 2-Step RSV method and learning-based algorithms such as logistic regression or neural networks [9]. Training data must be available in order to fit the model. This a serious drawback, but this approach allows the integration of not only aligned and not aligned scores but also the original rank of the document.

3   Decompounding Algorithm

In some languages, such as Dutch, Finnish, German and Swedish, words are formed by the concatenation of others. These are the so-called *compound words* which, if untreated, may bias the performance of our multilingual system. In order to increase recall, compound words must be decompounded. Unfortunately there is no straightforward method for this due to the high number of possible decompositions exhibited by many compound words.

Chen [12] proposes an approach towards a maximal decomposition applied on German documents: decompositions with a minimal number of components and, in case of multiple options, the one with highest probability, are chosen. In this way, decompounding is performed with a minimal set of rules and a dictionary which must contain no compound words. Chen has applied this algorithm only to German corpora, so no data about its effectiveness on other languages is available. However, we find that applying decomposition to every compound word may not be desirable, since some of these words have a meaning which, when decomposed, is lost.

Hollink et al. [13] provide a review of compound words for Dutch, German and Swedish, giving the connectives used for compounding by each of these languages. They apply an existing recursive algorithm to find all possible decompositions, using a dictionary generated from the document collection. This study is very illustrative with respect to the decomposition of words, but lacks a proposal for selection.

The solution we have adopted is based mainly on the Chen approach, but preserves compound words in some cases and extends the algorithm to Dutch and Swedish. We establish three main rules as the core of our algorithm. First, the word is decompounded in all possible compositions as in [13]. Then, given a compound word cw formed by composites $w_1, w_2...w_n$, we select a decomposition by applying following rules:

1. **Rule 1.** We do not decompound if the probability of the compound word is higher than any of its composites.

   $P(cw) \le P(w_1) \wedge P(cw) \le P(w_2) \wedge ... \wedge P(cw) \le P(w_n) \longrightarrow cw$ is returned

2. **Rule 2.** Shortest decomposition (that one with the lowest number of composites) is selected. For example, if we find that cw can be decomposed into two forms $w_1 + w_2$ or $w_3 + w_4 + w_5$ the first decomposition would be selected.

3. **Rule 3.** In case several decompositions have the same number of composites, that one with highest probability will be chosen. The probability of a composition is the same as proposed by Chen: the product of the probabilities of its composites:

$$P(w_1 + w_2 + ... + w_n) = P(w_1) \cdot P(w_2) \cdot ... \cdot P(w_n)$$

where the probability for a word w_i in a collection is

$$P(w_i) = \frac{tfc(w_i)}{\sum_{j=1}^{N} tfc(w_j)}$$

where $tfc(w_i)$ is the number of occurrences of word w_i in a collection whose dictionary contains N different words.

Table 1. Length of wordlist used by the decompounding algorithm

Language	Main word sources	Size
Dutch	CLEF data, spelling dictionary, Babylon	387735
Finnish	CLEF data, spelling dictionary	359117
German	CLEF data, spell.dictionary, Babylon, MORPHIX	657452
Swedish	CLEF data, spelling dictionary, Babylon	294151

4   Experiments and Results

We participated in the Multi-4 and Multi-8 tasks. Each collection was pre-processed as usual, using stopword lists and stemming algorithms available on the Web[2]. Stopword lists were increased with terms such as "retrieval", "documents", "relevant".... Once the collections had been pre-processed, they were indexed with the Zprise IR system, using the OKAPI probabilistic model [14]. This OKAPI model was also used for the on-line re-indexing process required by the calculation of 2-step RSV.

The rest of this section describes our bilingual and multilingual experiments driven by query-translation with fully and partially aligned queries.

4.1   Translation Strategy and Bilingual Results

Our translation approach is very simple. We used Babylon[3] to translate English query terms. Since an English to Finnish dictionary is not available on the Babylon site, we used the *FinnPlace* online dictionary [4]. Both bilingual dictionaries

---

[2] http://www.unine.ch/info/clef
[3] Babylon is a Machine Readable Dictionary available at http://www.babylon.com
[4] available at http://www.tracetech.net/db.htm

may suggest more than one translation for the translation of each query term. In our experiments, we decided to take the first translation listed.

We retrieved documents using non-expanded and expanded queries (pseudo-relevance feedback, PRF). Non-expanded queries are fully aligned queries. By this we mean that a translation is obtained for each term in the query. Queries expanded by pseudo-relevance feedback are expanded with monolingual collection-depended words. Such words will usually not be aligned. The first type of queries was used when testing original 2-Step RSV. Mixed 2-Step RSV was tested by using the second type of queries.

Table 2 shows the bilingual precision obtained by means of both translation approaches. We have taken only *Title* and *Description* query fields into account.

Table 2. English and Bilingual experiments

	Avg. Prec. without PRF	Avg. Prec. with PRF
English → Dutch	0.251	0.310
English	0.464	0.453
English → Finnish	0.286	0.253
English → French	0.371	0.400
English → German	0.288	0.321
English → Italian	0.237	0.292
English → Spanish	0.310	0.348
English → Swedish	0.212	0.259

In this study, we adopted Robertson-Croft's approach to pseudo-relevance feedback (blind expansion) [15], where the system expands the original query with generally no more than 15 search keywords, extracted from the 10-best ranked documents.

4.2   Multilingual Results

The bilingual results list obtained were the starting point - the first step towards providing users with a single list of retrieved documents. In this section, we study the second step. Unfortunately, an implementation error damaged dramatically our own official runs based on the 2-Step RSV approach[5] In the following, we present the results of both official and corrected runs.

Our approach to merging combined several approaches: round-robin, raw scoring, normalized score and 2-step RSV approach. In addition, a theoretical

---

[5] The error was as follows: we use two indices per collection: Okapi index and term frequency (TF) index. The Okapi index was used by monolingual runs. The TF index was used by the second step of the 2-step RSV method: in order to re-weight the query terms, term-frequency statistics were obtained from the TF-index files. In some languages such as English, we made a mistake by taking the OKAPI-index files instead of the TF-index files.

optimal performance was calculated by using the procedure proposed in [12] (label "Optimal performance" in Table 3). This procedure computes the optimal performance that could be achieved by a CLIR System merging bilingual and monolingual results, under the constraint that the relative ranking of the documents in the individual ranked list is preserved. In this procedure, the relevance of documents must be known a-priori. Thus it is not useful to predict ranks of documents in the multilingual list of documents, but it gives the upper-bound performance for a set of ranked lists of documents, and this information is useful to measure the performance of different merging strategies. Note that 2-step RSV calculus does not guarantee the preservation of the relative ranking of documents, theoretically the upper-bound performance calculated by this procedure could be surpassed. A detailed description of the algorithm is available in [12].

Table 3. Multi-4 experiments with fully and partially aligned queries

	Avg. Prec. without PRF	Avg. Prec. with PRF
round-Robin	0.216	0.245
raw scoring	0.269	0.294
normalized scoring	0.232	0.283
2-step RSV (official)	0.1724	-
raw mixed 2-step RSV (official)	-	0.211
2-step RSV (fixed)	**0.291**	-
raw mixed 2-step RSV (fixed)	-	**0.335**
norm. mixed 2-step RSV (fixed)	-	0.315
optimal performance	*0.331*	*0.371*

Table 4. Multi-8 experiments with fully and partially aligned queries

	Avg. Prec. without PRF	Avg. Prec. with PRF
round-Robin	0.160	0.1815
raw scoring	0.213	0.239
2-step RSV (official)	0.1423	-
raw mixed 2-step RSV (official)	-	0.168
2-step RSV (fixed)	**0.242**	-
raw mixed 2-step RSV (fixed)	-	**0.296**
norm. mixed 2-step RSV (fixed)	-	0.266
optimal performance	*0.285*	*0.350*

The proposed 2-step RSV merging approach achieves a better performance than any of the other approaches. Raw mixed 2-step RSV and normalized mixed 2-step RSV were calculated by means of eq. 1 and eq. 2, with $\alpha = 0.75$. Mixed 2-step results using logistic regression and neural networks are not given in this paper because training data (relevance judgments) for this years new collections are not available.

The good performance of raw-mixed 2-step RSV is counterintuitive. However, not all of the terms to be added to the original query are new terms since some terms obtained by means of pseudo-relevance feedback are already in the initial query. On the other hand, as Table 3 shows, raw-scoring works relatively well for this experiment. Thus, the percent (0.25) of local RSV added to each document score is partially comparable. However, normalized mixed 2-step RSV should improve raw mixed 2-step RSV results when collections are very different in size or very different weighting schemas are used for each collection. Finally, experiments carried out with CLEF 2001 (training) and CLEF 2002 (evaluation) relevance judgments show that learning-based algorithms perform slightly better than raw-scoring as a way to integrate both available values when mixed 2-step is used [11]. In any case, the mixing of both the local and global scores obtained for each document by means of mixed 2-step RSV is an open problem with respect to the integration of several sources of information, and again refers to the collection fusion problem.

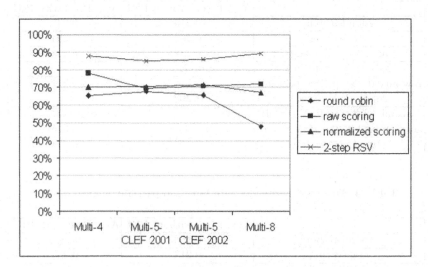

Fig. 1. Performance of traditional merging strategies with respect to several sets of languages (fully aligned queries). The 100% case represents *optimal performance*

Perhaps our most interesting result this uear is shown in Figures 1 and 2. As we suspected last year, the perfomance of round-robin and raw-scoring decreases as the number of languages increases. On the other hand, 2-step RSV maintains about 85% of optimal performance.

5   Conclusion and Future Work

At CLEF 2003 we focused on merging approaches and decompounding algorithms. We have tested 2-step RSV and mixed 2-step RSV in the Multi-4 and

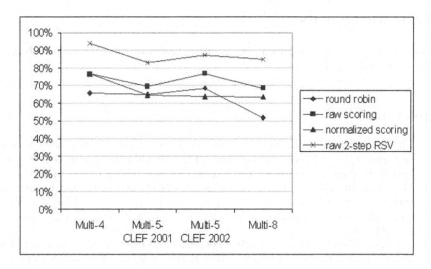

Fig. 2. Performance of traditional merging strategies with respect to several sets of languages (partially aligned queries using PRF). The 100% case represents *optimal performance*

Multi-8 tasks. Results show that the proposed method scales well with four, five and eight languages, overcoming traditional approaches.

Our next efforts will be aimed in a number of directions:

- Since our decompounding algorithm is highly dependent on the wordlists used, we intend to obtain a better wordlist.
- We mean to test the method described here using other translation strategies such as Machine Translation or Multilingual Similarity Thesaurus.
- The index terms used in the experiments reported here are basically obtained by means of stemming. We are very interested in the application of an n-gram indexing approach. However, while stemming terms are directly assimilable as feasible representations of concepts, n-grams cannot be assimilated directly as concepts since a given n-gram is usually contained by several unrelated terms. We have carried out some preliminary experiments, and the results obtained so far confirm that an n-gram cannot function as a direct representation of a concept.
- Finally, we will keep on studying strategies in order to deal with aligned and not-aligned query terms. The integration of both types of terms by means of neural networks (although these structures require training data) and the development of global pseudo-relevance feedback procedures, and not locally for each monolingual collection, should be interesting areas for investigation.

Acknowledgments

This work has been supported by Spanish Government (MCYT) with grant FIT-150500-2003-412.

References

1. Chen, A.: Multilingual Information Retrieval using English and Chinese Queries. In Peters, C., ed.: Proceedings of the CLEF 2001 Cross-Language Text Retrieval System Evaluation Campaign. LNCS 2406, Springer Verlag (2002) 44–58
2. Martínez-Santiago, F., Martin, M., Ureña, L.: SINAI at CLEF 2002: Experiments with merging strategies. In Peters, C., ed.: Proceedings of the CLEF 2002 Cross-Language Text Retrieval System Evaluation Campaign. LNCS 2785, Springer Verlag (2003) 187–198
3. Savoy, J.: Report on CLEF-2001 Experiments. In Peters, C., ed.: Proceedings of the CLEF 2001 Cross-Language Text Retrieval System Evaluation Campaign. LNCS 2406, Springer Verlag (2003) 27–43
4. Gey, F., Jiang, H., Chen, A., Larson, R.: Manual Queries and Machine Translation in Cross-language Retrieval and Interactive Retrieval with Cheshire II at TREC-7. In Voorhees, E.M., Harman, D.K., eds.: Proceedings of the Seventh Text REtrieval Conference (TREC-7). (2000) 527–540
5. Nie, J., Jin, F.: Merging Different Languages in a Single Document Collection. In Peters, C., ed.: Proceedings of the CLEF 2001 Cross-Language Text Retrieval System Evaluation Campaign. LNCS 2406., Springer Verlag (2003) 59–62
6. McNamee, P., Mayfield, J.: JHU/APL Experiments at CLEF: Translation Resources and Score Normalization. In Peters, C., ed.: Proceedings of the CLEF 2001 Cross-Language Text Retrieval System Evaluation Campaign. LNCS 2406., Springer-Verlag (2002) 193–208
7. Calvé, L., A., Savoy, J.: Database merging strategy based on logistic regression. Information Processing & Management. 36 (2000) 341–359
8. Savoy, J.: Cross-language information retrieval: experiments based on CLEF 2000 corpora. Information Processing & Management 39 (2003) 75–115
9. Martín, M., Martínez-Santiago, F., Ureña, L.: Aprendizaje neuronal aplicado a la fusión de colecciones multilingües en CLIR. Procesamiento del Lenguaje Natural (2003) In press.
10. Martínez-Santiago, F., Ureña, L.: SINAI experience at CLEF. Revista Iberoamericana de Inteligencia Artificial (2003) In press.
11. Martínez-Santiago, F., Ureña, L.: A merging strategy proposal: the 2-step retrieval status value method. Technical report, University of Jaén (2003)
12. Chen, A.: Cross-language Retrieval Experiments at CLEF-2002. In Peters, C., ed.: Proceedings of the CLEF 2002 Cross-Language Text Retrieval System Evaluation Campaign. LNCS 2785. (2003) 5–20
13. V. Hollink, J. Kamps, C.M.M.d.R.: Monolingual retrieval for European languages. Information Processing Retrieval 7(1-2) (2004)
14. Robertson, S.E., Walker., S., Beaulieu, M.: Experimentation as a way of life: Okapi at TREC. Information Processing and Management 36(1) 1 (2000) 95–108
15. Harman, D.: Relevance feedback revisited. In: Proceedings of the 15th International ACM SIGIR Conference on Research and Development in Information Retrieval (SIGIR-92). (1992) 1–10

Merging Results by Predicted Retrieval Effectiveness

Wen-Cheng Lin and Hsin-Hsi Chen

Department of Computer Science and Information Engineering,
National Taiwan University, Taipei, TAIWAN
denislin@nlg.csie.ntu.edu.tw; hh_chen@csie.ntu.edu.tw

Abstract. In this paper we propose several merging strategies to integrate the
result lists of each intermediate run in distributed MLIR. The prediction of retrieval effectiveness was used to adjust the similarity scores of documents in the
result lists. We introduced three factors affecting the retrieval effectiveness,
i.e., the degree of translation ambiguity, the number of unknown words and the
number of relevant documents in a collection for a given query. The results
showed that the normalized-by-top-k merging with translation penalty and collection weight outperformed the other merging strategies except for the raw-
score merging.

1 Introduction

Multilingual Information Retrieval abbreviated as MLIR facilitates the uses of queries
in one language to access documents in various languages. Most of the previous approaches [7] focused on how to unify the language usages in queries and documents.
The adaptation of traditional information retrieval systems has been considered.
Query translation and document translation methods have been introduced. The resources used in the translation have been explored.

In the real world, multilingual document collections are distributed in various resources, and managed by information retrieval system of various architectures. How
to integrate the results from heterogeneous resources is one of the major issues in
MLIR. Merging result lists of individual languages is a commonly adopted approach.
Document collections of each language are indexed and retrieved separately, and the
result lists of each document collection are merged into a multilingual result list. The
goal of result lists merging is to include as many relevant documents as possible in
the final result list and to ensure that relevant documents have higher ranks. Several
attempts have been made on this problem [8]. The simplest merging method is *raw-
score merging*, which sorts all the documents by their original similarity scores, and
then selects the top ranked documents. The second approach, *round-robin merging*,
interleaves the results of each run based on the rank of each document. The third approach is *normalized-score merging*. For each topic, the similarity score of each
document is divided by the maximum score in each result list. After adjusting scores,
all results are put into a pool and sorted by the normalized score.

Lin and Chen [4, 5] proposed *normalized-by-top-k merging* to avoid the drawback
of normalized-score merging. Translation penalty is also considered during merging
result lists. The performance of normalized-by-top-k with translation penalty is simi-

C. Peters et al. (Eds.): CLEF 2003, LNCS 3237, pp. 202–209, 2004.
© Springer-Verlag Berlin Heidelberg 2004

lar to that of raw-score merging. Moulinier and Molina-Salgado [6] proposed collection-weighted normalized score to merge result lists. The normalized collection score is used to adjust the similarity score between a document and a query. Collection score only reflects the similarity of a (translated) query and a document collection. This method could fail if a query is not translated well. Savoy [11] used logistic regression to predict the relevance probability of documents according to the document score and the logarithm of the rank. Again, this method does not consider the quality of query translation. Furthermore, the relationship between the rank and the relevance of a document is not strong. Braschler, Göhring and Schäuble [1] proposed feedback merging that interleaves the results according to the propositions of the predicted amount of relevant documents in each document collection. The amount of relevant information was estimated by the portion of overlap between the original query and the ideal query constructed from the top ranked documents. The experimental results showed that feedback merging had little impact.

In this paper, we will explore several merging strategies. The basic idea of our merging strategies is: adjusting the similarity scores of documents in each result list to make them more comparable and to reflect the confidence in retrieval effectiveness. We assume that the importance of each intermediate run depends on their retrieval performance. We introduced three factors affecting the retrieval effectiveness, i.e., the degree of translation ambiguity, the number of unknown words and the number of relevant documents in a collection for a given query. The rest of this paper is organized as follows. Section 2 describes our merging strategies. Section 3 shows the IR model and query translation technique. Section 4 discusses the experimental results. Section 5 provides concluding remarks.

2   Merging Strategies

We aim to include as many relevant documents as possible in the final result list and to make relevant documents have higher ranks during merging. If a result list contains many relevant documents in the top ranks, i.e., it has good performance, the top ranked documents should be included in the final result list. On the other hand, if a result list has few or even no relevant documents, the final result list should not contain many documents from this list. Thus, the higher the performance of an individual run, the more important it is. However, without a priori knowledge of a query, the prediction of the performance of an individual run for each document collection is a difficult challenge. The similarity score between a document and a query is one of a few clues that are commonly used. A document with higher similarity score seems to be more relevant to a specific query. Because there are several document collections and the underlying IR systems may be different, the similarity scores of a query with different collections cannot be compared directly. The basic idea of our merging strategies is: to adjust the similarity scores of documents in each result list to make them more comparable and to reflect the confidence in retrieval effectiveness. The characteristics of the underlying IR model, the effects of the query translation and the statistics of individual document collection will be addressed in the following subsections.

2.1 Normalized by Top K

Similarity scores reported by different information retrieval systems may differ considerably from each other. In vector-based IR models, the similarity score defined by the cosine formula ranges from 0 to 1, but the score may be much larger than 1 when the Okapi system [9] is used. It is obvious that the scores cannot be compared directly. Thus, similarity scores have to be normalized to the same range to make them comparable at the first step. The approach of normalized-score merging maps the similarity scores of different result lists to the values within the same range. The major drawback is: if the maximum score is much higher than the second one in the same result list, the normalized-score of the document at rank 2 would be made lower even if its original score is high. Thus, the final rank of this document might be lower than that of the top ranked documents with similar original scores in another result list. A revised score normalization method is proposed as follows. The original score of each document is divided by the average score of top k documents instead of the maximum score. We call this *normalized-by-top-k* approach.

2.2 Translation Penalty

The similarity score reflects the degree of similarity between a document and a query. A document with higher similarity score seems to be more relevant to the given query. However, if the query is not formulated well, e.g., inappropriate translation of a query, a document with a high score may still not meet the users' information needs. When the result lists are merged, those documents that have high, but incorrect scores should not be included in the final result list. Thus, the effectiveness of each individual run has to be considered in the merging stage.

When a query translation method is used to deal with the unification of languages in queries and documents, queries are translated into the target language and then the target language documents are retrieved. We can predict the multilingual retrieval performance based on the translation quality. Intuitively, using English to access an English collection is expected to have better performance than using it to access other collections. Similarly, using a bilingual dictionary with greater coverage is expected to be better than using dictionary with less coverage. Less ambiguous queries have also higher tendency to achieve better translation than more ambiguous queries. Normalization in Section 0 just reflects the same comparison basis, but does not consider the above issues. Two factors, i.e., the degree of translation ambiguity and the number of unknown words, are used to model the translation performance. For each query, we compute the average number of translation equivalents of query terms and the number of unknown words in each language pair, and use them to compute the weights of each cross-lingual run. The following formula is proposed to determine the weights.

$$W_i = c_1 + \left[c_2 \times \left(\frac{51 - T_i}{50} \right)^2 \right] + \left[c_3 \times \left(1 - \frac{U_i}{n_i} \right) \right]. \tag{1}$$

where W_i is the merging weight of query i in a cross-lingual run,

T_i is the average number of translation equivalents of query terms in query i,
U_i is the number of unknown words in query i,
n_i is the number of query terms in query i, and
c_1, c_2 and c_3 are tunable parameters, and $c_1+c_2+c_3=1$.

The best case of query translation is that each query term has only one translation, that is, the average number of translation equivalents is 1 and the number of unknown words is 0. In such a case, a query will be translated correctly, thus the value of merging weight W is 1 and the similarity scores of documents remain unchanged. As the number of unknown words or average number of translation equivalents increases, the translation quality and retrieval performance are more likely to be worse. Therefore, the value of merging weight decreases towards 0 to reduce the importance of this intermediate run.

2.3 Collection Weight of Individual Document Collections

The number of relevant documents in a collection for a given query is also an important factor for measuring retrieval effectiveness. If a document collection contains more relevant documents, it could have a greater contribution to the final result list. Since the number of relevant documents in a document collection is not known a priori, we have to predict it. Callan, Lu and Croft [2] proposed CORI net to rank distributed collections of the same language for a query. Moulinier and Molina-Salgado [6] used collection score to adjust the similarity score between a document and a query.

In our approach, the similarity between a document collection and a query is used to predict the number of relevant documents contained in the document collection. For a given query, a document collection that is more similar to it has a higher likelihood to contain more relevant documents. The similarities are used to weight document collections. For each document collection, a collection weight, which is defined as follows, is computed to indicate its similarity to a query. A document collection is viewed as a huge document and represented as a collection vector. The ith element in a collection vector is the document frequency df of the ith index term in the collection. Similarly, the ith element in a query vector is the frequency of the ith index term in the query. Since document collections are in different languages, we do not use inverse collection frequency icf, which is analogous to idf. The cosine similarity formula shown below is used to compute the collection weight, which is added to the merging weight.

$$W_i^{'} = W_i + c_4 \times CW_i \cdot \qquad (2)$$

$$CW_i = \frac{\sum_{j=1}^{m} qtf_{ij} \times df_j}{\sqrt{\sum_{j=1}^{m} qtf_{ij}^2} \times \sqrt{\sum_{j=1}^{m} df_j^2}} \cdot \qquad (3)$$

where W_i' is the new merging weight of query i in an intermediate run,

W_i is the merging weight described in Section 0,

CW_i is the collection weight of a target collection for query i,

c_4 is a tunable parameter,

qtf_{ij} is the term frequency of index term j in query i,

df_j is the document frequency of index term j in a target collection, and

m is the number of index terms.

2.4 Predicting Retrieval Effectiveness by Linear Regression

Three factors, i.e., the degree of translation ambiguity, the number of unknown words and the number of relevant documents for a given query in a document collection, are now proposed to determine retrieval effectiveness. We use linear regression to predict the retrieval effectiveness according to the three factors. The original similarity score of a document is normalized by normalized-by-top-k method, and the score of the predicted precision is added to the normalized score. Documents from all collections are sorted according to the adjusted similarity scores and the top ranked documents are reported.

3 Query Translation and Document Indexing

In the experiments, the Okapi IR system was adopted to index and retrieve documents. The weighting function was BM25 [9]. The document set used in the CLEF 2003 small-multilingual task consists of English, French, German and Spanish. The numbers of documents in the English, French, German and Spanish document sets are 169,477, 129,806, 294,809 and 454,045, respectively. The <HEADLINE> and <TEXT> sections in English documents were used for indexing. For Spanish documents, the <TITLE> and <TEXT> sections were used. While indexing French and German documents, the <TITLE>, <TEXT>, <TI>, <LD> and <TX> sections were used. The words in these sections were stemmed, and stopwords were removed. All letters were transformed to the lower cases. We adopted stopword lists and stemmers developed by University of Neuchatel[1] [10].

English queries were used as the source language queries and translated into target languages, i.e., French, German and Spanish. A dictionary-based approach was adopted. For each English query term, we found its translation equivalents by looking up a dictionary. The first two translation equivalents with the highest occurrence frequency in the target language documents were considered as the target language query terms. If a query term does not have any translation equivalents, the original English query term was kept in the translated query. The dictionaries we used are the Ergane English-French, English-German and English-Spanish dictionaries. They are available at http://www.travlang.com/Ergane.

---

[1] http://www.unine.ch/info/clef/

4 Experiments

We submitted four runs in the CLEF 2003 small-multilingual task. All runs used topic title and description fields. The details of each run are described in the following.

1. NTUm4Topn
   The result lists were merged by normalized-by-top-k merging strategy. The average similarity score of the top 100 documents was used for normalization.
2. NTUm4TopnTp
   In this run, translation penalty was considered. The similarity scores of each document were first normalized by the average similarity score of the top 100 documents and then multiplied a weight determined by formula (1). The values of c_1, c_2 and c_3 were 0, 0.4 and 0.6, respectively. In query translation, an English query term that had no translation equivalent was also used to retrieve target language documents. If such an English term occurs in the target language documents, it can be viewed as a word similar to the other translated words when the merging weight is computed. Table 1 lists the number of English query terms that have no translation, but occur in target language collection.
3. NTUm4TopnTpCw
   In this run, the collection weight was also considered. We used formula (2) to adjust the similarity score of each document. The values of parameters were the same as run NTUm4TopTp. The value of c_4 was 0.5.
4. NTUm4TopnLinear
   We used linear regression to determine the weights of the three variables, including the average number of translation equivalents of query terms, the portion of unknown words in a query and the collection weight of the target collection, to predict the performances of each intermediate run. CLEF 2001 and 2002 test sets were used as training data to estimate the parameters. The original similarity score of a document was normalized by normalized-by-top-k method, and the score of the predicted precision was added to the normalized score.

The results of official runs are shown in Table 2. To compare the effectiveness of our approaches with the past merging strategies, we also conducted several unofficial runs that used raw-score merging, normalized-score merging and round-robin merging strategies. The average precision of optimal merging proposed by Chen [3] was regarded as an upper-bound, which was used to measure the performances of our merging strategies. The performances of the unofficial runs are also shown in Table 2. The performance relative to optimal merging is enclosed in parentheses. The results show that the performances of the merging strategies we proposed were better than normalized-score merging and round-robin merging, but worse than raw-score merging. The experimental results in CLEF 2002 and NTCIR3 [4, 5] showed that normalized-by-top-k merging overcomes the drawback of normalized-score merging. In CLEF 2003, the performance of normalized-by-top-k merging was still better than normalized-score merging. The performance dropped down slightly after considering translation penalty. From Table 3, the performance of English-Spanish runs was worse than the other intermediate runs, but the merging weights of three cross-lingual runs were similar. This is because the average number of translation equivalents and the number of unknown words of three cross-lingual runs did not differ too much. After considering the collection weights of each document collection, the performance was improved and was about 7.12% increase to normalized-by-top-k merging. The performance of using the merging weight predicted by linear regression was slightly better than normalized-by-top-k merging, but worse than normalized-by-top-k with translation penalty and collection weight.

Table 1. Number of English query terms without translation but in target language corpora

Language	French	German	Spanish
# query terms	891	891	891
# query terms without translation equivalents	326	322	251
# query terms without translation equivalents but in target language corpora	209 (64.11%)	230 (71.43%)	147 (58.57%)

Table 2. Performances of merging strategies

Run	Average precision
NTUm4Topn	0.1489 (60.97%)
NTUm4TopnTp	0.1478 (60.52%)
NTUm4TopnTpCw	0.1595 (65.32%)
NTUm4TopnLinear	0.1516 (62.08%)
Raw score merging	0.1691 (69.25%)
Normalized score merging	0.1366 (55.94%)
Round-robin merging	0.1412 (57.82%)
Optimum merging	0.2442

Table 3. Performances of intermediate runs

Run	# Topic	Average precision
English -> English	54	0.5063
English -> French	52	0.2568
English -> German	56	0.2574
English -> Spanish	57	0.0797

5 Conclusion

The merging problem is critical in distributed multilingual information retrieval. In this paper, we proposed several merging strategies to integrate the result lists of collections in different languages. We assume that the importance of each intermediate run depends on their retrieval performance. We introduced three factors affecting the retrieval effectiveness, i.e., the degree of translation ambiguity, the number of unknown words and the number of relevant documents in a collection for a given query. Normalized-by-top-k avoids the drawback of normalized-score merging. The experimental results show that considering translation penalty and collection weight improves performance. We also used linear regression to predict the retrieval effectiveness. The performance of the merging weight predicted by linear regression is similar to normalized-by-top-k. The performances of our merging strategies were better than normalized-score merging and round-robin merging, but were worse than raw-score merging in single IR system environment. However, raw-scoring merging is not workable if different information retrieval systems are adopted.

References

1. Braschler, M., Göhring, A. and Schäuble, P.: Eurospider at CLEF 2002. In: Peters, C. (Ed.): Working Notes for the CLEF 2002 Workshop. (2002) 127-132.
2. Callan, J.P., Lu, Z. and Croft, W.B.: Searching Distributed Collections With Inference Networks. In: Fox, E.A., Ingwersen, P. and Fidel, R. (Eds.): Proceedings of the 18th Annual International ACM SIGIR Conference on Research and Development in Information Retrieval. ACM Press (1995) 21-28.
3. Chen, A.: Cross-language Retrieval Experiments at CLEF-2002. In: Peters, C. (Ed.): Working Notes for the CLEF 2002 Workshop. (2002) 5-20.
4. Lin, W.C. and Chen, H.H.: NTU at NTCIR3 MLIR Task. In: Kishida, K., Ishida, E. (Eds.): Working Notes of the Third NTCIR Workshop Meeting. Part II: Cross Lingual Information Retrieval Task. Tokyo, Japan: National Institute of Informatics (2002) 101-105.
5. Lin, W.C. and Chen, H.H.: Merging Mechanisms in Multilingual Information Retrieval. In: Peters, C. (Ed.): Working Notes for the CLEF 2002 Workshop. (2002) 97-102.
6. Moulinier, I. and Molina-Salgado H.: Thomson Legal and Regulatory experiments for CLEF 2002. In: Peters, C. (Ed.): Working Notes for the CLEF 2002 Workshop. 91-96.
7. Oard, D. and Diekema, A.: Cross-Language Information Retrieval. Annual Review of Information Science and Technology, Vol. 33. (1998) 223-256.
8. Peters, C. (Ed.): Working Notes for the CLEF 2002 Workshop. (2002)
9. Robertson, S.E., Walker, S. and Beaulieu, M.: Okapi at TREC-7: automatic ad hoc, filtering, VLC and interactive. In: Voorhees, E.M. and Harman, D.K. (Eds.): Proceedings of the Seventh Text REtrieval Conference (TREC-7). National Institute of Standards and Technology (1998) 253-264.
10. Savoy, J.: Report on CLEF-2001 Experiments: Effective Combined Query-Translation Approach. In: Peters, C., Braschler, M., Gonzalo, J. and Kluck, M. (Eds.): Evaluation of Cross-Language Information Retrieval Systems. Lecture Notes in Computer Science, Vol. 2406. Springer (2001) 27-43.
11. Savoy, J.: Report on CLEF-2002 Experiments: Combining Multiple Sources of Evidence. In: Peters, C. (Ed.): Working Notes for the CLEF 2002 Workshop. (2002) 31-46.

MIRACLE Approaches to Multilingual Information Retrieval: A Baseline for Future Research

José L. Martínez[1], Julio Villena[2,3], Jorge Fombella[3], Ana G. Serrano[4],
Paloma Martínez[1], José M. Goñi[5], and José C. González[3,5]

[1] Computer Science Department, Universidad Carlos III de Madrid,
Avda. Universidad 30, 28911 Leganés, Madrid, Spain
{pmf,jlmferna}@inf.uc3m.es
[2] Department of Telematic Engineering, Universidad Carlos III de Madrid,
Avda. Universidad 30, 28911 Leganés, Madrid, Spain
jvillena@it.uc3m.es
[3] DAEDALUS – Data, Decisiond and Language,
S.A. Centro de Empresas "La Arboleda", Ctra. N-III km. 7,300 Madrid 28031, Spain
{jvillena,jfombella,jgonzalez}@daedalus.es
[4] Artificial Intelligence Department, Universidad Politécnica de Madrid,
Campus de Montegancedo s/n, Boadilla del Monte 28660, Spain
{agarcia,aruiz}@isys.dia.fi.upm.es
[5] E.T.S.I. Telecomunicación, Universidad Politécnica de Madrid,
Avda. Ciudad Universitaria s/n, 28040 Madrid, Spain
jmg@mat.upm.es

Abstract. This paper describes the first set of experiments defined by the MIRACLE (Multilingual Information RetrievAl for the CLEf campaign) research group for some of the cross language tasks defined by CLEF. These experiments combine different basic techniques, linguistic-oriented and statistic-oriented, to be applied to the indexing and retrieval processes.

1 Introduction

It is well known that the amount of Internet pages is expanding rapidly; more and more encyclopaedia, newspapers and specialised sites related to almost every topic appear on-line and this has brought about the development and commercialization of a variety of tools devoted to facilitating information location and extraction from the billions of pages that make up the web. Among these tools we can find famous web search engines such as Google, Yahoo!, Altavista, etc. The need to process this huge amount of data has lead to important innovations in the field of Information Retrieval, most of them implemented into the aforementioned web search engines. Moreover, information is not only present in different kinds of formats but also in almost all languages used around the world.

There are currently three main trends in the field of the characterization of documents and queries which affect the information retrieval process: *semantic*

C. Peters et al. (Eds.): CLEF 2003, LNCS 3237, pp. 210–219, 2004.
© Springer-Verlag Berlin Heidelberg 2004

approaches try to implement some degree of syntactic and semantic analysis of queries and documents, reproducing in a certain way the understanding of the natural language text; *statistical approaches* retrieve and rank documents according to the match of documents-query in terms of statistical measures and *mixed approaches* that combine both of them, trying to complement the statistical approach with semantic approaches by integrating natural language processing (NLP) techniques, in order to enhance the representation of queries and documents and, consequently, to produce adequate levels of recall and precision. Of course, there are other proposals concerning the Semantic Web that include a new layer on top of the search systems which is in charge of extracting information from web pages. Although the Semantic Web promises to be the future of text search systems, the work presented in this paper does not include this information representation subsystem.

The MIRACLE approach focuses on the mixed approach dealing with a combination of statistical and linguistic resources to enable the multilingual search to be carried out.

2 System Architecture

Several, free distribution and proprietary, components have been used to built the system architecture. These components are:

- *Retrieval Engine:* The information retrieval engine at the base of the system is the Xapian system [9]. This engine is based on the probabilistic retrieval model and includes a variety of functionality, useful for experiment definitions, e.g., stemmers based on the Porter algorithm [11].
- *Linguistic Resources:* Stemmers based on the Porter algorithm, included in the Xapian engine have been applied. Ad hoc tokenizers have also been developed for each language, standard stopword lists have been used and a special word decompounding module for German has been applied. Using EuroWordNet [10] to apply semantic query and index term expansions was not considered due to previous results obtained in CLEF campaigns. Retrieval precision fell to very low values.
- *Translation Tools:* For translation purposes, several different translation tools have been considered: Free Translation [6], for full text translations, LangToLang [7] and ERGANE [8], for word by word translations. Other available tools such as Google Language Tools [4] and Altavista Babel Fish [5], were tested but discarded.

The modular approach followed to build the architecture has provided the necessary flexibility and scalability to carry out the different defined experiments.

3 Experiment Definition

As is already known, Multilingual Information Retrieval (MIR) is the task of searching for relevant documents in a collection of documents in more than one language in response to a query, and presenting a unified ranked list of documents regardless of the language. Multilingual retrieval is an extension of bilingual retrieval, where the collection consists of documents in a single language that is different from the query language.

We have taken a number of factors which can dramatically influence system performance, into account when building our MIR system:

Combination Operator: As previously mentioned, our system is based on a probabilistic retrieval model, where several Boolean operators can be applied to construct a query. These are basically 'AND' operators and 'OR' operators, with the ability to assign weights to each operator. Another kind of operator investigated consists in the representation of the query as a document, indexing this new document and using acquired weights to build a new query. This operator is denoted with the suffix *doc* in our experiments, and tries to resemble a Vector Space Model Approach [3].

Stemming Algorithm: The stemming process is used to group together all words with related meanings under the same canonical representative. This grouping is guided by syntactical information, since words are arranged according to their stems. This dimension is used to take into account the effect of this stemming process on the use of original words to build the query. Of course, quality related to the stemming process is also relevant for system performance.

Techniques to Merge Retrieval Results: MIR systems are commonly based on three different approaches: the first translates the query into each target language and uses each translated query to search the independent collections according to the document language; in the second, all documents are translated to the language used to formulate the query, matching the query against the translated collection; in the third approach, the query is again translated to each target language, but all translations and the original query are used to build a multilingual one, which is applied to a unique document collection made up of documents in all languages. The MIRACLE contribution has taken into account the first and third approaches, but not the second due to the excessive resources needed to translate all the documents. With the first approach, techniques to merge the separate results lists obtained are needed. Techniques considered were:

- Round Robin, where results are merged taking into account positions in the results lists obtained for each language. So, if there are four target languages, the first element of each list is taken to obtain the four initial positions of the final results list, and so on.
- Normalization, where partial similarity measures are normalized (taking into account the number of documents in each collection) and ordered according to this normalized relevance value.

Of course, this dimension has no effect when monolingual or bilingual tasks are considered.

Translation Tools Used: Several on-line translation tools were considered for the experiments carried out by the MIRACLE team in the CLEF forum. These tools were:

Free Translation, for full text translations, LangToLang and ERGANE, for word by word translations. Different experiments have been defined according to the number of translation tools used. It is worth mentioning that retaining ambiguity often has a positive effect on MIR systems; in monolingual information retrieval there are several studies showing that dealing with lexical variation (discriminating word senses) is more beneficial for incomplete and relatively short queries, [2], due to the retrieval process itself carrying out a disambiguation process in extended queries (it is expected that a conjunction of terms would eliminate many of the spurious forms). Obviously, this dimension is not considered for monolingual experiments.

Query Section: As described in [14] queries are structured into three different fields: title, description and narrative. According to the query sections used, different experiments have been carried out, trying to take into account the relevance in performance introduced by long queries.

Relevance Knowledge: To improve the quality of retrieval results, knowledge on relevance of documents (supplied by the user) for a first query execution can be exploited. So, retrieved relevant documents can be used to remake the query expression and search again. The automatic relevance feedback process implemented consists of formulating a query, getting the first 25 documents, extracting the 250 most important terms for those documents, and constructing a new query to be carried out against the index database.

Tables 1, 2 and 3 show the different experiments submitted to CLEF 2003 for each task. Some details of these experiments should be commented:

- The *Tordirect* multilingual test applies the third approach described for MIR systems: the original query and its translations are used to build a query that is executed against a single index of all documents, regardless of the language.
- The *Tor3full* bilingual experiment includes the query in its original language to take into account the effect of erroneous translations.

Table 1. Monolingual Experiments

Exp. Identifier	Combination Operator	Stemming Applied	Query Section Used	Rel. Feed back
or (B)	OR	Yes	Title + Desc.	No
orand	AND for most frequent query stems, OR for the rest	Yes	Title + Desc.	No
Doc	DOC	Yes	Title + Desc.	No
Orfull	OR	Yes	Title + Desc. + Narr.	No
Orlem	OR	Yes + original query words	Title + Desc.	No
Orrf	OR	Yes	Title + Desc.	Yes

Table 2. Bilingual Experiments

Exp. Identifier	Combination Operator	Stemming Applied	Translators Used	Query Section Used	Rel. Feed back
Tor1 (B)	OR	Yes	FreeTranslation	Title + Desc.	No
Tor2	OR	Yes	FreeTranslation + LangToLang	Title + Desc.	No
Tor3	OR	Yes	FreeTranslation + Ergane	Title + Desc.	No
Tdoc	DOC	Yes	FreeTranslation	Title + Desc.	No
Tor3full	OR + original query words	Yes	FreeTranslation + Ergane	Title + Desc.	No

Table 3. Multilingual Experiments

Exp. Identifier	Combination Operator	Stemming Applied	Results Mixing Method	Translators Used	Query Section Used
Torall (B)	OR	Yes	Normalize	FreeTranslation	Title + Desc.
Torallrr	OR	Yes	Round Robin	FreeTranslation	Title + Desc.
Tor3	OR	Yes	Normalize	FreeTranslation +Ergane	Title + Desc.
Tdoc	DOC	Yes	Normalize	FreeTranslation	Title + Desc.
Tordirect	OR + original query words	Yes	Unique Index Database	FreeTranslation	Title + Desc.

4   Tasks and Results

This section contains the results obtained for tasks in which the MIRACLE consortium took part.

4.1 Multilingual-4

The languages selected by the MIRACLE research team were: Spanish, English, German and French. Four different experiments, all with Spanish as the query language, were carried out for this task, corresponding to those defined in the previous section.

Figure 1 shows Recall – Precision values obtained for each experiment. Best results correspond to *Tordirect*, followed by *Tor3*. Thus, we obtained better results when there is only one index database in which all languages are included. This can be due to variations in frequency of appearance of words that remain in the same form independently of the language considered, such us proper nouns.

The worst results were obtained by the approach where the retrieved documents list is put together taking into account the order of the results in the partial results list, i.e., when a round robin mixing technique is applied. This is not surprising taking into account that no method for considering the document collection as a whole to weight results is being applied.

If the values for average precision for all submissions are considered, the results of the MIRACLE approach are far from the best averages obtained. The baseline for our multilingual tasks was *Torall*, which has been improved by the *Tordirect*, *Tor3* and *Tdoc* experiments. Some conclusions could be drawn:

- The third approach for multilingual processing, where a single multilingual index is built for the document collections and for the query, could lead to better results than separately indexing the collections.
- If several translation tools are applied, precision can be improved, perhaps due to the inclusion of a great variety of translations for each query word.
- The *doc* technique can offer better results because the representation built for the query is closer to the document representations (remember that the query is indexed as part of the document collection)
- Our worst result was obtained for the *QTorallrr* experiment, due to the method applied to merge partial results list when constructing the final retrieved documents list.

4.2 Bilingual

For the bilingual task, three different language combinations were used: Spanish queries against the English document collection, French queries against the English document collection and Italian queries against the Spanish document collection. The experiments carried out for each language pair were very similar to those described for the previous task. This is the first time that the MIRACLE research team takes part in CLEF, so it was possible to choose English as one of the target languages for this task.

Figure 2 shows the results for each bilingual task. For technical reasons it was not possible to run *Tor1* or *Tor3* for the bilingual French – Spanish task. As the graphics show, the best results for all language combinations are obtained for *Tor1*. This result seems to show that using several translation tools does not improve the results, which appears to be inconsistent with the conclusions drawn from our multilingual experiments. The explanation is that, for multilingual experiments, three translations for each query are obtained and used to construct the query, which can lead to a more complete query representation, but for bilingual experiments, only one translation is obtained and only one document collection is searched. The narrative field for queries offers the worst retrieval performance, perhaps due to the excessive number of terms introduced when considering all query fields and translating them with all available tools.

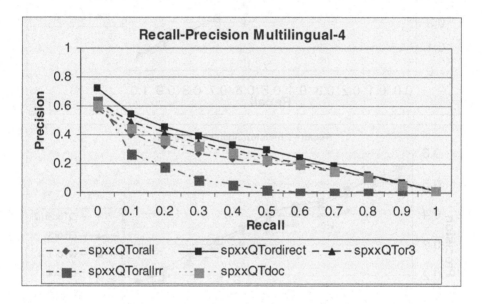

Fig. 1. Recall-Precision graph for the Multilingual-4 task

A comparison with the result of the rest of the participants in CLEF 2003 has been made using mean average precision values supplied with the result files. The results for the Italian–Spanish tasks are not as good as the rest of the submissions. Our best system is performing below the best of all submissions as is our mean precision value. Of course, it must be taken into account that our results are included in average precision values provided by the organisation. On the other hand, for the Spanish–English and the French–English tasks, the performance obtained is the best of all of the participants in this task.

4.3 Monolingual

In this task only one language was used to formulate queries which are processed against a document collection in the same language as the query. The MIRACLE research team submitted runs for the Spanish, English, French and German tasks.

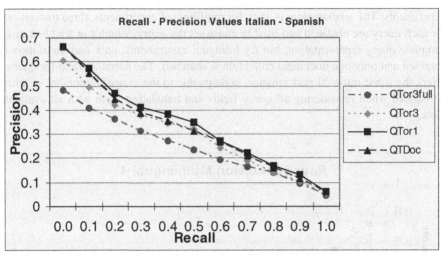

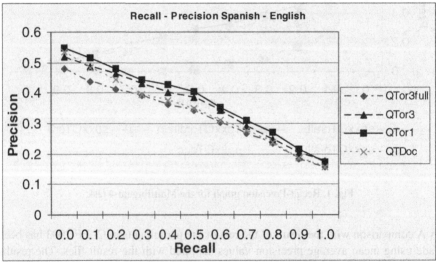

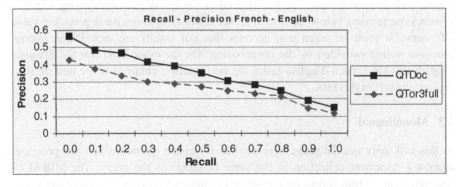

Fig. 2. Recall-precision graphs for bilingual tasks

Several different experiments were carried out for this task, as described in Table 1. Taking into account obtained results, only for the French – French task have we improved on the baseline experiment, consisting of an ORed expression made up of all words in the query. For the rest of the tasks, variations in the baseline experiment have not lead to better Recall- Precision values. Tasks where relevance feedback has been used always give the worst results, suggesting that our relevance feedback method should be changed. CLEF 2003 participants who applied relevance feedback improved their retrieval results. Experiments where the query is used to construct a document to be indexed and used as a query expression to be matched against the index document database, always resulted in lower performance values than the baseline. Again, this fact seems inconsistent with multilingual conclusions, but for this experiment only one language is being considered and, probably, the *doc* method has to be adapted for this particular case.

To compare MIRACLE results with all participants in CLEF, average precision values provided by the CLEF organisation are used. MIRACLE monolingual French – French results lead to low precision values. This can be due to the linguistic resources used for this language, e.g., the tokenizer used is not specific for the French language, producing low quality stems. Also, the French – French task is the only one where the best of our runs does not reach the mean value for all runs submitted. In the German – German task, results are not much better, maybe for a similar reason.

5   Conclusions and Future Directions

As a first conclusion from the experiments carried out, none of the different techniques applied improves results obtained for defined baseline experiments. Although the MIRACLE approach has obtained good results for bilingual tasks working on the English collection, the MIRACLE results do not improve the retrieval performance achieved by the best participants in the CLEF 2003 initiative. Nevertheless, the objectives of this research team have been accomplished. The main goal pursued with this first participation in the CLEF initiative was to establish a starting point for future research work in the field of cross-language retrieval. For later CLEF initiatives, according to results obtained, new experiments will be defined, aimed at looking deeply into the proposed mixed approach. Improvements will apply different retrieval models, in particular, the Vector Space Model, supported by a semantic approach, and will follow two basic lines ([1],[12],[13]):

- From the linguistic point of view, specific linguistic resources and techniques will be applied, such as shallow parsers, tokenizers, language specific entity recognition subsystems and semantic information, probably extracted from EuroWordnet.
- From the statistical perspective, ngram approaches will be implemented. Some of the CLEF 2003 participants have obtained good results with ngram techniques and the MIRACLE team will try to improve on these results combining some of the above mentioned linguistic techniques. Several weight assignment methods will also be explored.

Acknowledgements

This work has been partially supported by the projects OmniPaper (European Union, 5th Framework Programme for Research and Technological Development, IST-2001-32174) and MIRACLE (Regional Government of Madrid, Regional Plan for Research, 07T/0055/2003).

References

[1] Greengrass, E. Information Retrieval: A Survey, Internet Available (20.10.2003): http://www.csee.umbc.edu/cadip/readings/IR.report.120600.book.pdf, November (2000).

[2] Voorhees, E.: On expanding query vectors with lexically related words, 2nd Text Retrieval Conference, pp. 223-231, (1994).

[3] Karen Sparck Jones and Peter Willet: Readings in Information Retrieval, Morgan Kaufmann Publishers, Inc. San Francisco, California (1997).

[4] "Google Language Tools", www.google.com/language_tools.

[5] "Altavista's Babel Fish Translation Service", www.altavista.com.

[6] "Free Translation", www.freetranslation.com.

[7] "From Language To Language", www.langtolang.com.

[8] "Ergane Translation Dictionaries", http://dictionaries.travlang.com.

[9] "The Xapian Project", www.sourceforge.net.

[10] "Eurowordnet: Building a Multilingual Database with Wordnets for several European Languages." http://www.let.uva.nl/ewn/, March (1996).

[11] "The Porter Stemming Algorithm" page maintained by Martin Porter. www.tartarus.org/~martin/PorterStemmer/.

[12] Sparck Jones, K. Index term weighting. Informa. Storage and Retrieval, 9, 619-633, (1973).

[13] Salton, G., Yang,C. On the specification of term values in automatic indexing. Journal of Documentation, 29 (1973), 351-372.

[14] Braschler, M. and Peters, C. CLEF2003: Methodology and Metrics, this volume.

Experiments to Evaluate Probabilistic Models for Automatic Stemmer Generation and Query Word Translation

Giorgio M. Di Nunzio, Nicola Ferro, Massimo Melucci, and Nicola Orio

Department of Information Engineering,
University of Padova,
Via Gradenigo, 6/a – 35031 Padova – Italy
{dinunzio,nf76,melo,orio}@dei.unipd.it

Abstract. The paper describes statistical methods and experiments for stemming and for the translation of query words used in the monolingual and bilingual tracks in CLEF 2003. While there is still room for improvement in the method proposed for the bilingual track, the approach adopted for the monolingual track makes it possible to generate stemmers which learn directly how to stem the words in a document from a training word list extracted from the document collection, with no need for language-dependent knowledge. The experiments suggest that statistical approaches to stemming are as effective as classical algorithms which encapsulate predefined linguistic rules.

1 Introduction

The Information Management Systems (IMS)[1] research group of the Department of Information Engineering of the University of Padova participated in the CLEF monolingual track in 2002 for the first time; on that occasion experiments on graph-based stemming algorithms for Italian were specifically carried out. The graph-based stemmer generator proposed achieved a retrieval effectiveness comparable to that of Porter's stemmers.

The spectrum of languages covered has been increased to five and the theoretical framework underlying the stemmer generator has been redefined this year. Although our approach has shifted from a graph-based to a probabilistic framework, the characterizing notion of mutual reinforcement between stems and derivation has been preserved. A new approach to stemmer generation based on Hidden Markov Models has also been experimented and has achieved good results.

2 Monolingual Track

Our approach to monolingual retrieval is focused on the development of stemming algorithms for five languages – i.e., Dutch, French, German, Italian, and

---

[1] http://www.dei.unipd.it/~ims

C. Peters et al. (Eds.): CLEF 2003, LNCS 3237, pp. 220–235, 2004.

Spanish – that have been used as a testbed. Our aim has been to develop algorithms which do not exploit any linguistic knowledge about the morphology of a given language and the rules to form word derivations. To this end, the assumption was that the parameters of a statistical model can be inferred from the set of words of a given language and that they can be applied for stemming words. Two different approaches have been tested. A probabilistic framework for the notion of mutual reinforcement between stems and derivation is presented in Section 2.1, whereas a framework based on Hidden Markov Models (HMMs) is presented in Section 2.2.

2.1   A Probabilistic Framework for Stemmer Generation

The *Stemming Program for Language Independent Tasks* (SPLIT) is a language independent stemming procedure which was originally proposed in [1, 2] to automatically generate stemmers for some European languages. SPLIT is based on a suffix stripping paradigm and assumes that the stem of a word can be found by splitting the word and holding the first part as a candidate stem. Therefore, the problem of word stemming is reduced to the problem of finding the right split for the word. A probabilistic framework for SPLIT has been designed and experimented and the following results have been obtained:

- a technique based on the concept of *mutual reinforcement* between stems and derivations to estimate the probabilities of the framework;
- an algorithm that implements this technique and that generates a stemmer for a given language.

Probabilistic Framework. Given a finite collection W of words, a word $w \in W$ of length n can be split into $n - 1$ possible parts so that no empty substring is generated. Therefore each split is associated with a pair of substrings called *prefix* and *suffix* respectively. The concatenation of these substrings form the word w. In our probabilistic framework it is assumed that the prefix-suffix pairs are not equiprobable, but that the concatenation of a *stem* with a *derivation* is a more probable event than the concatenation of two generic prefixes and suffixes.

Thus a maximum likelihood criterion to identify the most probable pair of sub–strings, i.e. the stem and derivation, can be employed as shown in Figure 1. Let U be the set of substrings generated after splitting every word $w \in W$ of a given language into all the possible prefix-suffix pairs. If $x \in U$ and $y \in U$ are the prefix and the suffix of the word w respectively, then $w = xy$. Let $\Omega(w) = \{(x, y) \in U \times U : w = xy\}$ be the set of all the prefix-suffix pairs which form a given word w. Thus the pair $(x, y)^*$ which is the most probable split of a given word w can be found as follows:

$$(x, y)^* = \arg \max_{\Omega(w)} \Pr(x, y) \ . \tag{1}$$

Mutual Reinforcement Model. A mutual reinforcement relationship exists among substrings of a language and can be stated as follows:

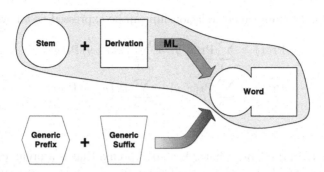

Fig. 1. Choice of the (stem, derivation) pair of a word within the probabilistic framework

> Stems are prefixes that are more likely to be completed by derivations, and derivations are suffixes that are more likely to complete stems.

Figure 2 gives an intuitive view of the mutual reinforcement relationship where, for the sake of clarity, only a small subset of prefixes and suffixes are reported. On the left of the figure a community of stems and derivations is shown. In the example shown `comput` is probably a stem because it refers to substrings which are in turn used to create other words: `ation` and `er` are referred to by `comput` and are used to create `compilation` or `reader`. On the right of the figure, a community of generic suffixes is depicted for prefix `c`; the prefix `c` is not likely to be a stem, because it forms words with suffixes, e.g. `omputer` or `ompilation`, that are not suffixes of any other words. This sort of *coupled frequent usage* allows

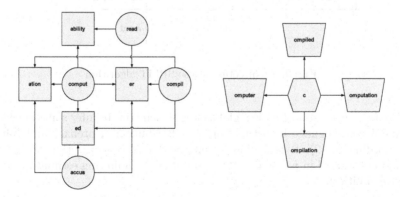

Fig. 2. Example of mutual reinforcement relationship

us to estimate the prefix and suffix probability distribution which is necessary to compute the probability distribution of the pairs so as to apply the probabilistic framework.

The mutual reinforcement relationship can be expressed as follows:

$$\Pr(x) = \sum_{y \in Y} \Pr(x, y) = \sum_{y \in Y} \Pr(x \mid y) \Pr(y) \ ,$$
$$\Pr(y) = \sum_{x \in X} \Pr(x, y) = \sum_{x \in X} \Pr(y \mid x) \Pr(x) \ ,$$

$$(2)$$

where:

- $\Pr(x)$ is the probability that x is a good prefix, that is a prefix candidate to be a stem. Similarly $\Pr(y)$ is the probability that y is a good suffix, that is a suffix candidate to be a derivation;
- $\Pr(y \mid x)$ is the conditional probability that a word ends with the suffix y given that it begins with the prefix x;
- $\Pr(x \mid y)$ is the conditional probability that a word begins with the prefix x given that it ends with the suffix y;
- $X \subseteq U$ is the set of all the prefixes and $Y \subseteq U$ is the set of all the suffixes.

The SPLIT Algorithm. Figure 3 shows the architecture of the SPLIT algorithm described below:

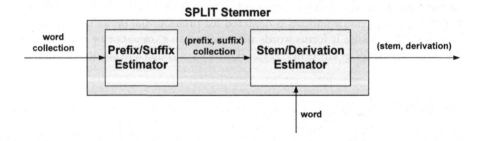

Fig. 3. Architecture of the SPLIT algorithm

- *Prefix/Suffix Estimation* is a global step which tries to infer some knowledge about the language by estimating the distribution of prefixes and suffixes, according to (2). It is a global step because it concerns the whole set U and not a word in particular. This step uses the following estimations of the probabilities:
    - $\Pr(x \mid y) = \frac{1}{|P(y)|}$, where $P(y) = \{x \in U : \exists w \in W, w = xy\}$ and $|P(y)|$ is the number of words which end with suffix y;
    - $\Pr(y \mid x) = \frac{1}{|S(x)|}$, where $S(x) = \{y \in U : \exists w \in W, w = xy\}$ and $|S(x)|$ is the number of words which begin with prefix x.

The algorithm iteratively computes:

$$\Pr^{(t)}(x) = \sum_{y \in Y} \Pr(x \mid y)\Pr^{(t-1)}(y) \ ,$$

$$\Pr^{(t)}(y) = \sum_{x \in X} \Pr(y \mid x)\Pr^{(t)}(x) \ ,$$

for $t = 0, 1, 2, \ldots$, where $\Pr^{(0)}(y)$ is a vector of uniform probabilities.

– *Stem/Derivation Estimation* is a local step, which tries to distinguish among all the pairs which lead to the same word, according to (1). It is a local step, because it concerns a particular word. Equation (1) is solved by considering two different cases:

1. $\Pr(x, y) = \Pr(x) \Pr(y \mid x)$,
2. $\Pr(x, y) = \Pr(x) \Pr(y)$.

Case 1 takes into account the possible stochastic dependence between x and y. On the other hand, case 2 considers x and y as independent events, because $\Pr(x)$ and $\Pr(y)$ have absorbed some knowledge about the morphology of the language through their estimation by (2), which already took into account the dependence between x and y.

In addition a little linguistic knowledge is injected by inserting a heuristic rule which forces the length of the prefix to be at least α characters and the length of the suffix to be at most β characters.

The CLEF 2002 collection has been used to train the algorithm and to set appropriate values for all the parameters. Once training was finished, the following parameters were chosen because they gave the best performances in each language:

- Dutch: case 2 with $\alpha = 4$, $\beta = 4$;
- French: case 1 with $\alpha = 1$, $\beta = 3$;
- German: case 2 with $\alpha = 4$, $\beta = 4$;
- Italian: case 1 with $\alpha = 1$, $\beta = 3$;
- Spanish: case 2 with $\alpha = 3$, $\beta = 3$.

2.2 An Approach Based on Hidden Markov Models for Stemmer Generation

Another statistical approach to stemming based on Hidden Markov Models (HMM) [3] has been experimented. HMMs are finite-state automata where transitions between states are ruled by probability functions. At each transition, the new state emits a symbol with a given probability. HMMs are called *hidden* because states cannot be directly observed; what is observed are only the symbols they emit. For each state the parameters that completely define an HMM are the probabilities of being the initial and the final state, the transition probabilities to any other state, and the probability that a given symbol is emitted.

HMMs as Word Generators. HMMs are particularly useful to model processes that are generally unknown but that can be observed through a sequence of symbols. For instance, the sequence of letters that forms a word in a given language can be considered as a sequence of symbols emitted by an HMM. The HMM starts in an initial state and performs a sequence of transitions between states by emitting a new letter at each transition until it stops at a final state. In general, several state sequences, or *paths*, can correspond to a single word. It is possible to compute the probability of each path, and hence to compute the most probable path corresponding to a word. This problem is normally addressed as *decoding*, for which an efficient algorithm exists: the Viterbi decoding.

In order to apply HMMs to the stemming problem, a sequence of letters that forms a word can be considered as the result of a concatenation of two subsequences of letters, a prefix and a suffix, as in the approach carried out for the SPLIT algorithm. A way to model this process is through an HMM where states are divided into two disjoint sets: states in the *stem-set* generate the first part of the word and states in the *suffix-set* can generate the last part, if the word has a suffix. For many languages, there are some assumptions that can be made on the model:

- an initial state belongs only to the stem-set, i.e. a word always starts with a stem;
- the transitions from states of the suffix-set to states of the stem-set have always a null probability, i.e. a word can be only a concatenation of a stem and a suffix;
- a final state belongs to both sets, i.e. a stem can have a number of different derivations, but it may also have no suffix.

A general HMM topology that fulfills these conditions is depicted in Figure 4. Once a complete HMM is available for a given language, stemming can

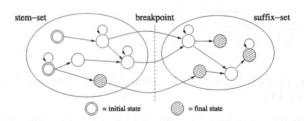

Fig. 4. HMM topology with the stem-set and the suffix-set highlighted

be straightforwardly carried out considering a word as a sequence of symbols emitted by the HMM. As a first step, the most probable path that corresponds to the observed word is computed using decoding. Then the analysis of this path highlights the transition from a state of the stem-set to a state of the suffix-set. We call this transition the *breakpoint*. If there is no breakpoint then the word has no suffix, otherwise the sequence of letters observed before the breakpoint is taken as the stem and the one observed after is taken as the suffix.

Training the HMM. The proposed topology defines the number of states, the labels indicating the sets to which the states belong, the initial and final states, and the allowable transitions. Yet all the probability functions that constitute the HMM parameters need to be computed. The computation of these parameters is normally achieved through *training*, which is based on the Baum-Welch expectation-maximization (EM) algorithm. As in the case of SPLIT, our goal is to develop fully automatic stemmers that do not require previous manual work. This means that we consider that neither a formalization of morphological rules nor a training set of manually stemmed words are available.

We propose performing an unsupervised training of the HMM using only a sample of the words of the considered language. The training set can be built at random from documents that are available at indexing time. It can be noted that an unsupervised training does not guarantee that the breakpoint of the most probable path has a direct relationship with the stem and the suffix of a given word. In order to create such a relationship, the injection of some more knowledge about the general rules for word inflection is proposed. Thus it has been reasonably assumed that the number of different suffixes for each language is limited compared to the number of different stems. Suffixes are a set of letter sequences that can be modeled by chains of states of the HMM. This assumption suggests a particular topology for the states in the suffix-set, which can be made by a number of state chains with different lengths, where transitions from the stem-set are allowed only to the first state of each chain; the transition from one state to the next has probability one: each chain terminates with a final state. The maximum length of state chains gives the maximum length of a possible suffix. Analogously, also the stem-set topology can be modeled by a number of state chains, with the difference that a state can have non-zero self-transition probability. The minimum length of a chain gives the minimum length of a stem. Some examples of topologies for the suffix-set are depicted in Figure 5, where the maximum length of a suffix is set to four letters, and the minimum length of a stem is set to three letters.

After the redefinition of the suffix-set topology, the HMM can be trained by performing the EM algorithm using a training set of words. Given the previous assumption, it is likely that a letter sequence that corresponds to a suffix will be frequently present in the training set. For this reason, the EM algorithm will give a high probability that the letters of frequent suffixes are emitted to the states in the suffix-set. For example the unique state of a suffix-set chain will emit the last letter of each word with the highest probability, the states in a two-state suffix-set chain will respectively emit the most frequent couple of final letters of each word, and so on. Once the model has been trained the path that terminates with the most frequent sequence is expected to have a high probability.

The STON Algorithm. An algorithm called STON has been developed to test the methodology and the changes in retrieval effectiveness depending on some of its parameters. STON needs an off-line training, while stemming can be performed on-line for any new word. Once training has ended, STON receives as input a sequence of letters corresponding to a word and gives as output the position of the breakpoint. Hence, STON performs in two steps:

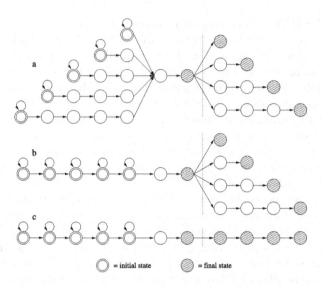

Fig. 5. Three topologies of the HMM that have been tested

- *Training/off-line*: STON computes through the EM algorithm:

$$\lambda_L^* = \arg\max_{\lambda} \prod_{w \in W_L} Pr(w \mid \lambda)$$

given a set of words $w \in W_L$ taken from a collection of documents written in a language L, and given an HMM with parameters λ which define the number of states and the set of allowable transitions. This step needs to be performed only once for each language, possibly using a sample of the words of a document collection.
- *Stemming/on-line*: STON computes the most probable path q across the states corresponding to w_L by using the Viterbi decoding:

$$q^* = \arg\max_{q} Pr(q \mid w_L, \lambda_L)$$

given a word w_L written in language L and a trained model λ_L, Decoding can be carried out also for words that were not part of the training set.
Once the most probable path q^* is computed, the position of the breakpoint, and hence the length of the stem, can be computed by a simple inspection of the path, that is considering when the path enters the suffix-set.

3   Cross-Language Retrieval Using Mutual Reinforcement

Our approach to bilingual retrieval aimed at testing whether the notion of mutual reinforcement relationship which has been successfully applied to stemming can effectively work also in the context of keyword translation based on machine readable dictionaries. It is assumed that any description of the context of a translation is absent in the dictionary. This way a dictionary is simply a list of records and a record relates a source word to the list of possible target words which are translations of the source.

One problem of dictionaries is the lack of entries for many words in the document collection. The problem of missing translations is especially acute whenever small or simple dictionaries are employed. If no translations are available for a source word, a solution is to translate the words which are most closely related to the source word. The set of words which are most related to another is called context.

A context of a word can be built using collocates. A collocate of a word is one that frequently occurs just before or just after the word in the documents of the collections. If collocates are available, and a source word cannot be translated, the translations of the collocates of the source word can be found. This way a source word might not be directly translated, but could be connected to the target language contexts which translate the context of the source word.

Thus translation is performed between source word contexts and target word contexts rather than between single words. As context translations are uncertain events, they have been modelled using a probability space.

Let Y be the set of target words, X be the set of source words, and $D \subseteq X \times Y$ be the dictionary. D is also the universe of the elementary events of the probabilistic model. Let us define $D'(r) = \{(x,y) \in D \mid x = r\}$ and $D''(t) = \{(x,y) \in D \mid y = t\}$ as the subset of translations of r to any target word and the subset of translations for which t is a target word respectively. The contexts have been defined as subsets $X(r) \subseteq X$ or $Y(t) \subseteq Y$ depending on whether they are of a source word or of a target word respectively.

A target context $Y(t)$ is a translation of the source context $X(r)$ if there is $(x,y) \in D$ such that $x \in X(r)$ and $y \in Y(t)$. Of course, there may be $0, 1, \ldots$ pairs (x,y) such that $x \in X(r)$ and $y \in Y(t)$ and then $Y(t)$ is a translation of the source context $X(r)$ to different degrees. Intuitively, the degree to which $Y(t)$ is a translation of $X(r)$ is directly proportional to the size of the set $D(r,t) = \{(x,y) \in D, x \in X(r), y \in Y(t)\}$ which is the set of translations found between the words of the context of r and those of context of t.

Using this probabilistic model the best target context, i.e. the most probable target context which is a translation of the source context can be found. The selection of the best translation can be formalized by $\Pr(Y(t)$ translates $X(r))$ and is approximated by the conditional probability:

$$\Pr(Y(t) \text{ translates } X(r)) \approx \Pr(Y(t) \mid X(r)).$$

Given that the probability that $Y(t)$ translates $X(r)$ is directly related to $|D(r,t)|$, the estimation formulas

$$\Pr(Y(t) \mid X(r)) = \frac{|D(r,t)|}{|D'(r)|} \qquad \Pr(X(r) \mid Y(t)) = \frac{|D(r,t)|}{|D''(t)|}$$

can be defined. At search time, all the target contexts $Y(t)$ corresponding to each possible translation t of r are considered for each source query word r. As there may be several candidate translation contexts $Y(t)$, a criterion to choose which translation context should be used is necessary.

The idea is that the best translations of a source context are the ones which are a translation of other source contexts and that can be conversely translated back to one of the source contexts. This mutual reinforcement relationship between contexts states that the best target translations of a source context are translated by the best source contexts, and viceversa. Thus the following mutual definition is considered:

$$\Pr(Y(t)) = \sum_{X(r)} \Pr(Y(t) \mid X(r)) \Pr(X(r)) \ ,$$

$$\Pr(X(r)) = \sum_{Y(t)} \Pr(X(r) \mid Y(t)) \Pr(Y(t)) \ ,$$

where $\Pr(Y(t))$ is the probability that $Y(t)$ is a translation of a source context, $\Pr(X(r))$ is the probability that $X(r)$ is a translation of a target context. The most probable $Y(t)$ has been taken as a translation of each query word b such that a translation of a word in $X(r)$ occurs in $Y(t)$.

4 Experiments

The aim of the experiments for the monolingual track was to compare the retrieval effectiveness of the language independent stemmers, illustrated in the previous sections, with that of an algorithm based on a-priori linguistic knowledge – we have chosen the widely used Porter's stemmers. The hypothesis was that the proposed probabilistic approaches generate stemmers that perform as effectively as Porter's stemmers. To evaluate stemming algorithms, the performances of different IR systems have been compared by changing only the stemming algorithms for different runs, all other things being equal.

Our aim was to test the following hypotheses:

H': stemming does not hurt and can enhance the effectiveness of retrieval,
H": the proposed statistical stemmers perform as effectively as Porter's ones.

Experiments were conducted for the following languages: Dutch, French, German, Italian and Spanish. For each track four different stemming algorithms were tested:

- **No Stem**: no stemming algorithm was applied;
- **Porter**: the stemming algorithms freely available at the Snowball Web site edited by Martin Porter for different languages have been used;
- **SPLIT**: the stemming algorithm based on the notion of mutual reinforcement has been used;
- **STON**: the stemming algorithm based on Hidden Markov models has been used.

As regards the stop-words used in the experiments, i.e. words which have little semantic meaning, the stop-lists available at `http://www.unine.ch/info/clef/`

Table 1. Relevant retrieved document number (recall) for 2003 Topics

Algorithm	Relevant Retrieved (Recall %)				
	Dutch	French	German	Italian	Spanish
No Stem	1,419 (89.98)	869 (91.86)	1,330 (72.88)	488 (60.32)	2,084 (88.01)
SPLIT	1,420 (90.04)	886 (93.66)	1,376 (75.40)	497 (61.43)	2,122 (89.61)
STON	1,386 (87.33)	891 (94.19)	1,384 (75.84)	503 (62.18)	2,148 (90.71)
Porter	1,416 (89.79)	911 (96.30)	1,434 (78.58)	492 (60.82)	2,202 (92.99)
Total Relevant Docs	1,577	946	1,825	809	2,368

have been used. These stop-lists are cross-linked by the CLEF consortium for the participants of the CLEF campaigns. The details of the retrieval system used for the experiments can be found in [4, 5].

For each language, the results over all the queries of the test collection have been summarized. Table 1 compares the number of relevant retrieved documents and the recall for the different algorithms under examination. Table 2 reports, for each language, the average precision attained by the system with the considered stemming algorithms. Table 3 reports the exact R-precision attained by the system, for each language. The exact R-precision is the precision after R documents have been retrieved, where R is the number of relevant documents for the topic.

In general stemming improves the recall. The Dutch language represents an exception to this note, since both the STON and the Porter stemmer retrieve less relevant documents than without any stemmer.

Note that for French, German, Italian and Spanish stemming positively affects the precision, thus improving the overall performance of the system, since the recall has also improved. Dutch stemming does not degrade the overall per-

Table 2. Average precision for 2003 Topics

Algorithm	Average Precision (%)				
	Dutch	French	German	Italian	Spanish
No Stem	42.11	42.86	34.92	34.76	39.27
SPLIT	42.84	45.60	37.11	38.17	38.25
STON	42.57	45.67	36.68	34.66	40.56
Porter	43.49	45.87	37.88	35.53	43.42

Table 3. Exact R-precision for 2003 Topics

Algorithm	Exact R-Precision (%)				
	Dutch	French	German	Italian	Spanish
No Stem	40.51	39.45	36.59	36.32	40.26
SPLIT	41.54	43.22	37.80	38.39	39.85
STON	39.66	42.20	37.53	33.26	39.90
Porter	40.55	41.68	38.73	34.79	42.70

formances of the system. Furthermore, when the stemming algorithms positively affect the performances, SPLIT and STON perform as effectively as Porter's stemmer.

Thus these figures gives a positive answer to both hypotheses H' and H'' since stemming does not hurt and sometimes improves the performance of an information retrieval system (IRS). The experimental evidence confirms the hypothesis that it is possible to generate stemmers using probabilistic models without or with very little knowledge about the language.

However the degree to which the observed differences are significant has to be measured using statistical testing methods. To test the hypotheses more soundly, the runs have been compared using the following measures: number of relevant retrieved documents (labelled Rel. Retr.), average precision (labelled Avg. Prec) and exact R-precision (labelled Exact R-Prec.), which are the same measures used previously. Furthermore the runs have also been compared using precision after 10, 20 and 30 retrieved documents (labelled, respectively, P @ 10 docs, P @ 20 docs and P @ 30 docs). These latter measures correspond to performance assessing from a more user-oriented point of view than a system-oriented one. If stemming is applied in an interactive context, such as that of a search engine or of a digital library, the ranking used to display the results to the user acquires great importance: in fact, it would more interesting to know if the user finds the relevant document after 10 or 20 retrieved documents instead of knowing if successful retrieval is reached after 50% retrieved documents.

Table 4 allows us to answer question H'. As far as the Dutch language is concerned, with our approach stemming does not exhibit significant differences with respect to the case of no stemming. For French, stemming shows significant differences with respect to the case of no stemming in terms of number of relevant retrieved documents, but not for the other measures. For German, stemming exhibits an impact on the performances for all the considered measures with the exception of the exact R-precision. In the case of Italian, there is no clear indication whether the null hypothesis should be rejected or not. Finally for Spanish, stemming clearly influences the performances in terms of number of relevant retrieved documents and average precision; for the other measures there is no strong evidence for accepting the null hypothesis.

Thus, in general, the hypothesis that stemming influences the performances of an IRS cannot be rejected. The impact of the stemming depends on both the language and the considered measure: stemming for the Dutch language is little effective.

Table 5 allows us to answer hypothesis H'' for the SPLIT algorithm. The results show that in general the hypothesis that SPLIT is as effective as Porter's algorithm cannot be rejected. However, there is some exception to this observation: with French and German, there are some significant differences in terms of number of relevant retrieved documents; for Spanish Porter's stemmer significantly performs better than SPLIT in terms of average precision, P @ 20 docs and P @ 30 docs.

Table 4. Comparison of No Stem and Porter runs for different measures

Measure		Dutch	French	German	Italian	Spanish
Rel. Retr.	No Stem > Porter	6	1	4	3	6
	No Stem = Porter	43	41	33	41	28
	No Stem < Porter	7	10	19	7	23
	Signed Rank Test (p–value)	83.94%	0.49%	0.09%	43.16%	0.06%
Avg. Prec.	No Stem > Porter	26	23	20	18	22
	No Stem = Porter	4	6	1	11	1
	No Stem < Porter	26	23	35	22	34
	Signed Rank Test (p–value)	73.61%	39.72%	0.89%	53.64%	1.07%
Exact R-Prec.	No Stem > Porter	10	12	16	16	12
	No Stem = Porter	34	28	18	25	22
	No Stem < Porter	12	12	22	10	23
	Signed Rank Test (p–value)	79.51%	52.96%	16.17%	34.73%	6.66%
P @ 10 docs	No Stem > Porter	12	11	11	13	12
	No Stem = Porter	34	26	23	28	23
	No Stem < Porter	10	15	22	10	22
	Signed Rank Test (p–value)	89.60%	33.16%	4.96%	53.16%	31.06%
P @ 20 docs	No Stem > Porter	7	14	8	9	14
	No Stem = Porter	33	25	22	29	18
	No Stem < Porter	16	13	26	13	25
	Signed Rank Test (p–value)	10.49%	71.81%	2.59%	51.26%	17.72%
P @ 30 docs	No Stem > Porter	13	12	9	12	9
	No Stem = Porter	28	25	24	30	27
	No Stem < Porter	15	15	23	9	21
	Signed Rank Test (p–value)	25.34%	12.63%	1.21%	62.63%	6.10%

Table 6 allows us to answer to hypothesis H″ for the STON algorithm. The results show that in general the hypothesis that STON is as effective as Porter's algorithm cannot be rejected. However, German is an exception with significant differences between STON and Porter's stemmers in terms of number of relevant retrieved documents, where Porter's algorithm performed better than STON. It is worth noting that the reliability of the statistical test might be affected by the presence of a high number of tied values for some measures, such as for example the number of relevant retrieved documents. In particular the omission of tied observations which is performed by both the sign test and the signed rank test introduces bias toward the rejection of the null hypothesis, as reported by [6].

Bilingual Experiments. Free dictionaries available on the Web at http://www.travlang.com/Ergane and http://www.freedict.com/ have been used. Source words have been stemmed and the dictionaries have been merged after stemming. Porter's stemmers have been used because they are considered to be standard algorithms. Stemming increased the number of translations but reduced the number of entries. The five most frequent collocates of each keyword were computed to create word contexts for each language collection. Table 7

Table 5. Comparison of SPLIT and Porter runs for different measures

		Dutch	French	German	Italian	Spanish
	SPLIT > Porter	6	1	2	6	11
	SPLIT = Porter	44	39	38	43	27
Rel. Retr.	SPLIT < Porter	6	12	16	2	19
	Signed Rank Test (p–value)	96.97%	0.24%	0.11%	46.09%	5.88%
	SPLIT > Porter	24	22	22	25	19
	SPLIT = Porter	3	9	3	12	1
Avg. Prec.	SPLIT < Porter	29	21	31	14	37
	Signed Rank Test (p–value)	71.99%	72.17%	25.53%	5.59%	0.43%
	SPLIT > Porter	10	13	16	15	14
	SPLIT = Porter	29	31	19	28	21
Exact R-Prec.	SPLIT < Porter	17	8	21	8	22
	Signed Rank Test (p–value)	82.88%	56.62%	41.96%	3.86%	12.95%
	SPLIT > Porter	12	10	13	12	11
	SPLIT = Porter	34	29	29	31	25
P @ 10 docs	SPLIT < Porter	10	13	14	8	21
	Signed Rank Test (p–value)	70.47%	62.52%	47.61%	13.35%	14.61%
	SPLIT > Porter	5	11	13	14	9
	SPLIT = Porter	34	31	22	33	20
P @ 20 docs	SPLIT < Porter	17	10	21	4	28
	Signed Rank Test (p–value)	8.44%	98.61%	2.28%	2.25%	0.07%
	SPLIT > Porter	10	6	13	16	9
	SPLIT = Porter	33	31	24	28	19
P @ 30 docs	SPLIT < Porter	13	15	19	7	29
	Signed Rank Test (p–value)	24.69%	11.72%	2.96%	30.73%	0.02%

summarizes the size and the coverage after stemming and merging the two dictionaries.

The experimental results were rather disappointing. Porter's stemming algorithm used on a source language was rather aggressive and was thus detrimental to retrieval performance because many translations were erroneously mixed. Furthermore, the procedure to generate the contexts was not very effective because many contexts contained unrelated words. The average precision was between 15% and 20%. However, we believe that the approach will stimulate further research.

5   Conclusions and Future Work

This year the IMS research group has carried out many experiments and developed methodologies for both automatic stemmer generation and query translation. The first methodology has been tested in the monolingual track of CLEF, while the second has been tested in the bilingual track. The idea underlying both automatic stemmer generation and query translation has been the use of diverse

Table 6. Comparison of STON and Porter runs for different measures

		Dutch	French	German	Italian	Spanish
Rel. Retr.	STON > Porter	3	5	3	6	9
	STON = Porter	45	43	37	40	30
	STON < Porter	8	4	16	5	18
	Signed Rank Test (p–value)	10.16%	100.00%	0.92%	46.48%	31.42%
Avg. Prec.	STON > Porter	24	21	22	21	28
	STON = Porter	7	10	4	11	1
	STON < Porter	25	21	30	19	28
	Signed Rank Test (p–value)	62.95%	98.50%	12.38%	74.70%	23.37%
Exact R-Prec.	STON > Porter	13	15	16	9	20
	STON = Porter	28	28	21	26	16
	STON < Porter	15	9	19	16	21
	Signed Rank Test (p–value)	34.46%	75.33%	39.89%	57.20%	25.14%
P @ 10 docs	STON > Porter	7	10	8	8	13
	STON = Porter	38	28	36	27	30
	STON < Porter	11	14	12	16	14
	Signed Rank Test (p–value)	19.56%	51.90%	60.06%	23.70%	54.73%
P @ 20 docs	STON > Porter	12	10	7	16	18
	STON = Porter	32	28	30	23	21
	STON < Porter	12	14	19	12	18
	Signed Rank Test (p–value)	96.57%	43.17%	7.28%	66.77%	57.61%
P @ 30 docs	STON > Porter	9	9	13	14	16
	STON = Porter	30	29	27	25	23
	STONh < Porter	17	14	16	12	18
	Signed Rank Test (p–value)	6.29%	22.31%	30.37%	75.07%	25.14%

Table 7. A summary of the dictionaries employed

Language	No. of entries	Av. No. of translations
German	67889	3.69
French	29819	2.97
Spanish	15697	3.52
Italian	8958	3.93

probabilistic models. Whereas the probabilistic models for stemmer generation have confirmed the positive results observed last year, those employed for query translation need further experiments and refinement.

Acknowledgments

The work reported in this paper has been conducted in the context of a joined program between the Italian National Research Council (CNR) and the Ministry of Education (MIUR), under the law 449/97-99.

References

1. Agosti, M., Bacchin, M. Ferro, N., Melucci, M.: Improving the automatic retrieval of text documents. In Peters, C., Braschler, M., Gonzalo, J., Kluck, M., eds.: Proceedings of Cross Language Evaluation Forum 2002. LNCS 2785, Springer-Verlag (2003) 279–290
2. Bacchin, M., Ferro, N., Melucci, M.: The effectiveness of a graph-based algorithm for stemming. In: Proceedings of the Internation Conference on Asian Digital Libraries, Singapore (2002) 117–128
3. Rabiner, L., Juang, B.: Fundamentals of speech recognition. Prentice Hall, Englewood Cliffs, NJ (1993)
4. Di Nunzio, G.: The CLEF2003 lexer. (`http://www.dei.unipid.it/~dinunzio/CLEF2003Lexer.pdf`)
5. Di Nunzio, G., Ferro, N., Melucci, M., Orio, N.: The University of Padova at CLEF 2003: Experiments to evaluate probabilistic models for automatic stemmer generation and query word translation. In Peters, C., Borri, F., eds.: Working Notes for the CLEF 2003 Workshop. (2003) 211–223
6. Gibbons, J.D.: Nonparametric Statistical Inference. 2nd edn. Marcel Dekker, Inc., New York, USA (1985)

Clairvoyance CLEF-2003 Experiments

Yan Qu, Gregory Grefenstette, and David A. Evans

Clairvoyance Corporation,
5001 Baum Boulevard, Suite 700,
Pittsburgh, PA 15213-1854, USA
{yqu,grefen,dae}@clairvoyancecorp.com
http://www.clairvoyancecorp.com

Abstract. In CLEF 2003, Clairvoyance participated in the bilingual retrieval track with the German and Italian language pair. As we did not have any German-to-Italian translation resources, we used the Babel Fish translation service provided by altavista.com for translating German topics into Italian, with English as a pivot language. Then the translated Italian topics were used for retrieving Italian documents from the Italian document collection. The translated Italian topics and the document collections were indexed using three different kinds of units: (1) linguistically meaningful units, (2) character 6-grams, and (3) a combination of 1 and 2. We submitted three automatic runs, one for each of the three different indexing units.

1 Introduction

At some point in any cross-language retrieval system, terms from a query in one language must be matched up to terms drawn from documents in another language. This matching involves bilingual resources, from either aligned texts or from some type of translation dictionary. Possessing no direct German-to-Italian or Italian-to-German bilingual resources, we at Clairvoyance participated in the CLEF 2003 bilingual retrieval track using the German and Italian language pair to examine whether using a third language as a pivot language could yield reasonable results. If pivot language translation provides good results, this approach will have many advantages; for example, translation between M languages necessitates $M \times (M-1)$ bilingual resources if each language is translated directly into each other but only $2 \times M$ bilingual resources if each language can be translated into a pivot language. Though many proposals have been made for creating a universal pivot language for translation, none has become used for open-text machine translation. But information retrieval, though covering non-restricted domains, is easier than machine translation since grammar need not be preserved under translation but only relevant terms. As we did not have German-to-Italian translation resources, we used the free Babel Fish translation service provided by Altavista.com for translating German topics into Italian, with English as a pivot language. The resulting translated Italian topics were used in our experiments for retrieving Italian documents from the Italian document collection. Since our linguistic resources for processing Italian (morphological analyzer and part-of-speech tagger)

C. Peters et al. (Eds.): CLEF 2003, LNCS 3237, pp. 236–241, 2004.

were primitive, we wanted to test whether using n-grams could allow us to circumvent missing analyses, since at least part of an incorrectly analyzed word could match an n-gram. The translated Italian topics and the document collections were thus indexed using three different kinds of features: (1) linguistically meaningful units (e.g., words and NPs recognized by our morphological analyzer), (2) character 6-grams, and (3) a combination of 1 and 2. We submitted the results of three automatic runs, each based on one combination of the indexing units. In the following sections, we describe the details of our submission and present the performance results.

2 CLARIT Cross-Language Information Retrieval

In CLEF 2003, we adopted query translation as the means for bridging the language gap between the query language and the document language for cross-language information retrieval (CLIR). For German-to-Italian CLIR, the German topics were translated into Italian via Babel Fish; the resulting translated topics were then used for retrieving Italian documents from the Italian document collection. For query and document processing, we used the CLARIT system [1], in particular, those components encompassing a newly developed Italian NLP module (for extracting Italian phrases), indexing (term weighting and phrasal decomposition), retrieval, and "thesaurus extraction" (for extracting terms to support pseudo relevance feedback).

2.1 Query Translation Via a Pivot Language

The Babel Fish translation service (altavista.com) provides translation between selected language pairs including German-to-English and English-to-Italian. It does not provide translation service between German and Italian directly. So we used English as a pivot language, first translating the German topics to English and then translating the English topics into Italian. As an illustration of typical results for this process, Figure 1 provides the translations from Babel Fish for Topic 141.

Even though some errors were introduced into the queries by translation, we felt that, except for translation of proper names, the quality of the translation from German to English and from English to Italian by Babel Fish was adequate for CLIR purposes. We quantitatively evaluate this impression in Section 3.

2.2 Italian Topic Processing

Once the topics were translated into Italian, we extracted two alternative types of terms from the topics: linguistically meaningful units or character n-grams.

To extract linguistically meaningful units, we used CLARIT Italian NLP. This NLP module makes use of a lexicon and a finite-state grammar for extracting phrases such as NPs. The lexicon is based on the Multext Italian lexicon[1], which was expanded by adding punctuations and special characters. In addition, entries with accented vowels were duplicated by substituting the accented vowels with their

---

[1] http://www.lpl.univ-aix.fr/projects/multext/LEX/LEX.SmpIt.html

(1) Original German topic from CLEF-2003:
Briefbombe für Kiesbauer .
Finde Informationen über die Explosion einer Briefbombe im Studio der Moderatorin Arabella Kiesbauer beim Fernsehsender PRO7.

(2) English translation of (1) by Babel Fish:
Letter bomb for gravel farmer. Find information about the explosion of a letter bomb in the studio of the host Arabella gravel farmer with the television station PRO7.

(3) Ideal English topic from CLEF-2003:
Letter Bomb for Kiesbauer
Find information on the explosion of a letter bomb in the studio of the TV channel PRO7 presenter Arabella Kiesbauer.

(4) Italian translation of (2) by Babel Fish:
Bomba della lettera per il coltivatore della ghiaia. Trovi le informazioni sull'esplosione di una bomba della lettera nell'studio del coltivatore della ghiaia di Arabella ospite con la stazione PRO7 della televisione.

(5) Ideal Italian topic from CLEF-2003:
Lettera Bomba per Kiesbauer
Recupera le informazioni relative all'esplosione di una lettera bomba nello studio della presentatrice della rete televisiva PRO7.

Fig. 1. Topic 141 and its translations from Babel Fish

corresponding unaccented vowels followed by an apostrophe ("''"). The final lexi-concontained about 135,000 entries. An Italian stop word list[2] of 433 items was used to filter out stop words. The grammar specified the rules for constructing phrases, especially NPs, and morphological normalization rules for normalizing morphologi-cal variants to their root forms, e.g., "previsto" to "prever". In CLEF 2003 experi-ments, we extracted Adjectives, Verbs, and NPs as indexing terms.

Another way to construct terms is to use overlapping character n-grams. We have observed that our lexicon-based term extraction did not have complete coverage for morphological normalization. The n-gram approach we adopted was aimed at mitigat-ing such shortcomings. For the submissions, we used overlapping 6-grams, as these were previously reported to be effective [2]. Spaces and punctuations were included in the character 6-grams.

2.3 CLARIT Indexing and Retrieval

CLARIT indexing involves statistical analysis of a text corpus and construction of an inverted index, with each index entry specifying the index word and a list of texts. CLARIT allows the index to be built upon full documents or variable-length sub-documents. We used subdocuments as the basis for indexing and document scoring in our experiments. The size of a subdocument was in the range of 8 sentences to 12 sentences.

---

[2] Obtained from http://www.unine.ch/Info/clef/

CLARIT retrieval is based on the vector space retrieval model. Various similarity measures are supported in the model. For CLEF 2003, we used the dot product function for computing similarities between a query and a document:

$$sim(P,D) = \sum_{t \in P \cap D} W_P(t) \bullet W_D(t) \ . \tag{1}$$

where $W_P(t)$ is the weight associated with the query term t and $W_D(t)$ is the weight associated with the term t in the document D. The two weights were computed as follows:

$$W_D(t) = TF_D(t) \bullet IDF(t) \ . \tag{2}$$

$$W_P(t) = C(t) \bullet TF_P(t) \bullet IDF(t) \ . \tag{3}$$

where IDF and TF are standard inverse document frequency and term frequency statistics, respectively. $IDF(t)$ was computed with the target corpus for retrieval. The coefficient $C(t)$ is an "importance coefficient", which can be modified either manually by the user or automatically by the system (e.g., updated during feedback).

2.4 Post-translation Query Expansion

Query expansion through (pseudo) relevance feedback has proved to be effective for improving CLIR performance [3]. We used pseudo relevance feedback for augmenting the queries. After retrieving some documents for a given topic from the target corpus, we took a set of top ranked documents, regarding them as relevant documents to the query, and extracted terms from these documents. The terms were ranked based on the following formula:

$$Prob2(t) = \log(R_t + 1) \bullet \left(\log(\frac{N - R + 2}{N_t - R_t + 1} - 1) - \log(\frac{R + 1}{R_t} - 1) \right) \ . \tag{4}$$

where N is the number of documents in the target corpus, N_t is the number of documents in the corpus that contain term t, R is the number of documents for feedback that are (presumed to be) relevant to the topic, and R_t is the number of documents that are (presumed to be) relevant to the topic and contain term t.

3 Experiments

We submitted three automatic runs to CLEF 2003. All the queries used the title and description fields (Ttitle+Description) of the topics provided by CLEF 2003. The results presented below are based on relevance judgments of 42 topics, which have relevant documents in the Italian corpus. The three runs were:

- ccwrd: with linguistically meaningful units as indexing terms
- ccngm: with character 6-grams as indexing terms
- ccmix: a combination of linguistic and character 6-grams as indexing units

With the ccmix run, the combinations were constructed through a simple concatenation of the terms nominated by ccwrd and ccngm. We ran Italian monolingual experiments to obtain the baseline with ideal translations after obtaining the relevance judgments from CLEF 2003.

All the experiments were run with post-translation pseudo relevance feedback. The feedback-related parameters were based on training over CLEF 2002 topics. The settings for German-to-Italian retrieval were: extracting $T=80$ terms from the top $N=25$ retrieved documents with the Prob2 method. For the n-gram based indexing and the mixed model, an additional term cutoff percentage was set to $P=0.01$. For the word-based indexing, the percentage cutoff was set to $P=0.25$. For Italian monolingual retrieval with words as indexing terms: $T=50$, $N=50$, $P=0.1$. For Italian monolingual retrieval with n-grams and the mixed model as indexing terms: $T=80$, $N=25$, $P=0.05$.

Table 1 presents the results for our submitted runs; Table 2 presents results for our training runs with CLEF 2002 topics. The monolingual baselines for the ccwrd*, ccngm*, and ccmix* runs are the optimal monolingual runs based on word indexing, 6-gram indexing, and mixed indexing, respectively. While the 6-gram based indexing produced higher average precision compared with the word based indexing for the CLEF 2002 topics, it significantly underperformed word based indexing for CLEF 2003 topics. Further examination is required to account for the difference in behavior of the two indexing methods for the two top sets.

Table 1. German-to-Italian retrieval performance with CLEF 2003 topics. All three runs are our submitted runs

Run ID	Indexing Units	Recall	AP	% Mono AP
ccwrd	Adj+VP+NPs	541/809	0.2303	67.2% (of 0.3428)
ccngm	Character 6-grams	456/809	0.1624	54.3% (of 0.2993)
ccmix	Adj+VP+NPs, character 6-grams	505/809	0.2098	61.7% (of 0.3402)

Table 2. German-to-Italian retrieval performance with CLEF 2002 topics

Run ID	Indexing Units	Recall	AP	% Mono AP
ccwrd2002	Adj+VP+NPs	643/1072	0.1823	61.6% (of 0.2959)
ccngm2002	Character 6-grams	648/1072	0.2133	68.1% (of 0.3132)
ccmix2002	Adj+VP+NPs, character 6-grams	675/1072	0.2147	60.1% (of 0.3574)

Table 3 presents a comparison between different versions of the Italian topics for CLEF 2002 and CLEF 2003 topic sets. The average precision statistics were computed with word based indexing and with no feedback. Even though comparing different topic statements is not justified methodologically [4], the comparison gives us a rough estimate of the quality of the translation module. Translation from English to Italian decreased performance in the range of 16.4% to 34.8%, while adding another layer of translation from German to English decreased performance further by 16.1% to 24.2%. This shows that translation service such as Babel Fish still needs to be improved for better CLIR performance.

Table 3. Performance comparison between different versions of topics

Topics	2002 Avg. Prec	2003 Avg. Prec
(1) Translated English (from German) to Italian	0.1549	0.1748
Performance change compared with (2)	(-24.2%)	(-16.1%)
Performance change compared with (3)	(-36.7%)	(-45.3%)
(2) Ideal English to Italian	0.2048	0.2083
Performance change compared with (3)	(-16.4%)	(-34.8%)
(3) Ideal Italian	0.2449	0.3197

4   Conclusions

Due to the lack of resources, our participation in CLEF 2003 was limited. We succeeded in submitting three runs for German-to-Italian retrieval, examining word based indexing and n-gram based indexing. Our results with CLEF 2002 and CLEF 2003 did not provide firm evidence of which indexing method is better. Future analysis is required in this direction.

References

1. Evans, D.A., and Lefferts, R.G.: CLARIT–TREC Experiments. Information Processing and Management. 31(3) (1995) 385–395
2. McNamee, P., and Mayfield, J: Scalable Multilingual Information Access. In Peters, C., Braschler, M., Gonzalo, J., and Kluck, M. (eds.): Advances in Cross-Language Information Retrieval, Third Workshop of the Cross-Language Evaluation Forum, CLEF 2002. Revised Papers, Lecture Notes in Computer Science 2785, Springer (2003)
3. Ballesteros, L., and Croft, W. B: Statistical Methods for Cross-Language Information Retrieval. In Grefenstette, G. (ed): *Cross-Language Information Retrieval*, Chapter 3. Kluwer Academic Publishers, Boston (1998) 23–40
4. Voorhees, E.: The Philosophy of Information Retrieval Evaluation. In Peters, C., Braschler, M., Gonzalo, J., and Kluck, M. (eds): Evaluation of Cross-Language Information Retrieval Systems: CLEF 2001 Workshop Revised Papers, Lecture Notes in Computer Science 2406, Springer (2002) 355–370

Simple Translations of Monolingual Queries Expanded Through an Association Thesaurus
X-IOTA IR System Used for CLIPS Bilingual Experiments

Gilles Sérasset[1] and Jean-Pierre Chevallet[2]

[1] Laboratoire CLIPS-IMAG* Grenoble France
Gilles.Serasset@imag.fr
[2] IPAL-CNRS, I2R A*STAR, National University of Singapore
viscjp@i2r.a-star.edu.sg

Abstract. In this paper we present the use of an association thesaurus for monolingual query expansion and a basic translation of this query for the bilingual CLEF task. An association thesaurus is based on the corpus itself, and we expect to enhance the results of both monolingual and bilingual querying.

1 Introduction

The easiest way to express knowledge is still natural language. For Information Retrieval purposes, one of the privileged sources of knowledge are documents themselves. In fact, this point of view is our paradigm for developing solutions to the problem of IR query reformulation. In our participation in CLEF, we want to test the use of natural language techniques, namely dependency analysis, in conjunction with statistical extraction techniques of term relations, to enhance recall. We have used classical co-occurrences information for query expansion before translation. The use of term co-occurrence data for query expansion is an old and debatable method [6], but we think is must be revisited using more NLT techniques. However, in this first experiment, we have not really exploited the full potential of the information available after the Natural Language Processing stage, so we are not able to provide an exhaustive assessment of these preliminary results.

2 Building an Association Thesaurus

An association thesaurus [7] is a graph computed using term co-location information. The main characteristic of such a structure is the reflection of the actual corpus content. We would like to exploit this information about the actual corpus

---

* This work is part of the PRISM-IMAG project devoted to high level indexing representation using interlingual graph formalism.

C. Peters et al. (Eds.): CLEF 2003, LNCS 3237, pp. 242–252, 2004.
© Springer-Verlag Berlin Heidelberg 2004

content, in order to guide and enhance the process of query translation. Our experience in managing this sort of thesaurus [2, 3] has taught us the usefulness of global knowledge extraction for Information Retrieval purposes. Thus, we would like to experiment this approach in a multi-lingual context.

The association thesaurus is computed using two simple dependency rules:

$$S(x, y) = \frac{|x \text{ and } y|}{|x \text{ or } y|}$$

This rule is the support S of the association between x and y expressed by the ratio of the number of occurrences where x and y appear together against the total number of occurrences of theses terms.

$$C(x, y) = \frac{|x \text{ and } y|}{|x|}$$

The confidence C rule is in fact the conditional presence of y knowing x. The confidence is 1 if y appears every times x appears. This is thus a dependency from x to y. These rules belongs to data mining domains [4, 1].

We can then build a thesaurus graph by computing and filtering these two values for all possible terms, and given a co-occurrence window which is often the document itself. Such a thesaurus is oriented due to the rule C. The support rule S is used as a threshold filter. This threshold means that under a given value, statistics are not enough informative to take into account this relation. Roughly, the more data treated and the higher we set the thresholds for these two measures, the more we seem to have meaningful associations from raw texts. We have also noticed that Natural Language pre-treatment can drastically reduce the amount of noise produced, i.e. the meaningless associations. We have already used this technique with success in [5].

In CLEF experiments, we have built such an association thesaurus on the French document side only, in order to use it for French query expansion. We have used the document themselves as windows boundaries for this co- occurrence matrix computation. This computation is a time consuming process, and the only difficulty is the size of the matrix: this matrix has the square size of the number of terms in use. We have solved this problem by first doing this computation in main memory using one hash coded table for this hollow matrix; and second by processing the corpus several times, doing the computation slice by slice, and merging the partial results in the final matrix file.

For the results presented here, all computations are done only on the sda95 corpus. In this corpus, the vocabulary is composed of 26, 921 terms: this is also the dimension of the matrix. Thus, this matrix represents a possible graph of $26, 921^2 = 480, 530, 241$ links. There are two links (direct and reverse) between a couple of terms if the couple appears at least once in a document. After producing co-occurrence relation, we count 16, 314, 078 non null value in this matrix witch are candidate relation for the thesaurus. So, only 3.4% of the matrix is non empty.

For the construction of the final association thesaurus, we have set an absolute threshold for the support S to 10 documents. This value means that the couple must appear at least in ten documents to be possibly stored in the thesaurus. We have then kept only couples which C values are above 0.5, and we have kept the order induced by the confidence rule: the produced association graph is the oriented graph. After this filtering there are only 6055 relations left from the $16,314,078$ initial candidate relations. So we have finally kept for the thesaurus only 0.037% of the candidate relations!

In this first experiment, we have not correlated the monolingual thesaurus building to the translation. We surely would have some interesting results, comparing two association thesauri on two corpora in different languages, but with a 'comparable' content.

3   Topic Translation

The query translation is thus uncorrelated with the data built from the association thesaurus. We have just tried much as possible to merge sets of translation links that were available to us as.

3.1   French to English Dictionary Preparation

The French to English dictionary we used for topics translation is an XML file containing 318276 entries in XML format:

```
<entry id="voiture">
  <eng_equiv>wagon</eng_equiv>
  <eng_equiv>carriage</eng_equiv>
  <eng_equiv>vehicle</eng_equiv>
  <eng_equiv>passenger vehicle</eng_equiv>
  <eng_equiv>automobile</eng_equiv>
  <eng_equiv>coach</eng_equiv>
  <eng_equiv>passenger coach</eng_equiv>
  <eng_equiv>(motor) car</eng_equiv>
  <eng_equiv>passenger car</eng_equiv>
  <eng_equiv>car</eng_equiv>
</entry>
```

This dictionary was built automatically by merging existing bilingual dictionaries:

- the "BTQ" (Banque Terminologique du Québec) available at CLIPS,
- the Bilingual French-English dictionary from the University of Rennes 1, freely available at http://sun-recomgen.med.univ-rennes1.fr/Dico/,
- the FeM dictionary (French English Malay), freely accessible athttp://www-clips.imag.fr/cgi-bin/geta/fem/fem.pl?lang=fr,
- the French English dictionary available for the participants on the CLEF web site.

Banque Terminologique du Québec: Each entry of the BTQ is used if it contains at least a French and an English equivalent. If the entry contains syn-

Original BTQ entries	Resulting entries

1087794 13 bowing
1087794 41 déformation en arc
1087794 48 arcure
 	
1857962 13 tying down
1857962 41 arcure
 	
1915051 13 bow
1915051 41 arcure
	`<entry id="arcure">`
	  `<eng_equiv>bow</eng_equiv>`
	  `<eng_equiv>bowing</eng_equiv>`
	  `< eng_equiv>tying down</eng_equiv>`
	`</entry>`
	
	`<entry id="déformation en arc">`
	  `<eng_equiv>bowing</eng_equiv>`
	`</entry>`

Fig. 1. Duplication of entries with alternate translations in French or English

onyms, alternate writings or abbreviations, it is duplicated accordingly. All other information is discarded in the process. Figure 1 gives an example of the process.

French-English Dictionary from Rennes University: The French to English dictionary of Rennes University gives English translations of French *forms*. However, in this experiment, we are working with lemmas instead of forms. Hence we had to extract translations of lemmas from this dictionary. For this, we used the dictionary of common words from ABU (Association des Bibliophiles Universels). This monolingual dictionary associates French forms with their lemma and corresponding morphological information. Using this dictionary, we were able to filter and keep all entries from Rennes dictionary:

1. that are proper nouns, or
2. where the form is equal to the lemma AND categories of the form and lemma match.

Figure 2 gives an example of the filtering process.

French-English-Malay Dictionary from GETA and USM: The French-English-Malay dictionary has been built in cooperation between the GETA (Groupe d'Étude pour la Traduction Automatique) from Université Joseph Fourier - Grenoble I and UTMK (Unit Terjemahan Melalui Komputer) from Universiti Sains Malaysia with the help of the French Embassy and of the Dewan Bahasa dan Pustaka. It consists in an XML dictionary of 19252 entries

Rennes' dictionary entries	ABU entries	Resulting entries
abbé=abbot (n.m.)	abbé abbé Nom:Mas+SG	abbé=abbot
abcés=abcess (n.m.)	abcès abcès Nom:Mas+InvPL	abcés=abcess
abdiqué=abdicated (v.)	abdiqué abdiquer Ver:...	
abdiquent=abdicate (v.)	abdiquent abdiquer Ver:...	
abdiquer=abdicate (v.)	abdiquer abdiquer Ver:Inf	abdiquer=abdicate

Fig. 2. Filtering of entries from Rennes University dictionary

```
<FEM-ENTRY>
  <ENTRY>répart|ir</ENTRY>
  <FRENCHPRON>re-partir</FRENCHPRON>
  <FRENCHCAT>v.tr.</FRENCHCAT>
  <ENGLISHEQU>distribute</ENGLISHEQU>
  <MALAYEQU>mengagihkan</MALAYEQU>
  <FRENCHGLOSS>(partager)</FRENCHGLOSS>
  <ENGLISHEQU>share out</ENGLISHEQU>
  <MALAYEQU>membahagi-bahagikan</MALAYEQU>
  <FRENCHGLOSS>(étaler)</FRENCHGLOSS>
  <ENGLISHEQU>spread</ENGLISHEQU>
  <MALAYEQU>membentangkan</MALAYEQU>
  <MALAYEQU>membukakan (selama beberapa waktu)</MALAYEQU>
  <FRENCHGLOSS>(classer)</FRENCHGLOSS>
  <ENGLISHEQU>&lt;&lt;</ENGLISHEQU>
  <MALAYEQU>mengelaskan</MALAYEQU>
  <MALAYEQU>mengklasifikan</MALAYEQU>
</FEM-ENTRY>
```

Fig. 3. An example entry from the FeM dictionary

linked to 30069 translations in English and Malay. The English is currently incomplete, (about 4800 translations are missing). Figure 3 shows an example of such a FeM entry.

Building Our Bilingual Dictionary: Our bilingual dictionary gathers all translation equivalences extracted from BTQ, RENNES, FeM and also from the dictionary available on the CLEF web site.

BTQ dictionary gave us 307189 entries linked to 488828 translations. (i.e. about $1,591$ translation per entry) with a maximum of 58 translation for a single entry (like "plateau").

After adding the RENNES dictionary, we count 311381 French entries leading to 496571 English equivalents, with a maximum of 60 translations for a single entry (like "support").

After adding the FeM dictionary, we count 316450 different French entries linked to 514593 English equivalents (i.e. about $1,626$ translation per entry).

After adding the CLEF dictionary, we count 318276 different French entries linked to 519748 English equivalents (i.e. about $1,633$ translation per entry).

4   Processing Details

In this section, we give some details on the processing that has been applied to documents and to queries. Except for the POS analysis, all other procedures were executed using our local X-IOTA IR system. This is an experimental modular IR system based on XML files. The choice of using XML for all processing stages enables us to quickly build an experimental data flow by just piping small, often generic, XML modules. We believe we obtain a good balance between ease of use and efficiency. For example, below we show an excerpt from a script that has been used in a loop across all documents to produce ready-to-index sets of documents:

```
cat $coll/$c.xml/$i |  xmlDel2Root -root DOC -t DOCNO I |
xmlwordend -trunc -t I -k SUBC SUBP ADJQ VBCJ VBPA VBPP |
xmlextrtxt I >> $coll/$c.doc/$name;
```

The xmlDel2Root module selects the XML sub trees to be moved to the root of the XML tree : at this stage, only DOCNO (doc identification) and I (analyzed document content in our IOTA POS format) XML sub trees are kept. The result is passed thought xmlwordend that deletes the POS tag at the end of words into the I sub trees and keeps only the selected one (the -k option). Finally, the remaining text is extracted from all sub trees from the I tag to be ready for the matrix construction which is our final indexing stage.

4.1   Collection Processing

The collections were processed in the following way. At first, all documents were analyzed using the Xerox Incremental Parser (XIP) [8, 9] for French and English. For latter processing with X- IOTA, the internal XIP format was transformed to XML. The next step is the classical term/document matrix construction. We have not used the dependency information provided by XIP for these experiments, but only the part of speech (POS) information. This POS information is used to filter meaningful terms: thus we do not need any stop-list, however, we still have used one in order to correct any mistakes in the analysis. We kept the following POS: all nouns, adjectives, and verbs in all forms. Notice that we have selected the lemmatized form of the analyzed word by the XIP parser and then we do not do any other stemming. This word transformation should be much more correct than the classical stemming done in IR. The final step is the matrix construction using the classical 'ltc' weighting scheme from the SMART system.

4.2   Query Processing

Only French queries have been processed. The queries are processed in the same way as the documents, and the XIP parser is used again. For example, here is the original query No 141:

```
Une lettre piégée pour Arabella Kiesbauer
Trouvez   des informations sur l'explosion d'une lettre
piégée dans le studio de la présentatrice Arabella Kiesbauer
de la chaîne de télévision PRO 7.
```

We have added a post filter that deletes all words that do not belong to the query itself such as 'trouver information'. The following XML is produced from this query:

```
<DOC>
  <DOCNO>C141</DOCNO>
  lettre piéger Arabella Kiesbauer explosion lettre piéger studio
  présentateur
  Arabella Kiesbauer chaîne télévision pro
</DOC>
```

The following initial vector is then produced:

```
<vector id="C141" size="10">
<c id="arabella" w="2"/>
<c id="chaîne" w="1"/>
<c id="explosion" w="1"/>
<c id="kiesbauer" w="2"/>
<c id="lettre" w="2"/>
<c id="piéger" w="2"/>
<c id="pro" w="1"/>
<c id="présentateur" w="1"/>
<c id="studio" w="1"/>
<c id="télévision" w="1"/>
</vector>
```

Each query term is then extended using the association thesaurus computed only on the SDA95 collection. The terms added have the arbitrary value of 0.1 because of the possible topic shift induced by this massive addition of terms. For this query, we obtain the following vector:

```
<vector id="C141" size="28">
<c id="arabella" w="2"/>
<c id="chaîne" w="1"/>
<c id="discount"  w="0.1"/>
<c id="rai"  w="0.1"/>
<c id="Telepiu"  w="0.1"/>
<c id="explosion" w="1"/>
<c id="wagon-citerne"  w="0.1"/>
<c id="déflagration"  w="0.1"/>
<c id="comète"  w="0.1"/>
<c id="kiesbauer" w="2"/>
<c id="lettre" w="2"/>
<c id="missive"  w="0.1"/>
<c id="piéger" w="2"/>
<c id="pro" w="1"/>
<c id="présentateur" w="1"/>
<c id="studio" w="1"/>
<c id="télévision" w="1"/>
<c id="sponsoring"  w="0.1"/>
<c id="vor"  w="0.1"/>
```

```
<c id="télé"   w="0.1"/>
<c id="téléspectateur"   w="0.1"/>
<c id="direct"   w="0.1"/>
<c id="rediffusion"   w="0.1"/>
<c id="retransmission"   w="0.1"/>
<c id="téléjournal"   w="0.1"/>
<c id="divertissement"   w="0.1"/>
<c id="radiodiffusion"   w="0.1"/>
<c id="décodeur"   w="0.1"/>
</vector>
```

Due to a processing error, there may be multiple versions of the same term with different weights in a query. This is possible because many thesaurus associations have a non-empty overlapping associated terms set. The result is that only the maximum weight is taken into account in the matching process. We probably should investigate a clever combination choice for this.

In this query example, the following very good associations have been used from the association thesaurus:

```
<entry id="lettre">
  <equiv>missive</equiv>
</entry>
```

Some other words like 'chaîne' (TV channel) are associated with both some good terms like 'rai', 'téléspectateur', 'télévision', and also with terms that are out of the query context like 'discount'.

```
<entry id="chaîne">
  <equiv>discount</equiv>
  <equiv>rai</equiv>
  <equiv>téléspectateur</equiv>
  <equiv>télévision</equiv>
  <equiv>Telepiu</equiv>
</entry>
<entry id="explosion">
  <equiv>wagon-citerne</equiv>
  <equiv>déflagration</equiv>
  <equiv>comète</equiv>
</entry>
```

We have not measured the objective quality of this fully automatic built association thesaurus, but a lot of examples we have looked at, tend to demonstrate that associations are of a surprising good quality and seem to be very meaningful. For the bilingual experiment, we have translated the French extended query using the merged dictionary. Here is part of the final English query vector.

```
<vector id="C141" size="145" >
<c id="arabella" w="2"/>
<c id="warp"  w="0.1"/>
<c id="pull chain"  w="0.1"/>
<c id="chain"  w="0.1"/>
<c id="P.C."  w="0.1"/>
<c id="lengthwise grain"  w="0.1"/>
<c id="catena"  w="0.1"/>
<c id="range"  w="0.1"/>
<c id="shackles"  w="0.1"/>
<c id="sequence"  w="0.1"/>
<c id="sound system"  w="0.1"/>
<c id="string"  w="0.1"/>
<c id="high-fidelity system"  w="0.1"/>
<c id="network"  w="0.1"/>
<c id="chain letter"  w="0.1"/>
<c id="polyline"  w="0.1"/>
<c id="channel"  w="0.1"/>
<c id="audio system"  w="0.1"/>
<c id="shackle"  w="0.1"/>
<c id="warp for yarn-beam"  w="0.1"/>
<c id="train"  w="0.1"/>
<c id="discount" w="0.1"/>
<c id="rai" w="0.1"/>
<c id="TViewer"  w="0.1"/>
<c id="viewer"  w="0.1"/>
<c id="color-TV viewer"  w="0.1"/>
<c id="television viewer"  w="0.1"/>
<c id="televiewer"  w="0.1"/>
<c id="TV"  w="0.1"/>
<c id="Tee-Vee"  w="0.1"/>
<c id="television broadcasting"  w="0.1"/>
<c id="tellies"  w="0.1"/>
<c id="telly"  w="0.1"/>
....
<c id="explosion"  w="0.1"/>
<c id="shot"  w="0.1"/>
<c id="burst"  w="0.1"/>
<c id="tank wagon"  w="0.1"/>
<c id="rail tanker"  w="0.1"/>
<c id="tanker"  w="0.1"/>
<c id="rail tank car"  w="0.1"/>
<c id="tank car"  w="0.1"/>
<c id="air blast"  w="0.1"/>
```

```
<c id="explosion"  w="0.1"/>
<c id="flash fire"  w="0.1"/>
<c id="deflagration"  w="0.1"/>
...
```

This method tends to produce very large queries, so we expect more to emphasis recall than precision.

5   Runs and Results

We submitted two runs for our participation: monolingual French queries[1] and bilingual French queries[2] for English documents. The average precision for the monolingual run (0.3287) is much lower than the best result of Neuchâtel (0.5450). Results for the bilingual task are also low. The loss of quality using the translated query (from 0.3287 to 0.1438 average precision), is not surprising because of the uncontrolled translation of the extended original French query using a big dictionary. However, we have used the classical vector space model, and this does not seem to be a correct choice compared with the results of other modeling approaches.

The recall for the monolingual task is quite high with 92% of documents retrieved. It falls down to 71% with the cross-lingual part, but this a good score compared to some other participants. In fact, we have tested massive query expansion rather than precise query translation. Thus, our approach supports recall better than precision. Concerning classical IR text treatment, we deliberately do not use any stem reduction except the one provided by the XIP analyzer. We have certainly missed some possible morphological links, and would like to have a better control of the 'link' produced by strong words suffix truncation. These links could be added to the computed thesaurus, by a contextual morphological derivation.

6   Conclusion

We have chosen to test monolingual query expansion followed by a translation of the extended query. Despite we are not among the best, we still believe in the introduction of NLP methods in the IR indexing process with global statistical measures like the one used in an association thesaurus. Our results cannot be considered as conclusive, as we do not take into account the influence of the model, and we have not done anything special for the translation. We would like to further investigate our approach by building and aligning multilingual association thesauri with other good sources of information.

---

[1] 2003CLIPSMONFR01.
[2] 2003CLIPSFRENG01.

References

1. Rakesh Agrawal and Giuseppe Psaila: Fast algorithms for mining association rules. In 20th Conference on Very Large Databases, Santiago, Chile, (1994) 487–499.
2. Chevallet, Jean-Pierre: Building thesaurus from manual sources and automatic scanned texts. In 2nd International Conference Adaptive Hypermedia and Adaptive Web Based Systems, Malaga, Spain (2002) 95–104.
3. Chevallet, Jean-Pierre: Technical aspects of thesaurus construction in TIPS. Technical report (2002).
4. Usama M. Fayyad, Gregory Piatetsky-Shapiro, Padhraic Smyth, and Ramasamy Uthurusamy: Advances in Knowledge Discovery and Data Mining. AAAI Press, ISBN 0-262-56097-6, (1996).
5. Mohamed Hatem Haddad, Jean Pierre Chevallet, and Marie France Bruandet: Relations between terms discovered by association rules. In 4th European conference on Principles and Practices of Knowledge Discovery in Databases PKDD'2000, Workshop on Machine Learning and Textual Information Access, Lyon France (2000).
6. Peat Helen J and Peter Willett. The limitation of term co-occurrence data for query expension in document retrieval systems. Journal of the American Society for Information Science (JASIS), 5(42):378–383, 1991.
7. Yufeng Jing and Bruce Croft. An association thesaurus for information retrieval. In Proceedings of RIAO'94 (1994) 146– 160.
8. Salah A t Mokhtar and Jean-Pierre Chanod. Incremental finite-state parsing. In Proceedings of Applied Natural Language Processing, Washington (1997).
9. Salah A t Mokhtar, Jean-Pierre Chanod, and Claude Roux. A multi-input dependency parser. In Seventh International Workshop on Parsing Technologies, Beijing (2001) 17–19.

Two-Stage Refinement of Query Translation in a Pivot Language Approach to Cross-Lingual Information Retrieval: An Experiment at CLEF 2003

Kazuaki Kishida[1] and Noriko Kando[2]

[1] Surugadai University, 698 Azu, Hanno, Saitama 357-8555, Japan
kishida@surugadai.ac.jp
[2] National Institute of Informatics (NII), Tokyo 101-8430, Japan
kando@nii.ac.jp

Abstract. This paper reports experimental results of cross-lingual information retrieval from German to Italian. The authors are concerned with CLIR in cases where available language resources are very limited. Thus transitive translation of queries using English as a pivot language was used to search Italian document collections for German queries without any direct bilingual dictionary or MT system for these two languages. In order to remove irrelevant translations produced by the transitive translation, we propose a new disambiguation technique, in which two stages of refinement of query translation are executed. Basically, this refinement is based on the idea of pseudo relevance feedback. Our experimental results show that the two-stage refinement method is able to significantly improve search performance of bilingual IR using a pivot language.

1 Introduction

This paper aims at reporting our experiment in cross-language IR (CLIR) from German to Italian at CLEF 2003. A fundamental interest of our research group is in CLIR between two languages with very limited translation resources since it is not yet easy to obtain sufficient language resources for direct translation between East Asian languages (i.e., Chinese, Japanese and Korean). Therefore, for our challenge at CLEF 2003, it was supposed that there is:

- no bilingual dictionary between German and Italian
- no machine translation (MT) system between German and Italian
- no parallel corpus between German and Italian
- no corpus written in the language of query (i.e., no German corpus)

We thus decided to explore a method for dictionary-based query translation using English as a pivot language because translation resources between English and other languages are often easily obtained, not only in the European environment, but also in the East Asian environment. In this study, only two relatively small dictionaries of German to English (G to E) and English to Italian (E to I), which are readily available on the Internet, are employed as resources.

C. Peters et al. (Eds.): CLEF 2003, LNCS 3237, pp. 253–262, 2004.
© Springer-Verlag Berlin Heidelberg 2004

The possibility of some extraneous or irrelevant translations being unjustly produced by the dictionary-based approach is well-known [1]. Particularly, in the case of the pivot language approach, two consecutive steps of translation (e.g., German to English and English to Italian) often yield many irrelevant translation candidates because of double replacements of each word. This means that we need to use a translation disambiguation technique.

According to the assumption of our study, the only resource to be used for translation disambiguation is the target document collection (i.e., Italian document sets included in the CLEF test collection). We propose a new disambiguation technique in which pseudo relevance feedback is repeated in two stages to refine query translations using only target language collections. The purpose of this paper is to experimentally verify the effectiveness of this two-stage refinement technique using the test collection of CLEF 2003.

This paper is organized as follows. In Section 2, we will review some previous work on the translation disambiguation techniques and the pivot language approach. In Section 3, the technique of two-stage refinement of query translation will be introduced. Section 4 will describe our system used in the experiment of CLEF 2003. In Section 5, the results will be reported.

2 Previous Works

2.1 Translation Disambiguation Techniques

In the CLIR field, various ideas or techniques for translation disambiguation have been proposed. Some proposals have regarded the exploration of methods that employ target language documents to identify extraneous or irrelevant translations. A typical approach is to use co-occurrence statistics of translation candidates according to the assumption that "the correct translations of query terms should co-occur in target language documents, and incorrect translations should tend not to co-occur" (Ballesteros and Croft [2]). Many studies have been attempted in line with this basic idea [3-9].

The fundamental procedure is as follows:

- Compute similarity degrees for all pairs of translation candidates based on co-occurrence frequencies in the target document collection.
- Select "correct" pairs of translation candidates according to the similarity degrees.

One of the difficulties in implementing the procedure is that computational complexity in selecting correct translations increases as the number of translation candidates grows. To alleviate this problem, Gao et al.[4] proposed an approximate algorithm for choosing optimal translations.

2.2 Pivot Language Approach

While so many languages are spoken in the world, bilingual resources are limited. There is no guarantee that useful resources will always be available for the combination of two languages that we need in a real situation. For example, it may be difficult to find bilingual resources in machine-readable form between Dutch and

Japanese. One of the solutions is to employ English as an intermediate (pivot) language, since English is an international language, and it is reasonably expected that bilingual dictionaries or MT systems with English are prepared for many languages.

The basic approach is transitive translation of a query using two bilingual resources (see Ballesteros [10]). If two MT systems or two bilingual dictionaries of Dutch to English and English to Japanese are available, we can translate a Dutch query into Japanese without a direct Dutch-Japanese resource. This approach has already been attempted by some researchers [11-15].

When using two bilingual dictionaries successively for query translation, it is crucial to solve translation ambiguity because of the possibility of many extraneous or irrelevant search terms being generated by the two translation steps. Suppose that an English term obtained from a bilingual dictionary of the source language to English was an irrelevant translation. Inevitably, all terms listed under the English term in the bilingual dictionary from English to the target language would also be irrelevant. Therefore, more irrelevant translations are generated in the pivot language approach than in the standard single-step translation process.

In order to solve the ambiguity, Ballesteros [10] attempted to apply the co-occurrence frequency-based method, query expansion, and so on. Meanwhile, Gollins and Sanderson [16] proposed a technique called "lexical triangulation" in which two pivot languages are used independently, and they attempted to remove erroneous translations by taking only translations in common from two ways of transitive translation using two pivot languages.

3 Two-Stage Refinement of Translations

3.1 Translation Disambiguation Stage

Translation disambiguation techniques based on term co-occurrence statistics may be useful in the situation that our study is presupposing, since the technique makes use of only the target document collection as a resource for disambiguation. However, as already mentioned, computational complexity is fairly high. Also, it should be noted that term co-occurrence frequencies can be considered as macro-level statistics of the entire document collection. This means that disambiguation based on the statistics may lead to false combinations of translation candidates (see Yamabana et al. [3]). Even if two terms A and B are statistically associated in general (i.e., in the entire collection), the association is not always valid in a given query.

Therefore, in this study, the authors decided to use an alternative disambiguation technique, which is not based on term co-occurrence statistics. First, we define mathematical notations such that:

s_j : terms in the source query ($j = 1,2,...,m$)

T_j : a set of translations in the pivot language for the j-th term s_j

T'_j : a set of translations in the target language for all terms included in the set T_j

By the transitive translation process using two bilingual dictionaries, it is easy to obtain a set of translated query terms in the target language with no disambiguation such that:

$$T = T_1' \cup T_2' \cup ... \cup T_m' \qquad (1)$$

The procedure of disambiguation we propose is to search the target document collection for the set of terms T, and then select the most frequently appearing term in the top-ranked documents from each set of T_j' ($j = 1,2,...,m$) respectively. The basic assumption is that a "correct" combination of each translation from distinct original search terms tends to occur together in a single document in the target collection. If so, such documents are expected to be ranked higher in the result of a search for the set T.

Suppose that we have three sets of translations in the target language as follows:

- T_1': term A, term B, term C
- T_2': term D, term E
- T_3': term F, term G

It is also assumed that a combination of term A, D and F is correct, and the other terms are irrelevant. In such a situation, we can reasonably expect that the irrelevant terms will not appear together in each document because of the low probability of such irrelevant terms being related. Meanwhile, the "correct" combination of term A, D and F would tend to appear in documents more frequently than any combinations including irrelevant translations. Therefore, the documents containing the "correct" combination should have a higher score for ranking.

To detect such a combination from the result of the initial search for the set T, it would be sufficient to use document frequencies of each translation in the set of top-ranked documents. That is, we can choose a term $\tilde{t}_j$ for each T_j' ($j = 1,2,...,m$) such that

$$\tilde{t}_j = \arg\max_t r_t, \ t \in T_j', \qquad (2)$$

where r_t is the number of top-ranked documents including the term t. Finally, we obtain a set of m translations through the disambiguation process, i.e.,

$$\tilde{T} = \{\tilde{t}_1, \tilde{t}_2, ..., \tilde{t}_m\}. \qquad (3)$$

Ideally, we should make use of co-occurrence frequencies of all combinations of translation candidates in the set of top-ranked documents. However, the computational cost is expected to be higher since we need to compile the statistics dynamically for each search run. A solution for avoiding the complexity is to count only simple frequencies instead of co-occurrences. That is, if the "correct" combination of translations appears often, the simple frequencies of each translation would naturally also become high. Equation (2) is based on this hypothesis.

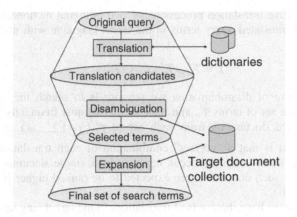

Fig. 1. Two-stage refinement of translation

3.2 Query Expansion Stage

In the previous stage, translation ambiguity was resolved, and the final m search terms in the target language were determined. We can consider this stage as a process for improving search precision. In the next stage, enhancement of recall should be attempted since some synonyms or related terms will have been removed in the previous stage.

According to Ballesteros and Croft [1,2], we execute a standard post-translation query expansion using a pseudo relevance feedback (PRF) technique in which new terms to be added to the query are selected on the basis of weight indicating the degree of importance of the term. In this study, we use a standard formula based on the probabilistic model for estimating the weight such that

$$w_t = r_t \times \log \frac{(r_t + 0.5)(N - R - n_t + r_t + 0.5)}{(N - n_t + 0.5)(R - r_t + 0.5)} \tag{4}$$

where N is the total number of documents, R is the number of relevant documents, and n_t is the number of documents including term t. It should be noted that, in PRF, the set of relevant documents is assumed to be the set of some top-ranked documents from the initial search. Therefore, r_t is defined as the same as before (see Equation (2)). We denote the expanded term set by the method as $\tilde{T}'$.

To sum up, the method we propose for refining the result of query translation consists of two stages: (a) translation disambiguation and (b) post-translation query expansion. The detailed procedure is as follows (see also Fig. 1):

1. Obtain a set of translations T (see Equation (1)) by transitive translation
2. Search the target document collection for the set T (i.e., initial search)
3. Select a single translation from each set of candidates respectively according to the document frequency in the top-ranked documents from the initial search, and obtain a new set $\tilde{T}$ (see Equation (3)) *(disambiguation stage)*
4. Search the target document collection for the set $\tilde{T}$ (i.e., second search)

5. Add terms according to each weight shown as Equation (4) (*query expansion stage*)
6. Finally, search the target document collection for the expanded set of terms $\tilde{T}'$ (i.e., third search)

4 System Description

4.1 Text Processing

Both German and Italian texts (in documents and queries) were basically processed by the following steps: (1) identifying tokens (2) removing stopwords (3) lemmatization (4) stemming. In addition, for German texts, decomposition of compound words was attempted on the basis of an algorithm for longest matching against headwords included in the German to English dictionary in machine readable form. For example, a German word, "Briefbombe," is broken down into two headwords listed in the German to English dictionary, "Brief" and "Bombe," according to a rule that only the longest headwords included in the original compound word are extracted from it. If a substring of "Brief" or "Bombe" is also listed in the dictionary, the substring is not used as a separated word.

We downloaded free dictionaries (German to English and English to Italian) from the Internet[1]. Also, stemmers and stopword lists for German and Italian were available through the Snowball project[2]. Stemming for English was performed using the original Porter's algorithm [17].

4.2 Transitive Translation Procedure

Before executing transitive translation by two bilingual dictionaries, all terms included in the bilingual dictionaries were normalized using the same stemming and lemmatization procedures as were applied to the texts of documents and queries. The actual translation process is a simple replacement, i.e., each normalized German term in a query was replaced with a set of corresponding normalized English words, and similarly, each English word was replaced with the corresponding Italian words. As a result, for each query, a set of normalized Italian words, i.e., T in Equation (1), was obtained. If no corresponding headword was included in the dictionaries (German-English or English-Italian), the unknown word was transmitted directly to the next step without any change.

Next, refinement of the set T through the two stages described in the previous section was executed. The number of top-ranked documents was set to 100 in both stages, and in the query expansion stage, the top 30 terms, ranked in decreasing order of term weights (Equation (4)), were added.

---

[1] http://www.freelang.net/
[2] http://snowball.tartarus.org/

Let y_t be the frequency of a given term in the query. If the top-ranked term was already included in the set of search terms, the term frequency in the query was changed to $1.5 \times y_t$. If not, the term frequency was set to 0.5 (i.e., $y_t = 0.5$).

Furthermore, in order to comparatively evaluate the performance of our two-stage refinement method, we decided to use commercial MT software provided by a Japanese company, "Jx9 for Windows."[3] In this case, first of all, the original German query was entered into the software. The software automatically executes German to English translation and then English to Italian translation (i.e., a kind of transitive translation). The resulting Italian text from the software was processed according to the procedure described in section 4.1, and finally, a set of normalized Italian words was obtained for each query. In the case of MT translation, only post-translation query expansion was executed with the same procedure and parameters as the case of dictionary-based translation.

4.3 Search Algorithm and Runs

The well-known BM25 of the Okapi formula [18] was used for computing each document score in all searches of this study. We executed three runs in which only the <DESCRIPTION> field in each query was used, and submitted the results to the organizers of CLEF 2003.

5 Experimental Results

5.1 Basic Statistics

The Italian collections include 157,558 documents in total. The average document length is 181.86 words.

5.2 System Error

Unfortunately, a non-trivial system error was detected after submission of results, i.e., a bug in our source code, only the last term within the set of search terms contributed to the calculation of document scores. Inevitably, search performance of all runs we submitted was very low.

5.3 Results of Runs Conducted After Submission

Therefore, the authors corrected the source code and attempted again to perform some search runs after submission of results to the organizers of CLEF. Six types of runs were conducted as shown in Table 1, which also indicates each mean average precision value calculated by using the relevance judgment file. The recall-precision curves of the six runs are presented in Figure 2. It should be noted that each value represented in Table 1 and Figure 2 was calculated for 51 topics for which one or more relevant documents are included in the Italian collections.

---

[3] http://www.crosslanguage.co.jp/english/

As shown in Table 1, MT outperforms dictionary-based translation significantly. It also turns out that the disambiguation technique based on term frequency moderately improves effectiveness of the dictionary-based translation method, i.e., the mean average precision with disambiguation is .207 in comparison with .190 in the case of no disambiguation. Specifically, Table 1 indicates that our technique of two-stage refinement has a strong effect on enhancement of search performance since the mean average precision of search with no disambiguation and no expansion by PRF is only .143, which is significantly lower than .207 in the case of searches through the two-stage refinement.

However, we can also point out that there is a large difference in performance between MT and the two-stage refinement. The reason may be attributed to differences in quality and coverage of vocabulary between the commercial MT software and free dictionaries downloaded from the Internet. Even if this is true, we need to modify the two-stage refinement method so that its performance level approaches that of MT.

For example, in Figure 2, at the levels of recall over 0.7, the search with expansion and no disambiguation is superior to that with disambiguation. This may be due to the fact that our disambiguation method selects only one translation and consequently may remove some useful synonyms or related terms. A simple solution might be to choose two or more translations instead of directly using Equation (2). Although it is difficult to determine the optimal number of translations to be selected, multiple translations for each source term may improve search recall.

Table 1. Mean average precison of runs executed after submission (51 topics)

Translation method		Expansion by PRF	
		done	none
MT		.301	.281
Dictionary	With disambiguation	.207	.181
	Without disambiguation	.190	.143

6 Concluding Remarks

This paper reports the results of our experiment in CLIR from German to Italian, in which English was used as a pivot language. In particular, two-stage refinement of query translation was employed to remove irrelevant terms in the target language produced by transitive translation using two bilingual dictionaries in succession.

It resulted that

- our two-stage refinement method significantly improves retrieval performance of
- dictionary-based bilingual IR using a pivot language, and
- the performance is inferior to that of MT-based searches.

By choosing two or more search terms in the disambiguation stage, it is possible that our method would become more effective.

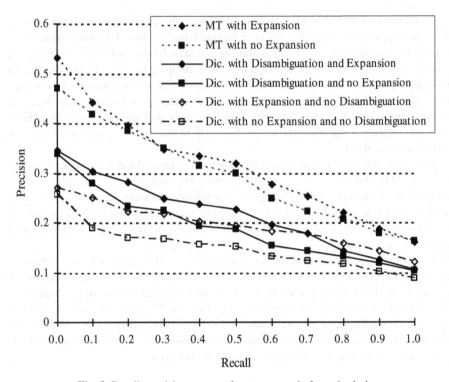

Fig. 2. Recall-precision curves of runs executed after submission

References

1. Ballesteros, L.A., Croft, W. B.: Phrasal translation and query expansion techniques for cross-language information retrieval. In Proceedings of the 20th ACM SIGIR conference on Research and Development in Information Retrieval (1977) 84-91
2. Ballesteros, L., Croft, W.B.: Resolving ambiguity for cross-language retrieval. In Proceedings of the 21st ACM SIGIR conference on Research and Development in Information Retrieval (1988) 64-71
3. Yamabana, K., Muraki, K., Doi, S., Kamei, S.: A language conversion front-end for cross-language information retrieval. In G. Grefenstette (Ed.) Cross-Language Information Retrieval, Kluwer, Boston (1998) 93-104
4. Gao, J., Nie, J. Y., Xun, E. X., Zhang, J., Zhou, M., Huang, C.: Improving query translation for cross-language information retrieval using statistical models. In Proceedings of 24th ACM SIGIR conference on Research and Development in Information Retrieval (2001) 96-104
5. Lin, C. J., Lin, W. C., Bian, G. W., Chen, H. H.: Description of the NTU Japanese-English cross-lingual information retrieval system used for NTCIR workshop. In Proceedings of the First NTCIR Workshop on Research in Japanese Text Retrieval and Term Recognition, National Institute of Informatics, Tokyo (1999) http://research.nii.ac.jp/ntcir/workshop/

6. Sadat, F., Maeda, A., Yoshikawa, M., Uemura, S.: Query expansion techniques for the CLEF Bilingual track. In C. Peters et al. (Eds.) Evaluation of Cross-Language Information Retrieval Systems. Lecture Notes in Computer Science, Vol.2406 Springer-Verlag, Berlin Heidelberg New York (2002) 177-184

7. Adriani, M.: English-Dutch CLIR using query translation techniques. In C. Peters et al. (Eds.) Evaluation of Cross-Language Information Retrieval Systems. Lecture Notes in Computer Science, Vol.2406 Springer-Verlag, Berlin Heidelberg New York (2002) 219-225

8. Qu, Y., Grefenstette, G., Evans, D. A.: Resolving translation ambiguity using monolingual corpora: a report on Clairvoyance CLEF-2002 experiments. In Working Notes for the CLEF-2002 Workshop (2002) 115-126.

9. Seo, H. C., Kim, S. B., Kim, B. I., Rim, H. C., Lee, S. Z.: KUNLP system for NTCIR-3 English-Korean cross-language information retrieval. In Proceedings of the Third NTCIR Workshop on Research in Information Retrieval, Automatic Text Summarization and Question Answering, National Institute of Informatics, Tokyo (2003) http://research.nii.ac.jp/ntcir/workshop/

10. Ballesteros, L. A.: Cross-language retrieval via transitive translation. In W.B.Croft (Ed.) Advances in Information Retrieval: Recent Research from the Center for Intelligent Information Retrieval, Kluwer, Boston (2000) 203-234

11. Franz, M., McCarley, J. S., Roukos, S: Ad hoc and multilingual information retrieval at IBM. In Proceedings of the TREC-7, National Institute of Standards and Technology, Gaithersburg (1999) http://trec.nist.gov/pubs/

12. Gey, F. C., Jiang, H., Chen, A., Larson, R. R.: Manual queries and machine translation in cross-language retrieval at TREC-7. In Proceedings of the TREC-7, National Institute of Standards and Technology, Gaithersburg (1999) http://trec.nist.gov/pubs/

13. Hiemstra, D., Kraaij, W.: Twenty-one at TREC-7: ad-hoc and cross-language track. In Proceedings of the TREC-7, National Institute of Standards and Technology, Gaithersburg (1999) http://trec.nist.gov/pubs/

14. Chen, A., Gey, F. C.: Experiments on cross-language and patent retrieval at NTCIR-3 workshop. In Proceedings of the Third NTCIR Workshop on Research in Information Retrieval, Automatic Text Summarization and Question Answering. National Institute of Informatics, Tokyo (2003) http://research.nii.ac.jp/ntcir/workshop/

15. Lin, W. C., Chen, H.H.: Description of NTU approach to Multilingual Information retrieval. In Proceedings of the Third NTCIR Workshop on Research in Information Retrieval, Automatic Text Summarization and Question Answering. National Institute of Informatics, Tokyo (2003) http://research.nii.ac.jp/ntcir/workshop/

16. Gollins, T., Sanderson, M.: Improving cross language information retrieval with triangulated translation. In Proceedings of the 24th ACM SIGIR conference on Research and Development in Information Retrieval (2001) 90-95

17. Porter, M.F.: An algorithm for suffix stripping. Program. 14 (1980) 130-137

18. Robertson, S. E., Walker, S., Jones, S., Hancock-Beaulieu, M. M., Gatford, M.: Okapi at TREC-3. In Proceedings of TREC-3. National Institute of Standards and Technology, Gaithersburg (1995) http://trec.nist.gov/pubs/

Regular Sound Changes for Cross-Language
Information Retrieval

Michael P. Oakes and Souvik Banerjee

University of Sunderland, School of Computing and Technology,
Sir Tom Cowie Campus at St. Peter's, Sunderland SR6 0DD, United Kingdom
{Michael.Oakes, Souvik.Banerjee}@sunderland.ac.uk

Abstract. The aim of this project is the automatic conversion of query terms in
one language into their equivalents in a second, historically related, language,
so that documents in the second language can be retrieved. The method is to
compile lists of regular sound changes which occur between related words of a
language pair, and substitute these in the source language words to generate
target language words. For example, if we know *b* in Italian often corresponds
with a *v* in Spanish, an unaccented *o* in Italian with *ó* in Spanish, and a terminal
e in Italian is replaced with a null in Spanish, we can construct the Spanish
word *autómovil* (car) from the Italian *automobile*.

1 Introduction

Buckley et al. [1] wished to determine how effective cross-lingual information retrieval (CLIR) could be with a minimal amount of linguistic information. They made
no use of dictionaries, but instead treated the English query words as "potentially misspelled French words". In order to use a set of English query words to retrieve French
documents, they first stored all the distinct vocabulary (word types) found at least five
times in the entire set of French documents in a trie. They considered two equivalence
classes of characters, one being vowels, where any combination of vowels could be
substituted for any other, the other being *k* sounds, where any combination of *c-k-qu*
could substitute for any other. Thus *music* and *musique* would be considered equivalent. If it was possible to transform any of the English query words into any of the
words in the trie of French words using either of the allowable substitutions, or by
adding or deleting one letter, those French words were added to the query. The
method proposed in this paper is novel in that it also incorporates regular, linguistically attested, sound changes between historically related languages.

2 First Experimental Run: Cognates Sought by Edit Distance

For our basic method, we assume that cognate words are vocabulary items which
occur in two or more languages, such that they have both similar meanings and simi-

C. Peters et al. (Eds.): CLEF 2003, LNCS 3237, pp. 263–270, 2004.

lar orthography. The degree to which two words, one Italian and its Spanish equivalent, are orthographically similar can be estimated using edit distance, which has for some time been used for automatic spelling correction [2]. Character level alignment may be performed by the technique of dynamic programming. The difference between two word forms (called the edit distance) is taken to be the smallest number of operations required to transform one word into the other. The allowable operations include substitution (a single character in one word is replaced by a single character in the other), deletion of a single character from the first word, and insertion of a single character into the second word. For example, we can align the words *automobile* and *automóvil* as shown in Figure 1.

```
e     -> 0    deletion :
l     -> l    match :
i     -> i    match :
b     -> v    substitution :
o     -> ó    substitution :
m     -> m    match :
o     -> o    match :
t     -> t    match :
u     -> u    match :
a     -> a    match :
edit distance = 3
```

Fig. 1. Character-level alignment of *automobile* and *automóvil*

In order to transform the Italian *automobile* into the Spanish *automóvil*, three operations (two substitutions and a deletion) are required, and thus the edit distance is 3. The technique of dynamic programming finds the alignment which minimises the edit distance. To convert the edit distance into a measure of the closeness between two words, we use formula (1) [3]. This matching coefficient will be 1 for two identically spelled words, and 0 for two words with no characters at all in common.

$$matching\_coefficient = 1 - \frac{edit\_dis\tan ce}{length\_of\_longer\_word} \tag{1}$$

A vocabulary list of over 56,000 words was produced consisting of all the Spanish words occurring twice or more in a subset of the Spanish document set. Program clef5.c was written to align each word in the Italian query sets with each Spanish word in the lexicon in turn, using dynamic programming. A subjectively assigned threshold of 0.8 was chosen, such that any word in the Spanish lexicon with a matching coefficient of 0.8 or more with respect to the Italian query word was assumed to be a possible translation of that query word. This method is similar to that used by the Kantrowitz et al. stemmer [4], an edit distance stemmer with complex edits corresponding to the most common suffixes. The first five Italian queries are shown in Figure 2.

```
*c141 lettera bomba per kiesbauer
*c142 christo impacchetta parlamento tedesco
*c143 conferenza pechino sulle donne
*c144 ribellioni sierra leone diamanti
*c145 importazioni giapponesi riso
```

Fig. 2. Five original Italian queries

```
*c141
[bomba] [bomba] match = 1.000000
[bomba] [bombas] match = 0.833333
[bomba] [bombay] match = 0.833333
*c142
[christo] [christa] match = 0.857143
[christo] [christi] match = 0.857143
[christo] [cristo] match = 0.857143
[christo] [hristo] match = 0.857143
[parlamento] [apartamento] match = 0.818182
[parlamento] [palamento] match = 0.900000
[parlamento] [parlament] match = 0.900000
[parlamento] [parlamento] match = 1.000000
[parlamento] [parlamentos] match = 0.909091
*c143
[conferenza] [conferencia] match = 0.818182
[donne] [donner] match = 0.833333
*c144
[sierra] [cierra] match = 0.833333
[sierra] [pierra] match = 0.833333
[sierra] [serra] match = 0.833333
[sierra] [sierra] match = 1.000000
[sierra] [tierra] match = 0.833333
[leone] [leone] match = 1.000000
[leone] [leonel] match = 0.833333
[leone] [leones] match = 0.833333
[diamanti] [diamant] match = 0.875000
[diamanti] [diamante] match = 0.875000
*c145
[importazioni] [importacion] match = 0.833333
```

Fig. 3. Translation of Italian queries into Spanish queries

The Italian query sets were "translated" into Spanish using program clef5.c, as shown in figure 3. Query words of fewer than 4 characters were stoplisted. Query c141 shows three types of Spanish terms picked up in response to the Italian query word *bomba* (bomb). Firstly, we find an exact match with *bomba*, the correct Spanish equivalent. We also get an above threshold match with *bombas*, a grammatical variant (plural) of *bomba*. Finally we pick up the incorrect translation *Bombay*, a source of noise in our system. The overall Spanish query to be presented to the search engine is *bomba, bombas, Bombay*. No Spanish query terms were found corresponding to the Italian words *lettera* or *Kiesbauer*.

3   Second Experimental Run: Cognates Sought by Regular Sound Changes

For the second experimental run, we used a more linguistically accurate definition of cognates, namely that cognate words are vocabulary items which occur in two or more historically related languages, such that they have similar meanings, and one can be transformed into the other by a predictable series of phonological changes. For example, Nothofer [5] has manually produced tables showing the sound equivalences which occur in four languages spoken in or near the Indonesian island of Java, namely Javanese, Madurese, Malay and Sundanese, all of which originate from the common ancestor language Proto-Malayo-Javanic (PMJ). One example of such an equivalence is Javanese *d* = Madurese *jh* = Malay *j* = Sundanese *j*, as in the words for *road, dalan, jhalan, jalan* and *jalan* respectively. Such a system of sound correspondences was first described for Indo-European languages where it is referred to as Grimm's Law, and it was later shown that such systems are found in all language families [6]. The task of identifying regular sound changes in bilingual word lists has been described by Guy [7] as "Given a sample word list from two related languages, extract the probable rules for predicting any word of one language from that of the other".

To find the regular sound changes found in a given language pair, the starting point is a bilingual word list where each word in one language is aligned with its translation. Single character substitutions can be identified using the Wagner & Fischer edit distance algorithm described in section 1. However, in their work on bilingual sentence alignment, Gale & Church [8] introduced additional operations into the dynamic programming algorithm. While the original algorithm allows only for single character insertions, deletions and substitutions, Gale and Church also con-sidered for example 2:1 correspondence, denoting that two sentences of one language correspond with just one of the other. They also allowed for the fact that some opera-tions are more commonly encountered in real data that others, by assigning higher edit distances to less frequently encountered operations. In program Jakarta.c [9] the allowed operations correspond to the list of the types of sound change which typically occur between related languages throughout the world given by Crowley

abbreviazione	abreviatura
aggettivo	adjetivo
amministrazione	administración
avverbio	adverbio
agricoltura	agricultura
anatomia	anatomía
architectura	arquitectura
automobile	automóvil
biologia	biología
botanica	botánica

Fig. 4. Sample word pairs examined for regular sound changes

[10] in Chapter 2. These include single character operations, operations with higher cardinality, operations which can only involve certain characters such as vowels, and operations which can only take place at certain positions (such as initial) in the two words. Program Jakarta.c was used to collate the sound changes discovered in a list of 63 word pairs taken from the introductions to Collins Gem Italian and Spanish dictionaries, examples of which are shown in Figure 4 below:

The sound changes found in the word pair *aggetivo* and *adjetivo* are shown in figure 5. These changes were a fusion of the double *t* in Italian to a single *t* in Spanish, and the dissimilation of the *gg* (producing a single sound) into *dj* (producing two separate sounds) in Spanish. All word pairs in the bilingual list were compared in this way, and the changes were collated to produce the list shown in figure 6, which includes the number of instances where a character remained as itself. *0* represents a null character. Pairs of words which require an above threshold edit distance of three to transform one into the other are deemed not to be cognate (such as *abbreviazione* and *abbreviatura*), and do not contribute to the tally of discovered sound changes.

```
o    -> o  match :
v    -> v  match :
i    -> i  match :
tt   -> t  fusion :
e    -> e  match :
gg   -> dj dissimilation :
a    -> a  match :
cost = 2
```

Fig. 5. Alignment of *aggettivo* and *adjetivo*

Based on the sound changes seen in Figure 6, the basic edit distance program used for the first experimental run (clef5.c) was amended to form program sounds5.c which implements the following metric: a cost of 1 is assigned for each insertion, deletion or single character substitution not recognised as being regular, and a cost of 0 for each exact character match, deletion or single character substitution listed as being regular. The transformations regarded as being regular are shown in Figure 7. As for the first experimental run, each Italian query term was matched against the Spanish lexicon, and all Spanish terms matching the Italian terms with an above threshold coefficient were included as Spanish query terms. A slightly higher threshold of 0.85 was used for the second experimental run, as the incorporation of the regular sound changes meant that true cognates matched with slightly higher coefficients, and raising the threshold would reduce the noise caused by false cognates being selected. The first five Spanish query sets produced for the second experimental run are shown in Figure 8.

```
a    -> a    : 50
a    -> o    : 1
az   -> ac   : 1
b    -> b    : 6
c    -> c    : 18
d    -> d    : 1
e    -> é    : 1
e    -> 0    : 9
e    -> e    : 29
f    -> f    : 10
g    -> g    : 19
gg   -> dj   : 1
gg   -> uj   : 1
i    -> í    : 12
i    -> i    : 47
l    -> l    : 23
m    -> m    : 13
mm   -> m    : 1
n    -> n    : 23
o    -> ó    : 3
o    -> 0    : 1
o    -> o    : 35
o    -> u    : 4
p    -> p    : 6
q    -> q    : 1
r    -> r    : 26
s    -> s    : 8
ss   -> s    : 1
st   -> s    : 1
t    -> d    : 1
t    -> t    : 26
tt   -> ct   : 1
tt   -> t    : 1
u    -> ú    : 1
u    -> o    : 1
u    -> u    : 7
v    -> v    : 9
vv   -> dv   : 1
z    -> z    : 1
za   -> te   : 1
0    -> 0    : trivial
```

Fig. 6. Sound substitutions found in the bilingual word list

```
z -> c not initial
o -> u not initial
t -> c not initial
v -> d not initial
i -> í
o -> ó
u -> ú
g -> j not first or second character
delete terminal o
delete terminal e
```

Fig. 7. Sound changes used in the second experimental run

```
*c141
[lettera] [lectura] match = 0.857143
[lettera] [lecturas] match = 0.875000
[bomba] [bomba] match = 1.000000
[bomba] [bombas] match = 1.000000
*c142
[christo] [chris] match = 0.857143
[christo] [christa] match = 0.857143
[christo] [christi] match = 0.857143
[christo] [cristo] match = 0.857143
[christo] [hristo] match = 0.857143
[parlamento] [palamento] match = 0.900000
[parlamento] [parlament] match = 1.000000
[parlamento] [parlamento] match = 1.000000
[parlamento] [parlamentos] match = 1.000000
*c143
[conferenza] [conferencia] match = 0.909091
[conferenza] [conferencias] match = 0.916667
[donne] [dunn] match = 1.000000
*c144
[sierra] [sierra] match = 1.000000
[sierra] [tierras] match = 0.857143
[leone] [leon] match = 1.000000
[leone] [león] match = 1.000000
[leone] [leone] match = 1.000000
[leone] [leones] match = 1.000000
[diamanti] [diamant] match = 0.875000
[diamanti] [diamante] match = 0.875000
[diamanti] [diamantes] match = 0.888889
*c145
[importazioni] [importacion] match = 0.916667
[importazioni] [importación] match = 0.916667
[importazioni] [importaciones] match = 0.923077
```

Fig. 8. Translation of Italian queries into Spanish queries using regular sound changes

4 The Search Engine

For both experimental runs, the task was to translate the Italian query sets to Spanish query sets, then match the Spanish query sets against the Spanish document set using a search engine. Our search engine uses a very simple algorithm. The Spanish query sets are submitted in turn, and for each document in the Spanish document set, a score of 1 is given for each word in the document which matches a word in the query set. The overall score for each document is normalised by dividing it by the number of words in the document, and the documents are ranked, so that those with the best normalised matching score are presented first.

5 Conclusions

We believe that our results could be improved in future in a number of ways. Firstly a larger Spanish vocabulary could be produced using the entire Spanish document set.

Secondly, we need to determine optimal matching coefficient thresholds which best discriminate between true and false word translations. Thirdly, we need a much larger bilingual word list to better determine the set of sound changes found in Italian and Spanish cognate words. Finally, program sounds5.c could be enhanced to allow regular multiple character substitutions.

We have demonstrated a method of generating target language query words using source language keywords and a list of regular sound changes, if the source and target languages are historically related, as they are in the case of Italian and Spanish, which share many cognate words. The differences with respect to Buckley et al.'s approach are firstly that linguistically motivated sound substitutions are used, and secondly that regular sound substitutions are used rather than just orthographic substitutions for homophones.

References

1. Buckley, C., Walz, J., Mitra, M. and Cardi, C.: Using Clustering and Super Concepts Within SMART. NIST Special Publication 500-240: The Sixth Text Retrieval Conference (TREC6), (2000). http://trec.nist.gov/pubs/trec6/t6_proceedings.html
2. Wagner, R. A. and Fischer, M. J.: The String to String Correction Problem. Journal of the ACM 21 (1974) 168
3. McEnery, A. M. and Oakes, M. P.: Sentence and Word Alignment in the CRATER Project. In: Thomas, J. and Short, M. (eds.): Using Corpora for Language Research. (1996) 211-231
4. Kantrowicz, M., Behrang, M. and Mittal, V.: Stemming and its Effects on TFIDF Ranking. Proceedings of the 23rd ACM SIGIR Conference, Athens, Greece. (2000)
5. Nothofer, B.: The Reconstruction of Proto-Malayo-Javanic. 's-Gravenhage:Martinus Nijhoff, (1975)
6. Bloomfield, L: On the Sound System of Central Algonquian. Language 1 (1925) 130-156
7. Guy, J. B. M.: An Algorithm for Identifying Cognates in Bilingual Word Lists and its Applicability to Machine Translation. Journal of Quantitative Linguistics 1(1) 34-42 (1994)
8. Gale, W. and Church, K. A.: Program for Aligning Sentences in Bilingual Corpora. Computational Linguistics 19(1) (1993) 75-102
9. Oakes, M. P.: Computer Estimation of Vocabulary in a Protolanguage from Word Lists in Four Daughter Languages. Journal of Quantitative Linguistics 7(3) (2000) 233-244
10. Crowley, T.: An Introduction to Historical Linguistics. Oxford University Press (1992)

Exeter at CLEF 2003: Experiments with Machine Translation for Monolingual, Bilingual and Multilingual Retrieval

Adenike M. Lam-Adesina and Gareth J. F. Jones*

Department of Computer Science,
University of Exeter EX4 4QF,
United Kingdom
{A.M.Lam-Adesina, G.J.F.Jones}@exeter.ac.uk

Abstract. The University of Exeter group participated in the monolingual, bilingual and multilingual-4 retrieval tasks this year. The main focus of our investigation this year was the small multilingual task comprising four languages, French, German, Spanish and English. We adopted a document translation strategy and tested four merging techniques to combine results from the separate document collections, as well as a merged collection strategy. For both the monolingual and bilingual tasks we explored the use of a parallel collection for query expansion and term weighting, and also experimented with extending synonym information to conflate British and American English word spellings.

1 Introduction

This paper describes our experiments for CLEF 2003. This year we participated in the monolingual, bilingual and multilingual-4 retrieval tasks. The main focus of our participation this year was the multilingual-4 task (being our first participation in this task), our submissions for the other two tasks build directly on our work from our past CLEF experiments [1][2]. Our official submissions included monolingual runs for Italian, German, French and Spanish, bilingual German to Italian and Italian to Spanish, and the multilingual-4 task comprising English, French, German and Spanish collections.

Our general approach was to use translation of both document collections and search topics into a common language. Thus the document collections were translated into English using Systran Version:3.0 Machine Translator (Sys MT), and all topics translated into English using either Systran Version:3.0 or Globalink Power Translation Pro Version 6.4 (Pro MT) machine translation (MT) systems.

Following from our successful use of Pseudo-Relevance Feedback methods in past CLEF exercises [1][2] and supported by past research work in text retrieval exercises

---

* Now at School of Computing, Dublin City University, Ireland.
  email: Gareth.Jones@computing.dcu.ie

C. Peters et al. (Eds.): CLEF 2003, LNCS 3237, pp. 271–285, 2004.

[3][4][5], we continued to use this method with success for improved retrieval. In our previous experimental work [6][1] we demonstrated the effectiveness of a new PRF method of term selection from document summaries, and found it to be more reliable than query expansion from full documents, this method is again used in the results reported here.

Following from last year, we again investigated the effectiveness of query expansion and term weight estimation from a parallel (pilot) collection [7], and found that caution needs to be exercised when using the collections to achieve improved retrieval performance for translated documents.

The remainder of this paper is structured as follows: in Section 2 we present our system setup and the information retrieval methods used, Section 3 describes the pilot search strategy, Section 4 presents and discusses experimental results and Section 5 concludes the paper with a discussion of our findings.

2 System Setup

The basis of our experimental system is the City University research distribution version of the Okapi system. The documents and search topics were processed to remove stopwords from a list of about 260 words; suffix stripped using the Okapi implementation of Porter stemming [8] and terms were indexed using a small set of synonyms. Since the English document collection for CLEF 2003 incorporates both British and American documents, the synonym table was expanded this year to include some common British words that have different American spelling.

2.1 Term Weighting

Document terms were weighted using the Okapi BM25 weighting scheme developed in [9] and further elaborated in [10] and calculated as follows,

$$cw(i, j) = \frac{cfw(i) \times tf(i, j) \times (K1 + 1)}{K1 \times ((1 - b) + (b \times ndl(j))) + tf(i, j)} \tag{1}$$

where $cw(i,j)$ represents the weight of term i in document j, $cfw(i)$ is the standard collection frequency weight, $tf(i,j)$ is the document term frequency, and $ndl(j)$ is the normalized document length. $ndl(j)$ is calculated as $ndl(j) = dl(j)/avdl$ where $dl(j)$ is the length of j and $avdl$ is the average document length for all documents. $k1$ and b are empirically selected tuning constants for a particular collection. $k1$ is designed to modify the degree of effect of $tf(i,j)$, while constant b modifies the effect of document length. High values of b imply that documents are long because they are verbose, while low values imply that they are long because they are multi-topic. In our experiments values of $k1$ and b are estimated based on the CLEF 2002 data.

2.2 Pseudo-Relevance Feedback

Retrieval of relevant documents is usually affected by short or imprecise queries. Relevance Feedback (RF) via query expansion aims to improve initial query statements by addition of terms from user assessed relevant documents. Expansion terms are selected using document statistics and aim to describe the information request better. Pseudo-Relevance Feedback (PRF) whereby relevant documents are assumed and used for query expansion is on average found to give improvement in retrieval performance although this is usually smaller than that observed for true user based RF.

The main implementation issue for PRF is the selection of appropriate expansion terms. In PRF problems can arise if assumed relevant documents are actually non-relevant thus leading to selection of inappropriate terms. However, the selection of such documents might suggest partial relevance, thus term selection from a relevant section or at least a related one might prove more beneficial.

Our query expansion method selects terms from summaries of the top 5 ranked documents. The summaries are generated using the method described in [6]. The summary generation method combines Luhn's keyword cluster method [11], a title terms frequency method [6], a location/header method [12] and the query-bias method from [13] to form an overall significance score for each sentence. For all our experiments we used the top 6 ranked sentences as the summary of each document. From this summary we collected all non-stopwords and ranked them using a slightly modified version of the Robertson selection value (rsv) [14] reproduced below. The top 20 terms were then selected in all our experiments.

$$rsv(i) = r(i) \times rw(i) \qquad (2)$$

where r(i) = number of relevant documents containing term i

rw(i) = the standard Robertson/Sparck Jones relevance weight [14] reproduced below

$$rw(i) = \log \frac{(r(i)+0.5)(N-n(i)-R+r(i)+0.5)}{(n(i)-r(i)+0.5)(R-r(i)+0.5)} \ .$$

where n(i) = the total number of documents containing term i

r(i) = the total number of relevant documents term i occurs in

R = the total number of relevant documents for this query

N = the total number of documents

In our modified version, potential expansion terms are selected from the summaries of the top 5 ranked documents, and ranked using statistics from assuming that the top 20 ranked documents from the initial run are relevant.

3 Pilot Searching

Query expansion is aimed at improving initial search topics in order to make them a better expression of the user's information need. This is normally achieved by adding terms selected from relevant or assumed relevant documents retrieved from the test collection to the initial query. However, it has been shown [15] that if additional documents are available these can be used in a pilot set for improved selection of expansion terms. The underlying assumption in this method is that a bigger collection than the test collection can help to achieve better term expansion and/or more accurate parameter estimation, and hopefully better retrieval and document ranking. Based on this assumption we explore the idea of pilot searching in our CLEF experiments.

The Okapi submissions for the TREC-7 [7] and TREC-8 [15] ad hoc tasks used the TREC disks 1-5, of which the document test set is a subset, for parameter estimation and query expansion. The method was found to be very effective. In order to explore the utility of pilot searching for our experiments, we used the TREC-7 and TREC-8 ad hoc document test collection itself for our pilot runs. This collection was used on its own for pilot searching without combination with the current CLEF test collections. The TREC and CLEF document collections are taken from the same time period, and the U.S. English CLEF 2003 English documents also appear within the TREC collection. The pilot searching procedure is carried out as follows:

1. Run the unexpanded initial query on the pilot collection using BM25 without feedback.
2. Extract terms from the summaries of the top R assumed relevant documents.
3. Select top ranked terms using (2) based on their distribution in the pilot collection.
4. Add desired number of selected terms to initial query.
5. Store equivalent pilot cfw(i) of search terms.
6. Either apply expanded query to the test collection and estimate term weights based on test collection, or apply expanded query with term weights estimated from pilot collection from the test collection.

4   Experimental Results

This section describes the establishment of the parameters of our experimental system and gives results from our investigations for the CLEF 2003 monolingual, bilingual and multilingual-4 tasks. We report procedures for system parameters selection, baseline retrieval results for all languages and translation systems without the application of feedback, and corresponding results after the application of different methods of feedback including results for term weight estimation from pilot collections. The CLEF 2003 topics consist of three fields: Title, Description and Narrative. All our experiments use the Title and the Description fields of the topics. For all runs we present the average precision results (Av.P), the % change from results for baseline no feedback runs (% chg.), and the number of relevant documents retrieved out of the total number of relevant in collection (Rel-Ret).

4.1   Selection of System Parameters

To set appropriate parameters for our runs development runs were carried out using the CLEF 2002 collections. For CLEF 2003 more documents were added to all individual collections, and thus we are assuming that these parameters are suitable for these modified collections as well. The Okapi parameters were set as follows k1=1.4 b=0.6. For all our PRF runs, 5 documents were assumed relevant for term selection and document summaries comprised the best scoring 6 sentences in each case. Where the length of sentence was less than 6, half of the total number of sentences was chosen. The rsv values to rank the potential expansion terms were estimated based on the top 20 ranked assumed relevant documents. The top 20 ranked expansion terms taken from these summaries were added to the original query in each case. Based on results from our previous experiments, the original topic terms are upweighted by a factor of 3.5 relative to terms introduced by PRF. Since the English document collection for CLEF 2003 includes documents taken from both American and British English sources in our development runs we experimented with updated synonym information to conflate British and American English word spellings. This method resulted in a further 4% improvement in average precision compared to the baseline no feedback results for our English monolingual unofficial run for CLEF 2002[1]. We anticipate this being a useful technique for CLEF 2003 as well, and the updated synonym list is again used for all our experiments reported here.

In the following tables of results the following labeling conventions are adopted for the selection of topic expansion terms and cfw(i) of the test collection:

TCow(i): topic expansion using only the test collection.
PCow(i): topic expansion using the TREC document pilot collection.
CCow(i): topic expansion using the combined multilingual-4 collection.
TopCow(i): topic expansion using a translated collection in the topic language.
TCcfw(i): cfw(i) values taken from the test collection in the final retrieval run.
PCcfw(i): cfw(i) values taken from the TREC document pilot collection in the final retrieval run.
CCcfw(i): cfw(i) values taken from the combined multilingual-4 collection in the final retrieval run.
TopCcfw(i): cfw(i) values taken from a translated collection in the topic language.

4.2 Monolingual Runs

We submitted runs for four languages (German, French, Italian and Spanish) in the monolingual task. Official runs are marked with a * and additional unofficial runs are presented for all languages. In this section we include results for the native English document collection as well for comparison. In all cases results are presented for the following:

1. Baseline run without feedback.
2. Feedback runs using expanded query and term weights from the test collection.
3. Feedback runs using expanded query from pilot collection and term weights from test collection.
4. Feedback runs using expanded query and term weights from pilot collection.

---

[1] Given that the CLEF 2002 English collection contains only American English documents, we found this improvement in performance from spelling conflation a little surprising for the CLEF 2002 task, and we intend to carry our further investigation into the specific sources of this improvement in performance.

5. An additional Feedback run is presented where query is expanded using a pilot run on a merged collection of all four text collection comprising the small multilingual collections, with the terms weights being taken from the test collection.
6. As 5, but with the term weights taken from the combined small multilingual pilot collection.

Results are presented for both Sys and Pro MT systems.

4.2.1 German Monolingual Runs

Table 1. Retrieval results for topic translation for German monolingual runs for both Sys MT and Pro MT topic translation

	Sys MT			Pro MT		
Run-ID	Av.P	% chg.	Rel_Ret	Av.P	% chg.	Rel_Ret
1. Baseline	0.488	-	1706	0.441	-	1580
2. TCow(i), TCcfw(i)	**0.568***	+16.4%	1747	0.511*	+15.9%	1657
3. PCow(i), TCcfw(i)	0.512*	+4.9%	1727	0.457	+3.6%	1616
4. PCow(i), PCcfw(i)	0.458	-6.1%	1665	0.431	-2.3%	1575
5. CCow(i), TCcfw(i)	0.550	+12.7%	1751	0.494	+12.0%	1663
6. CCow(i), CCcfw(i)	0.551	+12.9%	1750	0.512	+16.1%	1672

4.2.2 French Monolingual Runs

Examination of Tables 1 to 4 reveals a number of consistent trends. Considering first the baseline runs. In all cases Sys MT translation of the topics produces better results than use of Pro MT. This is not too surprising since the documents were also translated with Sys MT, and the result indicates that consistency (and perhaps quality) of translation is important. All results show that our PRF method results in improvement in performance over the baseline in cases.

The variations in PRF results for query expansion for the different methods explored are very consistent. The best performance is observed in all cases, except Pro MT Spanish, using only the test collection for expansion term selection and collection weighting. Thus although query expansion from pilot collections has been shown to be very effective in other retrieval tasks [2], the method did not work very well for CLEF 2003 documents and topics. Perhaps more surprising is the observation that term weight estimation from the pilot collection actually resulted in average precision in most cases lower than that of the baseline no feedback run. This result is very unexpected particularly since the method has been shown to be very effective and has been used with success in our past research work for CLEF 2001 [1] and 2002 [2].

Query expansion from the merged document collection (used for the multilingual task) of Spanish, English, French, and German also resulted in improvement in retrieval performance, in general slightly less than that achieved in the best results for French, German and Spanish using only the test collection. The result for this method is lower for Italian run, this is probably arises due to the absence of the Italian document collection from the merged collection. The use of the combined collection cfw(i) has mixed impact on performance.

Table 2. Retrieval results for topic translation for French monolingual runs for both Sys MT and Pro MT topic translation

Run-ID	Sys MT			Pro MT		
	Av.P.	% chg.	Rel_Ret	Av.P	% chg.	Rel_Ret
1. Baseline	0.487	-	918	0.422	-	885
2. TCow(i), TCcfw(i)	0.521*	+6.9%	933	0.457*	+8.3%	897
3. PCow(i), TCcfw(i)	0.491*	+0.8%	921	0.403	-4.5%	890
4. PCow(i), PCcfw(i)	0.489	+0.4%	920	0.426	+0.9%	885
5. CCow(i), TCcfw(i)	0.519	+6.6%	931	0.446	+5.7%	893
6. CCow(i), CCcfw(i)	**0.553**	+13.6%	931	0.467	+10.7%	891

4.2.3 Italian Monolingual Runs

Table 3. Retrieval results for topic translation for Italian monolingual runs for both Sys MT and Pro MT topic translation

Run-ID	Sys MT			Pro MT		
	Av.P	% chg.	Rel_Ret	Av.P	% chg.	Rel_Ret
1. Baseline	0.419	-	761	0.387	-	742
2. TCow(i), TCcfw(i)	**0.494***	+17.9%	787	0.449*	+16.0%	759
3. PCow(i), TCcfw(i)	0.432*	+3.1%	762	0.402	+3.89%	745
4. PCow(i), PCcfw(i)	0.393	-6.2%	754	0.387	0%	735
5. CCow(i), TCcfw(i)	0.456	+8.8%	771	0.452	+16.8%	759
6. CCow(i), CCcfw(i)	0.454	+8.4%	770	0.481	+24.3%	761

4.2.4 Spanish Monolingual Runs

Table 4. Retrieval results for topic translation for Spanish monolingual runs for both Sys MT and Pro MT topic translation

Run-ID	Sys MT			Pro MT		
	Av.P	% chg.	Rel_Ret	Av.P	% chg.	Rel_Ret
1. Baseline	0.422	-	2163	0.393	-	2111
2. TCow(i), TCcfw(i)	**0.470***	+11.3%	2195	0.452*	+15.0%	2145
3. PCow(i), TCcfw(i)	0.426*	+0.9%	2114	0.415	+5.6%	2081
4. PCow(i), PCcfw(i)	0.372	-11.8%	1973	0.397	+1.0%	2039
5. CCow(i), TCcfw(i)	0.462	+9.5%	2200	0.466	+18.6%	2148
6. CCow(i), CCcfw(i)	**0.470**	+11.3%	2167	0.462	+17.6%	2142

4.2.5 English Monolingual Runs

Table 5 shows the results for runs 1-6 for the native English document collection with native English topic statements. Again in this case the best performance is achieved using test collection expansion and term weighting. Expansion from the pilot collection is again unsuccessful with corresponding term weighting giving improved results for these expanded topic statements. Expansion from the combined collection is successful, but using the corresponding term weights degrades performance below the baseline. These results for the pilot collection are again surprising, particularly in the case of the use of the TREC document collection. The pilot collection and the test collection are both original English documents. Thus, based on previous results we might expect this to be more reliable than the earlier results for the translated documents in Tables 1-4.

Table 5. Retrieval results English monolingual runs

Run-ID	Av.P	% chg.	Rel_Ret
1. Baseline	0.456	-	982
2. TCow(i), TCcfw(i)	**0.483**	+5.9%	998
3. PCow(i), TCcfw(i)	0.425	-6.8%	994
4. PCow(i), PCcfw(i)	0.472	+3.5%	995
5. CCow(i), TCcfw(i)	0.477	+4.6%	992
6. CCow(i), CCcfw(i)	0.434	-4.8%	986

4.2.6 Native English Topic Runs

Table 6 shows an additional set of baseline results for the different translated language collections with the untranslated native English language topic statements. These runs were carried out without any feedback or alternative test collection weights to explore the impact of topic translation without interfering effects from these additional techniques.

The results show that in general retrieval performance is best for Sys MT topics rather than for the original English topics. This is perhaps surprising since the original English statements will be more "accurate" readings of the topics in English, however the vocabulary match between the documents and topics into English using the same resources is more effective for retrieval. By contrast the original English topics

Table 6. Baseline retrieval results for translated documents with native English topics

			Sys MT		Pro MT	
Original Document Language	Av.P	Rel_Ret	Av. P. % chg.	Rel_Ret chg.	Av.P. % chg.	Rel_Ret chg.
French	0.469	868	-3.7%	-17	+11.1%	-17
German	0.465	1619	-4.7%	-87	+5.4%	+39
Italian	0.400	751	-4.5%	-10	+3.4%	+9
Spanish	0.480	2045	+13.7%	-118	+22.1%	-66

perform better then the topic translations using Pro MT. Overall the trends here are consistent with our monolingual and bilingual retrieval results submitted to CLEF 2002 [2].

4.3 Bilingual Runs

For the Bilingual task we submitted runs for both the German-Italian and Italian-Spanish tasks. Official runs are again marked with a * and additional unofficial runs are presented. In all cases, results are presented for the following experimental conditions:

7. Baseline run without feedback.
8. Feedback runs using expanded query and term weights from the target collection.
9. Feedback runs using expanded query from pilot collection and term weights from test collection.
10. Feedback runs using expanded query and term weights from pilot collection.
11. We investigated further the effectiveness of pilot collection and the impact of vocabulary differences for different languages. This is done by expanding initial query statement from the topic collection and then applying the expanded query on the target collection (i.e. for German-Italian bilingual runs initial German query statement is expanded from the German collection and applied on the test collection).
12. Additionally both the expanded query and the corresponding term weights are estimated from the topic collection.
13. The topics were expanded using method 11 and then further expanded using method 8. The term weights in the target language are estimated from the test collection.
14. As 13 with the term weights estimated from the topic collection.

Results are again presented for both Sys MT and Pro MT topic translations.

4.3.1 Bilingual German to Italian

Table 7. Retrieval results for topic translation for Italian bilingual runs for Sys MT and Pro MT

Run-ID	Sys MT			Pro MT		
	Av.P	% chg	Rel_Ret	Av.P	% chg	Rel_Ret
7. Baseline	0.311	-	725	0.314	-	668
8. TCow(i),TCcfw(i)	0.370	+18.9%	748	0.359	+14.3%	701
9. PCow(i),TCcfw(i)	0.339	+9.0%	724	0.334	+6.4%	671
10. PCow(i),PCcfw(i)	0.327	+5.1%	715	0.335*	+6.7%	659
11. TopCow(i),TCcfw(i)	0.365	+17.4%	743	0.355*	+13.1%	691
12. TopCow(i),TopCcfw(i)	0.415*	+33.4%	750	0.397*	+26.4%	702
13.TopC>TCow(i), TCcfw(i)	0.433	+39.2%	750	0.418	+33.1%	735
14 TopC->TCow(i), TopCcfw(i)	**0.441**	+41.8%	749	0.421	+34.1%	733

4.3.2 Bilingual Italian to Spanish

Tables 7 and 8 show results for our bilingual runs. For the bilingual runs topic expansion and weighting using the test collection is shown to be better than using the TREC pilot collection for both tasks. Query expansion and term weight estimation from pilot collection resulted in improvement in average precision ranging from 1.2% to 9% for both results, although it failed to achieve comparable performance to other methods, which is again surprising but consistent with the monolingual results.

Table 8. Retrieval results for topic translation for Spanish bilingual runs for Sys MT and Pro MT

	Sys MT			Pro MT		
Run-ID	Av.P	% chg	Rel_Ret	Av.P	% chg	Rel_Ret
7. Baseline	0.327	-	1938	0.349	-	1923
8. TCow(i),TCcfw(i)	0.376	+14.9%	2042	**0.417**	+19.5%	2064
9. PCow(i),TCcfw(i)	0.331	+1.2%	1915	0.365	+4.6%	1940
10. PCow(i),PCcfw(i)	0.339	+3.7%	1870	0.364*	+4.3%	1872
11. TopCow(i),TCcfw(i)	0.389	+18.9%	2071	**0.417***	+19.5%	2011
12. TopCow(i),TopCcfw(i)	**0.391***	+19.6%	2051	0.385*	+10.3%	2004
13. TopC->TCow(i), TCcfw(i)	0.389	+19.0%	2064	0.379	+8.6%	1968
14.TopC->TCow(i), TopCcfw(i)	0.382	+16.8%	2059	0.367	+5.2%	1932

For our bilingual runs we also tried a new method of query expansion and term weight estimation from the topic language collection. For this condition the topic was first applied on the translated test collection associated with the topic language, i.e. translated German topics were applied to the translated German documents. We experimented with cfw(i) values taken from the test collection and from the topic collection. Interestingly using the topic collection cfw(i) improves results, dramatically so in the case of the German to Italian task. For the German to Italian task this method resulted a +33% improvement in average precision over the baseline when using test collection cfw(i). It also worked well for the Spanish bilingual run giving about 19% improvement in average precision. The use of term weights from the topic collection gives a large improvement over the result using test collection weights in the case of the German-Italian task, but for the Italian-Spanish task this has a negligible effect in the case of Systran MT and makes performance worse for Globalink MT. It is not immediately clear why these collections should behave differently, but it may relate to the size of the document collections, the Italian collection being much smaller than either of the German or Spanish collections.

We also explored a further strategy of double topic expansion. The topic is first expanded using the topic collection and then further expanded using the test collection. For the German to Italian task the result is further improved, resulting in a +41.8% in average precision for the Sys MT topics when the topic collection weights were used. However, this strategy is not effective for the Italian to Spanish task, but it can be noted that, unlike the German to Italian task, using test collection cfw(i) is still more effective than using the topic collection cfw(i).

4.4 Multilingual Retrieval

Multilingual information retrieval presents a more challenging task in cross-lingual retrieval experiments. A user submits a request in a single language (e.g. English) in order to retrieve relevant documents in different languages e.g. English, Spanish, Italian, German, etc. We approached the multilingual-4 task in two ways. First, we retrieved relevant documents using the English topics individually from the four different collections and then explored merging the results together using different techniques (described below). Secondly we merged the translated document collections with the English collection to form a single collection and performed retrieval directly from this collection without using a separate merging stage.

Different techniques for merging separate result lists to form a single list have been proffered and tested. All of the techniques suggest that making assumptions that the distribution of relevant documents in the results set for retrieval from individual collection is similar is not true [16]. Hence, straight merging of relevant documents from the sources will result in poor combination.

Based on these assumptions we examined four merging techniques for combining the retrieved results from the four collections to form a single result list as follows:

$$u = \frac{doc\_wgt}{g\max\_wt * rank} \tag{3}$$

$$p = doc\_wgt \tag{4}$$

$$s = \frac{doc\_wgt}{g\max\_wt} \tag{5}$$

$$d = \frac{doc\_wgt - \min\_wt}{\max\_wt - \min\_wt} \tag{6}$$

where u, p, s and d are the new document weight for all documents in all collections and corresponding results are labeled mult4* where * can be u, p, s or d depending on the merging scheme used. The variables in (3)-(6) are defined as follows:

doc_wgt = the initial document matching score
$gmax\_wt$ = the global maximum matching score i.e. the highest document from all collections for a given query
max_wt = the individual collection maximum matching score for a given query
min_wt = the individual collection minimum matching score for a given query
$rank$ = a parameter to control the effect of size of collection - a collection with more documents gets a higher rank (value ranges between 1.5 and 1).

To test the effectiveness of the merging schemes, we merged the 4 text collection into a single large combined collection. Expanded queries from this combined test collection (CCow(i),CCcfw(i)) and from the TREC data pilot collection (PCow(i),CCcfw(i)) were then applied on the resultant merged collection. For all official runs (mult4*) English queries are expanded from the TREC-7 and 8 pilot collections and then applied on the test collection.

Table 9. Retrieval results for small Multilingual task before and after applications of different erging strategies

Run-ID	Av.P	P10	P30	%chg.	Rel_Ret
Baseline	0.383	0.593	0.476	-	4613
Pcow(i),CCcfw(i)	**0.438***	**0.623**	**0.524**	**+14.3%**	**4828**
Ccow(i),CCcfw(i)	0.425	0.617	0.517	+10.9%	4853
Pcow(i),TCcfw(i)mult4u	0.351*	0.520	0.434	-8.4%	4574
Pcow(i)TCcfw(i)mult4p	0.356*	0.532	0.438	-7.0%	4457
Pcow(i)TCcfw(i)mult4s	0.356*	0.518	0.438	-7.0%	4428
PCow(i)TCcfw(i)mult4d	0.331*	0.525	0.433	-13.5%	4609
CCow(i),TCcfw(i)mult4s	0.400	0.593	0.486	+4.4%	4675

An additional run CCow(i),CCcfw(i)mult4s was conducted whereby the expanded query was estimated from the merged document collection and applied on the individual collection before being merged using equation 5 above.

The baseline result for our multilingual run (Baseline) perhaps might not present a realistic platform for comparison with the feedback runs using the different merging strategies (PCow(i),TCcfw(i)mult4*). This is because it was achieved from a no feedback run from the merged multilingual collection.

The multilingual-4 results show that the different merging strategies for combining the retrieved lists from the separate collections provide similar retrieval performance. The result for merging strategy using (6) (which has been shown to be effective in past retrieval tasks) however resulted in about 14% loss in average precision compared to the baseline run. The more sophisticated merging strategies failed to show any improvement over raw score merging (4), although the merging strategy using (6), gave the highest number of relevant document retrieved for all the merging strategies.

Both our bilingual and monolingual runs show that retrieval results using query expansion and term weight estimation from pilot collection resulted in loss in average precision compared to baseline no feedback run in most cases. This might have contributed to the poor result from the different merging techniques for the multilingual runs (PCow(i),TCcfw(i)mult4*) where the expanded topic statement was calculated from the TREC pilot collection. For the multilingual results using the merging techniques (PCow(i),TCcfw(i)mult4*), we expanded the initial English queries and then applied these to the individual collections, the term weights were estimated from the individual test collections. However, results from our monolingual runs using this query expansion method were not very encouraging, and this might perhaps have contributed to the poor results after the application of the different merging techniques compared to the method whereby all the collections are merged to form one big collection.

To test this hypothesis, we conducted an additional run whereby we used the merged collection as the pilot collection and expanded the initial query from it (CCow(i),TCcfw(i)mult4s). The expanded topic was then applied on the individual collections and resultant result file merged using (5). The result showed an improvement of about 4% compared to that achieved from the baseline no feedback run from the merged collection (Baseline). It also resulted in about 11% increase in average precision over result from query expansion from the pilot collection (PCow(i),TCcfw(i)mult4s).

The best result for the multilingual task was achieved by expanding the initial query from the pilot collection and applying it on the merged collection. Query expansion from the merged collection (CCow(i),CCcfw(i)) also resulted in about 10% improvement in average precision. These results suggest that merging a collection in a multilingual task can be more beneficial than merging the result lists taken from the retrieval from individual collections. This result is presumably due to the more robust and consistent parameter estimation in the combined document collection. In many operational situations combining collections in this way will not be practical either due to the physical separation of the collections or the lack of opportunity to translate them into a common pivot language. From this perspective Multilingual IR can be viewed as distributed information retrieval task where there may be varying degrees of cooperation between the various collections. In this environment list merging is an essential component of the multilingual retrieval process. Results for the combined collection illustrate that better retrieval results than achieved using the currently proposed merging strategies is easily available using these documents, and further research is clearly required to develop distributed merging strategies that can approach combined collection retrieval performance.

5 Conclusions

For our participation in the CLEF 2003 retrieval tasks we updated our synonym information to include common British and American English words. We explored the idea of query expansion from pilot collection and got some disappointing results which are contrary to past retrieval work utilizing the use of expanded queries and term weight estimation from pilot collections. This result may be caused by vocabulary and term distribution mismatch between our translated test collection and the native English pilot collection, however this trend was also observed for the native English document collection, and further investigation is needed to ascertain whether this or other reasons underlie this negative result.

For the bilingual task we explored the idea of query expansion from a pilot collection in the topic language. This method resulted in better retrieval performance. Although we are working in English as our search language throughout, this result is related to the ideas of pre-translation and post-translation feedback explored in earlier work on CLIR [4], and the effectiveness of combining pre- and post-translation feedback appears to be related to the properties of the document collections.

The different merging strategies used for combining our results for the multilingual task failed to perform better than raw score merging. Further investigation is needed to test these methods, particularly as some of them have been shown to be effective in past research. Merging the document collections resulted in better average precision than merging separate retrieval result lists. However, it will often not be possible to merge the various collections together, in this case an effective method of merging the result list is needed. Further investigation will be conducted to examine the possibility of improving the results achieved from merging result lists.

References

1. Jones, G.J.F., Lam-Adesina, A.M.: Exeter at CLEF 2001. In: Peters, C., Braschler, M., Gonzalo, J., Kluck, M. (eds.): Evaluation of Cross-Language Information Retrieval Systems: Second Workshop of the Cross-Language Evaluation Forum, CLEF 2001, Darmstadt, Germany, September 3-4, 2001. Revised Papers. Lecture Notes in Computer Science, Vol. 2406 Springer-Verlag Berlin Heidelberg New York (2002) 59-77
2. Lam-Adesina, A.M., Jones, G.J.F.: Exeter at CLEF 2002: Cross-Language Spoken Document Retrieval Experiments. In: Peters, C., Gonzales, J., Braschler, M., Kluck, M. (eds.): Advances in Cross- Language Information Retrieval: Third Workshop of the Cross-Language Evaluation Forum, CLEF 2002, Rome, Italy, September 19 - 20, 2002. Revised Papers. Lecture Notes in Computer Science; Vol. 2785. Springer-Verlag, Berlin Heidelberg New York (2003) 127-146
3. Jones, G.J.F., Sakai, T., Collier, N. H., Kumano, A., Sumita, K.: A Comparison of Query Translation Methods for English-Japanese Cross-Language Information Retrieval. In: Proceedings of the 22nd Annual International ACM SIGIR Conference on Research and Development in Information Retrieval, San Francisco. ACM (1999) 269-270
4. Ballesteros, L., Croft, W. B.: Phrasal Translation and Query Expansion Techniques for Cross-Language Information Retrieval. In: Proceedings of the 20th Annual International ACM SIGIR conference on Research and Development in Information Retrieval, Philadelphia. ACM (1997) 84-91
5. Salton, G., Buckley, C.: Improving Retrieval performance by Relevance Feedback. In: Journal of the American Society for Information Science, (1990) 288-297
6. Lam-Adesina, A.M., Jones, G.J.F: Applying Summarization Techniques for Term Selection in Relevance Feedback. In: Proceedings of the 24th Annual International ACM SIGIR Conference on Research and Development in Information Retrieval, New Orleans, ACM (2001) 1-9
7. Robertson, S.E., Walker, S., Beaulieu, M.M.: Okapi at TREC-7: automatic ad hoc, filtering, VLS and interactive track. In: Voorhees, E., Harman, D.K. (eds.): Overview of the Seventh Text REtrieval Conference (TREC-7). NIST (1999) 253-264
8. Porter, M.F. An algorithm for suffix stripping. In: Program, 14 (1980) 130-137
9. Robertson, S.E, Walker, S.: Some simple effective approximations to the 2-Poisson model for probabilistic weighted retrieval. In: Proceedings of the 17th Annual International ACM SIGIR Conference on Research and Development in Information Retrieval, Dublin, ACM (1994) 232-241
10. Robertson, S.E, Walker, S., Jones, S., Hancock-Beaulieu, M.M., Gatford, M.: Okapi at TREC-3. In: Harman, D.K. (ed.): Proceedings of the Third Text REtrieval Conference (TREC-3),. NIST (1995) 109-126
11. Luhn, H.P.:The Automatic Creation of Literature Abstracts. In: IBM Journal of Research and Development, 2 (1958) 2, 159-165
12. Edmundson, H.P.: New Methods in Automatic Abstracting. In: Journal of the ACM, 16 (1969) 2, 264-285

13. Tombros, A., Sanderson M.: The Advantages of Query-Biased Summaries in Information Retrieval. In: Proceedings of the 21st Annual International ACM SIGIR Conference Research and Development in Information Retrieval, Melbourne. ACM (1998) 2-10
14. Robertson, S.E. : On term selection for query expansion. In: Journal of Documentation, 46 (1990) 359-364
15. Robertson, S.E., Walker, S.: Okapi/Keenbow. In: Voorhees, E., Harman, D.K. (eds.): Overview of the Eighth Text REtrieval Conference (TREC-8). NIST (2000) 151-162
16. Savoy, J.: Report on CLEF-2002 Experiments: Combining Multiple Sources of Evidence. In: Peters, C., Gonzales, J., Braschler, M., Kluck, M. (eds.): Advances in Cross- Language Information Retrieval: Third Workshop of the Cross-Language Evaluation Forum, CLEF 2002, Rome, Italy, September 19 - 20, 2002. Revised Papers. Lecture Notes in Computer Science; Vol. 2785. Springer-Verlag, Berlin Heidelberg New York (2003) 66-90

Lexical and Algorithmic Stemming Compared for 9 European Languages with Hummingbird SearchServer™ at CLEF 2003

Stephen Tomlinson

Hummingbird,
Ottawa, Ontario, Canada
stephen.tomlinson@hummingbird.com
http://www.hummingbird.com/

Abstract. Hummingbird participated in the monolingual information retrieval tasks of the Cross-Language Evaluation Forum (CLEF) 2003: for natural language queries in 9 European languages (German, French, Italian, Spanish, Dutch, Finnish, Swedish, Russian and English), find all the relevant documents (with high precision) in the CLEF 2003 document sets. SearchServer produced the highest mean average precision score of the submitted automatic Title+Description runs for German, Finnish and Dutch, the CLEF languages for which SearchServer could find words which are parts of compounds. In a comparison of experimental SearchServer lexical stemmers with Porter's algorithmic stemmers, the biggest differences (most of them significant) were for languages in which compound words are frequent. For the other languages, typically the lexical stemmers performed inflectional stemming while the algorithmic stemmers often additionally performed derivational stemming; these differences did not pass a significance test.

1   Introduction

Hummingbird SearchServer[1] is an indexing, search and retrieval engine for embedding in Windows and UNIX information applications. SearchServer, originally a product of Fulcrum Technologies, was acquired by Hummingbird in 1999. Founded in 1983 in Ottawa, Canada, Fulcrum produced the first commercial application program interface (API) for writing information retrieval applications, Fulcrum® Ful/Text™. The SearchServer kernel is embedded in many Hummingbird products, including SearchServer, an application toolkit used for knowledge-intensive applications that require fast access to unstructured information.

SearchServer supports a variation of the Structured Query Language (SQL), SearchSQL™, which has extensions for text retrieval. SearchServer conforms

---

[1] Fulcrum® is a registered trademark, and SearchServer™, SearchSQL™, Intuitive Searching™ and Ful/Text™ are trademarks of Hummingbird Ltd. All other copyrights, trademarks and tradenames are the property of their respective owners.

C. Peters et al. (Eds.): CLEF 2003, LNCS 3237, pp. 286–300, 2004.

to subsets of the Open Database Connectivity (ODBC) interface for C programming language applications and the Java Database Connectivity (JDBC) interface for Java applications. Almost 200 document formats are supported, such as Word, WordPerfect, Excel, PowerPoint, PDF and HTML.

SearchServer works in Unicode internally [4] and supports most of the world's major character sets and languages. The major conferences in text retrieval evaluation (CLEF [2], NTCIR [5] and TREC [8]) have provided opportunities to objectively evaluate SearchServer's support for natural language queries in more than a dozen languages.

This paper looks at experimental work with SearchServer for the task of finding relevant documents for natural language queries in 9 European languages using the CLEF 2003 test collections. For the experiments described in this paper, an experimental post-5.x version of SearchServer was used.

2   Methodology

2.1   Data

The CLEF 2003 document sets consisted of tagged (SGML-formatted) news articles (mostly from 1994 and 1995) in 9 different languages: German, French, Italian, Spanish, Dutch, Swedish, Finnish, Russian and English. Compared to last year, Russian was new, and there were more documents in Spanish, German, Italian, French and English. The English documents included some British English for the first time. Table 1 gives the sizes.

Table 1. Sizes of CLEF 2003 Document Sets

Language	Text Size (uncompressed)	Number of Documents
Spanish	1,158,177,739 bytes (1105 MB)	454,045
German	704,523,506 bytes (672 MB)	294,809
Dutch	558,560,087 bytes (533 MB)	190,604
English	601,737,745 bytes (574 MB)	169,477
Italian	378,831,019 bytes (361 MB)	157,558
Swedish	374,371,465 bytes (357 MB)	142,819
French	344,961,357 bytes (329 MB)	129,806
Finnish	143,902,109 bytes (137 MB)	55,344
Russian	68,802,653 bytes (66 MB)	16,716

The CLEF organizers created 60 natural language "topics" (numbered 141-200) and translated them into many languages. Each topic contained a "Title" (subject of the topic), "Description" (a one-sentence specification of the information need) and "Narrative" (more detailed guidelines for what a relevant document should or should not contain). The participants were asked to use the Title and Description fields for at least one automatic submission per task this year to facilitate comparison of results.

For more information on the CLEF test collections, see the CLEF web site [2].

2.2   Indexing

A separate SearchServer table was created for the documents of each language. For details of the SearchServer syntax, see last year's paper [9].

Unlike last year, we used SearchServer's default of not indexing accents for all languages, except for Russian, for which we indexed the combining breve (Unicode 0x0306) so that the Cyrillic Short I (0x0419) was not normalized to the Cyrillic I (0x0418).

We treated the apostrophe as a word separator for all languages except English.

Typically, a couple hundred stop words were excluded from indexing for each language (e.g. "the", "by" and "of" in English). The Porter web site [6] contains stop word lists for most European languages. We used its list for Russian, but our lists for other languages may contain differences.

SearchServer internally uses Unicode. A different option to SearchServer's translation text reader was specified for Russian (UTF8_UCS2) than for the other languages (Win_1252_UCS2) because the Russian documents were encoded in the UTF-8 character set and the documents for the other languages were encoded in the Latin-1 character set (a custom text reader, cTREC, was also updated to maintain support for the CLEF guidelines of only indexing specifically tagged fields; the new British and Russian collections necessitated the update).

By default, the SearchServer index supports both exact matching (after some Unicode-based normalizations, such as decompositions and conversion to uppercase) and matching of inflections.

2.3   Lexical Stemming

For many languages (including all 9 European languages of CLEF 2003), SearchServer includes the option of finding inflections based on lexical stemming (i.e. stemming based on a dictionary or lexicon for the language). For example, in English, "baby", "babied", "babies", "baby's" and "babying" all have "baby" as a stem. Specifying an inflected search for any of these terms will match all of the others. The lexical stemming of the experimental development version of SearchServer used for the experiments in this paper was based on Inxight LinguistX Platform 3.5. Unlike the previous two years, the lexical stemming was conducted in an "expanded" mode which tolerates missing accents (e.g. unlike last year, "bebes" stems to "bébé" in French) and handles more plural cases (e.g. unlike last year, "PCs" stems to "PC" in English).

For all languages, we used inflectional stemming which generally retains the part of speech (e.g. a plural of a noun is typically stemmed to the singular form). We did not use derivational stemming which would often change the part of speech or the meaning more substantially (e.g. "performer" is not stemmed to "perform").

SearchServer's lexical stemming includes compound-splitting (decompounding) for compound words in German, Dutch and Finnish (but not for Swedish in this version, and not for the other languages as it is not generally applicable). For example, in German, "babykost" (baby food) has "baby" and "kost" as stems.

SearchServer's lexical stemming also supports some spelling variations. In English, British and American spellings have the same stems, e.g. "labour" stems to "labor", "hospitalisation" stems to "hospitalization" and "plough" stems to "plow".

Lexical stemmers can produce more than one stem, even for non-compound words. For example, in English, "axes" has both "axe" and "axis" as stems (different meanings), and in French, "important" has both "important" (adjective) and "importer" (verb) as stems (different parts of speech). Search-Server records all the stem mappings at index-time, but at search-time, for the experiments in this paper, we arbitrarily just used the inflections from one stem (except for compounds) by specifying the '/noalt' option in the VEC-TOR_GENERATOR set option (e.g. 'word!ftelp/lang=french/base/noalt | * | word!ftelp /lang=french/inflect' was the setting for finding French inflections).

2.4   Intuitive Searching

For all runs, we used SearchServer's Intuitive Searching, i.e. the IS_ABOUT predicate of SearchSQL, which accepts unstructured natural language text. For example, for the German version of topic 41 (from a previous year), the Title was "Pestizide in Babykost" (Pesticides in Baby Food), and the Description was "Berichte über Pestizide in Babynahrung sind gesucht" (Find reports on pesticides in baby food). A corresponding SearchSQL query would be:

```
SELECT RELEVANCE('V2:3') AS REL, DOCNO
FROM CLEF03DE
WHERE FT_TEXT IS_ABOUT 'Pestizide in Babykost Berichte über
Pestizide in Babynahrung sind gesucht'
ORDER BY REL DESC;
```

For the Russian queries, the statement "SET CHARACTER_SET 'UTF8C' " was previously executed because the queries were in UTF-8 instead of Latin-1.

2.5   Statistical Relevance Ranking

SearchServer's relevance value calculation is the same as described last year [9]. Briefly, SearchServer dampens the term frequency and adjusts for document length in a manner similar to Okapi [7] and dampens the inverse document frequency using an approximation of the logarithm. SearchServer's relevance values are always an integer in the range 0 to 1000.

SearchServer's RELEVANCE_METHOD setting can be used to optionally square the importance of the inverse document frequency (by choosing a REL-EVANCE_METHOD of 'V2:4' instead of 'V2:3'). The importance of document length to the ranking is controlled by SearchServer's RELEVANCE_DLEN_IMP setting (scale of 0 to 1000). For all runs in this paper, RELEVANCE_METHOD was set to 'V2:3' and RELEVANCE_DLEN_IMP was set to 750.

2.6   Query Stop Words

We automatically removed words such as "find", "relevant" and "document" from the topics before presenting them to SearchServer, i.e. words which are not stop words in general but were commonly used in the CLEF topics as general instructions. For the submitted runs, the lists were developed by examining the CLEF 2000, 2001 and 2002 topics (not this year's topics). An evaluation in last year's paper [9] found this step to be of only minor impact.

2.7   Query Expansion from Blind Feedback

For one of the submitted runs for each language (the runs with identifiers ending with 'e', e.g. humDE03tde), the first 3 rows from the other submitted run for the language (e.g. humDE03td) were used to find additional query terms. Only terms appearing in at most 5% of the documents (based on the most common inflection of the term) were included. Mathematically, the approach is similar to Rocchio feedback with weights of one-half for the original query and one-sixth for each of the 3 expansion rows. See section 5.2 of [10] for more details. This is the first time we have used a blind feedback technique for CLEF submissions. We did not use it for any of the diagnostic experiments.

3   Official Results

The evaluation measures are expected to be explained in detail in [1]. Briefly: "Precision" is the percentage of retrieved documents which are relevant. "Precision@n" is the precision after n documents have been retrieved. "Average precision" for a topic is the average of the precision after each relevant document is retrieved (using zero as the precision for relevant documents which are not retrieved). "Recall" is the percentage of relevant documents which have been retrieved. "Interpolated precision" at a particular recall level for a topic is the maximum precision achieved for the topic at that or any higher recall level. For a set of topics, the measure is the mean of the measure for each topic (i.e. all topics are weighted equally).

The Monolingual Information Retrieval tasks were to run 60 queries against document collections in the same language and submit a list of the top-1000 ranked documents to CLEF for judging (in May 2003). CLEF produced a "qrels" file for each of the 9 tasks: a list of documents judged to be relevant or not relevant for each topic. (For Swedish, this paper still uses the preliminary set of qrels.)

For some topics and languages, no documents were considered relevant. The precision scores are just averaged over the number of topics for which there was at least one relevant document.

For tables focusing on the impact of one particular difference in approach (such as a stemming method as in Table 4), the columns are as follows:

- "Experiment" is the language and topic fields used (for example, "-td" indicates the Title and Description fields were used).

- "AvgDiff" is the average (mean) difference in the precision score.
- "95% Confidence" is an approximate 95% confidence interval for the average difference calculated using Efron's bootstrap percentile method[2] [3] (using 100,000 iterations). If zero is not in the interval, the result is "statistically significant" (at the 5% level), i.e. the feature is unlikely to be of neutral impact, though if the average difference is small (e.g. <0.020) it may still be too minor to be considered "significant" in the magnitude sense.
- "vs." is the number of topics on which the precision was higher, lower and tied (respectively) with the feature enabled. These numbers should always add to the number of topics for the language (as per Table 5).
- "2 Largest Diffs (Topic)" lists the two largest differences in the precision score (based on the absolute value) with each followed by the corresponding topic number in brackets (the topic numbers range from 141 to 200).

For tables providing multiple precision scores (such as Table 5), listed for each run are its mean average precision (AvgP), the mean precision after 5, 10 and 20 documents retrieved (P@5, P@10 and P@20 respectively), the mean interpolated precision at 0% and 30% recall (Rec0 and Rec30 respectively), and the mean precision after R documents retrieved (P@R) where R is the number of relevant documents for the topic. The number of topics with at least one relevant document is also included in this table, though it is a property of the test collection, not of the run.

3.1   Submitted Runs

In the identifiers for the submitted runs (e.g. humDE03tde), the first 3 letters "hum" indicate a Hummingbird submission, the next 2 letters are the language code, and the number "03" indicates CLEF 2003. "t", "d" and "n" indicate that the Title, Description and Narrative field of the topic were used (respectively). "e" indicates that query expansion from blind feedback was used. The submitted runs all used inflections from SearchServer's lexical stemming.

The following language codes were used: "DE" for German, "EN" for English, "ES" for Spanish, "FI" for Finnish, "FR" for French, "IT" for Italian, "NL" for Dutch, "RU" for Russian, and "SV" for Swedish.

For each language, we submitted a "td" and "tde" run (e.g. "humDE03td" and "humDE03tde" for German). Note that monolingual English submissions were not allowed. For Russian, additional runs were requested for the judging pools, so we also submitted Title-only runs ("humRU03t" and "humRU03te") and full topic runs ("humRU03tdn" and "humRU03tdne"). For 3 other Russian submissions ("humRU03tm", "humRU03tdm", "humRU03tdnm"), the "m" was meant to indicate that morphology (stemming) was disabled, but by accident for

---

[2] See last year's paper [9] for some comparisons of confidence intervals from the bootstrap percentile, Wilcoxon signed rank and standard error methods for both average precision and Precision@10.

Table 2. Precision of Submitted Runs

Run	AvgP	P@5	P@10	P@20	Rec0	Rec30	P@R	Topics
humES03td	0.466	59.7%	52.3%	42.6%	0.827	0.598	46.2%	57
humES03tde	0.529	61.1%	56.3%	48.1%	0.831	0.644	50.2%	57
humDE03td	0.546	67.9%	57.0%	46.4%	0.850	0.655	52.5%	56
humDE03tde	0.584	70.4%	61.1%	50.7%	0.868	0.693	53.6%	56
humNL03td	0.507	55.7%	46.4%	37.1%	0.787	0.615	48.0%	56
humNL03tde	0.531	57.9%	50.5%	40.2%	0.758	0.658	48.4%	56
(humEN03td)	0.502	46.3%	37.4%	30.1%	0.722	0.619	44.8%	54
(humEN03tde)	0.555	48.1%	41.9%	33.2%	0.747	0.668	50.4%	54
humSV03td	0.388	39.3%	30.4%	22.4%	0.702	0.506	37.8%	53
humSV03tde	0.431	40.8%	34.3%	26.3%	0.714	0.550	41.1%	53
humFR03td	0.518	49.2%	37.9%	28.1%	0.783	0.612	47.3%	52
humFR03tde	0.543	50.4%	39.8%	31.7%	0.782	0.626	49.0%	52
humIT03td	0.474	49.4%	38.6%	28.0%	0.813	0.591	43.3%	51
humIT03tde	0.518	53.3%	42.4%	33.2%	0.764	0.625	47.2%	51
humFI03td	0.588	46.7%	37.1%	27.4%	0.807	0.723	53.2%	45
humFI03tde	0.602	51.1%	39.8%	29.7%	0.796	0.718	52.0%	45
humRU03td	0.325	25.0%	17.9%	11.4%	0.587	0.452	31.1%	28
humRU03tde	0.319	25.7%	17.9%	11.4%	0.558	0.428	31.5%	28

these runs the CHARACTER_SET was set to Latin-1 instead of UTF-8, which led to precision scores of almost zero.

Table 2 lists the precision scores of the submitted runs (except the additional Russian runs) and also includes unofficial English runs produced at the same time (the runs are in descending order by number of topics for the language). The humDE03tde, humNL03tde and humFI03tde runs were the highest-scoring Title+Description runs in mean average precision of those submitted for the German, Dutch and Finnish monolingual tasks, respectively.

3.2 Impact of Query Expansion from Blind Feedback

Table 3 shows the impact of query expansion from blind feedback on the average precision score. For example, the impact for Spanish ("ES-exp-td") is based on subtracting the scores of the "humES03td" run from the scores of the "humES03tde" run. For 8 of the 9 languages (all except Russian), this technique increased the mean average precision score. For 6 of the 9 languages, this impact was statistically significant at the 5% level (i.e. zero was not in the approximate 95% confidence interval). The impact may have been least on Russian because it generally had the fewest relevant documents fed back in (as suggested by the relatively low precision scores in Table 2). In practice, users can decide which terms to add to a query rather than working blindly.

Table 3. Impact of Blind Feedback on Average Precision

Experiment	AvgDiff	95% Confidence	vs.	2 Largest Diffs (Topic)
ES-exp-td	0.063	(0.041, 0.087)	42-13-2	0.333 (192), 0.270 (200)
(EN-exp-td)	0.053	(0.024, 0.086)	30-14-10	0.500 (196), 0.352 (192)
IT-exp-td	0.044	(0.010, 0.074)	35-10-6	−0.500 (165), 0.417 (192)
SV-exp-td	0.043	(0.020, 0.068)	32-11-10	0.285 (199), 0.271 (179)
DE-exp-td	0.037	(0.001, 0.067)	44-10-2	−0.667 (172), 0.313 (200)
FR-exp-td	0.026	(−0.005, 0.053)	29-12-11	−0.500 (141), 0.308 (186)
NL-exp-td	0.025	(0.002, 0.047)	39-12-5	0.265 (179), 0.218 (186)
FI-exp-td	0.014	(−0.031, 0.052)	25-13-7	−0.667 (166), 0.392 (192)
RU-exp-td	−0.006	(−0.032, 0.017)	12-12-4	−0.246 (193), 0.144 (181)

4   Comparison of Lexical and Algorithmic Stemming

The experimental version of SearchServer used for these experiments allows plugging-in of custom stemming modules. As a test for this feature, we have experimented with plugging-in Porter's algorithmic "Snowball" stemmers [6]. For English, the Porter2 version was used.

Table 4 contains the results of a diagnostic experiment comparing average precision for the short (Title-only) queries when the only difference is the stemmer used: the experimental SearchServer lexical stemmer or Porter's algorithmic stemmer. Positive differences indicate that the SearchServer stemmer led to a higher score and negative differences indicate that the algorithmic stemmer led to a higher score. SearchServer's stemmer scored significantly higher for Finnish and German and significantly lower for Swedish. The differences for the other languages didn't pass the significance test.

(Table 4 is based on subtracting the "alg-t" run from the corresponding "lex-t" run in Table 5. Table 5 also lists a "none-t" run for each language, a run with stemming disabled. Table 6 isolates the impact of lexical stemming (i.e. subtracts

Table 4. Lexical vs. Algorithmic Stemming for Average Precision, Title-only queries

Experiment	AvgDiff	95% Confidence	vs.	2 Largest Diffs (Topic)
FI-stem-t	0.131	(0.032, 0.231)	28-14-3	−0.998 (185), 0.929 (196)
DE-stem-t	0.104	(0.054, 0.159)	39-13-4	0.833 (174), 0.596 (158)
NL-stem-t	0.035	(−0.009, 0.082)	28-20-8	0.635 (174), 0.494 (165)
RU-stem-t	0.013	(−0.009, 0.043)	8-3-17	0.338 (177), −0.111 (149)
ES-stem-t	0.005	(−0.008, 0.017)	29-14-14	−0.183 (186), 0.170 (151)
FR-stem-t	−0.004	(−0.027, 0.017)	18-14-20	−0.359 (145), 0.254 (177)
EN-stem-t	−0.005	(−0.025, 0.019)	13-23-18	0.469 (180), −0.225 (179)
IT-stem-t	−0.028	(−0.078, 0.006)	22-18-11	−1.000 (161), −0.287 (157)
SV-stem-t	−0.030	(−0.060,−0.005)	14-24-15	−0.500 (188), −0.333 (144)

the "none-t" run from the corresponding "lex-t"run for each language). But the focus of this section is Table 4.)

To try to better understand the differences between the lexical and algorithmic approaches to stemming, we look at the topics for each language with the two biggest differences in the average precision score (in some cases we look at more than two). We just look at the shorter Title-only topics for ease of analysis (fewer words in the query makes it easier to see what caused the difference) and because shorter queries are preferred by users anyway.

4.1   English Stemming

English topics 180 (Bankruptcy of Barings), 179 (Resignation of NATO Secretary General), 175 (Everglades Environmental Damage) and 168 (Assassination of Rabin) show that the algorithmic stemmer often performs derivational stemming (whereas the SearchServer stemmer is known to just do inflectional stemming as described earlier). In the case of topic 180, derivational stemming lowered the average precision score because it was harmful for this topic to match "Barings" with "bare", "bares" and "barely". But for topic 179, deriving "resign" and "resigned" from "resignation" was apparently helpful. Likewise, for topic 175, deriving "environment" from "environmental" was apparently helpful, and in topic 168 deriving "assassin" from "assassination" was apparently helpful. SearchServer's stemmer internally has the option of derivational stemming for English (and handles all of these cases similarly), but there is not currently an option to enable it. It might make for an interesting future experiment to try it.

English topic 200 (Flooding in Holland and Germany) illustrated that another difference for English is the handling of apostrophe-S. Perhaps surprisingly, the algorithmic stemmer never removes apostrophe-S. The SearchServer stemmer does remove it in some cases, e.g. it appears SearchServer scored higher on topic 200 because it matched "Holland's" with "Holland" and "Germany's" with "Germany". In topic 179, SearchServer matched "NATO's" with "NATO" and "general's" with "general". But in topic 168, "Rabin's" was not matched with "Rabin", so SearchServer is not using a simple rule (a more familiar case is that SearchServer does not match "Parkinson's" to "Parkinson"). For the other languages, we treated the apostrophe as a word separator, so handling of apostrophes won't be an issue.

4.2   French Stemming

French topics 145 (Le Japon et ses importations de riz (Japanese Rice Imports)) and 177 (La consommation de lait en Europe (Milk Consumption in Europe)) illustrate that the French algorithmic stemmer also does some derivational stemming. In topic 145, the algorithmic stemmer matched the noun "importations" with non-nouns such as "importé" and "importer", which apparently was helpful to the average precision score (though additionally deriving the unrelated terms "importance" and "important" might be disconcerting to a user). It also derived "Japonais" from "Japon". In topic 177, deriving "consommateurs" (consumers) and "consommateur" (consumer) from "consommation" (consumption) apparently hurt average precision.

French topic 162 (l'Union Européenne et les douanes turques (EU and Turkish Customs)) shows that sometimes SearchServer handles irregular inflections that the algorithmic stemmer does not. SearchServer matched "turques" with "turc" and "turcs", unlike the algorithmic stemmer. Both matched "turques" with "turque". The algorithmic stemmer additionally derived "turquie" which appears to be why it scored higher on this topic. Overall, for the French topics, Table 4 shows that neither stemmer scored significantly higher than the other (the confidence interval contains zero).

4.3   Italian Stemming

In Italian topic 161 (Diete per Celiaci (Diets for Celiacs)), the algorithmic stemmer found the one relevant document by matching "celiaci" with "celiaca". SearchServer stemmed "celiaci" to "celiare" and "celiaca" to itself and so did not make this match. We should investigate this case further.

In Italian topic 157 (Campionesse di Wimbledon (Wimbledon Lady Winners)), both stemmers matched "campionesse" with "campionessa", but SearchServer additionally matched "campioni" and "campione", which hurt average precision in this case.

In Italian topic 187 (Trasporto Nucleare in Germania (Nuclear Transport in Germany)), SearchServer scored higher, apparently from matching "nucleare" with "nucleari", unlike the algorithmic stemmer.

4.4   Spanish Stemming

In Spanish topic 186 (Coalición del gobierno holandés (Dutch Coalition Government)), SearchServer matched "holandés" with "holandeses" and "holandesa", unlike the algorithmic stemmer, and SearchServer scored a good 0.57 average precision, but the algorithmic stemmer derived "holandés" to "holanda", which apparently helped it score higher (0.75).

In Spanish topic 151 (Las maravillas del Mundo Antiguo (Wonders of Ancient World)), the algorithmic stemmer derived more terms from "maravillas" (wonders) such as "maravilloso" (wonderful) which hurt precision. Both stemmers matched "Antiguo" with "antiguos" and "antigua" (among others), and SearchServer additionally matched "antiquísima" which may have been helpful.

4.5   German Stemming

For German topic 174 (Bayerischer Kruzifixstreit (Bavarian Crucifix Quarrel)), SearchServer split the compound word "Kruzifixstreit" and found many relevant documents by matching terms such as "Kruzifix", "Kruzifixen" and "Kruzifixe" (and also "Streit", though it seemed less important in this case). The algorithmic stemmer does not support compound-splitting, and "Kruzifixstreit" did not itself appear in the document set (nor did any inflection of it), so it scored dramatically lower for this topic as can be seen in Table 4.

For German topic 158 (Fußball-Rowdys in Dublin (Soccer Riots in Dublin)), even though there was no compound word in the query, the relevant documents used compound words such as "Fussballrowdies" and "Fussballfans" which SearchServer successfully matched but the algorithmic stemmer did not.

German topic 190 (Kinderarbeit in Asien (Child Labor in Asia)) shows that compound-splitting is not always helpful. In this topic it hurt precision a lot to split "Kinderarbeit", presumably because the term was typically used in that form in the relevant documents, and a lot of other documents used the German words for 'children' and 'work' in other contexts. (This happens a lot in information retrieval; a technique that works well on average can still have a substantial percentage of cases for which it is harmful. While there may be room for automatic improvement, it's a good idea for applications to let the user override the defaults when desired.)

Overall for German, Table 4 shows that the SearchServer stemmer scored significantly higher on average, presumably because of compound-splitting.

4.6   Dutch Stemming

Dutch topic 174 (Beierse Kruisbeeldstrijd (Bavarian Crucifix Quarrel)) is the Dutch version of the crucifix query examined earlier for German. SearchServer scores highly for similar reasons, i.e. SearchServer splits the compound and matches "kruisbeeld" and "strijd" among other forms. "Kruisbeeldstrijd" did not itself appear in the document set and the algorithmic stemmer scored dramatically lower.

Dutch topic 165 (Golden Globes 1994 (Golden Globes 1994)) is a case for Dutch in which a large difference in average precision did not result from compound handling differences. SearchServer apparently scored higher from matching "Globes" with "Globe" and perhaps also from matching "golden" with "gelden". If compound words aren't as frequent in Dutch as German, that may be why the overall differences between the stemmers did not quite pass the significance test.

4.7   Finnish Stemming

For Finnish topic 185 (Hollantilaisten valokuvat Srebrenicasta (Dutch Photos of Srebrenica)), SearchServer did not match any of "Srebrenicassa", "Srebrenica" and "Srebrenican", variants of "Srebrenicasta" in the relevant document matched by the algorithmic stemmer. Srebrenica is a proper noun. Porter mentions in [6] that "in a language in which proper names are inflected (Latin, Finnish, Russian ...), a dictionary-based stemmer will need to remove i-suffixes independently of dictionary look-up, because the proper names will not of course be in the dictionary." We should investigate if we are handling proper nouns adequately for languages such as Finnish and Russian.

Finnish topic 196 (Japanilaisten pankkien fuusio (Merger of Japanese Banks)) also illustrates how inflective a language Finnish is. SearchServer matched several terms in the two relevant documents that the algorithmic stemmer did not such as "Japanilaisen", "Japaniin", "Japanilaiset", "japanilaisia", "japanilaispankin" (a compound) and "pankin", apparently helping it to score much higher.

Finnish topic 147 (Öljyonnettomuudet ja linnut (Oil Accidents and Birds)) is a case showing the importance of compounding to Finnish. SearchServer matched terms such as "Onnettomuuksien", "linturyhmä", "öljyonnettomuuksien", "lintuvahinkojen", "Öljykatastrofi", "öljy" and "lintuja" (just to name a few) which appeared to be missed by the algorithmic stemmer (though not all of these were from compound-splitting) and SearchServer scored substantially higher.

4.8   Swedish Stemming

Swedish topic 188 (Tysk stavningsreform (German Spelling Reform)) shows that when a lexicon-based stemmer does not support compound-splitting for a language with frequent compounds (which is currently the case for SearchServer regarding Swedish), a secondary penalty is that inflections of compounds can be missed. In this topic, SearchServer did not match "stavningsreform" to "stavningsreformen", even though it matches "reform" to "reformen", presumably because the lexicon does not contain most compound words. The algorithmic stemmer did match "stavningsreformen" which apparently is why it scored higher on this topic.

For Swedish topic 144 (Uppror i Sierra Leone och diamanter (Sierra Leone Rebellion and Diamonds)), it appears the difference in the score was from SearchServer matching "uppror" with "upproret" while the algorithmic stemmer did not. SearchServer's behaviour looks reasonable but it appears it was not helpful in this case just by chance (the top retrieved documents had similar relevance scores and the small shift caused by this difference happened to move down a relevant document).

Swedish topic 187 (Kärnavfallstransporter i Tyskland (Nuclear Transport in Germany)) is another case like topic 188. SearchServer did not match the Swedish compound word "Kärnavfallstransporter" with "kärnavfallstransport" nor "kärnavfallstransporten" (even though SearchServer does match "transporter", "transport" and "transporten" with each other). The algorithmic stemmer handled all of these cases and scored higher on this topic.

Swedish topic 179 (NATO:s generalsekreterares avsked (Resignation of NATO Secretary General)) is a case in which the opposite happened. SearchServer matched "generalsekreterares" with "generalsekreterare" while the algorithmic stemmer did not. Perhaps this word is handled because even though it looks like a compound, it probably is better not to split it because it has a different meaning as one word than it does if split in two. SearchServer scored higher on this topic.

4.9   Russian Stemming

For Russian, the submitted runs and the lexical diagnostic runs in the draft version of this paper were affected by a mishandling of words whose stem contained a breve accent (Russian support was very new in SearchServer and had not been

Table 5. Precision with Lexical, Algorithmic and No Stemming, Title-only queries

Run	AvgP	P@5	P@10	P@20	Rec0	Rec30	P@R	Topics
FI-lex-t	0.553	47.6%	35.3%	26.0%	0.762	0.682	52.5%	45
FI-alg-t	0.422	37.8%	27.8%	21.0%	0.682	0.539	40.9%	45
FI-none-t	0.301	30.2%	23.8%	17.8%	0.555	0.398	29.1%	45
DE-lex-t	0.424	59.6%	51.1%	40.8%	0.780	0.557	42.5%	56
DE-alg-t	0.319	47.5%	40.2%	31.5%	0.666	0.402	32.9%	56
DE-none-t	0.267	44.6%	35.7%	27.8%	0.635	0.333	28.6%	56
RU-lex-t	0.310	28.6%	21.1%	13.2%	0.546	0.444	26.9%	28
RU-alg-t	0.297	28.6%	20.7%	13.2%	0.510	0.420	26.0%	28
RU-none-t	0.254	25.0%	17.5%	10.4%	0.493	0.389	23.1%	28
SV-lex-t	0.338	35.5%	26.0%	19.2%	0.665	0.439	32.6%	53
SV-alg-t	0.368	35.5%	27.4%	20.2%	0.706	0.487	36.5%	53
SV-none-t	0.286	31.3%	23.2%	17.3%	0.593	0.352	28.2%	53
NL-lex-t	0.422	45.4%	38.0%	32.1%	0.671	0.514	40.3%	56
NL-alg-t	0.388	44.6%	34.8%	29.0%	0.652	0.505	37.6%	56
NL-none-t	0.372	42.9%	33.9%	28.1%	0.649	0.487	37.1%	56
FR-lex-t	0.447	40.4%	31.5%	24.5%	0.689	0.549	41.5%	52
FR-alg-t	0.451	40.4%	31.7%	25.0%	0.672	0.559	41.1%	52
FR-none-t	0.413	38.1%	29.2%	23.3%	0.671	0.518	38.7%	52
ES-lex-t	0.405	51.9%	44.0%	36.1%	0.803	0.535	40.1%	57
ES-alg-t	0.400	50.9%	43.2%	35.9%	0.783	0.521	39.6%	57
ES-none-t	0.374	46.7%	42.6%	34.4%	0.762	0.494	37.4%	57
IT-lex-t	0.394	40.4%	30.2%	21.9%	0.683	0.487	36.2%	51
IT-alg-t	0.422	41.2%	30.8%	22.4%	0.727	0.526	40.0%	51
IT-none-t	0.367	35.7%	25.9%	19.7%	0.649	0.445	34.1%	51
EN-lex-t	0.448	38.5%	34.4%	27.8%	0.676	0.550	43.4%	54
EN-alg-t	0.453	38.5%	34.3%	27.2%	0.678	0.547	43.2%	54
EN-none-t	0.435	40.0%	32.4%	27.1%	0.676	0.542	42.8%	54

Table 6. Impact of Lexical Stemming on Average Precision, Title-only queries

Experiment	AvgDiff	95% Confidence	vs.	2 Largest Diffs (Topic)
FI-lex-t	0.252	(0.149, 0.360)	32-11-2	1.000 (147), 0.999 (187)
DE-lex-t	0.157	(0.103, 0.213)	43-10-3	0.843 (174), 0.627 (192)
RU-lex-t	0.056	(0.016, 0.098)	19-5-4	0.302 (148), 0.264 (197)
SV-lex-t	0.051	(0.023, 0.085)	23-15-15	0.507 (195), 0.479 (192)
NL-lex-t	0.050	(0.001, 0.102)	30-19-7	0.709 (174), 0.487 (188)
FR-lex-t	0.034	(−0.023, 0.091)	25-18-9	0.923 (175), −0.875 (141)
ES-lex-t	0.031	(0.011, 0.052)	33-19-5	0.240 (164), 0.228 (181)
IT-lex-t	0.027	(0.006, 0.050)	24-18-9	0.317 (171), 0.202 (200)
EN-lex-t	0.013	(−0.007, 0.038)	23-21-10	0.417 (144), 0.262 (158)

officially released). For this paper, the diagnostic runs have been updated and there are more ties in the scores.

Table 7. HTML for Russian (Cyrillic) Words Mentioned in Text

English	HTML (hexadecimal Unicode) for Russian
M1: "milk" in topic 177	(Молока)
M2: inflection of "milk"	(молоко)
"Roman" in topic 149	(Римского)
"Roman-Catholic"	(римско-католической)
"visit" in topic 149	(Визит)
inflection of "visit"	(визита)

The author's LATEX setup does not yet support Cyrillic. Table 7 gives the HTML numeric character references for the characters of the Russian words referred to below (the numbers are the Unicode values of the Cyrillic characters in hexadecimal) so that the reader can know exactly which words are being referenced (just enter the HTML syntax into an HTML file and view it with an up-to-date web browser; alternately, look up the Unicode values in the Unicode Standard [11]).

Russian topic 177 (Milk Consumption in Europe) is a case where the decision to arbitrarily just match the inflections of one stem (as per the '/noalt' option mentioned earlier) made a difference (in this case, beneficial). The Russian word for "milk" in topic 177 (word M1 in Table 7) had two stems: itself (M1) and a second stem (M2). The second stem just had itself (M2) as a stem. The /noalt option caused just the first stem to be used, so SearchServer did not match M2, unlike the algorithmic stemmer (which always produces just one stem per word internally). In the case of this topic, it turned out to be helpful not to match that inflection and SearchServer scored higher. Although it is not very common, we should investigate this scenario further.

For Russian topic 149 (Pope's Visit in Sri Lanka), the Russian version of the topic contained the Russian word for "Roman" (but not the Russian phrase for "Roman-Catholic"). The algorithmic stemmer matched the variation of "Roman" used in the Russian for "Roman-Catholic", unlike SearchServer. Search-Server matched an inflection of the Russian word for "visit" which the algorithmic stemmer did not, but overall the algorithmic stemmer scored higher for this topic. We should investigate this case further.

Overall for Russian, as Table 4 shows, SearchServer scored higher on 8 topics, lower on 3, and tied 17, but the differences were not statistically significant (i.e. zero is in the approximate 95% confidence interval).

References

1. M. Braschler and C. Peters. CLEF2003: Methodology and Metrics. This volume.
2. Cross-Language Evaluation Forum web site. http://www.clef-campaign.org/
3. Bradley Efron and Robert J. Tibshirani. An Introduction to the Bootstrap. 1993. Chapman & Hall/CRC.
4. Andrew Hodgson. Converting the Fulcrum Search Engine to Unicode. In Sixteenth International Unicode Conference, Amsterdam, The Netherlands, March 2000.
5. NTCIR (NII-NACSIS Test Collection for IR Systems) Home Page. http://research.nii.ac.jp/~ntcadm/index-en.html
6. M. F. Porter. Snowball: A language for stemming algorithms. October 2001. http://snowball.tartarus.org/texts/introduction.html
7. S. E. Robertson, S. Walker, S. Jones, M. M. Hancock-Beaulieu, M. Gatford. (City University.) Okapi at TREC-3. In D. K. Harman, editor, Overview of the Third Text REtrieval Conference (TREC-3). NIST Special Publication 500-226. http://trec.nist.gov/pubs/trec3/t3_proceedings.html
8. Text REtrieval Conference (TREC) Home Page. http://trec.nist.gov/
9. Stephen Tomlinson. Experiments in 8 European Languages with Hummingbird SearchServer™ at CLEF 2002. In C. Peters, M. Braschler, J. Gonzalo and M. Kluck (eds): Advances in Cross-Language Information Retrieval. CLEF 2002 workshop. Revised papers. LNCS 2785 Springer (2003).
10. Stephen Tomlinson. Hummingbird SearchServer™ at TREC 2001. In E. M. Voorhees and D. K. Harman, editors, Proceedings of the Tenth Text REtrieval Conference (TREC 2001). NIST Special Publication 500-250. http://trec.nist.gov/pubs/trec10/t10_proceedings.html
11. The Unicode Standard Version 3.0. The Unicode Consortium. 2000. Addison-Wesley.

Océ at CLEF 2003

Roel Brand, Marvin Brüner, Samuel Driessen, Pascha Iljin, and Jakob Klok

Océ-Technologies B.V., P.O. Box 101,
5900 MA Venlo, The Netherlands
{rkbr,mbru,sjdr,pi,klok}@oce.nl

Abstract. This report describes the work done at Océ Research for the Cross-Language Evaluation Forum (CLEF) 2003. This year we participated in seven mono-lingual tasks (all languages except Russian). We developed a generic probabilistic model that does not make use of global statistics from a document collection to rank documents. The relevance of a document to a given query is calculated using the term frequencies of the query terms in the document and the length of the document. We used the BM25 model, our new probabilistic model and (for Dutch only) a statistical model to rank documents. Our main goals were to compare the BM25 model and our probabilistic model, and to evaluate the performance of a statistical model that uses 'knowledge' from relevance assessments from previous years. Furthermore, we give some comments on the standard performance measures used in the CLEF.

1 Introduction

This is our third participation in the Cross-Language Evaluation Forum (CLEF). In 2001 we have only participated in the Dutch monolingual task. Last year we participated in all mono-lingual tasks, in some of the cross-lingual and in the multi-lingual task. The goal for this year was to concentrate on mono-lingual tasks. We aimed to compare the models we constructed during the last two years and get more insight into the possibilities of using 'knowledge' from relevance assessments from previous years in order to construct information retrieval systems for this year. (Due to problems with indexing and a restriction on the maximum number of mono-lingual runs, the runs for Russian language were not carried out.)

2 Methods

2.1 Ranking Systems

Three different approaches were used to rank documents:

1. The BM25 model (for seven languages)
2. A probabilistic model (for seven languages)
3. A statistical model (for the Dutch language only)

C. Peters et al. (Eds.): CLEF 2003, LNCS 3237, pp. 301–309, 2004.
© Springer-Verlag Berlin Heidelberg 2004

The BM25 model was used again this year, just like in CLEF 2002 [1]. The probabilistic and statistical models appeared as a result of internal research done last year [2].

2.2 Query

Queries were constructed automatically from the *title* and *description* fields by splitting topics on non-alphanumerical characters to obtain terms. All single characters were removed afterwards. Furthermore, all remaining terms were converted to lower case. The expansion of query terms was carried out for the statistical approach only. For that model, the morphological collapse (dictionary based stemming) of Knowledge Concepts' Content Enabler semantic network was used to obtain root forms of (not necessarily all) query terms. The root forms were then expanded with the semantic network. The morphological variants of the root form (such as plural form, etc.) were added to the query.

Related Terms and Synonym Expansion. Research was done on using related terms and synonyms. We found that Knowledge Concepts' Content Enabler is not good enough to create related terms and synonyms for our models. A measure of 'similarity' between two terms is needed in order to rank the proposed list of related terms and synonyms. Only terms that are very 'similar' in their meaning to a query term should be added during query expansion.

Different Parts of the Topic. Last year we experimented with generating queries using different parts of the topics. All possible combinations of one to three parts (title, description, and narrative) were investigated. Both results of the runs for probabilistic and statistical models) and the statistical information indicate that using the narrative makes the performance of the information retrieval engine worse. We suppose that the narrative part contains too many irrelevant terms that add 'noise' to the query. A clever selection of terms from the narrative is needed. However, an automatic selection of 'proper' terms is not an easy task. We did not aim to solve it this year.

2.3 Indexing

The indexes were built for each of the languages by splitting documents on non-alphanumerical characters. Single character terms were removed from the indexes. Stop words were left in the indexes because it is very difficult to construct a universal set of stop words. If such a set is based on the frequencies within a document collection, it is highly probable that the set of stop words will not be the same for two different document collections. In case it is based on human decisions, a number of important terms from the document collection and/or query will be removed. For example, consider the terms 'new' and 'year' as stop words (they are used in this role quite often). After removing these terms from the document collection and from the queries, it becomes difficult to find a set of relevant documents for the query '*A New Year tree*'. In order to show that stop word removal is not always beneficial, consider the query '*Who said "To be or not to be?"*'. In this case *all* terms from the query could be defined as stop words. Nevertheless, stop word terms must be treated different than other terms. This year the following stop word lists were used:

- Dutch
  - internally developed stop word list
  - http://www.unine.ch/Info/clef/
- Spanish
  - http://www.unine.ch/Info/clef/
  - ftp://ftp.cs.cornell.edu/pub/smart/spanish.stop
- Finnish, Italian, French, Swedish, and German
  - http://www.unine.ch/Info/clef/

3 Ranking Models

3.1 BM25 Model

The general description of the BM25 model (without query expansion) is as follows:

- Let q_i be a query term in query q.
- Let $tf(q_i, d)$ be the term frequency of term q_i in document d.
- Let $df(q_i)$ be the document frequency of q_i.

Then for document d, and query q, the relevance of d with regard to q is calculated as:

$$\text{Rel}(d,q) = \sum_{q_i \in q} \frac{\log(N) - \log(df(q_i)) \cdot tf(q_i, d) \cdot (k_1 + 1)}{k_1 \cdot ((1-b) + (b \cdot nld(d))) + tf(q_i, d)}, \tag{1}$$

in which $nld(d)$ is the length of the document d, divided by the average document length.

Last year we observed that the performance of the BM25 ranking algorithm depends greatly on the choice of values for the parameters $k1$ and b. However, the estimation of those values for the optimal performance is only possible when the document collection, the set of queries and the set of relevance assessments are all available beforehand. Because the relevance assessments are not known in advance, a choice should be made for the parameters. For this year we chose $k1=1.2$ and $b=0.6$ for all seven languages. This pair of values was optimal for the Dutch document collection, set of queries and relevance assessments in 2001.

3.2 Probabilistic Model

The probabilistic model has been selected as the result of theoretical research conducted in 2002. It contains some innovations with respect to the standard probabilistic approach. The urn model (balls in an urn = terms in a document) was selected as a basis for the probabilistic model.

We calculate the degree of relevancy without making use of collection statistics (like document frequency). The sparse data problem is commonly solved using the linear interpolation method or other smoothing techniques that are based on collection statistics. However, Robertson showed that "relevance of a document to a request should not depend on the other documents in the collection" in order to guarantee "optimality of ranking by the probability of relevance" [3]. Hence, the selection of the complete document collection as a smoothing element is not strongly motivated and not even supposed to exist according to the basic principle of the probabilistic approach in information retrieval. We found experimentally that under certain distributions of terms over documents in the document collection, the linear interpolation approach will give illogical results for ranking. A standard solution to the sparse data problem is to assign non-zero values for query terms that do not exist in a document. The most natural and easy way to solve the sparse data problem is to assign a constant positive value α to the terms that do not exist in the document. We named this '**the α-method**'.

For the query without term expansion:

$$\text{Rel(d,q)}= \prod_{q_i \in q}[\frac{1}{2} \cdot (\frac{tf(q_i,d)}{L_D} + \alpha)], \tag{2}$$

where L_d is the length (not normalized) of the document d.

α should be selected less than [the length of the longest document in the document collection]$^{-1}$. This guarantees coordination level ranking.

3.3 Statistical Model

In 2002 we aimed to implement a set of clues (that we defined) in a '*mathematically correct*' model, i.e. a model without internal contradictions or violations of axioms.

Examples of clues are:

- presence of terms in a document that are synonyms to the terms from the query;
- importance of a topic's tag;
- part of speech of the query terms;
- query terms of certain document frequency;
- presence of proper nouns in the query;
- length of a document.

We found that a set of defined clues could not be entirely incorporated in the currently known information retrieval models while maintaining mathematical correctness. However, we have succeeded to construct a statistical approach that allows incorporation of these clues. For each clue, a value expressing its expected '*significance*' is calculated. *Significance* values are based on relevance assessments from previous years for (document, topic) pairs.

For every clue we test whether its incorporation makes a statistically significant contribution to the overall performance of an information retrieval system.

Let us select a *clue*[1] to investigate its contribution to the improvement of the performance. The following procedure is carried out for the set of queries. Let us consider a query q in order to describe the procedure:

- From q we determine those components that can be tested for contribution of *clue* with respect to the total performance of an information retrieval system.

---

[1] Taking two or more clues simultaneously is very complex.

Let us denote by $Comp_c(q, clue)$ the cth component in the query q that is tested, where $c = \overline{1, C(q, clue)}$, and $C(q, clue)$ is the total number of components from the query q that can be tested on *clue*.

Example 1. In case *clue* is 'presence of query terms in a document', all query terms are components.

Example 2. In case *clue* is 'noun', the components from the query 'Crocodiles living in the lake' are 'crocodiles', and 'lake'.

The following notation will be used:

$|R(J,q)|$ - the number of documents from document collection (Dc) that have got values *relevant* from the relevance assessments for the query q.

$|I(J,q)|$ - the number of documents from Dc that have got values *irrelevant* from the relevance assessments for the query q.

$\left|R_{Comp_c(q,clue)}\right|$ - the number of documents from Dc that have got values *relevant* from the relevance assessments for the query q and that contain $Comp_c(q, clue)$.

$\left|I_{Comp_c(q,clue)}\right|$ - the number of documents from Dc that have got values *irrelevant* from the relevance assessments for the query q and that contain $Comp_c(q, clue)$.

- Calculate for every component $Comp_c(q, clue)$:

$$R_c(clue,q) = \frac{\left|R_{Comp_c(q,clue)}\right|}{|R(J,q)|} \tag{3}$$

$$I_c(clue,q) = \frac{\left|I_{Comp_c(q,clue)}\right|}{|I(J,q)|} \tag{4}$$

The pair $(R_c(clue,q), I_c(clue,q))$ indicates how often a component $Comp_c(q, clue)$ occurs in relevant and irrelevant documents respectively. In case $R_c(clue,q) > I_c(clue,q)$, the component $Comp_c(q, clue)$ occurs more often in relevant documents than in irrelevant ones.

After $(R_c(clue,q), I_c(clue,q))$ are calculated for each component c of each query q, a set of pairs $\{(R_1(clue), I_1(clue)), (R_2(clue), I_2(clue)), \ldots, (R_t(clue), I_t(clue))\}$ is obtained, where $t = \sum_{q=1}^{|Q|} C(q, clue)$ is the number of all components for *clue* from all $|Q|$ queries in the test collection.

In case $\sum_{\substack{i=1 \\ \{R_i(clue)>I_i(clue)\}}}^{t} 1 > \sum_{\substack{i=1 \\ \{R_i(clue)<I_i(clue)\}}}^{t} 1$, one can state that after incorporating

clue, the components of q occur more often in relevant documents than in irrelevant ones. This statement implies that the incorporated clue is expected to improve the performance of the information retrieval system.

In order to decide if a clue may improve performance, the set of pairs $\{(R_1(clue), I_1(clue)), (R_2(clue), I_2(clue)),..., (R_t(clue), I_t(clue))\}$ should be statistically investigated. The statistical method called the Sign Test is used in order to compare two sets of pairs. It is the only method that can be used for our purpose.

The Sign Test is used to test the hypothesis that there is "no difference" between two probability distributions (in our case, $R(clue)$ and $I(clue)$). In case of the statistical model it tests whether the presence of *clue* has an influence on the distribution of components from the query in relevant and irrelevant documents.

Theory requires:

1. The pairs should be mutually independent.
2. Both $R_i(clue)$ and $I_i(clue)$ should have continuous probability distributions.

Because of the assumed mutual independence between queries, mutual independence between query terms, and mutual independence between terms in documents, pairs $(R_i(clue), I_i(clue))$ are mutually independent (point 1). A continuous distribution is defined as a distribution for which the variables may take on a continuous range of values. In the considered case, the values of both $R_i(clue)$ and $I_i(clue)$ take any value from the closed interval $[0,1]$, and so their distributions are continuous (point 2). Hence, the necessary conditions for the Sign Test hold.

The hypothesis implies that for given a pair of measurements $(R_i(clue), I_i(clue))$, both $R_i(clue)$ and $I_i(clue)$ are equally likely to be larger than the other. The zero hypothesis H_0: $P[R_i(clue) > I_i(clue)] = P[R_i(clue) < I_i(clue)] = 0.5$ is tested for every $i = \overline{1,t}$. Applying the one-sided Sign Test means that rejecting H_0, we accept the alternative hypothesis H_1: $P[R_i(clue) > I_i(clue)] > 0.5$. A one-sided 95% confidence interval is taken to test H_0 hypothesis. If H_0 is rejected, the incorporation of *clue* is expected to improve the performance of an information retrieval system.

Remark. Using the Sign Test described for a certain clue, we conclude whether its incorporation into an information retrieval system can improve the performance. This conclusion is based on theoretical expectations only.

Two criteria are defined to estimate the possible contribution of a clue to a system from a practical point of view.

In case there are t components for all the queries, $\forall i = \overline{1,t}$ calculate for *clue*

1. $\#(R(clue))$ – the number of components for which $R_i(clue) > I_i(clue)$
2. $\#(I(clue))$ – the number of components for which $R_i(clue) < I_i(clue)$

According to the theoretical issues of the Sign Test, one has to ignore the statistics of the components for which $R_i(clue) = I_i(clue)$. Thus, when a component of a certain clue is found in both relevant and irrelevant documents, and the relative frequency of $R_i(clue) = I_i(clue)$, this is neither good nor bad. Such an observation should not influence the total statistics.

However, the other theoretical issue will not be taken into account. According to the theory of the Sign Test, when one observes more than one component with the same values of $R_i(clue)$ and $I_i(clue)$, all but one component should be ignored too. However, this claim cannot be valid in the area of linguistics due to the following reasons:

1. The influence of each component to the clue has to be calculated. Even in the case the same statistics are obtained for different terms, all terms will make a contribution to the performance of the system. So, every component will be an extra observation for a clue.
2. In case a term is used in more than one query, it has multiple influences on the performance. For each query different statistics should be obtained. Hence, each component should be considered separately for every query used.
3. In case the same component is used more than one time for the same query, it is considered multiple times.

For estimating the significance of a certain clue, the ratio $\dfrac{\#(R(clue))}{\#(I(clue))}$ is calculated. The larger this ratio, the higher the significance is. After calculating these ratios for all clues, they can be ranked in a decreasing order, where the top value will correspond with the most significant clue.

- *Not all clues have the same contribution to the ranking function.*

The contribution of a certain clue depends on the level of improvement to the performance of an information retrieval system.

- *Not all clues should be implemented in the statistical model.*

A clue is implemented into a model if the ratio $\dfrac{\#(R(clue))}{\#(I(clue))}$ has a value higher than one. Only in this case one can expect that the selected clue can improve the performance of the system.

Experiments with the Statistical Model. Last year we experimented with the Dutch document collection, the set of queries and the relevance assessments for 2001 and 2002. The statistics for each of these two years were obtained. Two runs were submitted for the Dutch language using the statistical model, each run using the statistics of one of the two years. Different statistics were chosen depending on their degree of significance to obtain better performance results.

The experiments with the statistical model for CLEF data from 2001 and 2002 resulted in improvements of performance compared to the BM25 and probabilistic models. The proper choice of features to be selected and their 'significance' values lead to better results. However, this model is strongly dependent on the data collection, queries and relevance assessments. Hence, the results for a set of new documents, new queries and new relevance assessments are unpredictable.

4   Runs for 2003

This year we submitted 16 mono-lingual runs:

- for each of the following languages two runs (using BM25 and probabilistic ranking principles): Finnish, French, German, Italian, Spanish and Swedish;

- for Dutch BM25 ranking, probabilistic ranking, and two statistical rankings (one is based on statistics for 2001 and another one is based on statistics for 2002).

Numerical results of Océ at CLEF 2003

Name of the run	Number of retrieved relevant documents	Average precision	R-precision
Swedish BM25	729 out of 889	0.3584	0.3585
Swedish probabilistic	633 out of 889	0.2716	0.2743
Italian BM25	759 out of 809	0.4361	0.4287
Italian probabilistic	731 out of 809	0.3805	0.3865
French BM25	894 out of 946	0.4601	0.4273
French probabilistic	865 out of 946	0.4188	0.4044
Finnish BM25	417 out of 483	0.3570	0.3230
Finnish probabilistic	407 out of 483	0.3031	0.2624
Spanish BM25	2109 out of 2368	0.4156	0.4094
Spanish probabilistic	2025 out of 2368	0.3500	0.3696
German BM25	1482 out of 1825	0.3858	0.3838
German probabilistic	1337 out of 1825	0.3017	0.3088
Dutch BM25	1438 out of 1577	0.4561	0.4438
Dutch probabilistic	1336 out of 1577	0.4049	0.3652
Dutch statistical 2001	1375 out of 1577	0.4253	0.3940
Dutch statistical 2002	1378 out of 1577	0.4336	0.3983

5 Proposal of a Different Evaluation Measure

We want to propose a different evaluation measure for the CLEF. Therefore, we first recall the standard CLEF evaluation measure (taking the Dutch data from 2001as an example):

- There are 190,604 documents in the document collection. For each query, every participating information retrieval system provides a ranking of these documents and provides the top 1000 documents as the result. Assessors select the top N ($N<1000$) documents from this ranked list.
- Suppose that there are M participating information retrieval systems. At most $N*M$ documents are read by assessors and receive relevance assessments. In case the same document is in the top N for at least two participating systems, less than $N*M$ obtain relevance assessment values.
- There are 16774 relevance assessment values for 50 queries, so an average of 335 relevance assessments per query. There are 1224 documents known to be relevant for 50 queries, so an average of 25 relevant documents per query.

Looking at the above, we think that the *common evaluation measure can be improved*. The very simple reason is that we know the relevance assessment values for much less than 1000 documents. About 60-70% of all documents in the top 1000 have unknown relevance values. They are not retrieved by any of the participating IR systems, and are *irrelevant* by definition; even if in fact they are *relevant*. Paradox!

Proposal 1. For a *robust comparison* between s information retrieval systems based on the top N documents, all s systems must obtain relevance assessments for all N documents.

Proposal 2. By reducing N it is easier to achieve a *robust comparison*.

It is even gives better simulation of a real-life situation. Given a collection of not domain-specific newspaper articles, one can hardly expect that a user will look through all 1000 retrieved documents. A choice of $N=100$ or $N=200$ seems to be much more realistic. Another option is to derive N from a predetermined number of mutually different documents that should obtain relevance assessments and the amount of overlap in the submitted results.

6 Conclusions

We developed and tested a generic probabilistic model that does not make use of the global statistics from the document collection to rank the documents. We compared it with the BM25 model on the base of mono-lingual runs. The BM25 model systematically outperforms the probabilistic one. This indicates that striving for mathematical correctness is not the best guideline to obtain better retrieval performance. At the same time we have observed that the developed probabilistic model has a satisfactory performance. Furthermore, we conclude that (the construction of) a better retrieval model needs 'knowledge' about the data collection, and the way the user formulates the topics and assesses the documents. All this information is needed in order to tune the statistical retrieval engine.

References

1. Brand, R., Brüner, M.: Océ at CLEF 2002. Lecture Notes on Computer Science, Springer-Verlag Heidelberg (2003)
2. Iljin, P.: Modeling Document Relevancy Clues in Information Retrieval Systems. SAI (to appear in 2004)
3. Hiemstra, D.: Using Language Models for Information Retrieval. Ph.D. Thesis. Centre for Telematics and Information Technology, University of Twente (2001)

Comparing Weighting Models for Monolingual Information Retrieval

Gianni Amati, Claudio Carpineto, and Giovanni Romano

Fondazione Ugo Bordoni, via B. Castiglione 59,
00142 Rome, Italy
{gba,carpinet,romano}@fub.it

Abstract. Motivated by the hypothesis that the retrieval performance of a weighting model is independent of the language in which queries and collection are expressed, we compared the retrieval performance of three weighting models, i.e., Okapi, statistical language modeling (SLM), and deviation from randomness (DFR), on three monolingual test collections, i.e., French, Italian, and Spanish. The DFR model was found to consistently achieve better results than both Okapi and SLM, whose performance was comparable. We also evaluated whether the use of retrieval feedback improved retrieval performance; retrieval feedback was beneficial for DFR and Okapi and detrimental for SLM. Besides relative performance, DFR with retrieval feedback achieved excellent absolute results: best run for Italian and Spanish, third run for French.

1 Introduction

Although the choice of the weighting model may crucially affect the performance of any information retrieval system, there has been little work on evaluating the relative merits and drawbacks of different weighting models in the CLEF environment. The main goal of our participation in CLEF 2003 was to help fill this gap.

We consider three weighting models with a different theoretical background that have proved their effectiveness on a number of tasks and collections. The three models are Okapi [9], statistical language modeling [11], and deviation from randomness [2].

We study the retrieval performance of the rankings produced by each weighting model with and without retrieval feedback, on three monolingual test collections, i.e., French, Italian and Spanish. The collections are indexed with standard techniques and the retrieval feedback stage is performed using the method described in [5].

In the following we first describe the three weighting models, the method used for retrieval feedback, and the experimental setting. Then we compare the retrieval performance of the three methods, performing also a query-by-query analysis. Finally, we summarize the main results of the experiments.

C. Peters et al. (Eds.): CLEF 2003, LNCS 3237, pp. 310–318, 2004.

2 The Three Weighting Models

To assist clarity and comparison, the document ranking produced by each weighting model is represented using the same general expression, namely as the product of a document-based term weight by a query-based term weight:

$$sim(q,d) = \sum_{t \in q \wedge d} w_{t,d} \cdot w_{t,q}$$

This formalism also allows a uniform application of the subsequent retrieval feedback stage to the first-pass ranking produced by each weighting model, as we will see in the next section. Before giving the expressions for $w_{t,d}$ and $w_{t,q}$ for each weighting model, we report the complete list of variables that will be used:

f_t	the number of occurrences of term t in the collection
$f_{t,d}$	the number of occurrences of term t in document d
$f_{t,q}$	the number of occurrences of term t in query q
n_t	the number of documents in which term t occurs
D	the number of documents in the collection
T	the number of terms in the collection
λ_t	the ratio between f_t and T
l_d	the length of document d
l_q	the length of query q
avr_l_d	the average length of documents in the collection

2.1 Okapi

To describe Okapi, we use the expression given in [9]. This formula has been used by most participants in TREC and CLEF over the last years.

$$w_{t,d} = \frac{(k_1 + 1) \cdot f_{t,d}}{k_1 \cdot \left[(1 - b) + b \dfrac{l_d}{avr\_l_d} \right] + f_{t,d}}$$

$$w_{t,q} = \frac{(k_3 + 1) \cdot f_{t,q}}{k_3 + f_{t,q}} \cdot log_2 \frac{D - n_t + 0.5}{n_t + 0.5}$$

2.2 Statistical Language Modeling (SLM)

The statistical language modeling approach has been proposed in several papers, with many variants (e.g., [6], [7]). Here we use the expression given in [11], with Dirichlet smoothing.

$$w_{t,d} = log_2 \frac{f_{t,d} + \mu \lambda_t}{l_d + \mu} - log_2 \frac{\mu}{l_d + \mu} - log_2 \lambda_t + \frac{l_q}{|q \wedge d|} \cdot log_2 \frac{\mu}{l_d + \mu}$$

$$w_{t,q} = f_{t,q}$$

2.3   Deviation from Randomness (DFR)

Deviation from randomness has been successfully used at CLEF 2002, for the Italian monolingual task [2], and at TREC, for the Web and Robust tracks ([1], [4]). It is best described in [3].

$$w_{t,d} = (log_2(1 + \lambda_t) + f_{t,d}^* \cdot log_2\frac{1+\lambda_t}{\lambda_t}) \cdot \frac{f_t + 1}{n_t \cdot (f_{t,d}^* + 1)}$$

with

$$f_{t,d}^* = f_t \cdot log_2(1 + \frac{c \cdot avr\_l_d}{l_d})$$

3   Retrieval Feedback

As retrieval feedback has been incorporated in most recent systems participating in CLEF, it is interesting to also evaluate the performance of the different weighting models when they are enriched with retrieval feedback.

To perform the experiments, we used information-theoretic query expansion [5]. At the end of the first-pass ranking, each term in the top retrieved documents was assigned a score using the Kullback-Leibler distance between the distribution of the term in such documents and the distribution of the same term in the entire collection, and the terms with the highest scores were selected for expansion. The KLD scores are given by:

$$KLD_{t,d} = f_{t,d} \cdot log_2\frac{f_{t,d}}{f_t}$$

At this point, the KLD scores were also used to reweight the terms in the expanded query. As the weights for the unexpanded query (i.e., SLM, Okapi, and DFR) and the KLD scores had different scales, we normalized both the weights of the original query and the scores of the expansion terms by the maximum corresponding value; then the normalized values were linearly combined. The new expression for computing the similarity between an expanded query q_{exp} and a document d becomes:

$$sim(q_{exp}, d) = \sum_{t \in q \wedge d} w_{t,d} \cdot (\alpha \frac{w_{t,q}}{Max_q w_{t,q}} + \beta \frac{KLD_{t,d}}{Max_d KLD_{t,d}})$$

4   Experimental Setting

4.1   Test Collections

The experiments were performed using three CLEF 2003 monolingual test collections, namely the French, Spanish, and Italian collections. For all collections, the title+description topic statement was considered.

4.2 Document and Query Indexing

We identifed the individual words occurring in the documents, considering only the admissible sections and ignoring punctuation and case. The system then performed word stemming and word stopping. For word stemming, we used the French, Italian, and Spanish versions of the Porter stemming algorithm [8], which have been made available on the Snowball web site (http://snowball.tartarus.org) To remove common words, we used the stop lists provided by Savoy [10]. Thus, we performed a strict single-word indexing; furthermore, we did not use any ad hoc linguistic manipulation such as expanding or removing certain words from the query text or using lists of proper nouns.

4.3 Choice of Experimental Parameters

The final document ranking is affected by a number of parameters. To perform the experiments, we set the parameters using values that have been reported in the literature. Here is the complete list of parameter values:

Okapi $k_1 = 1.2$, $k_3 = 1000$, $b = 0.75$
SLM $\mu = 1000$
DFR $c = 2$
Retrieval feedback 10 pseudo-rel. docs., 40 exp. terms, $\alpha = 1$, $\beta = 0.5$

5 Results

For each collection and for each query, we computed six runs: two runs for each of the three weighting modesl, one without and one with retrieval feedback (RF). Table 1, Table 2, and Table 3 show the retrieval performance of each method on the French, Italian, and Spanish collection, respectively. Performance was measured using average precision (AV-PREC), precision at 5 retrieved documents (PREC-AT-5), and precision at 10 retrieved documents (PREC-AT-10). For each collection we show in bold the best result with retrieval feedback and the best result without retrieval feedback.

Note that for the French and Italian collections the average precision was greater than the early precisions; this is due to the fact that for these collections

Table 1. Retrieval performance on the French collection

	AV-PREC	PREC-AT-5	PREC-AT-10
Okapi	0.5030	0.4385	**0.3654**
Okapi + RF	0.5054	0.4769	0.3942
SLM	0.4753	0.4538	0.3635
SLM + RF	0.4372	0.4192	0.3462
DFR	**0.5116**	**0.4577**	**0.3654**
DFR + RF	**0.5238**	**0.4885**	**0.3981**

Table 2. Retrieval performance on the Italian collection

	AV-PREC	PREC-AT-5	PREC-AT-10
Okapi	0.4762	0.4588	0.3510
Okapi + RF	0.5238	0.4824	0.3902
SLM	0.5027	**0.4941**	**0.3824**
SLM + RF	0.5095	0.4824	0.3863
DFR	**0.5046**	0.4824	0.3725
DFR + RF	**0.5364**	**0.5255**	**0.4137**

Table 3. Retrieval performance on the Spanish collection

	AV-PREC	PREC-AT-5	PREC-AT-10
Okapi	0.4606	0.5684	0.5175
Okapi + RF	0.5093	0.6105	0.5491
SLM	0.4720	**0.6140**	0.5157
SLM + RF	0.5112	0.5825	0.5316
DFR	**0.4907**	0.6035	**0.5386**
DFR + RF	**0.5510**	**0.6140**	**0.5825**

the mean number of relevant documents per query is, on average, small, and that there are many queries with very few relevant documents.

The first main finding of our experiments is that the best absolute result for each collection and for each evaluation measure was always obtained by DFR with retrieval feedback, with notable improvements on several data points. The excellent performance of the DFR model is confirmed when comparing the weighting models without query expansion, although in the latter case DFR did not always achieve the best results (i.e., for PREC-AT-5 and PREC-AT-10 on Italian, and for PREC-AT-5 on Spanish).

Neither of the other two models (i.e., Okapi and SLM) was clearly superior to the other. They achieved comparable results on Spanish, while Okapi was slightly better than DFR on French and slightly worse on Italian. However, when considering the first retrieved documents, the performance of SLM was usually very good and sometimes even better than DFR.

The results in Table 1, Table 2, and Table 3 show also that retrieval feedback improved Okapi and DFR runs and mostly hurt SLM runs. In particular, the use of retrieval feedback improved the retrieval performance of Okapi and DFR for all evaluation measures and across all collections, whereas it usually decreased the early precision of SLM and on one occasion (i.e., for French) it hurt even the average precision of SLM. The unsatisfying performance of SLM + RF may be explained by considering that the experiments were performed using long queries.

We would like to emphasize that the DFR runs shown here correspond to actually submitted runs, although they were not our best runs. In fact, our best submitted runs had language-specific optimal parameters tuned using the past

CLEF collections. We also submitted for each language a run with the same experimental parameters, obtained by averaging the best parameters.

The parameters of our best runs were as follow. For French, $c = 2$, number of pseudo-relevant documents = 8 , number of expansion terms = 30, $\alpha = 1$, $\beta = 0.25$; run *fub03fr3*, average precision = 0.5377, ranked as the third absolute run. For Italian, $c = 2$, number of pseudo-relevant documents = 10 , number of expansion terms = 40, $\alpha = 1$, $\beta = 0.5$; run *fub03itB*, average precision = 0.5707, ranked as the first absolute run. For Spanish, $c = 2$, number of pseudo-relevant documents = 5 , number of expansion terms = 50, $\alpha = 1$, $\beta = 0.5$; run *fub03itB*, average precision = 0.5533, ranked as the first absolute run.

We also performed a query-by-query analysis. For each query, we computed the difference between the best and the worst retrieval result, considering average precision as the performance measure. Figure 1, Figure 2, and Figure 3 show the results for French, Italian, and Spanish, respectively.

Thus, the length of each bar depicts the range of performance variations attainable by the three methods (with retrieval feedback) for each query. The results show that the inter-method variations on single queries were considerable, but does not tell us which method performed best.

To get a more complete picture, for each collection, we counted the number of queries for which each method achieved the best, median, or worst performance. The results, shown in Table 4, confirm the better retrieval effectiveness of DFR over the other two models. The superiority of DFR over Okapi and SLM was clear for Spanish, while DFR and Okapi obtained more comparable results on the other two test collections. For French and Italian, the number of best results obtained by DFR and Okapi was similar, but, on the whole, DFR was ranked ahead of Okapi for a much larger number of queries.

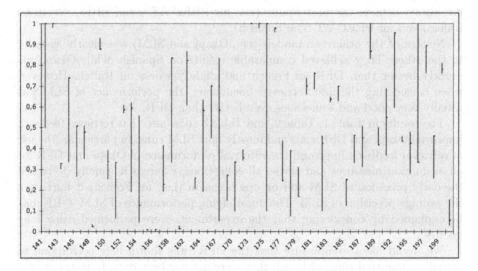

Fig. 1. Performance variation on individual queries for French

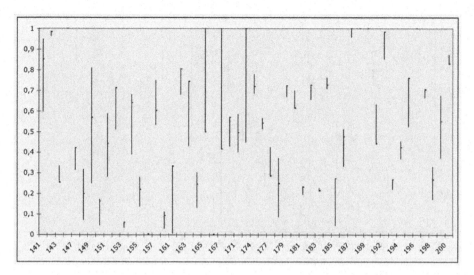

Fig. 2. Performance variation on individual queries for Italian

Table 4. Ranked performance

	French			Italian			Spanish		
	SLM	Okapi	DFR	SLM	Okapi	DFR	SLM	Okapi	DFR
1st	11	20	21	10	21	20	16	16	25
2nd	11	17	24	9	16	26	10	22	25
3rd	30	15	7	32	14	5	31	19	7

6   Conclusions

The main conclusion of our experiments is that the DFR model was more effective than both Okapi and SLM, which achieved comparable retrieval performances. In particular, DFR with query expansion obtained the best average absolute results for any evaluation measure and across all test collections.

The second conclusion is that retrieval feedback always improved the performance of Okapi and DFR, whereas it was often detrimental to the retrieval effectiveness of SLM, although the latter finding may have been influenced by the length of the queries used in the experiments.

These results seem to suggest that the retrieval performance of a weighting model is only moderately affected by the choice of the language, but this hypothesis should be taken with caution, because our results were obtained under specific experimental conditions.

Although there are reasons to believe that similar results might hold also across different experimental situations, in that we chose simple and untuned parameter values and made typical indexing assumptions, the issue needs more

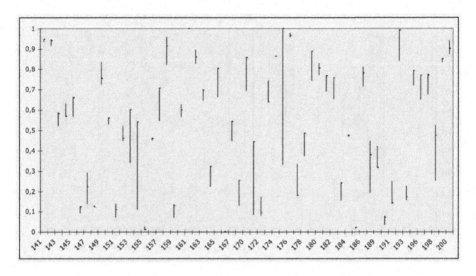

Fig. 3. Performance variation on individual queries for Spanish

investigation. The next step of this research is to experiment with a wider range of factors, such as the length of queries, the values of each weighting model's parameters, and the combination of parameter values for retrieval feedback. It would also be useful to experiment with other languages, to see if the hypothesis that the retrieval performance of a weighting model is independent of the language receives further support.

References

1. Amati, G., Carpineto, C., Romano, G.: FUB at TREC-10 Web Track: A Probabilistic Framework for Topic Relevance Term Weighting. In Proceedings of the 10th Text REtrieval Conference (TREC-10). NIST Special Publication 500-250. Gaithersburg, MD, USA (2001) 182–191.
2. Amati, G., Carpineto, C., Romano, G.: Italian monolingual information retrieval with PROSIT. In Peters, C., Braschler, M., Gonzalo, J., Kluck, M. (eds.): Advances in Cross-Language Information Retrieval. Third Workshop of the Cross Language Evaluation Forum, CLEF 2002, Rome, Italy, September 2002, Revised Papers. LNCS 2785. Springer (2003) 257–264.
3. Amati, G., van Rijsbergen, C. J.: Probabilistic models of information retrieval based on measuring divergence from randomness. ACM Transactions on Information Systems 20(4) (2002) 357–389.
4. Amati, G., Carpineto, C., Romano, G.: Fondazione Ugo Bordoni at TREC 2003: Robust and Web track. In Proceedings of TREC 2003. Gaithersburg, MD, USA (2003) 210–219.
5. Carpineto, C., De Mori, R., Romano, G., Bigi, B.: An Information Theoretic Approach to Automatic Query Expansion. ACM Transactions on Information Systems 19(1) (2001) 1–27.

6. Hiemstra, D., Kraaij, W.: Twenty-one at TREC-7: Ad hoc and cross-language track. In Proceedings of the 7th Text REtrieval Conference (TREC-7). NIST Special Publication 500-242. Gaithersburg, MD, USA (1998) 227–238.
7. Ponte, J., Croft, W. B.: A language modeling approach to information retrieval. In Proceedings of the 21st Annual International ACM SIGIR Conference on Reasearch and Development in Information Retrieval (1998) 275–281.
8. Porter, M. F.: An algorithm for suffix stripping. Program 14 (1980) 130–137.
9. Robertson, S. E., Walker, S., Beaulieu, M. M.: Okapi at TREC-7: Automatic Ad Hoc, Filtering, VLC, and Interactive track. In Proceedings of the 7th Text REtrieval Conference (TREC-7), NIST Special Publication 500-242. Gaithersburg, MD, USA (1998) 253–264.
10. Savoy, J.: Reports on CLEF-2001 experiments. In Peters, C., Braschler, M., Gonzalo, J., Kluck, M. (eds.): Evaluation of Cross-Language Information Retrieval Systems. Second Workshop of the Cross Language Evaluation Forum, CLEF 2001. Revised Papers. LNCS 2406. Springer (2002) 257–264.
11. Zhai, C., Lafferty, J.: A study of smoothing methods for language models applied to ad hoc information retrieval. In Proceedings of the 24th Annual International ACM SIGIR Conference on Research and Development in Information Retrieval (2001) 334–342.

Pruning Texts with NLP and Expanding Queries with an Ontology: TagSearch

Gil Francopoulo
www.tagmatica.com

Abstract. The basic lines of our system is first to use natural language processing to prune the texts and the query, and secondly to use an ontology to expand the queries.

1 Last Year

The system described here is based on the one used last year for CLEF 2002. But most components have been improved since last year and some new steps have been added.

The system, known as TagSearch, is based on three main components:

- A chunker, named TagChunker[1].
- Lucene, a good OpenSource search engine written by Doug Cutting and his friends[2].
- An ontology, named TagDico[3].

The first two components were used last year. The use of an ontology is new.

2 Objectives

Our main objective was to find the right documents by deducing implicit information and avoiding noise. The task is divided in two steps: indexing the texts and searching in the index.

3 Main Ideas for Indexing

The idea is that instead of indexing characters strings, the texts are parsed and only the results of the parsing are indexed[4]. So we are able to prune the wrong parts of speech. That means that is possible to:

---

[1] TALN-2003 (Batz-Sur-Mer) Francopoulo TagChunker: mécanisme de construction et évaluation.
[2] See: http://jakarta.apache.org/lucene/docs/index.html for details.
[3] See "www.tagmatica.com + Produits et services" for details.
[4] Only the part of speech tagging is used. The chunker produces also chunk grouping and chunk labelling, but this information is not used.

C. Peters et al. (Eds.): CLEF 2003, LNCS 3237, pp. 319–321, 2004.
© Springer-Verlag Berlin Heidelberg 2004

a) insert only the right part of speech inside the index. For instance, in the sentence : "the chair is there" the word "chair" is identified as a noun and not as a verb. So in the index, the pair "chair" + Noun is inserted. The goal is to avoid noise during searching.

b) insert only the part of speech we want. We insert only adjectives, nouns and verbs. Grammatical words and adverbs are not inserted, because we are not going to search against their meanings.

c) use word segmentation to group correctly compound words. And the segmentation is controlled by a French lexicon where a lot of compound words are described. For instance, if the compound word "pomme de terre" (potatoes in English) appears in a text, the whole string is inserted. In French, the words "pomme" and "terre" have nothing to do with "pomme de terre", so the three words "pomme", "terre" and "pomme de terre" must considered as being completely different words.

d) correct mistakes in the texts. TagChunker has a module called TagCorrector that is specialized in this task.

4 Main Ideas for Searching

When the index is constructed, we use it to evaluate the query against it.

First, we parse the query with the same chunker as for indexing. That means that, of course, the part of speech tagging and word segmentation is exactly the same. The result is scanned and only the nouns, adjectives and verbs are retained. If a compound noun appears in the query it is recognized correctly.

Searching is done as follows, until 1000 documents are produced:

Step-1: a Lucene query with an AND between the query words is automatically built and evaluated.

Step-2: all the words are expanded through three types of links in the ontology: synonymy, meronymy[5] and derivation[6]. Each initial word of step-1 is grouped by an OR with its expansion. The various groups are still connected by an AND. But instead of building one big query, the combination of each expansion is built, producing a lot of queries. For each query, the number of terms is computed and the evaluation starts with the queries that have less terms.

Step-3: a query is built as for in step-1, but instead of using AND, we use OR between words.

Step-4: queries are built like as for step-2, but instead of using AND, we use OR between groups.

---

[5] "meronymy" is the relation "is part of", for instance "Italy is a part of Europe".

[6] "derivation" is the relation that permits to link two related meanings with a different part of speech, for instance from a verb to a noun, by a link like "this is a name of the action" or "this is the name of the result of the action".

5 Expansion

The goal of expansion is to find documents that are on the subject we search but without exactly the word we have in the query. For instance, in a query like "Les syndicats en Europe[7]" (query C156). Imagine a text in the pool of documents that is about "syndicats en Italie" but without the word Europe. If the word "Europe" is not expanded, you cannot find this document. So meronymy expansion is the only possibility to find this document.

6 Document Ranking

The documents must be ranked. And a document that is found during step-1 must have a higher rank than one computed during step-2 or 3.

We use the ranking produced by Lucene as a basis and we multiply this ranking by a number less than that one in order to reflect the query ranking.

7 Results

Our results seem to be not so bad. We are not among the worst results, we are just after the five first results.

8 The Future

The lexicon being rather rich, a problem occurs: in case of polysemy, the system does not prune the meanings that are described in the lexicon but which are not in the context of the sentence. That means that sometime the expansion is noisy.

The system could be improved by a semantic disambiguation component.

9 Conclusion

The system has not been tailored specially to the task: only the query ranking has been adapted for CLEF 2003. We used the system in its current state and, our resources being limited, we did not spend too much time on the evaluation.

What is important, is that we learned in what direction we will improve the system: adding a semantic disambiguation component.

---

[7] Straightforward translation in English: «the syndicates in Europe».

Report on CLEF-2003 Monolingual Tracks: Fusion of Probabilistic Models for Effective Monolingual Retrieval

Jacques Savoy

Institut interfacultaire d'informatique, Université de Neuchâtel,
Pierre-à-Mazel 7, 2001 Neuchâtel, Switzerland
Jacques.Savoy@unine.ch
http://www.unine.ch/info/clef/

Abstract. For our third participation in the CLEF evaluation campaign, our first objective was to propose more effective and general stopword lists for the Swedish, Finnish and Russian languages, along with an improved, more efficient and simpler stemming procedure for these three languages. Our second goal was to suggest a combined search approach based on a data fusion strategy that would work with various European languages. Included in this combined approach is a decompounding strategy for the German, Dutch, Swedish and Finnish languages.

1   Introduction

Based on our experiments of the previous year [11], in CLEF 2003 we participated in the French, Spanish, German, Italian, Dutch, Swedish, Finnish and Russian monolingual tasks without relying on a dictionary. This paper presents the approaches we used in the monolingual track and is organized as follows. Section 2 contains an overview of the nine test collections used while Section 3 describes our general approach to building stopword lists and stemmers for use with languages other than English. In Section 4, we suggest a simple decompounding algorithm that can be used for German, Dutch, Swedish and Finnish. Section 5 evaluates two probabilistic models and nine vector-space schemes using the nine test collections. Finally, Section 6 evaluates various data fusion operators, and presents our official runs.

2   Overview of the Test Collections

The corpora used in our experiments included newspapers such as the *Los Angeles Times* (1994, English), *Glasgow Herald* (1995, English), *Le Monde* (1994, French), *La Stampa* (1994, Italian), *Der Spiegel* (1994/95, German), *Frankfurter Rundschau* (1994, German), *NRC Handelsbald* (1994/95, Dutch), *Algemeen Dagblad* (1995/95, Dutch), *Tidningarnas Telegrambyrå* (1994/95, Swedish), *Aamulehti* (1994/95, Finnish), and *Izvestia* (1995, Russian). Additional sources of

C. Peters et al. (Eds.): CLEF 2003, LNCS 3237, pp. 322–336, 2004.
© Springer-Verlag Berlin Heidelberg 2004

information consisted of news agency documents such as *EFE* (1994/95, Spanish) and the Swiss news agency (1994/95, available in French, German and Italian but without parallel translation).

As shown in Tables 1 and 2, these corpora are of various sizes, with the Spanish collection being the biggest and the German, English and Dutch collections next in size. Ranking third are the French, Italian and Swedish corpora, then somewhat smaller is the Finnish collection and finally the Russian collection is clearly the smallest. Across all the corpora the mean number of distinct indexing terms per document is relatively similar (around 112), although this number is slightly larger for the English collection (156.9) and smaller for the Swedish corpus (79.25).

Table 1. Test collection statistics

	English	French	German	Spanish
Size (in MB)	579 MB	331 MB	668 MB	1,086 MB
# of documents	169,477	129,806	294,809	454,045
# of distinct terms	426,757	355,691	1,666,538	774,263
Number of distinct indexing terms / document				
Mean	156.9	118.5	111.9	112.9
Standard deviation	118.77	95.72	100.06	55.75
Median	129	89	84	100
Maximum	1,881	1,621	2,424	642
Minimum	2	3	1	5
Number of queries	54	52	56	57
Number of rel. items	1,006	946	1,825	2,368
Mean rel. items / request	18.63	18.19	32.59	41.54
Standard deviation	28.61	33.16	36.95	57.37
Median	7	8	24	22
Maximum	139	193	226	303
Minimum	1	1	1	1

Tables 1 and 2 also compare the number of relevant documents per request, with the mean always being greater than the median (e.g., for the English collection, the average number of relevant documents per query is 18.63 with the corresponding median being 7). These findings indicate that each collection contains numerous documents, yet only a rather small number of relevant items are found per query. For each collection, 60 queries were created. However, relevant documents are not found for each request and each language. For the English collection, Queries #149, #161, #166, #186, #191, and #195 do not have any relevant items; for the French corpus, requests with no relevant documents are #146, #160, #161, #166, #169, #172, #191, #194; for the German collection: Queries #144, #146, #170, #191; for the Spanish collection: Queries #169, #188, #195; for the Italian collection: Queries #144, #146, #158, #160, #169, #170, #172, #175, #191; for the Dutch collection: Queries #160, #166, #191, #194; for the Swedish collection: Queries #146,

Table 2. Test collection statistics

	Italian	Dutch	Swedish	Finnish	Russian
Size (in MB)	363 MB	540 MB	352 MB	137 MB	68 MB
# of documents	157,558	190,604	142,819	55,344	16,716
# of distinct terms	560,087	883,953	767,504	1,444,232	345,728
Number of distinct indexing terms / document					
Mean	116.4	110	79.25	114	124.5
Standard deviation	88.24	107.03	64.00	91.35	124.53
Median	84	77	62	87	41
Maximum	1,395	2,297	1,547	1,946	1,769
Minimum	1	1	1	1	1
Number of queries	51	56	54	45	28
Number of rel. items	809	1,577	1,006	483	151
Mean rel. items / request	15.86	28.16	18.63	10.73	5.39
Standard deviation	20.32	43.10	28.35	15.78	7.11
Median	8	14.5	11.5	5	3
Maximum	110	226	170	82	31
Minimum	1	1	1	1	1

#160, #167, #191, #194, #198; for the Finnish corpus: Queries #141, #144, #145, #146, #160, #167, #169, #175, #182, #186, #188, #189, #191, #194, #195. The Russian corpus appeared for the first time in a CLEF evaluation campaign and only 28 requests actually found relevant documents.

During the indexing process of our automatic runs, we retained only the following logical sections from the original documents: <TITLE>, <HEADLINE>, <TEXT>, <LEAD>, <LEAD1>, <TX>, <LD>, <TI>, and <ST>. From the topic descriptions we automatically removed certain phrases such as "Relevant document report ...", "Find documents that give ...", "Trouver des documents qui parlent ...", "Sono valide le discussioni e le decisioni ...", "Relevante Dokumente berichten ..." or "Los documentos relevantes proporcionan información ...".

3   Stopword Lists and Stemming Procedures

In order to define general stopword lists, we first accounted for the top 200 most frequent words found in the various languages, together with articles, pronouns, prepositions, conjunctions or very frequently occurring verb forms (e.g., to be, is, has, etc.). With respect to the stopword lists we used last year [11], we only modified those for Swedish and Finnish, and created a new list for Russian (these lists are available at www.unine.ch/info/clef/). For English we used the list provided by the SMART system (571 words), while for the other European languages, our stopword list contained 430 words for Italian, 463 for French, 603 for German, 351 for Spanish, 1,315 for Dutch, 747 for Finnish, 386 for Swedish and 420 for Russian.

Once it removes high-frequency words, an indexing procedure generally applies a stemming algorithm in an attempt to conflate word variants into the same stem or root. In developing this procedure for various European languages, we first removed only inflectional suffixes such as singular and plural word forms, and also feminine and masculine forms, so that they conflate to the same root. Our stemmers also try to reduce various word declensions to the same stem, such as those used in the German, Finnish and Russian languages.

More sophisticated schemes have already been proposed for the removal of derivational suffixes (e.g., "-ize", "-ably", "-ship" in the English language), as can be seen in the stemmer developed by Lovins [8] (based on a list of over 260 suffixes), or that of Porter [9] (which looks for about 60 suffixes). For the French language only, our stemming approach tried to remove some derivational suffixes (e.g., "communicateur" → "communiquer", "faiblesse" → "faible"). For the Dutch language we used Kraaij & Pohlmann's stemmer [7]. Our various stemming procedures can be found at www.unine.ch/info/clef/. Currently, it is not clear whether a stemming procedure such as ours that removes only inflectional suffixes from nouns and adjectives is sufficient, or whether better retrieval effectiveness may be achieved by a stemming approach that also accounts for verbs or that removes both inflectional and derivational suffixes.

Finally diacritic characters, not usually not present in English collections (with some exceptions, such as " résumé"), but very common in Italian, Dutch, Finnish, Swedish, German, Spanish and Russian, were replaced by their corresponding non-accentuated letter. For this last language, we converted and normalized the Cyrillic Unicode characters into the Latin alphabet (the Perl script is available at www.unine.ch/info/clef/).

4   Decompounding Words

Most European languages manifest other morphological characteristics in addition to inflection, with compound word constructions being just one example (e.g., handgun, worldwide). In German, for example, compound words are widely used and can cause more difficulties than in English. For example, an insurance company would be "Versicherungsgesellschaft" ("Versicherung" + "s" + "Gesellschaft"). However the morphological marker ("s") is not always present (e.g., "Atomtests" built as "Atom" + "Tests"), and sometimes the letter "S" belongs to the decompounded word (e.g., "Wintersports" for "Winter" + "Sports"). In Finnish, we also encounter similar constructions as such as "rakkauskirje" ("rakkaus" + "kirje" for love & letter) or "työviikko" ("työ" + "viikko" for work & week). Recently, Braschler [3] showed that decompounding German words may significantly improve retrieval performance.

Our proposed decompounding approach shares some similarity with Chen's algorithm [5]. Before using it, we create a word list composed of all words appearing in the given collection (without stemming). Associated with each word, we also store the number of its occurrences in the collection (some examples are given in Table 3).

Table 3. Examples of German words included in our word list

computer	2,452	port	1,091
computers	79	ports	2
sicherheit	6,583	sport	1,483
sicher	4,522	sports	199
heit	4		
		winter	1,643
bank	9,657	winters	148
bund	7,032	wintersport	44
bundes	2,884	wintersports	2
bundesbank	1,453		
präsident	24,041		

In order to present an overview of our decompounding approach, we will take as an example the German word "Computersicherheit," composed of "Computer" + "Sicherheit" (security). This compound word does not appear in our German word list as shown in Table 3, so our algorithm starts the decompounding process by attempting to split a word following the $k = 4$ last letters (given the two strings "computersicher" and "heit"). During the entire procedure, we only consider words having a length greater than a given threshold (fixed at 3 for all languages in our experiments). If both components appear in the word list, then we have a candidate for decompounding; otherwise the k limit is increased by one. Since, in our case, the string "computersiche" does not appear in the German word list, splitting is rejected. When $k = 9$, our algorithm will find the word "computers" in the word list, but will fail to find the word "icherheit". With $k = 10$, our algorithm will find both the word "computer" and "sicherheit" in the German word list (see Table 3) and this solution becomes the top level decompounding suggestion. Recursively, the system now tries to decompose the two parts, namely the words "computer" and "sicherheit". During this recursive process, the system is allowed to ignore some short sequences of letters at the end of a word (such as "-s" or "-es" in German, or "-s" for the Swedish language) because such morphological markers may indicate the genitive form (such as "'s" in the noun phrase "John's book").

After this generative part, the system responds with a tree of possible ways in which the compound construction can be broken down and for each component, we find the number of its occurrences in the corpus. In our example, the answer will be (computer 2452, sicherheit 6583 (sicher 4522, heit 4)). Thus, from this result, we know that the word "Sicherheit" appears 6,583 times in the corpus, and we can consider decomposing this term into the words "sicher" and "heit". From this we can add (or replace) the compound word in the document (or in the request) by all possible candidates ("computer" + "sicherheit", and "computer" + "sicher" + "heit" in our case) or by decompounding only the minimum number of terms ("computer" + "sicherheit" in our case).

However, when faced with multiple candidates, our algorithm will try to select the single "best" one. To achieve this, our system considers the total number of occurrences for the component words and, if this value is greater than the number of occurrences for the compound construction, the candidate will be selected. In our example, the system will not decompound the word "Sicherheit" because the number of occurrences of the words "sicher" (4,522) and "heit" (4) will not produce a total (4,526) greater than the number of occurrences of the word "sicherheit" (6,583).

If we consider the German word "Bundesbankpräsident" (president of the (German) federal bank), the generative part of our algorithm would return (bundesbank 1453 (bund 7032, bank 9657), präsident 24041) and the final decompounding approach would return (bund 7032, bank 9657, präsident 24041). In this case, the number of occurrences of "bundesbank" (1,453) is smaller than the sum of the occurrences of the words "bund" and "bank". However, our approach does not always generate the appropriate components of a compound term. For example, faced with the compound construction "wintersports", the system answers with (winter 1643, port 1091) instead of (winter 1643, sport 1483). This problem is due to the fact that the first part of our approach ignores backtracking and will stop when it encounters the first splitting of the compound into two parts.

5   Indexing and Searching Strategy

In order to obtain a broader view of the relative merits of various retrieval models, we first adopted a binary indexing scheme by which each document (or request) is represented by a set of keywords, without any weight. To measure the similarity between documents and requests, we computed the inner product (retrieval model denoted "doc=bnn, query=bnn" or "bnn-bnn"). In order to weight the presence of each indexing term in a document surrogate (or in a query), we can compute the term occurrence frequency (retrieval model notation: "doc=nnn, query=nnn" or "nnn-nnn") or we can compute the term frequency in the collection (or more precisely the inverse document frequency, denoted by idf_j). Cosine normalization can prove beneficial and each indexing weight can vary within the range of 0 to 1 (retrieval model notation: "ntc-ntc", Table 4 shows the exact weighting formulation).

Other variants might also be created. For example, the tf component may be computed as $0.5 + 0.5 \cdot [tf$ / max tf in a document] (retrieval model denoted "doc=atn"). We might also consider whether a term's presence in a shorter document provides stronger evidence than it does in a longer document, leading to more complex IR models; for example, the IR model denoted by "doc=Lnu" [4], "doc=dtu"[12]. In addition to the previous models based on the vector-space approach, we also considered probabilistic models. In this respect, we used the Okapi probabilistic model [10]. In Table 4, n denotes the number of documents in the collection, nt_i indicates the number of distinct indexing terms included in the representation of D_i, l_i the length of D_i measured as the sum of tf_{ij}, and $avdl$ the mean document length.

Table 4. Weighting schemes

bnn	$w_{ij} = 1$	npn	$w_{ij} = tf_{ij} \cdot ln\left[\frac{n - df_j}{df_j}\right]$
nnn	$w_{ij} = tf_{ij}$		
ntc	$w_{ij} = \dfrac{tf_{ij} \cdot idf_j}{\sqrt{\sum_{k=1}^{t}(tf_{ik} \cdot idf_k)^2}}$	atn	$w_{ij} = idf_j \cdot \left[\dfrac{0.5 + 0.5 \cdot tf_{ij}}{max\ tf_{i.}}\right]$
lnc	$w_{ij} = \dfrac{ln(tf_{ij})+1}{\sqrt{\sum_{k=1}^{t}(ln(tf_{ik})+1)^2}}$	dtn	$w_{ij} = (ln(ln(tf_{ij}) + 1) + 1) \cdot idf_j$
ltn	$w_{ij} = (ln(tf_{ij}) + 1) \cdot idf_j$	ltc	$w_{ij} = \dfrac{(ln(tf_{ij})+1) \cdot idf_j}{\sqrt{\sum_{k=1}^{t}[(ln(tf_{ik})+1) \cdot idf_k]^2}}$
Okapi	$w_{ij} = \dfrac{(k_1+1) \cdot tf_{ij}}{K + tf_{ij}}$ with $K = k_1 \cdot \left[(1 - b) + b \cdot \frac{l_i}{avdl}\right]$		
dtu	$w_{ij} = \dfrac{(ln(ln(tf_{ij})+1)+1) \cdot idf_j}{(1-slope) \cdot pivot + (slope \cdot nt_i)}$		
Lnu	$w_{ij} = \dfrac{\frac{ln(tf_{ij})+1}{ln\left(\frac{l_i}{nt_i}\right)+1}}{(1-slope) \cdot pivot + (slope \cdot nt_i)}$		

As a second probabilistic approach, we implemented the Prosit (PRObabilistic Sift of Information Terms) approach [1], [2] which is based on the following indexing formula:

$$w_{ij} = Inf_{ij}^1 \cdot Inf_{ij}^2 = (1 - Prob_{ij}^1) \cdot Inf_{ij}^2 \text{ with}$$
$$Prob_{ij}^1 = tfn_{ij} / (tfn_{ij} + 1)$$
$$tfn_{ij} = tf_{ij} \cdot \log_2\left[1 + ((C \cdot mean\ dl) / l_j)\right]$$
$$Inf_{ij}^2 = -\log_2\left[1/(1+l_j)\right] - tfn_{ij} \cdot \log_2\left[l_j/(1+l_j)\right] \text{ with } l_j = tc_j/n$$

where tc_j indicates the number of occurrences of term t_j in the collection and n the number of documents in the corpus. In our experiments, the constants b, k_1, $avdl$, C and $mean\ dl$ are fixed according to values listed in Table 5 while the constant $pivot$ is fixed at 100, and $slope$ at 0.1.

To evaluate our approaches, we used the SMART system as a test-bed running on an Intel Pentium III/600 (memory: 1 GB, swap: 2 GB, disk: 6 x 35 GB). To measure the retrieval performance, we adopted the non-interpolated mean average precision (computed on the basis of 1,000 retrieved items per request by the TREC-EVAL program, see ftp://ftp.cs.cornell.edu/pub/smart/). We indexed the English, French, Spanish and Italian collections using words as indexing units. The evaluation of our two probabilistic models and nine vector-space schemes is given in Table 6.

In order to represent German, Dutch, Swedish, Finnish and Russian documents and queries, we considered the n-gram, decompounding and word-based indexing schemes. The resulting mean average precision for these various indexing approaches is shown in Table 7 (German and Dutch corpora), in Table 8 (Swedish and Finnish languages) and in Table 9 (Russian collection).

Table 5. Parameter setting for the various test collections

Language	Index	b	k_1	$avdl$	C	$mean\ dl$
English	word	0.8	2	800	1.5	167
French	word	0.75	3	900	1.25	182
Spanish	word	0.4	1.2	400	1.75	157
German	word	0.5	1.5	600	3	152
German	5-gram	0.3	1	500	2.5	475
Italian	word	0.55	1.5	800	1.25	165
Dutch	word	0.8	3	600	2.25	110
Dutch	5-gram	0.6	1.2	600	1.75	362
Finnish	word	0.75	2	900	1.25	114
Finnish	5-gram	0.6	1.2	800	2	539
Swedish	word	0.7	2	500	3	79
Swedish	4-gram	0.75	2	900	1.75	292
Russian	word	0.7	2	800	1.5	124
Russian	5-gram	0.75	1.2	750	1.75	451
Russian	4-gram	0.75	1.2	750	1.75	468

Table 6. Mean average precision of various single searching strategies (monolingual)

	Mean average precision			
Query TD Model	English 54 queries	French 52 queries	Spanish 57 queries	Italian 51 queries
Prosit	48.19	**52.01**	47.23	47.17
doc=Okapi, query=npn	**48.83**	51.64	**48.85**	**48.80**
doc=Lnu, query=ltc	44.51	48.26	45.79	45.32
doc=dtu, query=dtn	43.17	46.58	45.03	45.71
doc=atn, query=ntc	45.55	45.48	44.04	45.77
doc=ltn, query=ntc	34.68	39.01	42.40	42.56
doc=ntc, query=ntc	27.12	32.74	27.08	28.90
doc=ltc, query=ltc	28.14	34.41	29.74	28.63
doc=lnc, query=ltc	33.89	37.98	33.52	32.68
doc=bnn, query=bnn	15.97	24.01	26.48	25.33
doc=nnn, query=nnn	6.50	12.27	19.84	22.36

It was observed that pseudo-relevance feedback (blind-query expansion) seems to be a useful technique for enhancing retrieval effectiveness. In this study, we adopted Rocchio's approach [4] with $\alpha = 0.75$, $\beta = 0.75$ whereby the system was allowed to add m terms extracted from the k best ranked documents from the original query. To evaluate this proposition, we used the Okapi and the Prosit probabilistic models and enlarged the query by the 10 to 175 terms provided by the 3 or 10 best-retrieved articles.

The results shown in Tables 10, 11, 12, and 13 (giving our best results) indicate that the optimal parameter setting seems to be collection-dependent. Moreover, performance improvement also seems to be collection dependent (or

Table 7. Mean average precision of various single searching strategies (German & Dutch collections)

Query TD	Mean average precision					
Model	German words 56 queries	German decomp. 56 queries	German 5-gram 56 queries	Dutch words 56 queries	Dutch decomp. 56 queries	Dutch 5-gram 56 queries
Prosit	42.14	45.53	42.88	**47.15**	48.36	39.41
Okapi-npn	**44.54**	**46.93**	**44.27**	46.86	**48.73**	**40.23**
Lnu-ltc	40.64	45.44	39.63	43.38	45.08	33.63
dtu-dtn	42.60	43.95	39.08	42.69	43.78	33.82
atn-ntc	40.98	43.67	40.36	41.92	43.52	36.43
ltn-ntc	39.07	39.32	38.57	38.45	39.51	32.47
ntc-ntc	27.40	32.64	31.59	29.27	30.36	29.42
ltc-ltc	28.85	36.02	32.76	30.97	32.41	28.24
lnc-ltc	30.16	35.93	32.10	31.39	33.15	28.53
bnn-bnn	23.63	23.31	21.07	26.14	26.80	21.16
nnn-nnn	15.97	10.85	9.78	11.35	10.64	9.82

Table 8. Mean average precision of various single searching strategies (Swedish & Finnish collections)

Query TD	Mean average precision					
Model	Swedish words 54 queries	Swedish decomp. 54 queries	Swedish 4-gram 54 queries	Finnish words 45 queries	Finnish decomp. 45 queries	Finnish 5-gram 45 queries
Prosit	39.80	41.38	**40.66**	46.35	46.96	**49.03**
Okapi-npn	**40.54**	**41.97**	40.49	46.54	46.61	48.97
Lnu-ltc	38.56	40.32	38.22	**48.73**	**47.31**	46.03
dtu-dtn	38.71	40.85	36.91	44.44	44.78	43.54
atn-ntc	37.21	38.47	40.50	42.91	43.99	48.56
ltn-ntc	34.47	36.12	36.65	42.47	43.11	42.94
ntc-ntc	25.74	27.45	26.52	32.73	33.46	35.64
ltc-ltc	26.93	29.26	25.91	37.27	38.34	37.72
lnc-ltc	27.46	29.67	29.28	36.93	39.18	37.21
bnn-bnn	20.21	22.33	25.79	17.95	15.17	20.06
nnn-nnn	11.87	12.06	12.70	13.85	13.21	14.83

language dependent), with no improvement for the English corpus (see Table 10), a small enhancement for the French collection (+0.5% from 51.64 to 51.91), yet an increase of 8.5% for the Spanish corpus (from a mean average precision of 48.85 to 53.02), and 9.4% for the Italian language (48.80 to 53.39). In Table 11, the improvement for the German collection is around 8.6% (words indexing, from 44.54 to 48.39) and of 15.5% for the Dutch corpus (from 46.86 to 54.14). As shown in Table 12, the enhancement is around 16% (from 39.80 to 46.17) for the Swedish collection, and of 13.7% with the Finnish language (from 46.35

Table 9. Mean average precision of various single searching strategies (Russian collection)

Query TD	Mean average precision			
	Russian words extended stemmer	Russian words light stemmer	Russian 5-gram	Russian 4-gram
Model	28 queries	28 queries	28 queries	28 queries
Prosit	36.69	34.89	30.44	**34.43**
Okapi-npn	34.26	34.58	30.31	32.51
Lnu-ltc	36.34	**36.30**	27.36	29.75
dtu-dtn	32.67	32.95	28.49	30.55
atn-ntc	**37.06**	33.22	**31.29**	31.41
ltn-ntc	29.55	30.89	23.83	22.05
ntc-ntc	33.47	30.14	28.69	27.39
ltc-ltc	32.34	28.74	26.40	27.52
lnc-ltc	32.58	24.47	20.65	21.88
bnn-bnn	14.84	15.23	13.13	9.05
nnn-nnn	12.27	11.41	7.95	5.83

Table 10. Mean average precision using blind-query expansion

Query TD	Mean average precision			
Model	English 54 queries	French 52 queries	Spanish 57 queries	Italian 51 queries
doc=Okapi, query=npn	**48.83**	51.64	48.85	48.80
5 docs / 10 terms	48.79	51.33	52.74	52.97
5 docs / 15 terms	48.15	**51.91**	52.87	**53.39**
5 docs / 20 terms	47.37	51.30	**53.02**	52.35
10 docs / 10 terms	45.70	49.81	52.51	51.33
10 docs / 15 terms	44.10	48.59	52.55	51.17
10 docs / 20 terms	45.62	49.68	52.79	51.94

to 52.71). For the Russian corpus, the improvement shown in Table 13 is slight (+1.6% from 34.26 to 34.81).

6   Data Fusion

For the English, French, Spanish, Italian and Russian languages, we assumed that the n-gram indexing and word-based document representation approaches serve as distinct and independent sources of evidence regarding the content of documents. For the German, Dutch, Swedish and Finnish languages, we added the decompounding indexing approach in our documents (and queries) representation scheme.

Table 11. Mean average precision using blind-query expansion (German & Dutch collections)

Query TD	Mean average precision					
	German words	German decomp.	German 5-gram	Dutch words	Dutch decomp.	Dutch 5-gram
Model	56 queries	56 queries	56 queries	56 queries	56 queries	56 queries
Okapi-npn	44.54	46.93	44.27	46.86	48.73	40.23
k doc. /	5/10 46.46	5/10 50.32	5/50 **47.26**	5/10 52.32	5/10 54.60	5/100 43.12
m terms	5/20 47.83	5/20 51.40	5/100 46.96	5/30 53.39	5/30 54.79	5/150 43.32
	5/40 **48.39**	5/50 **51.64**	5/125 46.88	5/50 **54.14**	5/40 **55.56**	5/200 **43.90**
	10/10 45.98	10/15 50.32	10/40 46.46	10/15 51.26	10/15 53.07	10/100 42.34
	0/15 46.31	10/30 50.20	10/100 46.50	10/20 51.14	10/20 52.81	10/150 42.67
	10/20 46.08	10/40 50.33	10/125 46.59	10/40 51.72	10/30 53.77	10/200 42.54

Table 12. Mean average precision using blind-query expansion (Swedish & Finnish collections)

Query TD	Mean average precision					
	Swedish words	Swedish decomp.	Swedish 4-gram	Finnish words	Finnish decomp.	Finnish 5-gram
Model	54 queries	54 queries	54 queries	45 queries	45 queries	45 queries
Prosit	39.80	41.38	40.66	46.35	46.96	49.03
k doc. /	3/20 **46.17**	3/10 **48.22**	3/30 42.48	3/20 52.50	3/10 52.03	3/15 50.98
m terms	3/30 44.68	3/15 46.46	3/40 42.51	3/30 **52.71**	3/20 **53.37**	3/50 49.44
	3/60 42.76	3/40 43.73	3/50 **42.92**	3/40 50.04	3/30 52.93	3/125 49.06
	5/20 43.61	5/30 47.35	5/30 39.89	5/20 49.69	5/10 48.82	5/30 52.45
	5/30 44.12	5/40 46.80	5/40 41.53	5/30 47.90	5/15 47.85	5/60 **52.92**
	5/40 43.60	5/50 46.36	5/50 41.79	5/50 49.77	5/20 48.85	5/75 52.67

Table 13. Mean average precision using blind-query expansion (Russian collection)

Query TD	Mean average precision			
	Russian words extended stemmer	Russian words light stemmer	Russian 5-gram	Russian 4-gram
Model	28 queries	28 queries	28 queries	28 queries
Okapi-npn	34.26	34.58	30.31	32.51
5 docs / 20 terms	**34.81**	32.68	29.27	30.76
5 docs / 30 terms	32.46	34.69	29.10	30.45
5 docs / 40 terms	31.87	**34.81**	29.64	30.62
10 docs / 20 terms	30.84	31.30	30.25	29.92
10 docs / 30 terms	29.24	33.00	30.07	30.17
10 docs / 40 terms	29.28	30.24	30.03	29.84
10 docs / 50 terms	27.99	28.88	29.32	29.46

Table 14. Data fusion combination operators

combMAX	$\max (\alpha_i \cdot RSV_k)$
combMIN	$\min (\alpha_i \cdot RSV_k)$
combSUM	$\sum (\alpha_i \cdot RSV_k)$
combANZ	$\sum (\alpha_i \cdot RSV_k) / \#of nonzero(RSV_k)$
combNBZ	$\sum (\alpha_i \cdot RSV_k) \cdot (\#of nonzero(RSV_k)$
combRSV%	$\sum (\alpha_i \cdot (RSV_k/MaxRSV^i))$
NormN	$\sum \left[\alpha_i \cdot \left[(RSV_k - MinRSV^i)/(MaxRSV^i - MinRSV^i)\right]\right]$

Table 15. Mean average precision using different combination operators ($\alpha_i = 1$, with blind-query expansion)

	Mean average precision				
Query TD	English	French	Spanish	Italian	Russian
Model #doc/#term	54 queries	52 queries	57 queries	51 queries	28 queries
Okapi-npn	0/0 48.83	10/10 49.81	10/10 52.51	10/20 51.94	10/20 31.30
Prosit	3/15 50.99	5/30 52.30	10/10 50.19	10/50 50.82	5/30 35.41
combMAX	48.83	52.27	50.19	50.82	35.41
combMIN	2.88	42.77	8.21	18.62	24.96
combSUM	51.13	53.58	51.89	51.87	**35.68**
combANZ	37.95	53.25	43.97	50.05	35.60
combNBZ	51.11	53.66	51.89	51.86	35.65
combRSV%	**53.60**	54.50	53.30	53.58	34.43
NormN	53.25	**54.69**	**53.49**	54.37	34.30
round-robin	50.24	52.61	53.16	**54.47**	34.11

Table 16. Mean average precision using different combination operators ($\alpha_i = 1$, with blind-query expansion)

	Mean average precision			
Query TD	German	Dutch	Swedish	Finnish
Model	56 queries	56 queries	54 queries	45 queries
Prosit word #doc/#term	5/20 48.40	10/20 51.14	3/60 42.76	5/30 47.90
Prosit decomp. #doc/#term	10/40 51.40	10/20 51.81	3/40 43.73	5/15 47.85
Prosit n-gram #doc/#term	5/175 49.46	10/150 44.23	3/40 42.51	3/125 49.06
combMAX	49.97	44.23	43.29	50.22
combMIN	35.54	6.30	33.80	33.36
combSUM	53.71	50.24	47.85	54.51
combANZ	47.85	31.90	41.32	49.25
combNBZ	53.70	50.81	47.57	**55.60**
combRSV%	54.46	53.99	48.23	54.49
NormN	**54.58**	**54.30**	**48.41**	54.16
round-robin	50.83	50.65	44.44	48.73

Table 17. Description and mean average precision (MAP) of our official runs

Run name	Query	Index	Model	Query expansion	Combined	MAP
FR	TD	word	Okapi	10 docs / 10 terms	round-	
UniNEfr	TD	word	Prosit	5 docs / 30 terms	robin	52.61
FR	TD	word	Okapi	10 docs / 10 terms		
UniNEfr2	TD	word	Prosit	5 docs / 30 terms	RSV%	**54.50**
SP	TD	word	Okapi	10 docs / 10 terms		
UniNEsp	TD	word	Prosit	10 docs / 10 terms	RSVnorm	**53.80**
SP	TD	word	Okapi	5 docs / 10 terms		
UniNEsp2	TD	word	Prosit	10 docs / 10 terms	RSVnorm	53.69
DE	TD	word	Prosit	5 docs / 20 terms		
UniNEde	TD	decomp.	Prosit	10 docs / 40 terms	RSVnorm	54.58
	TD	5-gram	Prosit	5 docs / 175 terms		
DE	TD	word	Pro+Oka	5 docs / 20 terms		
UniNEde2	TD	decomp.	Pro+Oka	10 docs / 40 terms	RSVsum	**56.03**
	TD	5-gram	Pro+Oka	5 docs / 175 terms		
IT	TD	word	Okapi	10 docs / 20 terms		
UniNEit	TD	word	Prosit	10 docs / 50 terms	RSV%	**52.23**
IT	TD	word	Okapi	10 docs / 20 terms		
UniNEit2	TD	word	Prosit	10 docs / 50 terms	RSVsum	51.56
NL	TD	word	Okapi	10 docs / 20 terms	round-	
UniNEnl	TD	decomp.	Okapi	10 docs / 20 terms	robin	**50.65**
	TD	5-gram	Prosit	10 docs / 150 terms		
NL	TD	word	Okapi	10 docs / 20 terms		
UniNEnl2	TD	decomp.	Okapi	10 docs / 20 terms	RSVsum	50.24
	TD	5-gram	Prosit	10 docs / 150 terms		
SV	TD	word	Pro+Oka	3 docs / 15 terms		
UniNEsv	TD	decomp.	Pro+Oka	3 docs / 15 terms	RSV%	48.53
	TD	4-gram	Pro+Oka	3 docs / 40 terms		
SV	TD	word	Pro+Oka	5 docs / 30 terms		
UniNEsv2	TD	decomp.	Pro+Oka	5 docs / 50 terms	RSVnorm	**49.03**
	TD	4-gram	Pro+Oka	5 docs / 30 terms		
FI	TD	word	Prosit	5 docs / 30 terms		
UniNEfi	TD	decomp.	Prosit	5 docs / 15 terms	RSVsum	**54.51**
	TD	5-gram	Prosit	3 docs / 125 terms		
FI	TD	word	Prosit	5 docs / 30 terms		
UniNEfi2	TD	decomp.	Prosit	5 docs / 15 terms	RSVsum	53.55
	TD	5-gram	Prosit	3 docs / 125 terms		
RU	TDN	word	Okapi	10 docs / 20 terms		
UniNEru	TDN	word	Prosit	5 docs / 30 terms	RSVsum	35.32
RU	TD	word	Okapi	10 docs / 20 terms		
UniNEru1	TD	word	Prosit	5 docs / 30 terms	RSVsum	31.83
RU	TD	5-gram	Okapi	10 docs / 50 terms		
UniNEru2	TD	5-gram	Prosit	5 docs / 40 terms	RSVsum	**32.77**
	TD	4-gram	Okapi	10 docs / 50 terms		
	TD	4-gram	Prosit	5 docs / 40 terms		
RU	TDN	word	Okapi	10 docs / 10 terms		
UniNEru3	TDN	word	Prosit	5 docs / 20 terms	RSVsum	**42.24**

In order to combine these two and three point indexing schemes respectively, we evaluated various fusion operators, as suggested by Fox and Shaw [6]. Table 14 shows their precise description. For example, the combSUM operator indicates that the combined document score (or the final retrieval status value) is simply the sum of the retrieval status value (RSV_k) of the corresponding document D_k computed by each single indexing scheme. CombNBZ specifies that we multiply the sum of the document scores by the number of those retrieval schemes able to retrieve the corresponding document. In Table 14, we can see that both the combRSV% and NormN apply a normalization procedure when combining document scores. When combining the retrieval status value (RSV_k) for various indexing schemes, we may multiply the document score by a constant α_i (usually equal to 1) in order to attribute a different weight to each retrieval scheme according to its overall performance. In addition to using these data fusion operators, we also considered the round-robin approach, where in turn we take one document from all individual lists and remove duplicates, keeping the most highly ranked instance.

Table 15 and Table 16 show the evaluation of various data fusion operators, comparing them to the single approach using the Okapi and the Prosit probabilistic models. As shown in these tables, the NormN or combRSV% fusion strategies usually improve retrieval effectiveness over the best single retrieval model.

7   Conclusion

In this fourth CLEF evaluation campaign, we proposed a general stopword list and stemming procedure for eight European languages. Currently it is not clear if a stemming procedure such as the one we suggested, where only inflectional suffixes are removed from nouns and adjectives, could produce better retrieval effectiveness than a stemming approach that takes both inflectional and derivational suffixes into account. We also suggested a simple decompounding approach for German, Dutch, Swedish and Finnish. In order to achieve better retrieval performance, we used a data fusion approach, one requiring that document (and query) representation be based on two or three indexing schemes.

Acknowledgments. The author would like to thank C. Buckley from SabIR for giving us the opportunity to use the SMART system. This research was supported by the Swiss National Science Foundation (grant #21-66 742.01).

References

1. Amati, G., Carpineto, C., Romano, G.: Italian Monolingual Information Retrieval with PROSIT. In: Peters, C., Braschler, M., Gonzalo, J., Kluck, M. (eds.): Advances in Cross-Language Information Retrieval. Lecture Notes in Computer Science, Vol. 2785. Springer-Verlag, Berlin Heidelberg New York (2003) 257–264
2. Amati, G., van Rijsbergen, C.J.: Probabilistic Models of Information Retrieval Based on Measuring the Divergence from Randomness. ACM Transactions on Information Systems, 20 (2002) 357–389.

3. Braschler, M., Ripplinger, B.: Stemming and Decompounding for German Text Retrieval. In Proceedings 25th European Conference in IR. Lecture Notes in Computer Science, Vol. 2633. Springer-Verlag, Berlin Heidelberg New York (2003) 177–192

4. Buckley, C., Singhal, A., Mitra, M., Salton, G.: New Retrieval Approaches Using SMART. In Proceedings TREC-4. NIST Publication #500-236, Gaithersburg (1996) 25–48

5. Chen, A.: Cross-Language Retrieval Experiments at CLEF 2002. In: Peters, C., Braschler, M., Gonzalo, J., Kluck, M. (eds.): Advances in Cross-Language Information Retrieval. Lecture Notes in Computer Science, Vol. 2785. Springer-Verlag, Berlin Heidelberg New York (2003) 28–48

6. Fox, E.A., Shaw, J.A.: Combination of Multiple Searches. In Proceedings TREC-2. NIST Publication #500-215, Gaithersburg (1994) 243–249

7. Kraaij, W., Pohlmann, R.: Viewing Stemming as Recall Enhancement. In Proceedings of the ACM-SIGIR'96. The ACM Press, New York (1996) 40–48

8. Lovins, J.B.: Development of a Stemming Algorithm. Mechanical Translation and Computational Linguistics 11 (1968) 22–31

9. Porter, M.F.: An Algorithm for Suffix Stripping. Program 14 (1980) 130–137

10. Robertson, S.E., Walker, S., Beaulieu, M.: Experimentation as a Way of Life: Okapi at TREC. Information Processing & Management 36 (2000) 95–108

11. Savoy, J.: Report on CLEF 2002 Experiments: Combining Multiple Sources of Evidence. In: Peters, C., Braschler, M., Gonzalo, J., Kluck, M. (eds.): Advances in Cross-Language Information Retrieval. Lecture Notes in Computer Science, Vol. 2785. Springer-Verlag, Berlin Heidelberg New York (2003) 66–90

12. Singhal, A., Choi, J., Hindle, D., Lewis, D.D., Pereira, F.: AT&T at TREC-7. In Proceedings TREC-7. NIST, Publication #500-242, Gaithersburg (1999) 239–251

Selective Compound Splitting of Swedish Queries for Boolean Combinations of Truncated Terms

Rickard Cöster, Magnus Sahlgren, and Jussi Karlgren

Swedish Institute of Computer Science, SICS,
Box 1263, SE-164 29 Kista, Sweden
{rick, mange, jussi}@sics.se

Abstract. In languages that use compound words such as Swedish, it is often neccessary to split compound words when indexing documents or queries. One of the problems is that it is difficult to find constituents that express a concept similar to that expressed by the compound. The approach taken here is to expand a query with the leading constituents of the compound words. Every query term is truncated so as to increase recall by hopefully finding other compounds with the leading constituent as prefix. This approach increases recall in a rather uncontrolled way, so we use a Boolean quorum-level search method to rank documents both according to a tf-idf factor but also to the number of matching Boolean combinations.

The Boolean combinations performed relatively well, taking into consideration that the queries were very short (maximum of five search terms). Also included in this paper are the results of two other methods we are currently working on in our lab; one for re-ranking search results on the basis of stylistic analysis of documents, and one for dimensionality reduction using Random Indexing.

1 Introduction: Compounds in Swedish

This year, we focused on the Swedish monolingual track. We submitted four runs, where the first two deal with the problem of using compound word splitting for query expansion. The other two runs test very different approaches: first, how to re-rank search results based on a stylistic analysis of the retrieved documents and, secondly, the effect of aggressive dimensionality reduction using Random Indexing.

Swedish is a compounding language. This means that new words are often formed by adjoining two or more separate words. Such words are called *closed* compounds. For example, the Swedish word "diamantgruva" is a closed compound of "diamant" (diamond) and "gruva" (mine). The other two forms of compound words are the *open* form ("post office") and the *hyphenated* ("long-term"). The closed form is common in Swedish (and languages such as German, Finnish and Danish) whereas the open form is more common in English.

C. Peters et al. (Eds.): CLEF 2003, LNCS 3237, pp. 337–344, 2004.

It is necessary for a retrieval system to split compounds into constituents, since a compound may be too specific and not suitable as an index term. One of the problems is that it is difficult to find constituents that express a concept [1] that is similar to that expressed by the compound.

For example, when indexing the compound word "Diamantgruva" it is probably useful to also include "Diamant" and "Gruva" as index terms. Consider instead the compound "Domstol" (Court). It consists of "Dom" (Judgement) and "Stol" (Chair). "Stol" is not very useful as an index term in the context of courts, whereas "Dom" probably is. Splitting "Domstol" thus potentially makes more harm than keeping the original compound.

Another problem is exemplified by splitting the compound "Riksdagshus" (Parliament building). The lemmatizer that we used split this into "Riks", "Dags" and "Hus". It did not find the word "Riksdag" (Parliament) which is desirable as separate index term in the context of parliament buildings. The error is that the words "Riks" and "Dags" are extracted as constituents, but "Riksdag(s)" is not a compound. It also seems that the lemmatizer does not make a morphological analysis of the constituents. This has the effect that sometimes a joining 's' is left at the end of words where there should be none. In summary, some of the problems with using constituents from compound splitting are that they

- may not express a concept similar to that expressed by the compound
- may be ambiguous
- may not always be valid words

2   Selective Compound Splitting and Boolean Combinations

Since compound splitting may not always yield constituents that improve a query, it is desirable to have a method for selecting only a subset of the constituents. Compounds are often very specific words, so one way to improve the query is to find constituents that boost recall. In our case, we selected only the leading constituent when expanding the query.

The leading constituent is sometimes a modifier to the last constituent, i.e. it determines something about the last constituent. For instance, the leading constituent "Ozon" (Ozone) in "Ozonlager" (Ozone layer) determines that the layer mentioned is the ozone layer. The word "Ozon" is useful as a search term, since documents about ozone layers probably also contain the separate word "Ozon". Such documents might also contain other compounds that begin with "Ozon" such as "Ozonhalt" (Ozone amount) and "Ozonhål" (Ozone hole), and using these words in an expansion might improve the query.

Expanding a query with the leading constituent of a compound search word will effectively increase the recall, and hopefully in such a way that the new doc-

---

[1] We assume each term expresses a concept the user is interested in.

uments that are found are related to the concept expressed by the compound. If we also expand the query with all terms that begin with the leading constituent, we will find new words that again, hopefully, are related. While doing so, we will also find terms that are not related to the concept at all, so there must be also be some way of narrowing the query.

To narrow the query, we used a Boolean quorum-level type of combination where documents were ranked according to both the tf-idf factor but also according to how many of the Boolean combinations that matched.

All search terms were truncated, not only the leading compounds. For instance, the truncation of "Diamant" found "Diamantexport" (Diamond export), "Diamantföretag" (Diamond corporation) and also the term "Diamantgruva" mentioned earlier.

2.1   Retrieval Engine and Model

The underlying retrieval engine we used is an experimental system developed at SICS. It currently supports Boolean, Vector Space and structured queries. It is designed to handle a large amount of documents and queries, using algorithms described in [8] and [1] to effectively manage large amounts of data. The system is described in more detail in our CLEF paper [5] from last year.

The Swedish document collection was parsed and normalized using a lemmatizer, but we did not use any compound splitting at indexing time. Also, we used a list of 285 stop words. For scoring documents, we used pivoted cosine normalization, or Lnu in Smart notation [7]. We set the slope to 0.3 after some informal experiments, and set the pivot to the average number of unique terms in a document, as suggested in [7].

2.2   Boolean Combinations of Truncated Terms

We decided to do compound splitting at query time, so that we could elaborate with how to select good constituents for improving the queries.

We tried two different automatic query formulation approaches. For `sicsSVtad` we selected words from the *Title* field only. For `sicsSVtmd`, we again used the *Title* words, but also added some words (those with lowest document frequency) from the *Desc* field up to a maximum of 5 words per query.

Each such base term was then truncated, and we performed a ranked Boolean AND between the base terms and a ranked Boolean OR between the terms found by truncating the base terms. In the case where there were less than 1000 documents in a result list, we appended the results of a standard vector space query using all words from the *Desc* field.

To illustrate the Boolean combination procedure, let a, b and c be three query terms, and let $a_1, \ldots, a_n$ be the expanded terms from the truncation of a (and $b_1, \ldots, b_m$, $c_1, \ldots, c_r$ for b and c). For each Boolean combination of the query terms, we constructed one query. In total this makes 7 queries, displayed in Table 1.

In general, the number of such Boolean query combinations is $\sum_{i=1}^{k} \binom{k}{i}$ where k is the number of terms in the query. This type of Boolean combination is some-

Table 1. The 7 possible Boolean combinations of three truncated words a, b and c

$$(a_1 \vee \ldots \vee a_n) \wedge (b_1 \vee \ldots \vee b_m) \wedge (c_1 \vee \ldots \vee c_r)$$
$$(a_1 \vee \ldots \vee a_n) \wedge (b_1 \vee \ldots \vee b_m)$$
$$(a_1 \vee \ldots \vee a_n) \wedge (c_1 \vee \ldots \vee c_r)$$
$$(b_1 \vee \ldots \vee b_m) \wedge (c_1 \vee \ldots \vee c_r)$$
$$(a_1 \vee \ldots \vee a_n)$$
$$(b_1 \vee \ldots \vee b_m)$$
$$(c_1 \vee \ldots \vee c_r)$$

times called quorum-level search [6], although the standard way of performing the search is to include all combinations of the same size in one and the same query, combined by the OR operator. This strategy was not appropriate, since then we would have normalized documents differently and would not have been able to merge the result lists in a straightforward way.

Since each Boolean combination was a single query, we simply set the RSV for each document to the sum of the RSV values from all queries in that combination. This has the desirable property that documents are not only ranked according to the tf-idf model, but also to the number of combinations of the search terms in the document. For instance, a document where all search terms are found would be at the top of the list, since that document would get positive RSV values from all queries in the combination.

3   Other Approaches

The Boolean combinations of truncated terms are designed to increase recall. To compensate for the attendant raise in noise level we investigate stylistic filtering of the retrieved documents: we boost the rank of news items with animate agents in the hope that this will reduce the average rank of obviously uninteresting items of statistical value only such as sport score tables and stock market reports.

3.1   Stylistic Filtering to Boost News Items with Animate Agents

As the text corpus was composed of news service items with longer, more textual pieces, short one-paragraph or one-sentence passages, as well as tables of sports or stock results, a filter to boost the rank of items more likely to be relevant to the textually oriented materials requested for CLEF was designed. The basic assumption of the filter was that items more likely to be relevant would contain more animate agents than others: texts with the personal agents present and with descriptions of actions taken by people or organizations or other animate entities were assumed to be of a higher information value than texts with completely impersonal and non-active constructions.

The style filter was constructed in a multi-step process. First, a set of prototypical animate agents was drawn up. The list used as a seed set can be seen in Table 2. Second, all verbs in the corpus were tabulated by their occurrence with a subject from the seed set of animate agents. Verbs which occurred at least once with one of the prototypically animate agents were noted to be personal verbs - comprising a set of over 2200 verbs. Third, for each textual item, the number of personal verbs was tabulated. This statistic was used as an animacy score for the text item. Fourth, the output from other retrieval runs was then reranked using the animacy score as a key. The reranking was done in one pass through the list. If an item has a low animacy score, operationalized as less than 75 per cent of the average animacy score of any text in the retrieved set, and the item just below it has a higher animacy score, their position is swapped. This method avoids large scale movement of items through the ranked list but shifts adjacent items from position to position.

Table 2. Seed word set for the prototypical animate agents

Swedish	English	Swedish	English
han	he	barn	child
hon	she	ungdom	youth
man	man	pojke	boy
kvinna	woman	flicka	girl

The parameters of the reranking algorithm given above – such as the swap window of two and the threshold of 0,75 – were not set in any principled way. While they provided promising results for the training data, the results for the actual experiment did not affect the results. Further experiments will be necessary to establish more powerful settings.

3.2   Dimensionality Reduction by Random Indexing

Dimensionality reduction is often important in information retrieval tasks, since the dimensionality of the search space induces constrains on the performance of the retrieval engine; very high-dimensional data will require large amounts of memory and processing time, and will severely limit the effciency of the system. This is especially important in real-world settings, where the user expects both accurate and, sometimes even more important, *fast* results. A common approach to reduce the dimensionality of the data in information retrieval systems is by using various forms of word filtering techniques, such as stop lists, frequency thresholding and morphological normalization.

An alternative method for dimensionality reduction in the Vector Space Model (VSM) [6] is to combine word filtering with the use of reduced representations for the vocabulary. Assuming the standard definition of the VSM, where the dimensionality of the document vectors is given by the size of the vocabulary, i.e. the number w of unique words in the data (normally after word filtering), we can define a reduced representation as vectors of dimensionality $d \ll w$. One way of producing such reduced representations is to use a random mapping method [4], where words are represented by *nearly* orthogonal random vectors of dimensionality $d \ll w$, and where document and query vectors are defined as the average (i.e. the vector sum) of the vectors of the words in the document or query. The point of this methodology is that the resulting search space will be significantly smaller than the original search space, while still containing approximately the same information.

In one of our CLEF 2003 runs (sicsSVind), we used the Random Indexing approach [2], [3] to assign nearly orthogonal sparse random vectors to each unique word in the data. The vectors, which we call *index vectors*, were 1,000-dimensional with 6 randomly distributed non-zero elements (three +1s and three -1s). We then produced 1,000-dimensional document and query vectors by simply summing the index vectors of the words in the documents and the queries (after aggressive word filtering[2]). The resulting 1,000-dimensional document and query vectors are much smaller than the standard VSM vectors that will be 121,545-dimensional for the Swedish data (after word filtering).

The retrieval was then performed by simply calculating the vector similarity between each query vector and all the document vectors. The documents with highest similarity score were ranked as most relevant to the query. As similarity measure, we used the cosine of the angles between the vectors, given by:

$$d_{cos}(x, y) = \frac{\boldsymbol{x} \cdot \boldsymbol{y}}{|\boldsymbol{x}||\boldsymbol{y}|} = \frac{\sum_{i=1}^{n} x_i y_i}{\sqrt{\sum_{i=1}^{n} x_i^2 \sum_{i=1}^{n} y_i^2}}$$

The results are somewhat disappointing; only 2 queries are above the median results, 3 are on the median, and 48 below. It is not clear at this point whether the results are an artefact of the dimensionality reduction, or if they depend on the simple and naive query formulation process used in these runs. Future experiments will investigate this matter more fully.

4   Results

We performed three experiments for this year's CLEF campaign. The experiments on stylistic reranking and on dimensionality reduction using random indexing did not deliver interesting results; we will here only give a detailed analysis for our experiments on Boolean query processing of compounds in query terms.

A summary of the results of the runs using the Boolean combination queries is displayed in Table 3. The Table shows the number of queries that were above, on, or below the median result as well as the number of queries that obtained the maximum or minimum score.

The overall results are encouraging but there are also many failed queries. Since we use a maximum of 5 search terms for each query, the misses are easily attributed to the small amount of query terms. However, we believe that it is interesting to evaluate what type of results that can be achieved when using few query terms, since it is well known that many users (especially web search engine users) typically use only three or four words to express their query.

---

[2] We used a stop list based on document frequencies together with ordinary word frequency thresholds (excluding low (< 3 occurrences) and high (> 12000 occurrences) frequency words).

Table 3. Number of queries above, on or below the median score for each run. The number of queries with max or min score is displayed in the last two columns

Run	Above	On	Below	Max	Min
sicsSVtad 14		10	29	6	5
sicsSVtmd 12		10	31	6	2

There is an interesting difference between the two runs; the number of queries above the median result and the number of queries that obtained the lowest score. Recall that in sicsSVtad, only terms from the *Title* field were used. When we added some terms from the *Desc* field in sicsSVtmd we got fewer (3) queries that obtained lowest score but also fewer queries (2) above the median.

The fewer number of queries that got lowest score is due to the fact that we added more search terms to the query in the sicsSVtmd run. For instance, the average precision of query 165 was improved from 0.3333 to 1.000. The query in sicsSVtad was "GOLDEN GLOBE" whereas in sicsSVtmd it was expanded to "GOLDEN GLOBE KATEGORI DRAMA FILM".

We noted that for the queries that were above median in sicsSVtad and then below median insicsSVtmd, the difference was very small in terms of average precision. For instance, the average precision of query 147 was changed from 0.0673 to 0.0619, and the median was 0.0639.

5 Discussion

For a compounding language such as Swedish, it is important to develop methods that can effectively manage compound words in information retrieval systems. The approach taken in this paper is to look at how the leading constituent of a compound word can be used to expand the query. These query terms were added to the query and all query terms were truncated to increase recall. To strike a balance between high recall and high precision, we used a Boolean quorum-level combination method where documents were ranked according to both the tf-idf factor but also according to how many of the Boolean combinations matched.

The Boolean combinations performed relatively well, taking into consideration that the queries were very short. This was our first attempt to tackle the problem of using compound word splitting for query expansion, and we will continue to pursue this line of research. What we would like to do to next is to use co-occurrence statistics and perhaps also clustering methods to find words that are related to the compound, so that we can have a more principled way of checking the relation between the concept expressed by the constituent and that expressed by the compound.

Acknowledgements

The work reported here is partially funded by the European Commission under contracts IST-2000-29452 (DUMAS) and IST-2000-25310 (CLARITY) which is hereby gratefully acknowledged. We thank Tidningarnas Telegrambyrå AB, Stockholm, for providing us with the Swedish text collection.

References

1. Folk, M. J., Zoellick, B., Riccardi, G.: File Structures: An Object-Oriented Approach with C++. Addison-Wesley, 3rd edition, (1998).
2. Kanerva, P., Kristofersson, J., Holst, A.: Random indexing of text samples for latent semantic analysis. In Proceedings of the 22nd Annual Conference of the Cognitive Science Society, Erlbaum, (2000) p. 1036.
3. Karlgren, J., Sahlgren, M.: From words to understanding. In Uesaka, Y., Kanerva, P., Asoh, H. editors, Foundations of Real World Intelligence, CSLI publications, (2001) 294–308.
4. Kaski, S.: Dimensionality reduction by random mapping: Fast similarity computation for clustering. In Proceedings of the IJCNN'98, International Joint Conference on Neural Networks, IEEE Service Center, (1998) 413–418.
5. Sahlgren, M., Karlgren, J., Cöster, R., Järvinen, T.: SICS at CLEF 2002: Automatic query expansion using random indexing. In C. Peters, M. Braschler, J. Gonzalo and M. Kluck (eds): Advances in Cross-Language Information Retrieval. CLEF 2002 workshop. Revised papers. LNCS 2785 Springer (2003).
6. Salton, G., McGill, M.: Introduction to Modern Information Retrieval. McGraw-Hill, (1983).
7. Singhal, A., Buckley, C., Mitra, M.: Pivoted document length normalization. In Proceedings of the 19th International Conference on Research and Development in Information Retrieval (1996) 21–29.
8. Witten, I.H., Frank, E.: Data Mining: Practical Machine Learning Tools and Techniques with Java Implementations. Morgan Kaufmann, San Francisco, (2000).

COLE Experiments at CLEF 2003 in the Spanish Monolingual Track

Jesús Vilares[1], Miguel A. Alonso[1], and Francisco J. Ribadas[2]

[1] Departamento de Computación, Universidade da Coruña,
Campus de Elviña s/n, 15071 La Coruña, Spain
{jvilares,alonso}@udc.es
[2] Escuela Superior de Ingeniería Informática, Universidade de Vigo,
Campus de As Lagoas, 32004 Orense, Spain
ribadas@ei.uvigo.es
http://www.grupocole.org/

Abstract. In this our second participation in the CLEF Spanish monolingual track, we have continued applying Natural Language Processing techniques for single word and multi-word term conflation. Two different conflation approaches have been tested. The first approach is based on the lemmatization of the text in order to avoid inflectional variation. Our second approach consists of the employment of syntactic dependencies as complex index terms, in an attempt to solve the problems derived from syntactic variation and, in this way, to obtain more precise terms. Such dependencies are obtained through a shallow parser based on cascades of finite-state transducers.

1 Introduction

In Information Retrieval (IR) systems, the correct representation of a document through an accurate set of index terms is the basis for obtaining a good performance. If we are not able to both extract and weight appropriately the terms which capture the semantics of the text, this shortcoming will have an effect on all the subsequent processing.

In this context, one of the major limitations we have to deal with is the linguistic variation of natural languages [5], particularly when processing documents written in languages with more complex morphologic and syntactic structures than those present in English, as in the case of Spanish. When managing this type of phenomena, the employment of Natural Language Processing (NLP) techniques becomes feasible. This has been our working hypothesis since our research group, the COLE Group, started its work on Spanish Information Retrieval.

As in our first participation in CLEF [23], our main premise is the search for simplicity, motivated by the lack of available linguistic resources for Spanish such as large tagged corpora, treebanks or advanced lexicons. This work is thus a continuation and refinement of the previous work presented in CLEF 2002, but

C. Peters et al. (Eds.): CLEF 2003, LNCS 3237, pp. 345–357, 2004.

centered this time on the employment of lemmatization for solving the *inflectional variation* and the employment of syntactic dependencies for solving the *syntactic variation*.

This article is outlined as follows. Section 2 describes the techniques used for single word term conflation. Section 3 introduces our approach for dealing with syntactic variation through shallow parsing. Official runs are presented and discussed in Section 4. Next, Section 5 describes the set of experiments performed after our participation in the workshop, in an attempt to eliminate some of the drawbacks detected. Finally, our conclusions and future developments are presented in Section 6.

2   Single Word Term Conflation

Our proposal for single word term conflation continues to be based on exploiting the lexical level in two phases: first, by solving the *inflectional variation* through lemmatization, and second, by solving the *derivational morphology* through the employment of morphological families.

The process followed for single word term conflation starts by tagging the document. The first step consists in applying our linguistically-motivated preprocessor module [12, 6] in order to perform tasks such as format conversion, tokenization, sentence segmentation, morphological pretagging, contraction splitting, separation of enclitic pronouns from verbal stems, expression identification, numeral identification and proper noun recognition. Classical approaches, such as stemming, rarely manage these phenomena, resulting in erroneous simplifications during the conflation process.

The output generated by our preprocessor is then taken as input by our tagger-lemmatizer, MrTagoo [9], although any high-performance part-of-speech tagger could be used instead. MrTagoo is based on a second order Hidden Markov Model (HMM), whose elements and procedures for the estimation of parameters are based on Brant's work [7], and also incorporates certain capabilities which led to its use in our system. Such capabilities include a very efficient structure for storage and search —based on finite-state automata [11]—, management of unknown words, the possibility of integrating external dictionaries in the probabilistic frame defined by the HMM [13], and the possibility of managing ambiguous segmentations [10].

Nevertheless, these kind of tools are very sensitive to spelling errors, as, for example, in the case of sentences written completely in uppercase —e.g., news headlines and subsection headings—, which cannot be correctly managed by the preprocessor and tagger modules. For this reason, the initial output of the tagger is processed by an *uppercase-to-lowercase* module [23] in order to process uppercase sentences, converting them to lowercase and restoring the diacritical marks when necessary.

Once text has been tagged, the lemmas of the content words (nouns, verbs and adjectives) are extracted to be indexed. In this way we solve the problems derived from inflection in Spanish. With regard to computational cost, the running cost of a lemmatizer-disambiguator is linear in relation to the length of the word, and cubic in relation to the size of the tagset, which is a constant. As we only need to know the grammatical category of the word, the tagset is small and therefore the increase in costs with respect to classical approaches (stemmers) becomes negligible.

Our previous experiments in CLEF 2002 showed that lemmatization performs better than stemming, even when using stemmers which also deal with derivational morphology.

Once inflectional variation has been solved, the next logical step consists of solving the problems caused by derivational morphology. For this purpose, we have grouped those words derivable from each other by means of mechanisms of derivational morphology; each one of these groups is a *morphological family*. Each one of the lemmas belonging to the same morphological family is conflated into the same term, a *representative* of the family. The set of morphological families are automatically generated from a large lexicon of Spanish words by means of a tool which implements the most common derivational mechanisms of Spanish [25]. Since the set of morphological families is generated statically, there is no increment in the running cost.

Nevertheless, our previous experiments in CLEF 2002 showed that the employment of morphological families for single word term conflation introduced too much noise in the system. Thus, we have chosen lemmatization as the conflation technique to be used with single word terms, while morphological families will only be used as a complement in multi-word term conflation, as shown in Section 3.

3   Managing the Syntactic Variation Through Shallow Parsing

Following the same scheme of our previous experiments, once we have established the way to process the content of the document at word level, the next step consists of deciding how to process, at phrase level, its syntactic content in order to manage the *syntactic variation* of the document. For this purpose, we will extract the pairs of words related through syntactic dependencies in order to use them as complex index terms. This process is performed in two steps: first, the text is parsed by means of a *shallow parser* and, second, the syntactic dependencies are extracted and conflated into index terms.

3.1   The Shallow Parser

When dealing with syntactic variation, we have to face the problems derived from the high computational cost of parsing. In order to maintain a linear complexity with respect to the length of the text to be analyzed, we have discarded the employment of full parsing techniques [16], opting for the application of *shallow parsing* techniques, also looking for greater robustness.

The theoretical basis for the design of our parser comes from formal language theory, which tells us that, given a context-free grammar and an input string, the syntactic trees of height k generated by a parser can be obtained by means of k layers of finite-state transducers: the first layer obtains the nodes labeled by non-terminals corresponding to left-hand sides of productions that only contain terminals on their right-hand side; the second layer obtains those nodes which only involve terminal symbols and those non-terminal symbols generated on the previous layer; and so on. It can be argued that the parsing capability of the system is, in this way, limited by the height of the parseable trees. Nevertheless, this kind of shallow parsing [4] has shown itself to be useful in several NLP application fields, particularly in Information Extraction. Its application in IR, which has not been deeply studied, has been tested by Xerox for English [14], showing its superiority with respect to classical approaches based on contiguous words.

This way, we have implemented a shallow parser based on a five layer architecture whose input is the output of our tagger-lemmatizer. Next, we will describe the function of each layer:

Layer 0: Improving the Preprocessing. Its function is the management of certain linguistic constructions in order to minimize the noise generated during the subsequent parsing. Such constructions include:

- *Numerals in non-numerical format.*
- *Quantity expressions.* Expressions of the type *algo más de dos millones* (a little more than two million) or *unas dos docenas* (about two dozen), which denote a number but with a certain vagueness about its concrete value, are identified as numeral phrases ($NumP$).
- *Expressions with a verbal function.* Some verbal expressions such as *tener en cuenta* (to take into account), must be considered as a unit, in this case synonym of the verb *considerar* (to consider), to avoid errors in the upper layers such as identifying *en cuenta* as a complement of the verb.

Layer 1: Adverbial Phrases and First Level Verbal Groups. In this layer the system identifies, on the one hand, the *adverbial phrases* ($AdvP$) of the text, either those with an adverbial head —e.g., *rápidamente* (quickly)—, or those expressions which are not properly adverbial but have an equivalent function —e.g., *de forma rápida* (in a quick way)—. On the other hand, non-periphrastic verbal groups, which we call *first level verbal groups*, are processed, in both their simple and compound forms, and in both their active and passive forms.

Layer 2: Adjectival Phrases and Second Level Verbal Groups. Adjectival phrases ($AdjP$) such as *azul* (blue) or *muy alto* (very high) are managed here, together with periphrastic verbal groups, such as *tengo que ir* (I have to go), which we call *second level verbal groups*. *Verbal periphrases* are unions of two or more verbal forms working as a unit, and attributing shades of meaning, such as obligation, degree of development of the action, etc., to the semantics of the main verb. Moreover, these shades cannot be expressed by means of the simple and compound forms of the verb.

Layer 3: Noun Phrases. In the case of noun phrases (NP), together with simple structures such as the attachment of determiners and adjectives to the noun, we have considered more complex phenomena, such as the existence of *partitive complements* (PC) —e.g., *alguno de* (some of), *ninguno de* (none of)—, in order to cover more complex nominal structures —e.g., *cualquiera de aquellos coches nuevos* (any of those new cars)—.

Layer 4: Prepositional Phrases. Formed by a noun phrase (NP) preceded by a preposition (P), we have considered three different types according to the preposition, in order to make the extraction of dependencies easier: those preceded by the preposition *por* (by) or $PPby$, those preceded by *de* (of) or $PPof$, and the remaining prepositional phrases or PP.

Each of the rules involved in the different stages of the parsing process has been implemented through a finite-state transducer, producing, in this way, a parser based on a cascade of finite-state transducers. Therefore, our approach maintains a linear complexity.

3.2   Extraction and Conflation of Dependencies

Once the text has been parsed, the system identifies the syntactic roles of the phrases recognized and extracts the *dependency pairs* formed by:

- A noun and each of its modifying adjectives.
- A noun and the head of its prepositional complement.
- The head of the subject and its predicative verb.
- The head of the subject and the head of the attribute. From a semantical point of view, copulative verbs are mere links, so the dependency is directly established between the subject and the attribute.
- An active verb and the head of its direct object.
- A passive verb and the head of its agent.
- A predicative verb and the head of its prepositional complement.
- The head of the subject and the head of a prepositional complement of the verb, but only when it is copulative (because of its special behavior).

Once such dependencies have been identified, they are conflated through the following conflation scheme:

1. The simple terms compounding the pair are conflated employing morphological families —see Section 2— in order to improve the management of the syntactic variation by covering the appearance of morphosyntactic variants of the original term [24, 15]. In this way, terms such as *cambio en el clima* (change of the climate) and *cambio climático* (climatic change), which express the same concept in different words —but semantically and derivatively related—, can be matched.
2. Conversion to lowercase and elimination of diacritical marks, as in the case of stemmers. Previous experiments show that this process eliminates much of the noise introduced by spelling errors [23].

The process of shallow parsing and extraction of dependencies is explained in detail in [21].

4   CLEF 2003 Official Runs

In this new edition of CLEF, the document corpus for the Spanish Monolingual Track has been enlarged with respect to previous editions. The new corpus is formed by the 215,738 news items (509 MB) from 1994 plus 238,307 more news items (577 MB) from 1995; that is, 454,045 documents (1086 MB). The set of topics consists of 60 queries (141 to 200).

Our group submitted four runs to the CLEF 2003 Spanish monolingual track:

— `coleTDlemZP03` (`TDlemZP` for short): Conflation of content words via lemmatization, that is, each form of a content word is replaced by its lemma. This kind of conflation only takes inflectional morphology into account. The resulting conflated document was indexed using the probabilistic engine ZPrise [3], employing the Okapi BM25 weight scheme [17] with the constants defined in [19] for Spanish ($b = 0.5$, $k_1 = 2$). The query is formed by the set of meaningful lemmas present in the *title* and *description* fields —i.e., short topics.
— `coleTDNlemZP03` (`TDNlemZP` for short): The same as before, but the query also includes the set of meaningful lemmas obtained from the *narrative* field —i.e., long topics.
— `coleTDNlemSM03` (`TDNlemSM` for short): As in the case of `TDNlemZP`, the three fields of the query are conflated through lemmatization. Nevertheless, this time the indexing engine is the vector-based SMART [8], with an `atn-ntc` weighting scheme [20]. This run was submitted in order to use it as baseline for the rest of runs employing long topics.
— `coleTDNpdsSM03` (`TDNpdsSM` for short): Text conflated via the combination of simple terms, obtained through the lemmatization of content words, and complex terms, obtained through the conflation of syntactic dependencies, as was described in Section 3. According to the results of a previous tuning phase described in [22], the balance factor between the weights of simple and complex terms was fixed at 4 to 1 –i.e., the weights of simple terms are quadrupled– with the aim of increasing the precision of the top ranked documents.

There are no experiments indexing syntactic dependencies with the Okapi BM25 weight scheme, since we are still studying the best way to integrate them into a probabilistic model. The conditions employed in the official runs were as follows:

1. The stopword list was obtained by lemmatizing the content words of the Spanish stopword list provided with SMART [1].
2. Employment of the uppercase-to-lowercase module to process uppercase sentences during tagging.
3. Elimination of spelling signs and conversion to lowercase after conflation in order to reduce typographical errors.
4. Except for the first run, `TDlemZP`, the terms extracted from the *title* field of the query are given double relevance with respect to *description* and *narrative*, since this field summarizes the basic semantics of the query.

Table 1. CLEF 2003: official results

	TDlemZP	TDNlemZP	TDNlemSM	TDNpdsSM
Documents	57k	57k	57k	57k
Relevant (2368 expected)	2237	2253	2221	2249
R-precision	.4503	.4935	.4453	.4684
Non-interpolated precision	.4662	.5225	.4684	.4698
Document precision	.5497	.5829	.5438	.5408
Precision at 0.00 Re.	.8014	.8614	.7790	.7897
Precision at 0.10 Re.	.7063	.7905	.6982	.7165
Precision at 0.20 Re.	.6553	.7301	.6331	.6570
Precision at 0.30 Re.	.5969	.6449	.5738	.6044
Precision at 0.40 Re.	.5485	.5911	.5388	.5562
Precision at 0.50 Re.	.4969	.5616	.5003	.5092
Precision at 0.60 Re.	.4544	.4871	.4457	.4391
Precision at 0.70 Re.	.3781	.4195	.3987	.3780
Precision at 0.80 Re.	.3083	.3609	.3352	.3191
Precision at 0.90 Re.	.2093	.2594	.2292	.2248
Precision at 1.00 Re.	.1111	.1512	.1472	.1525
Precision at 5 docs.	.5930	.6421	.5930	.5684
Precision at 10 docs.	.5070	.5596	.5018	.4965
Precision at 15 docs.	.4713	.4971	.4515	.4573
Precision at 20 docs.	.4307	.4614	.4281	.4202
Precision at 30 docs.	.3719	.4012	.3784	.3678
Precision at 100 docs.	.2316	.2393	.2316	.2305
Precision at 200 docs.	.1461	.1505	.1455	.1458
Precision at 500 docs.	.0726	.0731	.0718	.0719
Precision at 1000 docs.	.0392	.0395	.0390	.0395

According to Table 1, the probabilistic-based approach through a BM25 weighting scheme –TDlemZP and TDNlemZP– is shown to be clearly superior to the vector-based `atn-ntc` weighting scheme –TDNlemSM and TDNpdsSM–, even when only lemmatizing the text. As we can see, TDlemZP obtains similar or better results than TDNlemSM even when the latter also employs the extra information provided by the *narrative*.

With respect to the main contribution of this work, the use of syntactic dependencies as complex index terms, the results differ slightly from those obtained during the tuning phase [22], where syntactic dependencies clearly showed an improvement in the precision of the top ranked documents. With respect to global performance measures, the TDNpdsSM run obtains better results than TDNlemSM, except for average document precision. However, the behavior of the system with respect to ranking is not good, since the results obtained for precision at N documents retrieved when employing complex terms —TDNpdsSM— are worse than those obtained using only simple lemmatized terms —TDNlemSM—. On the other hand, the results for precision vs. recall continue to be better.

Table 2. Distribution of terms in CLEF 2003 collection

	[1..1]	[2..2]	[3..4]	[5..8]	[9..16]	[17..32]	[33..64]	[65..128]	[129..∞)
Lemmas	51.68	13.54	10.16	7.29	5.05	3.50	2.56	1.86	4.36
Dependencies	57.48	14.89	10.61	7.02	4.40	2.65	1.50	0.80	1.04

5   New Experiments with CLEF 2003 Topics

5.1   Re-tuning the Weight Balance Factor

Taking into account the possibility that the weight balance factor between lemmas and dependencies could be more collection-dependent than supposed, we decided to try different values in a range of 1 to 12. Preliminary experiments [22] showed that a balance factor of 10 could be more appropriate for this larger collection.

Nevertheless, in order to minimize the noise introduced by rare or misspelled terms, and also to reduce the size of the index, we decided to eliminate the most infrequent terms according to their *document frequency* (df) in the collection. Table 2 shows the percentage of different terms (lemmas or dependencies) which appear in only 1 document, in 2 documents, between 3 and 4 documents, between 5 and 8 documents, and so on. For example, we can observe that 52% of lemmas and 57% of dependencies only appear in one document of the collection. Taking into account these statistics, we decided to discard those terms which appear in less than five documents. This pruning of the index allowed us to eliminate 75% of the lemmas and 82% of the dependency pairs with minimal incidence on the performance of the system.

Table 3 shows the new results obtained. The first column, *lem*, shows the results for our baseline, lemmatization —as in the official run TDN1emSM—, whereas the next columns, *sdx*, contain the results obtained by merging lemmatized simple terms and complex terms based on syntactic dependencies (*sd*) when the weight balance factor between simple and complex terms, x to 1, changes —i.e., when the weight of simple terms is multiplied by x. As already stated in Section 4, *sd4* shows the results obtained with $x = 4$, the balance factor used in the official run TDNpdsSM. The column *opt* shows the best results obtained for *sdx*, written in boldface, whereas the column Δ shows the improvement of *opt* with respect to *lem*.

These new results corroborate those obtained in previous experiments [22], since *sd10* continues to be the best choice for our purpose, which is to increase the precision of the top ranked documents. It obtains the best results for precision at N documents, and non-interpolated and document precision, being slightly better than those obtained through lemmatization (*lem*). In the case of precision vs. recall, *sd4* is the best compromise in the range 0.00–0.40.

Table 3. CLEF 2003: Re-tuning the system a posteriori

	lem	sd1	sd2	sd4	sd6	sd8	sd10	sd12	opt	Δ
Documents	57k	57k	57k	57k	57k	57k	57k	57k	- -	- -
Relevant (2368 expected)	2221	2218	2241	**2248**	2243	2244	2242	2239	2248	27
Non-interpolated precision	.4681	.4014	.4413	.4613	.4656	.4696	**.4710**	.4705	.4710	.0029
Document precision	.5431	.4647	.5149	.5394	.5444	.5470	**.5475**	.5472	.5475	.0044
R-precision	.4471	.3961	.4415	**.4542**	.4480	.4463	.4454	.4450	.4542	.0071
Precision at 0.00 Re.	.7805	.7562	**.7940**	.7721	.7827	.7811	.7776	.7856	.7940	.0135
Precision at 0.10 Re.	.6994	.6428	.6817	.7036	.7032	**.7125**	.7109	.7104	.7125	.0131
Precision at 0.20 Re.	.6343	.5640	.6097	.6392	.6501	**.6526**	.6464	.6421	.6526	.0183
Precision at 0.30 Re.	.5736	.5144	.5614	**.5925**	.5913	.5922	.5912	.5867	.5925	.0189
Precision at 0.40 Re.	.5332	.4706	.5108	.5348	.5347	.5307	.5336	**.5357**	.5357	.0025
Precision at 0.50 Re.	.4987	.4222	.4647	.4931	.4936	.4975	**.5040**	.5032	.5040	.0053
Precision at 0.60 Re.	.4462	.3643	.4183	.4380	.4382	.4444	.4467	**.4468**	.4462	.0006
Precision at 0.70 Re.	.3969	.3122	.3466	.3758	.3884	.3941	**.3969**	.3958	.3969	.0000
Precision at 0.80 Re.	.3343	.2578	.2964	.3186	.3274	.3291	.3296	**.3299**	.3299	-.0044
Precision at 0.90 Re.	.2294	.1951	.2156	.2245	.2306	**.2333**	.2313	.2316	.2333	.0039
Precision at 1.00 Re.	.1470	.1316	.1499	**.1514**	.1493	.1501	.1488	.1489	.1514	.0044
Precision at 5 docs.	.5965	.4842	.5228	.5684	.5825	.6000	**.6070**	.5930	.6070	.0105
Precision at 10 docs.	.5000	.4333	.4825	.4947	.5018	.5035	**.5053**	**.5053**	.5053	.0053
Precision at 15 docs.	.4515	.3860	.4409	**.4561**	.4503	.4503	.4503	.4526	.4561	.0046
Precision at 20 docs.	.4281	.3632	.4009	.4193	.4184	.4211	**.4237**	**.4237**	.4237	-.0044
Precision at 30 docs.	.3813	.3205	.3497	.3673	.3760	.3772	**.3789**	**.3789**	.3789	-.0024
Precision at 100 docs.	.2314	.2053	.2221	.2309	.2332	**.2340**	.2337	.2333	.2340	.0026
Precision at 200 docs.	.1455	.1368	.1429	.1454	.1464	**.1465**	.1461	.1461	.1465	.0010
Precision at 500 docs.	.0718	.0692	.0711	.0718	.0719	.0719	**.0720**	.0719	.0720	.0002
Precision at 1000 docs.	.0390	.0389	.0393	.0394	**.0394**	.0394	.0393	.0393	.0394	.0004

5.2   Incorporating Pseudo-Relevance Feedback

A second set of experiments consisted in the application of pseudo-relevance feedback (blind-query expansion) adopting Rocchio's approach [18] in the case of lemmas indexed with SMART:

$$Q_1 = \alpha Q_0 + \beta \sum_{k=1}^{n_1} \frac{R_k}{n_1} - \gamma \sum_{k=1}^{n_2} \frac{S_k}{n_2}$$

where Q_1 is the new query vector, Q_0 is the vector for the initial query, R_k is the vector for relevant document k, S_k is the vector for non-relevant document k, n_1 is the number of relevant documents, n_2 is the number of non-relevant documents, and α, β and γ are, respectively, the parameters that control the relative contributions of the original query, relevant documents, and non-relevant documents. In the case of our system, it only takes into account relevant documents ($\gamma = 0$).

First, we explored the space of solutions searching for, on the one hand, the best relation α/β and, on the other hand, the most accurate number of documents and terms to be used in the expansion. Table 4 shows the non-interpolated precision when different values of α and different numbers of terms and documents are used. Preliminary experiments, not presented here so as not to tire the reader, had shown that the behaviour of our system improved when increasing the value of α; these experiments were made using a fixed value of $\beta = 0.10$

Table 4. Tuning the parameters for blind-query expansion ($\beta = 0.10$ fixed)

	Non-interpolated precision								
α	1.00		1.20		1.40		1.60		1.80	
no. of docs.	5	10	5	10	5	10	5	10	5	10
5 terms	.5175	.4986	.5176	.4988	.5181	.4987	.5180	.4986	.5172	.4984
10 terms	.5201	.5027	.5210	.5035	.5211	.5039	.5211	.5041	.5204	.5038
15 terms	.5205	.5055	.5218	.5064	.5225	.5070	.5226	.5071	.5227	.5069
20 terms	.5223	.5074	.5234	.5087	.5243	.5091	.5244	.5093	.5252	.5093

while varying α. The best results were obtained with a value of α in the range 1.40–1.80, finally opting for expanding the query with the best 10 terms of the 5 top ranked documents using $\alpha = 1.40$ and $\beta = 0.10$.

Table 5 contains the final set of results obtained for CLEF 2003 topics. The runs are the same as those submitted to the official track, except for the following changes:

1. Those terms which appear in less than five documents have been discarded.
2. The balance factor for the run TDNpdsSM has been increased to 10 —i.e., the weight of lemmas is multiplied by 10.
3. A new run has been considered, TDNlemSM-f. This run is the same as TDNlemSM, but applies Rocchio's approach for pseudo-relevance feedback. The initial query is expanded with the best 10 terms of the 5 top ranked documents using $\alpha = 1.40$ and $\beta = 0.10$.

The results and their interpretation are similar to those obtained in the official runs. Nevertheless, the use of a bigger balance factor in TDNpdsSM now leads to a slight improvement with respect to the baseline, TDNlemSM. On the other hand, as was expected, the employment of relevance feedback in TDNlemSM-f produces major improvement. We expect that the application of pseudo-relevance feedback to TDNpdsSM will produce a similar increase in performance. Currently, we are are investigating how to adapt Rocchio's approach to this case.

6   Conclusions and Future Work

Throughout this article we have studied the employment of Natural Language Processing techniques to manage linguistic variation in Spanish Information Retrieval. At word-level, inflectional variation has been solved through lemmatization whereas, at phrase-level, syntactic variation has been managed through the employment of syntactic dependencies as complex index terms. Such dependencies were obtained through a shallow parser based on cascades of finite-state transducers, and then conflated by means of derivational morphology.

Table 5. CLEF 2003: final results

	TDlemZP	TDNlemZP	TDNlemSM	TDNpdsSM	TDNlemSM-f
Documents	57k	57k	57k	57k	57k
Relevant (2368 expected)	2235	2253	2221	2242	2260
Non-interpolated precision	.4619	.5163	.4681	.4710	.5211
Document precision	.5478	.5818	.5431	.5475	.6086
R-precision	.4480	.4928	.4471	.4454	.4796
Precision at 0.00 Re.	.7894	.8429	.7805	.7776	.7760
Precision at 0.10 Re.	.7027	.7717	.6994	.7109	.7134
Precision at 0.20 Re.	.6447	.7161	.6343	.6464	.6636
Precision at 0.30 Re.	.5932	.6377	.5736	.5912	.6204
Precision at 0.40 Re.	.5401	.5895	.5332	.5336	.5925
Precision at 0.50 Re.	.4905	.5544	.4987	.5040	.5467
Precision at 0.60 Re.	.4544	.4844	.4462	.4467	.4932
Precision at 0.70 Re.	.3758	.4189	.3969	.3969	.4655
Precision at 0.80 Re.	.3042	.3570	.3343	.3296	.4095
Precision at 0.90 Re.	.2076	.2586	.2294	.2313	.3364
Precision at 1.00 Re.	.1145	.1539	.1470	.1488	.2306
Precision at 5 docs.	.5860	.6281	.5965	.6070	.6000
Precision at 10 docs.	.5053	.5561	.5000	.5053	.5421
Precision at 15 docs.	.4632	.4971	.4515	.4503	.4982
Precision at 20 docs.	.4272	.4605	.4281	.4237	.4640
Precision at 30 docs.	.3737	.4035	.3813	.3789	.4105
Precision at 100 docs.	.2321	.2404	.2314	.2337	.2461
Precision at 200 docs.	.1463	.1504	.1455	.1461	.1527
Precision at 500 docs.	.0726	.0731	.0718	.0720	.0742
Precision at 1000 docs.	.0392	.0395	.0390	.0393	.0396

The improvement obtained using syntactic information is not as great as expected, which suggests that our actual way of integrating such information must be improved. Our future work will focus on this goal in three different ways: first, its integration in a probabilistic retrieval model (e.g., using the Okapi BM25 weight scheme); second, testing its behaviour during feedback; third, investigating the possibility of storing simple and complex terms in separate indexes, combining them afterwards by means of *data fusion* techniques [26].

Acknowledgements

The research described in this paper has been supported in part by Ministerio de Ciencia y Tecnología (TIC2000-0370-C02-01, HP2001-0044 and HF2002-81), FPU grants of Secretaría de Estado de Educación y Universidades, Xunta de Galicia (PGIDIT03SIN30501PR, PGIDT01PXI10506PN, PGIDIT02PXIB30501PR and PGIDIT02SIN01E), Universidade de Vigo, and

Universidade da Coruña. The authors would also like to thank Darrin Dimmick, from NIST, for giving us the opportunity to use the ZPrise system, and Fernando Martínez, from Universidad de Jaén, for helping us to make it operative in our system.

References

1. ftp://ftp.cs.cornell.edu/pub/smart (site visited October 2003).
2. http://www.clef-campaign.org (site visited October 2003).
3. http://www.itl.nist.gov (site visited October 2003).
4. Abney, S.: Partial parsing via finite-state cascades. Natural Language Engineering, 2(4) (1997) 337–344.
5. Arampatzis, A., van der Weide, T., Koster, C., van Bommel, P.: Linguistically motivated information retrieval. In Encyclopedia of Library and Information Science. Marcel Dekker, Inc., New York and Basel (2000).
6. Barcala, F.M., Vilares, J., Alonso, M.A., Graña, J., Vilares, M.: Tokenization and proper noun recognition for information retrieval. In A Min Tjoa and Roland R. Wagner (eds.). Thirteenth International Workshop on Database and Expert Systems Applications. IEEE Computer Society Press (2002) 246–250.
7. Brants, T.: TnT - a statistical part-of-speech tagger. In Proceedings of the Sixth Applied Natural Language Processing Conference (ANLP'2000), Seattle (2000).
8. Buckley, C.: Implementation of the SMART information retrieval system. Technical report, Department of Computer Science, Cornell University. (1985). Source code available at [1].
9. Graña, J.: Técnicas de Análisis Sintáctico Robusto para la Etiquetación del Lenguaje Natural. PhD thesis, University of La Coruña, La Coruña, Spain (2000).
10. Graña, J., Alonso, M.A., Vilares, M.: A common solution for tokenization and part-of-speech tagging: One-pass Viterbi algorithm vs. iterative approaches. In Petr Sojka, Ivan Kopecek, and Karel Pala (eds.). Text, Speech and Dialogue. LNCS 2448. Springer-Verlag, Berlin-Heidelberg-New York (2002) 3–10.
11. Graña, J., Barcala, F.M., Alonso, M.A.: Compilation methods of minimal acyclic automata for large dictionaries. In Bruce W. Watson and Derick Wood (eds.) Implementation and Application of Automata. LNCS 2494. Springer-Verlag, Berlin-Heidelberg-New York (2002) 135–148.
12. Graña, J., Barcala, F.M., Vilares, J.: Formal methods of tokenization for part-of-speech tagging. In Alexander Gelbukh (ed.). Computational Linguistics and Intelligent Text Processing. LNCS 2276. Springer-Verlag, Berlin-Heidelberg-New York (2002) 240–249.
13. Graña, J., Chappelier, J.-C., Vilares, M.: Integrating external dictionaries into stochastic part-of-speech taggers. In Proceedings of the Euroconference Recent Advances in Natural Language Processing (RANLP 2001). Tzigov Chark, Bulgaria (2001) 122–128.
14. Hull, D. A., Grefenstette, G., Schulze, B. M., Gaussier, E., Schutze, H., Pedersen, J. O.: Xerox TREC-5 site report: routing, filtering, NLP, and Spanish tracks. In Proceedings of the Fifth Text REtrieval Conference (TREC-5)(1997) 167–180.
15. Jacquemin, C., Tzoukermann, E.: NLP for term variant extraction: synergy between morphology, lexicon and syntax. In Tomek Strzalkowski (ed.). Natural Language Information Retrieval, Vol.7 of Text, Speech and Language Technology. Kluwer Academic Publishers, Dordrecht/Boston/London (1999) 25–74.

16. Perez-Carballo, J., Strzalkowski, T.: Natural language information retrieval: progress report. Information Processing and Management 36(1) (2000) 155–178.
17. Robertson, S.E., Walker, S.: Okapi/Keenbow at TREC-8. In E. Voorhees and D. K. Harman (eds.). Proceedings of the Eighth Text REtrieval Conference (TREC-8), NIST Special Publication 500-264 (2000) 151–161.
18. Rocchio, J.J.: Relevance Feedback in Information Retrieval. In G. Salton (ed.). The SMART Retrieval System—Experiments in Automatic Document Processing. Prentice Hall, Englewood Cliffs, NJ (1971).
19. Savoy, J.: Report on CLEF 2002 Experiments: Combining Multiple Sources of Evidence. In C. Peters, M. Braschler, J. Gonzalo, and M. Kluck (eds.). Advances in Cross-Language Information Retrieval: Results of the CLEF 2002 Evaluation Campaign. LNCS 2785 Springer-Verlag, Berlin-Heidelberg-New York (2003) 66–90.
20. Savoy, J., Le Calve, A., Vrajitoru, D.: Report on the TREC-5 experiment: Data fusion and collection fusion. Proceedings of TREC'5, NIST publication #500-238, Gaithersburg, MD (1997) 489–502.
21. Vilares, J., Alonso, M.A.: A Grammatical Approach to the Extraction of Index Terms. In G. Angelova, K. Bontcheva, R. Mitkov, N. Nicolov and Ni. Nikolov (eds.). Proceedings of International Conference on Recent Advances in Natural Language Processing (RANLP 2003), Borovets, Bulgaria (2003) 500-504.
22. Vilares, J., Alonso, M.A., Ribadas, F.J.: COLE experiments at CLEF 2003 Spanish monolingual track. In C. Peters and F. Borri (eds.). Results of the CLEF 2003 Cross-Language System Evaluation Campaign, Working Notes for the CLEF 2003 Workshop (2003) 197–206. Available at [2].
23. Vilares, J., Alonso, M.A., Ribadas, F.J., Vilares, M.: COLE experiments in the CLEF 2002 Spanish monolingual track. In C. Peters, M. Braschler, J. Gonzalo, and M. Kluck (eds.). Advances in Cross-Language Information Retrieval: Results of the CLEF 2002 Evaluation Campaign. LNCS 2785 Springer-Verlag, Berlin-Heidelberg-New York (2003) 265–278.
24. Vilares, J., Barcala, F.M., Alonso, M.A.: Using syntactic dependency-pairs conflation to improve retrieval performance in Spanish. In Alexander Gelbukh (ed.) Computational Linguistics and Intelligent Text Processing. LNCS 2276. Springer-Verlag, Berlin-Heidelberg-New York (2002) 381–390.
25. Vilares, J., Cabrero, D., Alonso, M.A.: Applying productive derivational morphology to term indexing of Spanish texts. In Alexander Gelbukh (ed.). Computational Linguistics and Intelligent Text Processing, LNCS 2004. Springer-Verlag, Berlin-Heidelberg-New York (2001) 336–348.
26. Vogt, C., Cottrell, G. W.: Fusion via a linear combination of scores. Information Retrieval 1(3) (1999) 151–173.

Experiments with Self Organizing Maps in CLEF 2003

Javier Fernández, Ricardo Mones, Irene Díaz,
José Ranilla, and Elías F. Combarro*

Artificial Intelligence Center, University of Oviedo, Spain
ir@aic.uniovi.es

Abstract. In our first participation in the Cross Language Evalution Forum, we tested the performance of a clustering method which uses self organizing maps.

1 Introduction

Many approaches to Information Retrieval focus on the word level. Word indices are built, synonyms are used to expand queries, and so on.

In this work for the Cross Language Evaluation Forum we have tested an approach which focuses more on the document rather than the word level. First, we create clusters of similar documents and then we search for the cluster that is most similar to a given query. This method should have several advantages:

1. The search is faster, since the number of elements to compare with the query is less
2. Similar documents are clustered together and can be retrieved even if they contain no words of the query (without the use of a thesaurus)
3. In addition to an Information Retrieval system a hierarchy of the documents is built

In this paper we describe a very simple system of this kind, based on self organizing maps [1]. These maps have been used successfully for a series of tasks in Information Retrieval [2, 3, 4, 5].

We tested the performance of the system in the monolingual Spanish task of the 2003 edition of the Cross Language Evaluation Forum, which consists of searching for 60 different topics over the news published during 1994 and 1995 by the EFE agency.

The rest of the paper is organized as follows. In Section 2, we briefly describe similar approaches that can be found in the literature. Section 3 is devoted to describing the system. The experiments conducted to test the system are described in Section 4 and their results are presented in Section 5. Finally, in Section 6, we draw some conclusions and propose some ideas for further research.

---

* The research reported in this paper has been supported in part under FICYT grant PR-01-GE-15.

C. Peters et al. (Eds.): CLEF 2003, LNCS 3237, pp. 358–366, 2004.

2   Previous Work

Self-Organizing Maps ([1]) or simply SOMs, are methods for unsupervised clustering of elements. These elements are represented by numerical vectors which are used, in a training phase, to adjust the vectors associated with a set of neurons. The neurons are usually situated in a 2-dimensional topological map. This topology has influence in the training phase, since the values of a neuron are modified together with those of its neighbors.

These maps have been successfully used in a wide variety of tasks [6, 1], including document management [2, 3, 4] and Information Retrieval [5].

Here, we use SOMs to cluster similar documents together. The search is then performed over the neurons instead of over the documents themselves, the computational complexity can thus be reduced several orders of magnitude.

This clustering has also the advatange of disambiguating the meaning of words (since the context of the word is also considered) and this has been shown to give an improvement in the retrieval of relevant documents [5] at least compared with simple classical methods such as Salton's Vector Space Model [7] and Latent Semantic Indexing [8].

3   The System

The number of documents that use in the experiments (see section 4), is over 300 hundred times more than others used in the referred literature with the same system [5]. This makes infeasible the use of all the words of the corpus to represent the documents, and makes the selection of the most representative words or features necessary.

The main difference of our system with previous approaches (see Section 2) is the use of two different representations of the documents. Since we are dealing with documents which come from a news agency, we consider that proper nouns are specially important.

The frequencies and distribution over documents of proper nouns and other words are quite different. If we use just one lexicon, then most proper nouns will be dropped when we filter the words, resulting in a serious limitation in the retrieval phase. For this reason, we use two separate lexica: one of proper nouns and another general purpose one.

Each document is represented by two vectors (see [9]). The first has as components the number of times that each word from the vocabulary of proper nouns appear in the document; the second one is similar, but regards the lexicon of common words.

Two different groups of clusters are then constructed using the two different groups of vectors representing the documents. When we are given a query, it is matched against both groups of clusters and the results are combined to give the final set of documents considered relevant for the query.

The whole process involves the following steps:

1. Extraction of the lexica
2. Selection of the features representing the documents
3. Clustering of the documents
4. Comparison of the query with the clusters
5. Combination of the results

They are described in more detail in the following sections.

3.1   Extraction of the Lexica

We iterate through all the documents in the collection to get the two lexica: the one of proper nouns and the one of common words.

The first step consists of deciding whether a word is a proper noun or not. To this extent, some complex algorithms have been developed (the Named Entity Task of the Message Understanding Conferences was devoted to this problem) but we take advantage of the capitalization in Spanish language to use a simple method: a word which begins with capital letter and is not at the beginning of a sentence is a proper noun; a word all in lower case letters is a common word; any other word is declared ambiguous and its type is decided after all other words have been processed. If the ambiguous word appears somewhere else in the document as a proper noun then it is a proper noun. If not, it is considered a common word. This process is depicted in Figure 1.

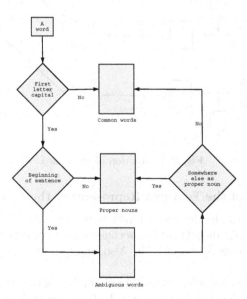

Fig. 1. Deciding whether a word is a proper noun

During this process, all words are normalized. They all are put in lower case and diacritical marks are eliminated[1]. Also, common words pass through a process of stemming, performed with a stemmer for the Spanish language based on that of Porter [10].

From the lexica, we eliminate all the stop-words. We consider two different lists of stop-words, one for proper nouns and another one for common words. The one for proper nouns is much shorter than the other, since there exist words that have empty meaning when used as common words but not when used as proper nouns. For instance, "más", is the Spanish for "more", and is a stop-word when used as common word, but it is also a surname, and thus should not be eliminated when used as proper noun.

The whole process is summarized in Figure 2.

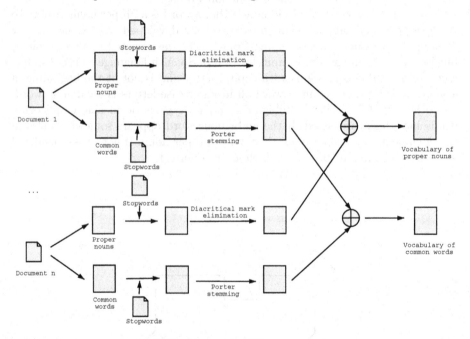

Fig. 2. Extraction of the lexica

3.2   Selection of the Features Representing the Documents

The number of words in the lexica tends to be very big. This makes it almost impossible to use certain algorithms because the dimension of the vectors that represent the documents is too high. Also, most of the words are really non-informative.

For these reasons, we select only a small number of the words in the lexica to actually represent the documents in which they appear. To choose the relevant

---

[1] As they are used by the stemmer, diacritical mark elimination for common words is delayed until the stemming phase has been finished.

words, we use two well-known filtering measures: *tfidf* (see [9]) for the lexicon of common words and *df* (the number of documents in which the word appears) for proper nouns.

We use two different measures for the lexica since their behavior is not the same. While a proper noun which appears in many documents is clearly important, frequent common words will likely be non-informative. That is why document frequency is considered important when selecting proper nouns but not for other words.

3.3   Clustering of the Documents

Since we have two different kinds of representations of the documents, we train two different networks, one with each representation (see Figure 3). For the training we do not use all the documents, but a number of them which contain sufficient occurrences of the words in the corresponding lexicon. If the word of the lexicon which appears in fewer documents has $df = x$ then we impose that the number of documents selected for the training must be big enough for all the words of the lexicon to appear in at least $\frac{1}{4}x$ training documents.

The size of the SOM can be varied in order to obtain bigger or smaller clusters.

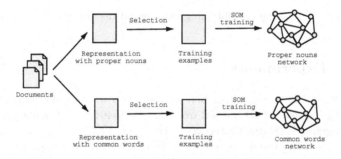

Fig. 3. Clustering the documents

3.4   Comparison of the Query with the Clusters

Given a query we represent it in the same way as we represent the documents. Thus, we will have two different vectors for each query. Each of them is compared to the corresponding network, finding the neuron which is closest to the vector according to the cosine distance defined by

$$d(q, v) = \frac{\sum_{i=1}^{n} q_i v_i}{\sqrt{\sum_{i=1}^{n} q_i^2} \sqrt{\sum_{i=1}^{n} v_i^2}}$$

where q_i are the components of the vector representation of the query, v_i are the components of the vector associated with the neuron and n is the size of the vectors.

All the documents mapped to the neuron are regarded as relevant to the query. If more documents are needed, the process is repeated with the next closest neuron.

3.5   Combination of the Results

We will then have a number of documents which have been found relevant to the query with the network of proper nouns and another set of documents which come from the network of common words. To combine the results obtained, we average the distances of the two representations of the documents to the corresponding vectors representing the query and retain those documents with lower values. This process is shown in Figure 4.

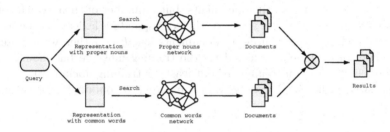

Fig. 4. Obtaining the relevant documents

4   The Experiments

We have used the system described in Section 3 for the monolingual Spanish task, which consists of 60 queries over all the 454042 documents published by the news agency EFE during the years 1994 and 1995.

After processing the documents, we have obtained 277196 proper nouns and 144652 common words. Of these, we have retained all the proper nouns that appear in at least 100 different documents and the 5% of common words with the highest $tfidf$. This makes a total of 9924 proper nouns and 7233 common words.

We have trained SOMs of three different sizes: 25x25, 50x50 and 75x75 neurons. Thus, we can test the influence of the number of documents in the clusters. This number was on average 726.467 for the 25x25 networks, 181.617 for 50x50 and 80.718 for 75x75.

5   The Results

5.1   Official Runs

After submitting the results of the official experiments, we detected a serious bug in the implementation of the algorithm that meant that the output of the system was completely wrong. In fact, the experiments carried out, with the networks of sizes 25x25 and 50x50, returned 60000 documents each, of which only four were relevant for any query.

5.2   Unofficial Runs

Once the bug was detected and corrected, we repeated the official experiments and also conducted some others to perform a more thorough test of the system.

Since it seems that the number of documents taken from each network is a very important parameter (see [5]), we have tested its influence in the first place. For that reason, we have fixed the set of the networks to 50x50 (neither too small, not too big) and performed experiments retrieving a number of documents from each network ranging from 2000 up to 30000. Then, the distances of all these documents to query are computed and only the 1000 closest ones are retained. In Table 1 we summarize the results of these runs.

Table 1. Influence of the number of documents

Documents per network	R-precision
2000	0.0454
3000	0.0459
4000	0.0461
5000	0.0498
6000	0.0509
7000	0.0530
8000	0.0507
9000	0.0498
10000	0.0496
15000	0.0629
20000	0.0621
25000	0.0618
30000	0.0619
All	0.0365

We can see that there is an improvement if we take more documents from the networks (though from 7000 to 10000 there is a small decrease), up to 15000 documents. Also, from 20000 documents the overall performance decreases again. Thus, we have decided to use 15000 documents from each of the networks in the rest of the experiments.

With this number of documents, we have perfomed experiments with the different sizes of networks. Results can be seen in Table 2.

In view of the results, one can argue that the performance could increase if the size of the network is set to 100x100 or even bigger (up to some point). Unfortunately, nowadays we lack the computer power needed to test the method with those settings. The amount of memory needed to load all the training documents and to store the neurons of the network is too big. A possible solution

Table 2. Influence of the size of the networks

Size of network	R-precision
25x25	0.0460
50x50	0.0629
75x75	0.0665

is to split the training documents into smaller subsets and train the neurons in a sort of batch process, where the output network of a training is the input of the next one. However, we have decided not to do this because it is not clear that the results obtained are really comparable.

Also notice that, in every case, the use of the SOMs to preselect a number of documents gets better results than the use of the traditional model in which simply the documents closest to the query are selected (see last row of Table 1). This confirms the results obtained in [5] for a much smaller collection.

However, it is clear that these results are still very poor and that the method needs considerable improvement in order to get satisfactory results.

6 Conclusions and Future Work

The experiments shown here suggest that the use of SOMs in IR can be of help (cf. [5]), even in situations when the amount of information is very big and the number of relevant documents is small.

To improve the results, we will study modifications of the method. It seems that the size of the networks used and the number of features selected for the representation of the documents have a crucial influence. For this reason, we plan to perform experiments with different values of this parameters (using batch mode for the biggest ones).

The way that the results of the two networks are combined is also important, thus we consider interesting to investigate other methods, including weighted averages and earlier combinations of the lexica and of the networks.

References

1. Kohonen, T.: Self-Organizing Maps. Volume 30 of Springer Series in Information Science. Springer Verlag (2001)
2. Lagus, K., Honkela, T., Kaski, S., Kohonen, T.: Self-organizing maps of document collections: A new approach to interactive exploration. In Simoudis, E., Han, J., Fayyad, U., eds.: Proceedings of the Second International Conference on Knowledge Discovery and Data Mining. AAAI Press, Menlo Park, California (1996) 238–243
3. Kohonen, T., Kaski, S., Lagus, K., Honkela, T.: Very large two-level SOM for the browsing of newsgroups. In von der Malsburg, C., von Seelen, W., Vorbrüggen, J.C., Sendhoff, B., eds.: Proceedings of ICANN96, International Conference on Artificial Neural Networks, Bochum, Germany, July 16-19, 1996. Lecture Notes in Computer Science, vol. 1112. Springer, Berlin (1996) 269–274

4. Kohonen, T., Kaski, S., Lagus, K., Salojärvi, J., Honkela, J., Paatero, V., Saarela, A.: Self organization of a massive text document collection. In Oja, E., Kaski, S., eds.: Kohonen Maps. Elsevier, Amsterdam (1999) 171–182
5. Lagus, K.: Text retrieval using self-organized document maps. Neural Processing Letters **15** (2002) 21–29
6. Kaski, S., Kangas, J., Kohonen, T.: Bibliography of self-organizing map (SOM) papers: 1981-1997. Neural Computing Surveys **1** (1998) 1–176
7. Salton, G., Wong, A., Yang, C.: A vector space model for automatic indexing. Communications of the ACM **18** (1975) 613–620
8. Deerwester, S., Dumais, S.T., Furnas, G.W., Landauer, T.K., Harshman, R.: Indexing by latent semantic indexing. Journal of the American Society for Information Science **41** (1990) 391–407
9. Salton, G., McGill, M.J.: An introduction to modern information retrieval. McGraw-Hill (1983)
10. Porter, M.F.: An algorithm for suffix stripping. Program (Automated Library and Information Systems) **14** (1980) 130–137

Ricoh at CLEF 2003

Yuichi Kojima, Hideo Itoh, Hiroko Mano, and Yasushi Ogawa

Software R&D Group, RICOH CO., Ltd.,
1-1-17 Koishikawa, Bunkyo-ku, Tokyo 112-0002, JAPAN
{ykoji,mano,hideo,yogawa}@src.ricoh.co.jp

Abstract. This paper describes RICOH's participation in the Monolingual Information Retrieval tasks of the Cross-Language Evaluation Forum (CLEF) 2003. We applied our system using the same kind of stemmer, the same options and different parameters to five European languages and compared the results for each langauge. Although the overall performance of the system was reasonable, there were two problems. The first was the lack of a compound splitter for German and the second was the failure of query expansion when there were few relevant documents.

1 Introduction

For the CLEF 2003 monolingual information retrieval task, RICOH submitted runs for French, German, Italian, Spanish and Dutch. We have worked on English and Japanese text retrieval in the past few years [2, 3, 4, 5]. The CLEF 2003 experiments were our first trials in European languages. Our focus in the experiments was:

1. to test our approach based on a probabilistic model for European languages
2. to find language-specific problems

Section 2 of this paper outlines our system, Section 3 describes the modifications made for the experiments, Section 4 gives the results, and Section 5 contains some conclusions.

2 Description of the System

Before describing our approach to European languages, we give an outline of the system as background information. The basic features of the system are:

- effective document ranking based on a probabilistic model [8] with query expansion using pseudo-relevance feedback [2]
- scalable and efficient indexing and searching based on an inverted file module [4]

This system has also been used for TREC and NTCIR experiments and has been shown to be effective.

In the following sections, we explain the processing flow of the system [5].

C. Peters et al. (Eds.): CLEF 2003, LNCS 3237, pp. 367–372, 2004.

2.1 Query Term Extraction

We used the "title" and "description" fields for each topic. An input topic string is transformed into a sequence of stemmed tokens using a tokenizer and stemmer. Stop words are eliminated using a stopword dictionary. Two kinds of terms are extracted from stemmed tokens for initial retrieval: a "single term" is each stemmed token and a "phrasal term" consists of two adjacent tokens in a stemmed query string.

2.2 Initial Retrieval

Each query term is assigned a weight w_t, and documents are ranked according to the score $s_{q,d}$ as follows:

$$w_t = \log\left(k_4' \bullet \frac{N}{n_t} + 1\right) \tag{1}$$

$$s_{q,d} = \sum_{t \in q} \frac{f_{t,d}}{K + f_{t,d}} \bullet \frac{w_t}{k_4' \bullet N + 1} \tag{2}$$

$$K = k_1\left((1-b) + b\frac{l_d}{l_{ave}}\right) \tag{3}$$

where N is the number of documents in the collection, n_t is the document frequency of the term t, $f_{t,d}$ is the in-document frequency of the term, l_d is the document length, l_{ave} is the average document length, and k_4', k_1 and b are parameters.

Weights for phrasal terms are set lower than those for single terms.

2.3 Query Expansion

As a result of the initial retrieval, the top 10 documents are assumed to be relevant (pseudo-relevance) to the query and selected as a "seed" for query expansion. Candidates for expansion terms are extracted from the seed documents in the same way as for the query term extraction mentioned above. Phrasal terms are not used for query expansion. The candidates are ranked on the Robertson's Selection Value [6], or RSV_t and the top-ranked terms are selected as expansion terms. The weight is re-calculated as $w2_t$ using the Robertson/Sparck-Jones formula [7]

$$RSV_t = w2_t \bullet \left(\frac{r_t}{R} - \frac{n_t}{N}\right) \tag{4}$$

$$w2_t = \alpha \bullet w_t + (1-\alpha) \bullet \log\frac{\frac{r_t + 0.5}{R - r_t + 0.5}}{\frac{n_t - r_t + 0.5}{N - n_t - R + r_t + 0.5}} \tag{5}$$

where R is the number of relevant documents, r_t is the number of relevant documents containing the term t, and α is a parameter.

The weight of the initial query term is re-calculated using the same formula as above, but with a different α value and an additional adjustment to make the weight higher than the expansion terms.

2.4 Final Retrieval

Using the initial query and expansion terms, the ranking module performs a second retrieval to produce the final result.

3 Experiments

Four items in the system must be adjusted depending on the language: (1) the tokenizer, (2) the stemmer, (3) the stopword dictionary, and (4) the training data. We used the same tokenizer originally developed for English for all the target languages. The others are as follows.

3.1 Stemming

We used Snowball stemmers [1] for all target languages because (1) we did not have stemmers for any European languages except English, (2) we are not familiar enough with these languages to develop specific stemmers, and (3) unlike the earlier result [9], Snowball stemmers were reasonably efficient in the preparatory experiments. Table 1 shows the results of using CLEF 2002 data with and without stemming.

Table 1. Average precision with and without stemming using title and description queries

	French	German	Italian	Spanish	Dutch
With stemming	0.4334	0.3701	0.4000	0.4936	0.4187
Without stemming	0.3841	0.3392	0.3899	0.4468	0.4023

3.2 Stopword Dictionary

We did not use stopword dictionaries because we did not have any.

3.3 Training

We trained the system by selecting the best parameter-set from 500 candidate parameter-sets for each language to get the highest average precision score.

However, there was a bug in our training scripts. The system was trained using CLEF 2002 queries and CLEF *2003* data collections, instead of CLEF *2002* data collections. This mismatch resulted in extra noise documents in the retrieved documents and adversely affected the tuning performance.

Table 2 shows the results with and without training.

Table 2. Average precision with and without training using title and description queries

	French	German	Italian	Spanish	Dutch
Without training	0.4334	0.3701	0.4000	0.4936	0.4187
With training using 2002 data	0.4493	0.3746	0.4088	0.5004	0.4371
With training using 2003 data	0.4493	0.3746	0.4018	0.4985	0.4371

4 Results

Table 3 gives a summary of our official results for CLEF 2003 and Table 4 gives a summary of our additional results using parameters trained with CLEF 2002 (correct) data collections. The additional result for Dutch is the same as the official one because the data collection was the same. The additional results for French and German are also the same as the official ones because the new parameters selected by the correct training scripts were unchanged from the official runs. Our query expansion is not effective for French and Italian with correctly tuned parameters in comparison to the average precision with and without query expansion. Query expansion is less effective for French and Italian runs. A common feature of these two runs is the small number of relevant documents.

Table 5 summarizes the comparison to the median by topic using our official runs. Each number in the table is the frequency of topics that caused differences in the average precision compared to the median for that topic from A to B. The result for Spanish with query expansion is the best of all the results and the French results are worst. The German result without query expansion is worst and the German result with query expansion is also unsatisfactory because it contains two badly failed queries and no successful query.

Table 3. Official runs for CLEF 2003

Language	Run	Relevant	Rel. ret.	Average Prec.	R-precision	Query Expansion
French	rfrtdp03	946	927	0.4916	0.4697	NO
	rfrtde03	946	928	0.4901	0.4634	YES
German	rdetdp03	1825	1583	0.4425	0.4230	NO
	rdetde03	1825	1693	0.4736	0.4385	YES
Italian	rittdp03	809	761	0.5200	0.4954	NO
	rittde03	809	782	0.5296	0.4868	YES
Spanish	restdp03	2368	2206	0.4727	0.4605	NO
	restde03	2368	2248	0.5174	0.4806	YES
Dutch	rnltdp03	1577	1415	0.4439	0.4206	NO
	rnltde03	1577	1421	0.4719	0.4498	YES

We checked the queries that resulted in differences from −1.0 to −0.5 to find the problems. We did not use the results for Italian and Spanish in this analysis because the results were modified from the official runs to the additional ones. The bracketed numbers in Table 5 are the topic numbers of the queries. Topic 174 of the German queries contains a compound word "Kruzifixstreit". We added the words "kruzifix" and "streit", decompounded from the compound word, to topic 174 by hand and got an improved result. The average precision changed to 0.8451 from 0.1893. Topic 175 of the French queries and topics 158 and 194 of the German queries had few relevant documents. Topic 175 had one relevant document, topic 158 had three, and topic 194 had two.

Table 4. Additional runs for CLEF 2003

Language	Run	Relevant	Rel. ret.	Average Prec.	R-precision	Query Expansion
French	rfrtdp03	946	927	0.4916	0.4697	NO
	rfrtde03	946	928	0.4901	0.4634	YES
German	rdetdp03	1825	1583	0.4425	0.4230	NO
	rdetde03	1825	1693	0.4736	0.4385	YES
Italian		809	767	0.5140	0.4874	NO
		809	779	0.5166	0.4829	YES
Spanish		2368	2207	0.4864	0.4719	NO
		2368	2285	0.5293	0.4906	YES
Dutch	rnltdp03	1577	1415	0.4439	0.4206	NO
	rnltde03	1577	1421	0.4719	0.4498	YES

Table 5. Number of topics in comparison to median for average precision using official runs

Language	From -1.0 to -0.5 (bad)	From −0.5 to 0.0	0.0	From 0.0 to 0.5	From 0.5 to 1.0 (good)	Query Expansion
French	0	19	24	17	0	NO
	1 [175]	15	31	13	0	YES
German	1 [174]	31	12	15	1	NO
	2 [158, 194]	20	8	30	0	YES
Italian	0	18	21	20	1	NO
	1	15	17	26	1	YES
Spanish	0	29	13	17	1	NO
	0	14	9	37	0	YES
Dutch	0	20	14	26	0	NO
	0	20	9	31	0	YES

5 Conclusions

Our approach was tested with reasonable results. According to "comparison to median by topic", the Spanish result was good, but the German and French results were less so. We compared the results for each language under the same conditions. This comparison raised questions for each language, e.g.:

- Why is query expansion not effective for French and Italian?
- Why did the retrieval of some queries fail badly in French and German?

It is likely that our query expansion does not work well when there are few relevant documents. There is a strong correlation between the effectiveness of our expansion and the number of relevant documents for each language and this correlation should be checked with each query.

We also consider that the failure of queries in French and German relates to different problems. For the German result, one of the main causes is probably that we have no German compound splitter. For the French and German results with query expansion, the main cause of failure of query expansion was probably the small number of relevant documents.

References

1. Snowball web site. At http://snowball.tartarus.org/ visited 7th November 2002.
2. Ogawa, Y., Mano, H., Narita, M., Honma, S.: Structuring and expanding queries in the probabilistic model. In The Eighth Text Retrieval Conference (TREC-8), pages 541-548, 2000.
3. Toyoda, M., Kitsuregawa, M., Mano, H., Itoh, H., Ogawa, Y.: University of Tokyo/RICOH at NTCIR-3 Web Retrieval Task. At http://research.nii.ac.jp/ntcir/workshop/OnlineProceedings3/NTCIR3-WEB-ToyodaM.pdf.
4. Ogawa, Y., Mano, H.: RICOH at NTCIR-2. In Proceedings of the Second NTCIR Workshop Meeting, pages 121-123, 2001.
5. Itoh, H., Mano, H., Ogawa, Y.: RICOH at TREC-10. In The Tenth Text Retrieval Conference (TREC-2001), pages 457-464, 2001.
6. Robertson, S.E.: On term selection for query expansion. Journal of Documentation, 46(4):359-364, 1990.
7. Robertson, S.E., Spark-Jones, K.: Relevance weighting of search terms. Journal of ASIS, 27:129-146, 1976.
8. Robertson, S.E., Walker, S.: On relevance weights with little relevance information. In Proceedings of the 20th Annual International ACM SIGIR Conference (SIGIR '97), pages 16-24, 1997.
9. MacFarlane, A.: Pliers and snowball at CLEF 2002. In Working Notes for the CLEF 2002 Workshop, Rome, Italy, September 2002.

MediaLab at CLEF-2003: Using Keyword Disambiguation

Peter van der Weerd

MediaLab BV, Schellinkhout, The Netherlands
pweerd@medialab.nl
http://www.medialab.nl

Abstract. This report describes the participation of MediaLab BV in the CLEF-2003 evaluations. This year we participated in the monolingual Dutch task, experimenting with a keyword disambiguation tool. MediaLab developed this tool to exploit human assigned keywords in the search engine in a better way than just blind searching with the keywords themselves. Although this tool was not planned to be used for CLEF-like applications it was fun to check if it could help boosting the search quality.

1 Disambiguation

In traditional search applications people are used to assign keywords to searchable items, and then let the user search via these assigned keywords. The main problem with this approach is that the searching user has to follow the same thoughts as the assigning people to let the correct keywords cross his/her mind. However, people invested lots of time in assigning keywords, so it is a pity not using this effort.

MediaLab developed a tool for ranking a list of keyword (or other items) given a full text query. This list is generated in 2 phases.

- During indexing we build a co-occurrence network of the used words in the item at one site and the assigned keywords at the other side.
- At retrieval time we split the query into words and for each query word its connected keywords from the co-occurrence network are collected.

Note that the tool uses the human assigned keywords, so it is fully dependant of the quality of the assigned keywords.

For example, using this tool in the library of Eindhoven querying for "jaguar" let to a top3 keyword list of:

- jaguar (auto); geschiedenis [jaguar (car); history]
- katachtigen [cat-likes]
- zuid-amerikaanse mythen [South American myths]

With the same library data we experimented feeding the tool normalised author names instead of keywords. Results were surprisingly good. For instance querying for "pesten" (nagging) the top3 authors all wrote children's books about nagging.

C. Peters et al. (Eds.): CLEF 2003, LNCS 3237, pp. 373–375, 2004.

MediaLab plans to use the tool in search applications. Except presenting the standard result list we present also a list of best keywords, authors, etc which can be used by the user to re-order the results. In this way the user has the ability to view several cross-sections of the result list.

2 Approach

The CLEF data-collection contains some extra fields with keyword information (HTR) and with geographical information (GEO). We used both extra fields to feed the disambiguation tool. The searching process is done in the following way:

- doing a "normal" search giving result R1
- determine the top5 of disambiguation items and search all these items giving result R2
- then recompute the weights in R1 by adding a fraction of the weights in R2
- the modified R1 is used as the submission

We submitted a base run, and for each field (HTR and GEO) we submitted 5 runs with different relative weights of the second result.

HTR-5 means: normal result combined with a 50% weight of the HTR-result.
HTR-2 means: normal result combined with a 20% weight of the HTR-result.

3 Results

The following table summarizes some measures of the runs.

Table 1. Results per run

Run	Rel_ret	Precision at 10 docs	Average prec. (non-interp.)	R-precision
Base	1248	0.4071	0.3959	0.3695
HTR1 (10%boost)	1265	0.4018	0.4044	0.3809
HTR2 (20%boost)	1282	0.4000	0.4095	0.3903
HTR3 (30%boost)	1292	0.3946	0.3939	0.3749
HTR4 (40%boost)	1285	0.3893	0.3737	0.3507
HTR5 (50%boost)	1257	0.3804	0.3520	0.3396
GEO1 (10% boost)	1258	0.4036	0.3983	0.3739
GEO2 (20% boost)	1282	0.3929	0.3916	0.3661
GEO3 (30% boost)	1271	0.3750	0.3783	0.3479
GEO4 (40% boost)	1264	0.3536	0.3577	0.3309
GEO5 (50% boost)	1222	0.3268	0.3383	0.3185

It is clear that blind boosting the results with HTR or GEO data helps a little bit to retrieve more relevant documents. In case of boosting the results by the HTR data the optimum is about 10% to 20%, increasing the average precision with 3%. However, the effect is rather small.

The profit of boosting by the GEO data is less convincing, probably caused by the quality of the GEO-data. Looking at the data made us already hesitate about using it.

4 Conclusion

Although MediaLab's disambiguation tool was not intended for blind boosting search results, it might be used for it. Probably better results are achieved by using these fields in a normal blind relevance feedback procedure as used McNamee and Mayfield and others [1].

Reference

1. McNamee, P. and Mayfield, J.: JHU/APL Experiments at CLEF: Translation Resources and Score Normalization. Evaluation of Cross-Language Information retrieval Systems. Lecture Notes in Computer Science, Vol.2406. Springer-Verlag, Germany (2002) 193-208.

The GIRT Data in the Evaluation of CLIR Systems – from 1997 Until 2003

Michael Kluck

Informationszentrum Sozialwissenschaften (IZ), Lennéstr. 30, 53113 Bonn, Germany
kluck@bonn.iz-soz.de

Abstract. The motivations behind the creation of the German Indexing and Retrieval Test database (GIRT) are described and an overview of the structure of
the different versions of GIRT is given. The way in which GIRT has been employed in various TREC and CLEF campaigns is then illustrated with a short
description of methods and procedures used. The paper concludes with a summary of the trends in the GIRT tracks of these evaluation campaigns.

1   GIRT in the Context of Cross-Language Information Retrieval (CLIR)

One of the main reasons for the creation of the GIRT test corpus (GIRT = German
Indexing and Retrieval Test database) was that GIRT should provide a framework for
a meaningful comparison of modern retrieval systems, enabling the capabilities of
these systems to be assessed and compared with those of conventional systems, as
used by the Social Science Information Centre in Bonn (IZ) or by the commercial
vendors of the IZ databases.

   Although the most comprehensive series of information retrieval system evaluations is carried out by the TREC initiative (TREC = Text REtrieval Conference)[1] and
has been repeated every year since 1992, up until 1998 it was not possible to directly
exploit the TREC results in the German scientific information domain. One reason for
this was that the main ad hoc retrieval tracks in TREC used English news collections
for IR system testing. General-purpose news documents require very different search
criteria than those used for reference retrieval in databases of scientific literature
items, and also offer no possibility for comparable test runs with domain-specific
terminology. There was thus a strong demand for resources that would allow research
into retrieval on German texts; groups wanted to test the insights accruing from the
TREC experience and the capability of morphological components derived from
English texts on German language material. At that time, most experiments in information retrieval had been on monolingual (mainly English) collections; and there had
been few experiments in multilingual information retrieval systems[2].

---

[1] The Text REtrieval Conference (TREC) is an initiative of the National Institute for Standards
   and Technology (NIST) in Gaithersburg (MD, USA). See http://trec.nist.gov/

[2] cf. the overview of Womser-Hacker [1], p. 19.

C. Peters et al. (Eds.): CLEF 2003, LNCS 3237, pp. 376–390, 2004.
© Springer-Verlag Berlin Heidelberg 2004

The development of the GIRT test database was intended to contribute to remedying these deficits and to provide a valid basis for a comparison of different domain-specific retrieval systems and techniques. We felt that it was necessary to acquire knowledge on the pros and cons of different retrieval systems through practical testing in order to be able to develop decision factors for the choice and combination of different approaches or modules in our own professional environment as information providers[3].

For this reason, IZ decided to make the GIRT collection available to system developers and the IR research community, first in the context of the CLIR track in TREC and later on in the context of the Cross-Language Evaluation Forum (CLEF). The retrieval systems to be tested were supplied with a collection of structured social science documents consisting of content-bearing information fields. The aim was to investigate the effect of the inclusion of indexing terms on retrieval efficiency[4].

It should be noted that the special meaning of domain-specific scientific language makes particular demands on indexing and retrieval systems. In particular, in-depth research shows the difficulty of clearly differentiating technical terms used in sociology from standard language concepts: "its [sociology] words are common words that are in general use such as community and immigrant"[5]. In the social sciences, there is a large overlap between domain-specific terminology and words from everyday language, and in many cases there is a clear deviation in the meaning of scientific terms from those in common use. There is also considerable differentiation of meanings because of different content-related connotations such as "schools", theories, political implications, ethical grounding etc, which makes the automatic extraction of keywords for indexing and searching quite difficult in this scientific area.

2 GIRT Versions: Structure and Contents

The GIRT collection consists of scientific documents, which have been taken from the databases of the IZ; this means that they have been gathered for domain-specific, scientific purposes, are then processed and made publicly available for a fee. The GIRT data is originally German; but the titles, abstracts or content descriptions and the descriptors of most of the recent documents have been translated into English, making international access easier. The GIRT corpus is formed by an integrated data-

---

[3] cf. also Womser-Hacker [1], especially p. 319 ff.

[4] Already in TREC4 (1995) there were a number of requests to be able to test systems on indexed collections: "... manually indexed fields were included in the test documents, though not in the learning documents. As can be seen, there is a 5% to 6% improvement ..., which is reasonably substantial." (Buckley et al. [2], 34).

[5] Haas [3] p. 74: "T tests between discipline pairs showed that physics, electrical engineering, and biology had significantly more domain terms in sequences than history, psychology, and sociology (...) the domains with more term sequences are those which may be considered the hard sciences, while those with more isolated domain terms tend to be the social sciences and humanities."

base consisting of extracts of whole documents (which have some more information elements) derived from the SOLIS[6] (social science literature) and FORIS[7] (current research in the field of social sciences) databases that are built by IZ. All versions of GIRT contain the following attributes extracted from the original documents: author, German title, document language, publication year. Additionally, for all documents, intellectually assigned descriptors (indexing terms) and classifiers (classifying text) are provided. Detailed information on the specific variants of the GIRT corpus is given in a technical report of IZ [4].

2.1 GIRT-1

The first version of GIRT contained about 13,000 documents published between1990 and 1996. These documents originated from the printed alerting service "soFid"[8] for the topics "sociology of work", "women's research" and "migration and ethnical minorities" and from the articles of two important German social science journals (Kölner Zeitschrift fü Soziologie und Sozialpsychologie, Soziale Welt). Full texts (not included in the test database but made available separately) have also been provided for a small subset of documents.

The GIRT-1 corpus has been used for internal testing of retrieval systems (Messenger, freeWAISsf, Fulcrum) by IZ [5, 6, 7, 8], and for several system evaluations and testing at German universities (Regensburg, Konstanz, Hildesheim, Düseldorf) [9, 10, 11, 12], where the data or the topics or the existing relevance judgments have been used. The GIRT-1 corpus was also used for further research at IZ on the visualisation of information retrieval result sets [13] and on the use of neural networks [14]; these results have been published as doctoral theses.

2.2 GIRT-2

GIRT-2 contained the documents of GIRT-1 plus an additional set of documents for the same topics published for 1978-1989. GIRT-2 thus consisted of about 38,000 publications for 1978 to 1996. GIRT-2 was made available for TREC-7 and TREC-8.

---

[6] SOLIS contains descriptions of social science literature from German speaking countries (Germany, Austria, Switzerland, Liechtenstein) or German speaking social scientists: books and compilations, journal articles and reader articles, technical and scientific reports, "grey literature", doctoral theses and dissertations, documents from the Internet. The total number of documents was approximately 285,000 at the end of 2003, with a yearly increase of about 12,000 documents. See http://www.gesis.org/Information/SOLIS/index.htm.

[7] FOLIS contains descriptions of current research projects in the social science field in German speaking countries (Germany, Austria, Switzerland, Liechtenstein). The total number of documents was approximately 40,000 at the end of 2003, with a yearly increase of about 6,000 documents. See http://www.gesis.org/Information/FORIS/Recherche/index.htm.

[8] soFid = sozialwissenschaftlicher Fachinformationsdienst is a printed alerting service for about 28 topical areas in the social sciences which are printed separately per topic twice a year.

2.3 GIRT-3

For GIRT-3 we added English translations of titles (only for SOLIS) and English indexing terms plus, for some of the documents, English abstracts and German free keywords (terms not from the thesaurus). We also increased the corpus again by adding documents from all other topic areas. Thus, GIRT-3 contained documents for the time span 1976 to 1996, from all areas of social sciences. This meant that we provided a representative cross-section of German social science literature and research for that period. The total number of documents in GIRT-3 was more than 76,000.

Table 1. Fields included in GIRT-3[9]

FIELD NAME	Number of occurrences of this field	In % of the GIRT-3 documents	Average number of entries in this field per document
DOC	76,128	100	1
DOCNO	76,128	100	1
LANGUAGE	76,128	100	1
PUBLICATION YEAR	76,128	100	1
TITLE	76,128	100	1
TITLE-ENG	54,275	71.29	-
TEXT	73,291	96.27	-
TEXT-ENG	6,063	7.96	-
CONTROLLED TERM	755,333	-	9.92
FREE TERM	6,588	-	0.09
CLASSIFICATION	169,064	-	2.22
AUTHOR	126,322	-	1.66

GIRT-3 was offered in CLEF 2000, 2001, and 2002.

2.4 GIRT-4

For GIRT-4 the data structure, the selection and number of documents have been revised totally. GIRT-4 has been divided into two language-distinct corpora: German (GIRT4-DE) and English (GIRT4-EN). The total number of documents in each collection is now 151,319, identical for content. The selection criterion was that for each document there had to be a corresponding German and English title. The time span has been changed to 1990 – 2000. Thus, there is only a partial overlap with GIRT-3 data, namely with respect to the publication years 1990-1996.

---

[9] From Kluck and Gey [15].

GIRT-4 was used in CLEF 2003 and is offered in CLEF 2004. With this pseudo-parallel collection[10] we take into account the multilingual nature of CLEF. In the following tables we give details of the contents of GIRT-4 (Table 2) and the use of the information fields in the documents of GIRT4-DE and GIRT4-EN (Tables 3 and 4).

Table 2. Contents of GIRT-4[11]

FIELD NAME	Number of entries per corpus: DE and/or EN	Number of entries in this field per document: GIRT4-DE	Number of entries in this field per document: GIRT4-EN
DOCS DE + EN	302,638		
DOC NUMBER DE = EN	151,319	1	1
AUTHOR DE = EN	237,301	1.75	1.75
TITLE DE = EN	151,319	1	1
DESCRIPTORS DE = EN	1,535,709	10.15	10.15
CLASSIFYING TEXTS DE = EN	305,504	2.02	2.02
METHODOLOGICAL DESCRIPTORS DE	354,968	2.35	-
METHODOLOGICAL DESCRIPTORS EN	292,387	-	1.93
ABSTRACT DE	145,941	0.96	-
ABSTRACT EN (HT + MT)	22,058	-	0.15
FREE KEY WORDS DE	38,505	0.25	-
METHODOLOGICAL TEXT DE	10,258	0.07	-

HT = human translation; MT = machine translation

2.4.1 GIRT4-DE
The following tagged data fields occur in the German GIRT4 data.

2.4.2 GIRT4-EN
In the table on the following page, we comment the tagged data fields occurring in the English GIRT-4 database.

---

[10] The collections are denoted pseudo-parallel, because the English variant is mainly the result of translations – mainly by professional translators who are native English speakers, is not a source English document and the English part comprises essentially of less text, as not all documents have a translation of German language abstracts. Occasionally, the English text is longer than the German one.

[11] Revised from: Kluck, M.: Introduction to the Monolingual and Domain-Specific Tasks of the Cross-language Evaluation Forum 2003. Talk at the CLEF 2003 Workshop, Trondheim 21-22 Aug 2003, see http://clef.iei.pi.cnr.it:2002/workshop2003/ presentations/kluck.ppt

Table 3. Information fields with their tags in GIRT4-DE

DOCNO	Original document number in the underlying data bases: SOLIS and FORIS
DOCID	unique identification number, equals DOCNO
AUTHOR	author(s) of the document
TITLE-DE	German title, in general the original title, if the document title exists in German language; otherwise the title has been translated by a human translator into German; applies to all documents
PUBLICATION-YEAR	publication year
LANGUAGE-CODE	language code, in this case DE
COUNTRY CODE	country of publication
CONTROLLED-TERM-DE	controlled German descriptor from the Thesaurus for the Social Sciences; each document has at least one controlled term, on average there are ten descriptors assigned per document
METHOD-TERM-DE	controlled German descriptor on the methodology used, when applicable
METHOD-TEXT-DE	German text on the methodology used and on the research design, when applicable (only for FORIS)
CLASSIFICATION-TEXT-DE	German text of the classification assigned to the document, one entry is mandatory, but there can be more
FREE-TERM-DE	additional free terms or keywords in German, not controlled thesaurus terms, available for less than 10 % of the documents[12]
TEXT-DE	description or abstract of the content of the document, available for 96.4 % of the documents

3 Description of the Thesauri Provided for GIRT

The machine-readable Thesaurus for the Social Sciences [16, 17] that was provided for GIRT in CLEF contains the following elements: the German descriptors with broader and narrower terms and related terms, the German non-descriptors and the respective English translations for all descriptors and most of the non-descriptors.

The machine-readable German-Russian term list that is taken from the respective German-English-Russian thesaurus [18] provides the Russian equivalents for German

---

[12] Those documents that were part of GIRT-1 or GIRT-2 contain the artificial descriptor GIRT or GIRT2 in this field.

descriptors, but no information on the thesaurus structure. To map the Cyrillic character set, this term list has been coded in UTF-8.

Table 4. Information fields with their tags in GIRT4-EN

DOCNO	Randomly generated document number, which does not equal the document number of the corresponding documents in GIRT4-DE [13]
DOCID	unique identification number, equals DOCNO
AUTHOR	author(s) of the document
TITLE-EN	translation of the title into English, if the original title was not available in English, or otherwise the original English title, applies to all documents
PUBLICATION-YEAR	publication year
LANGUAGE-CODE	language code, in this case EN
COUNTRY CODE	country of publication
CONTROLLED-TERM-EN	controlled English descriptor from the Thesaurus for the Social Sciences, each document has at least one controlled term, on average there are ten descriptors assigned per document
METHOD-TERM-EN	controlled English descriptor on the methodology used, when applicable
CLASSIFICATION-TEXT-EN	English text of the classification assigned to the document, one entry is mandatory, but there could be more
TEXT-EN-HT	human translation of the description or of the abstract of the content of the document into English, available for 9.1 % of the documents
TEXT-EN-MT	machine translation of the description or of the abstract of the content of the document into English, available for 5.5 % of the documents. This machine translation by SYSTRAN is sometimes inaccurate and may contain untranslated German terms or phrases, if the MT-system was not able to provide a satisfactory translation, but it is sufficient searching (only for FORIS)

4   The Evaluation Campaigns Using GIRT

GIRT data was first offered as a sub-task in the CLIR track in TREC. Later on, the
organisers of TREC focussed their CLIR work on non-European languages and the
evaluation of CLIR-systems with European languages was transferred to Europe and
established as CLEF. Nevertheless a strong coordination with TREC and the parallel
Japanese initiative NTCIR [19] has been maintained especially with respect to the
content and methodology of the evaluation. We also (partly) share collection data,
evaluation software, and topics.

---

[13] Thus a direct identification of the corresponding German and the English documents should
be impossible. A concordance list of the numbers of the identical documents is stored by IZ.

4.1 TREC-7 and 8

GIRT3-data was provided for the first time within the context of an international CLIR evaluation exercise at TREC-7 in 1998 [20]. The aim was to allow CLIR system testing in a specific domain with structured data. 28 domain-specific topics (statements of information needs) were developed and translated into 3 languages (German, English, French). The German-English Thesaurus for the Social Sciences was also provided in machine-readable form. Unfortunately, as the data was made available at a late stage in the campaign, no participating group took up this offer in that year. Therefore the same data and topics were offered for the CLIR track of TREC in 1999 [21]. That year two groups used this data for system evaluation: University of California, Berkeley (USA), and Eurospider (Switzerland).

The general retrieval model of the research group from Berkeley was based on a probabilistic method [22]. In the context of GIRT, Berkeley [23] made use of the bilingual German-English thesaurus to a large extent, using it for the translation of the English topics and for the expansion of the queries by their retrieval system. Comparing with results obtained using the Systran machine translation system (freely available as Babelfish on the Internet), Berkeley reported that a significant improvement in retrieval of relevant documents (more than double) could be achieved with the thesaurus terms. However, the additional expansion of the query with the narrower terms of the thesaurus also led to a decrease in precision of the results.

Eurospider [24] used their similarity thesaurus [25] for French-German and English-German retrieval; for French-German they also used Systran as an alternative. Furthermore they applied their own stemmer and a decompounding algorithm for German. They did not use the indexing terms from the Thesaurus for the Social Sciences explicitly as such, just as part of the document data.

4.2 CLEF 2000

In the CLEF 2000 campaign, GIRT-3 data was also offered for the evaluation of domain-specific CLIR-systems. 25 new topics were provided; they were created in German and then translated into English and Russian.

Three groups participated in the GIRT task in CLEF 2000: Xerox (France); University of California, Berkeley (USA); University of Dortmund (Germany).

The research group from Berkeley again used their probabilistic retrieval system and developed a German stemmer similar to the Porter stemmer; this already gave a considerable improvement in the results [26]. The topics were translated using several different methods or algorithms:

- thesaurus look-up: use of German-English thesaurus to create a dictionary.
- fuzzy matching with the thesaurus, to find terms in the thesaurus that have other spellings.
- entry vocabulary module: a method to map English terms in the English queries onto German thesaurus terms.
- machine translation (MT) using the Power Translator software package.

The combination of all these methods gave a significant improvement in the overall results, primarily because each single method discovered additional relevant hits for different topics.

The University of Dortmund [27] used the machine translation of Babelfish (= Systran) to translate the topics. It is interesting to note that their system achieved significantly worse results in the domain-specific area of GIRT than in the main task for news articles, where they achieved a performance in the multilingual part that was near to the monolingual results.

Xerox concentrated on monolingual search in German for GIRT, but they did not submit a report on their tests so no details are known.

4.3 CLEF 2001

GIRT-3 was offered again in the CLEF 2001 campaign. 25 topics were provided in German, English and Russian. This time only one group (University of California, Berkeley) used this data.

Berkeley [28] concentrated on bilingual search in Russian and used the Promt machine translation (MT) system and fuzzy matching for the Russian-German thesaurus [18] to catch variations and composites of Russian terms. As expected the Russian translation of the thesaurus and the transliteration [29] of the Cyrillic characters into Latin letters was shown to be useful. Berkeley also offered their transliteration of the Russian-German thesaurus to the CLEF community as an XML-file[14].

4.4 CLEF 2002

In 2002 GIRT was part of the CLEF track for "Mono- and Cross-Language Information Retrieval for Scientific Collections", which also contained the AMARYLLIS collection with 150.000 French bibliographic documents from all scientific disciplines.

The 25 GIRT topics for GIRT were offered in German, English and Russian. GIRT-3, the English-German thesaurus and the German-Russian term list were again been provided as test data.

Four groups participated in the GIRT task in this campaign: University of California, Berkeley (USA), University of Amsterdam (Netherlands), University of Hildesheim (Germany), Xerox (France).

The University of Amsterdam [30] used a CLIR system, called FlexIR, which was based on the standard vector space model. Vectors representing the occurrence of key words in the documents and in the topics were reduced to 10 dimensions and their similarity was calculated. The results were unsatisfactory and could only be improved by a combination with the base run without, however, reaching the scores for FlexIR in the general tasks of CLEF. For the English-German bilingual search, the Ding dictionary of TU Chemnitz was used to translate titles and abstracts of the documents.

The Berkeley group [31] participated with monolingual (German) and bilingual runs (English-German and Russian-German). For English-German they used a

---

[14] See http://otlet.sims.berkeley.edu/thesaurus/russian_thes_tr.xml

decompounding method, and a combination of Systran and Power Translator machine translation, integrated by the thesaurus. For German monolingual retrieval, significantly better results were obtained by using all fields of the document and the topics, but this was not true for bilingual Russian-German retrieval. For this task, they employed both Systran and Promt together with the thesaurus.

Xerox [32] extracted bilingual lexicons from parallel or comparable corpora and optimised the values of the constants in the formula for the calculation of the similarity of terms and documents. It was again shown that a combination of different methods leads to a further optimisation of results.

The University of Hildesheim [33] tested their adaptive concept system, MIMOR, with GIRT doing monolingual search in German. Their basic retrieval system was IRF[15], which was developed by NIST in the context of TREC and is available as open source. By defining different parameters, the use of two retrieval systems was simulated. With respect to the combination of results, experiments with different weightings were carried out, and this led to slight variations in the results.

4.5 CLEF 2003

In CLEF 2003, the "Mono- and Cross-Language Information Retrieval for Scientific Collections" track offered a new, enlarged GIRT collection . By offering GIRT-4 in two separate language versions, two parallel corpora could be provided: a German corpus (GIRT4-DE) and a pseudo-parallel English corpus (GIRT4-EN), which strictly speaking represents a translation of the German corpus into the English language and does not contain as much textual information as the original German corpus. Thus GIRT-4 consisted of two separate parallel corpora in different languages, whereas GIRT-3 had contained a mixture of information fields with German and English contents[16]. Again 25 topics were created in three languages (German, English, Russian) and the English-German thesaurus and the German-Russian term list were made available.

Four groups participated in the GIRT-task in 2003: University of California, Berkeley (USA), Distance University of Hagen (Germany), ENEA/University La Sapienza Rome[17] (Italy), University of Amsterdam (Netherlands).

The research group from the University of Amsterdam [34] continued their experiments of the preceding year using the FlexIR retrieval system and applied the vector space model but now with a 100-dimensional space. They also applied two methods: 1. a stemmer (but without decomposition) for re-ranking, 2. a 4-gram

---

[15] IRF (= Information Retrieval Framework) "is a freely available object-oriented framework for information retrieval (IR) applications. A framework is software which defines the architecture of a group of related applications and supplies many of the basic components out of which they can be built, allowing application developers to extend the basic components to meet their special needs." (http://www.itl.nist.gov/iaui/894.02/projects/irf/irf.html)

[16] Sometimes in GIRT-3 there was no clear distinction between German and English content within one information field (i.e. in the title).

[17] ENEA = Ente per le Nuove tecnologie, l'Energia e l'Ambiente, S. Maria di Galeria (Roma); Università degli Studi di Roma La Sapienza.

model. After translation of the topics into the respective language of the documents, the 4-gram method was used to identify equal character strings. Both methods significantly improved on the results of the preceding year, especially when used in combination. Thus, general multilingual CLIR methods were applied to domain-specific CLIR with the same success. However, we feel that additional improvements could have been achieved by using the intellectually assigned indexing terms contained in the documents.

The University of California Berkeley [35] carried out all tasks and sub-tasks of the GIRT track in CLEF 2003. Again they showed that including the thesauri implies a significant improvement in the results, although publicly available machine translation systems are also significantly better than in the past. The best results were achieved by a combination of two MT-systems plus the thesaurus. However, the abstracts were also of great importance for the results. The titles of the document are usually not significant enough to identify the content of the document correctly, and need at least the addition of thesaurus terms. Berkeley is intensively studying the effects of the use of thesaurus terms: "Documents that have controlled vocabulary terms added to the usual title and abstract information prove advantageous in retrieval because the thesaurus terms add valuable search terms to the index. An index containing titles, abstracts, and thesaurus terms will always outperform an index only containing title and abstract."[18]

ENEA and University of Rome La Sapienza [36] applied a totally different approach than is customary in CLIR. They used data compression, which makes it possible in their opinion to identify the syntactic and the semantic distance of character strings, without having or using any knowledge of the respective languages and their peculiarities. For the monolingual experiments in German and English the intellectually assigned descriptors (and in one case the abstract) were used to represent the content of the documents. The "Title" or the "Title" and "Description" fields were used to represent the topics. The results showed really good recall, but low precision. The research group attributed these unsatisfactory results to the shortness of the texts and the lack of term disambiguation. An expansion of the text basis for topics and documents could also be helpful.

The Distance University of Hagen [37] introduced another concept into CLIR system evaluation with GIRT, based on a natural language interface. To analyse the texts of the topics and the documents, this group used a lot of lexical and morphological information and resources, which supported in particular the disambiguation of meanings of single character strings and decompounding. In order to build a searchable database of the GIRT-4 data the software package Zebra was implemented; this offers a Z39.50-inteface, relevance operators and a ranking of results. The Thesaurus for the Social Sciences was also applied as a lexical resource in MultiNet-style. Only monolingual tests in German were made. The Distance University of Hagen expects to significantly improve the effectiveness of automatic retrieval by using further lexical information and background knowledge.

---

[18] Petras, Perelman and Gey [35] p. 243.

4.6 CLEF 2004 to 2007

The GIRT-4 pseudo-parallel corpus is also offered in the CLEF 2004 campaign, and 25 new topics and the German-English and German-Russian thesauri are provided. We intend to offer the GIRT-4 in CLEF campaigns until 2007.

5 Trends in the Development of Retrieval Components for Domain-Specific Document Collections

In the monolingual, bilingual and multilingual CLEF-tasks with more general data collections (newspapers, news agencies), robust stemming, the application of well-known and well-tested weighting schemes and the automatic expansion of queries (blind feedback) have been shown to be the most effective procedures. In addition a combination of translations based on different resources (machine-readable dictionaries or thesauri, corpus-based procedures, machine translation) is very often used with success by participating groups. The most commonly used machine translation system is Systran. Most research groups using any kind of translation procedure in the bilingual or multilingual tracks prefer to translate the topics rather than the documents [38].

For the GIRT tasks these methods have also been particularly successful. In addition the development of specific stemmers and of decompounding procedures for German have been applied, and have shown an improvement in results. Systems that made use of the indexing terms in the document or of the thesaurus for translation purposes have generally done well. Some other language independent methods, like the n-gram method or data compression have been applied, but with varying success. Finally a method for natural language processing that made use of several linguistic resources and procedures was experimented, but here the results are not yet convincing.

References

1. Womser-Hacker, C.: Das MIMOR-Modell. Mehrfachindexierung zur dynamischen Methoden-Objekt-Relationierung im Information Retrieval. Habilitationsschrift. Universität Regensburg (1996)
2. Buckley, C., Singhal, A., Mitra, M., Salton, G.: New Retrieval Approaches Using SMART. In: Harman, D. (ed.): The Fourth Text Retrieval Conference (TREC-4) [1995]. NIST, Gaithersburg (1996)
3. Haas, S.W.: Disciplinary Variation in Automatic Sublanguage Term Identification. In: Journal of the American Society for Information Science, 48 (1997) 1, 67-79
4. Kluck, M.: Die Evaluation von Cross-Language-Retrieval-Systemen mit Hilfe der GIRT-Daten des IZ. Ein Bericht über die Entwicklung im Zeitraum von 1997 bis 2003. Bonn: Informationszentrum Sozialwissenschaften (2003)
5. Frisch, E., Kluck, M.: Pretest zum Projekt German Indexing and Retrieval Testdatabase (GIRT) unter Anwendung der Retrievalsysteme Messenger und freeWAISsf. Bonn: Informationszentrum Sozialwissenschaften (1997) (2.ed.)

6. Kluck, M.: German Indexing and Retrieval Test Data Base (GIRT): Some Results of the Pre-test. In: Dunlop, M. D. (ed.): The 20th BCS IRSG Colloquium: Discovering New Worlds of IR (IRSG-98), Grenoble, France, 25-27 March 1998, Grenoble (1998) (= electronic workshops in computing) see: http://www.ewic.org.uk/ewic/workshop/view.cfm/IRSG-98

7. Krause, J., Mutschke, P.: Indexierung und Fulcrum-Evaluierung. Bonn: Informationszentrum Sozialwissenschaften (1999), see http://www.gesis.org/Publikationen/Berichte/IZ_Arbeitsberichte/pdf/ab17.pdf

8. Binder, G., Stahl, M., Faulbaum, L.: Vergleichsuntersuchung MESSENGER – FULCRUM. Bonn: Informationszentrum Sozialwissenschaften (2000) see http://www.gesis.org/ Publikationen/Berichte/IZ_Arbeitsberichte/pdf/ ab18.pdf

9. Womser-Hacker, C. (Ed.) u.a.: Projektkurs Informationsmanagement: Durchführung einer Evaluierungsstudie, Vergleich der Information-Retrieval-Systeme (IRS) DOMESTIC - LARS II - TextExtender. Universität Konstanz (1998)

10. Käter, T., Rittberger, M., Womser-Hacker, C.: Evaluierung der Text-Retrievalsysteme Domestic, Intelligent Miner for Text, Lars II und TextExtender. In: Semar, W., Kuhlen, R. (Eds.): Information Engineering. Proceedings des 4. Konstanzer Informationswissenschaftlichen Kolloquiums (KIK '99). Konstanz: UVK (1999) 63-73

11. Käter, T.: Evaluierung des Text-Retrievalsystems "Intelligent Miner for Text" von IBM - Eine Studie im Vergleich zur Evaluierung anderer Systeme, (1999) Universität Konstanz, http://www.ub.uni-konstanz.de/kops/volltexte/1999/283/

12. Griesbaum, J.: Evaluierung hybrider Suchsysteme im WWW, Diplomarbeit Informationswissenschaft Universität Konstanz (2000)

13. Eibl, M.: Visualisierung im Document Retrieval. Theoretische und praktische Zusammenführung von Softwareergonomie und Graphik Design. Bonn: Informationszentrum Sozialwissenschaften (2000)

14. Mandl, T.: Tolerantes Information Retrieval. Neuronale Netze zur Erhöhung der Adaptivität und Flexibilität bei der Informationssuche. Konstanz: UVK (2001)

15. Kluck, M., Gey, F.C.: The Domain-Specific Task of CLEF – Specific Evaluation Strategies in Cross-Language Information Retrieval. In: Carol Peters (Ed.): Cross-Language Information Retrieval and Evaluation. Workshop of Cross-Language Evaluation Forum, CLEF 2000, Lisbon, Portugal, September 21-22, 2000, Revised Papers. Berlin: Springer (2001) 48-56

16. Schott, H. (Ed.): Thesaurus Sozialwissenschaften – Thesaurus for the Social Sciences [Ausgabe – Edition] 1999. [Bd. 1:] Deutsch-Englisch – German-English, [Bd. 2] Englisch-Deutsch – English-German. Bonn: Informationszentrum Sozialwissenschaften (1999)

17. See also Schott, H. (Ed.): Thesaurus Sozialwissenschaften [Ausgabe] 1999. [Bd. 1:] Alphabetischer Teil, [Bd. 2] Systematischer Teil. Bonn: Informationszentrum Sozialwissenschaften (1999)

18. Basarnova, S., Magaj, H., Mdivani, R., Schott, H., Sucker, D. (Eds.): Thesaurus Sozialwissenschaften Bd.1: Deutsch-Englisch-Russisch, Bd. 2: Russisch-Deutsch-Englisch, Bd. 3: Register. Bonn/Moskau: Informationszentrum Sozialwissenschaften / Institut fü wissenschaftliche Information in den Gesellschaftswissenschaften (INION RadW) (1997)

19. Kando, N.: CLIR at NTCIR Workshop 3: Cross-Language and Cross-Genre Retrieval. In: Peters, C., Braschler, M., Gonzalo, J., Kluck, M. (eds.): Advances in Cross-Language Information Retrieval. Third Workshop of the Cross-Language Evaluation Forum, CLEF 2002, Rome, Italy, September 19-20, 2002, Revised Papers. Berlin: Springer (2003) 485-504

20. Harman, D., Braschler, M., Hess, M., Kluck, M., Peters, C., Schäuble, P., Sheridan, P.: CLIR Evaluation at TREC. In: Peters, C. (ed.): Cross-Language Information Retrieval and Evaluation. Workshop of Cross-Language Evaluation Forum, CLEF 2000, Lisbon, Portugal, September 21-22, 2000, Revised Papers. Berlin: Springer (2001) 7-23

21. Vorhees, E.M., Harman, D.K. (eds.): The Eighth Text Retrieval Conference (TREC8) [1999]. Gaithersburg: NIST (2000) at: http://trec.nist.gov/ pubs/trec8/t8_proceedings.html

22. Cooper, W., Chen, A., Gey, F.: Full Text Retrieval based on Probabilistic Equations with Coefficients fitted by Logistic Regression. In: Harman, D.K. (ed.): The Second Text Retrieval Conference (TREC-2). Gaithersburg: NIST (1994) 57-66

23. Gey, F.C., Jiang, H.: English-German Cross-Language Retrieval for the GIRT Collection - Exploiting a Multilingual Thesaurus, In: Vorhees, E.M., Harman, D.K. (eds.): The Eighth Text Retrieval Conference (TREC8) [1999]. Gaithersburg: NIST (2000) 301-306

24. Braschler, M. Schäuble, P., Kan, M-Y., Klavans, J.L.: The Eurospider Retrieval System and the TREC-8 Cross-Language Track, In: Vorhees, E.M., Harman, D.K. (eds.): The Eighth Text Retrieval Conference (TREC8) [1999]. Gaithersburg: NIST (2000) 367-376

25. Sheridan, P., Ballerini, J.P.: Experiments in Multilingual Information Retrieval Using the SPIDER System. In: Proceeding of the 19th Annual International ACM SIGIR Conference (1996) 58-65

26. Gey, F.C., Jiang, H., Petras, V., Chen, A.: Cross-Language Retrieval for the CLEF Collections – Comparing Multiple Methods of Retrieval. In: Peters, C. (ed.): Cross-Language Information Retrieval and Evaluation. Workshop of Cross-Language Evaluation Forum, CLEF 2000, Lisbon, Portugal, September 21-22, 2000, Revised Papers. Berlin: Springer (2001) 116-128

27. Gövert, N.: Bilingual Information Retrieval with HyREX and Internet Translations Services. In: Peters, C. (ed.): Cross-Language Information Retrieval and Evaluation. Workshop of Cross-Language Evaluation Forum, CLEF 2000, Lisbon, Portugal, September 21-22, 2000, Revised Papers. Berlin: Springer (2001) 237-244

28. Gey, F.C., Jiang, H., Perelman, N.: Working with Russian Queries for the GIRT, Bilingual, and Multilingual CLEF Tasks. In: Peters, C., Braschler, M., Gonzalo, J., Kluck, M. (eds.): Evaluation of Cross-Language Information Retrieval Systems. Second Workshop of the Cross-Language Evaluation Forum, CLEF 2001, Darmstadt, Germany, September 3-4, 2001.Revised papers. Berlin: Springer (2002) 235-243

29. Gey, F.C.: Research to Improve Cross-Language Retrieval – Position Paper for CLEF. In: Peters, C. (ed.): Cross-Language Information Retrieval and Evaluation. Workshop of Cross-Language Evaluation Forum, CLEF 2000, Lisbon, Portugal, September 21-22, 2000, Revised Papers. Berlin: Springer (2001) 83-88

30. Kamps, J., Monz, C., de Rijke, M.: Combining Evidence for Cross-Language Information retrieval. In: Peters, C., Braschler, M., Gonzalo, J., Kluck, M. (eds.): Advances in Cross-Language Information Retrieval. Third Workshop of the Cross-Language Evaluation Forum, CLEF 2002, Rome, Italy, September 19-20, 2002, Revised Papers. Berlin: Springer (2003) 111-126

31. Petras, V., Perelman, N., Gey, F.C.: Using Thesauri in Cross-Language retrieval for German and French. In: Peters, C., Braschler, M., Gonzalo, J., Kluck, M. (eds.): Advances in Cross-Language Information Retrieval. Third Workshop of the Cross-Language Evaluation Forum, CLEF 2002, Rome, Italy, September 19-20, 2002, Revised Papers. Berlin: Springer (2003) 349-362

32. Renders, J-M., Déjean, H., Gaussier, E.: Assessing Automatically Extracted Bilingual Lexicons for CLIR in Vertical Domains: XRCE Participation in the GIRT Track of CLEF-2002. In: Peters, C., Braschler, M., Gonzalo, J., Kluck, M. (eds.): Advances in Cross-Language Information Retrieval. Third Workshop of the Cross-Language Evaluation Forum, CLEF 2002, Rome, Italy, September 19-20, 2002, Revised Papers. Berlin: Springer (2003) 363-371

33. Hackl, R., Kölle, R., Mandl, T., Womser-Hacker, C.: Domain Specific Retrieval Experiments with MIMOR at the University of Hildesheim. In: Peters, C., Braschler, M., Gonzalo, J., Kluck, M. (Eds.): Advances in Cross-Language Information Retrieval. Third Workshop of the Cross-Language Evaluation Forum, CLEF 2002, Rome, Italy, September 19-20, 2002, Revised Papers. Berlin: Springer (2003) 343-348

34. Kamps, J., Monz, C., de Rijke, M., Sigurbjörnsson, B.: Language-Dependent and Language-Independent Approaches to Cross-Lingual Text Retrieval. In this volume.

35. Petras, V., Perelman, N., Gey, F.C.: UC Berkeley at CLEF 2003 – Russian Language Experiments and Domain-Specific Cross-Language Retrieval. In this volume

36. Alderuccio, D., Bordoni, L., Loretto, V.: Data Compression Approach to the Monolingual GIRT Task: An Agnostic Point of View. In this volume

37. Leveling, J.: University of Hagen at CLEF 2003: Natural Language Access to the GIRT4 Data. In this volume

38. Braschler, M., Peters, C.: Cross-Language Evaluation Forum: Objectives, Results, Achievements. In: Information Retrieval, 7 (2004) 1-2, 7-31

A Data-Compression Approach to the Monolingual GIRT Task: An Agnostic Point of View

Daniela Alderuccio[1], Luciana Bordoni[1], and Vittorio Loreto[2]

[1] ENEA - Uda/Advisor - Centro Ricerche Casaccia -Via Anguillarese,
301 - 00060 S. Maria di Galeria (Rome), Italy
{alderuccio, bordoni}@casaccia.enea.it
[2] "La Sapienza", Univ. in Rome, Physics Dept., P.le Aldo Moro, 2,
00185 Rome, Italy
loreto@roma1.infn.it

Abstract. In this paper we apply a data-compression IR method in the GIRT social science database, focusing on the monolingual task in German and English. For this purpose we use a recently proposed general scheme for context recognition and context classification of strings of characters (in particular texts) or other coded information. The key point of the method is the computation of a suitable measure of remoteness (or similarity) between two strings of characters. This measure of remoteness reflects the distance between the structures present in the two strings, i.e. between the two different distributions of elements of the compared sequences. The hypothesis is that the information-theory oriented measure of remoteness between two sequences could reflect their semantic distance. It is worth stressing the generality and versatility of our information-theoretic method which applies to any kind of corpora of character strings, whatever the type of coding used (i.e. language).

1 Introduction

Today Internet has become a powerful resource for accessing and gathering information in all areas of the public and private sector (education, research, e-commerce, advertising, marketing, banking, finance, etc.). The consequent exponential growth of available multilingual data has led to an increasing need for Cross-Language Information Retrieval Systems [1,2], facilitating equal access to information for all users without the limit of a multilingual knowledge.

The aim of CLIR techniques is to bridge the gaps related to the lack of linguistic knowledge of common users and to the ambiguity of language. For this purpose, techniques able to give a comparable representation of the user query and of the stored information are being developed, in order to retrieve and extract all documents matching the query.

Our aim is to estimate the degree of remoteness (or similarity) with which documents in a corpus reflect the distance with respect to the user's information need.

This paper is organised as follows. Section 2 describes the methodology adopted, while Section 3 presents the results of the monolingual experiments in English and German; Section 4 presents the conclusions as well as directions for future work.

C. Peters et al. (Eds.): CLEF 2003, LNCS 3237, pp. 391–400, 2004.
© Springer-Verlag Berlin Heidelberg 2004

2 Methodology

In this section we briefly describe the information-theoretic method we use.

Information extraction takes places via a two-step process. The first step is the syntactic step, where the structure of the message is identified (detected) without associating any specific meaning with it. The second step (the semantic step) adds common sense knowledge of the meaning to the syntactic information. This is a way of representing the method we use to identify the language in which a given text is written. In the first step we scan the text and identify the syntactic structure; in a second phase we extract the meaning of the sentence, applying real world knowledge and linguistic competence.

We hypothesise that we can extract and measure the syntactic information of a given sequence (e.g. a text). The question emerges as to whether we could obtain from this measure some information about the meaning of the sequence. The answer to this question is far from trivial.

With this hypothesis in mind, the first logical step is to provide ourselves with tools that can measure the amount of syntactic or structural information contained in a given string. We shall follow an Information Theoretic approach [3,4]. In Information Theory (IT) the word "information" acquires a very precise meaning, namely the "entropy" of a string of characters. In a sense, entropy measures the surprise the source emitting the sequences can give us. Suppose the surprise one feels upon learning that an event E has occurred depends only on the probability of E. If the event occurred with probability 1 (certainty) our surprise at its occurrence would be zero. On the other hand if the probability of occurrence of the event E were quite small our surprise would be proportionally larger.

It is possible to extend the definition of the entropy for a generic string of characters, without any reference to its source. This is what we need to analyze a text whose source and/or statistical properties are a priori unknown. Among the many equivalent definitions of entropy the best for this case is the so-called Chaitin-Kolmogorov complexity, or Algorithmic Complexity (see for instance [5]): *the algorithmic complexity of a string of characters is given by the length (in bits) of the smallest program which produces the string as output.* A string is called complex if its complexity is proportional to its length. This definition is really abstract: for one thing, it is impossible, even in principle, to find such a program [5]. Since the definition is not based on the time the best program should take to reproduce the sequence, one can never be sure that there might not exist a shorter program that could eventually output the string in a larger (eventually infinite) time.

Despite the intrinsic difficulty of measuring the algorithmic complexity of a generic string of characters, we note that there exist algorithms explicitly conceived to approach the theoretical limit of optimal coding. These are the file compressors or zippers. It is thus intuitive that a typical zipper, besides reducing the space a file occupies on a memory storage device, can be considered as an entropy meter. The better the compression algorithm, the closer the length of the zipped file to the minimal entropic limit, and hence the better will be the estimate of the algorithmic complexity provided by the zipper. It is indeed well known that compression algorithms provide a powerful tool for the measure of entropy and more generally for the estimation of more sophisticated measures of complexity [3,6].

Any algorithm that tries to estimate the entropy (or better the Algorithmic Complexity) of a string of characters (with arbitrary statistical properties) only carries out the syntactic step. To proceed to the semantic level we need to add other ingredients that could bridge the gap between the syntactic properties of a sequence (e.g. a text) and its semantic aspects. With this precise aim a general method has recently been proposed for context recognition and context classification of strings of characters or other coded information [7]. Based on data-compression techniques, the key point of the method is the computation of a suitable measure of remoteness between two bodies of knowledge. This idea has been used for authorship attribution and for defining a suitable distance between sequences in language phylogenesis.

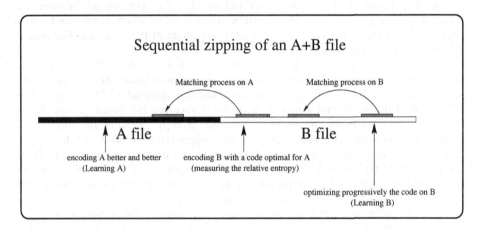

Fig. 1. Schematic description of how a sequential zipper optimizes its features at the interface between two different sequences A and B while zipping the sequence A+B obtained by simply appending B after A

The key point of the new method is simple. Suppose you want to estimate the "distance" (or similarity) between texts A and B in terms of their informatic content. For instance, for two texts written in different languages (e.g. English and Italian), their "distance" can be thought of as a measure of the difficulty experienced by a typical speaker of mother tongue A in understanding the text written in language B. More generally one can imagine to measure the remoteness between two languages by measuring the distance between two typical texts representative of the two languages. A possible way to estimate the remoteness between two texts has been proposed in [7] in terms of the so-called the relative entropy [8]. At the zero-th order of approximation we can describe the procedure as follows. We take a long English text and we append to it an Italian text, then we zip the resulting text. The zipper begins reading the file starting from the English text and after a while it is able to encode (almost) optimally the English file (this is the aim of the compression procedure). When the Italian part begins, the zipper starts encoding it in a way which is optimal for the English. So the first part of the Italian file is encoded with the English code. After a while the zipper "learns" Italian and changes its rules. Therefore if the length of the Italian file is "small enough", the difference between the length (in bits) of the zipped English+Italian text and the length (in bits) of the English text zipped alone will give a measure of the "distance" between the two texts. Figure 1 illustrates this *learning* process when using the LZ77 scheme [9], one of the best known compression algorithm. We do not enter in too many details here and we refer the reader to [7,10,11].

Once one has defined the entropy-based remoteness between two texts, or more generally between two strings of characters one has in his hands a powerful tool to implement suitable algorithms for recognizing the "context" of a given sequence (for example for a sequence of characters representing a text, we might like to recognize the language in which it is written, the subject treated, and its author).

3 Monolingual GIRT Experiments

In the framework of CLEF 2003 we applied our method to both the GIRT English and German tasks.

The German Indexing and Retrieval Data Base (GIRT) is a scientific text collection which covers the domain of social sciences. The GIRT collections contains 151,319 documents, available as two parallel corpora in German (GIRT4-DE) and English (GIRT4-EN). It is composed by two databases: FORIS (Social Science Research Information System), and SOLIS (Social Science Literature Information System). Both databases are in German. There are also English translations of the titles for nearly all documents and about 17% of the documents have an English abstract.

Reference documents contain: bibliographical information (author, language of the document, publication year); abstracts; controlled-terms; classification terms and free-terms (see Braschler, M. & Peters, C., CLEF2003: "Methodology and Metrics", this volume).

In our experiments we used ABSTRACTs and CONTROLLED-TERMs (indexing terms assigned by experts; each document has an average of 10 indexing terms).

The topics contains three main parts:

- TITLE: a short title;
- DESC: a one sentence description.
- NARR: a more complex narrative, specifying the relevance assessment criteria.

In our experiment we used TITLE and DESCR fields.

For the German Monolingual task we performed the following three runs (comparing the fields in parenthesis):

ENEASAPDTC: (Title Topic vs. Controlled Terms)
ENEASAPDTA: (Title Topic vs. Abstract)
ENEASAPDTDC: (Title + Desc. Topic vs. Controlled Terms)

For the English Monolingual task we performed the following two runs:

ENEASAPETC: (Title Topic vs. Controlled Terms)
ENEASAPETDC: (Title + Desc. Topic vs. Controlled Terms).

The equivalent of the ENEASADTA could not be performed because only 17% of the English documents contains an abstract. The retrieval would not be exhaustive because the documents without abstract would have been ignored.

3.1 Experiments with the German and English Collections

In the implementation of our method a text is considered as a unique sequence of characters (ASCII format). Texts have been pre-processed: all carriage returns and punctuation marks have been removed; additionally all the capital letters (even in German) have been converted into small letters (with advantages in the retrieval phase, see subsection 3.2).

For our experiments we need to select – for each run – only a few items of information contained in the topics and in database documents. For this reason, we need to create artificial topics and artificial reference documents, where an artificial text is supposed to have the original document's features needed for the specific run under consideration.

The construction of the artificial topics as well as of the artificial reference documents depends on the specific run.

German Runs:

ENEASAPDTC: Artificial topic texts are composed only by Topic Titles. Artificial reference texts are obtained by appending – for each original reference text – all the Controlled Terms.

ENEASAPDTA: Artificial topic texts are composed only by Topic Titles. Artificial reference texts are composed by the Abstracts of the original reference texts.

ENEASAPDTDC: Artificial topic texts are composed only by appending the Title and the Description of each Topic. Artificial reference texts are obtained by appending – for each original reference text – all the Controlled Terms.

English Runs:

ENEASAPETC: Artificial topic texts are composed only by Topic Titles. Artificial reference texts are obtained by appending – for each original reference text – all the Controlled Terms.

ENEASAPETDC: Artificial topic texts are composed only by appending Title and Description of each Topic. Artificial reference texts are obtained by appending – for each original reference text – all the Controlled Terms.

From the point of view of our method the GIRT task could be summarized as follows. We have a corpus of known documents D_i ($i = 1,...,151319$) and a corpus of topics T_j ($j = 76,...,100$).

For each run and for each topic T_j, we compare an artificial topic text AT_j with a corpus of artificial reference documents AD_i ($i = 1,...,151319$). For each topic, we are interested in: (a) detecting the artificial reference texts AD_i, which are closest (according to some rules) to the AT_j topic text, and (b) in ranking them. The procedure consists in measuring the cross-entropy between a text A and a text B, where cross-entropy is given by the minimal number of bits necessary to codify text A with a code which is optimal for text B (see [10, 11] for details).

In our case, for each artificial topic text AT_j we rank all other documents (restricting the list to the first 1000 documents), according to the value of the so-called cross-entropy per character between the artificial topic text AT_j and each artificial reference text.

3.2 Results

Before proceeding to the evaluation of the results, some remarks are in order.

Users of scientific collections are typically recall-oriented, that is they are more interested in retrieving all the relevant documents available in a database, rather than in extracting only some relevant documents. For this reason we base our algorithm on recall values.

GIRT is a scientific collection covering the domain of social science, therefore documents contain a lot of sociological terminology, expressed in common words but used in a specific meaning (e.g. "gender differences", "gender studies", etc.). IR systems return sets of relevant documents in response to a query, but IR performance can be negatively affected when there is a clear difference between the scientific meaning and the common meaning [13].

Our algorithm is sensitive to changes in string structure, therefore it can be influenced by differences in sentence structure, due to different writing style and documents sources. CLEF documents were written by different authors and come from heterogeneous sources (journal articles, monographs, grey literature, research projects), so the structure of the information contained in abstracts may reflect their different origin.

The use of controlled-terms can be a viable solution for overcoming this problem, even though this semantic tagging performed by human experts is subjective and error-prone. Furthermore, controlled terms have not been assigned in an homogeneous way, that is some documents have 2 or 3 controlled-terms, other more: the average is 10 controlled-terms for each document. As a consequence, our algorithm will retrieve documents and rank them, also on the basis of the number of occurrences of controlled-terms. For this reason, if a document has a multi-level interpretation, it will be tagged by an expert with more controlled-terms. In this way if we find a document with 12 controlled-terms, 4 of which are similar to the title of the topic, our algorithm will likely place this document at the top of the list, before other documents with 3 or 2 controlled-terms.

In the German run ENEASAPDTA (where Topic Titles have been compared against document Abstract) the completeness of results retrieved by our algorithm can be influenced by the lack of about 5.378 abstract (the German collection FO4D has 15.955 documents, and about 13.574 documents have abstracts; in the LI4D collection 132.367 documents have abstracts out of a total of 135.364 documents).

We tried to compare the results obtained in the two monolingual tasks in order to optimize them and to improve future cross-language applications, but we found some obstacles related to translations.

In general the topics translation into English is quite faithful to the original German text. Differences in results between the document retrieval in German with respect to that in English can depend on the variation with respect to the original version. As an example in Topic No. 88 we have the following translation:

Title-DE: SPORT IM NATIONALSOZIALISMUS
Title-EN: SPORTS IN NAZI GERMANY

the added word *"Germany"* in the title of the English translation will retrieve documents where this word occurs such as in "Federal Republic of Germany" on the one hand, but on the other hand can lead to ignoring documents where "Nazism" or "National Socialism" occur.

In the description field of Topic No. 88:

Desc-DE: Finde Dokumente ueber die Rolle des Sportes im Dritten Reich"
Desc-EN: Find documents about the role of sports in the German Third Reich"

the use of the word "German" is pleonastic, and this use of more words than necessary to denote sense, might influence the results.

Other differences in results are related to the grammatical, morphological and syntactical differences between the German and English languages (e.g. in German nouns are identified by capital letters; there is a wide use of compounding and of verbs with separable prefixes syntactically not bound to the verb-stem; in subordinated clauses the inflected verb is placed toward the end of the sentence, etc.).

One of the advantage of our algorithm is the faculty of recognizing sequences of similar characters within the strings. This allows for the extraction of texts where words or parts of words are embodied in compounds, for example our algorithm is able to find documents where the word *"Mitglieder"* (member) is contained in the word *"Parteimitglieder"* (party member) (Topic. No. 092). To achieve this, the texts have been pre-processed and all capital letters have been substituted by small letters.

One of the disadvantages is that some results may be partially altered if the sequence of characters occurs in more than a word.

This was particularly evident in:

- Topic No. 080, where the word "India" contains the sequence "*i n d*". In this case our algorithm found a lot more documents related to the term "*ind*ustr-y/ial/ie/iel" than related to the country of "*Ind*ia";
- and in Topic No. 099, where in the word "S*port*" the sequence of characters "*p o r t*" was detected in texts containing words like "re*port*ing", "De*port*ation", "Re*port*age", "Ex*port*", "Trans*port*".

In spite of some points of weakness, on average our algorithm performs quite well.

Table 1 reports the average recall (over all topics) for the different runs.

Figs. 2 and 3 report the results for the recall obtained for each single topic and for each run, for English and German respectively.

In Fig. 4 we report the results of the average precision obtained for each single topic and for each run, compared with the average performance.

Table 1. Average recall (averaged over all the topics) for our five runs. For each run, we report the ratio between the total number of relevant documents retrieved (independently of the position in the ranking) and the total number of existing relevant documents

RUN ID	ENEASAPDTC	ENEASAPDTDC	ENEASAPDTA	ENEASAPETC	ENEASAPETDC
RECALL	0.6528	0.6145	0.5904	0.7087	0.6996

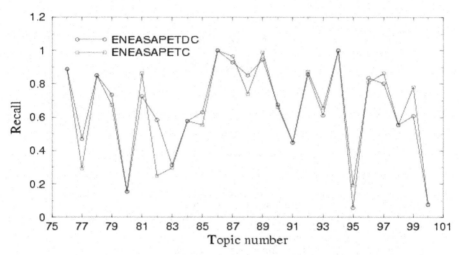

Fig. 2. English: recall obtained for each single topic and for each run

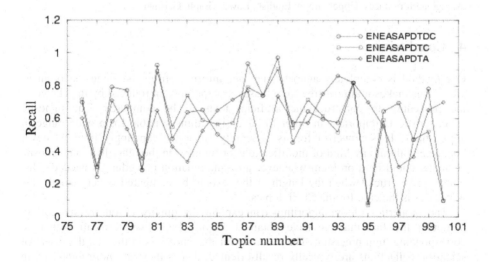

Fig. 3. German: recall obtained for each single topic and for each run

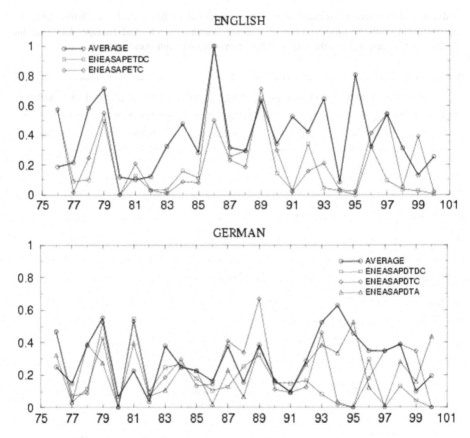

Fig. 4. Average precisions obtained for each single topic and for each run, compared with the average performances. Upper Graph: English. Lower Graph: German

4 Conclusions

Our method is completely agnostic, i.e. not informed from the linguistic point of view. This makes it almost free from biases, except those introduced by the choice of the procedure to construct the artificial texts to be compared. The agnostic characteristic is important in order to have algorithms suitable for a wide range of applications. It is powerful for its generality since we can apply it to whatever language without any kind of modifications or tuning. On the other hand its agnostic character could be a problem whenever a disambiguation procedure is needed. This point can be crucial when the length of the texts to be compared is very small (few words), as is the case for the CLEF topics.

The properties of our algorithm can explain the quality of our results and in particular the fact that we have obtained a quite high overall recall without a corresponding high precision. The rationale for this choice is in the fact that users of scientific collections are typically recall-oriented, that is they are more interested in retrieving all the relevant documents available in a database, rather than in extracting only some relevant documents.

Nevertheless, future work will be oriented in the direction of improving precision. We can imagine two possible directions. On the one hand we could perform some expansion procedures for the queries and/or the reference texts, in order to reduce the strong bias due to the extreme shortness of the documents to be compared. On the other hand we could develop some hybrid procedure able to balance the need to keep the method as agnostic as possible with the implementation of linguistically relevant tips.

References

[1]   Rijsbergen, C.J.: Information Retrieval, 2nd ed., Butterworths, London (1979)

[2]   Croft, B. (ed.): Advances in Information Retrieval – Recent Research from the Centre for Intelligent Information Retrieval. Kluwer Academic Publisher (2003)

[3]   Shannon, C.E.: A Mathematical Theory of Communication. The Bell System Technical Journal, 27:379-423 and 623-656 (1948)

[4]   Zurek, W.H. (editor): Complexity, Entropy and Physics of Information. Addison-Wesley, Redwood City (1990)

[5]   Li, M., Vitànyi, P.: An Introduction to Kolmogorov Complexity and its Applications. 2nd ed. Springer-Verlag, Berlin Heidelberg New York (1997)

[6]   Khinchin, A.I.: Mathematical Foundations of Information Theory. Dover, New York (1957)

[7]   Benedetto, D., Caglioti, E., Loreto, V.: Language Trees and Zipping, Physical Review Letters 88:048702-048705 (2002)

[8]   Ziv, J., Merhav, N.: A Measure of Relative Entropy between Individual Sequences with Applications to Universal Classification. IEEE Transactions on Information Theory, 39:1280-1292 (1993)

[9]   Ziv, J., Lempel, A.: A Universal Algorithm for Sequential Data Compression. IEEE Transactions on Information Theory, 23:337-343 (1977)

[10] Puglisi, A., Benedetto, D., Caglioti, E., Loreto, V., Vulpiani, A.: Data Compression and Learning Time Sequences Analysis, Physica D, 180:92-107 (2003)

[11] Benedetto, D., Caglioti, E., Loreto, V.: Zipping Out Relevant Information. Invited column "Computing Prescriptions" in the AIP/IEEE journal Computing in Science and Engineering, January-February issue (2003)

[12] Braschler, M., Ripplinger, B.: Stemming and Decompounding for German Text Retrieval. Advances in Information Retrieval – Proceedings of the 25th European Conference on IR Research, ECIR 2003, Pisa, Italy (2003)

[13] Kluck, M., Gey, F.C.: The Domain-specific Task of CLEF – Specific Evaluation Strategies in Cross-Language Information Retrieval. Proceedings CLEF 2000 Workshop, Springer-Verlag, Berlin Heidelberg New York (2001).

UC Berkeley at CLEF-2003 – Russian Language Experiments and Domain-Specific Retrieval

Vivien Petras[1], Natalia Perelman[1], and Fredric Gey[2]

[1] School of Information Management and Systems
{vivienp, perelman}@sims.berkeley.edu
[2] UC Data Archive & Technical Assistance,
University of California, Berkeley, CA 94720 USA
gey@ucdata.berkeley.edu

Abstract. As in the previous years, Berkeley's group 1 experimented with the domain-specific CLEF collection GIRT as well as with Russian as query and document language. The GIRT collection was substantially extended this year and we were able to improve our retrieval results for the query languages German, English and Russian. For the GIRT retrieval experiments, we utilized our previous experiences by combining different translations, thesaurus matching, decompounding for German compounds and a blind feedback algorithm. We find that our thesaurus matching technique compares to conventional machine translation for Russian and German against English retrieval and outperforms machine translation for English to German retrieval.

With the introduction of a Russian document collection in CLEF 2003, we participated in the CLEF main task with monolingual and bilingual runs for the Russian collection. For bilingual retrieval our approaches were query translation (for German or English as topic languages) and document translation (for English as the topic language). Document translation significantly underperformed query translation (using the Promt translation system).

1 Introduction

For several years, Berkeley's group 1 has experimented with domain-specific collections and investigated thesaurus-aided retrieval within the CLEF environment. We theorize that collections enhanced with subject terms from a controlled vocabulary contain more query-relevant words and phrases and, furthermore, that retrieval using a thesaurus-enhanced collection and / or queries enriched with controlled vocabulary terms will be more precise. This year's GIRT collection has been extended to contain more than 150,000 documents (as opposed to the 70,000 documents it contained in the previous years) and we investigated the usefulness of a thesaurus in a bigger document collection. The larger a document collection is, the more individual documents can be found for any chosen controlled vocabulary term. In a worst-case scenario, this effect could nullify the specificity of the thesaurus terms and have a negative outcome on the retrieval performance. However, our experiments show that incorporating the thesaurus data achieves performance improvements. Using the multilingual GIRT thesaurus (German, English, Russian) to translate query files for

C. Peters et al. (Eds.): CLEF 2003, LNCS 3237, pp. 401–411, 2004.
© Springer-Verlag Berlin Heidelberg 2004

bilingual retrieval has proven to be useful for performance improvement. Our *thesaurus matching technique* is comparable to machine translation for Russian and German, but outperforms the tested machine translation systems for English to German. However, the competitiveness of thesaurus matching versus machine translation depends on the existence of controlled vocabulary terms in the query fields and the size and quality of the thesaurus.

CLEF 2003 was the first time a Russian language document collection was available in CLEF. We have worked for several years with Russian topics in both the GIRT task and the CLEF main tasks, so we welcomed the opportunity to do Russian monolingual retrieval and bilingual retrieval No unusual methodology was applied to the Russian collection, however encoding was an issue and we ended up using the KOI-8 encoding scheme for both documents and topics.

For our retrieval experiments, the Berkeley group is using the technique of logistic regression as described in [1].

2   The GIRT Retrieval Experiments

2.1   The GIRT Collection

The GIRT collection (German Indexing and Retrieval Test database) consists of 151,319 documents in the social science domain. The documents contain titles, abstracts and controlled vocabulary terms describing reports and papers indexed by the GESIS organization (http://www.social-science-gesis.de). The GIRT controlled vocabulary terms are based on the Thesaurus for the Social Sciences [2] and are provided in German and English. The thesaurus terms have also been translated to Russian, so a German-Russian version of the thesaurus is available.

For the 2003 CLEF experiments, two parallel GIRT corpora were made available: (1) German GIRT 4 contains document fields with German text, and (2) English GIRT 4 contains the translations of these fields into English.

This year, we carried out the monolingual task in both the German and English corpus, testing which parts of the document (title, abstract, or thesaurus terms) will provide relevant input for retrieval.

We also experimented with the bilingual task by using German, English and Russian as query languages against both corpora.

For all runs against the German collection, we used our decompounding procedure to split German compound words into individual terms. The procedure is described in [3] and [4]. All runs used only title and description fields from the topics. Additionally, we used our blind feedback algorithm for all runs to improve performance. The blind feedback algorithm assumes the top 20 documents as relevant and selects 30 terms from these documents to add to the query. From our experience, using the decompounding procedure and our blind feedback algorithm increases the performance anywhere between 10 and 30%. The run BKGRMLGG1 (Table 1) for example, which reached an average precision of 0.4965 in the official run, would have yielded only 0.3288 average precision without decompounding and blind feedback.

2.2 GIRT Monolingual Retrieval

For the GIRT monolingual task, we performed two experiments for each of the German and English corpora: a monolingual run against an index containing all document fields and a monolingual run against an index without the controlled vocabulary fields. As was expected, the runs against the indexes containing all fields yielded better retrieval results than the runs against the smaller indexes. For comparison purposes, we also constructed two additional indexes containing only the controlled vocabulary terms and the controlled vocabulary terms and the titles respectively. The results for the German and English monolingual runs can be found in tables 1 and 2.

Table 1. Monolingual runs against the German GIRT 4 corpus. Official runs are BKGRMLGG1 and BKGRMLGG2

| Run Name | BKGRMLGG1 | BKGRMLGG2 | BKGRMLGG3 | BKGRMLGG4 |
Document Fields	All	Title, Abstract	Title, Thesaurus	Thesaurus
Retrieved	25000	25000	25000	25000
Relevant	2117	2117	2117	2117
Rel Ret	1860	1767	1624	1474
Avg. Precision	0.4965	0.4199	0.3530	0.2935

Judging from these results, the controlled vocabulary terms have a positive impact on the retrieval results, but not as big as the abstract. Runs without the thesaurus terms lose only about 16% of their average precision, whereas runs without the abstract lose about 29%. An index that only contains titles would only yield a performance of 0.1820 in average precision, which confirms the theory that most titles are not as expressive of an article's content as the controlled vocabulary terms or the abstract.

Comparing these results to last year's, the bigger collection size might have an impact. Last year, the indexes with title and abstract and title and thesaurus terms yielded about the same results. Both were about 23% worse than the general index containing all fields. This could mean that the thesaurus terms in the larger collection do not have as much expressive power and are not as discriminating as in a smaller collection. However, the results can also be explained by other influences: (i) the queries contain fewer terms found in the thesaurus, (ii) the abstracts are more expressive, (iii) there were fewer controlled vocabulary terms assigned to each document.

Table 2. Monolingual runs against the English GIRT 4 corpus. Official runs are BKGRMLEE1 and BKGRMLEE2

| Run Name | BKGRMLEE1 | BKGRMLEE2 | BKGRMLEE3 | BKGRMLEE4 |
Document Fields	All	Title, Abstract	Title, Thesaurus	Thesaurus
Retrieved	25000	25000	25000	25000
Relevant	1332	1332	1332	1332
Rel Ret	1214	763	1160	1092
Avg. Precision	0.5192	0.2484	0.4853	0.3207

For the English GIRT corpus, the results seem to be quite different. Here the index with only title and thesaurus term fields yields almost as good a result as the general index. The index without the thesaurus terms shows a performance only half as good as the general index. However, this result can probably be explained by the fact that there are far fewer abstracts in the English GIRT corpus than there are controlled vocabulary terms. The title and thesaurus terms seem to bear the brunt of the retrieval effort in this collection.

2.3   GIRT Bilingual Retrieval

We submitted 5 official runs for the GIRT bilingual task and used all query languages (German, English and Russian) available. Generally, the runs against the English GIRT collection (with translated query files from German and Russian) yielded better results than the runs against the German GIRT collection. This can be most probably attributed to the better quality of machine translation systems for the English language as opposed to the German language. However, there does not seem to be a high variation in the results between the Russian and the other query languages, which points to a rapid improvement in the machine translation for Russian, which can be seen in the definite increase of precision figures as compared to the detrimental results of last year.

We used two machine translation systems for each query language: L & H Power Translator and Systran for German and English; and Promt and Systran for the Russian language. We also used our thesaurus matching as one translation technique [5], which will be further discussed in part 2.4. For thesaurus matching, we identify phrases and terms from the topics files and search them against the thesaurus. Once we find an appropriate thesaurus term, we substitute the query term or phrase with the thesaurus term in the language used for retrieval.

The results for the bilingual runs against German and English and a comparison of the different translation techniques can be found in tables 3 & 4 for Russian to German and English to German respectively and table 5 & 6 for Russian and German to English respectively. All runs are against the full indexes containing all document fields.

Table 3. Bilingual Russian runs against the German GIRT 4 corpus. Official runs are BKGRBLRG1 and BKGRBLRG2

Run Name	BKGRBLRG3	BKGRBLRG4	BKGRBLRG1	BKGRBLRG5	BKGRBLRG2
Transl.			Sys	Thes.	Sys + Promt
Technique	Systran	Promt	+ Promt	Matching	+ Thes.
Retrieved	25000	25000	25000	25000	25000
Relevant	2117	2117	2117	2117	2117
Rel Ret	1264	1555	1547	1343	1577
Avg. Precision	0.1925	0.2798	0.3117	0.1983	0.3269

From the Russian runs against the German GIRT corpus, one can see the superior quality of the Promt translator (about 30% better results than the Systran Babelfish translating system). The Systran system is also handicapped in that it has no direct translation from Russian to German. English was used as a Pivot language and could have introduced additional errors or ambiguities. Nevertheless, a combination of both translating systems reaches an improvement in overall precision, but not in recall.

Our thesaurus matching technique – although with a much more restricted vocabulary – compares with the Systran translator in precision and reaches a better recall. This can be explained with the superior quality (in terms of relevance for retrieval) of the thesaurus terms in a search statement. Whereas in last year's experiment the combination of translation and thesaurus matching achieved a performance improvement of 30%, this year the combination achieves only marginal improvements in precision and recall. This can mostly be explained with the improved quality of the machine translation system Promt, so that our thesaurus matching technique does not add as many high-quality terms to the query as it did last year.

Table 4. Bilingual English runs against the German GIRT 4 corpus. Official run is BKGRBLEG1

Run Name	BKGRBLEG2	BKGRBLEG3	BKGRBLEG1	BKGRBLEG4	BKGRBLEG5
Transl. Technique	L+H Power	Systran	Sys + L+H	Thes. Matching	L+H + Thes.
Retrieved	25000	25000	25000	25000	25000
Relevant	2117	2117	2117	2117	2117
Rel Ret	1656	1488	1672	1712	1803
Avg. Precision	0.3886	0.3001	0.3669	0.4299	0.4606

For English to German retrieval, the L+H Power Translator system attains much better results in retrieval than Systran, so that the combination of both translations actually degraded the retrieval performance of the overall run (although recall increased slightly).

Two queries negatively impacted the retrieval results using machine translation: 94 (Homosexuality and Coming-Out) and 98 (Canadian Foreign Policy). Both were caused by wrong translations of critical search words. "Coming-Out" for query 94 was translated into "Herauskommen" (a direct translation of the English phrases), although the phrase remains as is in German as a borrowed construct. Query 98 contains the phrase "foreign policy", which was translated into "fremde Politik", a common mistake in word-for-word translation systems. Although "foreign" is most commonly translated with "fremd", in the phrase "foreign policy" it should become the compound "Aussenpolitik" – an error that dropped this query's precision to 0.0039. However, the phrase "foreign policy" is a controlled vocabulary term and was therefore correctly translated using our thesaurus matching technique. Using thesaurus matching improved this query's average precision to 0.3798.

For English to German retrieval, thesaurus matching proved to be most effective; this run outperformed the best machine translation run by roughly 10%. Combining machine translations and translations using our thesaurus matching improves performance even more: the BKGRBLEG5 run outperformed the best machine translation run by 18%.

Table 5. Bilingual Russian runs against the English GIRT 4 corpus. Official run is BKGRBLRE1

Run Name Transl. Technique	BKGRBLRE2 Systran	BKGRBLRE3 Promt	BKGRBLRE1 Sys + Promt	BKGRBLRE4 Thes. Matching	BKGRBLRE5 Promt + Thes.
Retrieved	25000	25000	25000	25000	25000
Relevant	1332	1332	1332	1332	1332
Rel Ret	997	1084	1042	935	1077
Avg. Precision	0.3420	0.4258	0.4111	0.3107	0.4524

Also for Russian to English retrieval, the Promt translator shows superior quality – even better than for Russian to German. It outperforms the Systran translator in a way that a combination of the translations actually proves to be disadvantageous to the retrieval outcome.

Our thesaurus matching run yielded the worst results of all runs – this is partly due to the fact that there is no direct mapping table between the Russian and English thesaurus version so that German had to be used as a pivot language. In the process of mapping the Russian queries to the German and then English thesaurus versions, information was lost and consequently two queries (93 & 95) could not be effectively translated and no documents were retrieved from the English collection.

Nevertheless, a translation using thesaurus matching adds new and relevant search terms to some queries so that a combination of machine translation plus thesaurus matching translation slightly outperformed the best machine translation run by 6%.

Table 6. Bilingual German runs against the English GIRT 4. Official run is BKGRBLGE1

Run Name Transl. Technique	BKGRBLGE2 L+H Power	BKGRBLGE3 Systran	BKGRBLGE1 Sys + L+H	BKGRBLGE4 Thes. Matching	BKGRBLGE5 L+H + Thes.
Retrieved	25000	25000	25000	25000	25000
Relevant	1332	1332	1332	1332	1332
Rel Ret	1067	1116	1121	1074	1197
Avg. Precision	0.4022	0.3748	0.4068	0.3977	0.4731

Once again, the L+H Power translator outperforms the Systran translator also for translations in the opposite direction of English to German retrieval. However, a combination of the two MT systems marginally outperforms L+H in precision and makes an impact on recall.

Thesaurus matching from German to English reaches a result similar to any of the machine translations systems but the combination of the L+H Power translation and our translation from thesaurus matching achieves a performance improvement of 17%.

2.4   The Effectiveness of Thesaurus Matching

Thesaurus matching is a translation technique where the system relies exclusively on the vocabulary of the thesaurus to provide a translation. The topic files are searched for terms and phrases that occur in the thesaurus and are then substituted by their foreign language counterparts. A more detailed description can be found in [5].

Due to this process, the translated query consists of controlled vocabulary terms in the appropriate language and untranslated words that were not found in the thesaurus.

This has the advantage of emphasizing highly relevant search terms (which will occur in the thesaurus term fields of the relevant documents) but also has a major drawback. The technique will only work when the queries contain enough words and phrases that occur in the multilingual thesaurus and when those terms and phrases represent the meaning of the search statement. Fortunately, almost all queries contain more than one term that can be found in the thesaurus and therefore translated.

Nevertheless, most of the variation in our retrieval results (comparing query by query to the machine translation results) can be accounted for by looking at which queries contain the most thesaurus terms and how many good phrases our algorithm can detect. A large general thesaurus should be able to provide a good translation approximation but specialized thesauri with highly technical vocabulary might not fare as well. However, depending on the nature of the query, specialized thesauri could help in identifying important search terms from a search statement.

Additionally, our thesaurus matching technique might be able to improve: (i) by allowing a better fuzzy match between query terms and thesaurus terms, (ii) by incorporating partial matching of query terms to thesaurus terms, (iii) by exploiting narrower and broader term relationships in the thesaurus when expanding the query, or (iv) by exploiting the use-instead and used-for relationships in the thesaurus (which we have ignored so far).

Further experiments should show whether our thesaurus matching technique can improve and – considering that its competitive advantage over the three investigated MT systems lies in its ability to translate phrases - whether it can compete against phrase dictionaries as well.

3   Russian Retrieval for the CLEF Main Task

CLEF 2003 marked the first time a document collection has been available and evaluated in the Russian language. The CLEF Russian collection consisted of 16,716 articles from *Izvestia* newspaper from 1995. This is a small number of documents by most CLEF measures (the smallest other collection of CLEF 2003, Finnish, has 55,344 documents; the Spanish collection has 454,045 documents). There were 37

Russian topics, which were chosen by the organizers from the 60 topics of the CLEF main multilingual task. In our bilingual retrieval we worked with English and German versions of these topics.

3.1 Encoding Issues

The Russian document collection was supplied in the UTF-8 unicode encoding, as were the Russian version of the topics. However, since the stemmer we employ is in the KOI8 format, the entire collection was converted into KOI8 encoding. In indexing the collection, we converted upper-case letters to lower-case and applied Snowball's Russian stemmer (http://snowball.tartarus.org/russian/stemmer.html) together with a Russian stopword list created by merging the Snowball list with a translation of the English stopword list.

In addition, the Promt translation system would also only work on KOI8 encoding which meant that our translations from English and German also would come in that encoding.

3.2 Russian Monolingual Retrieval

We submitted four Russian monolingual runs, the results of which are summarized below. All runs utilized blind feedback, choosing the top 30 terms from the top ranked 20 documents of an initial retrieval run. This was the same methodology used above in the GIRT retrieval. For the BKRUMLRR1 and BKRUMLRR2 runs we used the TITLE and TEXT document fields for indexing. BKRUMLRR3 and BKRUMLRR4 were run against an index containing the TITLE, TEXT, SUBJECT, GEOGRAPHY, and RETRO fields.

The results of our retrieval are summarized in Table 7. Results were reported by the CLEF organizers for 28 topics which had one or more relevant documents.

Table 7. Berkeley Monolingual Russian runs for CLEF 2003

Run Name	BKRUMLRR1	BKRUMLRR2	BKRUMLRR3	BKRUMLRR4
Index	Koi	Koi	Koi-all	Koi-all
Topic fields	TD	TDN	TD	TDN
Retrieved	28000	28000	28000	28000
Relevant	151	151	151	151
Rel Ret	125	127	146	148
Avg. Precision	0.3338	0.3655	0.3878	0.4395

Following the workshop we performed additional Russian experiments in order to determine the effect of combinations of methodologies on the retrieval results. The components tested were stemming / no stemming, blind feedback (BF) / no blind feedback for the various document and topic fields which were indexed. We also tested settings of blind feedback parameters other than the 30 terms selected from the top 20 documents of an initial retrieval which were parameters used for the official runs.

The results of these additional experiments are summarized in Table 8 below. In general the more techniques applied, the higher the overall average precision.

Table 8. Post-Workshop Russian Monolingual Runs for combinations of methodologies

Document fields Topic fields	Title, Text TD	Title, Text TDN	Title, text, subject geo, retro TD	Title, text, subject geo, retro TDN
No stemming No blind feedback	0.2592	0.2359	0.3377	0.3533
No stemming BF 10 docs 10 terms	0.2843	0.2450	0.3913	0.3757
Stemming / No blind feedback	0.3342	0.3674	0.3971	0.4306
Stemming / BF 10 docs 10 terms	0.3367	0.3747	0.4354	0.4306
Official Runs BF 20 docs 30 terms	0.3338	0.3655	0.3878	0.4395

3.3 Russian Bilingual Retrieval

We submitted six bilingual runs against the Russian document collection. These runs only indexed the TITLE and TEXT fields of the documents and are so directly comparable only to the monolingual runs BKMLRURR1 and BKMLRURR2 above. Four of these runs (BKRUBLGR1, BKRUBLGR2, BKRUBLER1, BKRUBLER2) utilized query translation from either German or English topics into Russian.

Table 9. Bilingual Russian runs

Run Name Language Topic fields	BKRU BLGR1 German TD	BKRU BLGR2 German TDN	BKRU BLER1 English TD	BKRU BLER2 English TDN	BKRU MLEE1 En TD	BKRU MLEE2 En TDN
Retrieved	28000	28000	28000	28000	28000	28000
Relevant	151	151	151	151	151	151
Rel Ret	121	122	125	126	119	121
Avg. Prec.	0.2809	0.3125	0.2766	0.3478	0.1604	0.2227

Translation to Russian was done using the Promt online translation facility at http://www.translate.ru The only difference between runs numbered one and two was the addition of the narrative field in topic indexing.

Two final runs (BKRUMLEE1 and BKRUMLEE2) utilized a technique developed by Aitao Chen, called 'Fast Document Translation'. Instead of doing complete document translation using a MT software, the MT system is used to translate the entire vocabulary of the document collection on a word-by-word basis without the contextualization of position in sentence with respect to other words. Using this technique will choose only one translation for a polysemous word, but this defect is compensated by extremely fast translations of all the documents into the target language. We submitted 246.252 unique Russian words from the Izvestia collection to the Promt translation system (this was done 5,000 words at a time) for translation to English and then used this to translate all the documents into English. Monolingual retrieval was performed by matching the English versions of the topics against the translated English document collection.

3.4 Brief Analysis of Russian Retrieval Performance

Bilingual retrieval was in all cases worse than monolingual (Russian-Russian) retrieval in terms of overall precision. German→Russian retrieval was comparable to English→Russian retrieval for TD runs, but the English→Russian TDN run was substantially better than its German→Russian counterpart. Speculation (without evidence) is that de-compounding the German narrative before translation would have improved the performance. Fast document translation runs significantly underperformed query translation runs.

Because of the nature of the retrieval results by query for the Russian collection (eleven of the 28 topics have 2 or fewer relevant documents) one has to be cautious about drawing conclusions from the results. In general, monolingual retrieval substantially outperformed bilingual retrieval over almost all topics. However, for Topic 169 the bilingual retrieval is much better (best precision 1.0 for German-to-Russian) than the monolingual, with the best run being German-to-Russian where the German topic contains the words CD-Brennern which translates to laser disc (лазерного диска) and music industry (Musikindustrie → музыкальной индустрии) instead of the use, in the Russian version of topic 169, of the words компакт-дисков (compact disk) and аудио-промышленности (audio industry) which aren't very discriminating. The German→Russian retrieval for Topic 187 (with one relevant document) fell victim to translation problems: "Radioactive waste" in English is expressed in German as " radioaktivem Mџ". The English "wast e" is translated correctly as "отходы" while the German "Mџ" is translated as " мусору," or "garbage". This and other differences in translation lead to a decrease from 1.0 precision for English bilingual to 0.25 for German bilingual for topic 187. Several other topics have the same disparity of translation.

4 Summary and Acknowledgments

Berkeley's group 1 participated in the CLEF GIRT tasks and CLEF Main tasks for Russian mono- and bilingual retrieval. We experimented with German, English and Russian as collection and query languages.

Within the GIRT domain-specific collection, we investigated the use of thesauri in document retrieval, document index enhancement and query translation. Documents that have controlled vocabulary terms added to the usual title and abstract information prove advantageous in retrieval because the thesaurus terms add valuable search terms to the index. An index containing titles, abstracts and thesaurus terms will always out-perform an index only containing title and abstract. However, the hypothesis that the-saurus terms might be able to substitute for abstracts because of their specificity was not borne out. Retrieval involving thesauri can be influenced by several factors: the size of the collection, the size of the controlled vocabulary and the nature of the queries.

For topic translations, we found that although a combination of different machine translation systems might not always outperform an individual machine translation system, a combination of a machine translation system and our thesaurus matching technique does. Thesaurus matching outperformed machine translation in English to German retrieval and added new and relevant search terms for all other query languages. For German and Russian queries, thesaurus matching yielded comparable re-sults to machine translation.

We experimented with the CLEF 2003 Russian document collection with both monolingual Russian and bilingual to Russian from German and English topics. In addition to query translation methodology for bilingual retrieval, we tried a fast document translation method to English and performed English-English monolingual retrieval, which did not perform as well as query translation.

We would like to thank Aitao Chen for supplying his German decompounding software and for performing the fast document translation from Russian to English. This research was supported in part by DARPA (Department of Defense Advanced Research Projects Agency) under contract N66001-97-8541; AO# F477: Translingual Information Detection Extraction and Summarization (TIDES) within the DARPA Information Technology Office.

References

1. Chen, A.,Cooper, W., Gey, F.: Full text retrieval based on probabilistic equations with coef-ficients fitted by logistic regression. In: Harman, D.K. (Ed.), The Second Text Retrieval Conference (TREC-2), 57-66 (1994)
2. Schott, H. (Ed.): Thesaurus for the Social Science. [Vol. 1:] German-English., [Vol. 2:] English-German. Informationszentrum Sozialwissenschaften, Bonn (2000)
3. Chen, A.: Multilingual information retrieval using English and Chinese queries. In Peters, C., Braschler, M., Gonzalo, J., Kluck, M. (eds.): Evaluation of Cross-Language Information Retrieval Systems: Second Workshop of the Cross-Language Evaluation Forum, CLEF-2001, Darmstadt, Germany, September 2001, 44–58, Lecture Notes in Computer Science, Vol. 2406. Springer-Verlag, Berlin Heidelberg New York (2002)
4. Chen, A.: Cross-Language Retrieval Experiments at CLEF 2002. In: Peters, C., Braschler, M., Gonzalo, J., Kluck, M. (eds.): Advances in Cross-Language Information Retrieval. Third Workshop of the Cross-Language Evaluation Forum, CLEF 2002, Rome, Italy, September 19-20, 2002, Revised Papers. Lecture Notes in Computer Science, Vol. 2785. Springer-Verlag, Berlin Heidelberg New York (2003) 44–58
5. V. Petras, N. Perelman and F. Gey. Using Thesauri in Cross-Language Retrieval of German and French Indexed Collections. In: Peters, C., Braschler, M., Gonzalo, J., Kluck, M. (eds.): Advances in Cross-Language Information Retrieval: Third Workshop of the Cross-Language Evaluation Forum, CLEF-2002, Rome, Italy, September 19-20, 2002, Revised Papers. Lecture Notes in Computer Science, Vol. 2785. Springer-Verlag, Berlin Heidelberg New York (2003) 349-362

University of Hagen at CLEF 2003:
Natural Language Access to the GIRT4 Data

Johannes Leveling

Applied Computer Science VII,
Intelligent Information and Communication Systems,
FernUniversität in Hagen,
58084 Hagen, Germany
johannes.leveling@fernuni-hagen.de

Abstract. A natural language interface to databases allows a natural formulation of information needs, requiring little or no previous knowledge about database intrinsics or formal retrieval languages. Aiming at a full understanding of unrestricted natural language queries, the transformation into database queries and search failures caused by a vocabulary mismatch between query terms and database index terms become major problems to solve. This paper investigates methods of constructing query variants and their use in automated retrieval strategies. Performance results for an experimental setup with a GIRT4 database are presented.

1   Introduction

Query processing in a natural language interface (NLI) for databases faces two major problems:

1. The first problem is how to transform a user's natural language query into a database query.
2. The second problem is how to treat vocabulary problems between terms in a user query and terms in a database index. Unrestricted natural language input can contain vague or ambiguous utterances and over- or underspecifications of a user's information need. This causes – from a user's point of view – search failures.

   This paper investigates the performance of automated retrieval strategies. The retrieval strategies create query variants from search terms linguistically related to the terms used in the natural language description of an information need, rank them according to semantic similarity and successively retrieve documents up to a fixed result set size. To find search term variants, orthographic and morphological, lexical and syntactical variants are looked up with natural language processing tools in lexicon resources.

   Before presenting the approach and setup for retrieval experiments with GIRT (German Indexing and Retrieval Test database, [8]) in detail, a short overview of the underlying infrastructure of our solution to the first problem, the transformation of natural language queries is given.

C. Peters et al. (Eds.): CLEF 2003, LNCS 3237, pp. 412–424, 2004.
© Springer-Verlag Berlin Heidelberg 2004

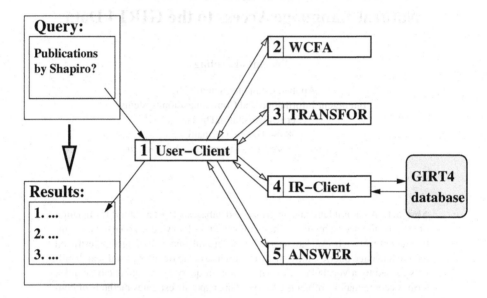

Fig. 1. The NLI architecture for the GIRT4 experiments. The arcs indicate a flow of data between system components

2   The NLI-Z39.50

The NLI-Z39.50 ([10]) is a natural language interface that supports searching in library databases with the standardized Internet protocol Z39.50 [11] for bibliographic data. The NLI-Z39.50 was developed as part of a project funded by the DFG (Deutsche Forschungsgemeinschaft). The Z39.50 (ANSI/NISO Z39.50) protocol is the de-facto standard in information retrieval targeting library databases, government or geospatial information resources and the basis of services for locating collections in digital libraries and for explaining database properties. Figure 1 gives an overview of the data and communication flow in the NLI-Z39.50. The transformation of a natural language query into a database query is divided into subsequent processing stages handled by five separate modules:

1. **User-Client:** The User-Client handles input and output and coordinates the processing steps and the communication between the system modules. It is accessible via a standard Internet browser, accepts natural language queries as input and displays the results in a readable form. For example, both the short and the longer query for GIRT topic 81 (topic title: *"Ausbildungsabbruch"/ "Vocational training dropout"* and topic description: *"Finde Dokumente, die über den Abbruch von Ausbildungsverhältnissen in Betrieben berichten."/ "Find documents on the dropout from vocational training in companies."*) is an acceptable and adequate input for the User-Client.

2. **WCFA:** By means of a Word Class Functional Analysis ([7], [4]), the natural language query is transformed into a well-documented knowledge and meaning representation, Multilayered Extended Semantic Networks (abbreviated as MultiNet) [6]. The natural language analysis is supported by HaGenLex [5], a domain-independent set of computer lexicons linked to and supplemented by external sources of lexical and morphological information, in particular CELEX [2] and GermaNet [9]. HaGenLex includes:

   - A lexicon with full morpho-syntactic and semantic information of about 20,000 lexemes.
   - A shallow lexicon containing word forms with morpho-syntactic information only. This lexicon contains about 50,000 entries.
   - Several lexicons with more than 200,000 proper nouns (including product names, company names, country and city names, etc.)

   Figure 2 shows the top layer of the MultiNet representation of the description of GIRT topic 81. The core MultiNet consists of concepts (nodes) and semantic relations and functions between them (edges). The relations and functions occuring in the example network are presented with a short description in Table 1. The Multi-Net Paradigm defines a fixed set of 93 semantic relations (plus a set of functions) to describe the meaning connections between concepts, including synonymy (SYNO), subordination, i.e. hyponymy and hypernymy (SUB), meronymy and holonymy (PARS), antonymy (ANTO), and relations for change of sorts between lexemes. For example the relation CHEA indicates a change from an event (verb) into an abstract object (noun).

   The WCFA provides powerful disambiguation modules, which use semantic and syntactic information to disambiguate lexemes and structures. MultiNet differentiates between homographs, polysemes, and meaning molecules (a regular polyseme with different meaning facets, for example *"Schule"/ "school"*).

   The semantic network in Figure 2 illustrates some features of the WCFA: the disambiguation of a verb (the correct reading represented by the concept node *"berichten.2.2"*), the inclusion of additional lexical information (the edge labelled CHEA between the nodes *"abbrechen.2.1"* and *"abbruch.1.1"*) and the decomposition of a compound noun by means of additional relations and concepts (the edges and nodes for *"ausbildung.1.1"* and *"verhältnis.1.1"*).

3. **TRANSFOR:** A rule system produces a database-independent query representation (DIQR) from the semantic query representation. The transformation process identifies structures in the MultiNet representation and key relations between concepts to return an intermediate query representation containing the core description of a user's information need. The transformation engine and transformation rules are described in greater detail in [10].

   A DIQR expression comprises common syntactical components to create database queries:

   - Attributes (so-called semantic access points), such as *"author"*, *"publisher"*, or *"title"*.

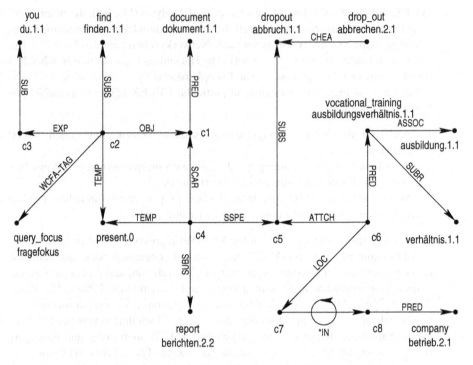

Fig. 2. The core MultiNet representation for the query *"Finde Dokumente, die über den Abbruch von Ausbildungsverhältnissen in Betrieben berichten."/ "Find documents on the dropout from vocational training in companies."* (GIRT topic 81)

Table 1. Overview of some important relations defined in the MultiNet paradigm

MultiNet relation	Short description
ASSOC	relation of association
ATTCH	attachment of object to object
CHEA	change of event to abstractum
LOC	relation specifying the location for a situation
PRED	predicative concept specifying a plurality
SCAR	carrier of a state
SSPE	entity specifying a state
SUB	conceptual subordination for objects
SUBR	metarelation for the description of relations
SUBS	conceptual subordination for situations
TEMP	relation specifying a temporal restriction for a situation
*IN	a location-producing function

- Term relations specifying how to search and match query terms. For example, the term relation $"<"$ indicates that a matching document must contain a term with a value less than the given search term (for numbers).
- Term types indicating a data type for a term. Typical examples for term types are *"number"*, *"date"*, *"name"*, *"word"*, or *"phrase"*.
- Search terms identifying the concepts searched for. Search terms include multi-word expressions such as adjective noun phrases (such as *"allgemeinbildende Schule"/ "general education school"*).
- Boolean operators for the combination of attributes, term relations, term types, search terms or expressions to construct more complex expressions, for example *"AND"* (conjunction) and *"OR"* (disjunction).

For example, when a descriptor search is limited to the title attribute, the semantic network from Figure 2 would be transformed into the DIQR

```
(AND (media_object = (word 'dokument.1.1'))
     (title = (AND (OR (word 'abbruch.1.1')
                       (word 'abbrechen.2.1'))
                   (OR (word 'ausbildungsverhältnis.1.1')
                       (AND (word 'ausbildung.1.1')
                            (word 'verhältnis.1.1')))
                   (word 'betrieb.2.1'))))
```

4. **IR-Client:** The IR-Client (Information Retrieval-Client) handles Z39.50 database access, database query processing, and document retrieval. The DIQR is transformed into queries of the Z39.50 protocol. After adapting a query to search features supported by a database it can be submitted to the database. The result set of document representations matching the query is retrieved.
5. **ANSWER:** The ANSWER module generates an answer representation in response to the natural language query (e.g., it processes the documents which are stored in the database in a bibliographic format, such as USMarc, to return a list of documents in a form readable by the user). The results found can then be presented to the user.

The GIRT4 retrieval experiments were performed on the basis of the existing module infrastructure of the NLI-Z39.50 (the User-Client, WCFA, TRANSFOR, IR-Client, and ANSWER module).

3   System Changes for the GIRT Experiments

The two major modifications to provide an experimental setup are the creation of a database in order to access the GIRT4 data via the Z39.50 protocol and enhancements of the IR-Client to support queries using the Z39.50 relevance operator and ranked results sets.

3.1   The Z39.50 GIRT4 Database

A GIRT4 database supporting access via the Z39.50 protocol was created using a free software kit, Zebra [3]. The default indexing strategy was applied to the data, which means that words are indexed as full forms. No additional indexing techniques and no morphological or syntactical preprocessing of the SGML data were employed (i.e. no stopword removal, stemming, or decomposition of compound nouns). Furthermore, the process for matching queries against documents remained unchanged in the Zebra software.

In contrast to most library databases, a Zebra database supports a relevance query operator and ranked result sets. The standard ranking algorithm implemented in Zebra is based upon a popular term weighting schema. A term weight is computed as the product of a term factor (tf) and an inverse document factor (idf). Combining tf and idf for terms in a document or in a query yields a term weight vector, which can be utilized to compute a score (see [12] for an overview of term weighting and ranking methods in information retrieval).

Two technical constraints affect the experimental setup: Firstly, a real world Z39.50 database accepts queries only up to a fixed length (e.g. the number of characters in the Z39.50 query string is limited). Secondly, disjunctions in a query (the Boolean OR operator) are restricted to a small number (about 3 or 4 operators in a query). Queries not meeting these constraints are rejected by the database with an error message. In the NLI-Z39.50, a query preprocessing step creates a set of disjunction-free queries by eliminating OR operators and decreasing the query length, thus removing the effect of these technical constraints.

3.2   IR-Client

Early test runs with the GIRT topics were performed with a single Boolean query obtained from the topic description. The recall for these test runs was close to zero. In order to find more documents, query construction and processing in the IR-Client were adapted. For the retrieval experiments, the IR-Client was modified to apply the query relevance operator and to deal with ranked result sets.

The DIQR serves as input format for the IR-Client. For example, the query *"Kennst du Bücher von Dörner über Komplexitätsmanagement?"* is represented as:

```
(AND (author = (name 'dörner.0'))
     (title = (OR  (word 'komplexitätsmanagement.1.1')
              (AND (word 'komplexität.1.1')
                   (word 'management.1.1'))))))
```

For a library database, disjunctions in this query are eliminated and the resulting queries are submitted to the target databases in parallel. A fixed number of results can be obtained by retrieving records and removing duplicate results until the result set contains the number of records wanted. In the DIQR, a disjunction already marks alternate search terms (in this case, a compound noun and its parts). Eliminating the disjunction yields two query variants[1]:

```
(AND (author = (name 'dörner.0'))
     (title = (word 'komplexitätsmanagement.1.1')))
```

---

[1] A query variant is a reformulation of the original query obtained by eliminating, adding, or substituting one or more query terms with other (linguistically related) terms.

and

```
(AND (author = (name 'dörner.0'))
     (title  = (AND (word 'komplexität.1.1')
                    (word 'management.1.1')))))
```

In order to improve recall, a set of query variants is constructed utilizing NLP tools and background knowledge represented in MultiNet. The query variants are ordered by their semantic similarity to the original query, OQ. The top ranked queries are used to either a) construct a single database query by collecting all search terms in the top ranked query variants in a word list and retrieve documents up to a given result set size or b) perform multiple searches in succession, starting with the top ranked query variants and retrieving a document only if it scores better than any document in the current result set[2]. Both methods are investigated with the GIRT retrieval experiments.

Search Term Variants: Search term variants are generated to increase the chance of matching query terms with database terms (the more different terms are matched, the higher the chance for finding a relevant document). The reverse approach, normalizing index terms and computing concept similarities for WordNet for linguistically motivated indexing is described in [1].

The WCFA and background knowledge represented as a large MultiNet provide a means to look up search term variants of the following types:

Orthographic Variants: Search terms may occur in different orthographic variants in a query or a document. Orthographic variants include terms in new German spelling (such as *"Schiffahrt"* and *"Schifffahrt"*), terms with German "Umlauts" expanded to their two-letter representation (e.g. "Bänke" and "Baenke"), and different hyphenations. The WCFA and a set of orthographic rules generate orthographic variants for a search term. For retrieval experiments, these variants are considered to be equal to the original orthographic search term.

Morphologic Variants: Morphology is concerned with the internal structure of words and consists of two subclasses:

- Inflectional morphology (for example plural forms for nouns (*"Stadt"*/ *"city"* vs. *"Städte"*/ *"cities"*) or comparative and superlative forms for adjectives (*"gut"*/ *"good"* vs. *"besser"*/ *"better"*). Inflectional variants are obtained via the WCFA which returns a list of full forms for a given lexeme. From this set of full forms, the forms with a prefix string match in the set are eliminated. For example, the full form lookup for the lexeme *"buch.1.1"*/ *"book"* returns a list containing the words *"Buch"*, *"Buchs"*, *"Buches"*, *"Buche"*, *"Bücher"*, and *"Büchern"*. The forms *"Buchs"*, *"Buches"*, *"Buche"*, and *"Büchern"* are eliminated as variants, because they match the prefix string *"Buch"* or *"Bücher"*. The remaining term variants, *"Buch"* and *"Bücher"*, are considered to be equal to the original concept.

---

[2] Disregarding technical constraints, a single query could be constructed from multiple query variants by syntactically combining the variants with disjunction operators, e.g. by joining them with an "OR".

- Derivational morphology (typically affecting the part-of-speech, for example *"Abbruch"/ "dropout"* vs. *"abbrechen"/ "drop_out"*). Derivational variations can be looked up in HaGenLex and in the MultiNet representation with background knowledge. Figure 2 contains a typical example for a derivational term variation.

Lexical Variants: The same meaning can be expressed using different words. Several knowledge and lexicon resources provide lexically and semantically related variants for a concept:

- A mapping of GermaNet to Hagenlex, in MultiNet representation, containing mostly synonymy and subordination relations (such as (*"ansehen.2.3"* SYNO *"betrachten.1.2"*) and (*"ansehen.1.1"* SUB *"wertschätzung.1.1"*)).
- HagenLex entries providing MultiNet relations between lexicalized concepts.
- A semantic network containing background knowledge for proper names (for example state names and their relations to inhabitants, language, and geographical information).
- A MultiNet representation of the GIRT thesaurus. The thesaurus entries were transformed semi-automatically into a large MultiNet. First, the text fields in the thesaurus entries were analyzed via the WCFA, obtaining a set of unconnected, disambiguated lexemes (concept nodes). Thesaurus relations were then transformed into MultiNet relations to connect the concepts (i.e. the *narrower-term* and *broader-term* relation correspond to the MultiNet relation SUB, *related-term* corresponds to ASSOC, and *use-instead* and *use-combination* correspond to SYNO) The combination of MultiNet representations for thesaurus entries forms a large network providing a semantic representation of the GIRT thesaurus.

Syntactic Variation: Some syntactic variations are normalized by the WCFA. For example, the MultiNet representation in Figure 2 contains a compound and parts of the compound.

A concept score (concept similarity) is assigned by computing the semantic similarity between a concept variation and the corresponding concept in OQ. The scores are computed by a formula from [1], adapted and extended for MultiNet relations. The semantic similarity between two concepts x and y for a subset of MultiNet relations is defined as follows:

$$
sim(x, y) = \begin{cases}
1 & : \text{if } (x \text{ EQU } y) \text{ or } (y \text{ EQU } x) \text{ exists (equal variants)} \\
0.9 & : \text{if } (x \text{ SYNO } y) \text{ or } (y \text{ SYNO } x) \text{ exists (synonymy)} \\
0.7 & : \text{if } (x \text{ SUB } y) \text{ exists (hyponymy)} \\
0.5 & : \text{if } (y \text{ SUB } x) \text{ exists (hypernymy)} \\
0.6 & : \text{if } (x \text{ PARS } y) \text{ exists (meronymy)} \\
0.4 & : \text{if } (y \text{ PARS } x) \text{ exists (holonymy)} \\
0.3 & : \text{if } (x \text{ ASSOC } y) \text{ or } (y \text{ ASSOC } x) \text{ exists (related concepts)} \\
\ldots & : \ldots
\end{cases}
$$

For concepts connected via a path of relations, the semantic similarity is computed as the product of similarities along the path connecting them.

To produce a ranked set of query variants, the semantic similarity (a measure to compare different concepts or queries) between the original query in DIQR (OQ) and a variant is computed as the product of semantic similarities of their concepts.

3.3   The Automated Retrieval Strategy

The general idea for the automated retrieval strategy is to generate and process a set of query variants differing in their search terms. Using the DIQR as a starting point, the following steps are carried out:

1. For each search term (multi-word lexemes and adjective noun phrases are counted as a single search term) in OQ, the set of linguistically related concepts is looked up (orthographic, morphologic, lexical, and syntactical variants). The MultiNet relation between two concepts x and y determines their semantic similarity, $sim(x, y)$, as defined above.
2. To generate a set of query variants, search term variants are computed and search terms in the original query are replaced by search term variants. The set of query variants is ranked, ordering queries by their score (the semantic similarity between a query variant and the original query representation).
3a. To construct a single database query, all search terms in the top ranked query variants are collected in a word list to form search terms in an extended query. The documents found are retrieved until the result set exceeds a fixed size.
3b. To perform multiple queries, the top ranked queries are used for retrieval. Documents scoring higher than the minimum score in the result set are retrieved and inserted into the result set.
4. For each document retrieved, the following information is known:
   - The *database score* for the document, determined by the database's ranking schema (the Zebra *tf-idf* score).
   - The *query score* for the current query variant, which is equivalent to the semantic similarity between the original query (OQ) and the current query variant.

   Document scores are computed as the product of database score and query score. If multiple instances of a document are found and retrieved for different query variants, the maximum of both scores is taken. For Boolean queries and databases not supporting the relevance operator, a database score of 1 is assumed to introduce a ranked result set for Boolean queries.

The ranked result set consists of the set of documents retrieved, ordered by their document score.

4   GIRT4 Retrieval Experiments

Retrieval results for five runs for the monolingual German GIRT task were submitted to the GIRT committee for relevance assessment. The parameters for these runs and for a baseline experiment, for which results were not submitted (included for comparison), are shown in Table 2.

The experimental parameters varied are:

Table 2. Overview of parameters and mean average precision for retrieval experiments

Run ID	topic fields	background knowledge used?	query type	ranking
Run1	TD	N	M	QD
Run2	T	Y	M	QD
Run3	D	Y	M	QD
Run4	TD	Y	S	QD
Run5	TD	Y	M	QD
Baseline	TD	Y	M (Boolean)	Q

- The topic fields used as a natural language query: title (T), description (D) or the combination of both (TD).
- Using lexicon and background knowledge, yes (Y) or no (N), as resources for generating term variants.
- Constructing multiple (M) queries or a single query (S) for retrieval.
- Ranking documents by a combination of query score and database score (QD) or by query score alone (Q).

Only search terms with a semantic similarity greater than 0.3 were used. The total number of query variants was reduced by limiting the number of variants for a search term to $1 + \frac{100}{2 \cdot \# concepts\ in\ OQ}$. As a default, search terms in a query were right-truncated and searched for in the abstract (TEXT) and title (TITLE) field of the documents. The 250 top ranked query variants were used for query construction and the maximum result set size was limited to 1000 documents. For experiments using the title and the description of a topic, both were analyzed and transformed separately and the resulting query representations were appended.

5   Results and Analysis

Experiments with the GIRT task for which results were submitted all rely on the use of the Z39.50 relevance operator. Because this operator is not supported by library databases, an additional experiment was conducted, which did not employ the relevance operator (the Baseline experiment).

The following observations can be made from the retrieval results:

- The Baseline experiment was performed with multiple Boolean queries for each topic and evaluated with the *trec_eval* program. For the 25 GIRT4 queries, 2117 documents are marked as relevant in the relevance assessments. A total of 883 documents were found and retrieved in the Baseline experiment, of which 200 documents are relevant (average precision for all retrieved documents: 0.0809). For twelve queries the result set was empty.

    The Baseline (a data retrieval experiment, because documents are found by exact matching) shows that recall for Boolean queries is low (compared to the information retrieval experiments). In comparison to the first experiments with near-zero recall,

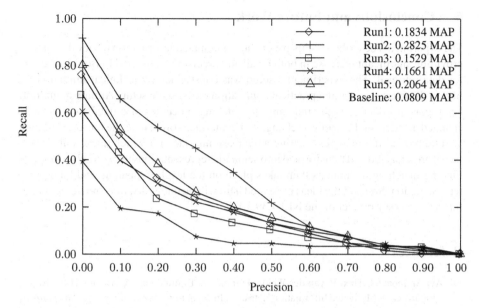

Fig. 3. Recall-Precision Graph and Mean Average Precision (MAP) for the GIRT4 (German-German) Retrieval Experiments

multiple query variants offer a considerable improvement in retrieval performance. For the NLI-Z39.50, this retrieval strategy is applicable without modification, because it does not require the (unsupported) relevance operator.

For data retrieval in very large databases, a Boolean retrieval model may still be adequate, because a database of several million documents usually contains documents matching exactly with a given query. Information retrieval tasks rely on the concept of relevance, in this case the Z39.50 relevance operator.

- The setup performs considerably better with shorter queries (Run2, title queries) than with longer queries (Run3, description queries). This is probably due to the fact that for shorter queries, more search term variants are employed to create the pool of query variants and the queries contain more terms different to the terms in OQ.
- The strategy with multiple queries seems to perform better than the strategy of constructing a single query (Run5 vs. Run4). This is evidence that multiple queries (and multiple scores for a document) allow a finer granularity for ranking documents.
- Using additional lexical information and background knowledge shows a small improvement in retrieval performance (Run5 vs. Run1). The results imply that sufficient background knowledge in MultiNet representation is not yet available to show the expected significant increase in retrieval performance.

Summarizing, the automated retrieval strategy combined with additional lexical information and background knowledge still offers a high potential to increase retrieval performance. Additional methods like pseudo-relevance feedback or other means to produce query variants (such as omitting or adding search terms) have not yet been explored in combination with this approach.

6   Conclusions and Future Work

The experiments described in this paper show automated information retrieval strategies providing significant increase in both recall and precision, compared to Boolean queries for data retrieval. The experimental setup was constrained by technical limitations of library databases to permit a practical application of the same setup. Aiming at multiple heterogeneous databases the indexing or matching processes of a database cannot be changed as easily and cheaply as changing the interface software or the retrieval strategy.

Future research involves creating a database interface for which queries and documents are analyzed and transformed into semantic representations using NLP techniques. Finding matching documents then takes place on the level of meaning and knowledge representation. Some of the ideas presented here will be integrated into and implemented for the successor project of the NLI-Z39.50.

References

1. Avi Arampatzis, Theo P. van der Weide, Patrick van Bommel, and Cornelius H. A. Koster. Linguistically Motivated Information Retrieval. In Allen Kent, editor, *Encyclopedia of Library and Information Science*, volume 69. Marcel Decker, New York, 2000.

2. R. Harald Baayen, Richard Piepenbrock, and Leon Gulikers. *The CELEX Lexical Database. Release 2 (CD-ROM)*. Linguistic Data Consortium, University of Pennsylvania, Philadelphia, Pennsylvania, 1995.

3. Sebastian Hammer, Adam Dickmeiss, Heikki Levanto, and Mike Taylor. *Zebra – User's Guide and Reference*. Index Data Aps, Ryesgade 3, Kopenhagen, 1995–2003.

4. Sven Hartrumpf. *Hybrid Disambiguation in Natural Language Analysis*. PhD thesis, Fern-Universität Hagen, Fachbereich Informatik, Hagen, Germany, 2002.

5. Sven Hartrumpf, Hermann Helbig, and Rainer Osswald. The semantically based computer lexicon HaGenLex – Structure and technological environment. *Traitement automatique des langues*, 44(2), 2003.

6. Hermann Helbig. *Die semantische Struktur natürlicher Sprache: Wissensrepräsentation mit MultiNet*. Springer, Berlin, 2001.

7. Hermann Helbig and Sven Hartrumpf. Word class functions for syntactic-semantic analysis. In *Proceedings of the 2nd International Conference on Recent Advances in Natural Language Processing (RANLP'97)*, pages 312–317, Tzigov Chark, Bulgaria, 1997.

8. Michael Kluck and Fredric C. Gey. The domain-specific task of CLEF — specific evaluation strategies in cross-language information retrieval. In Carol Peters, editor, *Cross-Language Information Retrieval and Evaluation. Workshop of the Cross-Language Information Evaluation Forum (CLEF 2000)*, volume 2069 of *LNCS*, pages 48–56, Berlin, 2001. Springer.

9. Claudia Kunze and Andreas Wagner. Anwendungsperspektiven des GermaNet, eines lexikalisch-semantischen Netzes für das Deutsche. In Ingrid Lemberg, Bernhard Schröder, and Angelika Storrer, editors, *Chancen und Perspektiven computergestützter Lexikographie*, volume 107 of *Lexicographica Series Maior*, pages 229–246. Niemeyer, Tübingen, 2001.

10. Johannes Leveling and Hermann Helbig. A robust natural language interface for access to bibliographic databases. In Nagib Callaos, Maurice Margenstern, and Belkis Sanchez, editors, *Proceedings of the 6th World Multiconference on Systemics, Cybernetics and Informatics (SCI 2002)*, volume XI, pages 133–138, Orlando, Florida, 2002. International Institute of Informatics and Systemics (IIIS).

11. Z39.50 Maintenance Agency (Library of Congress). *Information Retrieval (Z39.50): Application Service Definition and Protocol Specification for Open Systems Interconnection, ANSI/NISO Z39.50-1995 (version 3).* NISO Press, Bethesda, MD, 1995.
12. Justin Zobel and Alistair Moffat. Exploring the similarity space. *SIGIR Forum*, 32(1):18–34, 1998.

The CLEF 2003 Interactive Track

Douglas W. Oard[1] and Julio Gonzalo[2]

[1] College of Information Studies and Institute for Advanced Computer Studies,
University of Maryland, College Park MD 20740, USA
oard@umd.edu
[2] Departamento de Lenguajes y Sistemas Informáticos,
Universidad Nacional de Educación a Distancia,
E.T.S.I Industriales, Ciudad Universitaria s/n, 28040 Madrid, Spain
julio@lsi.uned.es

Abstract. The CLEF 2003 Interactive Track (iCLEF) was the third
year of a shared experiment design to compare strategies for cross-
language search assistance. Two kinds of experiments were performed: a)
experiments in *Cross-Language Document Selection*, where the user task
is to scan a ranked list of documents written in a foreign language, selecting those which seem relevant to a given query. The aim here is to compare different translation strategies for an "indicative" purpose; and b)
Full Cross-Language Search experiments, where the user task is to maximize the number of relevant documents that can be found in a foreign-
language collection with the help of an end-to-end cross-language search
system. Participating teams could choose to focus on any aspects of the
search task (e.g., query formulation, query translation and/or relevance
feedback). This paper describes the shared experiment design and briefly
summarizes the experiments run by the five teams that participated.

1 Introduction

A Cross-Language Information Retrieval (CLIR) system, as that term is typically
used, takes a query in some natural language and finds documents written in one
or more other languages. From a user's perspective, that is only one component of
a system to help a user search foreign-language collections and recognize relevant
documents. We generally refer to this situated task as *Multilingual Information
Access*. The Cross-Language Evaluation Forum interactive track (iCLEF) in
2003 was the third occasion on which a community of researchers have used a
shared experiment designed to compare strategies providing interactive support
for the Multilingual Information Access process. As was the case in 2002, iCLEF
2003 included two tasks from which participating teams could select:

- Experiments in Cross-Language Document Selection, where the user task is
  asked to scan a ranked list of documents that are written in a foreign language using some form of automated translation assistance, selecting those
  which seem to them to be relevant to a given topic. The aim here is to compare the degree to which different translation strategies are able to support
  the document selection process.

C. Peters et al. (Eds.): CLEF 2003, LNCS 3237, pp. 425–434, 2004.

- Full Cross-Language Search experiments, where the user is asked to to find as many relevant documents as possible with the help of a complete interactive CLIR system.

Seven teams registered for the track, from which five submissions were received. In Section 2 we describe the shared experiment design in detail, and in Section 3 we enumerate the participants and describe the hypotheses that they sought to test. Section 4 briefly recaps the official results; fuller analysis of these results can be found in each team's paper. Finally, in Section 5 we make some observations about this year's track and briefly discuss the prospects for the future of iCLEF.

2   Experiment Design

The basic design for an iCLEF 2003 experiment consists of:

- Two systems to be compared, one of which is usually intended as a reference system;
- A set of searchers, in groups of 8;
- A set of 8 topic descriptions, written in a language in which the searchers are fluent;
- A document collection in a different language (usually one in which the searchers lack language skills);
- A standardized procedure to be followed in every search session;
- A presentation order (i.e., a list of user/topic/system combinations which defines every search session and their relative order); and
- A set of evaluation measures for every search session and for the overall experiment, to permit comparison between systems.

Compared to iCLEF 2002, the main changes are the increase in the number of topics seen by each searcher from four to eight, the increase in the minimum number of searchers from four to eight, and (in order to keep the experiment duration reasonable) the decrease in the time per search from 20 minutes to 10. These changes reflect lessons learned in 2003, where statistical significance testing offered only a limited degree of insight with more limited numbers of topics and searchers. In the remainder of this section, we describe these aspects in detail.

2.1   Topics

Topics for iCLEF 2003 were selected from those used for evaluation of fully automated ranked retrieval systems in the CLEF 2002 evaluation campaign. The main reason that we selected a previous year's topics was that it offered insight into the number of relevant documents per topic and language, something that could not be guaranteed in advance with fresh CLEF 2003 topics.

The criteria for topic selection were:

– Select only broad (i.e., multi-faceted) topics.
– Select topics that had at least a few relevant documents in every document language, according to CLEF 2002 assessments.
– Discard topics that are too easy (for instance, when the presence of a proper noun is always correlated with relevance) or too difficult (for instance, when the accuracy of relevance judgments would depend on the order in which documents were assessed).

These are the English titles and descriptions of the selected topics (description fields were also available, but are not shown here for space reasons):

```
<top>
<num> C100 </num>
<iCLEF> 1 </iCLEF>
<EN-title> The Ames espionage case </EN-title>
<EN-desc> Find documents that show the impact of the Ames
espionage case on U.S.-Russian relations. </EN-desc>
</top>

<top>
<num> C106 </num>
<iCLEF> 2 </iCLEF>
<EN-title> European car industry </EN-title>
<EN-desc> Find documents which report about the situation in the
European car industry regarding the fall in sales (sales crisis)
and possible countermeasures. </EN-desc>
</top>

<top>
<num> C109 </num>
<iCLEF> 3 </iCLEF>
<EN-title> Computer Security </EN-title>
<EN-desc> What is the status of computer security in regard to
networked access? </EN-desc>
</top>

<top>
<num> C111 </num>
<iCLEF> 4 </iCLEF>
<EN-title> Computer Animation </EN-title>
<EN-desc> Find discussions of the impact of computer animation
on the film industry. </EN-desc>
</top>
```

```
<top>
<num> C120 </num>
<iCLEF> 5 </iCLEF>
<EN-title> Edouard Balladur </EN-title>
<EN-desc> What is the importance for the European Union of the
economic policies of Edouard Balladur? </EN-desc>
</top>

<top>
<num> C123 </num>
<iCLEF> 6 </iCLEF>
<EN-title> Marriage Jackson-Presley </EN-title>
<EN-desc> Find documents that report on the presumed marriage
of Michael Jackson with Lisa Marie Presley or on their
separation. </EN-desc>
</top>

<top>
<num> C133 </num>
<iCLEF> 7 </iCLEF>
<EN-title> German Armed Forces Out-of-area </EN-title>
<EN-desc> Find documents which report on political and juridical
decisions on out-of-area uses of the Armed Forces of
Germany. </EN-desc>
</top>

<top>
<num> C139 </num>
<iCLEF> 8 </iCLEF>
<EN-title> EU fishing quotas </EN-title>
<EN-desc> Find information about fishing quotas in the EU.
</EN-desc>
</top>
```

We did not impose any restriction on the topic language; participating teams could pick any topic language provided by CLEF, or could prepare their own manual translations into any additional language that would be appropriate for their searcher population.

2.2   Document Collection

We allowed participants to search any CLEF document collection (Dutch, English, French, German, Italian, Spanish, Finnish or Swedish). We provided standard Machine Translations of the Spanish collection (into English) and of the English collection (into Spanish) for use by teams that found those language pairs convenient, in each case using Systran Professional 3.0.

2.3   Search Procedure

For teams that chose the full (end-to-end) search task, searchers were given a topic description written in a language that they could understand and asked to use one of the two systems to find as many relevant documents as possible in the foreign-language document collection. Searchers were instructed to favor precision rather than recall by asking them to envision a situation in which they might need to pay for a high-quality professional translation of the documents that they selected, but that they wished to avoid paying for translation of irrelevant documents.

The searchers were asked to answer some questions at specific points during their session:

- Before the experiment, about computer/searching experience and attitudes, and their language skills.
- After completing the search for each topic (one per topic).
- After completing the use of each system (one per system).
- After the experiment, comparing the two systems and soliciting and general feedback on the experiment design.

Every searcher performed eight searches, half with one system, and then half with the other. Each search was limited to 10 minutes. The overall time required for one session was approximately three hours, including initial training with both systems, eight 10-minute searches, all questionnaires, and two breaks (one following training, one between systems).

For teams that chose to focus solely on document selection, the experiment design was similar, but searchers were asked only to scan a frozen list of documents (returned by for some standard query by some automatic system) and select the ones that were relevant to the topic description from which the query had been generated.

2.4   Searcher/Topic/System Combinations

The presentation order for topics, searchers and systems was standardized to facilitate comparison between systems. We chose an order that was counterbalanced in a way that sought to minimize user/system and topic/system interactions when examining averages. We adopted a Latin square design similar to that used in previous iCLEF evaluations. The presentation order for topics was varied systematically, with participants that saw the same topic-system combination seeing those topics in a different order. An eight-participant presentation order matrix is shown in Table 1. Additional participants could be added in groups of 8, with the same matrix being reused as needed.

2.5   Evaluation

In this section we describe the common evaluation measure used by all teams, and the data that was available to individual teams to support additional evaluation activities. These measures are identical to iCLEF 2002.

Table 1. Presentation order for topics, and association of topics with systems

Searcher	Block 1	Block 2
1	System A: 1,4,3,2	System B: 5,8,7,6
2	System B: 2,3,4,1	System A: 6,7,8,5
3	System B: 1,4,3,2	System A: 5,8,7,6
4	System A: 2,3,4,1	System B: 6,7,8,5
5	System A: 7,6,1,4	System B: 3,2,5,8
6	System B: 8,5,2,3	System A: 4,1,6,7
7	System B: 7,6,1,4	System A: 3,2,5,8
8	System A: 8,5,2,3	System B: 4,1,6,7

Data Collection. For every search (i.e., searcher/topic/system combination), two types of data were collected:

- The set of documents selected as relevant by the searcher. Optional attributes are the *duration* of the assessment process, the *confidence* in the assessment, and judgment values other than "relevant" (such as "somewhat relevant," "not relevant," or "viewed but not judged."
- The ranked lists of document identifiers created by the ranked retrieval system. One list was submitted by teams focusing on document selection; teams focused on query formulation and reformulation were asked to submit one ranked list for every query refinement iteration.

Official Evaluation Measure. The set of documents selected as relevant was used to produce the official iCLEF measure, an unbalanced version of van Rijsbergen's F measure that we called F_α:

$$F_\alpha = \frac{1}{\alpha/P + (1-\alpha)/R}$$

where P is precision and R is recall [1]. Values of α above 0.5 emphasize precision, values below 0.5 emphasize recall [2]. As in prior years, $\alpha = 0.8$ was chosen, modeling the case in which missing some relevant documents would be less objectionable than finding too many documents that, after perhaps paying for professional translations, turn out not to be relevant.

The comparison of average $F_{\alpha=0.8}$ measures across the two systems being tested provides a first order characterization of the effect of system differences on search effectiveness, but participating teams are encouraged to augment this comparison with additional measures based on the analysis of all available data (ranked lists for each iteration, assessment duration, assessment confidence, questionnaire responses, observational notes, statistical significance tests, etc.).

Relevance Assessments. We provided relevance assessments by native speakers of the document languages for at least:

- All documents for which judgments were made by searchers (to support reliable computation of $F_{\alpha=0.8}$).

- The top 20 documents in every ranked list produced during a search iteration with an end-to-end search system.

All iCLEF 2003 relevance judgments were done by CLEF assessors immediately after assessing the CLEF 2003 pools. Only documents that had not been previously assessed in CLEF 2002 were specifically judged for iCLEF 2003.

3   Participants

Seven teams expressed interest in participating, and five teams submitted experiment results: University of Alicante (Spain), SICS (Sweden), University of Maryland (UMD, USA), a team formed jointly by BBN Technologies and the University of Maryland (BBN/UMD, USA) and UNED (Spain). Three groups focused on document selection strategies:

- **SICS** (Sweden). The SICS iCLEF experiments were, as last year, centered on trying to measure differences between assessing texts in one's native language and one in which the searcher has a near-native competence. The hypothesis being tested was whether intra-subject differences between native and near-native languages were significantly different; it seemed reasonable to expect that assessment would be slower and less reliable in a foreign language, even one in which the subject is fluent on a professional level. This year SICS used a system developed as part of the CLARITY project, components of which were also used in last year's iCLEF experiments. One of the salient features of the interface is a panel in which the user can store results from the assessment process. Some debriefing questions were added to last year's protocol to investigate the user's confidence in their judgments.
- **University of Alicante** (Spain) compared a query-oriented passage extraction system (presented at iCLEF 2002) with a new automatic extraction approach based on syntactic and semantic patterns based on the main verb of the sentence and its arguments. Thus, such patterns show only the basic information of each sentence. The language best known by the searchers was Spanish; the document language was English, a language in which the searchers self-reported passive language abilities (i.e, recognition, but not production). The goal of the experiment was to discern which of the approaches would best support rapid and accurate selection of relevant documents.
- **BBN Technologies/University of Maryland** (USA) compared the use of brief summaries constructed using automatic headline generation with the use of the first 40 words from each story as the summary. The document language was Spanish, for which the eight searchers self-reported little or no fluency. The searchers were fluent in English, so the standard Systran translations were used as a basis for both conditions. Headlines were automatically produced for each document by removing grammatical constituents from a parse tree of the lead sentence of a document until a length threshold was met. The hypothesis being tested was that headlines could

support more rapid assimilation of the topic of a document without adverse effects on accuracy.

The other two groups experimented with full cross-language searches:

- **University of Maryland** (USA). The focus of Maryland's full-system experiment was on query formulation and iterative query reformulation. The hypothesis was that providing greater insight into and control over the query reformulation process could improve the usability of a search system, yielding greater accuracy with less reformulation effort. Participants interacted with two systems. One system provided descriptions for the available translations and allowed control over which translations were used, The other system performed fully automatic query translation. The query language was English and the document language was Spanish; searchers self-reported little or no fluency in Spanish.
- **UNED** (Spain). The UNED experiment tested whether document summaries based on phrase translation (which UNED used in document selection experiments in 2001 and in query reformulation experiments in 2002) could also be used as the basis for a document translation approach to interactive cross-language searching. The phrase translation summaries contained only 30% as many words as the original documents, and could be generated two orders of magnitude faster than full machine translation. Users performed searches with two systems. In one, the system generated possibly relevant noun phrases in response to a query, the user picked some of those phrases for automatic translation, and the system then used the translated phrases to search the documents. The nature of the user interaction in the second system was the same, but instead of translating the selected noun phrases, the search was performed on the phrase translation summaries in the query language. Spanish was the query language and English was the document language. The hypothesis was that searching phrase translation summaries (which were needed in any case for display) could yield comparable search effectiveness to the approach based on query translation.

4   Results and Discussion

The available official results for the $F_{\alpha=0.8}$ measure are shown in Table 2.[1]

5   Conclusion

The iCLEF design evolved rapidly over the first two years of the track; this year's design included only evolutionary improvements over last year's. Growth in the number of participating teams now seems to be leveling off; five teams participated in 2002 and in 2003, although participation by a sixth team would have been likely if we had been able to provide ranked lists for use in the document

---

[1] Difficulties with log file analysis precluded quantitative evaluation of SICS results.

Table 2. Official iCLEF 2003 results

Group	Experiment Condition	$F_{\alpha=0.8}$
Experiments in Query formulation and refinement		
Maryland	automatic query translation	.20
Maryland	user-assisted query translation	.23
UNED	query translation	.29
UNED	(summarized) document translation	.29
Experiments in Document selection		
SICS	foreign language docs	
SICS	native language docs	
Alicante	passages	.45
Alicante	patterns	.44
BBN/UMD	First 40	.47
BBN/UMD	Hedge	.38

selection task a bit sooner. This, therefore seems like a good time to think about the future of iCLEF.

First, we should make the point that iCLEF is not, and never has been, the only venue for evaluation of interactive CLIR; several individual researchers have run well designed studies to explore one aspect or another of this topic. Rather, the unique strength of iCLEF is in the community that it draws together. Advancing the state of the art in interactive CLIR requires expertise in several areas, including information retrieval, computational linguistics, and human-computer interaction. Few research teams can draw on such a broad range of expertise, iCLEF includes two or more teams with interests in each. Moreover, as with other specialized tracks, iCLEF serves to enrich the dialog at CLEF by bringing in researchers with new perspectives that might not otherwise participate. The evaluation framework that we have evolved is indeed a useful and important contribution, but we expect that the greatest legacy of iCLEF will result from the discussions we have had and the ideas we have shared.

Where next for iCLEF? One possibility is to continue the process we have started. Our assessment process leverages the work already being done for CLEF, and it has the felicitous side effect of contributing additional relevance judgments that may be useful to those who are interested in studying the assessment process. Research teams around the world are now working on interactive CLIR, and iCLEF provides a natural venue in which they can report their results and share their ideas. After iCLEF 2002 we discussed some related tasks that we might also try; searching narrow (single-aspect) topics and interactive cross-language question answering were two of the ideas we considered. Ultimately, we decided that the community's best interests would be served by a year of relative stability in the evaluation design, allowing the participating research teams to build on their results from last year. But there is no reason why we should not explore these ideas, and others, again.

The future of iCLEF is, of course, to some extent bound up with the future of CLEF itself. Here, there are two countervailing forces to consider. iCLEF adds a valuable dimension to CLEF, but it also competes for resources with other good ideas. In a world with constrained resources, choices will need to be made. A spirit of exploration has been one of the hallmarks of CLEF, and we should not be afraid to explore radical ideas that may take us in interesting new directions. If cross-language question answering yields interesting results, then perhaps we might try an interactive task within the question-answering track. If cross-language caption-based image retrieval works well, why not interactive caption-based searches for images? If cross-language spoken document retrieval goes in interesting directions, perhaps interactive searching for foreign-language speech would be the next natural challenge. Ultimately, each of these tracks seeks to meet the needs of real users, so it is natural to expect that each will want to involves users in their research at some point. The interactive CLIR community is still relatively small, so we can not hope to go in all of these directions at once. But is is said that a journey of a thousand li (a measure of distance in ancient China) begins with a single step. Over the past three years, we have taken that step, and as a group we have achieved some interesting and important results. Now is the time to think about the next step.

Acknowledgments

We are indebted to many people that helped with organization of this iCLEF track: Fernando López wrote the evaluation scripts and maintained the Web site and distribution list, Martin Braschler created the assessment pools; Ellen Voorhees, and Djuna Franzén coordinated relevance assessments, and Jianqiang Wang provided Systran translations for English and Spanish collections. Finally, we also want to thank Carol Peters for her continued support and encouragement.

References

1. van Rijsbergen, C.J.: Information Retrieval. Second edn. Butterworths, London (1979)
2. Oard, D.: Evaluating cross-language information retrieval: Document selection. In Peters, C., ed.: Cross-Language Information Retrieval and Evaluation: Proceedings of CLEF 2000. Springer-Verlag Lecture Notes in Computer Science 2069 (2001)

iCLEF 2003 at Maryland: Translation Selection and Document Selection

Bonnie Dorr,* Daqing He, Jun Luo, Douglas W. Oard, Richard Schwartz,**
Jianqiang Wang, and David Zajic

Institute for Advanced Computer Studies,
University of Maryland, College Park, MD 20742, USA
{dorr, daqingd, jun, oard, wangjq, dmzajic}@umiacs.umd.edu
schwartz@bbn.com

Abstract. Maryland performed two sets of experiments for the 2003 Cross-Language Evaluation Forum's interactive track, one focused on interactive selection of appropriate translations for query terms, the second focused on interactive selection of relevant documents. Translation selection was supported using possible synonyms discovered through back translation and two techniques for generating KeyWord In Context (KWIC) examples of usage. The results indicate that searchers typically achieved a similar search effectiveness using fewer query iterations when interactive translation selection was available. For document selection, a complete extract of the first 40 words of each news story was compared to a compressed extract generated using an automated parse-and-trim approach that approximates one way in which people can produce headlines. The results indicate that compressed "headlines" result in faster assessment, but with a 20% relative reduction in the $F_{\alpha=0.8}$ search effectiveness measure.

1   Introduction

The goal of Cross-Language Information Retrieval (CLIR) is to help searchers find relevant documents even when their query terms are chosen from a language different from the language in which the document are written. For the Cross-Language Evaluation Forum's (CLEF) interactive track (iCLEF), we have been exploring the most challenging such case—when the searcher's knowledge of the document language is so limited that they would be unable to formulate queries or recognize relevant documents in that language. Our challenge is thus to provide searchers with translation tools that are tuned to the tasks that they must perform during an interactive search process: choosing query terms and recognizing relevant documents. For iCLEF 2003, we ran two sets of experiments, one focusing on each aspect of this challenge.

---

* Authors names in alphabetical order, affiliations as shown except as noted.
** BBN Technologies, 9861 Broken Land Parkway, Suite 156, Columbia, MD 21046.

C. Peters et al. (Eds.): CLEF 2003, LNCS 3237, pp. 435–449, 2004.

Although query formulation for CLIR might appear on the surface to be similar to query formulation in monolingual applications, the iterative nature of the interactive search process results in a difference that is of fundamental importance. When searching within the same language, searchers seek to choose terms that authors actually used in documents. That is clearly not possible when using query translation for CLIR; instead, searchers must choose query terms that the *system* will translate into terms that were used by authors. In CLIR, searchers interact with a translation system, and not (directly) with documents. We know much about how users interact with documents in an iterative search process, but we know comparatively little about how they interact with translation systems for this purpose. That was the focus of our first set of iCLEF experiments this year.

Document selection might initially seem to be a more straightforward task; here, we want to support the searcher's decisions about relevance with the best possible translations. But, again, the iterative nature of the search process complicates the question; for interactive searching, assessment speed can be as important as assessment accuracy. The reason for this is simple; longer assessment times would mean either fewer documents read or few iterations performed, both of which can adversely affect the effectiveness of a search process. We therefore need translations that can be assessed rapidly and accurately. That was the focus of our second set of iCLEF experiments this year.

The remainder of this paper is organized as follows. We first introduce the design of our query translation experiments, present our results, and draw some conclusions. We then do the same for our document selection experiments. Finally, we conclude with some ideas for future work that have been inspired by the experiments reported in this paper.

2   Query Translation Experiments

Ultimately, we are interested in learning whether a searcher's ability to interactively employ a CLIR system based on query translation can be improved by providing greater transparency for the query translation process. Our experiments last year for iCLEF 2002 demonstrated the utility of user-assisted query translation in an interactive CLIR system [4]. With user-assisted query translation function, a CLIR system provides an additional interaction opportunity where the searcher can optionally select (or remove) translations of individual query terms before and/or after viewing the retrieved documents. Our experiment results demonstrate that the average scores of $F_{\alpha=0.8}$ obtained from searches on a system with user-assisted query translation appeared better than that of a system without it. However, due to the small sample size (four searchers), we did not obtain statistical significance. In addition, we believe that the quality of the search also lies in the whole process of the search, rather than the search outcome alone. This motivated us to design an iCLEF 2003 experiment to explore the following questions:

1. What strategies do searchers apply when formulating their initial query, and when reformulating that query? Would the availability of a translation selection function lead searchers to adopt different strategies? Can we observe any relationship between subject knowledge, search experience, or other similar factors on the choice of strategies in each condition?
2. Is there a statistically significant difference in search effectiveness (as measured by $F_{\alpha=0.8}$) between searches performed using a system with user-assisted query translation and a system that lacks that capability? Formally, we sought to reject the null hypotheses that there is no difference between the $F_{\alpha=0.8}$ for the manual and automatic conditions that are defined below.

2.1   System Design

We used the Maryland Interactive Retrieval Advanced Cross-Language Engine (MIRACLE) for the query translation experiments reported in this paper. MIRACLE is an improved version of the CLIR system that we used for iCLEF 2002. MIRACLE has recently evolved rapidly during the DARPA Surprise Language Exercise, but at the time of our iCLEF experiments the basic architecture of the system and the layout of the user interface were quite similar to that of our iCLEF 2002 system (see Figure 1). The system supports two conditions, an "automatic" condition, with a design similar to that of present Web search engines, and a "manual" condition, in which the user can participate in the construction of a translated query.

MIRACLE uses the InQuery text retrieval system (version 3.1p1) from the University of Massachusetts to implement Pirkola's structured query technique (which has been shown to be relatively robust in the presence of unresolved translation ambiguity) [9]. For the automatic condition, Pirkola's method is applied over all known translations; for the manual condition, only selected translations are used. A backoff translation strategy is used when the term to be translated is not known; first the term is stemmed, if translation still fails then a stemmed version of the term list is also used. This serves to maximize the coverage of the bilingual term list [8].

Since we are interested in the case in which searchers have no useful knowledge of the document language, we must provide the user with some evidence about the meaning of each translation in the manual condition. Optimally, we would like to provide query-language definitions of each document language-term. Although dictionaries that contain such definitions do exist for some language pairs, they are relatively rare in print, and extremely rare in an accessible electronic form. Therefore, we present searchers with as many of the following three sources of evidence as can be constructed for each term:

The Document-Language Term. For languages in the same writing system, this can sometimes be informative, since some translations may be cognates or loan words that the searcher can recognize. For example, one Spanish translation of "ball" is "fiesta;" clearly that is the "party" sense of ball (as in "to attend a ball").

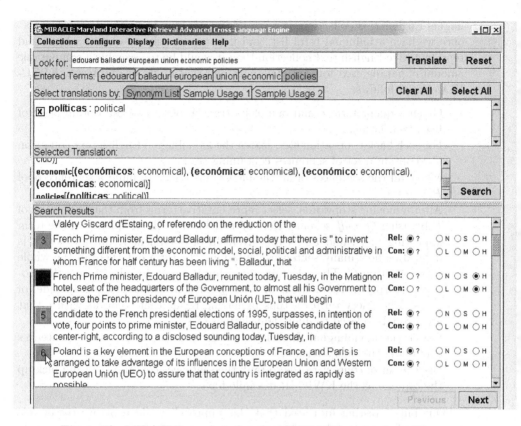

Fig. 1. The MIRACLE user interface for iCLEF 2003, manual condition

Possible Synonyms. Translations are cross-language synonyms, so round-trip translation can reveal useful synonyms. For example, one possible translation of "bank" into Spanish is "ribera." The following translations can be found for "ribera:" bank, shore, seashore, riverside, and waterfront. This leaves little question that "ribera" does not refer to a financial sense of "bank."

Examples of Usage. For iCLEF 2002, we found examples of usage (which we call "KeyWord in Context", or KWIC) in word-aligned parallel text. While examples found in this way are generally correct and often informative, the size and scope of available parallel text collections may not be sufficient to find examples for some terms in this way. We therefore added a second way of constructing KWIC examples of usage that we call KWIC-IR to our iCLEF 2003 system.

KWIC-IR. The searchers in iCLEF 2002 liked KWIC based on parallel text because it provided more context information than the possible synonyms that result from round-trip translation. We therefore sought to extend KWIC to additional cases using an approach based on round-trip translation and a monolingual English text collection. It is straightforward to obtain "back translations" once we have a bilingual term list, and it is much easier to obtain a large and representative English text collection than it would be to assemble a comparable amount of parallel text for every language pair that might be of interest. KWIC-IR works as follows:

- Given a query term e and one of its translations s, we can obtain a set of back translations;
- For each back translation bte_i, search the monolingual English text collection C to obtain a set of sentences containing bte_i.
- Merge all the sentences of all the back translations to build a sentence pool P;
- After removing stopwords, select representative terms from the sentence pool P by using $tf * idf$ scheme. Here tf is defined as the frequency of the term appearing in P; and idf is the inversion of document frequency, which is defined as how many sentences containing the term out there in the whole text collection C. The selection algorithm is tuned to select terms that co-occur sharply in the context of these back translations, (which include, of course, the query term e), thus preferring terms that co-occur with e that are strongly related to many translations of s;
- Search the monolingual English text collection to obtain a set of sentences containing the query term e;
- Use the set of context words to rank the sentences containing e, and pick up the top one as the KWIC-IR example for s.

Our initial testing indicated that this approach could generate reasonable examples of usage much of the time; our iCLEF 2003 experiments provided our first opportunity to try it in the context of an extrinsic (task-centered) evaluation.

2.2   Experiment Design

We followed the standard protocol for iCLEF 2003 experiments. Searchers were sequentially given eight topics (stated in English), four using the manual condition, and four using the automatic condition. Presentation order for topics and system was varied systematically across searchers as specified in the track guidelines. After an initial training session, they were given 10 minutes for each search to identify relevant documents using the radio buttons provided for that purpose in our user interface. The searchers were asked to emphasize precision over recall (by telling them that it was more important that the document that they selected be truly relevant than that they find every possible relevant document). We asked each searcher to fill out brief questionnaires before the first search (for demographic data), after each search, and after using each system. Each searcher used the same system at a different time, so we were able to observe each individually and make extensive observational notes. We also conducted a semi-structured interview (in which we tailored our questions based on our observations) after all searches were completed.

We conducted a small pilot study with a single searcher (umd00) to exercise our new system and refine our data collection procedures. Eight searchers (umd01-umd08) then performed the experiment using the eight-subject design specified in the track guidelines[1]. We submitted all eight runs (umd01-umd08) for use in forming relevance pools.

Resources. We chose English as the query language and Spanish as the document language. The Spanish document collection contained 215,738 news stores from EFE News Agency. We used the Spanish-to-English translations provided by the iCLEF organizers for construction of document surrogates and for viewing the full document translations. The translations were created by using Systran Professional 3.0.

We obtained our Spanish-English bilingual term list in our lab. It contains 24,278 words and was constructed from multiple sources [3]. We used the In-Query built-in Spanish stemmer to stem both the collection and the Spanish translations of the English queries. Our KWIC techniques (called "sample usages" in the MIRACLE system for easy understanding by the searchers) require parallel Spanish/English texts and a big monolingual English collection. We obtained the first one from the Foreign Broadcast Information Service (FBIS) TIDES data disk, release 2, and the second one from the TDT-4 collection English news part, which was collected and released by Linguistic Data Consortium (http://www.ldc.upenn.edu).

Measures. We computed the following measures in order to gain insight into search behavior and search results:

- $F_{\alpha=0.8}$, as defined in the track guidelines (with "somewhat relevant" documents treated as not relevant). We refer to this condition as "strict" relevance judgments. This value was computed at the end of each search session.
- $F_{\alpha=0.8}$, but with "somewhat relevant" documents treated as relevant. We refer to this condition as "loose" relevance judgments. This value was also computed for each session.
- The total number of query iterations for each search.

The F measure is an outcome measure; it cannot tell us what happened along the way. We therefore also used Camtasia Studio (www.techsmith.com) to record the searcher's activities during each session.

2.3   Results

Searcher Characteristics. There were four female and four male searchers. Otherwise, the searcher population was relatively homogeneous. Specifically, our searchers were:

Educated. Six of the eight searchers were either enrolled in a Masters program or had already earned at least a masters degree. The remaining two were

---

[1] http://terral.lsi.uned.es/iCLEF/2003/guidelines.html

one undergraduate student that was near graduation and one person with a Bachelors degree.

Mature. The average age over all eight searchers was 33, with the youngest of 21 and the oldest of 45.

Experienced Searchers. Five of the eight searchers held degrees in library science. The searchers reported an average of about 7 years of on-line searching experience, with a minimum of 3 years and maximum of 10 years. All searchers reported extensive experience with Web search services, and all reported at least some experience searching computerized library catalogs (ranging from "some" to "a great deal"). Seven of the eight reported that they search at least once or twice a day.

Inexperienced with Machine Translation. Seven of the eight searchers reported never having, or having only some, experience with any machine translation software or free Web translation services. The remaining one reported having more than "some experience" with machine translation software or services.

Not Previous Study Participants. None of the eight subjects had previously participated in a TREC or iCLEF study.

Native English Speakers. All eight searchers were native speakers of English.

Not Skilled in Spanish. Five of the eight searchers reported no reading skills in Spanish at all. Another three reported poor reading skills in Spanish.

Results for Relevance Judgments. Our official results are based on the $F_{\alpha=0.8}$ values averaged over all searchers that ran each condition. We use what we call *strict relevance*, i.e., treating "somewhat relevant" as "irrelevant" in the calculation of precision and recall. We found that the manual and automatic conditions achieved very nearly the same value for this measure when averaged over all eight topics (0.2272 and 0.2014, respectively). For comparison, we recomputed the same results with *loose relevance*, i.e., treating "somewhat relevant" as "relevant" in the calculation. Again, the difference in average values for $F_{\alpha=0.8}$ across all eight topics between the two conditions is small (0.3031 for manual, 0.2850 for automatic). According to Wilcoxon sign-rank test, neither of the differences is statistically significant.

Looking at the results by topic (see Figure 2), only Topic 5 exhibits a clear difference between the $F_{\alpha=0.8}$ values for the manual and automatic conditions, and only with strict relevance judgments. Topic 5 is about the economic policies of the French politician Edouard Balladur. It was neither the topic that the searchers felt was most difficult, nor the topic that they felt was easiest. We do not presently have an explanation for this effect. The reason that there is no difference on Topic 4 is that all the searchers did not find any official relevant document in both conditions, although they marked several. One possible explanation is that there are only 3 official relevant documents in the whole collection of 215,738 documents.

Similar values of $F_{\alpha=0.8}$ can mask offsetting differences in precision and recall, so we also examined precision and recall separately. As Figure 3 illustrates, precision seems to be more sensitive to the manual/automatic distinction than

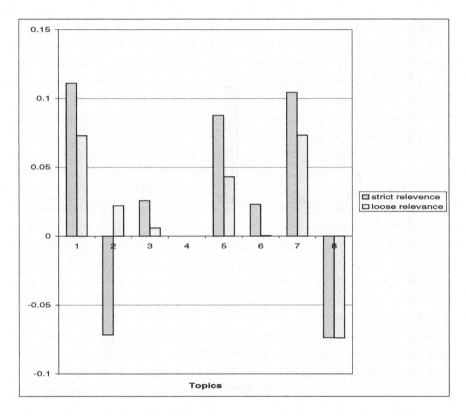

Fig. 2. Absolute improvement in $F_{\alpha=0.8}$ from the manual condition. Bars above the x axis favor the manual condition, below favor the automatic condition. Loose judgments treat "somewhat relevant" as relevant

recall, with the precision for Topic 5 strongly favoring the manual condition and the precision for Topic 8 (EU fishing quotas) strongly favoring the automatic condition. On the other hand, recall is somewhat sensitive to the manual/automatic distinction for Topics 1 (The Ames espionage case) and 7 (German Armed Forces out-of-area), in both cases favoring the manual condition. Since we would normally expect recall and precision to change in opposite directions, Topics 5 and 8 (which clearly lack this effect) and, to some degree, Topic 7, deserve further exploration.

One interesting comparison we can draw is between this year's results and those from last year. Although there is language difference (Spanish vs German), topic difference (one of this year's topic only has 3 relevant documents (Topic 4), another has 181 relevant documents (Topic 8)), and some small system differences, it is interesting to note that last year's searchers achieved $F_{\alpha=0.8} = 0.4995$ for the manual condition, and 0.3371 for the automatic condition. The manual condition thus achieved a 48% improvement in $F_{\alpha=0.8}$ over the automatic condition in last year's experiment, but we only saw a 13% improvement this year.

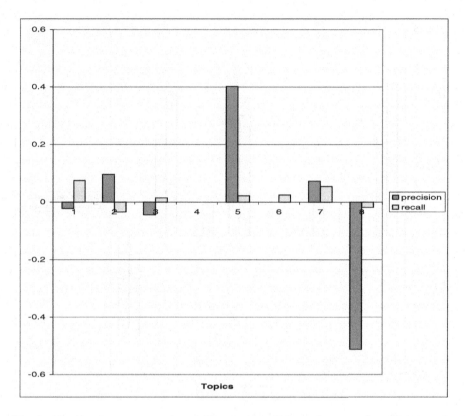

Fig. 3. Absolute improvement in precision and recall from the manual condition, strict judgement. Bars above the x axis favor the manual condition, below favor the automatic condition

Last year, searchers were allowed 20 minutes for each topic; this year they were allowed only 10. Perhaps user-assisted query translation is of greater value later in the search process, after some of the more obvious ways of formulating the query have already been tried.

Query Iteration Analysis. We obtained the number of iterations for each search session through log file analysis. On average, searches in the manual condition exhibited fewer query iterations than searches in the automatic condition (3.72 vs 5.22). Looking at individual topics, topic 4 (computer animation) has the largest average number of iterations (8.25) for the automatic condition, followed by topics 1 (5.75) and 7 (5.50), whereas topic 5 has the largest average number of iterations (6) in the manual condition, followed by topics 3 (4.5) and 8 (4.25).

Subjective Assessment. We analyzed questionnaire data and interview responses in an effort to understand how participants employed the systems and

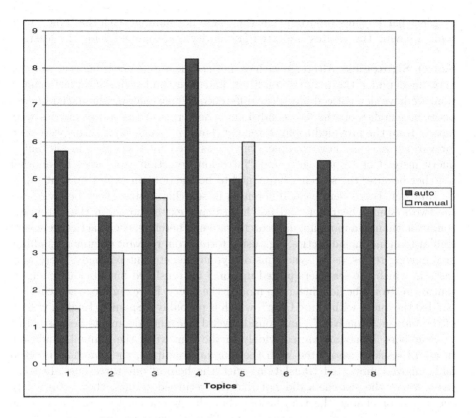

Fig. 4. Average number of query iterations, by topic

to better understand their impressions about the systems. The searchers reported that the manual and automatic conditions were equally easy to search with, but because the manual condition was under their control, they had a more satisfying overall experience under this condition.

When talking about the reasons for difficulty finding relevant documents, among the searchers using the manual condition, "unfamiliar topics" and "quality of the translation" were the most often mentioned (4 times each). The same general pattern was observed in the responses of searchers using the automatic condition: three mentions of "translation quality," two mentions of "unfamiliar topics," and two mentions of "no relevant documents returned."

For questions unique to the manual condition, all of the searchers reported that they could (somewhat or very) confidently select/remove translations, and all of them felt that it was (somewhat or very) useful to have the ability to modify the system's translation selections. However, there was no clear preference among the available indications of the meaning of each translation. Three searchers reported that the synonym list was the most useful cue, while two searchers found the examples of usage to be the most useful (three were not sure).

Most participants reported that they were not familiar with the topics, with topic 3 having the greatest reported familiarity and topic 8 having the least.

Search Strategies. Although we have noticed clear differences between searches performed under the manual condition and than under the automatic condition, we have not noticed any clear difference in constructing the initial queries between searches on the two conditions. The terms of the initial queries were mostly from the provided topic statement, however, some extra terms were used for various reasons. For example, "spy" was used by a searcher in the initial query instead of "espionage", and "intrusion detection" was used by another searcher because the searcher happened to be the domain expert on that topic.

However, there were clear differences in searchers' subsequent behaviors on the two systems. Searchers did not have many extra choices in the automatic condition than in a monolingual search system. Therefore, their tactics were very similar to monolingual tactics, e.g., using terms from relevant documents, adding or removing terms, using synonyms or hyponyms, etc. Interestingly, there were cases in which the searchers picked up some untranslated but obviously important terms from the documents to modify the query. For example, a searcher expanded the query with "king Leon", which is probably a Spanish/English variant of the phrase "Lion King", and found several relevant documents because of it.

Searchers' behaviors varied widely in the context of the manual condition. In all 12 sessions associated with the manual condition, the searchers checked and removed unwanted translations with the help of our three cues. In some cases where the searchers did not like the returned results, they returned to check and/or change the translations, but this happened less frequently than query changes. There were also cases in which searchers returned to change the queries after looking at the translations. In particular, one subject searched only once for topic 4 (computer animation) during the entire 10-minute session, but the searcher issued four different queries, of which the first three were changed based on only looking at translations. Another interesting observation is that translations provide an extra resource for generating query terms. For example, after getting frustrated with the query term "European Union" and its variants, a searcher decided to select one Spanish translation from each word of the term (i.e. "europeo" for european and "sindicato" for union) and put them directly into the query. This subject was able to mark two relevant documents based on this query.

While user-assisted translation selection has proved useful, there are a number of limitations. In particular, translation selection is only one step in the overall CLIR process. It provides an extra interaction anchor that searchers found to be helpful. However, its effect is not as great as query reformulation. We have found many more cases of query reformulation than translation re-selection. In addition, our use of cues to assist searchers limited the usefulness of user-assisted translation selection, to some degree, because our cues do not always provide the *best* explanations. Our goal was to give three different cues which provide *good* explanations—with the hope that the combination of these three would cover a wide range of situations. In practice, however, the searchers were sometimes confused by contradictory explanations and, as a result, they frequently decided to stick to one cue and ignore the other two.

3   Document Selection Experiments

In addition to the above investigation of the searcher's ability to choose queries using different techniques, we also ran an experiment to determine the user's ability to recognize relevant documents using different techniques. In particular, we compared the searcher's results using two different approaches to presenting document surrogates: (1) a complete extract of the first 40 (translated) words of each news story (2) a compressed extract generated using an automated parse-and-trim approach that approximates one way in which people can produce headlines. This section describes the parse-and-trim approach to headline generation and presents our results.

3.1   Parse-and-Trim Headline Generation

Headline generation is a form of text summarization in which the summarization is required to be informative and extremely short, and to mimic the condensed language features of newspaper headlines. Informative summaries answer the questions "what happened in this document?" or "what is claimed in this document?," rather than the question "what is this document about?"

Our headline generation system, *Hedge Trimmer*, constructs headlines automatically by selecting high-content words from the *lead* sentence of the document[2]. It does this by iteratively removing grammatical constituents from a parse of the lead sentence until a length threshold has been met. The parses are created by the BBN SIFT parser. As described in [6] the BBN SIFT parser builds augmented parse trees according to a process similar to that described in [2]. The BBN SIFT parser has been used successfully for the task of information extraction in the SIFT system [7].

The approach taken by Hedge Trimmer is most similar to that of [5], where a single sentence is shortened using statistical compression. However, Hedge Trimmer uses linguistically motivated heuristics for shortening the sentence. There is no statistical model, so prior training on a large corpus of stories and headlines is not required.

The input to Hedge Trimmer is a story. The first sentence of the story is passed through the BBN SIFT parser. The parse-tree result serves as input to a linguistically motivated module that selects story words to form headlines based on insights gained from observations of human-constructed headlines.

At present, Hedge Trimmer is applied to the problem of cross-language headline generation by translating the first sentence of a story into English and running the Hedge Trimmer process on the resulting translation.

---

[2] We currently take the first sentence to be the lead sentence of the document; but further investigation is currently underway for selecting the most appropriate lead sentence.

3.2   Use of Hedge Trimmer in iCLEF

We used Hedge Trimmer as the basis of forming document surrogates in the Interactive track for the 2003 Cross-Language Evaluation Forum. In this experiment two methods were used to produce English surrogates for Spanish documents. Surrogate A ("F40") consisted of the first 40 words of a machine translation of the document. Surrogate B ("HT") was a headline constructed by Hedge Trimmer from the machine translation of the first sentence. Eight subjects were shown surrogates for the results of IR searches on eight topics. The translations and search results were provided by iCLEF to all participants.

Each search result consisted of 50 documents. For each topic, the subjects were shown a description of the topic and surrogates for the 50 documents. The subjects were asked to judge whether the document was highly relevant, somewhat relevant or not relevant to the topic and whether they were highly confident, somewhat confident or not confident in their relevance judgment. The order of topics, and whether the subject saw F40 or HT for a particular topic was varied according to the Latin Square provided by iCLEF as part of the standard experiment design.

Our goal was to show that the two surrogates had close recall and precision, but that HT took the subjects less time to perform the task. Subjects were able to complete 1189 judgments in a total of 290:34 minutes with F40, while they completed 1388 judgments in 272:37 minutes with HT. That is, using F40 subjects made 4.09 judgments per minute, while with HT they made 5.09 judgments per minute. However the results of the experiment showed that over 32 searches F40 had an average precision of 0.5939, average recall of 0.3769 and average $F_{\alpha=0.8}$ of 0.4737, while HT had average precision of 0.4883, average recall of 0.2805 and average $F_{\alpha=0.8}$ 0.3798.

Inter-annotator agreement did not differ much between the two systems. We used Cohen's κ [1] to measure the pairwise inter-annotator agreement. κ is 0 when the agreement between annotators is what would be expected by chance, and is 1 when there is perfect agreement. Due to the experiment design, it was not possible to calculate system-specific inter-annotator agreement for each pair of annotators because some pairs of annotators never used the same surrogate for judging the same documents. The average overall κ score was for those cases in which subjects did see the same surrogate for the same document was 0.2455, while the average pairwise κ score for F40 was 0.2601 and the average pairwise κ score for HT was 0.2704.

After the subjects completed judging the documents for a topic, they were asked the following questions:

1. Were you familiar with this topic before the search?
2. Was it easy to guess what the document was about based on the surrogate?
3. Was it easy to make relevance judgments for this topic?
4. Do you have confidence in your judgments for this topic?

The subjects answered each question by selecting a number from 1 to 5, where 1 meant "not at all", 3 meant "somewhat" and 5 meant "extremely." The responses are shown in Table 1.

Table 1. Average Question Responses by System

	F40	HT
Question 1	2.09	1.97
Question 2	3.65	2.91
Question 3	3.75	3.28
Question 4	3.78	3.13

We do not take this result necessarily to mean that informative headlines are worse surrogates than the first forty words. It is likely that the headlines used in HT were not good enough headlines to make a conclusion about informative summaries in general. Also, the average length of the headlines used in HT was much shorter than forty words, giving F40 the advantage of including more topic information.

4   Conclusion and Future Work

We focused on testing the effectiveness of user-assisted translation selection in interactive CLIR application, and observing different search strategies/tactics that the searchers could used in their interaction with a CLIR system with user-assisted translation selection feature. Our analysis suggests the usefulness of the approach, and the diversity of tactics the searchers adapted to take advantage of the extra interaction opportunity provided by user-assisted translation selection. However, the effectiveness of the approach is dependent on the characteristics of the topic, the time pressure, and the quality of the cues. Further development of user-assisted translation selection will be on 1) finishing analyzing searchers search behaviors, and design better evaluation measures; 2) designing an easy-obtained and robust cue that can provide best explanation all the time.

In addition, we focused on the tasks of determining document relevance. Although the HT system shows some promise for this task, the results indicate that the system has not yet reached a point where better results are consistently obtained. Continued development on headline generation will focus on improving the quality of the outputs that are generated. In particular, the following improvements are planned for headline generation: (1) Use of an n-gram language model for selecting the best translation surrogate produced by the system; (2) Better selection of the window of words from the article from which the headline should be chosen; (3) Use of topic detection to identify words that should not be deleted. Moreover, one of our next steps is to use HT in the context of summarization of broadcast news. Experiments will compare how well headlines support human performance on an extrinsic task with respecto topic lists, sentence extraction, first-N-words, and other summarization approaches.

Acknowledgments

The authors would like to thank Julio Gonzalo and Fernando López-Ostenero for their tireless efforts to coordinate iCLEF, Nizar Habash for providing us theSpanish-English bilingual termlist, and Michael Nossal for developing the earlier version of the Miracle system. This work has been supported in part by DARPA cooperative agreements N660010028910 and BBNT Contract 9500004957.

References

1. Cohen, J.: A coefficient of agreement for nominal scales. Educational and Psychological Measures, **20** (1960) 37–46
2. Collins, M.: Three generative lexicalised models for statistical parsing. Proceedings of the 35th ACL (1997)
3. Habash, N. Y.:. Generation-heavy Hybrid Machine Translation. PhD thesis, Department of Computer Science, University of Maryland at College Park (2003)
4. He, D., Wang, J., Oard, D. W., Nossal, M.: Comparing user-assisted and Automatic Query Translation. In C. Peters, M. Braschler, J. Gonzalo and M. Kluck (eds): Advances in Cross-Language Information Retrieval. CLEF 2002 workshop. Revised papers. LNCS 2785 Springer (2003).
5. Knight, K., Marcu, D.: Statistics-based summarization step one; sentence compression. Proceedings of AAAI-2001 (2001)
6. Miller, S., Crystal, M., Fox, H., Ramshaw, L., Schwartz, R., Stone, R., Weischedel, R.: Algorithms that Learn to Extract Information; BBN: Description of the SIFT System as Used for MUC-7. Proceedings of the MUC-7 (1998)
7. Miller, S., Ramshaw, L., Fox, H., Weischedel, R.: A novel use of statistical parsing to extract information from text. Proceedings of the 1st Meeting of the North Amererican Chapter of the ACL, Seattle, WA (2000) 226–233
8. Oard, D. W., Levow, G., Cabezas, C.: CLEF Experiments at Maryland: Statistical Stemming and backoff translation. Peters, C. editor, Cross-Language Information Retrieval and Evaluation: Workshop of Cross-Language Evaluation Forum, CLEF 2000, Lisbon, Portugal (2000) 176-187
9. Pirkola, A.: The Effects of Query Structure and Dictionary Setups in Dictionary-Based Cross-Language Information Retrieval. Proceedings of the 21st Annual International ACM SIGIR Conference on Research and Development in Information Retrieval, Melbourne, Australia (1998)

UNED at iCLEF 2003: Searching Cross-Language Summaries

Fernando López-Ostenero, Julio Gonzalo, and Felisa Verdejo

Departamento de Lenguajes y Sistemas Informáticos,
Universidad Nacional de Educación a Distancia (UNED),
c/ Juan del Rosal, 16, Ciudad Universitaria, 28040 Madrid - Spain
{flopez,julio,felisa}@lsi.uned.es

Abstract. The UNED phrase-based cross-language summaries were first introduced at iCLEF 2001 as a translation strategy which permitted faster document selection with roughly the same accuracy than full Machine Translation. For our iCLEF 2003 participation, we tested the validity of our summaries as cross-language indexes for the retrieval stage of the interactive search process. We compared a reference system that performs query translation (and then retrieves target-language documents) with a system that directly retrieves cross-language summaries with the source-language query. The performance of both systems is very similar, confirming that UNED summaries are viable for cross-language indexing. This approach is trivially scalable to more than one target language, opening an interesting path for truly multilingual search assistance.

1 Introduction

For Cross-Language Information Retrieval (CLIR) purposes, query translation is normally preferred to document translation due to the high computational costs of performing Machine Translation (MT) on an entire document collection. However, document translation has, at least, two clear advantages over query translation: first, text can be translated more accurately, because there is more context; and second, merging of ranked results from different target languages is not necessary, because there is only one retrieval rank in the user's language. Unfortunately, the increase in computational costs (compared to query translation) is too dramatic for document translation to become a mainstream approach.

Nevertheless, from an interactive point of view, document translation has additional advantages:

– For the user of a CLIR system, some form of document translation is frequently unavoidable: the user needs some indication of the content of foreign-language documents in order to determine a) the relevance of the documents retrieved by the system, b) whether there is a need to refine the query and, if so, c) which terms should be added/removed from the original query.

C. Peters et al. (Eds.): CLEF 2003, LNCS 3237, pp. 450–461, 2004.

- If the user is involved in the query translation process, the interaction can become too complex when there is more than one target language. Moreover, previous research has shown that users prefer not to be involved in the query translation process [1, 2]. With a document translation approach to interactive CLIR, both problems simply disappear.

Therefore, in interactive CLIR the question is no longer whether we should translate documents or not, but *how* to translate documents in a way that *a*) facilitates the user search tasks (document selection and query refinement); *b*) minimizes the computational costs of translation, and *c*) provides optimal material for the automatic retrieval stage in the user's language (when the document translation approach is used).

In previous editions of iCLEF, we proposed a translation method that reasonably satisfies requisites *a* and *b*. The method generated summarized translations of target-language documents which rely essentially on noun phrase extraction and translation. While rather crude from a Computational Linguistics point of view, such summaries have excellent features for Multilingual Information Access:

- In iCLEF 2001, we obtained quantitative evidence that such cross-language summaries could be better for document translation purposes than full MT (users judgements were equally precise with both approaches, but summaries permitted faster judgments).
- In iCLEF 2002, our noun-phrase based summaries proved to be useful as a basis for query formulation and refinement.
- Phrase-based summaries can be generated more than one order of magnitude faster than full machine translations, and contain only 30% as many words as the original documents.

It thus seems reasonable to think of phrase-based summaries as good candidates for a document translation approach to Multilingual Information Access. This is the hypothesis that we sought to test in our iCLEF 2003 experiment. The challenge was to perform retrieval with phrase-based summaries as the only source of query-language indexes for target-language documents, because the size of the index set was just one third of its monolingual (or MT) counterparts.

In Section 2, we review the main features of our phrase-based summaries. In Section 3 we discuss the experimental design. In Section 4 we present the results of our experiment, and in Section 5 we draw some conclusions.

2   UNED Cross-Language Summaries

The UNED approach to *Cross-Language Search Assistance* (defined as the problem of assisting a user to search and detect relevant documents in a foreign-language text collection) is based on noun phrases as fundamental units for translation (both query and document translation) and formulation of user needs.

Cross-language pseudo-summaries are an essential part of the approach. They simply consist of the list of noun phrases present in the document, listed in order of appearance, and translated according to a simple greedy algorithm that makes use of a database of bilingual alignments between two and three-lemma phrases in the source and target languages [3]. The phrase alignment resource is built using a simple noun phrase extractor [4] on two comparable text collections (EFE 94 and LA Times 94 in our case) and an alignment algorithm based on co-occurrences of candidate translations (via bilingual dictionaries) and phrase frequency measures. The algorithm produces sets of phrases which are assumed to be *equivalent under translation*, and the most frequent phrase in each set is said to be the *canonical translation* for each member of the equivalent set (see Figure 1 for an example).

SPANISH	ENGLISH
acuerdo de libre comercio	**free trade agreement**
acuerdos de libre comercio	free trade accord
acuerdo libre comercio	free trade pact
acuerdo de libre cambio	free trade beyond the pact
acuerdos de libre cambio	free trade pacts
convenio de libre comercio	free trade agreements
convenios de libre comercio	free trade arrangements
compromiso de libre comercio	
...	

Fig. 1. Example of sets of noun phrases equivalent under translation

Table 1 lists the size of the bilingual noun phrase alignments as extracted from the EFE 1994 and LA Times 1994 corpora. In its current version, the alignment algorithms takes 17 hours to generate two-lemma alignments (8 hours of preprocessing and 9 hours of alignment) plus 60 hours to generate three-lemma alignments from these corpora.

Translation of non-aligned noun phrases (including phrases with more than three lemmas) is done with a greedy algorithm that translates, at each step, the two or three-lemma sub-phrase which has the best translation under the alignment resource, and uses overlapping phrases to translate the remaining words taking the context into account. The algorithm is described in detail in [3]. The translation of the whole LA Times 1994 collection (approx. 110.000 documents) takes a total of 14 hours (12 hours for summarization and 2 hours for translation). The average size of a summary is 30% the size of the original document.

A comparative example of translations provided by Systran and by our system can be seen in the Appendix.

Table 1. Aligned phrases resource

Language	2 lemmas	3 lemmas
English	1,700,183	288,872
Spanish	1,953,849	347,920

3   Experimental Design

The goal of the experiment is to test , in an interactive CLIR setting, whether searching cross-language summaries with the original query can match searching the original documents with a translated version of the query. As reference system, we have chosen the best of the two approaches tested in our iCLEF 2002 experiment. In this approach, users interact with the system to formulate an optimal query as a set of noun phrases. Query translation is then performed automatically (using the database of aligned phrases) and the retrieved set of documents can be examined via cross-language summaries. As the user does not have to deal with foreign-language expressions at any time, the translation and retrieval steps can be substituted for a direct retrieval on document translations without changing the user interface. This is very convenient for our experiment, because it permits a direct comparison of query translation versus document translation strategies without any additional interference.

A detailed description of the two systems to be compared follows:

1. **Initial Query Formulation:** the user reads the topic description and freely formulates an initial query. The time for reading and typing this initial query is not computed as searching time.
2. **Query Formulation by Phrases:** the system suggests a maximum of 10 phrases related to the initial user query. The user can either a) select a number of them and perform the initial search, or b) type in some additional words and ask the system to recompute the phrase suggestions.
3. **Document Retrieval:**
   - In the reference system (**Query Translation**), phrases are translated into English via the phrase alignment dictionary, and then a search is performed against the LA Times collection.
   - In the system being tested (**Document translation**), the original Spanish phrases are used to search the collection of Spanish summaries of LA Times documents.
4. **Document Ranking:** The result of the search is a ranked list of LA Times documents, with a colour code to indicate whether a document has been judged as relevant, not relevant, unsure, or has not yet been judged. Each document is displayed in the ranked list as a Systran translation of its title.
5. **Document Selection:** When the user clicks on a document title, its Spanish summary is shown to the user. The document can then be judged as relevant, not relevant or unsure.

6. **Query Refinement:** There are two ways of refining the query:
   - *Phrase Feedback*: If the user clicks on a phrase inside a document summary, the phrase is added to the query and the document ranking is updated with the enhanced query.
   - *Direct Reformulation*: at any point during the search, the user can select/deselect additional phrases to be included in the query, and can introduce new words to the phrase suggestion window.

Although the difference between both systems is transparent to the user, the architecture and implications of each are quite different. Figures 2 and 3 compare both approaches visually. The document translation approach can be trivially extended to more than one document language, as can be seen in Figure 4. Using phrase-based summaries, the document translation approach can be applied to a multi-language collection increasing its size by only 30% with respect to the original size per user language considered. For instance, a collection with four document/user languages would only double its size under this document translation approach. This is a challenge for the retrieval phase, because the set of indexes is much smaller than the original. Our hypothesis is that any possible difference in the quality of the rankings will not have an appreciable impact on the interactive searching task.

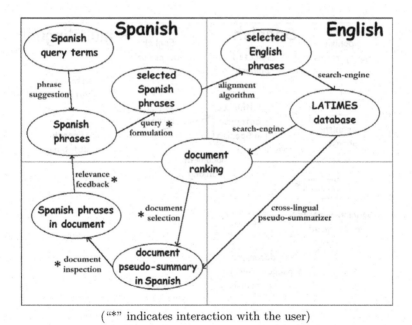

("*" indicates interaction with the user)

Fig. 2. Reference system: query translation approach

We have used eight native Spanish searchers for our experiment, the LA Times 1994 collection as the document set, and the eight official iCLEF topics

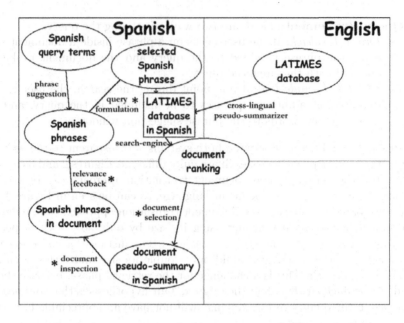

Fig. 3. Contrastive system: document translation approach

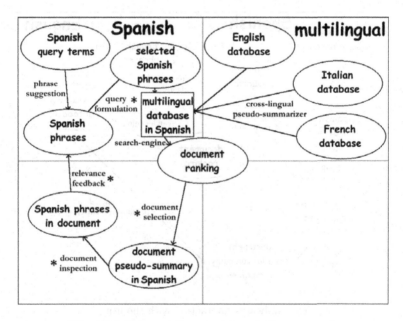

Fig. 4. Multilingual document translation approach

(in Spanish) extracted from the CLEF 2002 set. This year, our searchers did not interact with English at all, hence we were not particularly cautious with English proficiency when recruiting volunteers. We could thus focus on recruiting searchers with considerable experience with search engines (something that was not possible in previous years). In the end, all eight users had medium English skills (which were not put into practice in the experiment) and were highly experienced in web searching.

As specified in the track guidelines, each search session consisted in a unique user/system/topic combination according to a latin-square matrix design [5] that factors out the differences between individual topics (some topics are easier than others) and individual users (some users are better than others), so that a difference between systems can be established without bias. Both systems are identical to the user, therefore only one previous training phase was needed. Each user performed eight searches (on the eight iCLEF topics), with a limit of 10 minutes per search. Their goal was to retrieve as many relevant documents as possible, focusing on precision rather than recall (it is more important that selected documents are actually relevant, than finding every relevant item for a given topic).

4   Results and Discussion

4.1   Official Results

The official UNED results using Van Rijsbergen's $F_\alpha = 0.8$ measure ($\alpha = 0.8$ favors precision rather than recall) can be seen in Table 2. Both systems receive the same score, confirming our hypothesis that phrase-based summaries can be used for a cross-language indexing of the collection. Precision and recall are also almost identical for both approaches.

Table 2. Official UNED results

System	Precision	Recall	F_α
Query translation	.51	.14	.29
Document translation	.53	.14	.29

4.2   Dependence on User and Topic

Figure 5 separates results by searcher and by topic. Topics vary in difficulty as expected, with topics 3 and 4 being harder than the others. There is also variability between users, but part of this variability can be explained by the distribution of topics to systems assigned to each searcher. For instance, users 1 and 3 have opposite results (query translation is much worse for user 1 and much better for user 3), but they have an inverse assignment of topics and systems, and they do the two difficult topics with different systems. Overall, the detailed results are a good sample of how the latin-square design filters out possible topic/system/user combination bias.

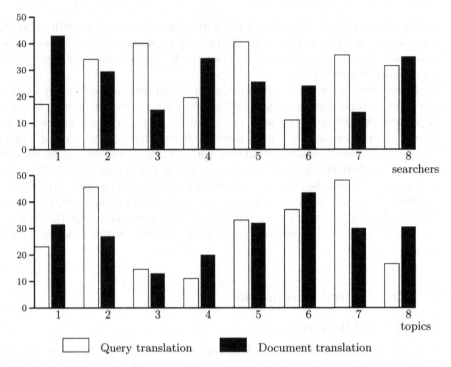

Fig. 5. F_α results by searcher and topic

Table 3. Average initial precision

System	Initial precision
Document translation	10%
Query translation	14% (+40%)

4.3   Initial Precision

Table 3 shows the initial precision, measured on the twenty first documents re-trieved by the system after initial query formulation by the user. Remarkably, the query translation approach performs 40% better than the document trans-lation one, indicating that the quality of batch retrieval might be better with a full document index than with an index based on the cross-language summary. But this initial difference is not reflected in the final retrieval results, suggesting that other interactive factors are predominant in the overall search results (for instance, facilities for query refinement).

4.4   Selections Across Time

Figure 6 shows the overall number of documents selected during the 10 minute searching time. Unlike our previous iCLEF 2002 experiment, this year there are no sensible differences between systems. In spite of the initial advantage in

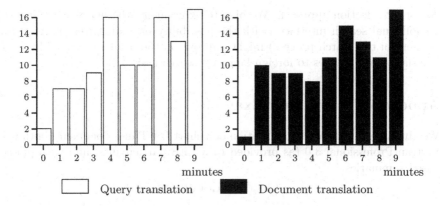

Query translation   ■ Document translation

Fig. 6. Number of selected documents across time

precision, the pattern of selections over time is basically equal for both systems. The growing curve of selections suggest that results would have improved with longer searches.

5   Conclusions

Document translation can be a viable approach to Multilingual Information Access once we find simplified, task-oriented ways of translating documents without the computational cost associated with commercial Machine Translation systems. In this experiment, we have proved that phrase-based summaries, although rather crude from a pure MT point of view, can be successfully used for Cross-Language searching. They can be generated much faster than full machine translations, and occupy only 30% of disk space. In these conditions, phrase-based summaries can be used to benefit from the main advantages of document-translation approaches to interactive CLIR:

– At document selection time, translations do not have to be generated on the fly, because all documents have been previously translated for indexing. Hence the interactive search process is not retarded by on-line translation.
– In a truly multilingual setting (with more than one target language), the complexity of translating the query to several languages (a big impediment if query translation is done interactively) and the problem of merging ranked results from different languages disappear.

In our present experiment, query formulation is somewhat restrained by the fact that the user has to formulate his/her query as a set of noun phrases that can in turn receive an appropriate automatic translation via the alignment resource. This makes perfect sense in the reference (query translation) system, as proved in our iCLEF 2002 experiment. But it might be an excessive constraint in the document selection approach. We plan to experiment whether a more classical, monolingual search interface (with the possibility of adding free terms at any moment of the search process) might improve on the results obtained by query translation approaches to foreign-language search assistance.

Appendix: Translation Example

We give an example of the translation of a short LA Times document, both with Systran Professional 3.0 (as provided to iCLEF participants) and with phrase-based summaries.

Original document

```
WORLD CUP SOCCER '94 / THE FIRST ROUND; SPOTLIGHT; NOT AGAINST BRAZIL

Reuters news  service sent a picture of Carlos Alberto Torres, the
captain of  Brazil's 1970  World  Cup  championship  team, talking
with Lothar Matthaeus,   captain   of Germany's  team, at a recent
practice at Southern Methodist University. The caption information
included with the photo identified Torres as a German fan. ELLIOTT
ALMOND
```

Systran translation

```
    FÚTBOL '94 / EL PRIMER REDONDO DE LA TAZA DEL MUNDO;
              PROYECTOR; NO CONTRA EL BRASIL

El  servicio  de  noticias  de  Reuters envió un cuadro de Carlos
Alberto Torres,  el  capitán  de Equipo 1970 del campeonato de la
taza del mundo del Brasil, hablando con Lothar Matthaeus, capitán
del equipo de Alemania,  en  una  práctica  reciente en Methodist
meridional Universidad. La información del subtítulo incluida con
la foto identificó  a  Torres como ventilador alemán. ALMENDRA DE
ELLIOTT
```

Cross-lingual pseudo-summary

```
copa del mundo de fútbol
primera ronda

reuters news service
ver carlos
campeón de la copa del mundo equipo
lothar matthaeus
práctica del reciente universidad metodista del sur
pie informacion
torres aficionados alemanes
elliott almendra
```

F_α measure

Searcher \ Topic	1	2	3	4	5	6	7	8	Avg.
1	0.13	0.32	0	0.24	**0.43**	**0.48**	**0.36**	**0.45**	0.3
2	**0.44**	**0.43**	**0.21**	**0.11**	0.37	0.43	0.56	0	0.32
3	**0.45**	0	**0.16**	0	0.56	0.37	0.68	0	0.28
4	0.09	0.33	0.16	0.2	0	**0.37**	**0.56**	**0.45**	0.27
5	0.58	**0.65**	**0.16**	0	**0.22**	0.37	0.68	0	0.33
6	0.13	0	0	0	**0.64**	0.32	0	**0.33**	0.18
7	**0.11**	0.53	0	**0.3**	0.22	**0.43**	0	0.67	0.28
8	**0.26**	0.65	0.43	**0.4**	0.18	**0.46**	**0.28**	0	0.33
Avg.	0.27	0.36	0.14	0.16	0.33	0.4	0.39	0.24	0.29

Precision

Searcher \ Topic	1	2	3	4	5	6	7	8	Avg.
1	0.17	0.3	0	0.4	1	1	1	**0.5**	0.55
2	**0.6**	**0.43**	**0.4**	**0.17**	0.67	0.75	1	0	0.5
3	**1**	0	**1**	0	1	1	1	0	0.63
4	0.1	0.5	1	1	0	1	1	**0.5**	0.64
5	1	**0.75**	1	0	**0.5**	1	1	0	0.66
6	0.17	0	0	0	1	0.67	0	**0.33**	0.27
7	**0.13**	0.67	0	**0.67**	0.5	**0.75**	0	0.67	0.42
8	**0.27**	0.75	0.8	**0.75**	0.33	**0.67**	0.5	0	0.51
Avg.	0.43	0.42	0.53	0.37	0.62	0.85	0.69	0.25	0.52

Recall

Searcher \ Topic	1	2	3	4	5	6	7	8	Avg.
1	0.07	0.43	0	0.1	**0.13**	**0.16**	0.1	**0.33**	0.16
2	**0.21**	**0.43**	**0.07**	**0.05**	0.13	0.16	0.2	0	0.16
3	**0.14**	0	**0.04**	0	0.2	0.11	0.3	0	0.1
4	0.07	0.14	0.04	0.05	0	**0.11**	**0.2**	**0.33**	0.12
5	0.21	**0.43**	**0.04**	0	**0.07**	0.11	0.3	0	0.14
6	0.07	0	0	0	**0.27**	0.11	0	**0.33**	0.1
7	**0.07**	0.28	0	**0.1**	0.07	**0.16**	0	0.67	0.17
8	**0.21**	0.43	0.15	**0.14**	0.07	**0.21**	0.1	0	0.16
Avg.	0.13	0.27	0.04	0.05	0.12	0.14	0.15	0.21	0.14

Fig. 7. Detailed results by topic and searcher (document translation in bold font)

Acknowledgments

We are indebted to Anselmo Peñas for the provision of the WTB phrase extraction software. This research has been funded by the Spanish Government, project *Hermes* (TIC2000-0335-C03-01) and the Spanish Distance University (UNED), project *iCLEF*.

References

1. Petrelli, D., Beaulieu, M., Sanderson, M., Demetriou, G., Herring, P.: Is query translation a distinct task from search? In: C. Peters, M. Braschler, J. Gonzalo and M. Kluck (eds): Advances in Cross-Language Information Retrieval. CLEF 2002 workshop. Revised papers. LNCS 2785 Springer. (2003)
2. López-Ostenero, F., Gonzalo, J., Peñas, A., Verdejo, F.: Phrases are better than words for interactive cross-language query formulation and refinement. In: C. Peters, M. Braschler, J. Gonzalo and M. Kluck (eds): Advances in Cross-Language Information Retrieval. CLEF 2002 workshop. Revised papers. LNCS 2785 Springer. (2003)
3. López-Ostenero, F., Gonzalo, J., Verdejo, M.F.: Noun Phrases as Building Blocks for Cross-Language Search Assistance. Information Processing and Management (to appear) (2004)
4. Peñas, A., Gonzalo, J., Verdejo, F.: Cross-language information access through phrase browsing. In: Applications of Natural Language to Information Systems. Lecture Notes in Informatics (2001) 121–130
5. Oard, D.W., Gonzalo, J.: The CLEF 2003 Interactive track. In: This volume. (2004)

Comparing Syntactic-Semantic Patterns and Passages in Interactive Cross Language Information Access (iCLEF at University of Alicante)

Borja Navarro, Fernando Llopis, and Miguel Ángel Varó

Departamento de Lenguajes y Sistemas Informáticos,
University of Alicante, Alicante, Spain
{borja, llopis, mvaro}@dlsi.ua.es

Abstract. We present the results of the interactive CLEF experiment at the University of Alicante. Our aim was to compare two interactive approaches: one based on passages (presented at iCLEF 2002), and a new interactive approach based on syntactic-semantic patterns. These patterns are composed by the main verb of a sentence plus its arguments, and are extracted automatically from the passages. Such patterns show only the basic information of each sentence. The objective was to investigate which of these approaches is faster and most useful in the selection of relevant documents by the user in a language different than that of the query (and of the user). The results show that both approaches are useful, but that the approach based on syntactic-semantic patterns is, in the majority of cases, faster. With these approaches it is possible to avoid the use of Machine Translation systems and the problems caused by their adoption in Interactive Cross-Language Information Access tasks.

1 Introduction

One of the most important aspects of Interactive Multilingual Information Access is the way in which the system shows the retrieved documents to the user; mainly, the way in which the system shows the relevant information. The user only has this information to decide whether the retrieved documents are relevant or not. This is a key point in order to ensure the correct selection of documents, and a key point for future refinements of the query.

The main problem is the multilingualism: the user formulates the query in one language, but the relevant documents are written in a different language. To deal with this situation, there are two main solutions: to show the relevant documents to the user in his/her own language, or to show the relevant documents in the language of the documents. In the first case, a translation of the document with a Machine Translation system is necessary. However, there are many problems related to Machine Translation. In the second case –showing the information

C. Peters et al. (Eds.): CLEF 2003, LNCS 3237, pp. 462–467, 2004.

in the language of the document–, the user may not be able to understand the information, and thus is unable to decide which documents are the relevant ones.

At iCLEF 2002, the University of Alicante proposed the use of passages for interaction with the user. In this approach, the system selects the most important passage of the retrieved documents. Each passage is translated into the language of the user with a Machine Translation system and, then, the translated passages are shown to the user.

The experiment concluded that this approach based on passages is faster and more precise than approaches based on the whole document. The user only has to read the relevant passage, not the whole document. This provides sufficient information to decide whether the document is relevant or not with high precision. However, there is an important problem with this approach: many passages could not be read/understood by the user due to problems with the English to Spanish machine translation [5].

This year we wanted to improve this approach in two respects: first, we wanted to improve the interaction speed –that is, the time consumed by the user from the uploading of a passage to the decision about its relevance–; and second, we wanted to improve the recall and precision in the selection of relevant documents. On other hand, we also wanted to solve the problems caused by Machine Translation systems.

To do this, we have defined an interactive approach based on syntactic-semantic patterns [7]. Each syntactic-semantic pattern is formed by a verb and the subcategorized nouns. From a semantic point of view, the main words of the sentence appear in each pattern. We think that it is both possible and effective to use these patterns in interaction with the user, because the patterns contain the main concepts of the document and their syntactic and semantic relations. Instead of showing the translated passage to the user, we only show the syntactic-semantic pattern of each sentence in the language of the document (without translation). As the users have passive abilities in the foreign language (English), we think that this is sufficient information to decide about the relevance of a document.

To conclude, the objectives of our experiment at iCLEF 2003 were:

- to investigate if it is possible for a searcher to decide whether a document is relevant or not with only the syntactic-semantic patterns extracted automatically from the passage;
- to investigate if the approach based on syntactic-semantic patterns is better than the approach based on passages only;
- to investigate if the approach based on syntactic-semantic patterns is better than the approach based on a machine translation of the passage.

In the next section, we will present two methods for interaction with the user: passage-based and pattern-based methods. We will briefly describe the experimental design and the results. In the final section we will make some conclusions and outline ideas for future work.

2   Two Methods for Interaction with the Users

2.1   Passage-Based Approach

The first method is passage-based. Passages are the most relevant pieces of text in a document. The main idea of this approach is that it is better to show only the relevant passage to the user, instead of the whole document. This approach was tested at iCLEF 2002 with good results (for more information, see [5]).

2.2   Syntactic-Semantic Pattern-Based Approach

The second method is based on syntactic-semantic patterns. These patterns are automatically extracted from the passage selected by the Information Retrieval system. The difference between the two methods is the way in which relevant information is shown to the user in a language different from that of the query: the passage in English only –method one–, or the syntactic-semantic patterns extracted from the passage, again in English –method two–.

From a theoretical point of view, a syntactic-semantic pattern is basically a linguistic pattern formed by three fundamental components:

1. A verb with its sense or senses.
2. The subcategorization frame of the sense.
3. The selectional preferences of each argument.

In order to define this kind of pattern we have considered the literature on the subcategorization frame and subcategorization acquisition ([1], [2]), about the relation between verb sense and verb subcategorization ([10], [9]), and about selectional preference ([8], [6]).

For the automatic extraction of these patterns, we have used the syntactic parser Minipar [3]. The extraction system looks for a verb. When a verb is located, it is extracted. The system then looks for a noun to the left of the verb. If a noun is located, it is extracted with the verb. The system then looks for a noun or preposition plus noun to the right of the verb. If a noun or preposition plus noun is located, it is extracted with the verb and the previous noun. Finally, the system looks for another noun or preposition plus noun to the right of this noun. If a noun or preposition plus noun is located, it is extracted with the verb and the previous nouns.

For example, from the passage:

"Primakov suggested that the Administration was using the Ames arrest to score domestic political points, to punish Russia for its independent stance on the conflict in Bosnia-Herzegovina and to provide a convenient excuse for cutting American aid to Russia, according to journalists who attended."

the system extracts patterns like these:

– Primakov suggest Administration
– administration use Ames arrest
– administration score domestic point
– Primakov punish Russia for its stance

- Primakov provide convenient excuse for
- Primakov cut American aid to Russia according to journalist
- journalist attend

With these syntactic-semantic patterns, only the most important information of each sentence is shown to the user: the most important words of each sentence –the verb and the subcategorized nouns– and the syntactic and semantic relation between them.

When the searchers are not fluent in and do not have a deep knowledge about the foreign language (English in our experiment), we think that it is better not to process the sentences completely. In order to decide on the relevance of a passage, it is easier to put the attention on the main words of the document only, that is, to put the attention on the syntactic-semantic patterns only.

Using such patterns, it would be difficult to understand a text written in a foreign language completely. However, this is not our objective. Our objective is to identify the topic of a text or passage and to decide whether it is relevant or not.

3   Description of the Experiment

We have focused our experiment in cross-language document selection on a searcher group with passive language abilities in the foreign language. The language of the user group is Spanish, and the foreign language is English.

The Information Retrieval system used is the IR-n system, developed at the University of Alicante [4]. The system uses the complete CLEF topic (title, description and narrative) to search for relevant documents. For each query, the IR-n system locates twenty five (possible) relevant documents.

Each retrieved document is shown to the user. The first system shows only the passages, and the second system shows the syntactic-semantic patterns extracted from these passages.

Each searcher must decide, on the basis of the passage or the patterns, whether the document retrieved is relevant or not. As we mentioned, the passages and patterns are written in English, a foreign language for the user. We have developed an HTML interface in order to help the user indicate whether he finds the document relevant or not. Together with the relevance judgments made by the user, we also save information on the time consumed to view each document.

4   Results

The results for the f-alpha average are shown in the Table 1.

These results show that it is possible to decide whether a text is relevant or not only from the the syntactic-semantic patterns. The result obtained for each system is very similar (only a difference of 0.0179371875). Thus we have achieved our first objective.

The time consumed by each searcher while deciding on the relevance of a document is shown in Table 2. Five of the eight searches consume less time with

Table 1. F-alpha average

SYSTEM	F-alpha average
Passages	0.45416703125
Patterns	0.43622984375

Table 2. Time consumed (seconds)

System	Searcher 1	Searcher 2	Searcher 3	Searcher 4
Passages	4359	5641	5361	5533
Patterns	3195	4840	5548	3063

System	Searcher 5	Searcher 6	Searcher 7	Searcher 8
Passages	1350	1707	1835	5287
Patterns	829	5046	7957	2555

patterns than with passages. Only in one case is the time consumed using the patterns very similar to that with the passages (searcher 3). Searchers 5 and 6 took much more time with the patterns than with the passages. However, we consider that they consumed an abnormal amount of time as the difference was very large. This was probably caused by problems during the experiment. Finally, the searcher that obtained the best result (searcher 4) consumed more time with the passages than with the patterns.

From this data, we conclude that the use of patterns in the interaction process improves the time consumed in the majority of cases. So the second objective has been achieved to a certain extent.

Finally, we have shown that with syntactic-semantic patterns it is possible to avoid the use of Machine Translation systems. In fact, the results obtained this year at iCLEF 2003 are better than the results obtained at iCLEF 2002, in which a Machine Translation system was used.

5   Conclusions

In this experiment, we have compared two methods for interaction with a IR system, the first one based on passages and the second on syntactic-semantic patterns. The results show that it is possible to decide whether a document is relevant or not using only the syntactic-semantic patterns. Furthermore, the time consumed by the searcher is less with the patterns than with the passages in the majority of cases. Finally, with these patterns it is possible to avoid the use of Machine Translation systems.

These syntactic-semantic patterns represent a simplification of the language: each pattern contains the main concepts and linguistic relations of a sentence. Due to this simplification, it is possible to use of these patterns in other cross-linguistic information access tasks such as, for example, indexing and searching documents by patterns, the alignment of patterns extracted from different languages (through the verb), or the refinement of the query with the patterns contained in the documents selected by the user.

Acknowledgements

We would like to thank the users (Belén, Raquel, Irene, Julio, Rafa, Ángel, Sonia and Yeroni) and Rubén, who implemented the pattern extraction system.

References

1. Briscoe, T., Carroll, J.: Automatic Extraction of Subcategorization from Corpora. In Workshop on Very Large Corpora, Copenhagen (1997).
2. Korhonen, A.: Subcategorization acquisition. Technical Report. University of Cambridge (2002).
3. Lin, D.: Dependency-based Evaluation of MINIPAR. In Workshop on the Evaluation of Parsing Systems, Granada (1998).
4. Llopis, F.: IR-n: Un sistema de recuperación de información basado en pasajes. PhD thesis, University of Alicante (2003).
5. Llopis, F., Ferrández, A., Vicedo, J. L., Díaz, M., Martínez, F.: Universities of Alicante and Jaen at iCLEF. Workshop of Cross-Language Evaluation Forum (CLEF 2002), LNCS 2785. Springer-Verlang (2002) 392–399.
6. McCarthy, D.: Lexical Acquisiton at the Syntax-Semantics Interface: Diathesis Alternations, Subcategorization Frames and Selectional Preferences. PhD thesis. University of Sussex (2001).
7. Navarro, B., Palomar, M., Martínez-Barco, P.: A General Proposal to Multilingual Information Access based on Syntactic Semantic Patterns. In Düsterhöft, A. and Thalheim, B. (eds.). Natural Language Processing and Information Systems - NLDB 2003. Lecture Notes in Informatics. GI-Edition. Bonn (2003) 186–199.
8. Resnik, Philip S.: Selection and Information: A Class-Based Approach to Lexical Relationships. PhD thesis, University of Pennsylvania (1993).
9. Roland, D.: Verb Sense and Verb Subcategorization Probabilities. PhD thesis. University of Colorado (2001).
10. Roland, D., Jurafsky, D.: Verb sense and verb subcategorization probabilities. In P. Merlo and S. Stevenson (eds.). The Lexical Basis of Sentence Processing: Formal, Computational, and Experimental Issues. John Benjamins, Amsterdam (2002) 325–346.

Continued Experiments on
Cross-Language Relevance Assessment

Jussi Karlgren and Preben Hansen

Swedish Institute of Computer Science, SICS,
Box 1263, SE-164 29 Kista, Sweden
{jussi,preben}@sics.se

Abstract. An experiment on how users assess document usefulness for an information access task in their native language (Swedish) versus a language they have near-native competence in (English).

Results show that relevance assessment in a foreign language takes more time and is prone to errors compared to assessment in the readers first language.

1 Cross-Linguality and Reading

For people in cultures all around the world competence in more than one language is quite common and the European cultural area is typical in that respect. Many people, especially those engaged in intellectual activities are familiar with more than one language and have some acquaintance with several.

1.1 Relevance Judgment in a Near-Native Language

We know that readers are excellent at making relevance assessments for texts. Both assessment efficiency and precision are very impressive. But judging trustworthiness and usefulness of documents in a foreign language is difficult and a noticeably less reliable process than doing it in a language and cultural context we are familiar with, as shown by last year's CLEF experiments [2]. To that experiment, we later added further subjects, bringing the total to 28 experimental subjects. The compounded results are briefly tabulated below.

Assessment Time. Assessment of documents in Swedish (20 s average) is faster[1] than assessement of documents in English (27 s average).

Agreement with Official Results. Assessments were judged by how well they correspond to the CLEF official assessments. The assessments in Swedish agreed with the CLEF assessments more often[2] (93 per cent agreement with official relevance judgments) than did the assessments in English (78 per cent agreement with official relevance judgments).

---

[1] Significant by Mann Whitney U; $p > 0.95$.
[2] Significant by Mann Whitney U; $p > 0.95$.

C. Peters et al. (Eds.): CLEF 2003, LNCS 3237, pp. 468–470, 2004.

1.2   Closing the Gap

This year we set ourself the task to examine what mechanisms might be introduced to the retrieval situation to close the gap between the two linguistic conditions. There are several intellectional or informational bottlenecks in the interaction situation which can be addressed for this purpose: the system understanding of the document, the user, the usage context or the expression of information need could all be enhanced. This year, however, we decided to focus on the interface itself and investigate the utility of an interface detail which invites the user to deliberate the selection of documents further.

2   Experiment Set-Up

Participants. The study involved 8 participants with self-reported high proficiency in English.

Language. The searches were always performed in Swedish. The retrieved set was variously in English or Swedish.

Queries. The eight CLEF queries used in this year's interactive track were used in both languages.

System. The system used was the first version of the CLARITY cross-lingual retrieval system, which accepts queries in any of Finnish, Swedish and English, and retrieves results in any or all of the three. The underlying search engine is built mostly at University of Tampere and the interface mostly at University of Sheffield with participation from SICS in Stockholm, Tilde in Riga, Alma Media in Tampere, and BBC in Reading [1].

Data. English news articles from Los Angeles Times and news wire items in Swedish from Tidningarnas Telegrambyrå.

Presentation. The retrieval results were presented in a ranked list with the news item headline visible in its original language.

Bookmark Panel. The interface allows the user to at any juncture during the retrieval process both to mark retrieved documents to be saved, which are then moved to a visible *bookmark panel* and to mark saved documents to be deleted, which are then removed from the panel.

Procedure. The participants were asked to answer some initial questions. They were given the TREC topic description and were allowed to formulate queries freely in Swedish, to inspect the resulting results, to select documents for reading, to reformulate the query, to save or delete documents from the bookmark panel, and whenever they felt they had exhausted the potential of the document set or felt satisfied with the resulting set to move on to the next query. Between each test query the participants were asked to answer a fixed set of questions related to the retrieval system; after the last query, participants were asked to answer a final set of questions.

3   Results

Unfortunately the logging functionality employed in the experiment was unreliable and some of the data we expected to be able to investigate did not materialize. The following data we were able to extract from the logs.

- Native (Swedish) documents were viewed for reading more often (9.5 per cent of Swedish documents viewed) than foreign documents (7.4 per cent)[3]. *Does the headline have an effect?*
- Foreign (English) documents were discarded from the bookmark panel more often after having first being saved (40 per cent, or 35 out of 80 saved documents) compared to native documents (15 per cent or 14 out of 90 saved documents)[4]. *Were users less confident in their first impressions of foreign-language documents?*
- Searches in native (Swedish) documents were reformulated more often. *Recycling terminology from the target set seems to have an immediate effect.*

4   To Take Home

- We know too little about human reading performance.
- We do know many each in themselves insignificant factors contribute: typography, perceived attitude, task context etc., etc., etc.
- Across languages new things crop up.
- These new things make a difference.

Acknowledgments

The work reported is partially funded by the European Commission under contracts IST-2000-29452 (DUMAS) and IST-2000-25310 (CLARITY) which is hereby gratefully acknowledged. We thank Tidningarnas Telegrambyrå AB, Stockholm, for providing us with the Swedish text collection. We also wish to thank our patient subjects for the time they spent reading really old news.

References

1. Hansen, H., Petrelli, D., Karlgren, J., Beaulieu, M., Sanderson, M.: User-centered interface design for cross-language information retrieval. In Proceedings of the 25th annual international ACM SIGIR conference on Research and development in information retrieval. ACM Press, (2002).
2. Karlgren, J., Hansen, P.: Cross language relevance assessment and task context. In C. Peters, M. Braschler, J. Gonzalo and M. Kluck (eds): Advances in Cross-Language Information Retrieval. CLEF 2002 workshop. Revised papers. LNCS 2785 Springer (2003).

---

[3] Significant by $\chi^2; p > 0.95$.
[4] Significant by $\chi^2; p > 0.999$.

The Multiple Language Question Answering Track at CLEF 2003

Bernardo Magnini*, Simone Romagnoli*, Alessandro Vallin*,
Jesús Herrera**, Anselmo Peñas**, Víctor Peinado**,
Felisa Verdejo**, and Maarten de Rijke***

*ITC-irst, Centro per la Ricerca Scientifica e Tecnologica,
Via Sommarive, 38050 Povo (TN), Italy
{magnini,romagnoli,vallin}@itc.it
**UNED, Spanish Distance Learning University,
Departamento de Lenguajes y Sistemas Informaticos, Ciudad Universitaria,
c./Juan del Rosal 16, 28040 Madrid, Spain
{jesus.herrera,anselmo,victor,felisa}@lsi.uned.es
***Language and Inference Technology Group, ILLC, University of Amsterdam,
Nieuwe Achtergracht 166, 1018 WV Amsterdam, The Netherlands
mdr@science.uva.nl

Abstract. This paper reports on the pilot question answering track that was carried out within the CLEF initiative this year. The track was divided into monolingual and bilingual tasks: monolingual systems were evaluated within the frame of three non-English European languages, Dutch, Italian and Spanish, while in the cross-language tasks an English document collection constituted the target corpus for Italian, Spanish, Dutch, French and German queries. Participants were given 200 questions for each task, and were allowed to submit up to two runs per task with up to three responses (either exact answers or 50 byte long strings) per question.

We give here an overview of the track: we report on each task and discuss the creation of the multilingual test sets and the participants' results.

1 Introduction

The question answering (QA) track at TREC-8 represented the first attempt to emphasize the importance and foster research on systems that could extract relevant and precise information rather than documents. Question answering systems are designed to find answers to open domain questions in a large collection of documents. QA development has acquired an important role among the scientific community because it entails research in both natural language processing and information retrieval (IR), putting the two disciplines in contact. Differently from the IR scenario, a QA system processes questions formulated into natural language (instead of keyword-based queries) and retrieves answers (instead of documents).

The past TREC conferences laid the foundations for a formalized and widely accepted evaluation methodology of QA systems, but the three tracks organized so far

C. Peters et al. (Eds.): CLEF 2003, LNCS 3237, pp. 471–486, 2004.

focused just on monolingual systems for the English language, which constitutes a drawback we tried to address. We were mainly interested in testing multilingual systems, and in particular to push the QA community into designing them. As the number of the participants and the results achieved by their systems show, we can argue that in the field of multilingual QA there is much work to do. Within the frame of planning and coordinating the research on question answering, outlined in Maybury's roadmap, multilingual QA has a pivotal role and should deserve much attention in the next years. Multilinguality represents a new area in QA research, and a challenging issue toward the development of more complex systems [8].

Multilinguality enables the user to pose a query in a language that is different from the language of the reference corpus. The cross-language perspective could be quite useful when the required information is not available in the user's language (as it often happens surfing the web) and in particular it fits the cultural situation in Europe, where different languages co-exist and are in contact, although English has become a widespread and standardized means of communication. In a multilingual environment, QA systems and other natural language processing resources could even contribute to conserve endangered languages that are progressively losing importance and prestige, in the effort to ensure their survival, as in the case of the 'Te Kaitito' bilingual question answering system for English and Maori [4].

Our activity, and in particular the production of two multilingual test sets that constitute reusable resources, can be regarded as a valuable contribution to the development of such cross-language systems [2]. The evaluation of cross-language resources is the key issue of the CLEF initiative, so our question answering track could not be limited to the English language. On the contrary, we attempted to raise interest on other European languages, like Italian, Spanish, Dutch, German and French. The basic novelty in comparison with the past TREC QA campaigns was the introduction of bilingual tasks, in which non-English queries are processed to find responses in an English document collection.

2 QA at CLEF

Our pilot question answering track was structured in both monolingual and bilingual tasks. We organized three monolingual tasks for Dutch, Italian and Spanish, in which the questions, the corpus and the responses were in the same language. In contrast, in the cross-language tasks we had Italian, Spanish, Dutch, French or German queries that searched for answers in an English document collection. In output, the systems had to retrieve English answers.

2.1 Monolingual Tasks

Unlike previous TREC QA tracks, we focused on the evaluation and on the production of reusable resources for non-English QA systems. The monolingual tasks were designed for three different languages: Dutch, Italian and Spanish. For each language we generated 200 queries, 180 of which were completely shared between all the three tasks. Participants were given the questions and the corresponding monolingual corpus: the task consisted in returning automatically, i.e. with no manual intervention, a ranked list of [docid, answer] pairs per question such that the retrieved document supported the answer. Participants were given 200 questions for each task, and were allowed to submit up to two runs per task with up to three responses per query. They could return either exact answers or 50 byte long strings that contained the answer, although they were not allowed to use both modalities within the same run. Following the TREC model, we formulated 20 questions that had no known answer in the corpora: systems indicated their belief that there was no answer in the document collection by returning "NIL" instead of the [docid, answer] pair.

The monolingual Italian question answering task was planned and carried out under the co-ordination of the Italian Centro per la Ricerca Scientifica e Tecnologica (ITC-irst), that was in charge for the supervision of the whole QA track. We could use the document collections released at CLEF 2002, made up of articles drawn from a newspaper (*La Stampa*) and a press agency (*SDA*) of the year 1994. The entire Italian target corpus was 200 Mb wide (about 27 millions words) and it was made available to registered participants at the end of last January, so that they could test their systems using the document collection well in advance.

The UNED NLP group (Spanish Distance Learning University), as Spanish member of the CLEF consortium, was in charge for the monolingual Spanish task. The collection we were allowed to employ was the one released at CLEF 2002, i.e. more than 200,000 news from *EFE Press Agency* of the year 1994.

The Language and Inference Technology Group at the University of Amsterdam took care of the monolingual Dutch task. The collection used was the CLEF 2002 Dutch collection, which consists of two full years of the *Algemeen Dagblad* and *NRC Handelsblad* newspapers, adding up to about 200,000 documents of 540 Mb.

2.2 Cross-Language Tasks

Our interest in developing QA systems for languages other than English was not the only achievement we pointed at: the great novelty introduced in the CLEF QA track was multilinguality, whose potentialities are currently out of the scope of the TREC competition. Cross-language QA systems are crucially important when the language of the query and the language of the document collection are different, and in multicultural situations such a possibility is far from being remote. Searching information in the World Wide Web for instance is often difficult because the document retrieved is in a language we cannot understand. In this sense the cross-language tasks we organized represent a good chance to push the QA community to design and evaluate multilingual systems.

The cross-language tasks consisted in searching an English corpus to find English responses to queries posed in a different language. The target document collection we used was a corpus made up of *Los Angeles Times* articles of the year 1994, that was the same employed in last year's CLEF campaign. We translated into five languages the original two hundred English questions we generated, so we were able to organize five different bilingual tasks: Dutch, French, German, Italian and Spanish. As in the monolingual tasks, participants had to process 200 questions (15 had no answer in the corpus) posed in one of the five languages and could choose to submit either exact answers or 50 byte strings, without mixing them in the same run.

2.3 Participants

Eight groups took part in this pilot question answering track, and a total of seventeen runs were submitted, three using 50 byte long strings as answers and the other fourteen, in compliance with last year's TREC conditions, returning exact answers. The fact that most participants chose to retrieve exact answers shows that many have made the transition from more or less long strings to precise responses.

Table 1 below shows the name of the participants, the task in which they participated and the filename of their runs. It is interesting to notice that all the participants except the DFKI group had already participated in some previous TREC QA campaigns.

Table 1. Participants in the CLEF Question Answering Track. Note that the fifth and sixth letters in the run names show whether the responses are exact answers (ex) or 50 byte long strings (st)

GROUP	TASK	RUN NAME
DLSI-UA U. of Alicante, Spain	Monolingual Spanish	alicex031ms alicex032ms
UVA U. of Amsterdam, the Netherlands	Monolingual Dutch	uamsex031md uamsex032md
ITC-irst Trento, Italy	Monolingual Italian	irstex031mi irstst032mi
	Bilingual Italian	irstex031bi irstex032bi
ISI U. of Southern California, USA	Bilingual Spanish	isixex031bs isixex032bs
/	Bilingual Dutch	/
DFKI Saarbruecken, Germany	Bilingual German	dfkist031bg
CS-CMU Carnegie Mellon U., USA	Bilingual French	lumoex031bf lumoex032bf
DLTG U. of Limerick, Ireland	Bilingual French	dltgex031bf dltgex032bf
RALI U. of Montreal, Canada	Bilingual French	udemst031bf udemex032bf

Three teams took part in the monolingual tasks, submitting a total of six runs. We had only one participant in each language, which is quite disappointing because no comparison can be made between similar runs. Anyway, since the question set for all the monolingual tasks was the same (except the NIL questions), the monolingual runs can be compared to some extent. Four teams initially registered for the monolingual Italian task, but unfortunately only one, the ITC-irst group, actually participated. Similarly, only the University of Alicante took part in the monolingual Spanish task submitting two runs of exact answers, although three other groups expressed their intention of participation. As for the monolingual Dutch task, the University of Amsterdam with its two runs of exact answers was the only participant.

Six groups participated in the cross-language tasks, submitting eleven runs. The challenging novelty of the cross-language question answering attracted more participants than the monolingual tasks: the bilingual French task was chosen by three groups, while no one tested their system in the bilingual Dutch.

3 Test Sets

From a potential user's point of view, a question answering system should be able to process natural language queries and return precise and unambiguous responses, drawn from a large reference corpus. Thus, in every evaluation campaign like the one we conducted, a set of well formulated questions is required. Since they should reflect real requests posed by humans, such questions must sound spontaneous and realistic. On the other hand, they must be clear, simple and factoid, i.e. related to facts, events, physical situations, so that the answers can be retrieved without inference. All the necessary information to answer the questions must be straightforwardly available and consequently included in the document collection searched by the systems. For this reason no external knowledge of the world should be required and the queries should deal with practical, concrete matters, rather than with abstract notions, that depend on personal opinion or reasoning.

The creation of the question sets for both the tasks entailed much work in terms of query selection and answer verification. In order to establish some common criteria of comparison between the several languages involved, we decided to provide the participants, independently from the language, with the same queries. Thus, we created two collections of two hundred questions each, translated into different languages: one for the monolingual tasks and the other one for the cross-language tasks. As a result, we put together two reusable linguistic resources that can be useful for the QA community but also for other NLP fields, such as Machine Translation. The test set for the monolingual tasks in particular represents a multilingual collection of queries with their answers in different corpora.

3.1 Gold Standard for the Monolingual Tasks

The benchmark collection of queries and responses for the Dutch, Italian and Spanish monolingual tasks was the result of a joint effort between the coordinators, who decided to share the test sets in the three languages. Our activity can be roughly divided into four steps:

1. *Production of a pool of 200 candidate questions with their answers in each language.* These queries were formulated on the basis of the topics released by CLEF for the retrieval tasks of the year 2000, 2001 and/or 2002. The CLEF topics, i.e. a set of concepts chosen with the aim of covering the main events occurred in the years 1994 and/or 1995, allowed us to pose questions independently from the document collection. In this way we avoided any influence in the contents and in the formulation of the queries. Questions were posed according to common

guidelines: they had to be generally short and fact-based, unrelated to subjective opinions. They could not ask for definitions (i.e. "Who is Bill Clinton") and they had to have just one unique and unambiguous item as response, which means that we avoided questions asking for multiple items like those used in the TREC list task. Three groups of native speakers, one for each language, were involved in this work and searched the correct answers. A question has an answer in the reference corpus if a document contains the correct response without any inference implying knowledge outside the document itself.

2. *Selection of 150 questions from each monolingual set.* Since our aim was to build a test set of shared queries that would find answers in all the monolingual corpora, each group chose 150 questions from its candidate pool and translated them into English, thus a larger collection of 450 queries was put together. English constituted a sort of inter-language we used to shift from one language to another, but in this phase we were aware that there was the risk of changing unwarily the content of the questions during the translation. Each group chose its 150 questions taking into consideration that they would be processed by the other two, so the most general queries, that were likely to find a response in the other two corpora, were selected. Those that were too strictly related to the specific issues of a country were discarded.

3. *Processing of the shared questions.* Once we had collected a pool of 450 questions that had response in one of the corpora, we detected the duplicates and eliminated them. Quite surprisingly, we found thirteen couples of queries that had an identical meaning, although the formulation could be slightly different. Then each group translated back from English the 300 questions provided by the other coordinators and verified whether they had an answer in its corpus.

4. *Selection of the final 200 questions.* At this point, about 450 different questions had been formulated and translated into Dutch, English, Italian and Spanish. All of them had at least one answer in at least one language (other than English), and more than 200, obtained by merging the data of the second cross-verification, proved to have at least one answer in all the three monolingual document collections. Our goal was to provide the QA participants with 200 questions, including a small rate of NIL queries, i.e. questions that do not have any known answer in the corpus. We agreed that the 10% of the test set was a reasonable amount of NIL questions, that were first introduced in QA evaluation at TREC-10 (2001). So we selected 180 questions from those that had a response in all the three corpora, and each group completed its monolingual test set adding 20 NIL questions, that were necessarily different for each task. Taking into consideration seven general classes of questions, we tried to balance the final test set of 180 questions, that is composed of: 45 entries that ask for the name or role of a PERSON, 40 that pertain a LOCATION, 31 a MEASURE, 23 an ORGANISATION, 19 a DATE, 9 a concrete OBJECT, while 13, due to their vagueness, can be labeled with OTHER.

The result of the question development phase is a useful and reusable multilingual question set, whose entries are structured in a XML format, as shown in the example of figure 1. More details are given in the paper "Creating the DISEQuA Corpus" (in this book).

```
<qa cnt="1" type="DATE">
    <language val="ITA" original="TRUE">
        <question assessor="Ale-irst">
            Quando è avvenuta la riunificazione delle due Germanie?
        </question>
        <answer n="1" idx="SDA19941115.00073">
            nel 1989
        </answer>
    </language>
    <language val="SPA" original="FALSE">
        <question assessor="Anselmo-UNED">
            ¿Cuándo se produjo la reunificación de Alemania?
        </question>
        <answer n="1" idx="EFE19941108-04388">
            1989
        </answer>
        <answer n="2" idx="EFE19941108-04508">
            1989
        </answer>
    </language>
    <language val="DUT" original="FALSE">
        <question assessor="LIT">
            Wanneer vond de Duitse hereniging plaats?
        </question>
        <answer n="1" idx="NH19940128-0161">
            in 1989
        </answer>
    </language>
    <language val="ENG" original="FALSE">
        <question assessor="">
            When did the reunification of East and West Germany take place?
        </question>
        <answer n="1" idx="-1">
            SEARCH[in 1989]
        </answer>
    </language>
</qa>
```

Fig. 1. Gold Standard format of a question for the monolingual tasks

3.2 Gold Standard for the Cross-Language Tasks

While in the monolingual tasks we had three different document collections and three sets of questions, all the bilingual tasks had one English target corpus. For this reason we generated 200 English queries and verified manually that each of them (except 15 NIL) had at least an answer. Then the questions were translated into each language. As in the monolingual test sets, translators were asked to be as faithful as possible to the original English version, in fact we were aware that every translation could be different from the source.

Because of organizational problems encountered shortly before the test set creation deadline, three Italian native speakers at ITC-irst had to take on the job, even though there was a high risk of inconsistencies that may have affected the quality of the question set as a resource.

Due to time constraints we could not compile a large pool of general questions independently from the corpus and then verify them. Instead, we chose an alternative approach: we randomly selected a document from the collection (while trying to select news with a worldwide importance, avoiding sections that deal with local politics or issues too strictly related to Los Angeles counties) and picked up a text snippet that was relevant, long and interesting enough to get a question out of it. For instance, from the following passage

> The government has banned foods containing intestine or thymus from calves because a new scientific study suggested that they might be contaminated with the infectious agent of bovine spongiform encephalopathy, commonly called "mad cow disease".

we drew the question 'What is another name for the "mad cow disease"?'.

Finally, we obtained a benchmark corpus in which each question appears in six languages, as the tag attribute <language val> in figure 2 shows:

```
<qa cnt="4" type="OTHER">
    <language val="ENG"  original="TRUE">
        <question assessor="Ale-irst">
            What is another name for the "mad cow disease"?
        </question>
        <answer n="1" idx="LA091194.0096">
            bovine spongiform encephalopathy
        </answer>
    </language>
    <language val="ITA"  original="FALSE">
        <question assessor="Ale-irst">
            Qual è un altro nome per la "malattia della mucca pazza"?
        </question>
        <answer n="1" idx="">
            SEARCH[bovine spongiform encephalopathy]
        </answer>
    </language>
    <language val="SPA"  original="FALSE">
        <question assessor="">
            ¿Qué otro nombre recibe la enfermedad de las vacas locas?
        </question>
        <answer n="1" idx="">
            SEARCH[bovine spongiform encephalopathy]
        </answer>
    </language>
    <language val="DUT"  original="FALSE">
        <question assessor="">
            Wat is een andere naam voor "gekke-koeienziekte"?
        </question>
        <answer n="1" idx="">
            SEARCH[bovine spongiform encephalopathy]
```

```
            </answer>
         </language>
         <language val="GER"  original="FALSE">
            <question assessor="">
                Was ist ein anderer Name fü "Rinderwahnsinn"?
            </question>
            <answer n="1" idx="">
                SEARCH[bovine spongiform encephalopathy]
            </answer>
         </language>
         <language val="FRE"  original="FALSE">
            <question assessor="">
                Quel autre nom donne-t-on à la "maladie de la vache folle"?
            </question>
            <answer n="1" idx="">
                SEARCH[bovine spongiform encephalopathy]
            </answer>
         </language>
      </qa>
```

Fig. 2. Gold Standard format of a question for the bilingual tasks

4 Results

Participants had one week to process the questions. Since no manual intervention of any kind was allowed, we asked participants to freeze their systems before downloading the queries from our "QA @ CLEF" website.[1] Before the start of the evaluation exercise, we released detailed guidelines with the necessary information about the required format of the submissions. We also put online a checking routine with which participants could make sure that their responses were in compliance with that.

4.1 Response Format

Since we allowed to submit both exact answers and 50 byte long strings, we could not evaluate these two formats together. For this reason, we divided our track into two subtasks with separated evaluations. The required format of the answers in both subtasks was the same, but we decided to draw up two separate results.

Table 2 shows an example of a participant's submissions, where the first column indicates the question number, provided by the organizers, and the string in the second one represents the unique identifier for a system and a run: the last two characters in this case show that the task is the bilingual Italian, and the fifth and sixth characters give information about the kind of responses retrieved in this run, i.e. exact answers.

The third field in the response format was the answer rank, which was crucially important for the evaluation of the system accuracy. Participants had to return the

---

[1] http://clef-qa.itc.it

questions in the same order in which they had been downloaded, i.e. unranked. On the contrary, they had to rank their responses by confidence, putting in the first place the surest answer.

The integer or floating point score number of the fourth column justified the answer ranking. This field was not compulsory, and the systems that had no scoring strategies could set the value to default 0 (zero).

The docid, i.e. the unique identifier of the document that supports the given answer, is placed in the fifth column. If the system maintained that there was no answer in the corpus or if it could not find one, the docid was replaced by the string "NIL".

The answer string had to be given in the last field of the response, that was left empty when the docid was substituted by "NIL".

Table 2. Examples of responses drawn from the first bilingual run submitted by ITC-irst

0001	irstex031bi	1	3253	LA011694-0094	Modern Art
0001	irstex031bi	2	1776	LA011694-0094	UCLA
0001	irstex031bi	3	1251	LA042294-0050	Cultural Center
0002	irstex031bi	1	9	NIL	
0003	irstex031bi	1	484	LA012594-0239	1991
0003	irstex031bi	2	106	LA012594-0239	Monday
0004	irstex031bi	1	154	LA072294-0071	Clark
0004	irstex031bi	2	117	LA072594-0055	Huber
0004	irstex031bi	3	110	LA072594-0055	Department

4.2 Judgments and Evaluation Measures

Each single answer was judged by human assessors, who assigned to each response a unique label: either right, or wrong, or unsupported or inexact. Assessors were told to judge the submissions from a potential user's point of view, because the evaluation should take into consideration the future portability of QA systems. They analyzed both the answers themselves and the context, i.e. the document that supported the answer, in which they appeared.

Answers were judged to be incorrect (W) when the answer-string did not contain the answer or when the answer was not responsive. In contrast, a response was considered to be correct (R) when the answer-string consisted of nothing more than the exact, minimal answer (or contained the correct answer within the 50 byte long string) and when the document returned supported the response. Unsupported answers (U) were correct but it was impossible to infer that they were responsive from the retrieved document. Answers were judged as non-exact (X) when the answer was correct and supported by the document, but the answer string missed bits of the response or contained more than just the exact answer.

In addition, we outlined some common criteria to distinguish and properly evaluate exact answers. We outlined general rules to apply in several cases: as regards the date of specific events that ended in the past, both day and year are normally required (unless the question refers only to the year), but if the day cannot be retrieved, the year is normally sufficient. For instance, if a system answered the question "When did Napoleon die?" returning "5th May", it would be judged as incorrect. On the other hand, both "May 5, 1821" and "1821" could be correct exact answers. Actually, no clear definitions of exact answer have been formalized, yet. Discussing the issue, we noticed that, generally speaking, articles and prepositions do not invalidate an "exact" answer. So, both "July, 9" and "on the 9th of July" are exact answers. Similarly, appositions should not represent a problem, as well. So for instance, "1957", "year 1957" and "in the year 1957" should be exact answers, though someone could object that (with dates) "year" is redundant. When a query asks for a measure, the unit of measure can be accepted, too. So, both "30" and "30 degrees" are exact.

Concerning NIL answers, they are correct if neither human assessors nor systems have found any answer before or after the assessment process. If there is an answer in the collection, NIL is evaluated as incorrect. A NIL answer means that the system *believes* that there is not an answer for that question in the collection. There is no way for systems to explicitly indicate that they do not know or cannot find the answer for a question.

In strict evaluation, only correct answers (R) scored points, while in lenient evaluation the unsupported responses (U) were considered to be correct, too. The score of each question was the reciprocal of the rank for the first answer to be judged correct, which means that each query could receive either 1, or 0, or 0.333, or 0.5 points, depending on the confidence ranking.

The basic evaluation measure was the Mean Reciprocal Rank (MRR), that represents the mean score over all questions. MRR takes into consideration both recall and precision of the systems' performance, and can range between 0 (no correct responses) and 1 (all the 200 queries have a correct answer at position one). Figures 6 and 7 below summarize the QA track results and show that the systems achieved better results in the monolingual than in the bilingual tasks, where the drop in performance is possibly due to the cross-language step. The QA system developed by ITC-irst proved to be the most accurate among those that participated, and the mean reciprocal rank scored in the monolingual Italian using 50 byte long strings as answers was the highest of the whole QA track.

Answer responsiveness and exactness were in the opinion of human assessors, whose judgment could be different, as in everyday life we have different criteria to determine whether a response is good or not. During the evaluation of most of the runs, two different assessors judged each single question (each question of the bilingual runs were judged by three NIST assessors) and in case of discrepancies, they discussed their opinion and tried to reach an agreement. Whenever they could not agree, another person took the final decision.

After the submission deadline had passed, we detected some mistakes in the questions. In particular, a blunder persisted in the Italian queries: we wrongly put an apostrophe after the contraction of the question word "quale" ("which"/"what"). We found 21 cases in the monolingual test set and 17 cases in the bilingual one. In the TREC campaigns the questions that contain mistakes are excluded from the evaluation, but, considering that the form "qual'e'/era" is quite common in Italian and that a QA system should be robust enough to recognize variant spellings, we decided to keep those queries. For the sake of completeness, we calculated precision and recall without the questions with that mistake, and we obtained just a very minor variation of the values (around 1%).

Table 3. Examples of judged responses drawn from the first bilingual run submitted by ITC-irst

Questions and judged responses						
What museum is directed by Henry Hopkins?						
W	1	irstex031bi	1	3252	LA011694-0094	Modern Art
U	1	irstex031bi	2	1773	LA011694-0094	UCLA
X	1	irstex031bi	3	1253	LA042294-0050	Cultural Center

Comment: The second answer was correct but the document retrieved was not relevant. The third response missed bits of the name, and was judged non-exact.

Where did the Purussaurus live before becoming extinct?						
W	2	irstex031bi	1	9	NIL	

Comment: The system erroneously "believed" that the query had no answer in the corpus, or could not find one.

When did Shapour Bakhtiar die?						
R	3	irstex031bi	1	484	LA012594-0239	1991
W	3	irstex031bi	2	106	LA012594-0239	Monday

Comment: In the questions that asked for the date of an event, the year was often regarded as sufficient.

Who is John J. Famalaro accused of having killed?						
W	4	irstex031bi	1	154	LA072294-0071	Clark
R	4	irstex031bi	2	117	LA072594-0055	Huber
W	4	irstex031bi	3	110	LA072594-0055	Department

Comment: The second answer, that returned the victim's last name, was considered sufficient and correct, since in the document retrieved no other people named "Huber" were mentioned.

Translation could be the source of mistakes, as well. In the monolingual Spanish questions collection, "minister of Foreign Affairs" was erroneously translated as "president of Foreign Affairs" during the question sharing between the Italian and the Spanish coordinators.

In tables 4 and 6 below, we give a general overview of the results achieved by participants. In the monolingual exact answers runs there was a certain homogeneity in the performance, in fact there was not a great gap between the average (81 questions answered correctly) and the best result (97 in strict evaluation).

Differently, the results of the bilingual exact answers runs show a clear drop in the systems' accuracy: the difference between the best result (90 queries with at least a right answer) and the average (51) seems to be significant.

Table 4. Summary statistics of the exact answers runs

EXACT ANSWERS RUNS

GROUP	TASK	RUN NAME	MRR		# of Q. with at least one right answer		NIL Answers	
			Str.	Len.	Str.	Len.	total	R
MONO-LINGUAL TASKS DLSI-UA	Monoling. Spanish	alicex031ms	.307	.320	80	87	21	5
		alicex032ms	.296	.317	70	77	21	5
ITC-irst	Monoling. Italian	irstex031mi	.422	.442	97	101	4	2
UVA	Monoling. Dutch	uamsex031md	.298	.317	78	82	200	17
		uamsex032md	.305	.335	82	89	200	17
CROSS-LANGUAGE TASKS ISI	Bilingual Spanish	isixex031bs	.302	.328	69	77	4	0
		isixex032bs	.271	.307	68	78	4	0
ITC-irst	Bilingual Italian	irstex031bi	.322	.334	77	81	49	6
		irstex032bi	.393	.400	90	92	28	5
CS-CMU	Bilingual French	lumoex031bf	.153	.170	38	42	92	8
		lumoex032bf	.131	.149	31	35	91	7
DLTG	Bilingual French	dltgex031bf	.115	.120	23	24	119	10
		dltgex032bf	.110	.115	22	23	119	10
RALI	Bilingual French	udemex032bf	.140	.160	38	42	3	1

Table 5. Number of correct answers at a given rank in the exact answers runs. As can be noticed, all the systems (except DLTG's one) returned more than one answer per question, and ranked the responses quite well (i.e. placing most of them at the first place)

RIGHT ANSWERS RANKING

RUN NAME	STRICT				LENIENT			
	1st	2nd	3rd	total	1st	2nd	3rd	total
alicex031ms	49	13	18	80 (40%)	49	15	23	87 (43.5%)
alicex032ms	51	12	7	70 (35%)	53	15	9	77 (38.5%)
irstex031mi	75	13	9	97 (48.5%)	79	13	9	101 (50.5%)
uamsex031md	47	14	17	78 (39%)	50	17	15	82 (41%)
uamsex032md	46	19	17	82 (41%)	50	25	14	89 (44.5%)
isixex031bs	53	13	3	69 (34.5%)	56	16	5	77 (38.5%)
isixex032bs	43	18	7	68 (34%)	48	21	9	78 (39%)
irstex031bi	55	13	9	77 (38.5%)	56	15	10	81 (40.5%)
irstex032bi	70	12	8	90 (45%)	71	13	8	92 (46%)
lumoex031bf	25	8	5	38 (19%)	28	9	5	42 (21%)
lumoex032bf	22	8	1	31 (15.5%)	25	9	1	35 (17.5%)
dltgex031bf	23	0	0	23 (11.5%)	24	0	0	24 (12%)
dltgex032bf	22	0	0	22 (11%)	23	0	0	23 (11.5%)
udemex032bf	20	12	6	38 (19%)	23	13	6	42 (21%)

Concerning the 50 byte long answers runs (tables 5 and 7), they do not allow many interpretations: we allowed to submit also these longer responses to facilitate and attract as many participants as possible, but in the end just three groups decided to return them, so we cannot make significant comparisons. The TREC workshops have probably pushed the QA community in tuning the systems on exact answers, and actually, it seems that there is not a great difference between exact and 50 byte answers. In next year's campaign we could keep both exact and longer answers, maybe expanding the latter to 200 bytes or more.

Table 6. Summary statistics of the 50 byte long answers runs

50 BYTE LONG ANSWERS RUNS

	GROUP	TASK	RUN NAME	MRR		# of Q. with at least one right answer		NIL Answers	
				Str.	Len.	Str.	Len.	total	R
MONO-LING.	ITC-irst	Monoling. Italian	irstst032mi	.449	.471	99	104	5	2
CROSS LANG.	DFKI	Bilingual German	dfkist031bg	.098	.103	29	30	18	0
	RALI	Bilingual French	udemst031bf	.213	.220	56	58	4	1

Table 7. Number of correct answers at a given rank in the 50 byte long answers runs

RIGHT ANSWERS RANKING

RUN NAME	STRICT				LENIENT			
	1st	2nd	3rd	total	1st	2nd	3rd	total
irstst032mi	83	9	7	99 (49.5%)	87	10	7	104 (52%)
dfkist031bg	13	8	8	29 (14.5%)	14	8	8	30 (15%)
udemst031bf	32	16	8	56 (28%)	33	17	8	58 (29%)

Tables 5 and 7 show that the systems were quite accurate in ranking their correct answers: in strict evaluation, about the 70% of the correct responses was returned at the first rank, on the average.

Strict and lenient evaluation results actually do not differ much. This suggests that the systems are quite precise in the correct answers they return: the unsupported responses were in fact a few. More strikingly, the performance of the cross-language systems turned out to be quite low, which suggests that multilinguality is a field that requires much more attention and investigation.

5   Conclusions and Future Perspectives

The first European evaluation of non-English QA systems has given rise to useful resources for future multilingual QA developments. It has allowed us to establish and test a methodology and criteria for both the test suit production and the assessment procedure. Unfortunately, the CLEF QA Track did not receive the expected attention in terms of participation, and in most tasks just one group submitted its results. Actually, twelve research groups registered and were interested into participating, but some of them could not adjust their system on time. This suggests that the debate and the activities on multilingual QA have a certain appeal on the community, even though much challenging work remains to be done. We can be pleased of the outcome of this pilot QA evaluation exercise, and we hope that the results and the resources we developed will encourage many other groups to participate in future campaigns.

Cross-linguality has always been out of the scope of the TREC QA tracks, and our pilot QA at CLEF hopefully represents a first step in the direction of more sophisticated evaluation campaigns of multilingual systems. In our track, we provided five non-English question sets but just one English target document collection: in the future we could have several reference corpora in different languages, many different question sets and answers translated into different languages. Multilinguality provides us with the opportunity to experiment with different approaches, exploring many potential applications: for instance, we could think about developing intelligent systems that taking into consideration the language and the text coverage, select the most useful target corpus to search the answer for a particular question posed in a particular language. The possibilities are manifold, and our cross-language tasks can be considered just a starting point.

Acknowledgements

The work described in this paper has been supported by the Autonomous Province of Trento, in the framework of the WebFAQ Project, by the Spanish Government (MCyT, TIC-2002-10597-E) and by the Netherlands Organization for Scientific Research (NWO) under project numbers 612-13-001, 365-20-005, 612.069.006, 612.000.106, 220-80-001, and 612.000.207.

The authors wish to acknowledge the contribution and support given by Franca Rossi, Elisabetta Fauri, Pamela Forner and Manuela Speranza at ITC-irst, who helped us in the generation and verification of the questions for both the monolingual and bilingual tasks.

Stephan Busemann at DFKI and Jian-Yun Nie at the University of Montreal took on the job of translating into German and French the questions for the bilingual tasks, and their contribution was fundamental.

We wish to thank the NIST, and in particular Ellen Voorhees and Donna Harman, for judging all the bilingual runs and for providing us with the necessary resources and feedback we needed to organize this pilot track.

We are also grateful to Carol Peters (ISTI-CNR) and Charles Callaway (ITC-irst) who, as English native speakers, edited the questions for the cross-language tasks.

We wish to thank Henry Chinaski, Vera Hollink, and Valentin Jijkoun for their help in the development and assessment of the monolingual Dutch task.

References

1. Braschler, M. and Peters, C.: The CLEF Campaigns: Evaluation of Cross-Language Information Retrieval Systems. UPGRADE (The European Online Magazine for the IT Professional), Vol. III, Issue no. 3, (June 2002).
   URL: http://www.upgrade-cepis.org/issues/2002/3/up3-3Braschler.pdf .
2. Burger, J., Cardie, C., Chaudhri, V., Gaizauskas, R., Harabagiu, S., Israel, D., Jacquemin, C., Lin, C.-Y., Maiorano, S., Miller, G., Moldovan, D., Ogden, B., Prager, J., Riloff, E., Singhal, A., Shrihari, R., Strzalkowski, T., Voorhees, E., Weishedel, R.: Issues Tasks and Program Structures to Roadmap Research in Question & Answering (Q&A), 2001.
   URL: http://www-nlpir.nist.gov/projects/duc/papers/qa.Roadmap-paper_v2.doc.
3. CLEF 2003 Question Answering Track: Guidelines for the Monolingual and Bilingual Tasks. URL: http://clef-qa.itc.it/guidelines.htm.
4. Knott A., Bayard I., de Jager S., Smith L., Moorfield J. and O'Keefe R.: A Question-Answering System for English and Maōri. Proceedings of the Fifth Biannual Conference on Artificial Neural Networks and Expert Systems (ANNES), University of Otago, November 2001.
5. Liddy, E.D.: Why are People Asking these Questions? A Call for Bringing Situation into Question-Answering System Evaluation. LREC Workshop Proceedings on Question Answering – Strategy and Resources, Grand Canary Island, Spain, 2002.
6. Magnini B., Negri M., Prevete R., Tanev H.: Multilingual Question/Answering: the DIOGENE System. Proceedings of the Tenth Text REtrieval Conference (TREC-2001), Gaithersburg, MD., 2001.
7. Magnini, B.: Evaluation of Cross-Language Question Answering Systems, proposal presentation held at the CLEF Workshop 2002.
   URL: http://clef.iei.pi.cnr.it:2002/workshop2002/presentations/q-a.pdf.
8. Maybury , M.: Toward a Question Answering Roadmap, 2002.
   URL:www.mitre.org/work/tech_papers/tech_papers_02/maybury_toward
9. Voorhees, E. M.: The TREC-8 Question Answering Track Report. Proceedings of the Eighth Text REtrieval Conference (TREC-8), Gaithersburg, MD., 1999.
10. Voorhees, E. M.: Overview of the TREC 2001 Question Answering Track. Proceedings of the Tenth Text REtrieval Conference (TREC-2001), Gaithersburg, MD., 2001.
11. Voorhees, E. M.: Overview of the TREC 2002 Question Answering Track. Proceedings of the Eleventh Text REtrieval Conference (TREC-2002), Gaithersburg, MD., 2002.
12. Voorhees, E. M., Tice, D. M.: Building a Question Answering Test Collection. Proceedings of SIGIR2000, Athens, Greece, 2000.

Creating the DISEQuA Corpus: A Test Set for Multilingual Question Answering

Bernardo Magnini*, Simone Romagnoli*, Alessandro Vallin*,
Jesús Herrera**, Anselmo Peñas**, Víctor Peinado**,
Felisa Verdejo**, and Maarten de Rijke***

* ITC-irst, Centro per la Ricerca Scientifica e Tecnologica,
Via Sommarive, 38050 Povo (TN), Italy
{magnini,romagnoli,vallin}@itc.it
** UNED, Spanish Distance Learning University,
Dpto. Lenguajes y Sistemas Informaticos,
Ciudad Universitaria, c./Juan del Rosal 16, 28040 Madrid, Spain
{anselmo,felisa,jesus.herrera,victor}@lsi.uned.es
*** Language and Inference Technology Group, ILLC,
University of Amsterdam, Nieuwe Achtergracht 166,
1018 WV Amsterdam, The Netherlands
mdr@science.uva.nl

Abstract. This paper describes the procedure adopted by the three coordinators of the CLEF 2003 question answering track (ITC-irst, UNED and ILLC) to create the question set for the monolingual tasks. Despite the few resources available, the three groups managed to formulate and verify a large pool of original questions in three different languages: Dutch, Italian and Spanish. Part of these queries was translated into English and shared between the three coordinating groups. A second cross-verification was then conducted in order to identify the queries that had an answer in all three monolingual document collections. The result of the joint efforts was the creation of the DISEQuA (Dutch Italian Spanish English Questions and Answers) corpus, a useful and reusable resource that is freely available for the research community. We report on the different stages of the corpus creation, from the monolingual kernels to the multilingual extension.

1 Introduction

Starting from the basis of the experience accumulated during the past TREC campaigns, the question answering (QA) track at CLEF 2003 focused on the evaluation of QA systems created for European languages other than English, and consequently promoted both monolingual (Dutch, Italian and Spanish) and cross-language tasks. Cross-linguality is a necessary step to push participants into designing systems that can find answers in languages different from the original language of the questions, thus depicting a possible scenario for future applications.

The document collections employed in this track were those used at CLEF 2002, i.e. articles drawn from newspapers and news agencies for 1994 (Dutch, Italian,

C. Peters et al. (Eds.): CLEF 2003, LNCS 3237, pp. 487–500, 2004.
© Springer-Verlag Berlin Heidelberg 2004

Spanish) and 1995 (Dutch). As coordinators of the monolingual tasks, we first needed to create a corpus of questions with related answers for the evaluation exercise, i.e. a replicable gold standard.

According to the CLEF QA guidelines, which are based on those of TREC 2002, the question set released to participants is made up of simple, mostly short, straightforward and 'factoid' queries. Systems should process questions that sound naturally spontaneous, and a good, realistic question set should consist of questions motivated by a real desire to know something about a particular event or situation. We could have extracted our questions directly from the document collection, simply turning assertive statements into interrogative ones. Such a procedure would have been reasonably quick and pragmatic, but would have undermined the original intentions of the QA track, which is to evaluate systems' performance in finding possible answers to open domain questions, independently of the target document collection used. Deriving the queries from the corpus itself would have influenced us in the choice of topics and words, and in the syntactic formulation of the questions.

The coordinators of the TREC 2002 QA track obtained their 500 questions corpus from question logs of WWW search engines (like the MSN portal). They extracted a thousand queries that satisfied pre-determined patterns from the millions of questions registered in the logs, and then, after correcting linguistic errors, they searched for the answers in a 3GB wide corpus. Similarly, the organizers of the TREC-8 QA (held in 1999) drew one hundred of the 200 final questions from a pool of 1,500 candidate questions contained in the FAQFinder logs [3].

This strategy leads to a well formed questions and answers corpus, but it requires a lot of resources, i.e. many native speakers for the verification of the questions, a huge document collection, access to the logs of search engine companies and - last but not least – a considerable amount of time. We had neither question logs nor a corpus big enough to permit the extraction of all kinds of answer. Thus, in order to cope with the lack of resources, we conceived an alternative approach for our QA corpus creation. Our aim was to preserve spontaneity of formulation and maintain independence from the document collections.

The monolingual tasks of the CLEF 2003 QA track required a test set of 200 fact-based questions. Our goal was to collect a heterogeneous set of queries that would represent an extensive range of subjects and have related answers in the three different corpora. The creation of the three test sets constituted the first step towards the generation of this multilingual corpus of questions and answers, which contains questions in four languages, with the related responses that the assessors extracted from the monolingual document collections during the verification phase.

Our activity can thus be roughly divided into four steps:

1. Formulation of a pool of 200 candidate questions with their answers in each language;
2. Selection of 150 questions from each monolingual set and their translation into English in order to share them with the other groups;
3. Second translation and further processing of each shared question in two different document collections;
4. Data merging and final construction of the DISEQuA corpus.

2   Question Generation

As stated, the reference corpora used when creating the questions for the monolingual tasks were three collections of newspaper and news agency documents in Dutch, Italian and Spanish, released in 1994 and 1995, and licensed by the Cross Language Evaluation Forum. These articles constituted a heterogeneous, open domain text collection. Each article had a unique identifier, i.e. a DOCID number, that participating systems had to return together with the answer string in order to prove that their responses were supported by the text. The text of the Italian collection was constituted by about 27 millions words (200 Mb) drawn from the newspaper *La Stampa* and the Swiss-Italian *SDA* press agency. The Spanish corpus contained more than 200,000 international news documents from the *EFE* press agency published during the year 1994. The Dutch collection was the CLEF 2002 Dutch collection, which consists of the 1994 and 1995 editions of *Algemeen Dagblad* and *NRC Handelsblad* (about 200,000 documents, or 540 Mb).

```
<DOC>
<DOCNO>EFE19940101-00001</DOCNO>
<DOCID>EFE19940101-00001</DOCID>
<DATE>19940101</DATE>
<TIME>00.28</TIME>
<SCATE>POX</SCATE>
<FICHEROS>94F.JPG</FICHEROS>
<DESTINO>ICX EXG</DESTINO>
<CATEGORY>POLITICA</CATEGORY>
<CLAVE>DP2403</CLAVE>
<NUM>736</NUM>
<TITLE>  GUINEA-OBIANG
        PRESIDENTE   SUGIERE   RECHAZARA   AYUDA   EXTERIOR
CONDICIONADA
</TITLE>
<TEXT>   Malabo, 31 dic (EFE).- El presidente de Guinea Ecuatorial, Teodoro Obiang
Nguema, sugirió hoy, viernes, que su Gobierno podría rechazar la ayuda internacional que
recibe si ésta se condiciona a que en el país haya "convulsiones políticas".
   En su discurso de fin de año, [......] conceptos de libertad, seguridad ciudadana y
desarrollo económico y social. EFE
   DN/FMR
   01/01/00-28/94
</TEXT>
</DOC>
```

Fig. 1. Format of the target document collection (example drawn from the Spanish corpus)

The textual contents of the Spanish collection, as shown in Figure 1, were not tagged in any way. The text sections of the Italian corpus on the contrary had been annotated with named entities tags such as <PERSON>, <LOCATION> and <AUTHOR>. The Dutch collections were formatted similarly.

Given these three corpora, our final goal was to formulate a set of 180 fact-based questions shared by all the three monolingual QA tasks. The goal of having the same queries in all the tasks was motivated by the need to compare system performance in different languages. Since the track was divided into many tasks and most of the groups participated in just one of them, by using the same test set, although translated into other languages, allows us to compare the accuracy of different runs. In addition to the 180 shared queries, we planned to include in each test set 20 questions with no answer in the corpora (the so-called NIL questions).

2.1 From Topics to Keywords

The key element that guided our activity through the first phase of question generation was the CLEF collection of topics. If we had asked people to generate questions without any restraint, we could have probably obtained just a few usable queries for our purpose. It would have been even more difficult to ask them to focus just on events occurred in 1994 or 1995, which is the time coverage of the articles in our text collections. Besides, we noticed that the mental process of conceiving fact-based questions without having any topic details can take a considerable amount of time: asking good questions can be as difficult as giving consistent answers. In order to cope with these drawbacks, to improve the relevance of the queries and to reduce the time necessary for their generation, we decided to use some CLEF topics.

Topics, that can be defined as "original user requests" [1], represent a resource developed for many NLP applications, included question answering. The team that generated the CLEF topics wanted to create a set of real life subjects which should meet the contents of the document collections. The main international political, social, cultural, economic, scientific and sporting issues and events occurring in 1994 and 1995 were included and topics were written in an SGML style, with three textual fields, as shown in Figure 2.

```
<top>
<num> C001
<I-title>Architettura a Berlino
<I-desc> Trova documenti che riguardano l'architettura a Berlino.
<I-narr> I documenti rilevanti parlano, in generale, degli aspetti architettonici di Berlino o,
in particolare, della ricostruzione di alcuni parti della città  dopo la caduta del Muro.
</top>1
```

Fig. 2. An Italian topic released by CLEF in the year 2000 (translation in the footnote)

The title field sketches straightforwardly the main content of the topic, the description field mirrors the needs of a potential user, presenting a more precise formulation in one sentence, and the narrative field gives more information concerning relevance.

In the very first experiment ITC-irst carried out to generate its questions set, two volunteers were provided with three CLEF topics structured as above, asking them to produce ten queries for each one. It took about forty-five minutes to conclude their task, and it was immediately noticed that the questions were too closely related to the

---

[1] <I-title>Architecture in Berlin
  <I-desc>Find documents on architecture in Berlin.
  <I-narr>Relevant documents report, in general, on the architectural features of Berlin or, in particular, on the reconstruction of some parts of the city after the fall of the Wall.

source topics. Therefore this pilot experiment showed the weaknesses and drawbacks of the strategy, which lead to overspecified questions, and underlined the need to improve the stimulating power of the topics reducing their specificity without losing relevance to the corpus.

The simplest way to expand the structure of the topics and widen the scope of activity for the people in charge of the question generation appeared to be to extract manually from each topic a series of relevant keywords that would replace the topics themselves. No particularly detailed instructions were given in that phase: we just isolated the most semantically relevant words. A keyword could be defined as an independent, unambiguous and precise element that is meant to rouse interest and stimulate questions over a specific issue. We also inferred keywords that were not explicitly present in the topic, assuming that even external knowledge, though related to the topic, could help to formulate pertinent questions. ITC-irst coordinators took into consideration the topics developed by CLEF in the years 2000, 2001 and 2002. Three people were involved in the extraction of keywords that were appended to each topic in form of a 'signature', as the tag in the following example shows. Thus, the topic entitled "Architecture in Berlin" (in Figure 2) was converted into a list of words that could appear unrelated to each other:

<IT-tsig>
architettura, Berlino, documenti, aspetti architettonici, ricostruzione, città, caduta del Muro, Muro
</IT-tsig>2

It is interesting to note that the keywords, even though derived from the topics, permitted a certain detachment from the restricted coverage of the topics themselves, without losing the connection with the important issues of the years 1994 and 1995, that constituted the core of the document collection. Thus the experiment was repeated and much better results in terms of variety and generality of the queries were achieved, in fact the people who were given the keywords instead of the topics were freer to range over a series of concepts without any restraint or need to adhere to a single specific and detailed issue. Although the existence of correlated keywords led to the generation of similar queries, this strategy was adopted with success.

The CLEF topics also had a pivotal role in the generation of the Spanish and Dutch queries. As preparatory work, the Spanish UNED NLP group studied the test set used at TREC 2002 and tried to draw some conclusions in terms of the formulation style of the questions and the necessary method to find the answer. Four people were then given the CLEF topics for 2000, 2001 and 2002 (but no keywords) with the task of producing 200 short, fact-based queries. The Dutch LIT group adopted the same strategy in its preparation. TREC QA topics (1-1893) were translated into Dutch, and old CLEF retrieval topics (1-140) were used to generate Dutch example questions, usually around 3 per topic.

2.2 From Keywords to Questions

Before generating the queries, the three groups agreed on common guidelines that would help to formulate a good and useful test set. Following the model of past TREC

---

[2] Architecture, Berlin , documents, architectural aspects, reconstruction, city, knocking down of the Wall, Wall.

campaigns, and particularly of the TREC 2002 QA track, a series of basic instructions were formulated.

Firstly, questions should be fact-based, and, if possible, they should address events that occurred in the years 1994 or 1995. When a precise reference to these two years was lacking in the questions, it had to be considered that systems would use a document collection of that year. No particular restraints were imposed on the length and on the syntactic form of the queries, but coordinators kept them simple.

Secondly, questions should ask for an entity (i.e. a person, a location, a date, a measure or a concrete object), avoiding subjective opinions or explanations. So, "Why-questions" were not allowed. Queries like "Why does Bush want to attack Iraq?" or "Who is the most important Italian politician of the twentieth century?" could not be accepted.

Since the TREC 2002 question set constituted a good term of comparison, and it did not include any definition question of the form "Who/What is X?", it was decided to avoid this question type, as well.

Thirdly, coordinators agreed that multiple-item questions, like those used in the TREC list-task, should be avoided. If the community is interested in processing list questions, we could propose them in next year's track, possibly together with definition queries. As a pilot evaluation exercise, we did not want to introduce too many difficulties that could have discouraged potential participants.

Similarly, the people in charge of the questions generation should not formulate 'double queries', in which there is a second indirect question subsumed within the main one (for instance, "Who is the president of the poorest country in the world?").

Finally, closed questions, known as yes/no questions, were also to be left out. Queries should be related to the topics or to the keywords extracted from the topics, without any particular restraint in the word choice. It was not necessary to know the answer before formulating a question: on the contrary, assessors had to be as close as possible to the information they found in the document collection. A prior knowledge of the answer could influence the search in the corpus.

Given these instructions, thirty people at ITC-irst were provided with two sets of keywords (extracted from two topics) and were asked to generate ten questions for each one. In this way, a large pool of 600 candidate queries was created. The examples shown in Figure 3 demonstrate that the keywords extended the limited scope of the topic "Architecture in Berlin", allowing people to pose questions related to history or even politics. Some questions, such as numbers 5 and 9, lost connection with the original form of the topic, introducing the name of a famous architect and asking for the number of inhabitants rather than focusing on the architectural features of the city. Adopting this strategy, we managed to preserve a certain adherence to the original content of the topic, while introducing some new elements. Inevitably, as a side effect, a number of queries turned out to be useless because they were almost totally unrelated to the keywords (and thus to the contents of the document collections) or badly formulated.

In spite of the guidelines defined before producing the candidate questions, some inconsistencies persisted. For instance, question 4 concerns a personal opinion rather than a fact: it is not clear how the importance of a place could be objectively measured. Similarly, question 7 deals with events that occurred later than 1994:

although the German government took the decision in 1991, Berlin officially became the capital city in 1999.

```
<num>C001</num>
<keyword> architettura, Berlino, documenti, aspetti architettonici, ricostruzione, città,
caduta del Muro, Muro </keyword>
<question n=1> Quando e' caduto il muro di Berlino? </question>
<question n=2> Chi ha costruito il Muro di Berlino? </question>
<question n=3> Quanto era lungo il muro di Berlino? </question>
<question n=4> Qual e' la piazza piu' importante di Berlino? </question>
<question n=5> Qual e' la professione di Renzo Piano? </question>
<question n=6> Quando e' stato costruito il muro di Berlino? </question>
<question n=7> Quando e' che Berlino e' ritornata ad essere capitale?</question>
<question n=8> Dove si trova Berlino? </question>
<question n=9> Quanti abitanti ha Berlino? </question>
<question n=10> Che cosa divideva il muro di Berlino? </question> [3]
```

Fig. 3. Questions generated from a list of keywords (translation in the footnote)

2.3 Verification of Questions

Once the candidate questions had been collected, it was necessary to verify whether they had an answer in the target document collection. This phase constituted the actual manual construction of the replicable gold standard for the CLEF QA track: systems would later process the questions automatically.

ITC-irst involved three native Italian speakers in this work. In order to cope with the large amount of candidate questions and with the possibility that many of them were not compliant with the generation guidelines and could not be used for the QA track, three different categories of queries were identified and each question was classified: the entries of list A were queries that respected the generation guidelines and whose answer was intuitively known, in list B were placed the relevant questions that, in the assessors' opinion, were more difficult to answer, while list C contained those that were badly formulated or did not respect the guidelines instructions. As expected, list B was the largest one, including 354 questions. At the end of the question verification phase, a total of 480 questions were processed manually, and the remaining 120, most of those included in list C, were eliminated.

Browsing a document collection in search of the answers can be a very exhausting activity without any tool that facilitates the detection of the relevant strings.

---

[3] <question n=1> When did the Berlin Wall fall? </question>
<question n=2> Who built the Berlin Wall? </question>
<question n=3> How long was the Berlin Wall? </question>
<question n=4> Which is the most important square in Berlin? </question>
<question n=5> What is Renzo Piano's job? </question>
<question n=6> When was the Berlin Wall built? </question>
<question n=7> When did Berlin become the capital again? </question>
<question n=8> Where is Berlin? </question>
<question n=9> How many inhabitants are there in Berlin? </question>
<question n=10> What did the Berlin Wall divide? </question

Fortunately, ITC-irst had a concordancer[4] available that allowed the three assessors to make selective searches within the corpus, to find the correct answers and to go back to the docid, i.e. the unique identifier, of the document that supported each answer. The common strategy employed by the assessors was to type parts of the query or parts of the known answer in the concordancer, and then browse the most relevant documents retrieved by the software in search of a text snippet that justified and supported the correct answer. The Dutch group developed a small number of grep-based shell scripts with the same purpose.

The problem of structuring data and finding a sensible format to describe both questions and answers arose during this first phase of the creation of DISEQuA. The issue was addressed by developing an XML syntax that would show the number of each question, the keyword set (or topic) from which it was generated, the person who verified it in the document collection and the type of entity to which it was related. Similarly, the answers found for each question needed to be numbered, and the docid of the document that supported each response had to be logged. The adoption of a precise format helped to solve the problem of losing trace of the changes that questions could undergo; new tags could be added to give more information. Secondly, structured data can be easily browsed and analyzed: for instance, the tag used to indicate the question type proved to be quite useful in balancing the test set. Thirdly, a common format for questions and answers was necessary to share them between the three groups that assembled the DISEQuA corpus.

Figure 4 shows an example drawn from the Italian question set: the attribute 'cnt' indicates the number assigned to the question, 'assessor' is the identifier of the person who processed the query, important in the case of inconsistencies. The attribute 'origin' gives the name of the file containing the keywords extracted from a single topic, while the attribute 'type' describes the category to which the answer belongs. Seven different question types were considered: PERSON, LOCATION, MEASURE, DATE, ORGANIZATION, OBJECT (i.e. concrete things) and OTHER (when the response could not be labeled with one precise type). The aim was to create a well-balanced test set, with a good coverage of all these categories.

Likewise, the attribute 'n' in the tag <answer> represents a progressive number of responses; in fact a single query could have several correct answers in the same document collection. Dates and numbers in particular change across different news reports for the same event. Sometimes earlier news items in the document collection are less precise than later ones, because they register a process that changes over a period. Since systems were expected to give an answer supported by a unique document, and not the final or best answer in the whole corpus, in such cases there were many correct responses. The attribute 'idx' gives the docid identifier of the document in which each single answer appears. Systems should return the docid as a justification of the answer, and in strict evaluation the unsupported responses were considered as incorrect.

When no answer was found in the target corpus, 'n' and 'idx' were labeled with 0 (zero), and the answer string was replaced by the string "NIL". Queries with no answer were not eliminated: on the contrary, twenty NIL questions were included in

---

[4] The "Toolbox for Lexicographers" developed by Claudio Giuliano.

the final version of each monolingual test set to evaluate systems' accuracy in recognizing that there was no response.

```
<qa>
    <question cnt="42" assessor="ALE" origin="keyword_C001.txt" type="MEASURE">
        Quanti abitanti ha Berlino?
    </question>
    <answer n="1" idx="SDA19940804.00147">
        3,5 milioni
    </answer>
</qa>
```

Fig. 4. Format of the verified questions (see question 9 in Figure 3)

Sometimes the responsiveness of the retrieved string was doubtful and the assessors could not decide whether it was acceptable. These cases required a deeper analyses and an agreement between different assessors. Doubts that emerged during the verification phase were indicated by inserting an asterix (*) before uncertain answers and a note explaining the doubt was appended to the question within the tag <rem>, as in the following example (see question 10 in figure 3):

```
<question n=5 origin=keyword_C001 type=LOCATION>
    Che cosa divideva il muro di Berlino ?
</question>
*<answer n="1" idx="LASTAMPA19941016.00038">
    Germania
</answer>
*<answer n="2" idx="LASTAMPA19941016.00038">
    mondo
</answer>
<rem>"Un evento inatteso, spettacolare, emozionante: sotto gli occhi del mondo cade il Muro di
Berlino, simbolomateriale della divisione della Germania e del mondo."</rem>5
```

A cut-and-pasted text snippet found in the document collection was usually placed in the tag <rem>, so that another assessor could take a decision without opening again the corpus in search of the necessary contextual information. In the example above, it was not clear whether the retrieved answers, which are metaphorical, could be accepted (actually, the Berlin Wall isolated West Berlin from the German Democratic Republic), so the first assessor that processed the question left the response undetermined. If a second assessor could not take a decision, the question was passed to a third person, who normally solved the doubts. Alternatively, badly formulated questions could be slightly modified in order to match the retrieved answer.

Some candidate questions asked for events occurring "in the year 1994" (or 1995), but since 1994 (and, for Dutch, 1995) was the year in which the target corpora were published, it was very improbable that the date would appear explicitly in the articles.

5 *<answer n="1"> Germany
  *<answer n="2"> the world
  <rem>"An unexpected, spectacular and exciting event: the eyes of the world are on the Berlin
  Wall that is falling, a concrete symbol of Germany's and the world's division."</rem>

For this reason, every explicit mention of the year 1994 (or 1995) had to be removed from the final version of the queries.

3   Sharing of Questions

At this point, each group had collected and verified 200 questions formulated in its own language. A small part of them (10%) had no answer in the document collections, while the rest had at least one supported response. Since the aim was to create a multilingual test set whose entries were formulated into three different languages, it was necessary to share the questions that had been generated independently. Thus, each group selected the 150 queries that seemed most likely to find an answer also in the other two document collections and translated them into English before sending them to the larger pool. Figure 5 shows the format chosen for the question sharing. Questions that were too strictly related to the issues or events of a particular country were skipped.

```
<qa cnt="20" type="MEASURE">
   <language val="ITA" original="TRUE">
           <question assessor="ALE">
                   Quanti abitanti ha Berlino?
           </question>
           <answer n="1" idx="SDA19940804.00147">
                   3,5 milioni
           </answer>
   </language>
   <language val="ENG" original="FALSE">
           <question assessor="">
                   How many inhabitants are there in Berlin?
           </question>
           <answer n="1" idx="-1">
                   SEARCH[3,500,000]
           </answer>
   </language>
</qa>
```

Fig. 5. Question sharing format

English was chosen as the intermediate language for two reasons: firstly to build a richer linguistic resource for further QA evaluation, considering that most question answering systems are currently designed for English applications; secondly, to simplify the passage from one language to another, without recurring to professional translators. Nevertheless, the translation into English required much attention because in the passage from one language to another, the syntactic formulation or even the meaning could change. It is important to underline that the 450 questions that form the DISEQuA corpus underwent three translations: one from the source language into English and then from English into the two target languages. Each translation could introduce some variations, with the risk that the four final versions would not be semantically equivalent and aligned. To avoid this problem, in the second translation both the English version and the original question in the source language were taken into consideration.

If we compare Figures 4 and 5, we see that changes in the format have been introduced in this phase. Though the question is the same in the two figures, it is numbered differently, in fact some questions that were placed before this one in the monolingual Italian test set were discarded because they had little chances of finding an answer in the Dutch and Spanish corpora.

The new tag <language> was added, with its attributes 'val' and 'original'. The former indicates the language in which the question appears ("DUT", "ITA", "SPA" or "ENG"). The latter keeps track of the source and the target language of each query: 'original' can have either "TRUE" or "FALSE" as Boolean values, where "TRUE" shows that the 'language val' is the source language, i.e. the language in which the question was first generated, while "FALSE" records that the query has been translated. Consequently, English questions, as intermediate versions, are always tagged "FALSE".

For the answer string format, a default negative value "-1" was assigned to the English version of each question, to distinguish it from the zero used in NIL questions. The string "SEARCH" followed by the translation within square brackets of the correct answer found in the source corpus was a valuable help for the assessors who would process the shared questions.

4   Data Merging

Thus, each group selected and translated 150 verified questions from its monolingual test set, so that a large pool of 450 queries formulated in English and a second source language was created. In the following phase, each group picked up the 300 questions submitted by the other two and translated them a second time from English into a new target language. As a consequence, all the questions had a translation in four different languages and could be processed again in the other two target document collections. When the second verification was concluded, the resulting data were merged. The different versions of the same questions were aligned, and the DISEQuA corpus was successfully assembled. Figure 6 shows how each question appears in the multilingual test set.

The merging revealed that 246 questions had at least one answer in all the three reference document collections, 111 had at least a response in two of them, and the remaining 93 just in the source corpus in which they were first processed. A subset of 180 shared questions with answer in all the three corpora was randomly extracted from the merged collection. Each group then added 20 NIL questions in order to create its final monolingual test set for the CLEF 2003 QA track. Due to lack of time, the 180 queries that the three test sets had in common could not be chosen manually and attentively, but fortunately they turned out to be quite balanced: 45 entries asked for the name or role of a PERSON, 40 referred to a LOCATION, 31 to a MEASURE, 23 an ORGANISATION, 19 a DATE, 9 a concrete OBJECT, and 13 were labeled with OTHER.

During the merging, it was noted that some questions had the same meaning: 13 duplicates were found, but since most of them were formulated in a slightly different way, which did not affect the semantic contents, it was decided to keep them in the DISEQuA corpus. Different formulations of the same question could be exploited in Machine Translation applications.

4.1   Availability of the DISEQuA Corpus

The DISEQuA corpus is the result of the joint efforts of three research groups; we aimed at creating not only a good test set for the CLEF QA track, but also a useful and reusable resource for further QA evaluation. It is freely available on the "QA @ CLEF" web site[6], together with the question set developed for the bilingual tasks of the CLEF competition. Both can be used for NLP applications, and everyone can download them and introduce further material, adding questions, answers or even queries in other languages.

Together with the DISEQuA corpus, another test set is available: a collection of 200 English questions translated into Dutch, French, German, Italian and Spanish. It is the test set created for the CLEF QA cross-language tasks. Unlike the DISEQuA, only one target corpus was used to verify the queries of this second resource. So, each question has six different translations, but the answers have been searched only in the *Los Angeles Times* document collection.

```
<qa cnt="20" type="MEASURE">
        <language val="ITA" original="TRUE">
            <question assessor="Ale-irst">
                        Quanti abitanti ha Berlino?
            </question>
            <answer n="1" idx="SDA19940804.00147">
                        3,5 milioni
            </answer>
        </language>
        <language val="SPA" original="FALSE">
                <question assessor="Víctor-UNED">
                        ¿Cuántos habitantes tiene Berlín?
                </question>
                <answer n="1" idx="EFE19940107-02622">
                        Casi cuatro millones
                </answer>
        </language>
        <language val="DUT" original="FALSE">
                <question assessor="LIT">
                        Hoeveel inwoners heeft Berlijn?
                </question>
                <answer n="1" idx="NH19950601-0163">
                        3,5 miljoen
                </answer>
        </language>
        <language val="ENG" original="FALSE">
                <question assessor="">
                        How many inhabitants are there in Berlin?
                </question>
                <answer n="1" idx="-1">
                        SEARCH[3,500,000]
                </answer>
        </language>
    </qa>
```

Fig. 6. Final question format in the DISEQuA corpus

---

[6] http://clef-qa.itc.it

5 Conclusions

In this paper we have outlined the procedure used for creating a multilingual corpus of questions and answers. The resource we developed constitutes a reusable source of information for many NLP fields. We translated 450 questions into four languages (Dutch, Italian, Spanish and English) and processed them in three different target corpora, retrieving the answers and the docid of the documents that support the answers. So the queries we generated can be employed to evaluate translingual QA in 12 different combinations.

In the future we could search for answers in an English document collection, for instance the Los Angeles Times corpus licensed by CLEF, and widen the scope of possible applications. DISEQuA could be updated by adding other questions in different languages or other target corpora. The focus of new queries need not be limited to simple factoid questions, but could address definitions or lists of items, as well. The small corpus we have built could be enriched in several ways.

A corpus of this type could also be used in Machine Translation, because questions have particular features, usually under-represented in other corpora, that deserve investigation. Any further development will constitute an enrichment of the resource.

Acknowledgements

The work described in this paper has been supported by the Autonomous Province of Trento, in the framework of the WebFAQ Project, by the Spanish Government (MCyT, TIC-2002-10597-E) and by the Netherlands Organization for Scientific Research (NWO) under project numbers 612-13-001, 365-20-005, 612.069.006, 612.000.106, 220-80-001, 612.000.207, and 612.066.302.

We would like to thank all the people at ITC-irst (TCC division) who formulated the questions for the monolingual Italian test set. We are grateful to Claudio Giuliano, who made his "Tool for Lexicographers" available, facilitating the search for answers in the corpora. We are also indebted to Franca Rossi and Elisabetta Fauri at ITC-irst, for their help in the verification of the questions. We also want to thank Henry Chinaski, Vera Hollink, and Valentin Jijkoun for their help in developing and assessing the questions for the monolingual Dutch task. Without their contributions, the DISEQuA corpus would not exist. Finally, we wish to thank Charles Callaway who, as English native speaker, edited the translation of the Italian questions.

References

1. Kluck, M., Womser-Hacker C.: Inside the Evaluation Process of the Cross Language Evaluation Forum (CLEF): Issues of Multilingual Topic Creation and Multilingual Relevance Assessment. Proceedings of the Third International Conference on Language Resources and Evaluation, (LREC 2002), Las Palmas de Gran Canaria 29-31 May 2002.

2. Magnini, B.: Evaluation of Cross-Language Question Answering Systems, proposal presentation made at the CLEF Workshop 2002.
URL: http://clef.iei.pi.cnr.it:2002/workshop2002/presentations/q-a.pdf.
3. Tice, D. M., Voorhees, E. M.: The TREC-8 Question Answering Track Evaluation. Proceedings of the Eighth Text REtrieval Conference (TREC-8), Gaithersburg, MD., 2000.

Bridging Languages for Question Answering: DIOGENE at CLEF 2003

Matteo Negri, Hristo Tanev, and Bernardo Magnini

ITC-irst, Centro per la Ricerca Scientifica e Tecnologica,
Via Sommarive, 38050 Povo (TN), Italy
{negri|tanev|magnini}@itc.it

Abstract. This paper presents the extension of the ITC-irst DIOGENE Question Answering system towards multilinguality. DIOGENE relies on a well tested three-components architecture built in the framework of our participation in the QA track at the Text Retrieval Conference (TREC 2002). The novelty factors are represented by the enhancement of the system with language-specific tools targeted to the Italian language (*e.g.* a module in charge of the answer-type extraction, and a named entities recognizer) and the introduction of a module for the translation of Italian queries into English queries. The overall architecture of the extended system, as well as the results obtained in the CLEF 2003 Monolingual Italian and Bilingual Italian/English QA tracks will be presented and discussed throughout the paper.

1 Introduction

Research in Question Answering (QA) has received a strong boost in recent years by the QA track organized within the TREC conferences [14], which aims at assessing the capability of systems to return exact answers to open-domain English questions. The success of the initiative has reflected on the tendency of system developers to focus their activity on issues raised by the track guidelines (*e.g.*. how to deal with particular types of questions, how to pinpoint exact answers within a text document, and how to rank them according to the system's confidence). Besides the many positive effects of the TREC experience, several aspects related to the QA problem have not been faced yet. For instance, even though multilinguality has been recognized as an important issue for the future [1], up to now little has been done to provide QA systems with the capability of handling languages other than English. However, multilinguality represents a promising direction for future developments for at least two reasons. First, allowing users to interact with machines in their native languages, it would contribute to an easier, faster, and more reliable information access. Second, cross-language capabilities enable the access to information stored in language-specific text collections that could hardly be captured by searching only through English documents.

In the framework of an increasing interest towards multilinguality testified by the set up of a multiple-language QA track within CLEF 2003, DIOGENE represents the first concrete attempt to develop a QA system capable of dealing with Italian and

C. Peters et al. (Eds.): CLEF 2003, LNCS 3237, pp. 501–513, 2004.
© Springer-Verlag Berlin Heidelberg 2004

English, both in monolingual and cross-language scenarios. In the former case, the Italian version of DIOGENE has been built upon the same well tested three-components architecture of the English version [8]. Figure 1 shows the main constituents of this common backbone: these are the *question processing* component (in charge of the linguistic analysis of the input question), the *search* component (which performs the query composition and the document retrieval), and the *answer extraction* component (which extracts the final answer from the retrieved text passages). Sharing the overall architecture, as well as a number of basic tools and resources, the two monolingual versions of DIOGENE provided us with a sufficiently flexible and reliable infrastructure for extensions towards cross-language QA within the CLEF 2003 framework. In particular, in order to retrieve English answers in response to Italian questions, the Italian *question processing* component has been extended with a module for keyword translation into English (also shown in Figure 1), and then combined with the *search* and the *answer extraction* components of the English version.

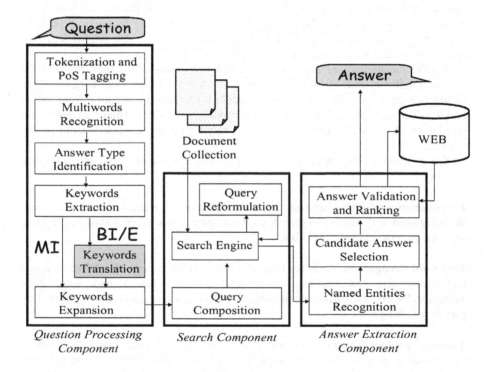

Fig. 1. The architecture of the DIOGENE system

The following sections will provide a general overview of our participation in the *monolingual Italian* (M-I) and *bilingual Italian/English* (B-I/E) tasks of the multiple-language QA track at CLEF 2003. In both the tasks of this new evaluation exercise systems were presented with a set of 200 Italian questions but, while for the M-I task answers had to be sought through an Italian document collection (the 193Mb corpus of the entire year 1994 of *La Stampa* newspaper and the 85Mb corpus of the 1994 *SDA* press agency), the target collection for the B-I/E task was composed of English texts (the 425Mb corpus of the entire year 1994 of *Los Angeles Times*). Focusing on the system's architecture, Section 2 will describe the *question processing* component, while Section 3 and 4 will describe in detail the *search*, and the *answer extraction* components, respectively. Finally, in Sections 5 and 6 the results of the different runs submitted for evaluation will be presented and some conclusions will be drawn.

2 Question Processing Component

The overall architecture set up for the ITC-irst participation in the multiple-language QA track at CLEF 2003 is an adaptation of the one described in [8], targeted to two specific tasks (*i.e.* M-I and B-I/E) of this new evaluation exercise. This adaptation was possible due to the general approach we took to develop the English version of DIOGENE, which relies on a cascade of simple, flexible and easily interchangeable modules and resources. In particular, the absence of any in-depth text analysis (most of the basic modules use a part of speech tagger as the only linguistic processor) meant that it was not necessary to find or develop from scratch crucial language specific tools such as, for instance, a full parser for Italian.

For the *question processing* component, both tasks required the substitution of the original English modules with language specific tools for dealing with Italian. In fact, for the bilingual task, the addition of a module for keyword translation from Italian into English was deemed a more reliable solution than performing an automatic translation of the whole question and then relying on the English version of the system.

The analysis of the input question is performed sequentially by the following modules.

Tokenization and PoS Tagging. First the question is tokenized and words are disambiguated with respect to their lexical category by means of a statistical part of speech tagger developed at ITC-Irst.

Multiword Recognition. As in the English version of the system, about five thousand multiwords (*i.e.* collocations, compounds and complex terms) have been automatically extracted from a monolingual Italian dictionary and are recognized by pattern matching rules.

Answer Type Identification. The answer type for a question represents the entity to be searched as answer. This information will be used to select the correct answer to an input question within the documents retrieved by the search engine. In particular, knowing the category of the entity we are looking for (*e.g.* PERSON, LOCATION, DATE, etc.) we can determine if any "candidate answer" found in a document is an appropriate instantiation of that category. Answer type identification relies on a manually defined taxonomy of *answer types* (*e.g.* "LOCATION", "PERSON", "ORGANIZATION" "TIME-PERIOD", "MEASURE", "TITLE", etc.), and a set of approximately 250 rules that check different features of an input question. These rules may detect the presence of a particular word, of words of a given part of speech, and of words belonging to a given semantic category. For instance, the rule described in (1) matches any question starting with "quale" ("*what*"), whose first noun, if any, is a person.

(1)   RULENAME: QUALE-CHI
        TEST: ["quale" [¬NOUN]* [NOUN:person-p]ⱼ +]
        OUTPUT: ["PERSON" J]

Rule (1) matches questions like "*Quale Primo Ministro Britannico visitò il Sud Africa nel 1960?*" ("*What British Prime Minister visited South Africa in 1960?*", which corresponds to Q-89 of the M-I task) since the first noun encountered after "quale" (*i.e.* "Prime_Minister") satisfies the person-p constraint. The same rule does not match the question: "*Quale paese invase il Kuwait nel 1990?*" ("*What country invaded Kuwait in 1990?*", Q-50 of the M-I task), since "country" does not satisfy the person-p predicate. Following the same methodology that proved to be successful in the development of the English version of DIOGENE, semantic predicates (*e.g.* person-p, location-p, organization-p, time-p) have been defined on the MULTIWORDNET taxonomy [13]. Each predicate checks if the sense of a word referred in a rule is subsumed by at least one high level synset manually selected for that predicate. As an example, the predicate person-p, for which the synset persona#1 ("human being") was selected, will be satisfied by any word subsumed by this synset (*e.g.* "Prime_Minister" "philosopher" "jazzman", etc.)

Keyword Extraction. At the end of the linguistic processing, a stop words filter is applied to isolate a set of "basic keywords", eliminating from the input question both non-content words and non-relevant content words.

Keyword Translation (Only for B-I/E). Bridging languages in a cross-language QA scenario requires dealing with the big issue of looking for answers through a target document collection that is in a different language with respect to the one of the question. Such a task can be accomplished following two different approaches: the translation of the input question by means of standard machine translation techniques [16], or the word by word translation [6] of the question keywords. At first glance, due to the availability of a well tested English version of the system, the first solution (*i.e.* automatically translate the Italian question and then perform the entire processing as in a monolingual English scenario) seems the most promising. Besides its simplicity, automatic question translation also seems favorable because it avoids the ambiguity problems inherent in the word-by-word translation, which are difficult to solve without relying on higher level linguistic analysis. However, state of the art machine translation systems still do not provide a sufficiently high quality and reliable output. Moreover, they are not optimized for translating questions, which are usually short and do not provide sufficient contextual information for a precise translation. Therefore, some approaches [4] combine dictionary-based word-by-word techniques with noun phrase extraction for an appropriate treatment of short questions. Adopting a similar perspective, we developed a word-by-word translation module which resorts to MULTIWORDNET and the Collins Italian/English dictionary, overcoming ambiguity difficulties by means of statistical techniques.

Our statistical dictionary-based approach to query translation is rather similar to the one described in [3], but does not require any training. The only resources that are needed are a bilingual dictionary, a search engine, the target corpus and, if available (but not essential), a text corpus in the source language (Italian in our case). Due to the relatively scarce resources needed, this translation technique could be easily extended to other languages.

The starting point of our methodology is the noisy-channel model [12]; according to this model, if we have a text in Italian i, its best translation in English (E) is found according to the formula:

$$(2) \qquad E = \arg \max_{e} (p(i \mid e).p(e))$$

We applied statistical techniques to calculate the two probabilities ($p(i|e)$ and $p(e)$), but further analysis of the results led us to the conclusion that $p(i|e)$ has a small impact on the final results. Therefore, in order to speed up the translation process, in the final version of the system we assigned a constant value to $p(i|e)$. However, in the following we will explain how both the probabilities were estimated.

The process is carried out through the following steps.

1. First, DIOGENE extracts all the possible translations for each of the Italian keywords using the Collins Italian/English dictionary. If the translation is not found (as in the case of multiwords), MULTIWORDNET is used to translate the word. If no translation is found and the word is capitalized, it is left as it is (this works for proper nouns, which are not listed in the dictionaries and whose coverage in MULTIWORDNET is rather limited). If the word is not capitalized and not found in Collins dictionary, nor in MULTIWORDNET, we skip it.

2. The next step is to estimate the probability of every translation in order to find the most plausible. Our algorithm has to deal with all the possible combinations of translations: even if sometimes the number of these combinations can be very large, our solution easily overcomes the problem. For ambiguity resolution, the main resources used by the algorithm are the target English text collection (indexed at paragraph level), and the DIOGENE search engine. Let us denote with $i=(i_1, i_2, i_3...i_n)$ a sequence of Italian keywords, and with $e=(e_{k1}, e_{k2},...e_{km})$ the set of English translations for every keyword i_k. We search in the target corpus using a Boolean query of the type:

$(e_{11}$ OR e_{12} OR ...) AND $(e_{21}$ OR e_{22} OR ...) AND ...AND $(e_{n1}$ OR e_{n2} OR ...)

This way we obtain paragraphs which contain at least one translation for every Italian keyword. If no paragraph is retrieved, a query relaxation algorithm is applied [8] which cuts off translations for Italian keywords which are less important. The process continues until a paragraph is found which contains at least one translation for each of the remaining keywords or one half of the initial keywords have been cut off (in this case the translation process fails and NIL is returned as the final answer).

3. Then, from the paragraphs obtained, we extract translation combinations and their frequency. The probability of each combination e is calculated by:

(3) $p(e = (e_{1i}, e_{2j}, e_{3k}, ...)) = frequency(e) / NumberParagraphsInCorpus$

Probability $p(i|e) = p(i_1, i_2, i_3|e_1, e_2, e_3, ...)$ was approximated using the trigram model. For example the conditional probability for five keywords has been calculated in the following way:

$p(i_1, i_2, i_3, i_4, i_5 \mid e_1, e_2, e_3, e_4, e_5) = p(i_1 \mid e_1) \, p(i_2 \mid e_2, i_1, e_1) \, p(i_3 \mid e_3, i_1, e_1, i_2, e_2) \, p(i_4 \mid e_4, i_2, e_2, i_3, e_3) \, p(i_5 \mid e_5, i_3, e_3, i_4, e_4)$

Our approach to the calculation of the conditional probabilities relies on the following assumption: If we have a word in English e and a set of its possible translations in Italian denoted by $TI(e)$, we assume that every word from $TI(e)$ in the Italian corpus can be translated in the word e when translating the corpus in English. Of course, this assumption is somewhat strong and influences the accuracy of the probabilities. We assume that the appearance of i implies that e appears in the English translation of the corpus. From this assumption it follows that the formula can be rewritten in the following way:

$p(i_1, i_2, i_3, i_4, i_5 \mid e_1, e_2, e_3, e_4, e_5) = p(i_1 \mid e_1) \, p(i_2 \mid e_2, i_1) \, p(i_3 \mid e_3, i_1, i_2) \, p(i_4 \mid e_4, i_2, i_3)$
$p(i_5 \mid e_5, i_3, i_4) = p(i_1) \, p(i_2, i_1) \, p(i_3, i_1, i_2) \, p(i_4, i_2, i_3) \, p(i_5, i_3, i_4) \cdot [p(e_1) \cdot p(e_2, i_1)$
$\cdot p(e_3, i_1, i_2) \cdot p(e_4, i_2, i_3) \cdot p(e_5, i_3, i_4)]^{-1}$

The probabilities in the previous formula can be calculated using the Italian corpus. Probability $p(i_1, i_2, i_3)$ can be calculated counting the number of paragraphs in the Italian corpus where these words occur together. This is acquired by just one query to the index of the corpus. Probability $p(e, i_1, i_2)$ is calculated by counting the paragraphs where at least one Italian translation of e appears (using again the above mentioned assumption) together with i_1 and i_2.
Using just frequencies counted in two corpora (Italian and English) we find the combination of English words E using the noisy-channel formula (2):

However, as stated before, to speed up the translation process we simplified the calculation of $p(i|e)$. In fact, our final experiments showed that the probability $p(i|e)$ has small impact on the translation quality, but significantly slows down the process. Therefore we changed the above formula into:

(4) $E = \arg\max_{e}(p(e)) = \arg\max_{e} frequency(e)$

This means that basically we choose combinations of English translations that have higher frequencies in the target corpus. Using the last formula, our method does not rely on any additional resource or training except for the bilingual dictionary, MULTIWORDNET (as addition to the bilingual dictionary), and the target English corpus.

As we will see in Section 5, the results achieved by DIOGENE in the B-I/E task were similar to those of the monolingual task. Assuming that the question sets in both the tasks have approximately equal level of difficulty, we may conclude that the quality of the translation achieved through this simple approach is more than satisfactory.

Keyword Expansion. In both the monolingual and the bilingual tasks, basic keywords are passed to an expansion phase which considers both morphological derivations and synonyms.

3 Search Component

Our participation in the QA tasks within CLEF 2003, relies on the same search component developed for the English version of DIOGENE, as described in [8]. The search component first combines the question keywords and their lexical expansions in a Boolean query; then performs document retrieval accessing the target document collections.

The search is performed by Managing Gigabytes (MG) [15], an open-source indexing and retrieval system for text, images, and textual images covered by a GNU public license and available via ftp from *http://www.cs.mu.oz.au/mg/*. Besides the speed of the document retrieval, the advantages derived from using MG are twofold. First, it allows for the customization of the indexing procedure. As a consequence, we opted to index the document collection at the paragraph level, using the paragraph markers provided in the SGML format of the documents. This way, although no proximity operator (*e.g.* the "NEAR" operator provided by AltaVista) is implemented in MG, the paragraph index makes the "AND" Boolean operator perform proximity search. In order to divide very long paragraphs into short passages, we set 20 text lines as the limit for paragraph length.

The other advantage derived from using MG concerns the possibility of performing Boolean queries, thus obtaining more control over the terms that must be present in the retrieved documents. Using the Boolean query mode, at the first step of the search phase all the basic keywords are connected in a complex "AND" clause, where the term variants (morphological derivations and synonyms) are combined in an "OR" clause. As an example, given the question "*Quando morì Shapour Bakhtiar?*" ("*When did Shapour Bakhtiar die?*", Q-3 of the B-I/E task), the translated basic keywords "die", " Shapour", and " Bakhtiar" are expanded and combined into:

[Shapour AND **Bakhtiar** AND **(die** OR **dies** OR **died** OR **dying** OR **death** OR **deaths)]**

However, Boolean queries often tend to return too many or too few documents. To cope with this problem, we implemented a feedback loop which starts with a query containing all the relevant keywords and gradually simplifies it by ignoring some of them. Several heuristics are used by the algorithm. For example, a word is removed if the resulting query does not produce more than a fixed number of hits (this probably means that the word is significant). Other heuristics consider the capitalization of the query terms, their part of speech, their position in the question, WORDNET class, etc. [10]. The algorithm stops when a maximum of 50 text paragraphs has been collected or a certain percentage of the question terms has been cut off. This way, the searching algorithm builds a set of the most significant words and narrows it until enough documents are retrieved. The efficiency of these kinds of feedback loops has been recently pointed out by [5].

Another problem we encountered using MG is related to the lack of language-specific stemming algorithms. Although it allows for different alternatives, derived from different combinations of case-folding and stemming modalities, English is the only language correctly handled while documents are indexed. As a consequence, as for the M-I task, the lack of an Italian stemming algorithm has reflected on a reduced precision of the document retrieval, which probably had some impact on the overall system performance.

4   Answer Extraction Component

Once the relevant paragraphs have been retrieved, the answer extraction component first performs a rough selection of candidate answers through named entity recognition. Then, automatic answer validation procedures are applied over the selected candidates to choose and rank, according to the CLEF QA track guidelines, the three final answers to be returned by the system.

4.1 Named Entity Recognition

The named entity recognition module is in charge of identifying all the entities that match the answer type category (*e.g.* person, organization, location, measure, etc.) within the relevant passages returned by the search engine. While the WORDNET-based named entity recognizer already developed for the English version of DIOGENE [11] was perfectly suitable for participating in the bilingual task, a language specific tool had to be developed from scratch to deal with Italian in the monolingual task. Also in this case, due to the availability of MULTIWORDNET and a PoS tagger for Italian, we could rely on the same approach adopted to handle English texts.

Each version of the system is based on the combination of a set of language dependent rules with a set of predicates, defined on the WORDNET/ MULTIWORDNET hierarchy for the identification of both proper names (i.e. person, location and organization names, such as "Galileo Galilei", "Rome", and "Bundesbank") and *trigger words* (i.e. predicates and constructions typically associated with named entities, such as "astronomer", "capital", and "bank"). The process of recognition and identification of the named entities present in a text is carried out in three phases. The first phase (*preprocessing*) performs tokenization, PoS-tagging, and multiword recognition of the input text. In the second phase, a set of *basic rules* (approximately 250 for the English language and 300 for Italian) is used for finding and marking with SGML tags all the possible named entities present in the text (e.g. <MEASURE><CARDINAL>200<\CARDINAL> *miles*<\MEASURE> *from* <LOCATION>*New York*<\LOCATION>). Finally, a set of higher level *composition rules* which is common to both the versions of the system is used to remove inclusions and overlaps among tags (e.g. <MEASURE>*200 miles*<\MEASURE> *from* <LOCATION>*New York*<\LOCATION>) as well as for co-reference resolution. The English version of the system has been tested using the test corpora and the scoring software provided in the framework of the DARPA/NIST HUB4 evaluation exercise [2]. Results achieved over a 365Kb test corpus of newswire texts vary among categories (ranging from an F-Measure score of 71% for the category MEASURE, to 96.5% for the category DATE), with an overall F-Measure score of 84%. For the Italian version, experiments carried out with the same scoring software over a 77Kb text corpus[1] revealed a comparable performance, with an overall F-Measure score of 83%.

4.2 Answer Validation

The automatic answer validation module used for our participation in CLEF 2003 is the same that we developed for the original English version of DIOGENE [8]. Its reusability (which is also one of its main strengths) is due to the fully statistical approach on which the module relies, which makes it completely language-independent.

Answer validation is in charge of evaluating and scoring a maximum of 60-90 answer candidates per question in order to find the exact answer required as the final output. The top 60 (for the B-I/E task) or 90 (for the M-I task) answer candidates are selected, among the named entities matching the answer type category, on the basis of their distance from the basic keywords and their frequency in the paragraphs retrieved by the search engine.

The basic idea behind our approach to answer validation is to identify semantic relations between concepts by mining for their tendency to co-occur in a large document collection. In this framework, considering the Web as the largest open domain text corpus containing information about almost all the different areas of human knowledge, all the required information about any existing relation between a question q and an answer a can be automatically acquired on the fly by exploiting Web data redundancy. In particular, given a question q and an answer a, it is possible to combine them in a set of *validation statements* whose truthfulness is equivalent to the degree of relevance of a with respect to q. For instance, given the question *"What is the capital of the USA?"*, the problem of validating the answer *"Washington"* is equivalent to estimating the truthfulness of the validation statement *"The capital of the USA is Washington"*. Therefore, the answer validation task could be reformulated as a problem of statement reliability. There are two issues to be addressed in order to make this intuition effective. First, the idea of a validation statement is still insufficient to catch the richness of implicit knowledge that may connect an answer to a question. Our solution to this problem relies on the definition of the more flexible idea of a *validation pattern*, in which the question and answer keywords co-occur closely. Second, we need an effective and efficient way to check the reliability of a validation pattern. With regard to this issue, our solution relies on a statistical count of Web searches. Given a question-answer pair $[q,a]$ we adopted the following generic four-step procedure for answer validation:

---

[1] Reference transcripts of two broadcast news shows, including a total of about 7,000 words and 322 tagged named entities, were manually produced for evaluation purposes and have been kindly provided by Marcello Federico and Vanessa Sandrini.

1) Compute the set of representative keywords *Kq* and *Ka* both from *q* and from *a*. This step is carried out using linguistic techniques, such as answer type identification (from the question) and named entities recognition (from the answer);
2) From the extracted keywords construct the validation pattern for the pair [*q,a*];
3) Submit the validation pattern to a search engine;
4) Estimate an *Answer Relevance Score (ARS)* considering the results returned by the search engine.

The retrieval on the Web is delegated to the AltaVista search engine (http://www.altavista.com), which allows for advanced search strategies using the proximity operator "NEAR" to retrieve only Web documents where the answer and the question keywords have closer (*i.e.* within a 10 token window) co-occurrences. The post-processing of the results is performed by HTML parsing procedures and a simple function which calculates the *ARS* for each [*q, a*] pair by analyzing the results page returned by the search engine. The *ARS* is calculated on the basis of the number of retrieved pages by means of a statistical co-occurrence metric called *corrected conditional probability* [10]. The formula we used is the following:

$$(5) \qquad ARS(a) = \frac{P(Ka \mid Kq)}{P(Ka)^{2/3}} = \frac{hits(Ka\,NEAR\,Kq)}{hits(Kq) * hits(Ka)^{2/3}} * |EnglishPages|$$

where:

- *hits(Ka NEAR Kq)* is the number of English-language pages returned by AltaVista, where the answer keywords (*Ka*) and the question keywords (*Kq*) are within distance of no more than 10 words of each other;
- *hits(Kq)* and *hits(Ka)* are the number of English-language pages where *Kq* and *Ka* occur respectively;
- *|EnglishPages|* is the number of English pages, indexed by AltaVista.

This formula can be viewed as a modification of the Pointwise Mutual Information formula, a widely used measure that was first introduced for identifying lexical relationships (in this case the co-occurrence of *Kq* and *Ka*).

In addition to the measurement of co-occurrence frequencies, for some question types (*e.g.* Where-location or When-event) we applied patterns for answer validation. For instance, given the question *"Where is Trento?"* and the candidate answer *"Italy"*, the phrases *"Trento in Italy"* and *"Trento Italy"* (which are some of the possible ways in which the answer to a question can be found in a text) are submitted to AltaVista. In these cases, the resulting number of pages is multiplied by 100 and added to the *ARS* improving its reliability.

5   Results and Discussion

The effectiveness of the extensions of DIOGENE towards multilinguality have been evaluated over four runs submitted to the monolingual Italian and the bilingual

Italian/English QA tasks at CLEF 2003. The results (*strict* statistics) achieved by each run are shown in Table 1.

Table 1. ITC-irst at CLEF

Run	A	R	W	U	X	Q I no corr. A	Q I corr. A	NIL	MRR
Irstex031mi	590	132	439	6	13	103	97	2/4	0.42
Irstst032mi	582	153	410	7	12	101	99	2/5	0.45
Irstex031bi	492	94	378	6	14	123	77	6/49	0.32
Irstex032bi	526	113	402	2	9	110	90	5/28	0.40

The first two rows of Table 1 refer to the *monolingual* task, while the other two are for the *bilingual* task. For each submitted run, columns 2-6 show the total number of answers (A) returned by the system (according to the CLEF QA guidelines, up to three ranked answers for each question could be output), and the number of answers that have been judged right (R), wrong (W), unsupported (U) and inexact (X). Columns 7 and 8 show the number of questions for which no correct answer was returned and the number of questions for which at least one answer was found by DIOGENE. The last two columns show the number of answers correctly marked as NIL out of the total of NIL returned, and the Mean Reciprocal Rank (MRR) obtained for each run. Differences among these figures are due to the adoption of different approaches to produce the final output. In particular, making the most of the opportunity to submit up to two runs for each task, we wanted to test the system's performance with different settings.

The monolingual version was tested in two evaluation scenarios, namely the *exact answer* task (*Irstex031mi*), where a TREC-like exact answer had to be returned for each question, and the *50 bytes* task (*Irstex032mi*), where response units with a maximal length of 50 bytes could be returned. In this second case, starting from each candidate answer, longer response units have been extracted by simply considering symmetric left and right windows covering the 50 bytes allowed. Our hypothesis was that in this way the impact of errors due to incorrect named entity tagging and, consequently, the number of inexact answers could have been reduced. Moreover, longer response units were expected to improve the quality of answers to particular classes of questions (*e.g.* non factoid questions, questions about acronyms, and those asking for entities which do not belong to the classes handled by our named entities recognizer, such as Q 127: "*Nomina un farmaco anti-malarico*" – "*Name an antimalaric drug*"), for which the system can only rely on heuristics considering the density of question keywords within the retrieved paragraphs. The evaluation of the 50 bytes run returned unexpected results, with an MRR improvement of only 3% with respect to the exact answer run. As for the number of inexact answers returned, the difference between the two runs is minimal (13 for the *exact answer* task vs. 12 for the *50 bytes* task), showing an acceptable overall performance of the named entity tagger in the detection of entities' boundaries. Unfortunately, also the total number of questions that received at least one correct answer and the number of NIL answers are almost the same.

The two runs of the bilingual version of the system were obtained by varying the answer validation algorithm described in the previous section, in order to test the impact of combining our statistical approach with traditional Information Retrieval metrics that also take into account the keywords density within the retrieved paragraphs. In particular, the significant improvement in the second run (*Irstex032bi*) results has been obtained by multiplying the *ARS* by a *keyword density coefficient* [7] which considers the distance of each candidate answer from the query keywords present in a paragraph.

6 Conclusion

In this paper we have provided an overview of the recent extensions of the DIOGENE QA system towards multilinguality. The system's backbone, built upon a cascade of simple and easily interchangeable modules, relies on a balance of shallow linguistic analysis and statistical techniques that drastically reduce the effort required to cross language barriers. This approach proved suitable both for handling languages other than English, and for bridging them in cross-language scenarios. In particular, it is worth noting how the absence of any in-depth text analysis (most of the basic modules use a part of speech tagger as the only linguistic processor) allows for multilingual extensions without developing crucial language specific tools from scratch. Moreover, two of the main system's components, namely the answer validation module and the keyword translator set up for working in cross-language mode, rely on purely statistical approaches without requiring any language-specific knowledge. Both the modules, in fact, simply use word co-occurrences (either in a document collection or in the Web) as the main source of "knowledge".

The results achieved at the CLEF 2003 Multiple Language QA task confirm the effectiveness of our approach: both the Italian and the Italian/English version of DIOGENE performed well, producing results that are comparable to the English version of DIOGENE (ranked fourth in the last TREC competition).

References

1. Burger, J., Cardie, C., Chaudhri, V., Gaizauskas, R., Harabagiu, S., Israel, D., Jacquemin, C., Lin, C.-Y., Maiorano, S., Miller, G., Moldovan, D., Ogden, B., Prager, J., Riloff, E., Singhal, A., Shrihari, R., Strzalkowski, T., Voorhees, E., Weishedel, R.: Issues, Tasks and Program Structures to Roadmap Research in Question & Answering (Q&A), 2001.
   URL: http://www-nlpir.nist.gov/projects/duc/papers/qa.Roadmap-paper_v2.doc.
2. Chinchor, N., Robinson, P., Brown, E.: Hub-4 Named Entity Task Definition (version 4.8). Technical Report, SAIC. http://www.nist.gov/speech/hub4_98.
3. Federico, M., and Bertoldi, N.: ITC-irst at CLEF 2002 Using N-best query translations for CLIR, CLEF 2002 Workshop, Rome, Italy, 2002.
4. Gao, Jianfeng, Jian Yun Nie, Endogan Xun, Jiang Zhang, Ming Zhou, Changning Huang: Improving Query Translation for Cross-Language Information Retrieval using Statistical Model. Proceedings of Conference on Research and Development in Information Retrieval (ACM SIGIR 01), New Orleans, Louisiana, USA, 2001.

5. Harabagiu, S., Moldovan, D., Pasca, M., Mihalcea, R., Surdeanu, M., Bunescu, R., Girjiu, R., Rus, V., Morarescu, P.: The Role of Lexico-Semantic Feedback in Open-Domain Question-Answering. Proceedings of the 39th Annual Meeting of the Association for Computational Linguistics (ACL-2001), Toulouse, France, 2001.
6. Hull, D., and Grefenstette, G.: A dictionary-based approach to multilingual information retrieval. In Proceedings of the 19th ACM SIGIR Conference on Research and Development in Information Retrieval, Zurich, Switzerland, 1996.
7. Magnini, B., Negri, M., Prevete, R., Tanev, H.: Multilingual Question Answering: the DIOGENE System. Proceedings of the Tenth Text Retrieval Conference 2001 (TREC-2001), Gaithersburg, MD., 2001.
8. Magnini, B., Negri, M., Prevete, R., Tanev, H.: Mining Knowledge from Repeated Co-occurrences: DIOGENE at TREC-2002 Proceedings of the Eleventh Text Retrieval Conference (TREC-2002), Gaithersburg, MD., 2002a.
9. Magnini, B., Negri, M., Prevete, R., Tanev, H.: Comparing Statistical and Content-Based Techniques for Answer Validation on the Web. Proceedings of the VIII Convegno AI*IA, Siena, Italy, 2002b.
10. Magnini, B., Negri, M., Prevete, R., Tanev, H.: Is It the Right Answer? Exploiting Web Redundancy for Answer Validation. Proceedings of the 40th Annual Meeting of the Association for Computational Linguistics (ACL-2002), Philadelphia, PA., 2002c.
11. Magnini, B., Negri, M., Prevete, R., Tanev, H.: A WORDNET-Based Approach to Named Entities Recognition. Proceedings of SemaNet02, COLING Workshop on Building and Using Semantic Networks, Taipei, Taiwan, 2002d.
12. Manning, C., Shutze, H.: Foundations of Statistical Natural Language Processing. MIT Press, 1999.
13. Pianta, E., Bentivogli, L., Girardi, C.: MULTIWORDNET: Developing an Aligned Multilingual Database. Proceedings of the 1st International Global WordNet Conference, Mysore, India, 2002.
14. Voorhees, E., Harman, D. K. Eds.: Proceedings of the Sixth Retrieval Conference (TREC-6) , Gaithersburg, MD., 1997.
15. Witten, I. H., Moffat, A., Bell T.: Managing Gigabytes: Compressing and Indexing Documents and Images (second ed.), Morgan Kaufmann Publishers, New York, 1999.
16. Zhiping Zheng. AnswerBus Question Answering System. *Proceeding of HLT* Human Language Technology Conference (HLT 2002). San Diego, CA., 2002.

Cross-Language Question Answering at the USC Information Sciences Institute

Abdessamad Echihabi, Douglas W. Oard*, Daniel Marcu, and Ulf Hermjakob

University of Southern California Information Sciences Institute,
4676 Admiralty Way, Marina Del Rey, CA 90292 USA
{echihabi, marcu, ulf}@isi.edu, oard@umd.edu

Abstract. The TextMap-TMT cross-language question answering system at USC-ISI was designed to answer Spanish questions from English documents. The system is fully automatic, including question translation from Spanish to English, question type determination, rewriting to generate expected answer structures, search in the target collection and on the Web as a side collection, and answer selection from among the plausible candidates that were found. A development test collection with answer patterns for 100 questions in English and Spanish was used to assess the effect of question translation on each processing stage, and some adjustments were made to the question translation process to minimize these effects. Two runs were submitted, both of which sought to return exact answers. For the better of the two runs (which omitted an additional Web-based answer validation stage), the top-ranked answer was scored as correct in 56 of 200 cases, 53 of which were judged to be supported by the content of the target collection.

1   Introduction

The goal of a Question Answering (QA) system is to find answers to questions in a large collection of documents. The QA track in the 2003 Cross-Language Evaluation Forum (CLEF) added a new wrinkle, with the question posed in one language (Spanish, in our case) and the documents written in another (for us, English). The challenge therefore was to identify answers to a Spanish question in a collection of English documents. The focus of the evaluation was on finding answers, so translation of the answer from English into Spanish was not required.

At the University of Southern California Information Sciences Institute we have been working on question answering in English for several years. We therefore adapted our existing TextMap English QA system [3] to perform Cross-Language question answering (CL-QA) by making the following changes:

- Question translation from Spanish to English using an off-the-shelf machine translation system, augmented with some simple postprocessing to correct observed systematic errors.

---

* Permanent address: College of Information Studies and Institute for Advanced Computer Studies, University of Maryland, College Park MD 20740 USA

C. Peters et al. (Eds.): CLEF 2003, LNCS 3237, pp. 514–522, 2004.
© Springer-Verlag Berlin Heidelberg 2004

- Candidate generation using the Inquery text retrieval system, to capitalize on cross-language search capabilities that can be constructed more easily using Inquery than with the MG system that we had previously used.
- Answer validation, using a second Web search to increase the score of answers found in the target collection that also have support on the Web.

Imperfect translation of questions can introduce new challenges for downstream components that vary with the design of each component. To assess the impact that imperfect translation may have on the accuracy of a question answering system, we prepared a 100-question development collection consisting of questions in English, human translations of those questions into Spanish, and answer patterns that facilitated automated scoring in English. In the next section, we describe a set of experiments using this collection and explain how those experiments informed the design of our CL-QA system. Section 3 describes the architecture and main components of our system; Section 4 presents our results for both one-best and three-best scoring. Finally, we draw some conclusions from this first experience with CL-QA in Section 5, along with some comments about directions that we may explore in the future.

2   Measuring Question Translation Effects

There are many alternatives one can use to build a CL-QA system that accepts questions in one language, L_1, and returns answers found in another language, L_2. We enumerate below some of these alternatives.

1. One can, for example, use a translation system to translate questions from L_1 into L_2 and an end-to-end question-answering system capable of operating in language L_2. Such a system would contain all stages of a monolingual QA system, from answer type identification and information retrieval through answer selection.
2. Alternatively, one could identify the expected answer type for a question in L_1; use L_1 to generate queries to a CLIR system that searched L_2 using some means other than one-best query translation; then translate L_1 into L_2; and finally perform answer pinpointing in L_2.
3. Or one can translate all L_2 documents into L_1; use an end-to-end question-answering system that operates in language L_1; and then project the answers back into L_2.

Several other alternatives are obviously possible.

From the beginning of our work, we had access to TextMap, a complete end-to-end English QA system that makes extensive use of parsing and syntactic/semantic transformations that have been tuned using large collections of English question-answer pairs [3]. The CL-QA track at CLEF 2003 offered an English document collection with Spanish questions, which tilted our preference towards the first two approaches in the above list. However, before proceeding with an implementation, we thought it would be wise to assess the impact that such a design choice would have on the accuracy of our CL-QA system.

Because the overall accuracy of a QA system is directly affected by its ability to correctly analyze the questions it receives as input, a CL-QA system could be quite sensitive to errors introduced during question translation. In order to assess the potential effect of such errors, we created a development test collection using the QA test collection from the 2002 Text Retrieval Conference (TREC). The first 100 questions from that collection (numbered 1394-1493) were independently translated from English into Spanish by two fluent speakers of Spanish that were also fluent in English. A native speaker of Spanish then reviewed the two sets of translations, selected the better of the two, and corrected a few errors that were observed in that set. The resulting Spanish questions could then be used in conjunction with the answer patterns that were provided with the TREC 2002 QA collection to automatically assess the accuracy of a CL-QA system[1].

The 100 Spanish questions were given as input to three CL-QA systems.

1. One system (TextMap-SMT) used a Statistical Machine Translation (SMT) system trained on a European Parliament parallel corpus [6] to translate Spanish questions into English; and TextMap to find answers to the translated questions.
2. A second system (TextMap-TMT) used a commercial off-the-shelf Transfer-method Machine Translation (TMT) system (the Systran Web-based system, www.systransoft.com) to translate Spanish questions into English; and TextMap to find answers to the translated questions.
3. A third system (TextMap-English) used a simple lookup table to produce perfect English translations for the Spanish questions in our development collection; and TextMap to find answers to these questions.

Statistical MT systems can be very effective when large quantities of representative translation-equivalent sentences are available for training. Unfortunately, disappointing results were obtained with TextMap-SMT (6/100 correct vs. 35/100 correct with TextMap-English), which led us to abandon this option for CLEF 2003. We believe that at least one reason for these poor results is the difference in genre between the data used to train the statistical MT system (European Parliament Proceedings) and the data used in the context of our evaluation (factoid questions).

TextMap-TMT found correct English answers to Spanish questions about 60% as often as the third system (20/100 correct for TextMap-TMT vs. 35/100 correct for TextMap-English). Our failure analysis process revealed one important improvement that we could make to question translation, however. We observed that Systran translation errors exhibited some clear regularities for certain question types, as might be expected from a rule-based system. For example, Systran exhibited a propensity to produce "whichever" rather than "how many" as a translation for the Spanish word "cuanto." We were able to automatically correct some of these mistakes using a few easily written regular expressions that we developed by inspection on our development collection. Overall,

---

[1] We provided these translations to the CLEF CL-QA track organizers for use by other teams.

our experiments with the development collection showed that translation quality significantly affects the accuracy of our system.

In order to attribute errors to specific processing stages, we built systems that combined components of TextMap-English and TextMap-TMT. When we used TextMap-TMT only for Answer Pinpointing (described below), 31 of 100 answers were correct (4 below what we get with TextMap-English). When we used TextMap-TMT only for search (both Web Search and Target Collection Search), 28 of 100 answers were correct (7 below what we get with TextMap-English). From this we conclude that while additional work in both cross-language retrieval and answer pinpointing could be useful, improvements in cross-language search may offer somewhat greater potential for improving the overall accuracy of our CL-QA system. We therefore started an effort to incorporate the best available cross-language information retrieval technology into TextMap-TMT; unfortunately, this work could not be completed before the submission deadline.

3   System Design

The experiments described in the previous section suggested that TextMap-TMT was the best system we could produce under the given time constraints. For the sake of completeness, we briefly review here the main components and data flow in the TextMap-TMT system (see Fig. 1 for an illustration of the data flow and [3] for a more detailed presentation of the TextMap system).

3.1   Using Question Translation for CL-QA

Our TextMap-TMT QA system includes the following major processing stages:

Question Translation. Spanish questions are automatically translated using Systran. A postprocessing module corrects some of the systematic errors that are produced by the translation software, as described above.

Question Analysis. Syntactic analysis is performed using the CONTEX parser developed at USC-ISI [4], and 143 types of named entities are tagged (e.g., PERSON, ISLAND, SPEED-QUANTITY, BASEBALL-SPORTS-TEAM, and DATE) using an extended version of the BBN IdentiFinder [1].

Answer Type Determination. The results of question analysis are used to automatically classify each question into one of 180 types that describe the expected nature of an appropriate answer (e.g., WHY-FAMOUS, PERSON-NAME, or DISEASE) [5]. Reformulation rules are then used to generate plausible ways of rewriting each question into forms in which an answer might be found (e.g., one rewriting for the question "Where is Devil's Tower?" would be "Devil's Tower, in LOCATION, ...").

Web Search. We use a large set of reformulation patterns and query expansion techniques to produce queries for the Google search engine. For example, the question "¿Cuándo se convirtió Alaska en un estado?" is translated to "When became Alaska a state?" This yields the following Web query:

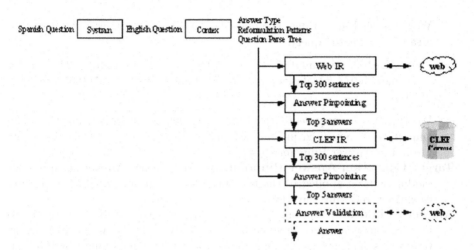

Fig. 1. TextMap-TMT Architecture

("Alaska" AND "state" AND "became") OR "Alaska became a state" OR "Alaska became a state on" OR "Alaska became a state in" OR "Alaska became a state about"

Similarly, "Where is Devil's Tower?" yields the following Web query:

("Devil" AND "Tower") OR ("location of Devil's Tower is") OR ("Devil's Tower is located ")

We retrieve the 10 top-ranked documents over the Web, rank each sentence found in that set of documents using a set of locally developed heuristics, and select the top 300 sentences.

Web Answer Pinpointing. The top 300 sentences retrieved by the Web retrieval stage are each then parsed. The reformulation patterns are used here to pinpoint and score answer constituents. Each answer is scored using a wide range of heuristics that measure the degree of overlap between questions and answers; the specificity of the match between the expected answer type and the syntactic/semantic category of the answer; the redundancy of the answer in the answer set; and a number of other factors (see [3] for details).

Target Collection Search. We use the same set of reformulation patterns as Web Search and a similar set of query expansion techniques to produce Inquery queries for the CLEF 2003 CL-QA track English collection (Los Angeles Times articles from 1994). These documents were indexed by Inquery with stopwords retained and the standard stemmer (kstem) enabled. Our use of Inquery for Target Collection Search (rather than MG, which we had previously used) was motivated by the facilities it provides for cross-language search using structured queries, but the cross-language search capability was not ready by the submission deadline. All processing therefore used the same set of translated questions from TMT. The query is expanded by rewarding the presence of at least one of the top three answers from

Web Answer Pinpointing. The question "¿Cuándo se convirtió Alaska en un estado?" yields the query.

> #passage100(#wsum(10 7 #wsum(49.049 6.730 #1(state) 7.242 #1(be-came) 35.077 #1(alaska)) 3 #or(#1(January 3 1959) #1(1867) #1(1959))))

We then rank every sentence in the top 1000 documents using the same heuristics as were used in Web search and select the top 300 sentences for use in the Answer Pinpointing stage.

Target Collection Answer Pinpointing. The same Answer Pinpointing module is then applied to the top 300 sentences from the CLEF collection to extract and rank the answers.

Answer Validation. Optionally, we can look back to the Web search results to increase our confidence in some potential answers by giving greater weight to answers that are also present in the top ten sentences found by the Web search stage. As many as five answers can have their confidence raised in this way, and the increase in confidence is proportional to the number of occurrences of that answer in the ten sentences.

Most stages of our original (English) TextMap system could be used unchanged, although we made some relatively minor changes to decouple Web Search from the parsing-based reformulation strategy and to accommodate the presence of Latin-1 characters from above the 7-bit ASCII character set.

4   Results

Figure 2 shows our official results. The center ring depicts the better of the two runs we submitted (which omitted Answer Validation), the top-ranked answer was scored as correct in 56 of 200 cases, 53 of which were judged to be supported by the content of the target collection. As shown on the inner ring, answer validation had the effect of increasing the number of unsupported correct answers (from 3 to 5) and reducing the overall number of correct answers (from 56 to 48). From this we conclude that our present approach to Answer Validation was not helpful in this case.

When used in interactive applications, it can be useful to display multiple candidate answers to the user. Accuracy within the top three answers was therefore chosen as the official measure of effectiveness for the CLEF 2003 CL-QA evaluation. By that measure, shown on the outer ring, our best run found 77 correct answers out of 200, 69 of which were judged to be supported by the content of the target collection.

5   Conclusions and Future Work

The complexity of present QA systems makes cross-language question answering a challenging task; many interacting components must be tuned to work together

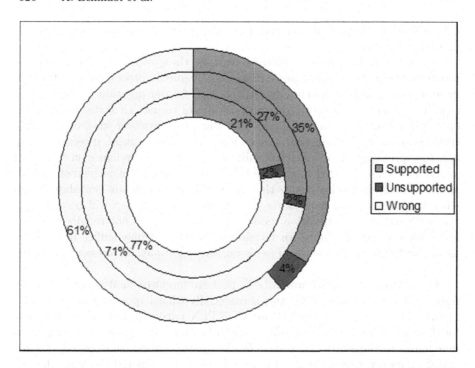

Fig. 2. Official Results. Inner ring: top-1 with Answer Validation; Middle ring: top-1 without Answer Validation; Outer ring: top-3 without Answer Validation

in new ways. We were therefore pleased to learn that TextMap-TMT found the right answer in better than one out of every four cases, for questions that we had never seen before. Moreover, in the course of our work we identified several promising directions for future work. We observed, for example, that Systran sometimes translates names that should be left untranslated; "Marcos" was translated to "Marks" in our development collection, for example. This would be easily prevented using a Spanish named entity tagger. Another obvious step is to build in more sophisticated approaches to cross-language search than we are presently using.

The most important things we have learned from this experience are not answers, however, they are questions. CL-QA creates a fundamental tension between the design of our best QA systems and the design of our best translation systems. The best QA systems that we are presently able to build rely on relatively deep analysis and a substantial amount of knowledge engineering. These systems are highly tuned to the characteristics we observe in the human use of language. With translation, however, we produce language using a machine. Moreover, the best presently available machine translation systems make extensive use of statistical analysis. If we use these statistics well, there will be no exploitable regularities in their error characteristics (indeed, if there were, then we could have made better use of the statistics!). Put simply, statistical translation developed using texts in one domain and deep linguistic analysis produced with a system designed to perform well in a different domain don't presently play well together.

Given this fundamental tension, we can see three ways to proceed. One alternative would be to move away from deep linguistic processing and towards greater use of statistical techniques as the basis for our question answering system. This is not an all-or-nothing proposition, of course; all statistics are done on symbols that have linguistic meaning. But as we discover ways of acquiring the large quantities of representative training data that we need, it seems reasonable to expect that the balance will shift in favor of greater reliance on statistical analysis. We have started to explore this direction using noisy-channel models, and we are now achieving results that are competitive with our TextMap system when suitable training data exists [2]. The obvious next step will be to couple this with statistical translation models. Notably, we may not require that our translation models be tuned for fact-based question; it may suffice to tune the model for the typical contents of news stories (essentially, an answer translation strategy).

The obvious alternative would be to perform linguistic analysis in a common framework for both languages; this is essentially what happens inside a transfer method MT system. Versions of our CONTEX parser [4] have been produced for Japanese and Korean as well as English, and parsing for eight languages in a common framework is available from Connexor (www.connexor.com). Ultimately, however, this approach can probably best be explored by those who can leverage the large investments that have already been made in transfer method MT systems. Of course, the best solution will likely ultimately be found somewhere in the middle ground, drawing together the best of the statistical techniques and the deeper linguistic analysis. It may be some time before we can see the shape of these solutions, but our experience at CLEF 2003 has started us on that path.

Acknowledgments

This work has been supported in part by ARDA contract MDA908-02-C-0007 (AQUAINT), DoD contract MDA904-02-C-0406 (LAMP) and DARPA cooperative agreement N660010028910 (TIDES).

References

1. Bikel, D.M., Schwartz, R., Weischedel, R.M.: An algorithm that learns what's in a name. Machine Learning, 34(1/3), February 1999.
2. Echihabi, A., Marcu, D.: A noisy-channel approach to question answering. In: Proceedings of the 41st Annual Meeting of the Association for Computational Linguistics, Sapporo, Japan, July 7-12 2003.
3. Hermjakob, U., Echihabi, A., Marcu, D.: Natural language based reformulation resource and web exploitation for question answering. In: Proceedings of the Text Retrieval Conference (TREC–2002). November 2002.

4. Hermjakob, U.: Rapid parser development: A machine learning approach for Korean. In: Proceedings of the North American chapter of the Association for Computational Linguistics (NAACL-2000), 2000. http://www.isi.edu/~ulf/papers/kor_naacl00.ps.gz.
5. Hovy, E.H., Gerber, L., Hermjakob, U., Lin, C.-Y., Ravichandran, D.: Toward semantics-based answer pinpointing. In: Proceedings of the DARPA Human Language Technologies Conference (HLT), San Diego, CA, 2001.
6. Koehn, P.: Europarl: A multilingual corpus for evaluation of machine translation. Available at http://www.isi.edu/~koehn/publications/europarl/, 2003.

How Frogs Built the Berlin Wall

A Detailed Error Analysis of a
Question Answering System for Dutch

Valentin Jijkoun, Gilad Mishne, and Maarten de Rijke

Language & Inference Technology Group, University of Amsterdam,
Nieuwe Achtergracht 166, 1018 WV Amsterdam, The Netherlands
{jijkoun, gilad, mdr}@science.uva.nl

Abstract. The paper describes the University of Amsterdam's participation in the Question Answering track at CLEF 2003, our system and the results produced by it. A thorough analysis of the wrong answers given by our system is provided, including a discussion of each type of error and possible strategies for handling them. We outline our current efforts for improvement of the system, and propose additional research directions and procedures to reduce errors of the presented types.

1   Introduction

In this year's CLEF evaluation exercise we participated in the *Dutch Question Answering* task, new on the CLEF agenda, building on and extending our earlier work on question answering at TREC [1]. We experimented with a multi-stream architecture for question answering, in which the different independent streams, each a complete Question Answering (QA) system in its own right, compete with each other to provide the system's final answer.

In this paper, we chose to focus on the errors made by our system. We give a detailed breakdown of the types of wrong answers we encountered and discuss their causes; additionally, we propose possible solutions for these errors, some of which are currently being implemented by us in our ongoing QA work. We hope that the paper may benefit both QA system researchers and QA engineers: we suggest areas on which to focus research, possible caveats, and directions to explore.

The paper is organized as follows. In Section 2 we give a general overview of our system and briefly present our results in CLEF 2003. Section 3 includes a classification of the errors, a diagnosis of their causes as well as a discussion of possible strategies to address them. We summarize and conclude in section 4.

2   System Description

The general architecture of a QA system, shared by many systems, can be summed up as follows. A question is first associated with a *question type*, out of

C. Peters et al. (Eds.): CLEF 2003, LNCS 3237, pp. 523–534, 2004.

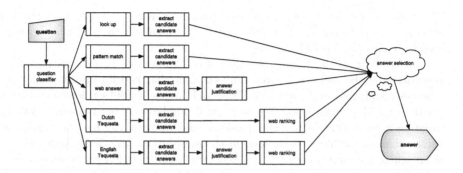

Fig. 1. The University of Amsterdam's Dutch Question Answering System

a predefined set such as DATE-OF-BIRTH or CURRENCY. Then a query is formulated based on the question, and a retrieval engine is used to identify documents that are likely to contain the answer. Those documents are sent to an *answer extraction* module, which identifies candidate answers, ranks them, and selects the final answer. On top of this basic architecture, numerous add-ons have been devised, ranging from logic-based methods [2] to ones that rely heavily on the redundancy of information available on the World Wide Web [3].

2.1   Multi-stream Architecture

During the design of our QA system, it became evident that there are a number of distinct approaches for the task; some are beneficial for all question types, and others only for a subset. For instance, abbreviations are often found enclosed in brackets, following the multi-word string they abbreviate, as in *"Verenigde Naties (VN)."* This suggests that for abbreviation questions the text corpus can be mined to extract multi-word strings with leading capitals followed by capitalized strings in brackets; the results can then be stored in a table to be consulted when an abbreviation (or an expansion of an abbreviation) is being asked for. Similar table-creation strategies are applicable for questions that ask for capitals, dates-of-birth, etc., whereas the approach seems less appropriate for definition questions, why-questions, or how-to questions. It was therefore decided to implement a *multi-stream* system: a system that includes a number of separate and independent subsystems, each of which is a complete standalone QA system that produces ranked answers, but not necessarily for all types of questions; the system's answer is then taken from the combined pool of candidates.

Scientifically, it is interesting to understand the performance of each stream on specific question types and in general. On the practical side, our multi-stream architecture allows us to modify and test a stream without affecting the rest of the system. A general overview of our system is given in Figure 1. The system consists of 5 separate QA streams and a final answer selection module that combines the results of all streams and produces the final answers.

Question Answering Streams. We now provide a brief description of the five streams of our QA system: Table Lookup, Pattern Match, English Tequesta, Dutch Tequesta, and Web Answer.

The *Table Lookup* stream uses specialized knowledge bases constructed by preprocessing the collection, exploiting the fact that certain information types (such as country capitals, abbreviations, and names of political leaders) tend to occur in the document collection in a small number of fixed patterns. When a question type indicates that the question might potentially have an answer in these tables, a lookup is performed in the appropriate knowledge base and answers which are found there are assigned high confidence. For example, to collect abbreviation-expansion pairs we searched the document collection for strings of capitals in brackets; upon finding one, we extracted sequences of capitalized non-stopwords preceding it, and stored it in the "abbreviation knowledge base." This approach answered question such as:

Q084. Waar staat GATT voor?	
(English	What does GATT stand for?)
Knowledge Base	Abbreviations
Table Entry	GATT: Overeenkomst over Tarieven en Handel
Extracted Answer	**Overeenkomst over Tarieven en Handel**

For a detailed overview of this stream, see [4].

In the *Pattern Match* stream, zero or more regular expressions are generated for each question according to its type and structure. These patterns indicate strings which contain the answer with high probability, and are then matched against the entire document collection. Here's a brief example:

Q002. In welke stad is het Europese Parlement?	
(English	In which city is the European Parliament located?)
Generated pattern	`Europese Parlement\s+in\s+(\S+)`
Match	...voor het **Europese Parlement in Straatsburg**, dat ...
Extracted Answer	**Straatsburg**

The *English Tequesta* stream translates the Dutch questions into English using Worldlingo's translation service available at http://www.worldlingo.com/. The auto-translated questions are then fed to *Tequesta*, an existing QA system for English developed at the University of Amsterdam [1]. The system uses the English CLEF corpus, and is extended with an Answer Justification module to anchor the answer in the Dutch collection.

The *Dutch Tequesta* is an adaptation of English Tequesta to Dutch and used as an independent stream, provided with the original Dutch newspaper corpus. The modifications to the original system included replacing (English) language specific components by Dutch counterparts; for instance, we trained TNT [5] to provide us with Part-of-Speech tags using the *Corpus Gesproken Nederlands* [6]; a named entity tagger for Dutch was also developed.

The *Web Answer* stream looks for an answer to a question on the World Wide Web, and then attempts to find justification for this answer in the collection. First, the question is converted to a web query, by leaving only meaningful keywords and (optionally) using lexical information from EuroWordNet. The query is sent to a web search engine (for the experiments reported here we used Google); if no relevant Web documents are found, the query is translated to English and sent again. Next, if the query yields some results, words and phrases appearing in the snippets of the top results are considered as possible answers, and ranked according to their relative frequency over all snippets. The Dutch named entity tagger and some heuristics were used to enhance the simple counts for the terms (e.g., terms that matched a TIME named entity were given a higher score if the expected answer type was a date). Finally, justifications for the answer candidates are found in the local Dutch corpus.

While each of the above streams is a "small" QA system in itself, many components are shared between the streams, including, for instance, an *Answer Justification* module that tries to ground externally found facts in the Dutch CLEF corpus, and a *Web Ranking* module that uses search engine hit counts to rank the candidate answers from our streams in a uniform way, similar to [7].

2.2   Results

Table 1 shows the evaluation results of our CLEF 2003 submissions and two post-submission runs, which resulted from very minor bug fixes. Besides the standard *Strict* and *Lenient* measures, we also evaluated our runs using a more "generous" *Lenient, Non-exact* measure that accepts non-exact answers as correct. For more details about the runs and a discussion of the results, see [8].

Table 1. Results on the CLEF 2003 test set

Run	Strict		Lenient		Lenient, Non-exact	
	# correct	MRR	# correct	MRR	# correct	MRR
uamsex031md	78 (39%)	0.298	82 (41%)	0.317	96 (48%)	0.377
uamsex032md	82 (41%)	0.305	89 (44.5%)	0.335	102 (51%)	0.393
uamsex031md.fixed	84 (42%)	0.335	87 (43.5%)	0.352	100 (50%)	0.407
uamsex032md.fixed	88 (44%)	0.349	95 (47.5%)	0.375	107 (53.5%)	0.428

3   Error Analysis

We now turn to a discussion of the incorrect answers given by our system, give examples of each, and suggest strategies for reducing the amount of wrong answers of these types. Some of these strategies are being implemented or tested as part of our ongoing QA work; others are offered as possible research areas in the QA domain.

Out of 200 questions, we answered 88 correctly (in this context we refer to the "fixed" strict runs, i.e., inexact and unsupported answers are regarded as incorrect ones). For the remaining 112 questions, we consider 2 wrong answers

Table 2. Breakdown of errors

Error type	Retrieval	Table	Justification	Tile	Confidence	Patterns	Lookup	Unit	Quest. classif.	Named entity	Answer selection
Absolute number of errors	2	2	5	6	8	9	12	12	20	51	97
Fraction of errors	1%	1%	2%	3%	4%	4%	5%	5%	9%	23%	43%

per question — the two top answers given by our system. Our third answer for all questions was NIL, as a simple strategy for answering the 10% questions with no known answer in the document collection. In total, we look at 224 wrong answers (also referred to as "errors"). Table 2 provides a breakdown of the errors according to type.

3.1   Answer Selection Errors

This large group of errors — 97 in total (43%) — is rather loosely-defined and revolves around the answer extraction process. Answer extraction, one of the critical stages of the Web Answer and the Tequesta streams, includes identifying possible answers from documents which were retrieved as relevant for the question. The extraction is composed of labeling terms which are likely to be answers (using named entity, part-of-speech tags and other techniques), and ranking these terms according to various measures, mostly based on proximity to query words. Some of these errors also originate from non-optimal top-ranking documents returned by our retrieval engine. Examples of such errors, where the answers given by the system are of the correct answer type and appear frequently in the relevant articles, are listed in Table 3.

Most of the errors stem from our simple ranking approach for the candidate answers, which is almost exclusively based on the proximity of the terms to the query words in the documents and their frequencies, with shallow NE tagging techniques. For example, for question 60 shown in Table 3, *Frogs* is a repeating entity in documents discussing a construction of a wall in Berlin for protecting frogs from car accidents; the construction was in debate at the time of the CLEF experiments, resulting in many web pages containing relevant terms, and referring to frogs as the reason for a construction of a Berlin wall.

This issue of *linking* entities of the right type to input questions is one of the most critical ones for QA systems. A number of partial solutions for this error class were proposed, ranging from usage of theorem provers for justification of the answer [2], rule based approaches [9] to the usage of parse tree similarity [10] and paraphrase dictionaries [11]. Recently, a noisy-channel approach was succesfully applied to address this issue [12]. Our research in this area is aimed at exploiting a range of light-weight reasoning methods, including some of the ones mentioned

Table 3. Examples of errors

Q033. Welke Russische president gaf opdracht tot de interventie in Tsjetsjenie?   (English: Which Russian president ordered the intervention in Chechnia?)   Answer: Gratsjov
Q037. Noem een Japanse stad die door een aardbeving is getroffen.   (English: Name a Japanese city hit by an earth quake.)   Answer: Los Angeles   Answer: Tokio
Q177. Wie stelde een embargo in tegen Irak?   (English: Who imposed an embargo against Iraq?)   Answer: Saddam Hussein
Q060. Wie heeft de Berlijnse Muur gebouwd?   (English: Who built the Berlin Wall?)   Answer: frogs

above; the lack of lexical resources for Dutch and the relative poverty of existing ones is an important bottleneck in this respect.

3.2   Table Lookup Errors

As noted earlier, our knowledge bases were constructed by preprocessing the document collection, searching for facts which tend to appear in fixed, repeating patterns. For this extraction process we used a small number of hand-crafted regular expression patterns; although these patterns also pick up noise from the text, we assumed that the amount of "real" facts extracted will be much higher, so we used frequency counts of the facts to filter out the noisy ones. This approach was very successful, and indeed the number of wrong answers given by the Table stream is low. They can be grouped into two classes: *Construction Errors* and *Lookup Errors*.

Construction Errors occurred when the selected answer was one of the "noisy facts" picked up during the preprocessing; A small number of inexact answers are derived similarly. For example:

Q022. Wie is de voorzitter van de Europese Commissie?   (English: Who is the president of the European Committee?)   Answer: **Jacques Santer. Volgens**

Out of our 224 errors, only 2 (1%) were Construction Errors.

Lookup Errors occurred when the lookup process in the table produced a wrong fact. The tables we constructed are simple text files, containing one fact per line. During the lookup process we search for lines containing all keywords from the question in a certain column, and then consider the data in another column as a candidate answer. For example, for question 93, *Wie is de leider van Sinn Fein?* (English: Who is the leader of Sinn Fein?), we search the Leaders table for a line containing the words (leider, Sinn, Fein) in the "description" column, and then consider the data in the "name" column (Gary Adams) to be an answer. If we do not find such a line, we start to omit some of the words we are looking for, based on heuristics such as capitalization and frequency of the word in the language (omitting high frequency words first). In most cases this process produces good results; however, in 12 cases (5%) incorrect answers were found using this lookup, either because the lookup words were found but had other semantics than that we intended, or because we omitted too many keywords and received irrelevant results. An example (of the first type of error):

Q118. Wie is de president van Joegoslavie?	
(English:	Who is the president of Yugoslavia?)
Answer:	**Vitaly Tsjoerkin**
Table Entry	Vitaly Tsjoerkin, president Jeltsins speciale afgezant voor het voormalige Joegoslavie

Our ongoing work for addressing these types of errors includes involving more linguistic resources in the table construction phase. For example, we now build our table using an NE-tagged version of the corpus, eliminating many noisy patterns; we also use dependency parsing for locating facts in the text, rather than just simple patterns. In future work, we intend to further enhance the construction process by using machine learning techniques to learn the patterns that store useful data in the document collection.

To address the lookup errors, we enhanced the lookup mechanism to support separate lists of stopwords and "keepwords" (words which should not be omitted during the lookup) per table. These lists help to avoid lookup errors such as supplying a former or vice president instead of a current one etc. Additionally, we plan to convert the simple text tables to real databases, allowing much more flexibility and accuracy with SQL querying (as well as increased efficiency).

3.3   Pattern Match Errors

In the Pattern Match stream, regular expression patterns were formulated using the question keywords and the question, in such a way that text which matches them contains the answer in a known position; the patterns were then matched against the document collection. As with the patterns used for constructing the tables, these patterns matched noisy elements, usually as a result of a pattern which is not strict enough; another problem was generation of non-grammatical patterns, but these did not yield any wrong answers since no text was matched at all. The following is an example of a mismatch for such a pattern:

Q021. Waar is Chiapas?	
(English:	Where is Chiapas?)
Generated Pattern	`Chiapas\s+is\s+([\^.]+)`
Match	de indiaanse boeren in Chiapas is zelfs verslechterd
Extracted Answer	**zelfs verslechterd**

In total, we encountered 9 (4%) pattern match errors; to handle them, we are experimenting with the use of part-of-speech tags in the pattern formulation process, to generate patterns which are more strict and thus less likely to match irrelevant text. A different approach to creation of the patterns involves learning them from data collected on the Web [13].

3.4 Question Classification Errors

Our question classifier, based on a set of manually constructed pattern-based rules, achieved 86% accuracy for about 20 question types. Of the questions not classified correctly, most were not classified at all and only a small number of questions was classified incorrectly. In some cases, incorrect or no classification still produces reasonable answers (using the Web, for example); for other cases, a wrong question type implies various other failures along the system pipeline that result in wrong answers. In total, about 20 (9%) of our errors are directly attributed to mis-classifications, but deeper analysis may reveal that other errors are also derived from an incorrect question type. For example, question *138. Onder welke naam is het EFA-project ook wel bekend?* (English: The EFA project is also known under which name?) was not classified at all; had it been classified as EXPAND-ABBREVIATION or even ALSO-KNOWN-AS, it would possibly contain much better candidate answers than the ones which were actually selected.

Since our participation at CLEF, we have improved our question classifier to use part-of-speech tags and WordNet for classifying questions not classified by the rule-based approach. We are currently reformulating the classifier, moving from the rule-based approach to a machine learning approach, using features such as ngrams of words from the question, subtrees of the question parse tree, and part-of-speech tags, in a manner similar to [14].

3.5 Justification Errors

Two of our streams obtained candidate answers from external resources rather than the Dutch document collection: the Web Answer stream used (Dutch and English) documents on the Web, and the English Tequesta stream used the English CLEF document collection, which contained English newspaper articles from the same dates as the Dutch one. Once an answer was found in one of these resources, justification of the answer — a document from the Dutch collection supporting the answer — was needed for a complete answer. For this justification process (sometimes referred to as "answer projection" [3]) we used an IR system to select the top ranking document from the Dutch collection, where the query was composed of keywords from the question and the answer, similarly to [15]. This approach sometimes failed for various reasons: English-Dutch translation problems and spelling variations, different formulations of the answer in the external resource and the document collection (synonymous words) and so on. In total, justification errors account for 5 (2%) of our errors.

To address this problem, we experimented with different IR models for retrieval of the answer justification; in the future we intend to also incorporate synonyms from WordNet for enriching our justification queries. Other answer justification methodologies, that we have not experimented with, include sliding windows on retrieved passages techniques [16].

3.6   Named Entity Errors

For our named entity classifier, we used TnT [5] trained on the *Corpus Gesproken Nederlands* [6], and some hand-made rules for fine-tuning. Although generally this approach provided good results, 51 (22%) of the wrong answers are attributed to incorrect NE classifications. For example, *Sensibiliseringscampagne* was classified as a location and given as an answer for *185. In welk land ligt het gebied van de Grote Meren?* (English: In which country is the area of the Great Lakes located?). The Web Answer stream had many named entity errors, mainly because web snippets tend to be ungrammatical phrases, which made the NE tagging task harder.

Constructing a reliable, robust NE tagger for Dutch is an ongoing effort [17]; as part of our revision of the question classification phase, we are currently looking into usage of a state-of-the-art NE tagger for reducing this type of errors.

3.7   Wrong Unit Errors

Questions for which the answer is a number or a quantity are sometimes answered with a number that common sense would rule out. For example, for question *32. Hoeveel landen nemen deel aan de Internationale Conferentie over Bevolking en Ontwikkeling?* (English: How many countries take part in the International Conference on Population and Development?), the system produced the answer *miljard* (English: a billion). There are 12 such errors (5%), some of which may be handled by various sanity-checks and world-knowledge filters of the candidate answers, such as the usage of Cyc in [18]. We are currently building an ontology based type-checker for answer (currently for LOCATION questions only) that will address some of these problems.

3.8   Voting Errors

In the final stages of the QA pipeline, final answers are selected from a pool of candidates provided by the different streams. Our selection process between the candidates was very naive, giving preference to the Table and Pattern streams which we considered highly reliable, and using the confidence level of the other streams to compare their candidates. However, these confidence levels were not always comparable, since they originated in different sources; 8 wrong answers (3% of errors) originated from mismatches in the confidence levels of the streams and the simplified answer selection process.

Since our CLEF experiments we have changed the voting mechanism thoroughly. We now use Web hit counts for all streams, to normalize the confidence scores given by them; moreover, the voting process now uses weights based on the question type and the stream for deciding between the candidates in the answer pool. The weights are learned from performance of the streams on a training set of questions, and initial experiments show significant improvements using this voting scheme.

3.9   Tiling Errors

Another step which is carried out at the final stages of the system is answer tiling. In this step, candidate answers which are similar (according to string similarity measures), or contain other candidates, or overlap with them, are joined to boost the confidence of the answer and to generate an answer which is more precise. For example, *Bill Clinton, president Clinton* and *former president Clinton* will be tiled to a single answer, *former president Bill Clinton*, which has higher confidence than any of the partial answers. In many cases the tiling process improves the answers given by the system, but 6 (3%) of the errors, mostly inexact ones, originate from this process:

Q031. Wat is de voornaam van Milosevic?	
(English:	What is Milosevic' first name?)
Candidate 1	Slobodan
Candidate 2	Slobodan Milosevic
Tiled Answer	Slobodan Milosevic

Addressing the tiling problem is tricky, since even humans will not necessarily agree whether *George Bush* and *George W. Bush* should be tiled to the same entity. We have done some refinement of our tiling process, but it is impossible to completely eliminate errors generated by it.

4   Conclusions

We presented our multi-stream question answering system and the runs it produced for CLEF 2003. Question answering is a multi-faceted problem, requiring contributions from information retrieval, natural language processing, and artifical intelligence. While addressing the question answering task will always leave room for improvement in most of the many modules required, an in-depth analysis of the types of wrong answers given by our system has revealed two major types: answer selection and named entity recognition. Both are on the language processing side of the spectrum, and both require a mixture of sufficient data and novel insights. In our ongoing QA research we are working on both of these long-term aspects. In our short-term work we are addressing the errors discussed with various strategies, and extending the various streams to handle them.

Acknowledgments

All three authors were supported by the Netherlands Organization for Scientific Research (NWO) under project number 220-80-001. In addition, Maarten de

Rijke was supported by grants from NWO, under project numbers 612-13-001, 365-20-005, 612.069.006, 612.000.106, 612.000.207, and 612.066.302.

References

1. Monz, C., de Rijke, M.: Tequesta: The University of Amsterdam's textual question answering system. In Voorhees, E., Harman, D., eds.: The Tenth Text REtrieval Conference (TREC 2001), National Institute for Standards and Technology. NIST Special Publication 500-250 (2002) 519–528
2. Moldovan, D., Harabagiu, S., Girju, R., Morarescu, P., Lacatusu, F., Novischi, A., Badulescu, A., Bolohan, O.: LCC Tools for Question Answering. [19]
3. et al., M.B.: AskMSR: Question answering using the Worldwide Web. In: Proc. EMNLP 2002. (2002)
4. Jijkoun, V., Mishne, G., de Rijke, M.: Preprocessing Documents to Answer Dutch Questions. In: Proc. 15th Belgian-Dutch Conference on Artificial Intelligence (BNAIC'03). (2003)
5. Brants, T.: TnT – a statistical part-of-speech tagger. In: Proc. 6th Applied NLP Conference, ANLP-2000. (2000)
6. Oostdijk, N.: The Spoken Dutch Corpus: Overview and first evaluation. In: Proc. LREC 2000. (2000) 887–894
7. Magnini, B., Negri, M., Prevete, R., Tanev, H.: Is it the right answer? exploiting web redundancy for answer validation. In: Proc. 40th Annual Meeting of the Association for Computational Linguistics (ACL). (2002) 425–432
8. Jijkoun, V., Mishne, G., de Rijke, M.: The University of Amsterdam at QA@CLEF 2003. In: Working Notes for the CLEF 2003 Workshop. (2003)
9. Xu, J., Licuanan, A., May, J., Miller, S., Weischedel, R.: TREC 2002 QA at BBN: Answer selection and confidence estimation. [19]
10. Ittycheriah, A., Roukos, S.: IBM's Statistical Question Answering System – TREC-11. In: Proc. 11th Text REtrieval Conference. (2002)
11. Duclaye, F., Yvon, F., Collin, O.: Learning paraphrases to improve a question-answering system. In: Proc. EACL 2003 Workshop on NLP for QA. (2003)
12. Echihabi, A., Marcu, D.: A Noisy-Channel Approach to Question Answering. In Hinrichs, E., Roth, D., eds.: Proc. 41st Annual Meeting of the Association for Computational Linguistics. (2003) 16–23
13. Ravichandran, D., Hovy, E.: Learning Surface Text Patterns for a Question Answering System. In: Proc. 40th ACL conference. (2002)
14. Zhang, D., Lee, W.: Question Classification using Support Vector Machines. In: Proc. 26th annual international ACM SIGIR conference on Research and development in information retrieval, ACM Press (2003) 26–32
15. Brill, E., Lin, J., Banko, M., Dumais, S., Ng, A.: Data-Intensive Question Answering. In: Text REtrieval Conference. (2001)
16. Lin, J., Fernandes, A., Katz, B., Marton, G., Tellex, S.: Extracting Answers from the Web Using Knowledge Annotation and Knowledge Mining Techniques (2002)
17. Sang, E.T.K., Meulder, F.D.: Introduction to the CoNLL-2003 Shared Task: Language-Independent Named Entity Recognition. In W. Daelemans and M. Osborne, ed.: Proc. of CoNLL-2003, Edmonton, Canada (2003) 142–147

18. Chu-Carroll, J., Prager, J., Welty, C., Czuba, K., Ferrucci, D.: A multi-strategy and multi-source approach to question answering. In: Proc. Eleventh Text REtrieval Conference (TREC 2002). (2002)
19. Voorhees, E., Harman, D., eds.: The Tenth Text REtrieval Conference (TREC 2002). In Voorhees, E., Harman, D., eds.: The Tenth Text REtrieval Conference (TREC 2002), National Institute for Standards and Technology. NIST Special Publication 500-251 (2003)

Cross Lingual QA: A Modular Baseline in CLEF 2003

Lucian Vlad Lita, Monica Rogati, and Jaime Carbonell

Carnegie Mellon University 5000 Forbes Ave. Pittsburgh, PA 15213
{llita, mrogati, jgc}@cs.cmu.edu

Abstract. We evaluate the feasibility of applying currently available research tools to the problem of cross lingual QA. We establish a task baseline by combining a cross lingual IR system with a monolingual QA system in a very short amount of time. A higher *precision* strategy involves applying the monolingual QA system to an automatically translated question, assumed to be correct. A higher *coverage* strategy consists of a term weighted proximity measure with varied query expansion, tuned for each individual question type.

1 Introduction

In our CLEF 2003 participation we evaluate the application of existing research modules to Cross-Lingual Question Answering (CLQA). The obvious first step towards solving this task is to combine cross lingual information retrieval with monolingual question answering. In order to set up a baseline with very little effort – one week's worth of work – we glued two existing off-the-(authors' research)-shelf components: a cross lingual information retrieval system and a monolingual question answering system, and tuned them on available question/answer datasets.

We have participated with two runs in the cross-lingual French-to-English CLEF task and we focused on quickly obtaining a system based on available tools and components.

2 Overview

Our CLEF system consists of two pre-existing components: a cross lingual information retrieval system (CLIR) and a monolingual question answering system (MQA), plus the necessary glue.

2.1 The CLIR Component

The cross lingual information retrieval component [4] is a system trained for the CLEF 2003 cross lingual retrieval task. It uses a parallel corpus to train a translation model, which is then used for query translation. The system uses GIZA++ [2] to train the translation model and a retrieval system based on Lemur [3]. No proprietary machine translation systems including SysTran, Google etc, have been used and the parallel corpus is freely available.

C. Peters et al. (Eds.): CLEF 2003, LNCS 3237, pp. 535–540, 2004.
© Springer-Verlag Berlin Heidelberg 2004

The CLIR system produces both a list of relevant documents as well as a translated expanded query with corresponding weights for each word.

2.2 The MQA Component

The monolingual question answering component is a high precision, pattern based QA system that relies on very few resources. The system is trained on the TREC [6] QA task datasets and has limited question type coverage.

The MQA system implements a simplified version of the widespread pipeline QA architecture. Initially, the questions are filtered and classified into question types and relevant question terms are extracted. A straightforward sentence-level retrieval follows, producing candidate sentences in tokenized form. In the answer extraction phase, high confidence finite state transducers (FSTs) are applied and candidate answers are produced with their corresponding confidence scores. Answers with similar surface forms are grouped and unified into a stronger representative answer with a higher score.

Currently, no answer verification is performed and no feedback loops are present. The MQA system was built to rely on as few resources as possible. Hence, the transducers are based on surface form, capitalization features, WordNet [7] based features, and a short list of grammatical constructs. Named entity taggers and gazetteers are the two ubiquitous elements in QA architectures that are missing from our system.

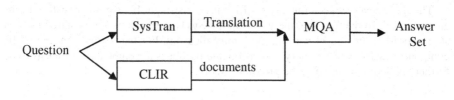

Fig. 1. High precision approach

2.3 Architecture

Our simple, ad-hoc architecture sets up an obvious baseline for the CLQA task. We approach the problem through two methods: a high precision method that is likely to answer few questions – especially given imperfect translations – and a higher recall method that covers most of the questions.

In our higher precision method, the source language question is first run through SysTran [5], a proprietary translation system with a free, limited, online interface. The un-altered English translation is then passed to the MQA component, which produces a list of answers, ordered by confidence scores. The documents used in answer extraction are produced by the CLIR component. If any answers are obtained via this strategy, the system offers them as the final set of answers. In case no answers were extracted, the higher recall method is activated.

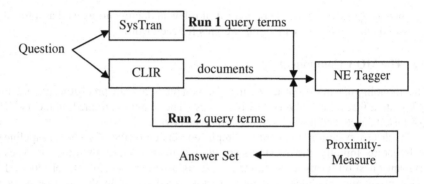

Fig. 2. High coverage approach. In RUN 1, the query terms are produced directly from the SysTran translation. In RUN 2, the query terms are produced by the CLIR component

Our higher coverage strategy also uses the CLIR component for document retrieval. A rudimentary question classification provides the mapping between the question text and answer types. The answer types correspond to entity types obtained by processing the relevant documents with a named entity tagger. Subsequently, given a set of question terms, we apply a term weighted proximity measure to candidate answers of the required type. Evidence for a particular answer is then combined with that of identical or similar answers in order to compute its final score.

The difference between our two CLEF runs consists in the way the question terms are produced. In the first run, the words in the SysTran translation are filtered using a stop word list, then used with the proximity measure. For the second run, the CLIR component takes over the query expansion and produces a weighted set of terms to be further applied in computing the proximity score.

3   Experiments

In the high precision approach experiments, the system first translates the question from French to English using the SysTran online interface. The un-altered, translated question is considered grammatically and semantically correct – i.e. a perfect translation – and is passed to the MQA component. Relevant documents are retrieved using the CLIR component and are also passed to the MQA component, which applies FSTs/patterns to identify candidate answers.

Using the higher coverage strategy, our system first classifies each question as one of the following types: location, temporal, person, numeric, quantity and other. We obtain the relevant documents using the CLIR component, we tokenize them, and we apply a simple sentence splitting algorithm. The BBN Identifinder [1] named entity tagger is applied to the processed documents. Entities corresponding to the required question type are identified as candidate answers. For each candidate answer, we compute a term weighted proximity score:

$$score = \Sigma_i (w_a * f(d_i) * w_{qi}) \tag{1}$$

where w_a is the term weight for the candidate answer, $f(d_i)$ is a function based on the distance between the candidate answer and i^{th} question term in its proximity, and w_{qi} is the term weight for the ith question term. The term weighting methods considered were: *okapi*, *idf*, and *ntc*. The distance functions explored were the linear, quadratic, and exponential functions.

3.1 Parameter Tuning

The training set consisted of approximately one hundred questions selected from TREC 9 & 10 question sets. Two French native speakers translated the original English questions*. The automatic SysTran translations were corrected in order to provide our system with reasonable training data. We used the limited data for parameter tuning for each individual question type. *Table 1.* shows the final parameter set used for the CLEF runs.

Table 1. Final parameters for the CLEF cross lingual QA task

Question Type	Term Weighting	Distance Function	# expansion terms	# documents
Location	NTC	Linear	10	20
Person	Okapi	Linear	50	20
Temporal	Okapi	Exponential	10	20
Quantity	Okapi	Quadratic	10	20
Numeric	Okapi	Exponential	10	20

The number of query expansion terms was varied from 5 to 200 for the second run. For the first run, the query terms considered were only the non-stopwords in the SysTran translation of the source question. The number of relevant documents retrieved by CLIR was varied from 1 to 30.

3.2 Performance at CLEF

The best MRR score we obtained was 0.1533 under the stricter policy, and 0.17083 under the looser. Our system did not offer any answer for nearly half of the questions, reflecting the fact that it is very conservative in terms of proposing answers with little evidence.

The monolingual component was trained on short, correct and meaningful English factoid questions. Out of 200 questions, the MQA approach worked on 11 questions, which were translated approximately correct. Out of these 11, it found correct answers for only 4 questions. For the other 7 questions it produced no answers.

---

* Many thanks to Antoine Raux.

Table 2. Final CLEF scores for both runs – test set contains 200 questions

	Strict MRR	% questions w/ a correct answer	Loose MRR	% questions w/ a correct answer	# NILs proposed	# NILs correct
Run 1	0.1533	19%	0.17083	21%	92	8
Run 2	0.1316	15.5%	0.14916	17.5%	91	7

4 Discussion

Our CLEF 2003 system combines the CLIR and MQA research modules into a CLQA baseline. There are several modifications, which could clearly improve the performance. We have employed no question analysis in French. Phrase detection, reformulation, classification by question type and answer type in the source language (French in our case) would clearly improve the performance. Since early errors propagate through the question answering pipeline, accurate question analysis before automatic translation would allow the system to select the appropriate answer extraction method.

The current question analysis in the target language (English) is a minimal classification into 6 question types. Since automatic translation is less than perfect, phrase identification and reformulation is almost always out of the question.

The training data consists of factoid questions and answers selected from TREC datasets. The CLEF question set appears to contain more complex questions and questions that contain more content words compared to the TREC style questions. However the fact that our system was tuned on *slightly* different data than the CLEF test data is not detrimental since it approaches a more likely real life test.

The retrieval step is tuned for the CLEF 2002 cross lingual IR task, and the query expansion is performed internally by the CLIR component. A document set of size 20 worked best for all question types. For fewer documents, there was not enough support for correct answers and for a larger document set size there was too much noise. The *person* question type required a wider query expansion.

The two runs showed that for this year's CLEF data, the CLIR-produced query expansion in English from the source question text in French is almost as good as using the question terms from the SysTran translation. This is particularly true for longer questions that involve more high-content words. The fact that proprietary components can play a more limited role in the system without drastic performance drops is certainly encouraging because it provides more control over the CLQA process.

The fact that the two runs were very similar in performance suggests that no question expansion – i.e. using the translated question terms in answer identification – is sufficient given our current basic methods. On the other hand, the lack of exact (SysTran) translation for the higher coverage strategy does not result in significant performance degradation.

5 Future Work

Our goal for this year's CLEF participation was to identify research issues for cross lingual question answering using a minimal baseline. In future research, we plan to address issues such as language independence and semi-automatic question analysis for CLQA.

References

1. Bikel, D.M., Miller, S., Schwartz R., and Weischedel R.: Nymble: A High-Performance Learning Name-Finder. In Proceedings ANLP (1997)
2. Och, F.J., Ney, H.: Improved Statistical Alignment Models. In Proceedings ACL (2000)
3. Ogilvie, P., Callan, J.: Experiments Using The Lemur Toolkit. In Proceedings TREC (2001)
4. Rogati, M., Yang, Y.: Multilingual Information Retrieval Using Open Transparent Resources in CLEF 2003 workshop notes (http://www.clef-campaign.org) (2003)
5. SysTran, http://babel.altavista.com/translate.dyn
6. Voorhees, E.: Overview of the TREC 2002 Question Answering Track. Text Retrieval Conference (2002)
7. Fellbaum, C. WordNet: An Electronic Lexical Database. MIT Press, Cambridge (1998)

Question Answering in Spanish

José L. Vicedo, Ruben Izquierdo, Fernando Llopis, and Rafael Muñoz

Departamento de Lenguajes y Sistemas Informáticos,
University of Alicante, Spain
{vicedo,rib1,llopis,rafael}@dlsi.ua.es

Abstract. This paper describes the architecture, operation and results
obtained with the Question Answering prototype for Spanish developed
in the Department of Language Processing and Information Systems at
the University of Alicante for the CLEF 2003 Spanish monolingual QA
evaluation task. Our system has been fully developed from scratch and
it combines shallow natural language processing tools with statistical
data redundancy techniques. The system is able to perform QA tasks
independently from static corpora or from Web documents. Moreover,
the World Wide Web can be used as an external resource to obtain
evidence to support and complement the CLEF Spanish corpora.

1 Introduction

Open domain QA systems are defined as tools capable of extracting the answer to user queries directly from unrestricted domain documents. Investigation
in question answering has been traditionally focussed to English language and
mainly fostered by Text REtrieval Conference (TREC[1]) evaluations. However,
the development of QA systems for languages other than English was considered
by the QA Roadmap Committee as one of the main lines for future investigations
in this field [1]. In particular, it recommended that systems should be developed
that perform QA from sources of information written in different languages.

As result of this interest, the Cross-Language Evaluation Forum[2] (CLEF
2003), has introduced a new task (*Multiple Language Question Answering*) for
the evaluation of QA systems in several languages. This evaluation offers several
subtasks: monolingual Spanish, Italian and Dutch QA and bilingual QA. The
bilingual subtask is designed to measure system performance when searching
answers in a collection of English texts to questions posed in Spanish, Italian,
Dutch, German or French.

The main characteristics of this first evaluation are similar to those proposed
in past TREC Conferences. For each subtask, the organisation provided 200
questions requiring short, factual answers whose answer is not guaranteed to
occur in the document collection. Systems should return up to three responses

---

[1] http://trec.nist.gov/
[2] http://clef-qa.itc.it/

C. Peters et al. (Eds.): CLEF 2003, LNCS 3237, pp. 541–548, 2004.

per question, and answers should be ordered by confidence. Responses have to be associated with the document in which they are found. A response can be either a [*answer-string, document-identifier*] pair or the string "NIL" when the system does not find a correct answer in the document collection. The "NIL" string is considered correct if there is no answer known to exist in the document collection; otherwise it is judged as incorrect. Two different kinds of answers are accepted: the exact answer or a 50 bytes long string that should contain the exact answer.

Our participation has been restricted to the Spanish monolingual task in the category of exact answers. Although we have experience in past TREC competitions [2, 3, 4], we decided to build a new system mainly due to the big differences between English and Spanish languages. Moreover, we designed a very simple approach (1 person month) that will facilitate later error analysis and will allow the detection of those basic language-dependent features that make Spanish QA different from English QA.

This paper is organised as follows: Section 2 describes the structure and operation of our Spanish QA system. Afterwards, we present and analyse the results obtained at CLEF QA Spanish monolingual task. Finally, we extract initial conclusions and discuss directions for future work.

2   System Description

Our system is organized in the three main modules of a general QA system architecture:

1. Question analysis.
2. Passage retrieval.
3. Answer extraction.

Question analysis is the first stage in the QA process. This module processes questions input to the system in order to detect and extract the useful information contained. This information is represented in a form that is easily processible by the remaining modules. The *Passage retrieval* module performs a first selection of relevant passages. This process is accomplished in parallel retrieving relevant passages from the Spanish EFE document collection and the Spanish pages in the World Wide Web. Finally, the *answer selection* module processes relevant passages in order to locate and extract the final answer. Figure 1 shows system architecture.

2.1   Question Analysis

The question analysis module carries out two main processes: *answer type classification* and *keyword selection*. The former detects the type of information that the question expects as answer (a date, a quantity, etc) and the latter selects those question terms (*keywords*) that will make it possible to locate those documents that are likely to contain the answer.

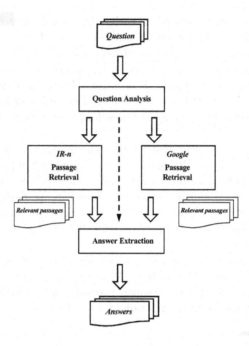

Fig. 1. System architecture

These processes are performed using a simple manually developed set of lexical patterns. Each pattern is associated with its corresponding expected answer type. Once a pattern matches the question posed to the system, this process returns both the list of keywords associated with the question and the type of the expected answer associated with the matched pattern. As our system lacks a named-entity tagger, it currently only copes with three possible answer types: NUMBER, DATE and OTHER. Figure 2 shows examples of the patterns and the output generated at the question analysis stage for test questions 002, 006 and 103.

2.2   Passage Retrieval

The passage retrieval stage is accomplished in parallel using two different search engines: IR-n [5] and Google[3].

IR-n is a passage retrieval system that uses groups of contiguous sentences as units of information. From the QA perspective, this passage extraction model allows us to benefit from the advantages of discourse-based passage retrieval models since self-contained information units of text, such as sentences, are used for building the passages. First, the IR-n system performs passage retrieval over the entire Spanish EFE document collection. In this case, keywords detected at

---

[3] http://www.google.com/

the question analysis stage are processed using the MACO Spanish lemmatiser [6] and their corresponding lemmas are used to retrieve the 50 most relevant passages from the EFE document database. These passages are made up of text snippets of 2 sentences. Second, the same keyword list (without lemmatisation) is input to the Google Internet search engine. For efficiency, relevant documents are not downloaded but the system just selects the 50 best short summaries returned in the main Google result pages. Figure 3 shows examples of retrieved passages for question 103. In this example, question keywords found in relevant passages are underlined.

```
Question 002  ¿Qué país invadió Kuwait en 1990?
Pattern       (qué|Qué)\s+([a-z|áéíóúñ]+)
Answer type   OTHER
Keywords      país invadió Kuwait 1990
Lemmas        país invadir Kuwait 1990


Question 006  ¿Cuándo decidió Naciones Unidas imponer el embargo sobre Irak?
Pattern       (cuándo|Cuándo)\s+
Answer type   DATE
Keywords      decidió Naciones Unidas imponer embargo Irak
Lemmas        decidir Naciones Unidas imponer embargo Irak


Question 103  ¿De cuántas muertes son responsables los Jemeres Rojos?
Pattern       (Cuántos|cuántos|Cuántas|cuántas)\s+([a-z|áéíóúñ]+)
Answer type   NUMBER
Keywords      muertes responsables Jemeres Rojos
Lemmas        muerte responsable Jemeres Rojos
```

Fig. 2. Question analysis example

2.3   Answer Extraction

This module processes in parallel both sets of passages selected at the passage retrieval stage (IR-n and Google) in order to detect and extract the three most probable answers to the query. The processes involved at this stage are the following:

1. *Relevant Sentence Selection.* Sentences in relevant passages are selected and scored.
   (a) Passages are split into sentences.
   (b) Each sentence is scored according to the number of question keywords they contain. Keywords appearing twice or more are only added once. This value (*sentence_score*) measures the similarity between each relevant sentence and the question.
   (c) Sentences that do not contain any keyword are discarded (*sentence_score* = 0).

Question 103   **¿De cuántas muertes son responsables los Jemeres Rojos?**

First retrieved passage from EFE Collection:

```
<DOCNO> EFE19940913-06889
... explotan los Jemeres Rojos, quienes no les preocupa que sus
ideas no sean respetadas por la comunidad internacional, que los
acusa de ser los responsables de la muerte de más de un millón de
camboyanos durante el genocidio de 1975 1978.
```

First retrieved passage from the World Wide Web:

```
<DOCNO> 1 Gooogle
   Los Jemeres Rojos fueron responsables de más de un millón de
muertes, mataron al menos a 20.000 presos políticos y torturaron a
cientos de miles de personas.
```

Fig. 3. Passages retrieved for question 103

2. *Candidate Answer Selection.* Candidate answers are selected from relevant sentences.
   (a) Relevant sentences are tagged using the MACO lemmatizer.
   (b) Quantities, dates and proper noun sequences are detected and are merged into single expressions.
   (c) Every term or merged expression in relevant sentences is considered a candidate answer.
   (d) Candidate answers are filtered. This process gets rid of those candidates that start or finish with a stopword or contain a question keyword.
   (e) From the remaining candidate set, only those whose semantic type matches the expected answer type are selected. When the expected answer type is OTHER, only proper noun phrases are selected as final candidate answers. Figure 3 shows (in boldface) the selected answer candidates for question 103.
3. *Candidate Answer Combination.* Each answer candidate is assigned a score that measures its probability of being the correct answer (*answer_frequency*). As the same candidate answer can probably be found in different relevant sentences, the candidate answer set may contain repeated elements. Our system exploits this fact by relating candidate redundancy with answer correctness as follows:
   (a) Repeated candidate answers are merged into a single expression that is scored according to its frequency in the candidate answer set.
   (b) Shorter expressions are preferred as answer to longer ones. This way, terms in long candidates that appear themselves as answer candidates boost shorter candidate answer scores by adding long candidate scores to the frequency value obtained by shorter ones.

Table 1. Spanish monolingual task results

Run	Strict		Lenient	
	MRR	Correct (%)	MRR	Correct (%)
alicex031ms	0,3075	40,0	0,3208	43,5
alicex032ms	0,2966	35,0	0,3175	38,5

4. *Web Evidence Addition.* At this point the system has two lists of candidate answers: one obtained from the EFE document set and another from available Spanish web documents. Next, both candidate answer lists are merged. This process consists of increasing the answer frequency of EFE list candidates by adding their corresponding frequency values from the web list. In this way, candidates appearing only in the web list are discarded.

5. *Final Answer Selection.* Answer candidates from previous steps are given a final score (*answer_score*) that measures two circumstances: (1) their redundancy through the answer extraction process (*answer_frequency*) and (2) the context in which they have been found (*sentence_score*). As the same candidate answer may be found in different contexts, an answer will maintain the maximum score for all the contexts they appear in. The final answer score is computed as follows:

$$answer\_score = sentence\_score \cdot answer\_frequency \qquad (1)$$

Answers are then ranked accordingly to their answer score and the first three answers are selected for presentation. Among the candidate answers for question 103 (example in Figure 3), the system selects *"un millón"* (one million) as the top ranked answer.

3   Results

We submitted two runs for the exact answer category. The first run (*alicex031ms*) was obtained applying the whole system as described above, while second run performed the QA process without activating Web retrieval (*alicex032ms*). Table 1 shows the results obtained for each run.

The result analysis may not be as conclusive as we would like, mainly due to the simplicity of our approach. Besides, the lack of the correct answers for test questions at this moment does not allow us to perform a correct error analysis. In any case, the results obtained show that using the World Wide Web as an external resource increases the percentage of correct answers retrieved by five percentage points. This fact confirms that the performance of QA systems for languages other than English can also benefit from this resource.

4   Future Work

This work has to be seen as a first and simple attempt to perform QA in Spanish. Consequently, there are several areas for future work to be investigated. Among them, we can indicate the following:

- Question analysis. Since the same question can be formulated in very diverse forms (interrogative, affirmative, using different words and structures,...), we need to study aspects such as recognizing equivalent questions regardless of the speech act or of the words, syntactic and semantic inter-relations or idiomatic forms employed.
- Answer taxonomy. An important part in the process of question interpretation resides in the system's ability to relate questions with the characteristics of their respective answers. Consequently, we need to develop a broad answer taxonomy that enables multilingual answer type classification. We expect to do this using the EuroWordNet[4] semantic net structure.
- Passage retrieval. An enhanced question analysis will improve passage retrieval performance by including question expansion techniques that make it possible to retrieve passages including relevant information expressed with terms that are different (but equivalent) to those used for question formulation.
- Answer extraction. Using a broad answer taxonomy involves using tools capable of identifying the entity that a question expects as answer. Therefore we need to integrate named-entity tagging capabilities that make it possible to narrow down the number of candidates to be considered as answers to a question.

Even though all these issues need to be investigated, it is important to note that this research needs to be developed from a multilingual perspective. Future investigations must address language-dependent and language-independent module detection in combination with the main long-term objective of developing a complete system capable of performing multilingual question answering.

Acknowledgements

This work has been partially supported by the Spanish Government (CICYT) with grant TIC2003-07158-C04-01.

References

1. Burger, J., Cardie, C., Chaudhri, V., Gaizauskas, R., Harabagiu, S., Israel, D., Jacquemin, C., Lin, C., Maiorano, S., Miller, G., Moldovan, D., Ogden, B., Prager, J., Riloff, E., Singhal, A., Shrihari, R., Strzalkowski, T., Voorhees, E., Weishedel, R.: Issues, Tasks and Program Structures to Roadmap Research in Question & Answering (Q&A). http://www-nlpir.nist.gov/projects/duc/papers/qa.Roadmap-paper_v2.doc (2000)

---

[4] http://www.dcs.shef.ac.uk/nlp/funded/eurowordnet.html

2. Vicedo, J., Ferrández, A.: A semantic approach to Question Answering systems. In: Ninth Text REtrieval Conference. Volume 500-249 of NIST Special Publication., Gaithersburg, USA, National Institute of Standards and Technology (2000) 511–516
3. Vicedo, J., Ferrández, A., Llopis, F.: University of Alicante at TREC-10. In: Tenth Text REtrieval Conference. Volume 500-250 of NIST Special Publication., Gaithersburg, USA, National Institute of Standards and Technology (2001)
4. Vicedo, J., Llopis, F., Ferrández, A.: University of Alicante Experiments at TREC-2002. In: Eleventh Text REtrieval Conference. Volume 500-251 of NIST Special Publication., Gaithersburg, USA, National Institute of Standards and Technology (2002)
5. Llopis, F., Vicedo, J., Ferrández, A.: IR-n system, a passage retrieval systema at CLEF 2001. In: Workshop of Cross-Language Evaluation Forum (CLEF 2001). Lecture notes in Computer Science, Darmstadt, Germany, Springer-Verlag (2001)
6. Atserias, J., Carmona, J., Castellón, I., Cervell, S., Civit, M., Màrquez, L., Martí, M., Padró, L., Placer, R., Rodríguez, H., Taulé, M., Turmo, J.: Morphosyntactic Analysis and Parsing of Unrestricted Spanish Text. In: Proceedings of First International Conference on Language Resources and Evaluation. LREC'98, Granada, Spain (1998) 1267–1272

Quantum, a French/English Cross-Language Question Answering System

Luc Plamondon and George Foster

RALI, Université de Montréal,
C.P. 6128, Succ. Centre-Ville
Montréal, Québec, Canada H3C 3J7
{plamondl,foster}@iro.umontreal.ca

Abstract. We describe a method for modifying a monolingual English question answering system to allow it to accept French questions. Our method relies on a statistical translation engine to translate keywords, and a set of manually written rules for analyzing French questions. The additional steps performed by the cross-language system lower its performance by 28% compared to the original system.

1 Introduction

A question answering (QA) system can be described as a particular type of search engine that allows a user to ask a question using natural language instead of an artificial query language. Moreover, a QA system pinpoints the exact answer in the document, while a classical search engine returns entire documents that have to be skimmed by the user.

Clarke [1] has shown that, for document collections smaller than 500 GB (100 billion words), the bigger the size of the collection, the better the performance of their QA system. If we suppose that an English speaker has access to about 10 times more digital documents — webpages, encyclopaedias on CDs, etc. — than a French speaker (estimation based on the number of pages on the web, see Fig. 1), there is no doubt that a QA system designed for French speakers but able to search English documents would open new possibilities both in terms of the quantity of topics covered and the quality of the answers.

We had previously developed the Quantum QA system [2] for the TREC evaluation campaigns. This system operates in English only: the question must be asked in English, the document collection is in English and the answer extraction is performed in English. For the purpose of a pilot project conducted with the National Research Council of Canada [3], we transformed Quantum into a bilingual system to allow French speakers to ask their questions in French and to get answers in French as well, but using an English document collection. We entered the cross-language QA track at CLEF 2003 with this bilingual system without further modifications.

C. Peters et al. (Eds.): CLEF 2003, LNCS 3237, pp. 549–558, 2004.

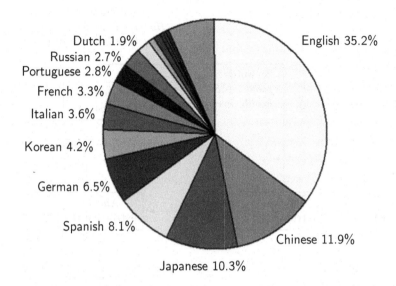

Fig. 1. Online language populations (March 2003), on a total of 640 million webpages. Source: http://www.glreach.com/globstats

2   Monolingual English System

Quantum was developped primarily for the TREC evaluation campaigns. It was designed to answer simple, syntactically well-formed, short and factual English questions such as the following from past campaigns: *What is pilates? Who was the architect of Central Park? How wide is the Atlantic Ocean? At what speed does the Earth revolve around the sun? Where is the French consulate in New York?* The document collection from which the answers are extracted are news from major newswires. For more details on the track and the system requirements, see the description of the TREC-11 QA track [4].

The architecture of the Quantum monolingual system is shown on Fig. 2, along with a sample question from the CLEF set. In the following sections, we describe only the elements that are relevant to the modifications we made in order to make the system cross-lingual.

2.1   Question Analysis

The goal of the question analysis phase is to determine the expected type of the answer to a particular question, and thus to determine the answer extraction mechanism — or extraction function — to use. Some of the extraction functions require an additional parameter called the question's *focus*. The focus is a word or group of words that appears in the question and that is closely related to the answer. For instance, the answer to *With what radioactive substance was Eda Charlton injected in 1945?* should be an hyponym of the question's focus *substance*. The answer to *In how many countries does Greenpeace have offices?*

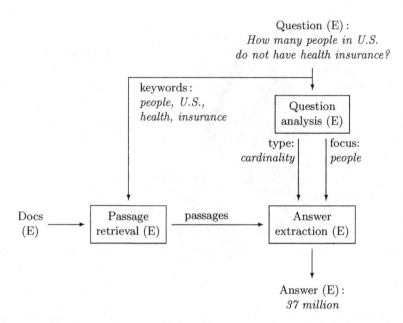

Fig. 2. Architecture of the monolingual version of Quantum. The question, the documents and the answer are all in English (E)

should contain a number followed by a repetition of the focus *countries*. Some types of questions such as *When was the Bombay Symphony Orchestra established?* do not require the identification of a focus because, in this case, we look for the time named entity that *when* stands for. All the words of the question, whether they are part of the focus or not, play a role in the process of finding the answer, at least through the information retrieval score (Sect. 2.2). We stress that our classification of questions, the interpretation of the question's focus and whether an extraction function requires a focus or not are all motivated by technical considerations specific to Quantum. A more rigorous study of questions based on psycho-linguistic criteria has been made by Graesser [5].

Before Quantum can analyze a question, it must undergo several operations: tokenization, part-of-speech tagging and NP-chunking. The analysis itself is performed via a set of 60 patterns and rules based on words, part-of-speech tags and noun-phrase tags. For example, Quantum uses the following pattern and rule to analyze the question in Fig. 2:

how many <noun-phrase NP_1> → type = *cardinality*, focus = NP_1

2.2 Retrieval of Relevant Passages

The answer extraction mechanisms are too complex to be performed on the entire document collection. For this reason, we employ a classical search engine to retrieve only the most relevant passages before we proceed with answer extraction. We use Okapi [6] because it allows for the retrieval of paragraphs instead of complete documents. We query it with the whole question and we let it stem the words and discard the stopwords. As a result, the query of the sample question in Fig. 2 would be a best match of *people, U.S., health* and *insurance.* We keep the 20 most relevant paragraphs along with their retrieval score as computed by Okapi.

2.3   Answer Extraction

The extraction function selected during question analysis (optionally parameterized with the focus) is applied on the most relevant paragraphs. Three techniques or tools are used, depending on the extraction function: regular expressions, WordNet (for hypernyms/hyponyms relations) and the Annie named entity extractor from the GATE suite [7]. For example, we would use WordNet to verify that *37 million Americans* can be an answer to the sample question in Fig. 2 because *Americans* is an hyponym of the question's focus *people.*

Each noun phrase in the relevant paragraphs is assigned an extraction score when it satisfies the extraction function criteria. This extraction score is combined with the retrieval score of the source paragraph to take into account the density of the question keywords surrounding the extracted noun phrase. The three best-scoring noun phrases are retained as answer candidates. We decided to consider noun phrases as base units for answers because we found that only 2% of the questions from the past TREC campaigns could not be answered with a single noun phrase.

3   Making the System Cross-Lingual

For Quantum as well as many other QA systems, the answer extraction phase is the most complex. Therefore, it was the impact on this phase which was decisive in selecting among strategies to transform our monolingual system into a cross-language bilingual system. Two factors were predominant: the availability of linguistic resources for answer extraction and the amount of work needed to transform the system.

Both factors argued in favour of an unmodified English answer extraction module (Fig. 3a) and the addition of a translation module for the question and the documents, instead of the creation of a new answer extraction module in French. On one hand, the quality and availability of linguistic resources is usually better for English than French. In fact, many good quality English resources are free, as it is the case for WordNet and the named entity extractor Annie used by Quantum. Furthermore, by retaining the answer extraction module in its original language, fewer modifications are required to transform the monolingual system. Indeed, in order to write a new answer extraction module in the same language as the questions (Fig. 3b), we would have to find linguistic resources for that language, adapt the system to the new resources' interfaces and then translate whole documents prior to extracting the answers, which is currently a time-consuming and error-prone process. On the other hand, it is more efficient to translate only the question and the extracted answer. We will show that a

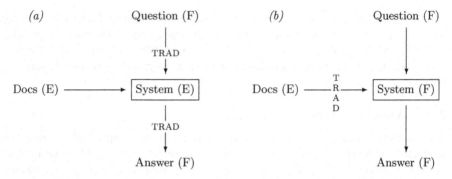

Fig. 3. Two approaches for the transformation of an English (E) monolingual system into a cross-language system for French (F) questions. In *(a)*, the system's core remains unmodified and better English linguistic resources can be used. In *(b)*, the core is transposed to French, new resources in French need to be found and whole documents need to be translated

full syntactically correct translation of the question is not mandatory and that the translation of the answer is facilitated by the particular context of QA.

In Fig. 3, we assume that the translation of the question and documents is perfect so that it is completely external to the blackbox system. Unfortunately, machine translation has not yet reached such a level of reliability. It is currently more efficient to *open* the system in order to make the translation steps easier. In our case, this allows us to avoid having to produce a complete and syntactically correct translation of the question. It also allows us to use different translation models depending on the task.

We first replaced the question analysis module by a new French version (Fig. 4) because the statistical techniques we use to translate the question are not reliable enough to produce syntactically correct sentences. Hence, our analysis patterns would seldom apply. Once the question is analyzed directly in French, the selected extraction function can be passed to the answer extraction module along with the question's focus, if any. However, the focus must be translated into English because we have retained the original English answer extraction module (among other things, the focus has to be known by WordNet). As for the passage retrieval module, we still use Okapi on the English document collection, which therefore requires translating the question keywords from French to English. Finally, the answer extraction module does not require any modification. Let us now examine each of the modified modules in more detail.

3.1 Converting the Question Analysis Module and Translating the Question's Focus

We use regular expressions that combine words and part-of-speech tags to analyze a question. The original English module uses around 60 analysis patterns. We wrote about the same number of patterns for French.

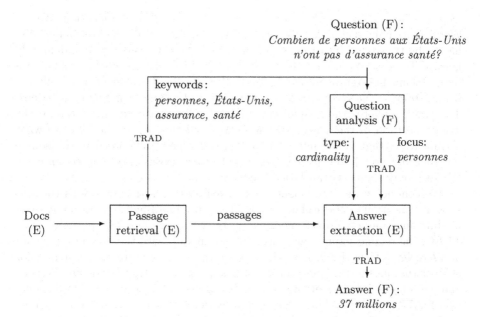

Fig. 4. Architecture of the bilingual version of Quantum (to be compared with the monolingual version in Fig. 2). The question and the answer are in French (F), while the documents are in English (E). The question analysis module operates in French and the other modules remain in English. Translation is required at three points: for the keywords, the focus and the answer

We found that French questions were more difficult to analyze because of the greater flexibility in the formulation of questions. For example, *How much does one ton of cement cost* can be formulated in two ways in French: *Combien coûte une tonne de ciment* or *Combien une tonne de ciment coûte-t-elle*. In addition, English question words — the base of the analysis — do not always map to a single equivalent in French: this is the case of *what*, which can be mapped to *qu'est-ce que* in *What is leukemia / Qu'est-ce que la leucémie*, to *que* in *What does "kain ayinhore" mean / Que signifie "kain ayinhore"*, to *quoi* in *Italy is the largest producer of what / L'Italie est le plus grand producteur de quoi* and to *quel* in *What party did Occhetto lead / Quel parti Occhetto dirigeait-il*. Among other difficulties there are the masculine/feminine and singular/plural agreements, the addition of an euphonic *t* in the interrogative form of certain verbs in the 3rd person singular (in *Combien une tonne coûte-t-elle* but not in *Combien deux tonnes coûtent-elles*), elisions (*Qu'appelle-t-on*) and two forms of the past tense (*Quand le mur de Berlin a-t-il été construit / Quand le mur de Berlin fut-il construit*, while the only appropriate form in English is *When was the Berlin Wall built*).

At the same time that the analysis rules select an extraction function, they also identify the question's focus. The focus semantics sometimes has an impact on the expected answer type. For instance, in *What is the longest river in Nor-*

way, the focus *river* indicates that the answer is the name of a location. We use WordNet to make such links. This means that the focus from the French question has to be translated into English before the expected answer type is definitely known. To do so, we use an IBM2 [8] statistical translation model trained on a set of documents composed of debates of the Canadian Parliament, news releases from *Europa - The European Union On-Line* and a sample of TREC questions. The IBM2 model is the simplest of the IBM series that takes into account the word's position in the source sentence. We need this feature because we want a translation that is the most probable given a particular word of the source sentence and, to a lesser degree, given all the other words of the source sentence. We keep only the best translation that is a noun.

We conducted an experiment on a sample set of TREC questions to measure the variation of performance between the original English question analysis module and the new French module [3]. Tested on a set of 789 questions from TREC, the regular expressions (used in conjunction with the semantic network of WordNet) of the English module select the correct extraction function for 96% of the questions. These questions were manually translated into French[1] and we found that the new French module selects the correct extraction function for 77% of them. This drop is due to two factors: the narrower coverage of the regular expressions and the incorrect translation of the focus (the focus is correctly translated half of the times). Most of these translation errors are due to the absence of the word in the training corpus, because many questions contain rare words, especially in definitions: *What is thalassemia, amoxicillin, a shaman*, etc. The translation of the focus is crucial to the question answering process. For example, it is almost impossible to determine that *37 million Americans* can properly answer the sample question in Fig. 4 if the focus *people* is wrongly translated into *flower*.

3.2   Translating the Keywords for Passage Retrieval

Cross-language information retrieval has been widely addressed outside the QA domain. State-of-the-art retrieval engines combine the translation model with the retrieval model [9]. However, since the search engine we use does not allow modifications to its retrieval model, we chose a simpler approach: we use an IBM1 translation model to get the best translations given the question and then we proceed as usual with Okapi. The selected target words are unordered and we retain only the nouns and verbs. Every word of the source sentence contributes equally to the selection of the best translations because the IBM1 model does not take the position of words into account, as the IBM2 model does. Hence, our method is slightly different from translating question keywords one by one. Our experiments showed that the best results are obtained when the query has as many non-stopwords as there are in the original question (5 on average for the CLEF questions).

---

[1] A French/English set of almost 2000 TREC questions is freely available on our website at http://www-rali.iro.umontreal.ca/LUB/qabilingue.en.html

We tested the cross-language passage retrieval module on the same TREC test set as for the question analysis module. We obtained an average precision of 0.570 with the original English module and an average precision of 0.467 with the cross-language module. Unlike in the question analysis module, a translation error does not compromise the location of the answer, as long as the query includes other keywords.

3.3   Translating the Answer

Even though it was not required at CLEF to translate the extracted answer back into the same language as the question, our pilot project included this step in order to make the QA process transparent to a French speaker. However, due to a lack of time, we were unable to complete the answer translation module. Nevertheless, we believe that the particular context of QA should make things easier than in typical machine translation. For one thing, a lot of answers are named entities that do not require a translation. On a random set of 200 questions from TREC, 25% have an answer that is a person or location name which is identical in both languages, or a number, a date, a company name or a title that does not require a translation. To translate other types of answers, it would be worth exploring the use of the question to help disambiguation.

3.4   Performance of the Complete System

We submitted two runs at CLEF: one with 50-byte answers and one with exact answers. The underlying QA process is the same in both, apart from additional checks performed on the 50-byte snippets to avoid submitting an answer a second time if it is already encompassed in a better ranking string. Statistics on the runs submitted at CLEF are listed in Table 1 (please refer to the CLEF 2003 Multiple Language QA track overview for details on the evaluation methodology). As expected, the 50-byte run performed better than the exact run, but the gap is wider than we anticipated: we estimated that only 2% of TREC questions could not be answered suitably by a single noun phrase but it appears that this number is higher for CLEF, given the number of inexact answers we obtained. As for the number of unsupported answers, they remain a lesser concern.

We wanted to compare the cross-language version of Quantum with the monolingual English version. We ran the monolingual version on the English CLEF questions and we obtained a MRR of 0.223 (exact answers, lenient evaluation). At CLEF, the cross-language version of our system obtained a MRR of 0.161 on the French questions. As mentioned above, the principal reasons for this 28% performance drop include the different French question analysis patterns, the focus translation and the keyword translation.

We also measured a drop of 44% after a similar experiment conducted on TREC data [3]. We believe that CLEF questions were easier to process because they included no definition questions, thus there were less focus words to translate. We have also tried to translate our TREC question set with Babelfish[2]

---

[2] http://world.altavista.com

Table 1. Statistics on the runs produced by Quantum on the French-to-English QA task at CLEF. *MRR* stands for *Mean Reciprocal Rank*. Strict evaluation considers only the *right* answers while lenient evaluation also considers *inexact* (too long or too short) answers and answers that are *unsupported* by the source document. *Inexact* and *unsupported* answers are not the total of inexact and unsupported answers in the whole run but the number of questions missed because the correct answer was inexact or unsupported

Run	Strict eval. (MRR)	Lenient eval. (MRR)	Inexact answers	Unsupported answers
50-byte	0.213	0.221	0	2
exact	0.140	0.161	11	5

and then use the original English system, but with this approach performance dropped even more (53%).

4   Conclusion

We have shown how it is possible to transform an English QA system into a cross-language system that can answer questions asked in a different language than the document collection. In theory, it is possible to translate only the system's input/output (with Babelfish, for example) and to make no modification to the English system itself. In practice, as long as machine translation will not produce perfect translations, it is more efficient to decompose the task and to plug in translation at different points in the system. For our QA system Quantum, we use an IBM1 translation model to get English keywords from the French question for passage retrieval. We then use a new set of French question analysis patterns to analyze the question, because the English patterns would hardly match a badly structured question translated automatically. The question's focus is the only part that needs to be translated. We use an IBM2 translation model for that purpose. Overall, on the CLEF questions, the performance of our cross-language system is 28% lower than the monolingual system.

We hope the cross-language QA systems that entered the CLEF campaign will give French, Dutch, German, Italian and Spanish speakers access to a greater amount of information sources. For French speakers in particular, we have measured that it is better to use a cross-language system (even one in a development stage) than to limit oneself to a monolingual French QA system on French documents and therefore to be confined to one tenth the amount of information available to English speakers.

Acknowledgements

This project was financially supported by the Bell University Laboratories, the Natural Science and Engineering Council of Canada and the National Research

Council of Canada. We would also like to thank Elliott Macklovitch and Guy Lapalme from the RALI, and Joel Martin from the NRC, for their help in conducting this research.

References

1. Clarke, C.L.A., Cormack, G.V., Laszlo, M., Lynam, T.R., Terra, E.L.: The Impact of Corpus Size on Question Answering Performance. In: Proceedings of the 25th Annual International ACM SIGIR Conference on Research Information Retrieval (SIGIR 02), Tampere, Finland (2002)
2. Plamondon, L., Lapalme, G., Kosseim, L.: The QUANTUM Question Answering System at TREC-11. In: Notebook Proceedings of the Eleventh Text Retrieval Conference (TREC-11), Gaithersburg, Maryland (2002)
3. Plamondon, L., Foster, G.: Multilinguisme et question-réponse: adaptation d'un système monolingue. In: Actes de la 10e conférence sur le traitement automatique des langues naturelles (TALN 2003). Volume 2., Batz-sur-Mer, France (2003)
4. Voorhees, E.M.: Overview of the TREC 2002 Question Answering Track. In: Notebook Proceedings of the Eleventh Text Retrieval Conference (TREC-11), Gaithersburg, Maryland (2002)
5. Graesser, A., Person, N., Huber, J. In: Mechanisms that Generate Questions. Lawrence Erlbaum Associates, Hillsdale, New Jersey (1992)
6. Robertson, S., Walker, S.: Okapi/Keenbow at TREC-8. In: Proceedings of the Eighth Text Retrieval Conference (TREC-8), Gaithersburg, Maryland (1998)
7. Cunningham, H., Maynard, D., Bontcheva, K., Tablan, V.: GATE: A Framework and Graphical Development Environment for Robust NLP Tools and Applications. In: Proceedings of the 40th Annual Meeting of the Association for Computational Linguistics (ACL 2002), Philadelphia, Pennsylvania (2002)
8. Brown, P.F., Pietra, S.A.D., Pietra, V.J.D., Mercer, R.L.: The mathematics of statistical machine translation: Parameter estimation. Computational Linguistics **19** (1993) 263–311
9. Kraaij, W., Nie, J.Y., Simard, M.: Embedding Web-based Statistical Translation Models in CLIR. Computational Linguistics **29** (2003)

A Cross–Language Question/Answering–System for German and English*

Günter Neumann and Bogdan Sacaleanu

LT–Lab, DFKI, Saarbrücken, Germany
neumann|bogdan@dfki.de
http://www.dfki.de/~neumann|bogdan

Abstract. This report describes the work done by the QA group of the Language Technology Lab at DFKI, for the 2003 edition of the Cross-Language Evaluation Forum (CLEF). We have participated in the new track "Multiple Language Question Answering (QA@CLEF)" that offers tasks to test monolingual and cross-language QA–systems. In particular we developed an open–domain bilingual QA–System for German source language queries and English target document collections. Since it was our very first participation at such kind of competition, the focus was on system implementation rather than system tuning.

1   Introduction

The basic functionality of an open–domain cross–language question/answering (QA) system is simple: given a Natural Language query in one language (say German) find answers for that query in textual documents written in another language (say English), and eventually express the found answers in the query language (The translation process of answers into the query language is currently not part of the QA@CLEF track, hence we will say nothing about this problem here.) In contrast to a standard cross–language IR system, the NL queries are usually well-formed NL–query clauses (instead of a set of keywords), and the identified answers should be textual fragments representing the answer (instead of complete documents containing the answer). Thus, for a question like "Welches Pseudonym nahm Norma Jean Baker an?" (*Which pseudonym did Norma Jean Baker use?*) the answer should be "Marilyn Monroe" rather than an English document containing this name.

At the Language Technology Lab of DVI we have begun the development of large–scale open–domain cross–language QA systems, currently with a focus on German and English. In [1] we have described a first prototype of a monolingual Web–based QA–system that processes German queries and Web pages (using Google for initial web page retrieval). On basis of this initial prototype we have

---

* The work presented in this paper has been funded by the BMBF project Quetal, FKZ 01 IW C02. Many thanks to Holger Neis and Hubert Schlarb for their implementation support.

C. Peters et al. (Eds.): CLEF 2003, LNCS 3237, pp. 559–571, 2004.

implemented BiQue a German–English bilingual textual QA–system. BiQue receives a German language query, parses and translates it into English, and searches for answers in a large English text collection maintained by the full–text search engine MG [2].

The main motivation for our participation at this year's CLEF was to foster development of an initial end–to–end cross–language QA–system enforced by external evaluation. Since we also plan to extend the system for English query and German document analysis (and to support mixed language mode), we have focused on the development of common LT-core components for bilingual query and answering processing that enable us to easily improve the system in the future. Thus, we also focused on the development of generic APIs (based on XML) and knowledge formalisms that helps us to systematically improve our system in next development cycles.

We start with an overview of the whole system, highlight some technical aspects, followed by a more detailed description of the methods we used for query translation and expansion. Finally, we present the results we have obtained for the task.

2   System Overview

The picture in Figure 1 displays the control flow between the major components of BiQue. The major control flow is basically state–of–the–art and — from a coarse–grained point of view — not novel. However, we think that we have realized a number of interesting "sub–issues" and an interesting "translation approach" (with hopefully fruitful future impacts, at least for us ;-) which is motivation enough to give some more details here.

2.1   Document Retrieval

We are using the MG system — a public–domain full–text retrieval engine, cf. [2] — for the selection of relevant paragraphs. MG is an easy useable software package that can handle text corpora of several Gigabytes very efficiently. In order to make use of the MG system in the context of the QA@CLEF track, we actually had to solve two problems:

 – How can we keep track of the document identifier?
 – How can we use MG for the selection of relevant short text passages?

The first issue is important because for each answer candidate one has to indicate the document from which the answer was extracted. Secondly, only a small fragment of the documents need to be processed more deeply in order to identify possible answer candidates. In order to fulfill both requirements when using MG, we performed a simple preprocessing of the text corpus: we attached to the front of each paragraph (identified by means of the SGML tag $\langle P \rangle$) of a document a status line which represents the document identifier and the number

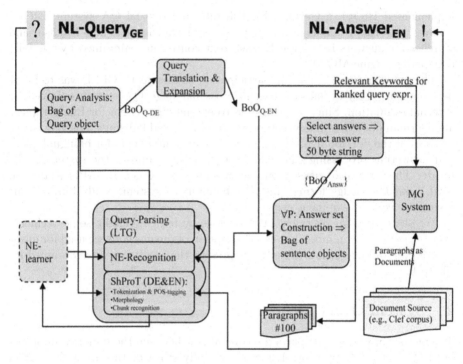

Fig. 1. A blueprint of BiQue's architecture

of the paragraph in the document. Each such extended paragraph is then treated as a single document by MG. Thus, given a set of keywords as input to MG it will return a set of paragraphs where each paragraph encodes its location within the original text document[1]. Here is example of a paragraph returned by MG for the query "leader, india":

```
######## LA110594-0041 10 ######## .
```
The official Indian position has changed a few times but basically has been that all the stones, or the most remarkable among them, should stay in India. India's leaders, however, haven't had the cash to purchase them.

MG supports document retrieval by either using a boolean query or a ranked query. We decided to use the ranked query because MG should only return paragraphs (see above), and hence a boolean query would be too restrictive already in an early processing phase. In case of ranked queries, MG computes for each paragraph a weight that we also make us of in later processing steps. Currently, we use the first 100 paragraphs returned by MG, basically because of performance reasons.

---

[1] By way: since the status line is part of a paragraph it can also be specified as part of the query. Hence, we also can use the status line information for reconstructing the whole document as well as for performing corpus navigation using MG.

2.2   Shallow Syntactic Processing

NL queries and documents are linguistically analyzed using ShProT, a shallow processing tool that consists of several integrated components: SPPC for tokenization and analysis of compound words (cf. [3]), TnT for part–of–speech tagging (cf. [4]), Mmorph for morphological analysis (cf. [5]) and Chunkie for phrase recognition (cf. [6]). TnT and Chunkie are statistical based components which derive the linguistic entities, rules and generalizations from annotated corpora. The language models are based on the Penn treebank (for English) and the Negra treebank (for German). ShProT receives as input an ascii text and returns a stream of sentences each consisting of a sequence of tagged phrases and tagged word forms. The tagged phrases actually define the type of the phrase (either NP or PP) and consists of a sequence of tagged word forms. A tagged word form contains the POS, and the lemma as determined by Mmorph. For unknown words (which also includes proper names) TnT tries to guess the POS. In case of a proper name, these are tagged with generic tags like NNP (for singular proper noun). Figure 2 shows the XML–representation of the shallow analysis of an example sentence.

2.3   Named Entity Recognition

Our Named Entity Recognition (NER) method is based on the unsupervised learning approach of [7]. A decision list of NER–rules (also represented in XML) is applied on the XML–output of ShProT and performs an additional annotation of relevant NPs with corresponding NE–type information (currently, we consider the NE–types PERSON, ORGANIZATION, LOCATION, TIME, and DATE). Currently, only NPs that contain at least one word recognized by ShProT as a proper noun or time/date expression will be considered as candidates for NE–typing[2]. All these NE candidate phrases are then further processed by the decision list matcher. Each element of the decision list is a simple IF–THEN rule. If a NP–candidate fulfills some spelling or contextual conditions (these are based on generic syntactic criteria of adjacent phrases like "capital of XXX") then it receives the NE–type as indicated by the rule (e.g., in the example case XXX is typed as LOCATION).

Our current NER–learner is still under development. Usually the decision list is automatically learned. However, for the QA@CLEF track we have not been able to perform a complete training phase because preprocessing of the QA–corpus turned out to be too expensive (it will be one future research issue to explore more efficient learning methods). For that reason a number of

---

[2] Note that this means that we perform NER after shallow parsing. Hence the accuracy of the NER depends on the accuracy of shallow parsing. In some sense the approach can also be viewed as a top–down classification approach, since NER–module actually performs a sub–typing of those generic NE types already recognized by the shallow processor.

```
<SENTENCE id="S4">
   <CHUNK id="H26" cat="NP">
   <W id="W99" PoS="DT" tclass="25" mclass="24" stems="[a]">
    <WORDFORM string="An" />
    <READINGS>
     <R id="R0" subtype="art_indef" category="Det" />
    </READINGS> </W>
   <W id="W100" PoS="NNP" tclass="22" mclass="-1" stems="[]">
    <WORDFORM string="FBI" /> <READINGS /> </W>
   <W id="W101" PoS="NN" tclass="24" mclass="29" stems="[informant]">
    <WORDFORM string="informant" />
    <READINGS>
     <R id="R0" subtype="char" category="Abbr" />
    </READINGS> </W>
   </CHUNK>
   <W id="W102" PoS="VBN" tclass="24" mclass="205" stems="[claim]">
    <WORDFORM string="claimed" />
    <READINGS>
     <R id="R0" subtype="main" tense="past" verbclass="intrans"
     category="Verb" vform="psp" />
    </READINGS> </W>
   <W id="W103" PoS="IN" tclass="24" mclass="-1" stems="[that]">
    <WORDFORM string="that" /> <READINGS /> </W>
   <W id="W104" PoS="NNS" tclass="25" mclass="-1" stems="[]">
    <WORDFORM string="Wilkins" /> <READINGS /> </W>
   <W id="W105" PoS="VBD" tclass="24" mclass="-1" stems="[be]">
    <WORDFORM string="was" /> <READINGS /> </W>
   <CHUNK id="H27" cat="NP">
    <W id="W106" PoS="DT" tclass="24" mclass="399" stems="[the]">
    <WORDFORM string="the" />
    <READINGS>
     <R id="R0" wh="no" subtype="gen" number="plural" category="Det" />
    </READINGS> </W>
    <W id="W107" PoS="NN" tclass="24" mclass="1" stems="[trig, German]">
    <WORDFORM string="triggerman" />
    <READINGS>
     <R id="R0" gender="neutrum" number="singular" category="Noun" />
    </READINGS> </W>
   </CHUNK>
   <W id="W108" PoS="$." tclass="1" mclass="-1" stems="[$PUNCTUATION]">
    <WORDFORM string="." /> <READINGS /> </W>
   </SENTENCE>
```

Fig. 2. The XML–representation of the shallow syntactic analysis for the sentence *An FBI informant claimed that Wilkins was the triggerman*

rules of the decision list were specified manually. In order to compensate possible (and actual) recall problems we combined the decision list with external Gazetters.

2.4   Internal Query and Document Representation

Internally, queries and documents are uniformly represented as weighted sets of structured (possibly linked) objects in order to facilitate a robust and efficient comparison between queries and answer candidates. More formally, we call the set $B := \{O_1, \ldots, O_n; \alpha\}$ a *Bag-of-Objects* or short BoO consisting of n objects O_i and weight α. Each object O_i is a tuple of the form $\langle WF, Stem, PoS, NE, \alpha_i \rangle$, i.e., a structured object consisting of a word form, a lemma, part–of–speech, named entity and weight α_i (note that for all elements but WF and α_i the actual value can be empty).

The weight of a BoO is determined during the matching phase of the query with a candidate answer sentence. The actual approach we are exploiting for comparing and merging two different BoOs is a variant of the *word overlap* method described in [8]. A word overlap (which is also a BoO in our case) is the subset of objects a query and an answer candidate have in common, i.e., the word overlap of two sentences s_1 and s_2 is $Ov_{s_1, s_2} := B_{s_1} \cap B_{s_2}$, where B_i is the BoO of s_i. The weight β of a word overlap Ov is determined as the sum over the weights α_i of the overlapping words. The weight of an individual object is currently specified a priori and is based on the word's Part–of–Speech. The weights are used as a measure for the utility of an answer. After Ov_{s_1, s_2} has been computed, the B_i obtain β as their weight, i.e., BoO with same word overlap have equal weight (however, this weight will later be updated using the expected answer type, see below).

We also define the *overlap set Os_q* of a query q as the set of all BoOs of all candidate answer sentences which have the same word overlap with q, i.e., $Os_q := \{B_{s_1}, \ldots, B_{s_n}\}$, with: $Ov_{q, s_i} = Ov_{q, s_j}$ for $i \neq j$. This means that the overlap sets define equivalence classes over the set of possible answer candidates wrt. the set of objects each answer has in common with the query, i.e., query and sentences with same word overlap (and hence, with equal weight, but see 2.6).

2.5   Query Processing

The main tasks of the query processor are the

1. parsing of a German (or English) NL query, and the
2. translation and expansion of the German query object to an English one.

A query object is a tuple $\langle EAT, BoO, Keys, L \rangle$ consisting of the expected answer type EAT, the BoO representation of the question, the set of relevant keywords used as query for the full–text retrieval engine MG (see 2.1), and the language identifier. We will now describe very briefly the different steps, and will only say a bit more on parsing in the subsection that follows.

The main goal of parsing a NL query in the context of open–domain QA is the identification of the question focus and the expected type (or concept) of the potential answer phrase (Expected Answer Type (EAT), cf. [9]). The question focus is a phrase or word in the question that can help to disambiguate it and — together with the question stem (e.g., *who, how much, where*) — can help to deduce the EAT.

After the parser has determined the EAT for the current question, a BoO representation is constructed on the basis of all content words of the question. (In principle, it is also possible to link the elements of the BoO based on the derivation tree computed during parsing (which corresponds roughly to a dependency tree, see next paragraph). However, we have not been able to finish implementation of this further step in due time which would have helped us to define more clever strategies for the identification of exact answers, see below 2.6.) So we currently have to live with a quite flat internal representation of the query. The set of relevant keywords is determined very simply from the BoO by collecting all stems of the content words (or word forms, if no such stem could have been computed).

Finally, query translation and expansion takes place in order to perform retrieval of English paragraphs and to allow for computation of overlap sets on basis of word overlap between the query and answer candidates. A description of details of this third step during the analysis of a question is postponed until section 3. The only thing worth mentioning here is that the German query BoO is basically translated to an English one (by keeping the EAT determined for the German query). Translation is basically realized by means of "merging" results from EuroWordNet with the results of externally available translation services, which we are using as a means for performing word sense disambiguation. Query expansion is performed simultaneously with query translation.

Query Parsing. Before going on in describing how answer processing is performed on basis of the translated query object, we describe some more details of our query parsing methods.

In our current system, we have specified manually a German and a English query grammar in form of a *Lexicalized Tree Grammar* (LTG). A query LTG consists of a set of syntax/semantics oriented tree patterns which express mutual constraints for the identification of a question focus and an EAT. Here is an example of such an elementary tree:

```
<tree id="6a" label="F-Wo" eat="LOCATION" freq="" prob="">
    <node label="PWAV">
        <node label="wo" type="TERM" anchor="YES"/>
    </node>
    <node label="VVFIN">
        <node label="schliessen" type="TERM" anchor="YES"/>
    </node>
    <node label="NE" nclass="PERSON" type="SUBST"/>
    <node label="NP" type="SUBST"/>
    <node label="PTKVZ">
        <node label="ab" type="TERM"/>
    </node>
</tree>
```

which would be applicable for a question like *Wo schloss Hillary Clinton das College ab?* (*Where did Hillary Clinton graduate college?*). A query grammar is applied on top of the shallow chunk analysis computed by first applying ShProT on the NL question. Note that nodes of type TERM are lexical anchors and nodes of type SUBST have to be expanded by substituting the node with a consistent (complete) phrase. Parsing of a query LTG is performed along the line of the method described in [10].

The major motivation why we have chosen a LTG approach is our future goal to automatically extract a linguistically expressive but specific *query sub-grammar* form a large–scale general source grammar following the approach described in [10], where we present a linguistically rich model of data–oriented parsing, called *HPSG–DOP*. The major idea behind HPSG–DOP is to automatically extract a *Stochastic* LTG from a Head-driven Phrase-Structure Grammar (HPSG) and a given corpus which can be processed much faster and robust than the original source grammar and which eases integration of domain knowledge more directly with syntactic constraints.

The current grammars (together with the possible supported EAT) have been defined on the basis of a manual translation of the QA–Trec 8 and 9 question corpus. Actually, it turned out that the current grammars have been defined a bit too Trec–8/9 specific concerning supported subcategorization. Hence, future work will focus on improving generalization without loosing the benefits of lexicalized tree structures. In some sense, the elementary trees of a LTG define clause–level patterns using lexical information about the question type and focus to constraint their applicability. Linguistically, an elementary tree of a LTG also describes a head–modifier relationship between the lexical anchors and the modifiers (basically the substitution nodes). Hence a derivation of a query analysis can also be used to uncover the dependency structure. Following a dependency reconstruction approach like the one described in [9], it would then be possible to construct a quasi logical form from the dependency relation in order to support theorem proving for answer validation.

2.6   Answer Processing

Paragraph Selection. The keywords of the translated query object are used to build a query expression for the MG system. Currently, we use the whole set of keywords (including the expanded terms) to form one MG–query. The ranked query mode of MG is then used to retrieve the N best paragraphs (see also 2.1). In the ranked query mode, MG actually ranks all documents according to some similarity measure applied on each document which specifies how close the document matches with the query. Thus seen, MG returns the N most similar documents with respect to the query.

Candidate Answer Selection. All retrieved paragraphs are analysed by Sh-ProT (see 2.2) which maps a paragraph into a sequence of sentence objects. A sentence object consists of the shallow syntactic XML–structure, the sentence BoO (constructed from it) and additional bookkeeping information (e.g., pointer to document identifier).

All sentence objects of every paragraph are collected into one container from which the overlap sets are constructed along the line described in 2.4. This means that a word overlap Ov_{q,s_i} is computed by merging the BoO of the query q with the BoO of every sentence object s_i, which is then used to construct and rank the overlap sets. In a next step, all sentence objects from the top five equivalence classes are collected into one list of answer candidate sentences. For each such sentence object it is then checked, whether it contains one element which is type–compatible with the expected answer type EAT of the query object. If so, the weight of the sentence is increased. Note that this means that a sentence whose corresponding word overlap weight is smaller than that of another sentence (which means that it is less similar wrt. to the query) might now receive a higher rank.

In a final step, each sentence is searched for an NP phrase which can serve as the exact answer of the question. The method that we have exploited so far, actually constructs a ranked list of all NPs (extracted from every sentences) that do not contain any element from the sentence's word overlap. Ranking is performed by taking into account the type of the NP (e.g., EAT–compatible, containing other NEs), and the number and distance of elements from the sentence's word overlap wrt. the NP (a similar method is described in [11]). By doing so we determine exact answer and 50bytes answer strings. Note that the underlying assumption made by our current method is that the strings of NPs serve as exact answers. Generally, this view is surely too restricted (and might only apply for certain kind of questions), and hence will be improved in the future.

3   Query Translation and Expansion

In this section we are going to describe in more detail how question translation and expansion is performed.

3.1   Background

Traditional approaches for cross–language information management systems can be classified as follows:

1. Systems that translate the queries into the target language, or
2. the document collection into the source language, or both,
3. queries and documents into an intermediate representation (inter–lingua).

Two types of translation services are well known within this context which are based on

- lexical resources (e.g., dictionaries, aligned word nets), or
- machine translation (e.g., example–based translation).

Each translation method has to deal with the following issues: *word sense disambiguation* (WSD) and *coverage*. WSD accounts for translating the appropriate meaning of a word, as suggested by its context, while coverage guarantees that source language words have a chance to be translated, to the extent to which it is intended (e.g., not all named entities should be translated). In retrieving the documents related to a formulated query, it is often useful to take into consideration words related to the query words. This *query expansion* method can be achieved either through syntactic or semantic variations. A query of the form "presidential election" could be extended with "election of the president", "the president was elected", "presidential vote", "presidency vote", etc. An issue in query expansion is the word sense disambiguation, too. As query words may be ambiguous, only the intended meanings of them should be targets of the expansion task.

3.2   Method

The system BiQue as used in this competition translates the German language question to the English language of the document collection by means of machine translation techniques. The system accounts for the above-mentioned coverage issue by using three different translation services: FreeTranslation, Altavista and Logos. The results of translating the original German question are used in generation of bag-of-object (BoO) collections of English open-class words, which are further on target of the query expansion module. Expansion is being achieved only through semantic variations using WordNet-like resources, whereby a pseudo word-sense-disambiguation task using the German original question and its English translations is being applied. Following we will describe the functioning of the question translation and expansion module by means of the example question:

Wo wurde das Militärflugzeug Strike Eagles 1990 eingesetzt?

Question Translation. Three different translation services have been considered for this purpose:

- FreeTranslation (via http://www.freetranslation.com/) yields:
  "Where did the military airplane become would strike used Eagles 1990?"
- Altavista (via http://babel.altavista.com/) yields:
  "Where was the military aircraft Strike Eagle used 1990?"
- Logos (off–line) yields:
  "Where was the soldier airplane Strike Eagles installed in 1990?"

Initial experiments using only one translation service unveiled the limitation imposed by the coverage problem: inadequate or no translations (e.g., some name of countries that were different in German and English). Extending the translation module with two further services, the results improved and pointed out the advantage of indirectly using it for question expansion as well, as different translations can generate synonym words. Moreover, the original German question and its English translations were used for question expansion too, as building blocks for our pseudo-WSD module.

Given the above-listed translations, a BoO collection of open-class normalized words has been created, with the following content (for convenience we abbreviate the object elements by means of their lexemes):

{SOLDIER, AIRPLANE, STRIKE, EAGLE, INSTALL, 1990, MILITARY, BE-
COME, STRIKE, USE, AIRCRAFT, EAGLE}.

This BoO is obtained as follows: from each English version of the question a
corresponding BoO is constructed by applying ShProT and the English question
grammar. The resulting different BoO's are then merged into one BoO which
represents the translated query object (re–using the expected answer type EAT
as computed for the German question analysis).

Question Expansion. For the expansion task we have used the German and
English wordnets aligned within the EuroWordNet lexical resource. Our goal
was to extend the English BoO collection with synonyms for the words that are
present in the wordnet.

Considering the ambiguity of words, a WSD module was required as part
of the expansion task. For this purpose we have used both the original question and its translations, leveraging the reduction in ambiguity gained through
translation. Our devised *pseudo-WSD algorithm* works as following:

1. look up every word from the translated BoO collection (see example above)
   in the lexical resource;
2. if the word is not ambiguous (which is, for example, the case for AIRPLANE,
   AIRCRAFT) then extend the BoO collection with its synonyms, e.g.,
   AIRPLANE ⟹ ⟨AEROPLANE, PLANE⟩
   AIRCRAFT ⟹ ⟨ ⟩ (i.e., in case of AIRCRAFT there are no synonyms);
3. if the word is ambiguous (e.g., USE) then
   (a) for every possible reading of it, get its aligned German correspondent
       reading (if it exists) and look up that reading in the German original
       question (i.e., in the BoO representation of the original German ques-
       tion "Wo wurde das Militärflugzeug Strike Eagles 1990 **eingesetzt?**"),
       e.g.,
       Reading-697925:
       EN: ⟨HANDLE, USE, WIELD⟩, DE: ⟨HANDHABEN, HANTIEREN⟩
       Reading-1453934:
       EN: ⟨BEHAVE TOWARD, USE⟩, DE: not aligned
       Reading-661760:
       EN: ⟨BE A USER OF, USE, USE REGULARLY⟩, DE: not aligned
       Reading-658041:
       EN: ⟨EXPEND, USE⟩, DE: ⟨AUFWENDEN⟩
       Reading-658243:
       EN: ⟨APPLY, EMPLOY, MAKE USE OF, PUT TO USE, USE, UTILISE,
       UTILIZE⟩
       DE: ⟨ANBRINGEN, ANWENDEN, BEDIENEN, BENUTZEN, **einsetzen**, . . . ⟩
   (b) if an aligned reading is found (e.g., Reading-658243) retain it and add
       the English synonyms of it to the BoO collection, i.e., expand it with:
       ⟨APPLY, EMPLOY, MAKE USE OF, PUT TO USE, USE, UTILISE, UTILIZE⟩.

Following the question expansion task, the BoO collection has been enriched
with new words that are synonyms of the un–ambiguous English words and by

synonyms of those ambiguous words, whose meaning(s) have been found in the original German question. Thus our expanded example looks as follows:

{SOLDIER, AIRPLANE, STRIKE, EAGLE, INSTALL, 1990, MILITARY, BE-COME, STRIKE, USE, AIRCRAFT, EAGLE, AEROPLANE, PLANE, APPLY, EMPLOY, MAKE USE OF, PUT TO USE, USE, UTILISE, UTILIZE}.

4   Results and Conclusion

We have participated for the first time in a QA track, and hence had to build BiQue from scratch, so the focus was on system implementation, rather than on system tuning (and actually we had no time to test different settings of critical system parameters, like the weighting values). We submitted only one run for the 50byte run, and obtained as result for the strict statistics 14.5% correct answers, and 15% for the lenient statistics. We had also planned to submit a second run by first preprocessing the whole corpus with ShProT, but it turned out that this was too time consuming. The major motivation was, that we wanted to perform a stemming of the complete corpus by using ShProT instead of the built in stemmer of MG which turned out to cause too much trouble in some cases. Anyway, this is surely a result that should and can be improved. (For example we were not able to process questions containing quoted terms, because we simply had not foreseen such questions. However, 20% of the test set contained such kind of questions.) Besides evaluation of the performance of the system wrt. different parametrization, important next steps for system improvement are, among others, the unsupervised online learning of more fine–grained NE rules, Machine Learning of query grammars, methods for determining the utility of answer candidates, development of ontology based answer validation methods, and more controlled query expansion by using fine–grained ontologies (following [12]).

References

1. Neumann, G., Xu, F.: Mining Answers in German Web Pages. In: Proceedings of The International Conference on Web Intelligence (WI 2003), Halifax, Canada (2003)
2. Witten, I.H., Moffat, A., Bell, T.C.: Managing Gigabytes: Compressing and Indexing Documents and Images. Morgan Kaufmann Publishers, San Francisco, CA (1999)
3. Neumann, G., Piskorski, J.: Shallow text processing core engine. Computational Intelligence 18 (2002) 451–476
4. Brants, T.: Tnt – a statistical part-of-speech tagger. In: Proceedings of the 6th Applied NLP Conference, ANLP-2000, Seattle, WA. (2000)
5. D., P., G., R.: Mmorph - the multext morphology program. Technical report, ISSCO, University of Geneva (1994)
6. Skut, W., Brants, T.: A maximum entropy partial parser for unrestricted text. In: 6th Workshop on Very Large Corpora, Montreal, Canada (1998)

7. Collins, M., Singer, Y.: Unsupervised models for named entity classification. In: In Proceedings of the Joint SIGDAT Conference on Empirical Methods in Natural Language Processing and Very Large Corpora., Association for Computational Linguistics (1999)

8. Light, M., Mann, G.S., Rilo, E., Breck, E.: Analysis for elucidating current question answering technology. Natural Language Engineering **7** (2001)

9. Harabagiu, S., Moldovan, D., Paşca, M., Mihalcea, R., Surdeanu, M., Bunescu, R., Gîrju, R., Rus, V., Morărescu, P.: FALCON: Boosting knowledge for answer engines. In: Proceedings of the Ninth Text REtrieval Conference (TREC-9). (2000)

10. Neumann, G.: Data-driven approaches to head-driven phrase structure grammar. In Bod, R., Scha, R., Sima'an, K., eds.: DATA-ORIENTED PARSING. CSLI Publications, University of Chicago Press (2003)

11. Radev, D., Fan, W., Qi, H., Wu, H., Grewal, A.: Probabilistic question answering on the Web. In: Proceedings of the Eleventh International World Wide Web Conference (WWW2002). (2002)

12. Hovy, E., Gerber, L., Hermjakob, U., Junk, M., Lin, C.Y.: Question answering in Webclopedia. In: Proceedings of the Ninth Text REtrieval Conference (TREC-9). (2000)

Cross-Language French-English Question Answering Using the DLT System at CLEF 2003

Richard F. E. Sutcliffe, Igal Gabbay, and Aoife O'Gorman

Documents and Linguistic Technology Group,
Department of Computer Science and Information Systems,
University of Limerick, Limerick, Ireland
{Richard.Sutcliffe, Igal.Gabbay, Aoife.OGorman}@ul.ie
www.csis.ul.ie/staff/richard.sutcliffe

Abstract. We describe the system built by the Documents and Linguistic Technology (DLT) Group at University of Limerick for participation in the French-English Question Answering Task of the Cross Language Evaluation Forum (CLEF). The starting point was our monolingual 2002 TREC system to which was added query classification working in French, machine translation of the query into English, and search of the document collection using a commercial engine. We then present the results of the runs carried out with this system before discussing our findings and proposed next steps.

1 Introduction

This article outlines the participation of the Documents and Linguistic Technology (DLT) Group in the Cross Language French-English Question Answering Task of the Cross Language Evaluation Forum (CLEF). Our aim was to make an initial study of cross language question answering (QA) by adapting the system we built for monolingual English QA for the Text REtrieval Conference (TREC) in 2002 [1]. Firstly, therefore, we outline the architecture of the TREC system which formed the basis of the work reported on here. Secondly, the many changes made to allow cross-language QA are described. Thirdly, the runs performed are presented together with the results we obtained. Finally, conclusions are drawn based on our findings.

2 Architecture of the TREC 2002 DLT System

2.1 Outline

In this section we summarise the structure of the DLT system used at TREC which formed the starting point for CLEF. Changes subsequently made are documented in the next section. Overall flow of control was as follows. Firstly, we identified the query type and hence decided upon the related named entities for which we would be searching. Secondly, we parsed the 50 TOPDOCS text files, dividing them into textual units using the markup. These files were supplied by the TREC organisers (at

C. Peters et al. (Eds.): CLEF 2003, LNCS 3237, pp. 572–580, 2004.
© Springer-Verlag Berlin Heidelberg 2004

the National Institute of Standards and Technology) and were generated by their PRISE retrieval system in response to the input query. Thirdly, we searched for instances of the named entities in the textual units and marked any which were found. Fourthly, we identified the winning instance using one of two possible strategies: highest-scoring or most-frequent. These stages are now dealt with in more detail.

2.2 Query Type Identification

We studied questions of each type and developed simple keyword-based heuristics to recognise them. This crude approach was surprisingly effective. In TREC 2002 425 of the 500 queries were correctly classified.

2.3 Text File Parsing

Each document within the TOPDOCS file was divided into a series of segments corresponding to a short passage of text. First, text within a HEADLINE tag was extracted. Second, text within a TEXT tag was extracted and divided up into separate Ps. Finally a P was divided wherever three contiguous blanks were found. This last stage was to approximate sentence recognition. The resulting textual units were used in subsequent processing.

2.4 Named Entity Recognition

The type of question identified in the first step determined the type of named entity or entities to be searched for, as is standard practice in QA systems. Each segment identified as above was therefore inspected and all instances of appropriate named entities were tagged.

2.5 Answer Entity Selection

Two methods were used: highest_scoring and most_frequent. In the first, we returned the named entity occurring in a textual unit which matched the keywords in the query best, chosen from any of the 50 TOPDOCS documents. In the second, we returned the named entity which most frequently occurred in the vicinity of query keywords, observed across all occurrences of the entity in the 50 TOPDOCS documents. Both strategies were unsophisticated but sometimes one or other of them can perform well on a particular query type.

In the next section we explain how the above architecture was adapted for CLEF.

3 Architecture of the CLEF 2003 DLT System

3.1 Outline

The CLEF system had many similarities with the TREC one but also differed in a number of important respects. Flow of control was as follows. Firstly, the type of the French input query was identified along with the appropriate named entities. Secondly, the query was translated and processed in order to produce a search expression for retrieval. Thirdly, the search expression was submitted to a text retrieval engine yielding a set of documents. Fourthly, appropriate named entities were recognised in these. Fifthly, the winning named entity was identified.

3.2 Query Type Identification

As the input query was in French, our existing type identifier had to be re-written. This was undertaken by the third author as part of a separate project in which a French monolingual version of our TREC system was developed [2]. The first step was removal of diacritical marks from the query, replacing each by the same letter minus the diacritic (e.g. 'á' becomes 'a' etc.). After this the query was converted to lower-case. Finally, simple keyword combinations were used to identify the query type. 19 query types were used and some of these can be seen in Table 1 together with an example of each.

3.3 Query Translation and Re-formulation

The next stage was translation of the French query into English. This was accomplished by submitting it to the Google translation service [3] with original capitalisation and diacritics. The result was then tokenised and stopwords were removed from any material not in double quotes.

3.4 Text Retrieval

Unlike in TREC, retrieval at CLEF was accomplished by indexing the documents ourselves. The document collection comprised 113,005 LA Times articles from 1994,

Table 1. Some of the Question Types used in the DLT system. The second column shows a sample question for each type. The translations resulting from submission to Google are listed in the third column

Question Type	Example Question	Google Translation
What_city	172 Quelle est la capitale de la Tchétchénie?	Which is the capital of Tchétchénie?
what_state	57 Quel est l'état indien qui a le plus grand nombre d'habitants?	Which is the Indian state which has the greatest number of inhabitants?
what_country	169 Dans quel pays le Mont Kilimanjaro se trouve-t-il?	In which country the Kilimanjaro Mount is it?
where	45 Où se trouve l'écosystème artificiel appelé "Biosphère 2"?	Where is the artificial ecosystem called "Biosphere 2"?
how_many3	76 Combien de salles de classe a-t-on construites en 1976 dans le district scolaire de Wilsona?	How many classrooms did one build in 1976 in the school district of Wilsona?
distance	164 Quelle est la longueur de la côte de la baie de Santa Monica?	Which is the length of the coast of bay of Santa Monica?
who	148 Qui est l'ambassadeur des États-Unis en Suisse?	Who is the ambassador of the United States in Switzerland?
when	178 Quand Shapour Bakhtiar est-il mort?	When Shapour Bakhtiar did he die?
unknown	160 Donner le nom d'un philosophe allemand.	To give the name of a German philosopher.

425MB in all. The search engine used was DTSearch [4]. Documents were indexed using the file segmentation option working with '<DOC>' tags. The engine supports a number of search operators including distance between words (e.g. Word1 w/1 Word2 meaning Word1 must occur within 1 word of Word2) and boolean operators AND and OR. The next step therefore was to produce a search query on the basis of the terms identified in the previous step as follows:

- A 'w/1' connector was inserted between two capitalised words. It specifies that the second word must occur within one word from the first (in either direction). This feature was helpful because French to English translation often reverses the order of proper nouns.
- Double quotes were removed and the string of text within the double quotes was retained, but only if the first word after the double quote was untranslated. This was verified by checking the membership of the word in the original query list in French. Untranslated quotations were searched for exactly.
- An AND connector was inserted between all other terms.
- If the query included the atom 'did', it was removed. If the rest of the query contained a verb which was among the list of verbs common to TREC questions, the verb was replaced with its past tense form. For example, 'die' in questions like 'How did X die?' was replaced with 'died'.

Table 2. Results by query type for correctly classified questions. The columns C and NC show the numbers of queries of a particular type which were classified correctly and not correctly. Those classified correctly are then broken down into Right, ineXact, Unsupported and Wrong for each of the two runs Run 1 and Run 2

Query Type	Classif.		Correct Classification							
			Run 1				Run 2			
	C	NC	R	X	U	W	R	X	U	W
what_city	9	0	5	0	0	4	5	0	0	4
what_state	0	1	0	0	0	0	0	0	0	0
what_country	2	0	1	0	0	1	1	0	0	1
what_continent	0	0	0	0	0	0	0	0	0	0
where	21	0	2	0	1	18	2	1	0	18
how_many3	17	1	0	0	0	17	0	0	0	17
distance	2	0	2	0	0	0	2	0	0	0
speed	0	0	0	0	0	0	0	0	0	0
temp	0	0	0	0	0	0	0	0	0	0
population	0	0	0	0	0	0	0	0	0	0
who	34	7	7	0	0	27	7	0	0	27
when	16	0	1	1	0	14	1	1	1	13
colour	0	0	0	0	0	0	0	0	0	0
what_river	0	0	0	0	0	0	0	0	0	0
what_water_mass	0	0	0	0	0	0	0	0	0	0
what_mountain	0	0	0	0	0	0	0	0	0	0
what_mountain_range	0	0	0	0	0	0	0	0	0	0
what_planet	0	0	0	0	0	0	0	0	0	0
unknown	58	32	4	0	0	55	3	0	0	55
Totals	159	41	22	1	1	136	21	2	1	135

The query was then submitted to the engine and the first n DOCs returned were used in subsequent processing. In most cases n was 10 while in one experiment it was 20. Before the named entity recognition stage, each DOC was subdivided into separate P elements where present. These were then further subdivided wherever three contiguous blanks were found – a process which approximates to sentence recognition.

3.5 Named Entity Recognition

The set of English named entities used and the methods for recognising them in CLEF were very similar to TREC [1]. Only two were added, general_name and planet. Type general_name recognises any sequence of up to five capitalised words interspersed by optional prepositions. It was inspired by Clarke et al. [5] and is used in cases where the question type can not be determined. Planet uses a simple list of the eight planets.

3.6 Answer Entity Selection

As previously, two forms of answer selection were used, highest-scoring and most-frequent. In the highest-scoring method the named-entity instance is selected which occurs in the vicinity of the maximum number of keywords taken from the translated query, across all document passages. In the most-frequent strategy the named-entity occurring most frequently overall across all passages is chosen.

Table 3. Results by query type for incorrectly classified questions. Once again, results are broken down into Right, ineXact, Unsupported and Wrong for each of the two runs Run 1 and Run 2

Query Type	Incorrect Classification							
	Run 1				Run 1			
	R	X	U	W	R	X	U	W
what_city	0	0	0	0	0	0	0	0
what_state	0	0	0	1	0	0	0	1
what_country	0	0	0	0	0	0	0	0
what_continent	0	0	0	0	0	0	0	0
where	0	0	0	0	0	0	0	0
how_many3	0	0	0	1	0	0	0	1
distance	0	0	0	0	0	0	0	0
speed	0	0	0	0	0	0	0	0
temp	0	0	0	0	0	0	0	0
population	0	0	0	0	0	0	0	0
who	0	0	0	7	0	0	0	7
when	0	0	0	0	0	0	0	0
colour	0	0	0	0	0	0	0	0
what_river	0	0	0	0	0	0	0	0
what_water_mass	0	0	0	0	0	0	0	0
what_mountain	0	0	0	0	0	0	0	0
what_mountain_range	0	0	0	0	0	0	0	0
what_planet	0	0	0	0	0	0	0	0
unknown	1	0	0	31	1	0	0	31
Totals	1	0	0	40	1	0	0	40

4 Runs and Results

4.1 Two Experiments

We submitted two runs. These only differed in respect of the answer selection strategy. The first run used the highest-scoring strategy working with the best 10 documents returned by the retrieval system. The second run adopted the most-frequent approach, also using the best 10 documents. The query classification module was the same for both runs.

4.2 Results

Results are summarised by query type in Tables 2 and 3. In respect of query classification it shows for each query type the number of queries assigned to that type which were correctly categorised along with the number incorrectly categorised. The overall rate of success was 79.5% which is broadly comparable to the 85% achieved in TREC. However, 90 queries were classified as unknown, i.e. nearly half of the set of 200. 58 of these were correctly classified. This shows the need to add further query types to the system in order to reduce unknown queries to a minimum. In addition various phrases which were frequently used in queries were not anticipated. Examples include 'à quelle époque' and 'à quel moment', both of which were classified wrongly as unknown rather than when.

The performance of question answering in Run 1 can be summarised as follows. Out of the 159 queries classified correctly, 21 were answered correctly. Out of the remaining 41 queries classified incorrectly a further 2 were answered correctly. Overall performance was thus 23 / 200 i.e. 11.5%. Results for Run 2 were very similar. 21 of the 159 queries were answered correctly along with one of the 41 queries giving a total of 22 / 200 i.e. 11%. In both runs 117 questions were answered NIL. We discuss these results below.

4.3 Platform

We used a Dell PC running Windows 2000 and having 256 Mb RAM. The whole system was written in Quintus Prolog Release 3.4.

5 Conclusions

5.1 Discussion of Results

Overall performance of our system was modest at 11.5% in Run 1 but this was not worse than that in TREC 2002 where the score was 10% in Run 1. The best performance was on queries of type what_city in which the system scored 5 / 9 i.e. 56%. Our system was simple, re-used as many components as possible and was constructed in a short timeframe. Our limited aim was to identify the key issues in cross-language QA and in this we were successful. We now consider the components of the system in turn before discussing our findings regarding the project in general.

Query categorisation was not a success with 90 queries classified as unknown. Performance on the remainder was 79.5%. To improve this, further examples need to be examined and appropriate keywords and phrases added. It is likely that our simple approach can give a better result even with such simple changes and without the need for complex analysis. Turning to query formulation and document retrieval, this was the first time we had used our own retrieval engine – for TREC we used the TOPDOCS and O'Gorman [2] searched the web with Google. The query formulation using Boolean operators and exact searches for untranslated quotations achieved much higher precision than was possible with the TOPDOCS where the PRISE engine no doubt uses a vector space type algorithm. On the other hand such an approach can lead to no documents being returned in the first instance, whereupon a query relaxation technique must be adopted in order to re-submit a slightly more general query. Unfortunately we had no such strategy and this was the main reason why so many NIL results were returned (117 / 200 queries, i.e. 58.5% overall).

For named entity recognition essentially the same module was used as for TREC. The main addition here was the entity general_name. In just two cases its use for processing queries of unknown type resulted in correct answers. For Query 106 'Of which political party Rudolf Scharping is member?' Run 1 returned the correct answer 'Social Democratic'. Run 2 returned the answer 'Kohl'. Run 2 returned the correct answer to Query 160 'To give the name of a German philosopher': 'Habermas'. Run 1 returned the answer 'Western'. Finally, in at least one case where the answer was wrong it was not nonsensical – Query 8 'Which is the largest exporting country of pétrole gross?' (system's answer: 'Kuwait'). The last component of the system is answer selection. The two strategies used (highest-scoring and most frequent) were the same as in TREC and did not perform well. No answer patterns such as Hovy et al. [6] are used and so the selection is just being made on non-structural correspondences between terms in a query and candidate answers such as co-occurrence measures.

5.2 Issues Raised

We now present our findings in terms of the specific issues of cross-lingual QA.

Translation of queries. Our approach is heavily reliant on obtaining a good translation. The results from Google were adequate but there were many errors which affected subsequent processing. A better strategy has to be worked out, perhaps involving a more detailed grammatical analysis of the query based on a specialised knowledge of query forms (rather than texts in general) followed by submission of individual query constituents for translation. In addition, several engines could be used and the results combined to overcome repeated errors of specific types committed by particular systems.

Translation of names within queries. Some names were recognised by Google (e.g. 'États-Unis') and hence translated correctly (e.g. 'United States'). However, many were left untranslated (e.g. Tchétchénie). The document collection refers to names in their American English form which can be radically different from the French term. For example the equivalent of Tchétchénie is Chechnya though it can appear in other variants. Generating the correct translation(s) for the whole range of names which might appear in a factoid question is a major task which we have not yet looked at in detail. Without accurate translations we will not answer questions mentioning such names correctly.

Diacritical marks. Our approach to these was to leave them in place for translation but to remove them entirely before question classification. This unsophisticated approach must surely lose important information. The processing of texts using diacritics raises issues which we have not previously encountered when working with English documents. The most obvious of these is the need to match a word containing the appropriate accents with its equivalent without, while at the same time giving priority to exact matches. The present cross-language system was essentially a monolingual English one with a French front end but in the context of monolingual French-French QA attention would have to be paid to query formulation unless the retrieval engine used explicitly supported a morphologically sophisticated model of multilingual documents.

Search queries returning no results. Intentionally narrow search expressions submitted to DTSearch could result in no matched document portions. This happened more often than we anticipated, the main reason being incorrectly translated (or not translated) parts of the input query. The answer is better translation together with query relaxation.

General names. Our experiment in recognising general names was not very successful. Part of the problem is accurate verification of candidates without knowing the question type. A better strategy has to be worked out for this as there will always be unknown questions.

5.3 Improvements and Next Steps

Following the conference the system was updated in a number of ways. Firstly, seven further query types were added and the classifier and named entity recogniser amended accordingly. Secondly, on examination of the translation produced by Google and comparing it with alternatives it was found that Reverso [7] generally gives a better result, so this was adopted instead. Thirdly the process of search expression formulation from the input query was augmented to allow recognition and appropriate treatment of compound names (e.g. titles) quoted expressions and numbers. Fourthly, progressive query relaxation was added to the document search engine to handle situations where the initial (or indeed subsequent) query yields no matching documents. Finally, a version of the web-based candidate answer re-ranking algorithm of Magnini et al. [8] was incorporated into the answer selection module.

From the cross-lingual perspective the most interesting areas for further work appear to be multilingual query classification, query translation by pre-analysis (rather than just by engine) and proper name translation (and indeed cultural localisation). We hope to experiment with some of these in the next CLEF.

References

1. Sutcliffe, R.F.E.: Question Answering using the DLT System at TREC 2002. In: Voorhees, E.M., Buckland, L. (eds.) Proc. of the Eleventh Text REtrieval Conference, Gaithersburg, Maryland, Nov. 19-22, 2002. NIST Special Publication 500-251 (2003) 677-685

2. O'Gorman, A.: Open Domain Question Answering in French. Undergraduate Final Year Project, University of Limerick, Ireland (2003)
3. Google Translation: www.google.ie/language_tools?hl=en (Accessed 2003)
4. DTSearch: www.dtsearch.com (Accessed 2000)
5. Clarke, C.L.A., Cormack, G.V., Kemkes, G., Laszlo, M., Lynam, T.R., Terra, E.L., Tilker P.L.: Statistical Selection of Exact Answers (MultiText Experiments for TREC 2002). In: Voorhees, E.M., Buckland, L. (eds.) Proc. of the Eleventh Text REtrieval Conference, Gaithersburg, Maryland, Nov. 19-22, 2002. NIST Special Publication 500-251 (2003) 823-831
6. Hovy, E. et al.: A Typology of over 140 Question-Answer Types. www.isi.edu/natural-language/projects/webclopedia/Taxonomy/taxonomy_toplevel.html (Accessed 2002)
7. Reverso: www.reverso.net (Accessed 2003)
8. Magnini, B., Negri, M., Prevete, R., Tanev H.: Is it the Right Answer? Exploiting Web Redundancy for Answer Validation. Proc. of the 40th Annual Meeting of the Association for Computational Linguistics, July 6-12, 2002, Philadelphia, PA (2002) 425-432

The CLEF 2003 Cross Language
Image Retrieval Track

Paul Clough and Mark Sanderson

Department of Information Studies, University of Sheffield, Regent Court,
211 Portobello Street, Sheffield, S1 4DP, UK
{p.d.clough, m.sanderson}@sheffield.ac.uk

Abstract. In this paper, we describe a pilot experiment run at CLEF 2003 for cross language image retrieval, called ImageCLEF. The task is this: given a user need expressed in a language different from the document collection, find as many relevant images as possible. To facilitate retrieval, textual captions are associated with each image, thereby enabling (but not limiting) retrieval using text-based retrieval methods. This paper describes our experiences of building a test collection for the ImageCLEF task, discusses the results from this campaign, and outlines our ideas for further ImageCLEF experiments.

1 Introduction

Retrieval from an image collection offers distinct characteristics from one in which the document to be retrieved is natural language text. For example, the way in which a query is formulated, the method used for retrieval (e.g. based on low-level features derived from an image, or based on an associated caption), the types of query, how relevance is assessed, the involvement of the user during the search process, and fundamental cognitive differences between the interpretation of visual versus textual media.

Within CLEF, the problem is further complicated by user queries being expressed in a language different to that of the document collection. This requires crossing the language barrier by translating the collection, the queries, or both into the same language. As multimedia collections grow and more organisations become responsible for managing large image repositories, the instigation of ImageCLEF addresses an important problem that is not dealt with by existing CLEF and iCLEF tasks. Furthering research in cross language image retrieval is appealing both academically and commercially as organisations would be able to offer the same collections to a wider and more diverse range of users with differing language backgrounds.

As a retrieval task, cross language image retrieval encompasses two main research areas: (1) image retrieval, and (2) cross language information retrieval (CLIR). Providing a suitable test collection for such different retrieval tasks is a tall order, therefore the primary aim of this test collection is to evaluate systems built to accept user requests formulated in a language different from the image

C. Peters et al. (Eds.): CLEF 2003, LNCS 3237, pp. 581–593, 2004.

captions to find relevant images. However, unlike searching text collections, previous research (see, e.g. [1]) has shown that image retrieval does have its own characteristics, e.g. that users tend to browse as well as perform specific searches, that users will often consult associated textual metadata to decide whether an image is relevant or not, that users search for both abstract and concrete concepts, that search requests tend to be more specific than textual searches, and that users request specific instances of objects rather than a general category, e.g. "London bridge" rather than just "bridges" (see also [2], and [3]). Of course, like text retrieval, search requests may vary: depending on the domain and the users searching ability.

Rather than make assumptions on which retrieval methods will be used on this test collection, e.g. combining both text-based and content-based retrieval methods, or the utilisation of relevance feedback, we aim to provide a test bed that can be used to evaluate a range of retrieval methods and for analysing the behavior of users during the search process, e.g. query formulation in both cross language and visual environments, iterative searching, and query reformulation. Goodrum [1] calls for a TREC-style test collection for image retrieval, which will provide a benchmark set of queries, relevance assessments and evaluation measures. We partially fulfill this call through ImageCLEF by creating a test collection of images and captions, and this year offered participants an ad hoc retrieval task for cross language image retrieval.

2   The Cross Language Image Retrieval Task

Two retrieval tasks were proposed for ImageCLEF: (1) ad hoc retrieval, and (2) an interactive search task. Because of a lack of interest in the latter task, in this paper we focus on the former ad hoc retrieval task. The exploratory nature of ImageCLEF also meant we concentrated our efforts on building a suitable test collection, rather than identifying and designing different retrieval tasks. The aim this year was to determine whether CLEF participants would be interested in this kind of retrieval task, rather than expend our efforts on identifying the characteristics of cross language image retrieval.

The aim of the ImageCLEF ad hoc retrieval task is this: given a multilingual statement describing a user need, find as many relevant images as possible using automatic or manual retrieval methods. This task is similar to the classic TREC ad hoc retrieval task in that we simulate the situation in which a system knows the set of documents to be searched, but cannot anticipate the user requests (i.e. queries are not known in advance). Participants are free to use whatever methods they wish to retrieve relevant images, including content or text-based retrieval methods, relevance feedback and any translation method. This retrieval task simulates when a user is able to express his/her need in natural language, but requires a visual document to fulfill their search request. While typical evaluation of content-based retrieval assumes the user performs "query-by-example" search using an exemplar of what it is they require, in ImageCLEF we provide search requests that consist of both a visual exemplar and textual description of the user need.

A question we might ask ourselves is whether this CLEF task is any different from the other CLEF tasks? At this stage in ImageCLEF, the answer has to be yes and no. In one respect the ad hoc retrieval task is the same as any other cross language task if retrieval is based on the captions only; however because the document to be judged is an image, approaches which exploit other features such as low-level content-based cues can also be used to enhance retrieval. Also, from our experiences of manually judging the relevance of images with respect to the ad hoc search requests, we also know that the image itself plays an important part in the judgment process. For example, a caption containing query terms may not be judged as relevant because the image is too small, too dark or not taken from the desired angle or view. On the other hand, an image may be relevant to the user but contain only a few or none of the query terms in the caption, perhaps because the caption is of poor quality, the language used by the annotator does not match the search request, or the caption is very short in length.

ImageCLEF aims to provide the necessary collection and framework in which to analyse the link between the image and text, and promote the discovery of alternative methods of retrieval for cross language image retrieval. We envisage that ImageCLEF will appeal to researchers from a variety of communities including image retrieval, CLIR, and user interaction.

3   The Test Collection

The classic means of measuring the performance of an information retrieval (IR) system is based on a test collection. This provides the necessary resources and framework in which to assess performance and is typically used to compare different retrieval methods or systems. The design of a standardised resource for IR evaluation was first proposed by Cleverdon [4] and has since been used in major IR conferences such as TREC [5], CLEF [6] and NTCIR [7].

Much work has taken place in addressing particular methods of collection construction including the kinds of documents to include, the types of requests users are likely to make on the collection, and how relevant documents should be defined based on such requests. Vorhees [8] discusses the main assumptions behind TREC's method of building an IR test collection (based on Cleverdon's ideas) and although critics have argued against this approach, over the years the creation of a standard test environment has proven invaluable for the design and evaluation of practical retrieval systems. So building upon previous research in test collection construction, the three main constituents of the ImageCLEF collection are:

1. **Document Collection:** a set of documents (i.e. texts and images).
2. **Topics:** a set of user information needs.
3. **Relevance Assessments:** a set of relevance judgments associated with the topics.

Voorhees and Harman [5] suggest that the set of texts used as the document collection is a sample which is likely to be encountered within an operational setting. Of course, it is not always possible to capture the entire population for a text collection (e.g. a constantly growing collection of news stories) therefore some kind of sampling is required to create a "representative" sample. Some test collections are built around specific domains (e.g. MEDLARS, CACM), or tasks (e.g. journalists finding images for an illustration task [3]), whereas other collections are more general (e.g. TREC). In ImageCLEF, we wanted to create a collection which represented a realistic domain, but on which a particular task was not imposed to create a more general collection suitable for further retrieval tasks and experiments in the future.

3.1   The Document Collection

Selecting a suitable collection for ImageCLEF proved to be a non-trivial task. Not only did we require a "large" collection of images, but also a collection with captions of high quality to facilitate text-based retrieval methods. Additional issues involving copyright were also encountered as typically photographs and images have a potentially high marketable value, thereby restricting permissible distribution. Our search was eased by our links with the library at St. Andrews University[1]. They hold one of the largest and most important collections of historic photographs in Scotland, exceeding over 300,000 photographs from a number of well-known Scottish photographers [9]. A cross-section of approximately 30,000 images from the main collection has been part of a large-scale digitisation project to enable public access to the collection via a web interface.

This collection was used as the basis for ImageCLEF because the collection represents a realistic image archive, high quality captions are associated with the images, and permission was granted by St. Andrews Library to downloaded and distribute the collection for use in ImageCLEF. Over a two day period, we automatically crawled the photographic collection, filtered out duplicate images and converted the captions into a TREC-style format. The collection consists of 28,133 images (a 368x234 large version and 120x76 thumbnail) and captions. The majority (82%) of images are in black and white (because of the historic nature of the collection) ranging between the years 1832 and 1992 (with a mean year of 1920). Images and captions of varying styles, presentation and quality exist in the collection from a diverse range of topics making it challenging for both image and text retrieval. Fig. 1 shows an example image and caption from the collection.

The captions, a vital part of the test collection, consist of data in a semi-structured format added manually by domain experts at St. Andrews University. The caption contains 8 fields, all or a combination of which can be used for text-based retrieval. Information in the caption ranges from specific date, location and photographer to a more general description of the image. Approximately 81% of captions have text in all fields, the rest are generally without a description. In most cases the description is a grammatical sentence of around 15 words enabling possible use of NLP technology to extract linguistic infor-

---

[1] http://www-library.st-andrews.ac.uk

Title: Old Tom Morris, golfer, St Andrews.
Short title: Old Tom Morris, golfer.
Location: Fife, Scotland
Description: Portrait of bearded elderly man in tweed jacket, waistcoat with watch chain and flat cap, hand in pockets; painted backdrop.
Date: ca.1900
Photographer: John Fairweather
Categories: `[golf - general]`, `[identified male]`,`[St. Andrews Portraits]`,`[Collection - G M Cowie]`
Notes: GMC-F202 pc/BIOG: Tom Morris (1821-1908) Golf ball and clubmaker before turning professional, later Custodian of the Links, St Andrews; golfer and four times winner of the Open Championship; father of Young Tom Morris (1851-1875).DETAIL: Studio portrait.

Fig. 1. An example image and caption from the ImageCLEF collection

mation, e.g. subject-object relations. The categories have been added manually by St. Andrews annotators and could be used for future image categorisation experiments. The captions exist only in British English, and the language tends to contain colloquial expressions.

3.2   Selecting Suitable Topics

System effectiveness for the ad hoc retrieval task is evaluated against a set of user needs called topics. Deciding on which topics to include in the test collection is crucial because if they are not representative of the collection, or if they differ from real user requests, effectiveness measured with the test collection will not be realistic of that one might expect to obtain in a practical setting. In TREC, NTCIR and CLEF, final topics are chosen from a pool of suggestions generated by searchers familiar with the domain of the document collection. This initial set is narrowed-down based on several conditions, including the estimated number of relevant documents for each topic, the variation of task parameters (e.g. for a multilingual task the topics are chosen to test different translation problems), the difficulty of the topic, and its scope (e.g. broad or narrow, general or specific). The goal is to "achieve a natural, balanced topic set accurately reflecting real world user statements of information needs" [10, pg. 1069].

The first author created a set of fifty topics that would test the capabilities of both a translation and image retrieval system, e.g. pictures of specific objects versus pictures containing actions, broad versus narrow concepts, topics containing proper names, compound words, abbreviations, morphological variants and idiomatic expressions. To determine potential subject areas for ImageCLEF topics, we first became familiar with the St. Andrews collection by browsing its contents, and analysing log files taken from the St. Andrews Library web server hosting the photographic collection over a two year period.

Results from a simple analysis of the log files (together with the subject categories used to group images) gave a set of 2796 distinct queries (of which 67% occur only once). Like previous results from examining image searches from Web search engines [11], we find on average that individual queries against the St. Andrews collection tend to be short and specific, i.e. requests for specific objects or locations. However, a more extensive click-through analysis would be necessary to verify our initial findings. By ranking queries by frequency, we were able to find the most common search requests and topics (e.g. from the top 15 most common queries, 60% of these were proper names).

After deciding the initial subject areas, we used combinations of keywords related to that area to explore possible topics by adding or removing words to make searches more specific or general. For example, the subject area "fishermen" might become "fishermen by the photographer Adamson", "churches" become "churches with tall spires", or "tay bridge railway disaster" might become "metal railway bridges". This results in finding more or less possibly relevant documents. The aim of this process was to create a set of topics that would test various issues involved with both query translation and image retrieval (and relevance assessment of visual information). The set of keywords used in this initial stage were used as the titles in the topic description, a few keywords describing the required topic. Table 1 lists the selected 50 topics and section 3.5 discusses some of the comments from assessors regarding those topics chosen for ImageCLEF.

3.3   Creating the Topic Statement

Given the fifty selected subject areas, we expressed the user's need using both a natural language statement and an example image. The topic defines to relevance assessors and participants what we expect a relevant and non-relevant image to be like. ImageCLEF topics consist of 2-3 keywords, the title, a short description of relevance, a narrative, and an example relevant image. Because the task involves image retrieval, we decided to supply an example image as part of the topic statement which would not typically accompany a topic definition for texts. Participants were free to use this image, maybe as part of a content-based search, or part of a relevance feedback cycle. Given the multilingual nature of ImageCLEF, topic titles were translated into Spanish, Dutch, German, French, and Italian by native speakers of each language [2]. We did not translate the narratives because of limitations in time and resources available to us. Translators were also given an example of a relevant image and also asked to specify alternative translations where appropriate (e.g. a colloquial version

---

[2] One of the participating groups, NTU, manually translated the topics into Chinese (traditional and simplified) and submitted Chinese to English runs.

of the translation). These translation variations were supplied as part of the ImageCLEF topic statement.

3.4   The Relevance Assessments

What turns a set of documents and queries into a test collection are the relevance judgments, manual assessments of which documents are relevant or not for each topic. There are two areas of concern with relevance assessments: (1) the quality or subjectivity of the judgments, and (2) their coverage or completeness. The first concern is based on disagreement between assessors about what constitutes a relevant document caused by subjectivity (e.g. knowledge of the topics or domain, different interpretations of the same document, and their experience of searching). This is not a trivial problem to solve, but we did two things to reduce this: (1) have two assessors judge each topic, and (2) capture information from the assessors about their judgments.

The second issue deals with the coverage of relevance assessments. Ideally every document in the collection would be judged for relevance for each topic, but with large collections this becomes infeasible as it requires too much manual effort (even though from ImageCLEF we find it is much quicker to judge the relevance of an image versus text). To make assessment feasible, pooling has been used in TREC, CLEF and NTCIR evaluations. In this technique, a set of candidate documents is created (the pool) by merging together the results of the top n documents from the ranked lists provided by participants. This assumes that highly ranked documents from each entry will contain relevant documents; questions left to deal with include what size of n is chosen, how many systems are used in the pooling process, and which systems are used to create the pool. Ideally, the ranked lists should come from a diverse range of systems to ensure maximal coverage, however because we had only 4 participants in ImageCLEF (resulting in 45 runs for each topic), the method proposed by Kuriyama et al. [7] and used in NTCIR, that of supplementing the pooling method with manual interactive searches, was applied (also known as *interactive search and judge* or ISJ). This was found to enhance recall and improve the coverage of relevant documents (particularly with queries requiring a more general image)- see Table 1.

To assess the topics, the topic creator assessed all fifty topics to provide a "gold" set of judgments (this involved assessing around 50,000 images); in addition, ten assessors from the University of Sheffield judged five topics each to provide a second judgment for each topic (enabling the agreement between assessors to be evaluated). Judging was made easier by creating a custom Web-based assessment tool which enabled the judgment of images in the pools (ranked by the proportion of systems which included the image in the top 100 documents), as well as providing an interactive search environment to supplement the pools as necessary. This tool enabled assessors to make judgments from any location; combined with term highlighting features in the Google toolbar, judgments were made quickly and easily. Assessors were asked to judge the relevance of *all* images from the topic pool based on the relevance description and using a ternary scheme: relevant, partially relevant, and not relevant. To convey the topic state-

ment to the assessors, they were provided with the topic as given to the participants and an example image. They were free to contact the first author with any
questions. Primary judgment was made on the image, but assessors were able to
also consult the image caption. Images were to be judged relevant if *any* part of
the image was deemed relevant.

The ternary scheme was adopted to deal with potential uncertainty in the assessor's judgment (i.e. it is possible to determine that the image is relevant, but
less certain whether it fulfils the need described by the topic exactly), and to enable evaluation based on a strict set of relevance judgments (i.e. those documents
marked as relevant only) and a more relaxed set (i.e. those marked as relevant
and partially relevant). We believe this is particularly important in practical image retrieval evaluation to deal with situations where a binary judgment might
be too restricting, e.g. only part of the image is relevant, the required object is
obscured (e.g. perhaps in the background), the image is too small, or the image
appears relevant, but the caption is unable to confirm its contents.

As assessment of images for relevance was found to be much faster than
assessment of text documents, *all* 45 submitted runs were assessed. By using all
runs for both monolingual and cross lingual entries (automatic and manual) to
create the pools and then using interactive searches to supplement the pools,
we hoped to find as many relevant images as possible from the collection and
maximise coverage. Rather than create a single set of relevant images (qrels)
for each topic, we created four sets based on the overlap of relevant images
between the assessors. We created the following four relevance sets from which
we evaluated participant's entries:

1. **Union-Strict:** the union of images judged as relevant by the two assessors
   and evaluated using only those marked as relevant.
2. **Union-Relaxed:** the union of images judged as relevant by the two assessors
   and evaluated using those marked as relevant or partially relevant.
3. **Intersection-Strict:** the intersection of images judged as relevant by the
   two assessors and evaluated using only those marked as relevant.
4. **Intersection-Relaxed:** the intersection of images judged as relevant by
   the two assessors and evaluated using those marked as relevant or partially
   relevant.

The strict relevance set can be contrasted with a high-precision task, and
the relaxed set providing an assessment that promotes higher recall. The most
stringent category of relevance assessment is intersection-strict as this produces
the smallest number of relevant documents, and most relaxed category is union
relaxed (see Table 1). Included in the pools are documents which were marked
as relevant or partially relevant using the interactive search. In summary, the
following procedure was used to assess relevance and evaluate participant's
entries:

1. Extracted the top 100 runs from each submission (45 submissions in total)
   for each topic.
2. Computed the union of documents from these runs to create the document
   pool.

Table 1. Topics used in ImageCLEF and their assessment characteristics

Topic	Title	Pool size	Added by ISJ	Strict ∩	Strict ∪	Relaxed ∩	Relaxed ∪
1	Men and women processing fish	504	0	9	14	15	25
2	A baby in a pram	908	3	5	16	25	64
3	Picture postcard views of St. Andrews	1312	118	23	100	25	136
4	Seating inside a church	1071	0	91	131	115	138
5	Woodland scenes	1239	0	137	300	238	502
6	Scottish marching bands	1145	5	5	8	7	16
7	Home guard on parade during World War II	772	2	5	8	7	16
8	Tea rooms by the seaside	1262	4	4	13	10	31
9	Fishermen by the photographer Adamson	601	0	4	6	4	7
10	Ships on the river Clyde	795	6	10	24	19	26
11	Portraits of Mary Queen of Scots	885	1	2	4	5	7
12	North Street St. Andrews	785	1	29	35	31	35
13	War memorials in the shape of a cross	803	6	12	27	14	31
14	Boats on Loch Lomond	1012	0	33	42	38	48
15	Tay bridge rail disaster	648	12	11	14	11	14
16	City chambers in Dundee or Glasgow	653	0	17	112	17	118
17	Great Yarmouth beach	937	1	9	11	10	13
18	Metal railway bridges	647	3	94	125	106	139
19	Culross abbey	643	0	3	3	3	3
20	Road bridges	1269	0	31	183	48	191
21	Animals by the photographer Lady Henrietta Gilmour	641	91	48	145	49	145
22	Ruined castles in England	698	41	42	85	53	114
23	London bridge	465	0	2	2	2	2
24	Damage due to war	695	4	12	14	12	17
25	Golf course bunkers	1383	3	12	18	22	37
26	Portraits of Robert Burns	831	4	6	6	6	6
27	Children playing on beaches	578	1	26	68	43	98
28	Pictures of golfers in the nineteenth century	1155	5	11	31	14	40
29	Wartime aviation	661	2	11	72	34	100
30	Glasgow before 1920	389	1	21	46	33	46
31	Exterior views of Indian temples	776	0	35	53	41	59
32	Male portraits	993	100	280	422	316	436
33	People using spinning machines	1192	1	7	10	8	10
34	Dogs rounding-up sheep	642	2	12	2	12	17
35	The mountain Ben Nevis	739	5	56	65	62	72
36	Churches with tall spires	1065	45	35	94	57	130
37	Men holding tennis racquets	736	0	2	3	3	4
38	Scottish fishing vessels by the photographer Thompson	929	1	14	16	14	19
39	Men cutting peat	881	0	5	5	5	7
40	Picture postcards by the Valentine photographic company	1218	266	104	726	194	899
41	A coat of arms	1006	6	10	25	13	46
42	University buildings	579	9	112	157	120	159
43	British Windmills	579	0	13	14	13	14
44	Waterfalls in Wales	731	0	24	27	24	28
45	Harvesting	595	2	14	22	18	24
46	Welsh national dress	1122	0	4	26	7	69
47	People dancing	882	5	10	19	12	19
48	Museum exhibits	467	7	17	37	25	49
49	Musicians and their instruments	440	3	7	17	7	21
50	Mountain scenery	1320	0	225	514	284	617
	Average	846	15	35	78	46	95

3. Two assessors manually judged each image in the document pool using the ternary scheme.
4. An interactive search was then performed to supplement the document pools with relevant images not found in the pool.
5. Four relevant document sets (qrels) for each topic were created from the pools.
6. Documents from each system run were compared against each set of qrels.
7. Measures of effectiveness were computed using trec_eval for each topic and across all 50.

3.5   Feedback from Translators and Assessors

The opinions of translators and assessors was sought for their views on the tasks they undertook. For the translators, some English queries were found to have no similar concepts in another language and therefore had to be expressed using different terms. Some of the ten relevance assessors spoke English as a second language (all albeit very well) and they struggled to understand some of the image captions due to colloquial or historic language usage, e.g. "perambulator" and "infant". Assessors noted that is was very easy to judge irrelevant images based on the image alone. The copies of the images in the collection were found to be sometimes not detailed enough to allow effective assessment to take place. Judging if an object was in the foreground or background was also not always straightforward. The partially relevant category was not well used by some of the assessors.

4   Evaluation

4.1   The Participants

Four groups participated in ImageCLEF 2003: the University of Surrey, National Taiwan University (NTU), Daedalus (Spain), and the University of Sheffield, exhibiting variety in the retrieval systems used and their methods for translating topic titles. None of the groups made use of content-based image retrieval methods during the retrieval process; all groups used information derived from the captions only. Sheffield and Surrey provided one automatic run for each language (including monolingual), whereas Daedalus submitted 25 runs based on different system parameters for all languages except Dutch. NTU translated the topic titles into Chinese and submitted 4 manual runs and 4 automatic runs for Chinese to English only.

NTU used the OKAPI retrieval system and two methods for translating Chinese queries into English based on dictionary lookup using four resources: the LDC Chinese-English dictionary, Denisowski's CEDICT, the BDC Chinese-English dictionary v2.2, and an in-house resource. Two methods were used to select translations: (1) a co-occurrence model, and (2) the two most frequent translations. In both cases, a backward transliteration model was used to translate person and location names not contained in the bilingual dictionary.

Table 2. Highest MAP and number of topics with no relevant image in the top 100 for each language and group (strict intersection)

Source	Surrey	NTU	Sheffield	Daedalus
MONO (MAP)	0.0624	-	0.5616	0.5718 (Qor)
(#failed topics)	27	-	1	1
IT	0.0539	-	0.4047	0.4043 (QTdoc)
	30	-	7	5
DE	0.0503	-	0.4285	0.4083 (QTdoc)
	29	-	8	5
NL	0.0289	-	0.3904	-
	32	-	7	-
FR	0.0529	-	0.4380	0.3710 (QTor1)
	30	-	3	5
ES	0.0320	-	0.4076	0.4323 (QTdoc)
	32	-	3	5
CN	-	0.2888 (NTUiaCoP)	0.2850	-
	-	12	12	-

Daedalus used a probabilistic IR system called Xapian and linguistic resources to deal with tokenisation, word decompounding, morphological variants and removal of stopwords. For translation, a dictionary-based lookup strategy was used based on three resources: FreeTranslation.com, LangToLang.com, and ERGANE (word-by-word translation). For English monolingual runs, WordNet was also used to expand queries with their synonyms, and in all retrieval experiments queries were constructed using an OR-ing approach.

Sheffield University also used a probabilistic system based on the BM25 weighting function for retrieval, but compared to the other groups used minimal language processing made possible through the use of Systran (on-line version). All fields in the caption were used for retrieval, and documents ranked by their BM25 score.

The University of Surrey used two free Internet translation resources and expanded queries using WordNet. Unfortunately, due to a misconfiguration problem with their system, the results submitted by them were not correct.

4.2   The Results

Systems are evaluated by comparing the output of submitted runs with the relevance sets (qrels) to determine how many relevant documents appear in the retrieval, and their rank position. We use a form of `trec_eval`[3] to compute retrieval effectiveness. Table 2 shows average precision for each participant's best run on a particular part of the ImageCLEF task. In addition, the number of topics for which no relevant images were returned in the top 100 is also shown; here it was assumed that users would be willing to examine the top

---

[3] We make use of the UMASS version of `trec_eval`.

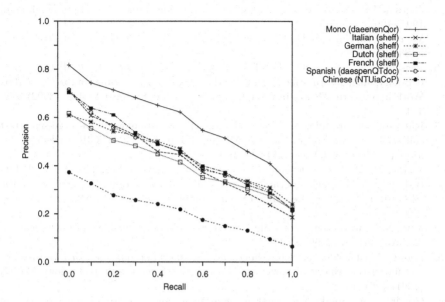

Fig. 2. Precision-Recall for best performing systems for each language (using strict intersection)

100 images from a topic and would regard finding no relevant images in that top set as a failure of the retrieval system for that topic. Somewhat unusually for effectiveness statistics, the two measures, especially between Sheffield and Daedalus, sometimes contradict each other: with one system scoring higher in average precision, while the other scores lower in number of failed topics.

Acknowledgments

The ImageCLEF track would not have run had it not been for St. Andrews University Library - in particular the curator of the St. Andrews image collection, Norman Reid - allowing a portion of the collection to be released for the track. This work was carried out within the Eurovision project at the University of Sheffield, funded by the EPSRC (Eurovision: GR/R56778/01).

References

1. Goodrum, A.: Image information retrieval: An overview of current research. Informing Science **Vol. 3(2)** (2000) 63–66
2. Armitage, L., Enser, P.: Analysis of user need in image archives. Journal of Information Science **Vol. 23(4)** (1997) 287–299
3. Markkula, M., Tico, M., Sepponen, B., Nirkkonen, K., Sormunen, E.: A test collection for the evaluation of content-based image retrieval algorithms - a user and task-based approach. Information Retrieval **Vol. 4(3/4)** (2001) 275–294

4. Cleverdon, C. In: The Cranfield tests on index language devices. In: K, Spark-Jones and P. Willett (eds), Readings in Information Retrieval, Morgan Kaufmann, 1997 (1997) 47–59
5. Voorhees, E., Harman, D.: Overview of TREC 2001. In: Proceedings of TREC2001, NIST. (2001)
6. Braschler, M., Peters, C.: CLEF methodology and metrics. In: C. Peters (Ed.), Cross-language information retrieval and evaluation: Proceedings of the CLEF2001 Workshop, Lecture Notes in Computer Science 2406, Springer Verlag. (2002) 394–404
7. Kuriyama, K., Kando, N., Nozue, T., Eguchi, K.: Pooling for a large-scale test collection: An analysis of the search results from the first NTCIR workshop. Information Retrieval **Vol. 5(1)** (2002) 41–59
8. Voorhees, E.: The philosophy of information retrieval evaluation. In: C. Peters (Ed.), Cross-language information retrieval and evaluation: Proceedings of the CLEF2001 Workshop, Lecture Notes in Computer Science 2406, Springer Verlag. (2002) 355–370
9. Reid, N.: The photographic collections in St Andrews University Library. Scottish Archives **Vol. 5** (1999) 83–90
10. Peters, C., Braschler, M.: Cross-language system evaluation: The CLEF campaigns. Journal of the American Society for Information Science and Technology **52(12)** (2001) 1067–1072
11. Goodrum, A., Spink, A.: Visual information seeking: A study of image queries on the World Wide Web. In: Proceedings of the 1999 Annual Meeting of the American Society for Information Science. (1999)

Assessing Translation Quality for Cross Language Image Retrieval

Paul Clough and Mark Sanderson

Department of Information Studies, University of Sheffield, Regent Court,
211 Portobello Street, Sheffield, S1 4DP, UK
{p.d.clough, m.sanderson}@sheffield.ac.uk

Abstract. Like other cross language tasks, we show that the quality of the translation resource, among other factors, has an effect on retrieval performance. Using data from the ImageCLEF test collection, we investigate the relationship between translation quality and retrieval performance when using Systran, a machine translation (MT) system, as a translation resource. The quality of translation is assessed manually by comparing the original ImageCLEF topics with the output from Systran and rated by assessors based on their semantic content. Quality is also measured using an automatic score derived from the mteval MT evaluation tool, and compared to the manual assessment score. Like other MT tasks, we find that measures based on the automatic score are correlated with the manual assessments for this CLIR task. The results from this short study formed our entry to ImageCLEF 2003.

1 Introduction

Translating a user's search request from the *source language* of the query into the language of the document collection, the *target language*, is a core activity in Cross Language Information Retrieval (CLIR). Bridging the source-target translation gap can be achieved using a variety of translation resources, including bilingual dictionaries, extracting word/phrase equivalents from parallel or comparable corpora, machine translation (MT) or a controlled vocabulary. There are advantages and disadvantages to each approach, but commonly CLIR involves specialised knowledge of both CLIR and translation methodologies, and familiarity with the source and target languages.

As an information retrieval task, image retrieval involves translation to match user requests expressed in natural language to captions associated with the images which act as semantic representations of an image's visual content. As a CLIR task, image retrieval involves matching queries in the source language with captions in the target language. However, because the ImageCLEF test collection is new and previously unused for evaluation, we cannot be sure of the degree to which translation affects retrieval per-

C. Peters et al. (Eds.): CLEF 2003, LNCS 3237, pp. 594–610, 2004.
© Springer-Verlag Berlin Heidelberg 2004

formance for the topics suggested in the proposed ad hoc retrieval task. As an image retrieval task there are other factors which affect whether retrieved images are relevant or
not, such as the quality or size of the image, the quality of the caption description, subjective interpretation of the image, and the short length of image descriptions.

For translation we use Systran, one of the oldest and most widely used commercial
machine translation systems, freely available via a Web-based interface. Experience
with this resource has shown that little or no multilingual processing is necessary as
would normally be required when dealing with cross language retrieval, e.g. tokenisation, case and diacritic normalisation, decompounding and morphological analysis,
therefore offering an attractive solution to problems involving translation. Systran has
been used widely for CLIR before, including cross language image retrieval [1], but
as a translation resource Systran presents limitations, such as one translation only for
a source query and no control over translation.

In this paper we show how the quality of Systran varies across language and
query, and illustrate some of the problems encountered when using Systran to translate the short ImageCLEF queries. These short texts of 2-3 words essentially use
Systran for dictionary-lookup as they carry little grammatical structure to help translation. Although much previous research has already been undertaken in MT evaluation, there appears less empirical evaluation of translation quality within CLIR as
translation quality is often judged based on retrieval performance. In this paper we
measure translation quality as distinct from the retrieval.

The paper divides into the following: in section 2 we present background material,
in section 3 the experimental setup, in section 4 the results, and in section 5 our conclusions and outline for future work.

2   Background

2.1 The ImageCLEF Task

ImageCLEF was a pilot experiment run at CLEF 2003 dealing with the retrieval of
images by their captions in cases where the source and target languages differ (see [2]
for further information about ImageCLEF). Because the document to be retrieved is
both visual and textual, approaches to this task can involve the use of both multimodal
and multilingual retrieval methods. The primary task at this year's ImageCLEF
was an ad hoc retrieval task in which fifty topics were selected for retrieval and described using a topic title and narrative. Only the title was translated into Dutch, Italian, Spanish, French, German, Spanish and Chinese (by NTU), and therefore suitable
for CLIR. As well as query-caption translation, further challenges for this task include: (1) captions which are typically short in length, (2) images that vary widely in
their content and quality, and (3) short user search requests which provide little
context for translation.

2.2 Systran

As a translation system, Systran is considered by many as a direct MT approach, although the stages resemble a transfer-based MT system because translation also involves the use of rules to direct syntax generation (see, e.g. [3]). There are essentially three stages to Systran: analysis, transfer and synthesis. The first stage, analysis, preprocesses the source text and performs functions such as character set conversion, spelling correction, sentence segmentation, tokenisation, and POS tagging. Also during the analysis phase, Systran performs partial analysis on sentences from the source language, capturing linguistic information such as predicate-argument relations, major syntactic relationships, identification of noun phrases and prepositional phrase attachment using their own linguistic formalism and dictionary lookup.

After analysis of the source language, the second process of transfer aims to match with the target language through dictionary lookup, and then apply rules to re-order the words according to the target language syntax, e.g. restructure propositions and expressions. The final synthesis stage cleans up the target text and determines grammatical choice to make the result coherent. This stage relies heavily on large tables of rules to make its decisions. For more information, consult [4] and [5].

2.3 MT Evaluation

Assessing how well an MT system works offers a challenging problem to researchers (see, e.g. [3] and [6]), and before evaluating an MT system, one must first determine its intended use and then evaluate the output based on whether the output is satisfactory for this purpose or not. MT evaluation is a subjective process and finding an objective measure is a non-trivial task. Dorr et al. [6] suggest that MT system evaluation can be treated similar to that of a software system where one evaluates the accuracy of input/output pairs (a *black-box* approach), or evaluates the data flow between internal system components (a *glass-box* approach).

In the black-box approach, a number of dimensions must be specified along which to evaluate translation quality (see, [6] for more information). In the glass-box approach, evaluation of system components might include linguistic coverage, or parsing accuracy. Organisations such as DARPA and NIST have established the necessary resources and framework in which to experiment with, and evaluate, MT systems as part of managed competitions, similar to the TREC (see, e.g. [7]) and CLEF (see, e.g. [8]) campaigns. For manual evaluation[1], three dimensions upon which to base judgments include translation *adequacy*, *fluency* and *informativeness*. Translation quality is normally assessed across an entire document when measuring fluency and informativeness, but adequacy is assessed between smaller units (e.g. paragraphs or sentences) which provide a tighter and more direct semantic relationship between bilingual document pairs. This is discussed further in section 3.1.

[1,2] See, e.g. TIDES: http://www.ldc.upenn.edu/Projects/TIDES/ [site visited: July 2003].

Test-suites can be used for both black-box and glass-box evaluation, and used to categorise the successes or failures of the system. The test-suite is often built for a specific application and type of evaluation in mind, and offers the research community a standardised resource within which different translation systems can be compared. Evaluation often takes the approach whereby the output of the MT system is captured and compared with a reference or gold-standard source and translation errors categorised and quantified, including lexical, grammatical and stylistic ones (see, e.g. [9]).

As well as manual methods of translation evaluation, there has also been much work in automating the task to reduce the amount of manual effort required, resulting in evaluation tools such as `mteval` which we discuss in section 3.2. The success of translation in CLIR is often based on retrieval performance and observations of translations, although previous work that does evaluate MT output as distinct from the retrieval process includes Patterson [10].

3   Experimental Setup

3.1   Manual Assessment of Translation Quality

In these experiments, we have used the evaluation framework as provided by NIST for both manual and automatic evaluation. To assess adequacy, a high quality reference translation and the output from an MT system are divided into segments to evaluate how well the meaning is conveyed between versions. Fluency measures how well the translation conveys its content with regards to how the translation is presented and involves no comparison with the reference translation. Informativeness measures how well an assessor has understood the content of a translated document by asking them questions based on the translation and assessing the number answered correctly.

Given topic titles from the ImageCLEF test collection, we first passed them through the on-line version of Systran to translate them into English, the language of the image captions. We then asked assessors to judge the adequacy of the translation by assuming the English translation would be submitted to a retrieval system for an ad hoc task. Translators who had previously been involved with creating the ImageCLEF test collection were chosen to assess translation quality because of their familiarity with the topics and the collection, each assessor given topics in their native language.

Translators were asked to assess topic titles[2] in the source language with the Systran English version and make a judgment on how well the translation captured the meaning of the original (i.e. how *adequate* the translated version would be for retrieval purposes). A five-point scale was used to assess translation quality, a score of 5 representing a very good translation (i.e. the same or semantically-equivalent words and syntax), to very bad (i.e. no translation, or the wrong words used altogether). Assessors were asked to take into account the "importance" of translation errors in the scoring, e.g. for retrieval purposes, mis-translated proper nouns might be considered worse than other parts-of-speech.

Table 1 shows an example topic title for each language and translation score for very good to good (5-4), okay (3) and bad to very bad (2-1) to provide an idea of the degree of error for these adequacy scores. We find that assessment varies according to each assessor; some being stricter than others, which suggests, further manual assessments may help to reduce subjectivity. In some cases, particularly Spanish, the source language title contains a spelling mistake which will affect translation quality. Some assessors allowed for this in their rating, others did not, therefore suggesting the need to manually check all topics for errors prior to evaluation.

Table 1 also highlights some of the errors produced by the MT system: (1) untranslated words, e.g. "*Muzikanten* and their instruments", (2) incorrect translation of proper nouns, e.g. "Bateaux sur Loch Lomond" translated as "Boats on Lomond *Log*" and "Il monte Ben Nevis" translated as "the mount *Very* Nevis", (3) mis-translations, e.g. "damage de guerre" translated as "*ramming* of war", and (4) wrong sense selection, e.g. "Scottish blowing chapels" where *kapelle* is mis-translated as chapel, rather than the correct word band. From this study, we found that many un-translated terms, however, were caused by mistakes in the original source texts. This might be seen as an additional IR challenge in which the queries reflect more realistic erroneous user requests. Systran was able to handle different entry formats for diacritics which play an important part in selecting the correct translation of a word, e.g. in the query "Casas de te' en la costa" (tearooms by the seaside), the word *te'* is translated correctly as *té* (sea) rather than *te* (you).

3.2 Automatic Assessment of Translation Quality

Although most accurate (and most subjective), manual evaluation is time-consuming and expensive, therefore automatic approaches to assess translation quality have also been proposed, such as the NIST `mteval`[3] tool. This approach divides documents into segments and computes co-occurrence statistics based on the overlap of word n-grams between a reference translation produced manually and an MT version. This method has been shown to correlate well with adequacy, fluency and informativeness because n-grams capture both lexical overlap and syntactic structure [3].

In the latest version of `mteval`, two metrics are used to compute translation quality: IBM's BLEU and NIST's own score. Both measures are based on n-gram co-occurrence, although a modified version of NIST's score has been shown to be the preferred measure [3]. These scores assume that the reference translation is of high quality, and that documents assessed are from the same genre. Both measures are influenced by changes in literal form. Translations with the same meaning but using different words score lower than those that appear exactly the same. This is justified in assuming the manual reference translation is the "best" translation possible and the MT version should be as similar to this as possible.

---

[3] We used mteval-v09.pl which can be downloaded from: http://www.nist.gov/speech/tests/mt [site visited: July 2003]

Table 1. Example adequacy ratings assigned manually

Source	Ade-quacy rating	Original source	Systran English	Reference English
Chinese (simplified)	4-5	圣安德鲁斯风景的明信片	Saint Andrews scenery postcard	Picture postcard views of St Andrews
	3	战争造成的破坏	The war creates destruction	Damage due to war
	1-2	大亚茅斯海滩	Asian Mao si beach	Great Yarmouth beach
Dutch	4-5	Mannen en vrouwen die vis verwerken	men and women who process fish	men and women processing fish
	3	Vissers gefoto-grafeerd door Adamson	Fisherman photographed Adamson	Fishermen by the photographer Adamson
	1-2	Muzikanten en hun instrumenten	Muzikanten and their instruments	Musicians and their instruments
German	4-5	Baby im Kinder-wagen	Baby in the buggy	A baby in a pram
	3	Portät der schot-tischen Königin Mary	Portraet of the Scottish Queen Mary	Portraits of Mary Queen of Scots
	1-2	Museumaustel-lungsstücke	Museumaustel-lungsstuecke	Museum exhibits
French	4-5	La rue du Nord St Andrews	The street of North St Andrews	North Street St Andrews
	3	Bateaux sur Loch Lomond	Boats on Lomond log	Boats on Loch Lomond
	1-2	Damage de guerre	Ramming of war	Damage due to war
Italian	4-5	Banda Scozzese in Marcia	Scottish band in march	Scottish marching bands
	3	Vestito tradizionale gallese	Dressed traditional Welshman	Welsh national dress
	1-2	Il monte Ben Nevis	The mount Very Nevis	The mountain Ben Nevis
Spanish	4-5	El aforo de la iglesia	Chairs in a church	Seating inside a church
	3	Puentes en la carret-era	Bridges in the high-way	Road bridges
	1-2	las montañas de Ben Nevis	Mountains of Horseradish tree Nevis	The mountain Ben Nevis

For n-gram scoring, the NIST formula is:

$$Score = \sum_{n=1}^{N} \left\{ \frac{\sum_{\substack{all\ w_i...w_n \\ that\ co\text{-}occur}} Info(w_1...w_n)}{\sum_{\substack{all\ w_i...w_n \\ in\ sys\ output}} (1)} \right\} \cdot exp\left\{ \beta \log^2 \left[min\left(\frac{L_{sys}}{L_{ref}} \right) \right] \right\}$$ (1)

where:

β is chosen to make the brevity penalty factor = 0.5 when the number of words in the system output is 2/3 of the average number of words in the reference translation.

N is the n-gram length.

$\overline{L_{ref}}$ is the average number of words in a reference translation, averaged over all reference translations.

L_{sys} is the number of words in the translation being scored.

$$Info(w_1...w_n) = \log_2 \left(\frac{number\ of\ occurrences\ of\ w_1...w_{n-1}}{number\ of\ occurrences\ of\ w_1...w_n} \right)$$

The NIST formula uses $info(w_1...w_n)$ to weight the "importance" of n-grams based on their length, i.e. that longer n-grams are less likely than shorter ones, and reduces the effects of segment length on the translation score. The information weight is computed from n-gram counts across the set of reference translations. The brevity penalty factor is used to minimise the impact on the score of small variations in the length of a translation. The mteval tool enables control of the n-gram length and maximises matches by normalising case, keeping numerical information as single words, tokenising punctuation into separate words, and concatenating adjacent non-ASCII words into single words.

To evaluate the translation produced by Systran with mteval, we compared the English ImageCLEF topic title (the reference translation) with the English output from Systran (the test translation). Within the reference and test translation files, each topic title is categorised as a separate segment within a document, resulting in a NIST score for each topic. An alternative approach would be to treat the topics as separate segments within one document, although in practice we found the scores to be similar to those obtained from the first approach. To minimise the effects of syntactic variation on the NIST scores, we use an n-gram length of 1 word. For example, the English topic title "North Street St Andrews" is translated into French as "La rue du Nord St Andrews" which translated literally into English is "The street of the North, St Andrews" which is rated as a good translation manually, but using an n-gram length > 1 would result in a low NIST score because of differences in word order.

3.3 The GLASS Retrieval System

At Sheffield, we have implemented our own version of a probabilistic retrieval system called GLASS, based on the "best match" BM25 weighting operator (see, e.g. [11]). Captions were indexed using all 8 fields, which include a title, description, photographer, location and set of manually assigned index categories, and the default settings of case normalisation, removal of stopwords and word stemming used by the retrieval system. To improve document ranking using BM25, we used an approach where documents containing *all* query terms were ranked higher than any other. The top 1000 images and captions returned for each topic title formed our entry to Image-CLEF. We evaluate retrieval effectiveness using *average precision* for each topic and across topics using *mean average precision* (or MAP) based on the ImageCLEF test collection.

4 Results and Discussion

4.1 Translation Quality

The average manual translation adequacy score across all languages for each topic is shown in Fig. 1. As one would expect, the average score varies across each topic, ranging from a minimum average score of 1.51 for topic 48 (Museum exhibits), to a maximum of 4.64 for topic 22 (Ruined castles in England), with an average manual score of 3.17 (i.e. okay).

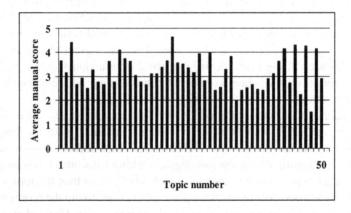

Fig. 1. Average manual adequacy score across the six languages for each topic

The six topics with an average score   4 are topics 3 (Picture postcard views of St Andrews), 12 (North Street St Andrews), 22 (Ruined castles in England), 43 (British windmills), 45 Harvesting), 47 (People dancing) and 49 (Musicians and their instruments). The topics with an average score ≥ 2 are 34 (Dogs rounding-up sheep) and 48 (Museum exhibits). Example translations of topics 34, 48 and 22 are given in Table 2.

Table 2. Example translations of topics 34, 48 and 22

English:	Dogs rounding up sheep	Museum exhibits	Ruined castles in England
Italian	Dogs that assemble sheep	Exposures in museums	Ruins of castles in England
German:	Dogs with sheep hats	Museumaustellungssteucke	Castle ruins in England
Dutch:	Dogs which sheep bejeendrijven	Museumstukken	Ruin of castles in United Kingdom
French:	Dogs gathering of the preois	Exposure of objects in museum	Castles in ruins in England
Spanish:	Dogs urging on ewes	Objects of museum	Castles in ruins in England
Chinese:	Catches up with the sheep the dog	*no translation*	Become the ruins the English castle

Not only do the average translation adequacy scores vary across topics as shown in Fig. 1, the scores also vary across language as shown by the bar charts in Fig. 2. Although from Fig. 1 one can determine on average which topics perform better or worse, the results of Fig. 2 show that between languages results can vary dramatically (e.g. topic 2) based on at least three factors: (1) the translation resource, (2) the assessor's judgment for that topic, and (3) the difficulty of the topic itself to translate (e.g. whether it uses colloquial language, or expresses a more general or specific concept). Some topics, such as topic 22 (Ruined castles in England) score similarly between all languages, but in general we observe that translation quality varies across topic and language (see also Table 1).

Table 3 summarises translation quality for both the manual and automatic assessment. On average Spanish, German and Italian translations are rated the highest manually indicating these are the strongest to-English Systran bilingual pairings; Chinese, Dutch and French are the lowest suggesting the weakest pairs. The Systran translations for Chinese are on average the shortest and 14% of topics get a rating very bad (the third highest), and 28% of topics a rating of very good (the lowest). French has the highest number of topics rated very poor, followed by Chinese and Italian. Upon inspection, many of these low scores are from words which have not been translated.

The bar chart in Fig. 3 shows the average NIST score across all languages for each topic, and immediately we see a much larger degree of variation across topics than for the manual scores shown in Fig. 1.

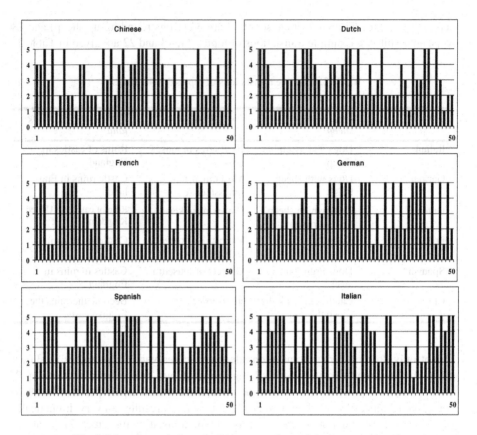

Fig. 2. Manual translation adequacy scores for each language and topic

Table 3. A summary of manual and automatic topic assessment for each source language

	Avg man score	Avg NIST score	man-NIST correlation	Mean translation length (words)	% topics man = 1	% topics man = 5	% topics NIST = 0
Chinese	3.34	1.68	0.268*	3.76	14%	28%	38%
Dutch	3.32	3.27	0.426*	4.32	8%	30%	12%
German	3.64	3.67	0.492*	3.96	8%	44%	10%
French	3.38	3.67	0.647*	4.78	24%	40%	8%
Italian	3.65	2.87	0.184	5.12	12%	50%	18%
Spanish	3.64	3.24	0.295*	4.38	6%	34%	10%

*Spearman's rho correlation significant at p<0.01

Overall, the highest automatic scores which are ≥ 5 are achieved with topics 1 (men and women processing fish), 23 (London bridge), 26 (Portraits of Robert Burns) and 49 (Musicians and their musical instruments). Topics with scores ≤ 1 are 5 (woodland scenes), 46 (Welsh national dress) and 48 (museum exhibits). Low scores are often the result of variation in the ways in which concepts are expressed in different languages. For example, in Chinese the query "coat of arms" is interpreted as "a shield" or "heraldic crest" because a direct equivalent to the original English concept does not exist. When translated back to English using Systran, more often than not the query is translated literally resulting in a low word overlap score.

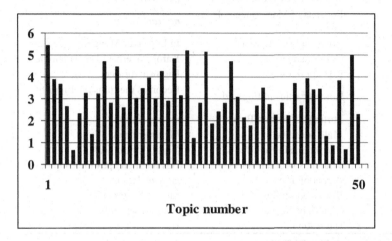

Fig. 3. Average automatic NIST adequacy score across all languages for each topic

From Table 3, Chinese also has the lowest average NIST score (1.68), which can be explained by the large proportion of topics with a zero score (38%) and the shorter average query length. Of these 38% of topics with a score of 0, 37% have no translation from Systran. From Table 3, German and French have the highest average NIST score, followed by Dutch and Spanish.

Contributing to the low Spanish scores is the high number of spelling errors in the source queries which result in non-translated words. Table 4 shows example translations with a 0 NIST score, i.e. where the reference and Systran translations have no words which overlap. In many cases, however, this is simply because different words are used to express the same concept, or lexical variations of the word (such as plurals) are used instead. For information retrieval, this is important because if a simple word co-occurrence model is used with no lexical expansion; the queries may not match documents (although in some cases stemming would help). This highlights the limitation of using mteval for assessing translation quality in CLIR because comparison is based on literal word overlap only.

These differences also contribute to the lack of statistical correlation for topics between the manual and automatic assessments (shown in Table 3). Using Spearman's rho to indicate in general whether the same topics are assigned a high or low score for both manual and automatic assessments at a statistical significance of $p<0.01$, we find that Chinese and Spanish have lowest significant correlation. For Chinese this is caused by the high number of topics with no translation, and Spanish because of spelling errors resulting in non-translated terms.

Table 4. Example translations with a NIST score of 0

	Reference translation	Systran version	Man score
Chinese	Woodland scenes	Forest scenery	5
	Scottish marching bands	*no translation*	1
	Tea rooms by the seaside	Seashore teahouse	5
	Portraits of Mary Queen of Scots	*no translation*	1
	Boats on Loch Lomond	In Luo river Mongolia lake ships	2
	Culross abbey	Karohs overhaul Daoist temple	3
	Road bridges	Highway bridge	5
	Ruined castles in England	Becomes the ruins the English castle	4
	Portraits of Robert Burns	*no translation*	4
	Male portraits	Men's portrait	5
	The mountain Ben Nevis	Nepali Uygur peak	2
	Churches with tall spires	Has the high apex the churches	4
	A coat of arms	*no translation*	1
	British windmills	England's windmill	4
	Waterfalls in Wales	Well's waterfall	2
	Harvesting	Harvests	5
French	Woodland scenes	Scenes of forests	1
	Waterfalls in Wales	Water falls to the country of Scales	1
	Harvesting	Harvest	5
	Mountain scenery	Panorama mountaineer	3
German	Glasgow before 1920	*no translation*	1
	Male portraits	Portraets of men	1
	Harvesting	Harvests	5
	Welsh national dress	Walisi tract	1
	Museum exhibits	Museumaustellungsstuecke	1
Italian	Woodland scenes	Scene of a forest	5
	Tea rooms by the seaside	It knows it from te' on lungo-mare	1
	Wartime aviation	Air in time of war	4
	British windmills	English flour mills	2
	Welsh national dress	Dressed traditional Welshman	3
	People dancing	Persons who dance	5
Spanish	Woodland scenes	A forest	5
	Wartime aviation	Aviators in time military	2
	Male portraits	Picture of a man	4
	Museum exhibits	Objects of museum	2
	Mountain scenery	Vista of mountains	1
Dutch	Woodland scenes	bunch faces	1
	Road bridges	Viaducts	4
	Men cutting peat	Turfstekers	1
	Mountain scenery	Mount landscapes	2

The correlation between scores for Italian is not significant which upon inspection is found to the use of different words from the original English to describe equivalent translations. Another contributing factor is the query length, which is generally longer (see Table 3) because of a more descriptive nature, e.g. "men cutting peat" (English) is translated as "men who cut the peat" (Italian). A further cause of non-correlation comes from words which are not translated, e.g. "Portraits of Robert Burns" (English) and "Ritratto of Robert Burns". Topics containing non-translated words are given a low manual score, but in the previous example 3 of the 4 original English terms are present which gives a high NIST score. For Dutch topics, erroneous translations are also caused by the incorrect translation of compounds (which also occurs in German). For example, the German compound "eisenbahnunglueck" is not translated.

4.2 Retrieval Performance

Fig. 4 shows a graph of recall versus precision across all topics and for each language using the *strict intersection* set of ImageCLEF relevance judgments. As with previous results for CLIR tasks, monolingual performance is the highest. Chinese has the lowest precision-recall curve, and is noticeably lower than the rest of the languages which group together and follow a similar shape. The French curve is the highest of the languages, which matches with Table 3 where French has the lowest NIST score, the least number of topics with a zero NIST score, and a high proportion of topics with a high manual assessment rating.

Fig. 5 provides a breakdown of retrieval performance across topics. The stacked bar chart shows monolingual average precision, and average precision across cross language results for each topic. Some languages perform better or worse for each topic (depending on the quality of translation), but the graph provides an overall indication of those topics which perform better or worse. Across all languages (excluding English) and topics, the MAP score is 0.420 (with a standard deviation of 0.23) which is on average 75% of monolingual performance (Table 5 shows the breakdown across languages).

Topics which perform poorly include 4 (seating inside a church), 5 (woodland scenes), 29 (wartime aviation), 41 (a coat of arms) and 48 (museum exhibits). These exhibit average NIST scores of 2.63, 0.64, 2.80, 3.71 and 3.83 respectively, and manual ratings of 3, 3.7, 4.17, 3.5 and 1.83 respectively. In some cases, the translation quality is high, but the retrieval low, e.g. topic 29, because relevance assessment for cross language image retrieval is based upon the image and caption. There are cases when images are not relevant, even though they contain query terms in the caption, e.g. the image is too small, too dark, the object of interest is obscured or in the background, or the caption contains words which do not describe the image contents (e.g. matches on fields such as the photographer, or notes which provide background meta-information).

Topic 29 (wartime aviation) and 4 (seating in a church) have very low monolingual average precision scores. For topic 29 this is because relevant images do not contain the terms "wartime" or "aviation", but rather terms such as "war", "planes", "runway" and "pilot". Relevant images for topic 29 relied on manual assessors using the interactive search and judge facility. We also find that the differences between the language of the collection and translated queries contribute to low average precision scores. This comes from two sources: (1) manual query translation and (2) the dictionary used by Systran. For example in Italian, the query "windmill" is translated manually as "mill of wind" which would match "wind" and "mill" separately. However, most captions only contain the term "windmill" and therefore do not match a query containing "wind" and "mill". The query "road bridge" is translated by Systran as "highway bridge" which will not match the collection because the only reference to a highway refers to a footpath and not a road.

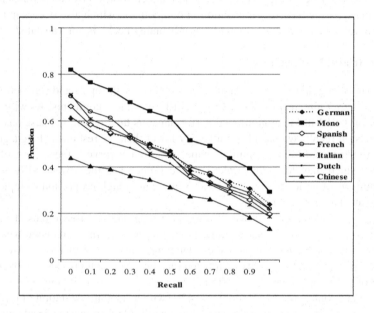

Fig. 4. Precision-recall graph for the Sheffield ImageCLEF entry

Table 5 summarises retrieval performance for each language and Spearman's rho between average precision and a number of possible influences on retrieval for each topic. We find that French has the highest MAP score (78% monolingual), followed by German (75% monolingual) and Spanish (73% monolingual). In general, average precision and translation quality is correlated (using Spearman's rho with p<0.01) for both the manual and automatic assessments which suggests that a higher quality of translation does give better retrieval performance, particularly for Chinese, German and French (manual assessments) and Spanish, French and Dutch (automatic assessments). The correlation between the manual scores and average precision scores is not significant and we find this is because of spelling errors in the Spanish source texts. In general the length of query and number of relevant document for a topic does not affect retrieval, although query length does obtain significant correlation for Chinese and Dutch. This corresponds with these languages generally having longer and more varied translation lengths (Table 3).

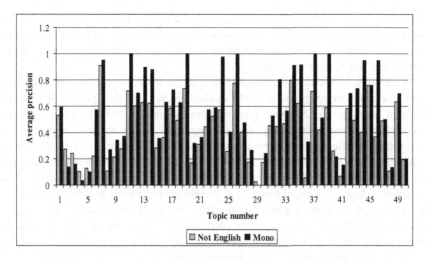

Fig. 5. Monolingual average precision and MAP across systems (excluding English)

Table 5. A summary of retrieval performance and possible influences on retrieval

	MAP	%mono	Avg Prec - man	Avg Prec - NIST	Avg Prec - query len	Avg Prec - #relevant
Chinese	0.285	51%	0.472*	0.384*	0.370*	0.159
Dutch	0.390	69%	0.412*	0.426*	0.374*	-0.165
German	0.423	75%	0.503*	0.324*	0.133	-0.281
French	0.438	78%	0.460*	0.456*	0.022	-0.046
Italian	0.405	72%	0.394*	0.378*	-0.011	-0.098
Spanish	0.408	73%	-0.061	0.462*	-0.025	0.025
Mono	0.562	-	-	-	-	-

*Spearman's rho correlation significant at p<0.01

We might expect the average precision scores to correlate well with the NIST score for the GLASS system because both are based on word co-occurrences, but it is interesting to note that retrieval effectiveness is correlated just as highly with the manual assessments (except Spanish), even though correlation between the manual and automatic assessments is not always itself high. This is useful as it shows that as a CLIR task, the quality of translation in the ImageCLEF cross language image retrieval task has a significant impact on retrieval thereby enabling, in general, retrieval effectiveness to indicate the quality of translation.

5   Conclusions and Future Work

We have shown that cross language image retrieval for the ImageCLEF ad hoc task is possible with little or no knowledge of CLIR and linguistic resources. Using Systran requires little effort, but at the price of having no control over translation or being able to recover when translation goes wrong. In particular, Systran provides only one translation version which is not always correct and provides only one alternative. There are many cases when proper names are mistranslated, words with diacritics not interpreted properly, words translated incorrectly because of the limited degree of context and words not translated at all.

We evaluated the quality of translation using both manual assessments, and an automatic tool used extensively in MT evaluation. We find that quality varies between different languages for Systran based on both the manual and automatic score which is correlated, sometimes highly, for all languages. There are limitations, however, with the automatic tool which would improve correlation for query quality in CLIR evaluation, such as resolving literal equivalents for semantically similar terms, reducing words to their stems, removing function words, and maybe using a different weighting scheme for query terms (e.g. weight proper names highly). We aim to experiment further with semantic equivalents using Wordnet and collection-based equivalents, and also assess whether correlation between the manual and automatic scores can be improved by using longer n-gram lengths.

Using GLASS we achieve cross language retrieval at 75% of the monolingual average precision score. Although Chinese retrieval is lowest at 51%, this would still provide multi-lingual access to the ImageCLEF test collection, albeit needing improvement. As the simplest approach possible, the challenge for ImageCLEF is what can be done to improve retrieval above the baseline set by Systran. Given that the task is not purely text, but also involves images, retrieval could be improved using content-based methods of retrieval, post-translation query expansion based on relevance feedback, and pre-translation query expansion based on EuroWordnet, a European version of Wordnet, and the ImageCLEF collection.

As a retrieval task, we have shown that translation quality does affect retrieval performance because of the correlation between manual assessments and retrieval performance, implying that in general, higher translation quality results in higher retrieval performance. We have also shown that for some languages, the manual assessments correlate well with the automatic assessment suggesting this automatic tool could be used to measure translation quality given a CLIR test collection.

Acknowledgments

We would like to thank members of the NLP group and Department of Information Studies for their time and effort in producing manual assessments. Thanks also to Hideo Joho for help and support with the GLASS system. This work was carried out within the Eurovision project at Sheffield University, funded by the EPSRC (Eurovision: GR/R56778/01).

References

1. Flank, S.: Cross-Language Multimedia Information Retrieval. In Proceedings of Applied Natural Language Processing and the North American Chapter of the Association for Computational Linguistics (ANLP-NAACL2000). (2000)

2. Clough, P. and Sanderson, M.: The CLEF 2003 cross language image retrieval task. This volume. (2004)
3. Hutchins, W.J. and Somers, H.: An Introduction to Machine Translation. Academic Press, London, England (1986)
4. Heisoft: How does Systran work? http://www.heisoft.de/volltext/systran/dok2/howorke.htm (2002)
5. Systran Ltd: The SYSRAN linguistics platform: A software solution to manage multilingual corporate knowledge. http://www.systransoft.com/Technology/SLP.pdf (2002)
6. Jordan, P.W., Dorr, B.J. and Benoit, J.W.: A First-Pass Approach for Evaluating Machine Translation Systems. Machine Translation, 8(1-2) (1993) 49-58
7. Voorhees, E.M. and Harman, D.: Overview of TREC 2001, In NIST Special Publication 500-250: Proceedings of TREC2001, NIST. (2001)
8. Peters, C. and Braschler, M.: Cross-Language System Evaluation: The CLEF Campaigns. In Journal of the American Society for Information Science and Technology 52(12) (2001) 1067-1072
9. Nyberg, M. and Carbonell, J.: Evaluation Metrics for Knowledge-Based Machine Translation. In Proceedings of Fifteenth International Conference on Computational Linguistics (COLING-94). (1994)
10. Patterson, C.: The Effectiveness of Using Machine Translators to Translate German and Portuguese into English when Searching for Images with English Captions. MSc dissertation for the degree of Masters of Arts in Librarianship, Department of Information Studies, University of Sheffield. (2002)
11. National Institute of Standards and Technology (NIST): Automatic Evaluation of Machine Translation Quality Using N-gram Co-Occurrence Statistics. http://www.nist.gov/speech/tests/mt/resources/scoring.htm (2002)

Foreign Name Backward Transliteration in Chinese-English Cross-Language Image Retrieval

Wen-Cheng Lin, Changhua Yang, and Hsin-Hsi Chen

Department of Computer Science and Information Engineering,
National Taiwan University, Taipei, Taiwan
denislin@nlg.csie.ntu.edu.tw
{d91013, hh_chen}@csie.ntu.edu.tw

Abstract. In this paper we propose an approach to deal with the Chinese-English cross-language image retrieval problem. Text-based image retrieval and query translation methods were adopted in the experiments. A similarity-based backward transliteration model with candidate filter was proposed to translate proper nouns that have no entries in a bilingual dictionary. The experimental results showed that using similarity-based backward transliteration increased retrieval performances.

1 Introduction

Multimedia data has an explosive growth nowadays, and more and more people are searching and using it. Searching in a large amount of data is not easy, thus the efficient retrieval of multimedia data becomes an important research issue. Two types of approaches, i.e., content-based and text-based approaches, are usually adopted. Content-based approaches use low-level visual features such as color, texture and shape to represent multimedia objects. Text-based approaches use collateral texts to describe the objects. Low-level visual features only show what the images or videos look like, but cannot tell us exactly what they are. On the other hand, text can describe the content of multimedia objects. Several hybrid approaches [12, 14, 15] that integrate visual and textual information have been proposed. Experimental results showed that the optimal technique depends on the query. The combined approach could outperform text- and content-based approaches in some cases.

Most of the previous work in image retrieval has focused on monolingual retrieval. Little work has been done on cross-language tasks. Sanderson and Clough [11] pointed out the need for cross-language image retrieval and discussed some issues in image CLIR. Images are good media in the context of cross language. People with no strong language skills can easily understand and judge the relevance of retrieved images. In this paper, we adopt a text-based approach to deal with the Chinese-English cross-language image retrieval problem. Query translation is adopted to unify the languages in queries and image captions. Proper noun processing plays an important role in query translation [1, 9]. IR systems must handle proper noun translation appropriately to achieve better performance. Bilingual dictionaries are usually

C. Peters et al. (Eds.): CLEF 2003, LNCS 3237, pp. 611–620, 2004.
© Springer-Verlag Berlin Heidelberg 2004

adopted to provide translations when translating query terms. However, proper nouns are often not listed in lexicons. We propose a similarity-based backward transliteration model to translate proper nouns not included in dictionaries.

The rest of this paper is organized as follows. Section 2 describes similarity-based backward transliteration. Section 3 shows the query translation methods. Section 4 discusses the experimental results. Finally, Section 5 provides concluding remarks.

2   Backward Transliteration

2.1   Similarity-Based Backward Transliteration

Lin and Chen [7, 8] proposed a similarity-based framework to model backward transliteration. In the similarity-based framework, the similarities of a transliterated word and candidate words are computed, and the candidate word with the highest similarity is chosen as the original word. The similarities can be measured at three levels, i.e. physical sounds, graphemes and phonemes. Comparing similarities at phoneme level has been shown to outperform the grapheme level [7, 8]. When comparing similarities at the phoneme level, the transliterated word and candidate words are first transformed into phonetic representations, i.e., International Phonetic Alphabet (IPA), and then the similarities between the IPA strings are measured.

The similarity score of two strings is the score of the optimal alignment. Given two strings S_1 and S_2, let Σ be the alphabet of S_1 and S_2, $\Sigma'=\{\Sigma, \text{'\_'}\}$, where '_' stands for space. Space could be inserted into S_1 and S_2 such that they are of equal length and denoted as $S_1{'}$ and $S_2{'}$. $S_1{'}$ and $S_2{'}$ are aligned when every character in either string has a one-to-one mapping to a character or space in the other string. The similarity score of an alignment is measured by the following formula.

$$Score = \sum_{i=1}^{l} s(S_1{'}(i), S_2{'}(i)) \tag{1}$$

where $s(a, b)$ is the similarity score between the character a and b in Σ,

$S'(i)$ is the ith character in the string S', and

l is the length of $S_1{'}$ and $S_2{'}$.

The similarity score $s(a, b)$ can be manually assigned or automatically learned. Lin and Chen [8] proposed a learning approach based on the Widrow-Hoff rule [6] to acquire phonetic similarities from a training corpus. The learning algorithm can capture subtle similarities that cannot easily be manually assigned based on phonological knowledge. The experimental results showed that learned similarities are more discriminative than manually assigned one.

The optimal alignment of two strings S_1 and S_2 can be computed efficiently using dynamic programming. Let T be an $n+1$ by $m+1$ table, where n and m are the lengths of S_1 and S_2 respectively. By filling table T row by row, we can obtain the optimal alignment and the similarity score of S_1 and S_2. The base condition is defined as follows.

$$T(i,0) = \sum_{1 \leq k \leq i} s(S_1(k),'\_') \cdot \tag{2}$$

$$T(0,j) = \sum_{1 \leq k \leq j} s('\_',S_2(k)) \cdot \tag{3}$$

The recurrence formula is defined as follows.

$$T(i,j) = \max \begin{bmatrix} T(i-1,j-1) + s(S_1(i),S_2(j), \\ T(i-1,j) + s(S_1(i),'\_'), \\ T(i,j-1) + s('\_',S_2(j)) \end{bmatrix} \cdot \tag{4}$$

where $1 \leq i \leq n$, $1 \leq j \leq m$.

2.2 Candidate Filter

Similarity based backward transliteration with automatically learned phonetic similarities works well, but will cost too much time if there are a lot of candidate words. This is not suitable for some applications like online IR systems. To reduce processing time, we use a pre-processing to decrease the number of candidates. A transliterated word and its original word should contain the same or similar phonemes, and the order of the phonemes should remain the same. In other words, if two IPA strings contain several identical or similar characters, their similarity may be higher. A vector space IR model is adopted to select the appropriate candidates for a transliterated word. The document set is the set of IPA strings of a list of proper nouns in the source language. Each proper noun is treated as one document. The query is the IPA string of the transliterated word. After retrieval, the top ranked documents (i.e., candidate words) are selected as the appropriate candidates of the transliterated word.

The transliterated word and its original word do not always contain the same phonemes due to the different pronunciation of different languages. For example, the English phoneme 'g' is usually transliterated into the Chinese phoneme 'k'[1]. If only the phonemes of the transliterated word are used as the query terms, the original word may not be retrieved. Thus, the query has to be expanded with the most co-transliterated phonemes. The co-transliterated Chinese-English phoneme pairs are trained from a Chinese-English personal name corpus, which has 51,114 pairs of Chinese transliterated names and the corresponding English original names. A variant Mutual Information is adopted to measure the strength of co-transliteration of two phonemes. The variant Mutual Information can solve the preference for rare terms problem of traditional Mutual Information [5]. Let x be a Chinese phoneme and y an English phoneme. The Mutual Information of x and y is defined as follows:

---

[1] All phonemes are represented in SAMPA, which can represent IPA in ASCII.

$$MI(x, y) = \log \frac{p(x, y)}{p(x)p(y)} \times \log(f(x, y)) \qquad (5)$$

where $p(x)$ is the occurrence probability of phoneme x in Chinese names,

$p(y)$ is the occurrence probability of phoneme y in English names,

$p(x, y)$ is the probability that x and y occur in a pair of transliterated and original names, and

$f(x, y)$ is the frequency of x and y occurring in a pair of transliterated and original names.

A phoneme x in a transliterated word will be expanded with the phonemes that have positive MI values with x. The augmented phonemes are weighted by *MI(x, y)/the number of augmented terms*.

3   Query Translation

In our experiments, Chinese queries were used as the source language queries. The Chinese queries are translated from English by native speakers. We adopted query translation to unify the languages used in queries and documents. First, the Chinese queries were segmented by a word recognition system, and tagged by a POS tagger. Name entities were then identified [3]. For each Chinese query term, we found its translation equivalents by looking up a Chinese-English bilingual dictionary. The bilingual dictionary is integrated from four resources, including the LDC Chinese-English dictionary, Denisowski's CEDICT[2], BDC Chinese-English dictionary v2.2[3] and a dictionary used in query translation in the MTIR project [1]. The dictionary contains 200,037 words, where a word may have more than one translation. We adopted the following two methods to select appropriate translations.

(1) CO model [2]

The CO model employed word co-occurrence information extracted from a target language text collection to disambiguate query term translations. We adopted traditional Mutual Information to measure the co-occurrence strength between words. The MI values of English words were trained on the TREC6 text collection [13]. For a query term, we compared the MI values of all the translation equivalent pairs (x, y), where x is the translation equivalent of this term, and y is the translation equivalent of another query term within a sentence. The word pair (x_i, y_j) with the highest MI value is extracted, and the translation equivalent x_i is regarded as the best translation equivalent of this query term. Selection is carried out on the basis of the order of the query terms.

---

[2] The dictionary is available at http://www.mandarintools.com/cedict.html

[3] The BDC dictionary is developed by the Behavior Design Corporation (http://www.bdc.com.tw).

(2) First-two-highest-frequency

The first two translation equivalents with the highest frequency of occurrence in the English image captions were considered as the target language query terms.

There are 150 distinct Chinese query terms in 50 topics. A total of 16 query terms could not be found in our dictionary. Of these 16 terms, 7 terms were tagged as personal names, and 5 terms were location names. These names are Chinese translations of foreign names. We can use a backward transliteration scheme to translate these names. First, we adopted the transformation rules [4] to identify the name part and keyword part of a name. The keyword parts are general nouns, e.g., "湖" (lake), "河" (river) and "橋" (bridge), and can be translated by looking up in the dictionary. We used the first-two-highest-frequency method to translate keywords. The name parts are transliterations of foreign names, and were transliterated into English in the following way.

(1) The personal names and the location names in the English image captions were extracted. We collected a list of English names that contained 50,979 personal names and 19,340 location names. If a term in the captions can be found in the name list, it was extracted. Total 3,599 names were extracted from the image captions.

(2) For each Chinese name, 300 candidates were selected from the 3,599 English names by using the candidate filter described in Section 2.2.

(3) The similarity-based backward transliteration approach described in Section 2.1 was adopted to translate the Chinese name. The top 6 candidates with the highest similarities were considered as the translations of the Chinese name.

In the segmentation and name identification stage, some terms were segmented or tagged incorrectly. These errors propagated to the translation stage and affected the performance of backward transliteration. In order to evaluate the real performance of similarity-based backward transliteration, we conducted manual runs in which the Chinese queries were segmented and tagged manually. In the manual runs, there are 136 distinct query terms and 18 terms have no translations. Among the 18 terms, 5 terms were tagged as person names, 9 terms were location names and 1 term was an organization name.

4 Experiments

In the experiments, we adopted a text-based approach. The captions were used to represent the images. The Okapi IR system [10] was adopted to index and retrieve the image captions. The weighting function was BM25. For each image, the caption text, <HEADLINE> and <CATEGORIES> sections were used for indexing. The words in these sections were stemmed, and stopwords were removed. The translated English queries were used to retrieve the image captions. Only the title sections of topics were used to construct queries.

We submitted eight runs in CLEF 2003 image track. The performances of two query translation methods with or without similarity-based backward transliteration were compared. The details of the submitted runs are shown in Table 1. The performances are shown in Table 2.

Table 1. Configurations of official runs

Run	Segmentation and Tagging	Query Translation	Backward Transliteration
NTUiaCo	Automatically	CO	No
NTUiaCoP	Automatically	CO	Yes
NTUiaF2hf	Automatically	First-two-highest-frequency	No
NTUiaF2hfP	Automatically	First-two-highest-frequency	Yes
NTUimCo	Manually	CO	No
NTUimCoP	Manually	CO	Yes
NTUimF2hf	Manually	First-two-highest-frequency	No
NTUimF2hfP	Manually	First-two-highest-frequency	Yes

Table 2. Results of official runs (Average Precision)

Run	Intersection Strict	Intersection Relaxed	Union Strict	Union Relaxed
NTUiaCo	0.1712	0.1876	0.1921	0.1869
NTUiaCoP	0.1892	0.2054	0.2103	0.2060
NTUiaF2hf	0.2635	0.2754	-	0.2496
NTUiaF2hfP	0.2888	0.3004	0.2852	0.2785
NTUimCo	0.1985	0.2210	0.2233	0.2219
NTUimCoP	0.2241	0.2459	0.2483	0.2475
NTUimF2hf	0.2821	0.3042	0.2808	0.2814
NTUimF2hfP	0.3143	0.3359	0.3148	0.3193

The results show that using similarity-based backward transliteration to translate proper nouns improves performance. In the automatic segmentation runs, twelve topics had proper nouns not contained in our dictionary. After applying the similarity-based backward transliteration model, the proper nouns in six topics were translated correctly, and the average precision for these topics increased dramatically. The performance of the twelve topics is shown in Table 3. Terms in square brackets are keywords extracted by transformation rules. In Topic 16, "丹地" (dan di), transliterated from "Dundee", was not translated correctly due to an error of keyword extraction. "丹地" was tagged as a location name, and "地" (di) was identified as a keyword according to the transformation rules. By dictionary look-up, "地" (di) was translated into "field" and "ground". Only "丹" (dan) was transliterated by similarity-based backward transliteration and the similarity between "丹" (dan) and "Dundee" is low. Five terms were segmented incorrectly, and thus were transliterated incorrectly.

Table 3. Performance of similarity-based backward transliteration in automatic runs (Intersection Strict)

Topic	Proper Noun	Translation Result Name	Keyword	NTUiaCo	NTUiaCoP	NTUiaF2hf	NTUiaF2hfP
3	安德魯斯 (Andrews)	Correct (rank 1)	-	0.0012	0.0216	0.0000	0.0123
9	亞當森 (Adamson)	Correct (rank 2)	-	0.0017	0.0271	0.0072	0.0477
10	克萊德 (Clyde)	Correct (rank 6)	-	0.0001	0.0870	0.0027	0.1019
12	安德魯斯 (Andrews)	Correct (rank 1)		0.0000	0.4314	0.0000	0.4293
	[北][街] (North street)	-	Correct				
14	蒙湖	Segmentation error	-	0.0188	0.0131	0.0025	0.0017
16	丹[地] (Dundee)	Keyword extraction error	-	0.0786	0.0573	0.1156	0.1165
17	茅斯	Segmentation error	-	0.0038	0.0034	0.0011	0.0011
19	卡羅斯大	Segmentation error	-	0.0000	0.0000	0.0063	0.0053
21	吉爾摩 (Gilmour)	Correct (rank 2)	-	0.0110	0.3227	0.0088	0.2416
27	灘上	Segmentation error	-	0.1425	0.0716	0.1020	0.1297
38	湯普森 (Thompson)	Correct (rank 1)	-	0.0104	0.1468	0.0444	0.4704
40	瓦倫	Segmentation error	-	0.0341	0.0185	0.0184	0.0165

In manual segmentation runs, the segmentation error problem is excluded. A total of 14 topics contain proper nouns which were not in our dictionary. The performances of seven and ten topics were increased after applying similarity-based backward transliteration model followed CO and first-two-highest-frequency models, respectively. The performances are shown in Table 4. Examining the results of backward transliteration, the original English words of about 50% Chinese proper nouns were in the top 6 ranks. Remember that the top 6 ranked terms were added to the query. One term at most was correct, the others were noise. Although noise was introduced, the performance of the topics in which the proper nouns were backward transliterated correctly improved. If the performance of backward transliteration is improved and fewer incorrect terms are added to the queries, the retrieval performance should be better. We also found that the original words of four Chinese transliterated words were not included in the name list. Thus, these original English words were not contained in the candidate lists. How to enlarge the coverage of the name list is also an important issue.

Table 4. Performances of similarity-based backward transliteration in manual runs (Intersection Strict)

Topic	Proper Noun	Translation Result		NTUimCo	NTUimCoP	NTUimF2hf	NTUimF2hfP
		Name	Keyword				
3	聖安德魯斯 (St Andrews)	Keyword extraction error	-	0.0012	0.0004	0.0002	0.0001
9	亞當森 (Adamson)	Correct (rank 2)	-	0.0017	0.0271	0.0072	0.0477
10	克萊德[河] (Clyde river)	Correct (rank 6)	Correct	0.0003	0.0974	0.0031	0.1019
12	聖安德魯斯 (St Andrews)	Keyword extraction error	-	0.0000	0.0678	0.0000	0.0678
	[北][街] (North street)	-	Correct				
14	洛蒙[湖] (Lomond loch)	Correct (rank 4)	Correct	0.0206	0.7295	0.0048	0.4463
15	泰[橋] (Tay bridge)	Has no entry in the name list	Correct	0.0210	0.0433	0.1119	0.1335
16	丹[地] (Dundee)	Keyword extraction error	-	0.0786	0.0573	0.1156	0.1165
17	[大]亞茅斯 (Great Yarmouth)	Has no entry in the name list	Wrong	0.0057	0.0025	0.0036	0.0011
19	卡羅斯 (Culross)	Has no entry in the name list	-	0.0072	0.0055	0.0044	0.0038
21	亨利耶塔 (Henrietta)	Has no entry in the name list	-	0.0233	0.3281	0.0133	0.2996
	吉爾摩 (Gilmour)	Correct (rank 2)	-				
26	勃恩斯 (Burns)	Correct (rank 3)	-	0.3571	0.3022	0.0119	0.2386
35	尼維[峰] (Nevis ben)	Wrong (rank 129)	Wrong	0.0000	0.0091	0.0000	0.0091
38	湯普森 (Thompson)	Correct (rank 1)	-	0.0104	0.1468	0.0444	0.4704
40	瓦倫坦 (Valentine)	Correct (rank 1)	-	0.0362	0.0253	0.0236	0.0175

Comparing the performances of two query translation models, surprisingly, the CO model was worse than the first-two-highest-frequency model. In the CO model, only one translation equivalent is selected for a query term. Since the image captions are very short, the suggested English translation may be not used in the captions. If we expand queries or captions, the performance may be better. On the other hand, the first-two-highest-frequency model selects the translations with the highest frequency in the target documents. Most of the English translated query terms present in the captions. The term usage is more consistent in the first-two-highest-frequency model.

5 Conclusion

In this paper we proposed an approach to deal with the Chinese-English cross-language image retrieval problem. Text-based image retrieval and query translation were adopted in the experiments. A similarity-based backward transliteration model with candidate filter was proposed to translate the proper nouns. The experimental results showed that using similarity-based backward transliteration increased the retrieval performance. The average precision of about 50% of topics containing proper nouns that are not included in dictionary were increased. The performance of the remaining topics decreased due to the failure of backward transliteration. The errors come from segmentation errors, named entity identification errors, keyword extraction errors, and the coverage of the list of names. Several methods such as learning phoneme similarity from larger data, extracting more named entities from the target document set, and improving the performance of candidate filter and keyword extraction will be further investigated to improve the performance of the similarity-based backward transliteration model.

The consistency of term usage is also an important issue. The image captions are usually short and the words used in captions are limited. Query expansion or document expansion could resolve this problem. We will experiment with various expansion approaches in the future.

References

1. Bian, G.W. and Chen, H.H.: Cross Language Information Access to Multilingual Collections on the Internet. Journal of American Society for Information Science, 51(3). (2000) 281-296.
2. Chen, H.H., Bian, G.W. and Lin, W.C.: Resolving Translation Ambiguity and Target Polysemy in Cross-Language Information Retrieval. In: Proceedings of 37th Annual Meeting of the Association for Computational Linguistics. Association for Computational Linguistics (1999) 215-222.
3. Chen, H.H., Ding, Y.W, Tsai, S.C. and Bian, G.W.: Description of the NTU System Used for MET2. In: Proceedings of 7th Message Understanding Conference. (1998).
4. Chen, H.H., Yang, C. and Lin, Y.: Learning Formulation and Transformation Rules for Multilingual Named Entities. In: Proceedings of ACL 2003 Workshop on Multilingual and Mixed Language Named Entity Recognition: Combining Statistical and Symbolic Models. Association for Computational Linguistics (2003) 1-8.

5. Church, K., Gale, W., Hanks, P. and Hindle, D.: Parsing, Word Associations and Typical Predicate-Argument Relations. In: Proceedings of International Workshop on Parsing Technologies. (1989) 389-398.
6. Duda, R.O., Hart, P.E. and Stork, D.G.: Pattern Classification. 2nd edition. Wiley-Interscience Publication (2001).
7. Lin, W.H. and Chen, H.H.: Similarity Measure in Backward Transliteration Between Different Character Sets and Its Application to CLIR. In: Proceedings of the Thirteenth Conference of Research on Computational Linguistics (ROCLING XIII). ROCLING (2000) 97-113.
8. Lin, W.H. and Chen, H.H.: Backward Machine Transliteration by Learning Phonetic Similarity. In: Proceedings of 6th Conference on Natural Language Learning. Association for Computational Linguistics (2002) 139-145.
9. Oard, D.W.: Issues in Cross-Language Retrieval from Document Image Collection. In: 1999 Symposium on Document Image Understanding Technology. (1999).
10. Robertson, S.E., Walker, S. and Beaulieu, M.: Okapi at TREC-7: Automatic ad hoc, Filtering, VLC and Interactive. In: Voorhees, E.M. and Harman, D.K. (Eds.): Proceedings of the Seventh Text REtrieval Conference (TREC-7). National Institute of Standards and Technology (1998) 253-264.
11. Sanderson, M. and Clough, P.: EuroVision - An Image-Based CLIR System. In: Proceedings of Cross-Language Information Retrieval: A Research Roadmap (Workshop at SIGIR 2002). (2002).
12. The Lowlands Team: Lazy Users and Automatic Video Retrieval Tools in (the) Lowlands. In: Voorhees, E.M. and Harman, D.K. (Eds.): Proceedings of The Tenth Text REtrieval Conference (TREC 2001). National Institute of Standards and Technology (2002) 159-168.
13. Voorhees, E.M. and Harman, D.K. (Eds.): Proceedings of the Sixth Text REtrieval Conference (TREC-6). National Institute of Standards and Technology (1997).
14. Westerveld, T.: Image Retrieval: Content versus Context. In: Proceedings of RIAO 2000, Vol. 1. (2000) 276-284.
15. Westerveld, T.: Probabilistic Multimedia Retrieval. In: Proceedings of the 25th Annual International ACM SIGIR Conference on Research and Development in Information Retrieval (SIGIR 2002). ACM Press (2002) 437-438.

Image Retrieval: The MIRACLE Approach

Julio Villena[1,2], José L. Martínez[1,3], Jorge Fombella[1], Ana G. Serrano[4],
Alberto Ruiz[4], Paloma Martínez[3], José M. Goñi[5], and José C. González[1,5]

[1] DAEDALUS, S.A.

Centro de Empresas "La Arboleda", Ctra. N-III, km 7,300 – 28031 Madrid, Spain
{jvillena,jfombella,jgonzalez}@daedalus.es

[2] Department of Telematic Engineering, Universidad Carlos III de Madrid,

Avda. Universidad 30 – 28911 Leganés, Madrid, Spain
jvillena@it.uc3m.es

[3] Computer Science Department, Universidad Carlos III de Madrid,

Avda. Universidad 30 – 28911 Leganés, Madrid, Spain
{jlmferna,pmf}@inf.uc3m.es

[4] Artificial Intelligence Department, Universidad Politécnica de Madrid,

Campus de Montegancedo s/n – 28660 Boadilla del Monte, Spain
{agarcia,aruiz}@isys.dia.fi.upm.es

[5] E.T.S.I Telecomunicación, Universidad Politécnica de Madrid,

Ciudad Universitaria s/n – 28040 Madrid, Spain
jmg@mat.upm.es, jgonzalez@dit.upm.es

Abstract. ImageCLEF is a pilot experiment run at CLEF 2003 for cross language image retrieval using textual captions related to image contents. In this paper, we describe the participation of the MIRACLE research team (Multilingual Information RetrievAl at CLEF), detailing the different experiments and discussing their preliminary results.

1 Introduction

There are two different approaches for image retrieval: content-based and text-based. Although during the last few years great efforts have been made in content-based image retrieval, it is commonly accepted that, up to now, the current state-of-the-art cannot solve the retrieval problem satisfactorily. Thus, we are focusing on text-based image retrieval, where the idea is to associate a text description with each image that describes its visual contents, and use it for the retrieval process. Cross Language Image Retrieval (CLIR) is the particular case where user queries are expressed in a language different to that of the image descriptions.

Image retrieval has its own characteristics that make it different from general text (or document) retrieval [1]. Image descriptions are usually incomplete, only showing partial aspects of the whole visual content and thus limiting the search options, and tend to be fairly short (typically image captions and/or a few keywords referring the most relevant characteristics of the image). User queries are generally more specific in image retrieval than in text retrieval [12] (users often look for images containing

C. Peters et al. (Eds.): CLEF 2003, LNCS 3237, pp. 621–630, 2004.
© Springer-Verlag Berlin Heidelberg 2004

specific contents –e.g., "fisherman in a boat"– instead of general categories –"boats"), and are even shorter than image descriptions (typically two or three words).

ImageCLEF [10] is a pilot experiment run at CLEF 2003 [11], which consists of cross language image retrieval using textual captions. A collection of nearly 30,000 black and white images from the Eurovision St Andrews Photographic Collection [10] was provided by the task coordinators. Each image had an English caption (of about 50 words). Sets of 50 topics in English, French, German, Italian, Spanish and Dutch were also provided. Non-English topics were obtained as a human translations of the original English ones, which also included a narrative explanation of what should be considered relevant for each image.

The proposed experiments were designed to retrieve the relevant images of the collection using different query languages, therefore having to deal with monolingual and bilingual image retrieval (multilingual retrieval is not possible as the document collection is only in one language). Although there are clear limitations in the current ImageCLEF task, both in the size of the collection and the number of possible experiments to be carried out (six – one monolingual and five bilingual), it represents an interesting starting point to get an idea of the performance of CLIR systems, both in monolingual and bilingual searches, and promote research into this information retrieval field.

The MIRACLE (Multilingual Information RetrievAl at CLEF) team is a joint effort of different research groups from two universities and one private company, with a strong common interest in all aspects of information retrieval and a long-lasting cooperation in numerous projects. In this paper we describe the different experiments that were submitted to the ImageCLEF 2003 campaign. The techniques applied vary from automatic machine translation, strategies for query construction, relevance feedback to topic term semantic expansion using WordNet [6]. The main objective behind the MIRACLE participation is to compare how these different retrieval techniques affect retrieval performance.

2 Description of the MIRACLE Experiments

The MIRACLE team submitted 25 runs to ImageCLEF, based on different system parameters: 5 for the monolingual English task, 6 for the bilingual Spanish to English and German to English tasks and 4 for the bilingual French to English and Italian to English tasks. All submitted runs are automatic (no human intervention in the whole retrieval process). As previously stated, all experiments are based on text-based image retrieval and make use of the image captions only.

This section contains a description of the tools, techniques and experiments that have been used for the different tasks.

The core information retrieval engine was Xapian [5], which is a free software/open source information retrieval library, released under the GPL and based on the probabilistic information retrieval model [1] [2]. We chose Xapian because it is designed to be a highly adaptable toolkit to allow developers to add advanced indexing and search facilities easily to their own applications. It integrates Snowball stemming algorithms [7] (based on the Porter algorithm [8]), and its complete implementation of the probabilistic information retrieval model allows term weighting and relevance feedback to be carried out.

In order to apply natural language processing to image descriptions and topics, ad-hoc tokenizers have been developed for each included language. They are used to identify different kinds of alphanumerical tokens such as dates, proper nouns, acronyms, etc., as well as recognising some of the common compound words from each language. Standard stopwords lists have also been used and a special word decompounding module for German has been applied. For English monolingual runs, (English) WordNet [6] has been used to expand queries with their synonyms.

Finally, for translation purposes, two available translation tools were considered: Free Translation Internet engine [3] for full text translations, and ERGANE dictionary lookup [4] for word by word translations.

At an initial stage common to all experiments, Xapian was used to index all the image descriptions in a single database. For each image, only the HEADLINE and TEXT fields were considered to create the image description, which was then tokenized, stemmed and stopword filtered with the English modules, before indexing it with Xapian.

We wanted our experiments to address the query construction and result merging issues. All of the previous modules were coupled in different ways, in order to evaluate different approaches for creating the query from the topic and to compare the influence of each one on the precision and recall of the image retrieval process. The name of each experiment reflects the techniques that were used in each case and the languages of the topics and the collection (always English).

2.1 Monolingual Experiments

In all cases, both the topic and the document language was English ("en"). Each of the 5 runs submitted consisted in one of the following base experiments (Q="query"):

- **Qor:** Intended as the baseline experiment to be compared with the results of other experiments, it consists of building the query with the combination of all the stemmed words appearing in the TITLE topic field, without stopwords, using an OR operator between them and including term weighting (the relative frequency of appearance of the stem in the topic).
- **Qorlem:** This experiment uses both the original words of the topic and the stemmed words, using the same OR operator and term weighting as before, i.e., it resembles the previous experiment but adds the original (non-stemmed) word forms. The idea behind this experiment is to try and measure the effect of inadequate word stemming.
- **Qorlemexp:** The idea behind this experiment is to perform synonym expansion of the terms and stems used in the previous Qorlem experiment, linking the newly obtained words with an OR operator, with the objective to retrieve a larger documents set (increase recall), despite a reduction in precision.
- **Qdoc:** For this experiment, a special feature of the Xapian system was used, which allowed the carrying out of queries based on documents in contrast to the indexed document collections. The query was first indexed as if it were another

image description, and then "similar documents" to this one were retrieved as results. This approach is similar to the idea of the Vector Space Model [1].

- **Qorrf:** This experiment carries out a blind relevance feedback (based on the results of a simple OR query as in the Qor experiment). The process consists of creating a query, getting the first 25 documents, extracting the 250 most important terms for those documents (top 10 keywords of each one), and constructing a new query to be carried out against the index database, which would provide the final results.

2.2 Bilingual Experiments

In all cases, the document language was English ("en"), but the topic language ranged from Spanish ("es"), German ("ge"), and French ("fr") to Italian ("it"). 20 different runs were submitted, consisting of the combination of the following base experiments with different languages (QT="query translation"):

- **QTor1:** Similar to the monolingual Qor experiment, but using the FreeTranslation tool: first, translate the full query from the source language to English with FreeTranslation, then apply the tokenizer to identify the different tokens in English, extract the stems, remove stopwords (in this case, stopstems) and finally generate a weighted-OR query with the resulting terms, as in the monolingual Qor experiment.
- **QTor3:** In this case, in addition to the translation of the complete query, a word by word translation is added, using the ERGANE dictionary lookup. The other steps (tokenizing, stemming and filtering) are the same as in the QTor1 experiment. The idea is to try to improve retrieval performance by putting together different translations for the words in the query.
- **QTdoc:** This is the bilingual equivalent of the monolingual Qdoc experiment. This time the query is first translated using FreeTranslation and the result obtained is indexed by the system as if it were just another image description. The information retrieval engine (Xapian) is then asked to retrieve similar documents to this newly added one.
- **QTor3exp:** This is the bilingual equivalent of the monolingual Qorlemexp experiment. It is basically the same as the QTor3 experiment, but adding a synonym expansion (using Wordnet) of the translated terms.
- **QTor3full:** Similar to the QTor3 experiment, but adding the original query (in the original language) to the terms used in the OR query. This way, query terms incorrectly translated or that have no proper translation into English are included in their original form (possibly being of little interest, but at least appearing).
- **TQor3fullexp:** This experiment is a combination of QTor3full and QTor3exp, using both translation engines together with the original query, adding synonym expansion for all the terms obtained.

All of these experiments were submitted for the bilingual Spanish to English and German to English tasks. For the bilingual French to English and Italian to English tasks, the semantic expansion was not included as a result of time limitations.

3 Evaluation of Results

To assess the defined experiments [10], the CLEF evaluation staff used the first 100 results of each submission (45 in all) to make a document pool (different for each query). In addition, the results of manually interactive searches were also added to each pool. Then, two different assessors evaluated all of the documents in the pools, taking into account a ternary scale: *relevant, partially relevant* and *not relevant*. The partially relevant judgment was used to pick up images which the judges thought were in some way relevant, but could not be entirely confident.

As a final step, four relevance sets were created using the relevance judgments of both judges: *union-strict* (the images of this set were the union of the ones judged as relevant by any assessor), *union-relaxed* (the union of the images judged as relevant or partially relevant by any assessor), *intersection-strict* (images judged as relevant by both assessors) and *intersection-relaxed* (images judged as relevant or partially relevant by both assessors). Strict relevance and intersection sets can be considered as high-precision results, while relaxed relevance and union sets can be thought of as results which promote higher recall.

In this section, we will present the results obtained in our experiments to reach some conclusions relative to the different approaches.

3.1 Monolingual Task

As stated before, the monolingual task consists of a set of queries in English, derived from a collection of image descriptions also in English. Figure 1 shows the recall vs. precision graph for each of the five runs we carried out for this task. The values presented correspond to the evaluation of the results, comparing them with the *intersection-strict* relevance set (the more stringent one).

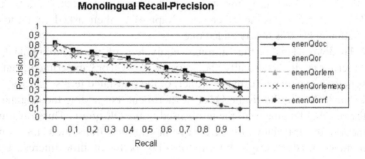

Fig. 1. Recall-Precision graph for the Monolingual task

The figure shows that the best runs have a fairly high precision value, specially taking into account that image retrieval is a difficult task. In fact, the results appear to be too high if we compare them with the monolingual document retrieval results that we obtained in the CLEF 2003 [9] monolingual tasks. Our interpretation is that the actual coverage of relevant documents was not as complete as it should have been, because of the way the relevant sets were established (based on the submissions of every group) and because only four groups took part in ImageCLEF this year. That could be the reason why such high precision values have been obtained.

The run using blind relevance feedback leads to considerably worse results than all the other strategies. A possible explanation could be that the parameter values used in the automatic relevance feedback were not appropriate to the kind of documents we were trying to retrieve. In fact, we used the top 250 terms from the first 25 images retrieved. Given that each image has a mean description field length of 50 words, it becomes quite apparent that the number of relevant terms retrieved could be excessive. Therefore, instead of helping to locate more relevant images, these terms only add noise that seriously diminishes the overall performance.

It is worth mentioning that, instead of increasing the performance of the system, using any kind of term expansion (adding original words from the topic or performing synonym expansion) only reduces the precision of the results. This could be due to the relatively low number of images in the collection, which would not make it necessary to use term expansion to minimize the effect of heterogeneous descriptions that would arise in larger collections from different sources. Perhaps this strategy could be of interest in next ImageCLEF track, which, probably, will include larger collections.

Figure 2 represents the average precision of each submitted run for all of the topics, ordered from best to worst. This graph is a simpler representation of the overall performance value for each experiment, allowing to compare the quantitative differences of each approach. It clearly shows the poor performance of our relevance feedback experiment, and the similarity of the other experiments, especially the simple weighted-OR query approach (Qor) and the query-indexing approach (Qdoc).

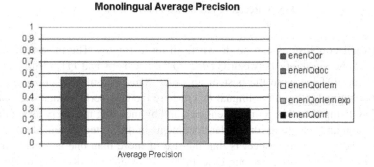

Fig. 2. Precision comparison of different runs

Although only *intersection-strict* relevance sets have been mentioned in this section, differences with the others are subtle, apart from a slight increase in the overall precision in all cases due to the larger number of relevant documents.

3.2 Bilingual Tasks

The bilingual tasks consist of the processing of queries in languages other than English, trying to retrieve relevant documents from a set of images described in English. Although queries in Spanish, Italian, German, French and Dutch were available, we only took part in tasks for the first four languages. Figure 3 shows the precision vs. recall graphs obtained for each of the runs carried out and for the language pairs (evaluating with *intersection-strict* relevance set).

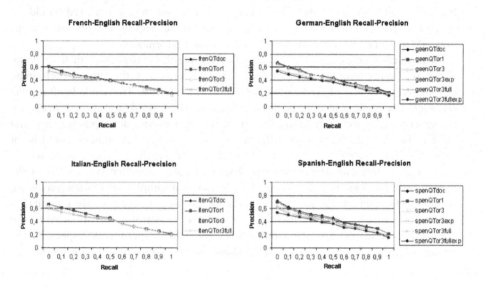

Fig. 3. Recall - Precision graphs for bilingual tasks

Several conclusions can be drawn from these figures. The most remarkable one could be the similarity between QTdoc, QTor1, QTor3 and QTor3full experiments. QTor1 and QTdoc were the best in all cases. This is somehow consistent with the results obtained in the monolingual task, where the best performance was obtained by simple OR-ing the topic terms (enenQor), and by indexing the query as another image description and searching for similar documents in the system (enenQdoc).

Another interesting aspect is that the use of more than one automatic translation has shown to be worse in our case than just using one of some quality (as the FreeTranslation has proved to be). The use of ERGANE as the word by word translator should be studied in more detail to see if it was the cause of this loss of quality (bad translations or incorporation of ambiguity of meanings) or whether this quality loss was due to the new values for the term weights modified after the inclusion of word by word translation. Our impression is that the longer the query, the worse the precision (but the better the recall, we hope). An example can be found in German to English and Spanish to English runs, in which synonym expansion is included (longer queries), leading, as expected, to worse precision values.

That precision values obtained in each task are quite similar, except for the French to English queries, which were slightly worse than the others. The explanation for this could be the poorer French to English translations provided by FreeTranslation, or the use of different terms (hardest to translate) in the French queries.

Figure 4 shows the average precision of every run, in descending order of precision and grouped by tasks. As in the case of the monolingual task, the results show little difference between the different approaches, although consistently outperformed the others. It is once more apparent that our French to English retrieval results are slightly worse than the others, while the Spanish to English has obtained the best individual results (while not the best average results in all runs).

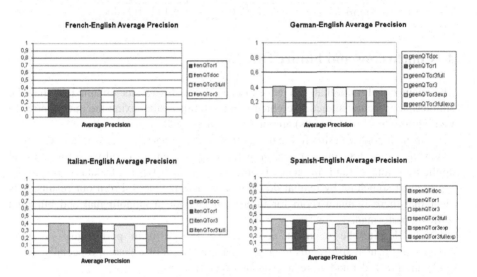

Fig. 4. Precision comparison between runs

3.3   Comparison with Other Participants

Three other groups participated in ImageCLEF 2003: the University of Surrey, the National Taiwan University (NTU), and the University of Sheffield, as the task coordinators. NTU translated the topic titles into Chinese and submitted runs for Chinese to English only, thus no comparison is possible. Although the University of Surrey submitted runs for each language, due to a misconfiguration problem with their system, the submitted results were not correct. Therefore, comparison is only fair between Sheffield and MIRACLE. The final results are shown in Table 1.

While MIRACLE obtained the best precision values in English (monolingual) and Spanish to English tasks, Sheffield exceeded our results in German and French to English. In Italian to English, the bilingual task results of the two groups were very similar.

Comparing the overall performance of the bilingual tasks with the monolingual one, there is a difference of about 10 to 15%, which is quite normal in typical CLIR nowadays. This is aligned with similar values that we have obtained in bilingual tasks of the CLEF 2003 core track [9] (as could be expected).

Table 1. Best Mean Average Precision values for each language and group

Source Language	Sheffield	MIRACLE
English	0.5616	0.5718 (Qor)
Italian	0.4047	0.4043 (QTdoc)
German	0.4285	0.4083 (QTdoc)
French	0.4380	0.3710 (QTor1)
Spanish	0.4076	0.4323 (QTdoc)

4 Conclusions and Future Directions

The main conclusion that can be extracted from the results obtained is that the simplest approaches studied (weighted-OR-ing terms and indexing the query and then looking for similar documents) are the ones which lead to better results.

Our main goal with this first participation in the ImageCLEF task was to establish a starting point for future research work in cross-language information retrieval applied to image (and in general other non-textual types of data that can be represented somehow by textual descriptions, such as video). From our results, it is clear that there is much room for improvement both in monolingual and bilingual retrieval performance.

Also, despite the apparent poor results derived from performing synonym expansion, for us it still seems to be an interesting field of research, especially for its application to wider and more heterogeneous collections.

Acknowledgements

This work has been partially supported by the projects OmniPaper (European Union, 5th Framework Programme for Research and Technological Development, IST-2001-32174) and MIRACLE (Regional Government of Madrid, Regional Plan for Research, 07T/0055/2003).

We would like to strongly thank Paul Clough for all of his support and encouragement. Furthermore, we acknowledge the great work of both the CLEF organization team, specially Carol Peters, and Sheffield University, for the coordination of ImageCLEF task.

References

1. Baeza-Yates, R., Ribeiro-Prieto B.: Modern Information Retrieval. Addison Wesley (1999).

2. SparckJones, K., Willet, P.: Readings in Information Retrieval, Morgan Kaufmann Publishers, Inc. San Francisco, California (1997).
3. Free Translation, http://www.freetranslation.com.
4. Ergane Translation Dictionaries, http://dictionaries.travlang.com.
5. The Xapian Project, http://www.sourceforge.net.
6. Miller, G.A.: WordNet: A Lexical Database for English. Communications of the ACM, 38(11):39-41 (1995).
7. Snowball Stemming Algorithms. http://snowball.tartarus.org/.
8. The Porter Stemming Algorithm. http://www.tartarus.org/~martin/PorterStemmer/.
9. Martínez, J.L., Villena, J., Fombella, J., García Serrano, A., Ruiz, A., Martínez, P., Goñi, J.M., González, J.C.: Evaluation of MIRACLE Approach Results at CLEF 2003. Working Notes for the CLEF 2003 Workshop (21-22 August, Trondheim, Norway), Vol 1 (2003).
10. Clough, P., Sanderson, M.: The CLEF 2003 Cross Language Image Retrieval Task. Working Notes for the CLEF 2003 Workshop (21-22 August, Trondheim, Norway), Vol 1 (2003).
11. Peters, C. Introduction. Working Notes for the CLEF 2003 Workshop (21-22 August, Trondheim, Norway), Vol 1 (2003).
12. Goodrum, A.A.: Image Information Retrieval: An Overview of Current Research. Informing Science, Vol 3(2):63-66 (2000).

Scene of Crime Information System:
Playing at St. Andrews

Bogdan Vrusias, Mariam Tariq, and Lee Gillam

Department of Computing, School of Electronics and Physical Sciences,
University of Surrey, Guildford, GU2 7XH, United Kingdom
{b.vrusias, m.tariq, l.gillam}@surrey.ac.uk

Abstract. This paper discusses the adaptation of the Scene of Crime Information System, developed within an EPSRC-funded project, to the collection of
data within the ImageCLEF track of the Cross Language Evaluation Forum
2003. The adaptations necessary to participate in this activity are detailed and
initial results are briefly presented.

1 The ImageCLEF Collection

ImageCLEF is concerned with the retrieval of images from a specific collection by
the captions associated to those images and is running in relation to an EPSRC-
funded project at Sheffield University (Eurovision, GR/R56778/01). The image collection consists of around 28,133 images from the photographic collection provided
by St Andrews University Library [1]. The 28,133 images are each referred to and
annotated by a single text file, and the full set of annotations is contained within one
SGML-based document[1]. Each annotation comprises identifiers to the text file and the
image files (DOCNO, SMALL_IMG, LARGE_IMG), the caption of the image
(HEADLINE), a set of categories that have been assigned to this image
(CATEGORIES), a database record identifier (RECORD_ID) and an unlabelled
chunk of text describing the image, denoted below in italics.

Example of an annotated section of the SGML-based document

```
<DOC>
<DOCNO>stand03_2093/stand03_27914.txt</DOCNO>
<HEADLINE>The Open Championship, St Andrews 1955. Dai
Rees and Max Faulkner fishing.</HEADLINE>
<TEXT>
<RECORD_ID>GMC-.000007.-.000009.-.000021</RECORD_ID>
```

---

[1] Although the file was proclaimed to be XML, a number of non-Unicode characters prevented
its parsing. It was necessary to replace these with their Hex sequences, ensuring full XML-
conformance, to use this collection.

C. Peters et al. (Eds.): CLEF 2003, LNCS 3237, pp. 631–645, 2004.
© Springer-Verlag Berlin Heidelberg 2004

Rees and Faulkner fishing. Three men in rowing boat
tied up at jetty, one holding two fishing rods, one
holding oar. July 1955 George Middlemass Cowie Fife,
Scotland GMC-7-9-21 mb/
```
<CATEGORIES>[piers and landing stages],[Fife all
views],[rowing boats],[golf - general],[golf - British
Open],[rowing],[angling],[battlefields],[fresh water
fishing],[fishing vessels],[fishing equip-
ment]</CATEGORIES>
<SMALL_IMG>stand03_2093/stand03_27914.jpg</SMALL_IMG>
<LARGE_IMG>stand03_2093/stand03_27914_big.jpg
</LARGE_IMG>
</TEXT>
</DOC>
```

The information encoded in the XML is intended for use in the retrieval task. By ranked retrieval matching, a set of up to 1000 images is to be retrieved for Task 1, automatic ad hoc retrieval, of the track, and for other purposes in Task 2, interactive image retrieval, of the track. The above XML fragment refers to the image shown below (Fig.1.), of three men in a boat.

Fig. 1. Example image from the ImageCLEF collection

From the above example, it is apparent that some of the categories assigned to the images may not be wholly reliable.

While some of the associations are clear as shown in Table 1., others could be associated to information that appears, but is not in the correct context – the combination of "Open Championship" and "St Andrews" being candidates for explaining the golfing categories – while the assignment of a "battlefields" category is less easily obvious.

Table 1. This table lists categories that can obviously be associated to specific features observed in the image shown above in Fig.1

Image feature	Category
jetty	piers and landing stages
Fife	Fife all views
rowing (boat)	rowing boats, rowing, fishing vessels
fishing (rods)	angling, fresh water fishing, fishing equipment

2 Task 1: Automatic Ad hoc Retrieval

The automatic ad hoc retrieval task aims at the ranked-retrieval of up to 1000 images from the Eurovision collection. The images are to be retrieved in response to a set of pre-formulated queries. The queries themselves comprise of 50 topics. Each topic has an English query, plus narrative description of the expected result of the query, and the English query has been translated into 5 other languages, French, German, Spanish, Italian and Dutch. Some queries have more than one translation for a given language.

The retrieval results are to be assessed by personnel from the University of Sheffield such that they can be evaluated using the trec_eval program with recall and precision metrics. Similar to TREC, the results will subsequently be published.

An example topic encoded in XML[2] is shown below:

```
<top>
<num>Number: 25</num>
<EN-title n="1">Golf course bunkers</EN-title>
<EN-narr>A relevant image will show a picture of a golf
course in which a bunker can be clearly identified. The
picture must be a photograph or a postcard, but not a
drawing, e.g. a plan of the golf course. A bunker is a
sandy hollow formed by wearing away of the turf, or
nowadays an artificial sand-hole with a built-up face.
An example relevant document is
[stand03_1714/stand03_7020].</EN-narr>
</top>
<top>
<num>Number: 25</num>
<DE-title n="1">Golfplatz Bunker</DE-title>
</top>
<top>
<num>Number: 25</num>
<FR-title n="1">Bunkers de terrain de golfe</FR-title>
</top>
```

---

[2] Similar character issues as reported previously were also fixed for this collection.

```
<top>
<num>Number: 25</num>
<IT-title n="1">Un bunker in un percorso di golf</IT-
title>
<IT-title n="2">bunkers in un campo di golf</IT-title>
</top>
<top>
<num>Number: 25</num>
<ES-title n="1">B&#x00FA;nkers en un campo de golf</ES-
title>
<ES-title n="2">Pista de golf</ES-title>
</top>
<top>
<num>Number: 25</num>
<NL-title n="1">Bunkers op een golfbaan</NL-title>
</top>
```

The example shown is for Topic 25, for which Golf course bunkers has been translated once into each of German, French and Dutch, and twice each for Spanish and Italian. With multiple translations for some languages for the 50 topics, we have the following number of queries for the various languages:

Table 2. The table below shows the number of queries for each language. These total 421 queries are to be made against the 28,133 annotations to retrieve images from the collection

Language	Number of Queries
Spanish	117
English	50
French	51
Italian	103
German	50
Dutch	50
Total	421

3 The SoCIS Archetype

The EPSRC-funded Scene of Crime Information System (SoCIS) project was run from October 1999 to March 2003. The aim of the project was to study the link between images and texts within a specialist domain context. A method has been outlined for developing an intelligent content-based image retrieval (CBIR) system, which can store and retrieve images based on the linguistic descriptions of the images. The corpus-based method uses the lexical and semantic properties of specialist texts for extracting key terms and for discovering the ontological organisation of the terms.

A prototype CBIR system was developed in the Java programming language for demonstrating the efficacy of the corpus-based method. The system, which is based on a 3-tier architecture of client, server, and database, can be accessed via a local intranet. SoCIS is an intelligent CBIR system that automatically: (a) labels (and *indexes*) images by keywords as well as relational facts extracted from the descriptions provided by domain experts; (b) extracts physical features of an image; (c) populates a database comprising domain-specific terminology, together with the semantic relationships between terms, starting from a random selection of collateral texts of the domain; and (d) learns to link image and text by using neural networks [2]. SoCIS has integrated modules from (a) System Quirk [3] - a set of tools for building and managing multilingual term bases with the use of powerful text analysis techniques, and (b) GATE [4] - a framework and graphical development environment comprising NLP tools. The main advantages that SoCIS can be said to have over other text-based and CBIR systems is its ability to extract information from both texts and images, to encode this information for indexing, and to build thesauri, all automatically.

The SoCIS prototype[3] was evaluated using images normally used for the training of Scene of Crime Officers (SoCOs) together with a description provided by the SoCOs as well as other collateral texts like crime scene reports and forensic science research papers and manuals. The question of (inter) indexer-variability, the variances in the output of different indexers for the same image, has been explored in the project [5]. This study further reinforced the need for automatic thesauri construction to aid in query expansion [6].

4 Adapting SoCIS

SoCIS was specifically targeted at the use of specialist languages – or Languages for Special Purposes (LSP) [3], [7]. The system has been built based on the knowledge gathered from Scene of Crime experts, from the testing and evaluation sessions performed with them, and from a domain-specific text corpus. The system had to be adapted to deal with multilinguality as well as structured data from a more general domain for the ImageCLEF collection. SoCIS does not have a translation tool so the translation of the queries from the other languages to English had to be carried out offline as discussed in section 4.1. A parser had to be written to extract the various fields containing textual information (in English) about the images from the provided XML document that could be used for indexing purposes. The indexing module was used to extract single and compound terms from the output of the parser. The main difficulty we encountered (see section 4.2) was the creation of a terminology dictionary and thesaurus related to the general domain, which is needed for the automatic indexing and query expansion modules. We decided to use WordNet (http://www. cogsci.princeton.edu/~wn/) for query expansion purposes but the indexing had to be carried out without using a terminology dictionary to filter out invalid terms. A new relevance ranking mechanism, which is briefly described in section 4.3, was adopted to handle the expanded terms retrieved from WordNet.

---

[3] http://www.surrey.ac.uk/socis.

4.1 Handling Multi-linguality

The first step necessary was the translation of the various queries to English. Without in-house software, we relied upon translation engines as found on the Internet. Some work was done in an attempt to exploit Google's translation tools for this purpose, however there were difficulties encountered in this. Eventually, Altavista's Babelfish was selected as the principal translation engine (http://babelfish.altavista.com/), however since this system does not translate Dutch, FreeTranslation.com (http://www.freetranslation.com/) was also used.

To translate the queries, Java code was used to wrap definitions of the query syntax used by these sites (with the HTTP POST command being used in both cases). Each query was posted to the site with its requested translation language pair, and the HTML result was retrieved. Using the Java JTidy utility, the resulting HTML was converted to XML [8], and XSLT [9] employed to strip out the end result of the translation.

Table 3. The results of translating the various languages for topic number 25 (Golf course bunkers) are shown in the table below

Language	Translation into English
German	Golf course shelter
French	Bunkers of ground of gulf
Italian (1)	A bunker in a distance of golf
Italian (2)	Bunkers in a golf course
Spanish (1)	B??nkers in a golf course
Spanish (2)	Track of golf
Dutch	Bunkers on a wave job

Immediately it can be seen that certain of these translations will cause problems with the retrieval. The topic identifies the image stand03_1714/stand03_7020 as being relevant. In the run, this was located only for English, Italian (2), and Dutch at ranks 798, 798 and 45 respectively. The quality of returned translation will therefore have a significant impact on the results being returned.

4.2 Synonymy and Morphology

The thesaurus construction module of SoCIS was developed to provide a query expansion facility for the system. There are general-purpose thesauri or lexicons available such as WordNet, which could be used but are inadequate in specialist domains due to a deficiency in specialized terminology. For example, the two key compound terms 'forensic science' and 'crime scene' are not present in WordNet. The method we developed was based on the analysis of a representative domain-specific text corpus to automatically extract key terms and relationships, which were then used to build the thesaurus [6] [10]. Since the ImageCLEF collection comprised of a wide range of mainly general topics such as buildings, golfers, animals, boats and so on, to apply our method we would have had to construct and analyze a corpus representing most of general knowledge, a clearly difficult and unpractical task. We decided that WordNet could be a possible resource to use for query expansion since its coverage is based on a general English dictionary.

A program was written to query a WordNet database to provide a set of synonyms and hyponyms for each of the query terms. In WordNet, English nouns, verbs, adjectives and adverbs are ordered into synonym sets (synsets). Each synset can be said to contain the words that represent a specific concept. The synsets are then linked to each other based on semantic relations such as antonymy, hyponymy and meronymy. Given a query term, the program returns all the words in the synset that the particular term is an element of, as well as all the hyponyms of each synset element to a specified level in the hierarchy. Initially we planned to go down 2 levels in the hierarchy but ended up using just the synonyms due to system performance issues related to the large number of expanded terms returned, which is discussed in section 5. Taking the query "Boats on Loch Lomond" as an example, the term 'boat' returned 53 expanded words going down one level in the hierarchy. Some synonyms returned were: *travel on water, sauceboat, gravy boat*; some hyponyms returned included *motorboat, mail boat, mailboat gondola, propel by oars, propel by paddles, yacht*, and so on. 'Loch' returned one synonym *lough* while 'Lomond' was not present since it is a proper noun. The very common term 'man' had 131 expanded words going down one level and 344 expanded words going down two levels with words such as *private, make swollen, belly out, candy striper, Homo erectus, clothes horse, ridicule with a satire*, and *gentleman*.

Some basic morphological analysis was also carried out for each query term to account for the use of variants such as singular or plural terms as well as the verb or adjective forms. The morphology module uses standard rules (for example if a word ends with 'ss' or 'h' then the plural form is usually derived by adding an 'es') as well as some common exceptions (for example the plural of ~man will be ~men). This was also important for the query expansion part since WorldNet only has singular forms of words as part of the synsets so a plural word used as the query term will return no results.

4.3 Relevance Ranking

For the query process, we considered three types of keywords: the original query keywords entered by the user, the expanded new keywords populated by WordNet, and the compound terms extracted from the stored captions that contain any of the query terms. Each keyword carried a proportion of its frequency in an annotation divided by the total number of terms allocated to this annotation. The query keyword frequency f was then multiplied with weight $w=1$, each expanded term (synonyms) returned by WordNet with weight $w=0.9$, and words (compound terms) containing substrings of the query keywords with weight $w=0.1$. The total ranking was then given by:

$$Rank = \sum \left(\frac{f_{td} \times w_t}{N_d} \right) \qquad (1)$$

Where f_{td} is the term frequency of term t in document d, w_t is the weight of a term t as described previously, and N_d is the total number of words in document d.

The choice on the weighting w of each type of keyword was decided when analyzing the results after several query trials, although the query keyword weighting was always kept at 1. The choice of an appropriate weight is very important as it affects the final results significantly. For instance decreasing the weights of the synonyms, and compound terms, will give more precision, whereas increasing these weights will give more recall.

5   Performance Issues

The main factor to have an effect on the performance of SoCIS was that the system has been designed for the analysis of free text in specialist domains whereas with the ImageCLEF collection we were dealing with structured texts in a general domain. This resulted in difficulties for SoCIS when indexing the images – the indices produced were relatively unreliable due to the different syntactic structure of the Image-CLEF text when compared to free text, which also affected the ranking. One example here is that the system considered all the category terms given by the ImageCLEF description in the XML document (since they where enclosed in square brackets) as a single compound term. Also due to the fact that we used WorldNet for query expansion, we encountered problems associated with polysemous words as well as different word forms (see the example of *boat* and *man* in section 4.2). Due to the amount of time it was taking to process the expanded queries (some times reaching up to 300 words, see section 4.2) we had to limit the expansion to just synonyms of the original query terms. Even so we had six computers running in parallel to finish the processing, which was taking approximately 8 hours per language.

6   Results and Evaluation

Although the combination of features outlined above would require significant efforts to develop as a usable real-world system (parallelization and optimization issues at least), the combination of technologies and techniques presented did enable participation in the ImageCLEF track. A system that in principle would allow a user to query a collection of images that have been annotated in English, using a query in one of six languages has been prototyped from this combination. According to the abstract from the Eurovision project, such a system had not been implemented or researched. Though far from perfect, the evaluation of the results obtained at this stage is important (Table 4).

From a selection of topics, we should evaluate where the exemplar image is ranked and the relevance of the top 10 images retrieved to the query.

Table 4. Across all languages, the following sets of results were obtained (missing topics and quantities for that topic are given in the third column)

Language	Query No.	Missing topic (Quantity)
Spanish	105 / 117	32 (3), 33 (1), 34 (1), 36 (1), 39 (2), 43 (3), 47 (1)
English	48 / 50	40, 46
French	47 / 51	7, 17, 25
Italian	91 / 103	13 (2), 17 (1), 27 (3), 29 (2), 31 (1), 39(1), 43 (1), 45 (1)
German	43 / 50	4, 7, 13, 27, 40, 46, 48
Dutch	38 / 50	5, 7, 13, 17, 18, 20, 27, 29, 36, 39, 40, 43
Total	372 / 421	

Table 5. This table shows the numbers of the 6 topics chosen with the captions and the 2 exemplar images for each of the topics

Query	Caption	Exemplar
7	Home guard on parade during World War II	stand03_1955/ stand03_24985
14	Boats on Loch Lomond	stand03_1346/ stand03_15600
21	Animals by the photographer Lady Henrietta Gilmour	stand03_1955/ stand03_5603
28	Pictures of golfers in the nineteenth century	stand03_2036/ stand03_7549
35	The mountain Ben Nevis	stand03_1643/ stand03_4692
42	University buildings	stand03_1853/ stand03_21431

Table 6. The table below shows the results from running the 6 queries through the system

Query	Language and Rank
7	Not found
14	Not found
21	Dutch [884], English [408], Spanish [408, 274, 884], French [408], German [764], Italian [408, 700]
28	Italian [179]
35	French [886], Italian [361]
42	Dutch [971]

For this selection of 6 topics, the exemplar image is only found for English for topic 21. This is an initially disappointing result. We consider, first, the top image being retrieved for each of these topics in the various languages. The next six tables (Table 7. to Table 12.) show the results obtained.

Table 7. The top images retrieved for English

Query	Image IDs	Image captions
7 (En)	stand03_1749/stand03_22144	Littlehampton. The **Parade**.
14 (En)	stand03_1502/stand03_16737	The Castle, **Loch** an Eilein
21 (En)	stand03_1675/stand03_22740	Engraving of a painting of a Biblical scene, [Noah, family and the Ark at Mount Ararat].
28 (En)	stand03_1714/stand03_7540	Old Tom Morris, **golfer**, St Andrews. (*ca 1900)*
35 (En)	stand03_1851/stand03_7899	Trossachs. Loch Achray, Trossachs Church and Ben An or Binnein (**Ben** A 'an).
42 (En)	stand03_1590/stand03_28349	Samuel Messieux, refugee from Paris and teacher of French at Madras **College**.

Table 8. The top images retrieved for French

Query	Image IDs	Image captions
7 (Fr)	No results	
14 (Fr)	stand03_1853/stand03_12134	**Boat** of Garten.
21 (Fr)	stand03_1675/stand03_22740	Engraving of a painting of a Biblical scene, [Noah, family and the Ark at Mount Ararat].
28 (Fr)	stand03_2046/stand03_13818	Kingsbarns. Old Grave Stone, Kingsbarns Churchyard.
35 (Fr)	stand03_1851/stand03_7899	Trossachs. Loch Achray, Trossachs Church and Ben An or Binnein (**Ben** A 'an).
42 (Fr)	stand03_1590/stand03_28349	Samuel Messieux, refugee from Paris and teacher of French at Madras **College**.

Table 9. The top images retrieved for German

Query	Image IDs	Image captions
7 (De)	No results	
14 (De)	stand03_1857/stand03_9586	View of **ship** at **sea**.
21 (De)	stand03_1675/stand03_22740	Engraving of a painting of a Biblical scene, [Noah, family and the Ark at Mount Ararat].
28 (De)	stand03_2046/stand03_13818	Kingsbarns. Old Grave Stone, Kingsbarns Churchyard.
35 (De)	stand03_1851/stand03_7899	Trossachs. Loch Achray, Trossachs Church and Ben An or Binnein (**Ben** A 'an).
42 (De)	stand03_2054/stand03_18895	Motherwell. Town Hall.

Table 10. The top images retrieved for Italian

Query	Image IDs	Image captions
7 (It)	stand03_1587/stand03_28525	[Walker family?] Untitled portrait of a man.
14 (It)	stand03_1502/stand03_16737	The Castle, **Loch** an Eilein
21 (It)	stand03_1675/stand03_22740	Engraving of a painting of a Biblical scene, [Noah, family and the Ark at Mount Ararat].
28 (It)	stand03_2046/stand03_13818	Kingsbarns. Old Grave Stone, Kingsbarns Churchyard.
35 (It)	stand03_1778/stand03_4502	Launch X.
42 (It)	stand03_2054/stand03_18895	Motherwell. Town Hall.

Table 11. The top images retrieved for Spanish

Query	Image IDs	Image captions
7 (Es)	stand03_1587/stand03_7524	Man in theatrical costume. [St Andrews ?].
14 (Es)	stand03_1853/stand03_12134	**Boat** of Garten.
21 (Es)	stand03_1675/stand03_22740	Engraving of a painting of a Biblical scene, [Noah, family and the Ark at Mount Ararat].
28 (Es)	stand03_2046/stand03_13818	Kingsbarns. Old Grave Stone, Kingsbarns Churchyard.
35 (Es)	stand03_2092/stand03_14170	Lochgilphead. Crinan Canal at
42 (Es)	stand03_1590/stand03_28349	Samuel Messieux, refugee from Paris and teacher of French at Madras **College**.

Table 12. The top images retrieved for Dutch

Query	Image IDs	Image captions
7 (Nl)	stand03_1587/stand03_7524	No results
14 (Nl)	stand03_1502/stand03_16737	The Castle, **Loch** an Eilein
21 (Nl)	stand03_1974/stand03_11773	Brompton Oratory. Altar of Our Lady of Good Counsel.
28 (Nl)	stand03_2046/stand03_13818	Kingsbarns. Old Grave Stone, Kingsbarns Churchyard.
35 (Nl)	stand03_1853/stand03_21295	Fettercairn. Cairn o' Mount and Clatterin' Brig
42 (Nl)	stand03_2054/stand03_18895	Motherwell. Town Hall.

These tables of results show some interesting features. For Topic 7, 3 of the queries returned no results, while those that did have a different first result. For topic 14, 5 of the 6 results refer to just 2 images. For topic 21, all but the Dutch results refer to the same image. For topic 28, all but the English result refer to the same image, however judging by the caption, the English result is the best. For topic 35, one image is referred to in 3 results. For topic 42, 2 images are equally referred to. For Topic 14, the top 5 results have been taken once for each language, and the similarity matrix between these results is shown in Table.

Table 13. Similarity matrix of results across the 6 languages

	En	Fr	De	Es	It	Nl	Total
16737	2	1		1	2		4
12134	1				1	1	3
14211	3				3	2	3
22301	4				4	3	3
16430	5				5	5	3
29031			3	3			2
16014			4	4			2
12138			5	5			2
16009		2					1
9586		3					1
9587		4					1
4618		5					1
13150			1				1
16833			2				1
5702				2			1
20573						4	1

The top 5 results show degrees of similarity between the English, Italian and Dutch results, with German and Spanish showing similarities, and French showing the most marked behavioural difference. This top 5 have captions as follows:

The Castle, Loch an Eilein
Boat of Garten.
Dunkeld. Loch of Craiglush and Creag nam Mial (Creagnam Hill).
Linlithgow Palace and Loch, from the air.
Bearsden. St Germain's Loch.

It would appear that a number of Lochs, apart from Loch Lomond with any boats on have been discovered in response to this query! Indeed, none of the 16 results above make mention of Lomond.

From this, it is apparent that although similar behaviour is achieved for certain language translations, the end result of retrieval is not correctly weighted. The initial concern that translation would have a significant bearing on retrieval is perhaps now not so relevant as the retrieval itself.

Taking a list of the exemplar images for retrieval, the ranking (where it exists) of that image within the 1000 results for each language was considered. For each language, if the exemplar image was retrieved within the first 1000, this was counted. If it was retrieved within the top 100 results, this was also noted. The following table presents the results obtained.

Table 14. Ranking obtained for the top 1000 and top 100 results

Lang.	top 1000	# queries	High	Low	Ave	top 100
Nl	20	50	17	971	319.55	7
De	21	50	11	973	309.05	11
En	28	50	8	798	257.96	12
Fr	33	51	11	995	337.52	11
It	42	103	1	967	353.14	14
Es	51	117	7	884	314.52	19

For two queries in Italian, both for Topic 19, the exemplar image was retrieved in first place. This is certainly a result of interest given the analysis of other results in this paper. In the above table, the first column represents the language code, the second the amount of exemplar images retrieved in the 1000 results, the third is the amount of queries, the fourth and fifth show the highest and lowest ranking of the exemplars, with the sixth column showing the average ranking. Column 7 shows the quantity of exemplars occurring in the first 100 retrieved results. This set of results tends to indicate that there is some value to the approach taken here, but how that compares to other approaches remains to be seen.

7 A Note on Text and Image Retrieval

Increasingly, images are being indexed and retrieved by both their visual content and by related texts such as captions that describe the image [11], [12], [13], [14]. Image descriptors extracted directly from image data (colour, texture and shape) tend to capture little of an image's semantic content [15], [16] – hence there is a need to extract information about the image content from *collateral* texts [6], [17], [18], [19].

8 Future Work

Numerous improvements suggest themselves, for example if the system could be grid-enabled then the different processing modules, as well as instances of the same module, could be run as a service, in parallel, which would significantly improve the processing time. The ranking mechanism needs to be further refined and tuned by carrying out more trial runs. WordNet was not very effective for the purpose of query expansion, as most of the expanded terms returned were conceptually irrelevant to the original query. To improve the query expansion one suggestion could be to use part-of-speech information from the query sentence to filter out some of the irrelevant expanded terms returned from WordNet – for example in the query "Boats on loch Lomond", the term boat is being used in the noun and not the verb form so the synonyms (*propel by oars, propel by paddles*) related to the verb form of *boat* would not be retrieved. Otherwise, an attempt could be made to analyze the British National Corpus (http://www.hcu.ox.ac.uk/BNC), which might perhaps yield only the more frequently used term associations.

Since the system deals with image retrieval, we are investigating methods of effectively combining text-based with image-based retrieval techniques. The physical features of an image such as colour, texture, and shape can be extracted and used in combination with the text features. This technique when incorporated into a system that learns how to index would result in a significant improvement in performance [20]. We are also investigating the creation of multimedia thesauri, based on Picard's initial work [21]. The premise here is that since specialist texts can be said to be a reflection of the ontological commitment of domain experts, specialist images may also reflect some form of ontological commitment on the part of the expert. Also, objects depicted in specialist images often represent the same concepts that are represented by lexical units in texts. The method discussed in [2] could help in establishing the link between an image and text.

Acknowledgements

This work was partially funded by the European Union through the Generic Information-based Decision Assistant (GIDA: IST-2000-31123) Projects and the EPSRC through the Scene of Crime Information System (SOCIS: GR/M89041/01) project.

References

1. Clough, P., Sanderson, S., Reid, N.: The Eurovision St Andrews Photographic Collection (ESTA). http://ir.shef.ac.uk/imageclef/guide.pdf (2003)
2. Ahmad, K., Vrusias, B., Tariq, M.: Co-operative neural networks and integrated classification. In: Proceedings of the International Joint Conference on Neural Networks. Hawaii, USA, May 2002. IEEE Press (2002)
3. Ahmad, K., Rogers, M.: Corpus linguistics and terminology extraction. In: Wright S.E., Budin G. (eds.): Handbook of Terminology Management, Vol. 2. Benjamins, Amsterdam/Philadelphia (2001) 725-760
4. Cunningham, H., Maynard, D., Bontcheva, K., Tablan, V.: GATE: A framework and graphical development environment for robust NLP tools and applications. In: Proceedings of the 40th Anniversary Meeting of the Association for Computational Linguistics (2002)
5. Handy, C.J., Ahmad, K.: Indexer Variability in Visual Domains. To appear in: Proceedings of the 13th LSP Conference, Guildford, Surrey, August 2003 (2003)

6. Ahmad, K., Tariq, M., Vrusias, B., Handy C.: Corpus-Based Thesaurus Construction for Image Retrieval in Specialist Domains. In: Sebastiani, F. (ed.): Proceedings of the 25th European Conference on Information Retrieval Research, ECIR-03. Lecture Notes in Computer Science, Vol. 2633. Springer-Verlag, Berlin Heidelberg New York (2003a) 502-510

7. Harris, Z.S.: Language and Information. In: Nevin, B. (ed.): Computational Linguistics, Vol. 14, No. 4. Columbia University Press, New York (1988) 87-90

8. Bray, T., Paoli, J., Sperberg-McQueen, C.M., Maler, E. (eds.): Extensible Markup Language (XML), Ver. 2.0. W3C Recommendation. http://www.w3.org/TR/REC-xml (2000)

9. Clark, J. (ed.): XSL Transformations (XSLT), Version 1.0. W3C Recommendation. http://www.w3.org/TR/xslt (1999)

10. Tariq, M., Manumaisupat, P., Al-Sayed, R., Ahmad, K.: Experiments in Ontology Construction from Specialist Texts. In: Proceedings of EUROLAN Workshop: Ontologies and Information Extraction, Bucharest, Romania, July 28 -August 08 (2003) 55-64

11. Srihari R.K.: Use of Collateral Text in Understanding Photos. Artificial Intelligence Review (Special Issue on Integrating Language and Vision), Vol. 8 (1995) 409-430

12. Srihari, R.K., Zhang, Z., Show&Tell: a Semi-Automated Image Annotation System. IEEE Multimedia, Vol.7, No. 3 (2000) 61-71.

13. Paek, S., Sable, C.L., Hatzivassiloglou, V., Jaimes, A., Schiffman, B.H., Chang, S-F., McKeown, K.R.: Integration of visual and text based approaches for the content labelling and classification of Photographs. ACM SIGIR'99 Workshop on Multimedia Indexing and Retrieval, Berkeley, California, USA (1999)

14. Barnard, K., Forsyth, D.: Learning the Semantics of Words and Pictures. International Conference on Computer Vision, Vol. 2. (2001) 408-415

15. Squire, McG.D., Muller, W., Muller, H., Pun, T.: Content-Based Query of Image databases: Inspirations from Text Retrieval. Pattern Recognition Letters, Vol. 21. No. 13-14. Elsevier Science, Netherlands (2000) 1193-1198

16. Eakins, J.P.: Towards intelligent image retrieval. Pattern Recognition, Vol. 35 (2002) 3-14

17. Smeulders, A.W.M., Worring, M., Santini, S., Gupta, A., Jain, R.: Content-Based Image Retrieval at the End of the early Years. IEEE Transactions on Pattern Analysis and Machine Intelligence, Vol. 22, No. 12. IEEE Press (2000) 1349-1380.

18. Gillam, L., Ahmad, K. Salway,.: Digital Heritage and the use of Terminology. Proceedings of 6th International Conference Terminology and Knowledge Engineering (TKE) (2002)

19. Salway, S., Frehen, J.: Words for Pictures: analysing a corpus of art texts. Proceedings of 6th International Conference Terminology and Knowledge Engineering (TKE) ISBN 2-7261-1217-X (2002)

20. Ahmad, K., Casey, M., Vrusias, B., Saragiotis, P.: Combining Multiple Modes of Information Using Unsupervised Neural Classifiers". In: Windeatt, T. Roli, F. (eds.): Proceedings of Multiple Classifier Systems 4th Int. Workshop. Lecture Notes in Computer Science, Vol. 2709. Springer-Verlag, Berlin Heidelberg New York (2003) 236-245

21. Picard, R.W.: Towards a Visual Thesaurus. In: Ian Ruthven (ed.): Springer-Verlag Workshops in Computing, MIRO 95, Glasgow, Scotland (1995)

The CLEF 2003 Cross-Language Spoken Document Retrieval Track

Marcello Federico[1] and Gareth J. F. Jones[2]

[1] ITC-irst, Trento, Italy
[2] Dept. of Computer Science, University of Exeter, U.K.

Abstract. The current expansion in collections of natural language based digital documents in various media and languages is creating challenging opportunities for automatically accessing the information contained in these documents. This paper describes the CLEF 2003 track investigation of Cross-Language Spoken Document Retrieval (CLSDR) combining information retrieval, cross-language translation and speech recognition. The experimental investigation is based on the TREC-8 and TREC-9 SDR evaluation tasks, augmented to form a CLSDR task. The original task of retrieving English language spoken documents using English request topics is compared with cross-language information retrieval using French, German, Italian, Spanish and Dutch topic translations.

1 Introduction

In recent years much independent research has been carried out on multimedia and multilingual information retrieval. The most extensive work in multimedia information retrieval has concentrated on spoken document retrieval from monolingual (almost exclusively English language) collections, generally using text search requests to retrieve spoken documents. Speech recognition technologies have made impressive advances in recent years and these have proven to be effective for indexing spoken documents for spoken document retrieval (SDR). The TREC SDR track ran for 4 years from TREC-6 to TREC-9 and demonstrated very good performance levels for SDR [2]. In parallel with this, there has been much progress in cross-language information retrieval (CLIR) as exemplified by the CLEF workshops. Good progress in these separate areas means that it is now timely to explore integrating these technologies to provide multilingual multimedia IR systems.

Following on from a preliminary investigation carried out as part of the CLEF 2002 campaign, a Cross-Language Spoken Document Retrieval (CLSDR) track was organized for CLEF 2003. Developing a completely new task for this track was beyond available resources, and so the track built on the work from the CLEF 2002 pilot track [3] and is mainly based on existing resources. These existing resources, kindly made available by NIST, were used for the TREC 8 and 9 monolingual SDR tracks [2]. Hence, the track results are closer to a benchmark than to a real evaluation.

C. Peters et al. (Eds.): CLEF 2003, LNCS 3237, pp. 646–652, 2004.
© Springer-Verlag Berlin Heidelberg 2004

In particular the NIST collection consists of:

- a collection of automatic transcripts (557 hours) of American-English news recordings broadcasted by ABC, CNN, PRI (Public Radio International), and VOA (Voice of America) made between February and June 1998. Transcripts are provided both with unknown story boundaries, and with known story boundaries (21,754 stories).
- two sets of 50 English topics (one each from TREC-7 and TREC-8) either in terse or short format.
- manual relevance assessments.
- scoring software for the known/unknown story boundary condition.

The TREC collections have been extended to a CLSDR task by manually translating with the short topics into five European languages: Dutch, Italian, French, German, and Spanish.

2   Track Specifications

The track aimed at evaluating CLIR systems on noisy automatic transcripts of spoken documents with known story boundaries. The following specifications were defined about the data and resources that participants were allowed to use for development and evaluation purposes.

Development Data (from TREC-8 SDR)

a Document collection: the B1SK Baseline Transcripts collection with known story boundaries made available by NIST.
b Topics: 50 short topics in English, French, German, Italian, Spanish and Dutch made available by ITC-irst.
c Relevance assessments: Topics-074-123.
d Parallel document collections (optional): available through LDC.

Evaluation Data (from TREC-9 SDR)

a Document collection: the B1SK Baseline Transcripts collection with known boundaries made available by NIST.
b Topics: 50 short topics in English, French, German, Italian, Spanish and Dutch.
c Relevance assessments: Topics-124-173
d Parallel document collections (optional): available through LDC.

Primary Conditions (Mandatory for All Participants)

- Monolingual IR without using any parallel collection (contrastive condition).
- Bilingual IR from French or German.

Secondary Condition (Optional)

- Monolingual IR using any available parallel collections.
- Bilingual IR from other languages.

Table 1. mAvPr results of CLSDR track at CLEF 2003

Official run	Site	Query	mAvPr
resultsEnconexp	UAlicante	EN	.3563
resultsEnsinexp	UAlicante	EN	.2943
aplspenena	JHU/APL	EN	.3184
exeengpl1.5	UExeter	EN	.3824
exeengpl3.5	UExeter	EN	.3696
Mono-brf	ITC-irst	EN	.3944
resultsFRconexp	UAlicante	FR	.2846
resultsFRsinexp	UAlicante	FR	.1648
aplspfrena	JHU/APL	FR	.1904
exefrprnsys1.5	UExeter	FR	.2825
exefrprnsys3.5	UExeter	FR	.2760
fr-en-1bst-brf-bfr	ITC-irst	FR	.2281
fr-en-sys-brf-bfr	ITC-irst	FR	.3064
aplspdeena	JHU/APL	DE	.2206
exedeprnsys1.5	UExeter	DE	.2744
exedeprnsys3.5	UExeter	DE	.2681
de-en-dec-1bst-brf-bfr	ITC-irst	DE	.2676
de-en-sys-brf-bfr	ITC-irst	DE	.2880
aplspitena	JHU/APL	IT	.2046
exeitprnpro1.5	UExeter	IT	.3011
exeitprnsys1.5	UExeter	IT	.2998
it-en-1bst-brf-bfr	ITC-irst	IT	.2347
it-en-sys-brf-bfr	ITC-irst	IT	.3218
aplspesena	JHU/APL	ES	.2395
exespprnpro1.5	UExeter	ES	.3151
exespprnsys3.5	UExeter	ES	.3077
es-en-1bst-brf-bfr	ITC-irst	ES	.2746
es-en-sys-brf-bfr	ITC-irst	ES	.3555
aplspnlena	JHU/APL	NL	.2269

3   Participants

Four research groups participated in this track:

University of Alicante (Spain) in addition to the mandatory monolingual run, this site submitted two runs with French as source language [5] . The system used performs query translation by means of several commercial off-the-shelf machine translation (MT) systems and performs query-document matching at the level of passage rather than of full document. These submissions adapted their existing document splitting algorithm developed for text data containing punctuation in order to identify passages in spoken data without punctuation marks on the basis of pauses contained in the transcripts. Finally, query expansion was just performed on the target collection.

Johns Hopkins University (USA) submitted one run for all available source languages: Dutch, French, German, Italian, and Spanish [6]. Their system employed n-gram decomposition for collection indexing, query translation, and query-document matching. Document retrieval was performed with a statistical language model. In particular, 5-grams were used in all the official bilingual runs. Query expansion just exploited the target collection.

University of Exeter (UK) submitted two runs for the following source languages: French, German, Italian, and Spanish [4]. The system used applied commercial MT systems for query translation and employed an Okapi retrieval method exploiting standard text preprocessing. In particular, query expansion is performed by using a parallel collection which is not truly contemporary to the searched documents.

ITC-irst (Italy) submitted two runs for the following languages: French, German, Italian, and Spanish [1]. The system used featured a statistical retrieval model integrating retrieval scores over multiple query translations. Query-document retrieval scores are computed with two methods: a statistical language model and an Okapi derived formula. Finally, the ITC-irst system employed a parallel collection for query expansion.

4 Results and Discussion

An overview of all submitted runs is reported in Table 1, which also shows performance in terms of average precision. Precision/recall plots of the primary condition runs are shown in Figures 1-3.

Interestingly, the ranking resulting from the contrastive monolingual run is almost preserved in both primary bilingual runs. In particular, the monolingual run shows performance by the pure retrieval systems, disregarding both the translation component and the query expansion on parallel corpora. However, it must be noticed that the latter feature was only exploited by the systems of U. Exeter and ITC-irst.

An interesting comparison between the system performance across the two conditions is given by the plot in Figure 4, which shows the ratio of mean-average-precisions between the bilingual and monolingual runs for different source languages. This plot points out that systems having better monolingual performance also show, in general, better bilingual retrieval performance. An exception was U. Alicante whose French-English shows the best ratio, despite the fact that its monolingual performance (`mavpr` .3563) was significantly lower than the best one (`mavpr` .3964 by ITC-irst). Comparing the methods used to achieve these results by U. Alicante and U. Exeter, it can be noted that Exeter use only a single MT system (Systran) to obtain this result, whereas Alicante use a combination of three MT systems (Babelfish (a version of Systran)), Power Translator and Freetranslator. It may be that Alicante's better relative performance is achieved due to greater coverage and possibly better selection of the translated terms arising from the use of multiple resources.

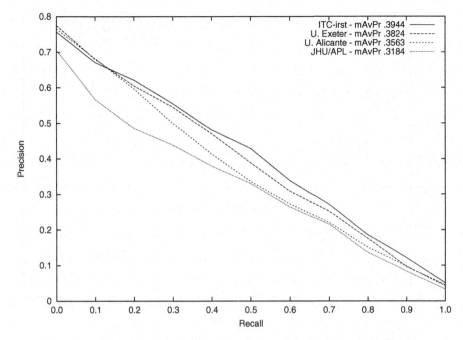

Fig. 1. Precision vs. recall of monolingual runs (primary condition)

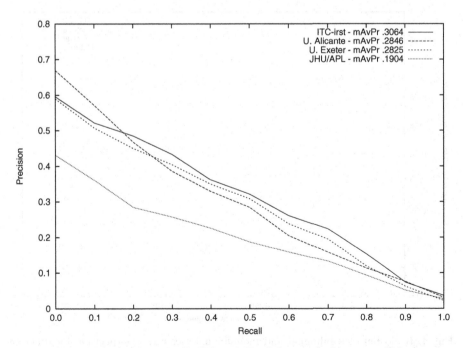

Fig. 2. Precision vs. recall of French-English runs (primary condition)

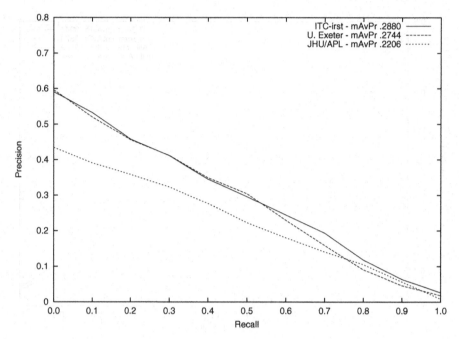

Fig. 3. Precision vs. recall of German-English runs (primary condition)

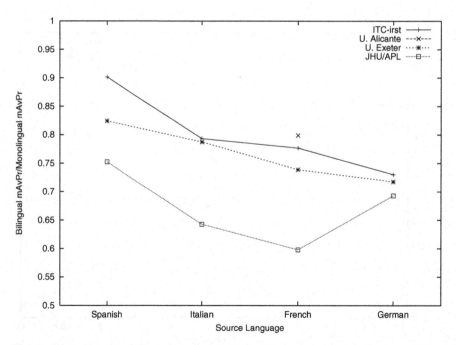

Fig. 4. Ratio between bilingual and monolingual mean-average-pecision for different source languages

Comparing the benefits of using large parallel text collections to improve retrieval performance explored by ITC-irst [1] and U. Exeter [4]. It can be seen that while using a contemporary text collection gives good improvement for ITC-irst, using a text collection from a period several years earlier is not beneficial for U. Exeter. This demonstrates the importance of using suitable text data to help compensate for the errorful transcriptions of the spoken documents.

The JHU submission [6] notes that using word stems performs better for their monolingual retrieval system whereas n-grams are better for bilingual retrieval. This is an interesting result and presumably relates to the translation accuracy and coverage of words vs n-grams for their system.

5   Concluding Remarks

Results from the CLEF 2003 CLSDR task show that as expected bilingual performance is lower for all participants than the comparative English monolingual run. However, the degree of degraded performance is shown to depend on the translation resources used. It has also been shown that different indexing units can be more effective for monolingual and bilingual retrieval on this data set. These are interesting observations and deserve further investigation.

References

1. Bertoldi, N. and Federico, M: ITC-irst at CLEF 2003: Cross-Language Spoken Document Retrieval. In this volume.
2. Garafolo, J. S., Auzanne, C. G. P. and Voorhees, E. M.: The TREC Spoken Document Retrieval Track: A Success Story. In Proceedings of the RIAO 2000 Conference: Content-Based Multimedia Information Access, Paris, 2000, 1–20.
3. Jones, G. J. F. and Federico, M.: CLEF 2002 Cross-Language Spoken Document Retrieval Pilot Track Report. In Proceedings of the CLEF 2002 Workshop on Cross-Language Information Retrieval and Evaluation, Rome, September 2002. Springer Verlag, 446–457.
4. Jones, G. J. F. and Lam-Adesina, A. M.: Exeter at CLEF 2003: Cross-Language Spoken Document Retrieval Experiments. In this volume.
5. Llopis, F. and Martinez-Barco, P.: Spoken Document Retrieval Experiments with the IR-n system. In this volume.
6. McNamee, P. and Mayfield, J.: N-grams for Translation and Retrieval in CL-SDR. In this volume.

Exeter at CLEF 2003: Cross-Language Spoken Document Retrieval Experiments

Gareth J. F. Jones[*] and Adenike Lam-Adesina

Department of Computer Science,
University of Exeter, EX4 4QF, U.K.
{G.J.F.Jones, A.M.Lam-Adesina}@exeter.ac.uk

Abstract. Cross-Language Spoken Document Retrieval (CLSDR) combines both the complexities of retrieval from collections characterized by speech transcription errors and language translation issues between search requests and documents. Thus achieving effective retrieval in this domain is potentially very challenging. For the CLEF 2003 SDR task we adopted a standard query translation strategy using commercial machine translation tools and explored pseudo-relevance feedback using a small contemporaneous collection and a much larger text collection from a different time period.

1 Introduction

Both Cross-Language Information Retrieval (CLIR) and Spoken Document Retrieval (SDR) are affected by limitations in language processing technologies. In the case of the former this relates to translation between the languages of queries and documents, and in the latter to the difficulties encountered in transcription of spoken data. These issues are analyzed in more detail in [1]. Spoken Document Retrieval (CLSDR) combines the difficulties of both CLIR and SDR. Thus retrieval in this domain is very challenging.

For the CLEF 2003 CLSDR task we adopted a query translation strategy and investigated the use of a small contemporaneous text collection and a large text document set from a different period to the test collection as pilot collections to augment the spoken document test set. All query statements were translated from the source language into English using two machine translation tools: Systran Version:3.0 (Sys MT) and Globalink Power Translation Pro Version 6.4 (Pro MT) machine translation (MT) systems. The task is based on the TREC 9 SDR task. A detailed description of the task is found in [2].

The remainder of this paper summarizes our retrieval system and gives results and analysis of our experimental results.

---

[*] Now at School of Computing, Dublin City University, Ireland.
email: Gareth.Jones@computing.dcu.ie

C. Peters et al. (Eds.): CLEF 2003, LNCS 3237, pp. 653–657, 2004.
© Springer-Verlag Berlin Heidelberg 2004

2 System Setup

The basis of the experimental system was the same as that used for our submissions to the monolingual, bilingual and multilingual tasks for CLEF 2003. The system combines Okapi BM25 term weighting with pseudo relevance feedback (PRF), and standard procedures of stop word removal and Porter stemming, full details are given in [3]. The parameters of the PRF system were set identically to those for the text retrieval system given in [3]. The Okapi parameters $K1$ and b were optimized for the SDR test collection.

3 Merged Collections

In our experiments for the CLSDR pilot track held at CLEF 2002 we experimented with the combination of the test collection with a small contemporaneous text document collection for term weight estimation [4]. This method aims to improve retrieval performance for the test set by better estimation of term weights. Our results for CLEF 2002 indicated that the method can give improvements in retrieval performance even when using only a small number of additional documents. Results for ITC-irst however showed that large improvements can be realized if a much larger number of contemporaneous text documents is used [5]. However, this large collection of truly contemporaneous documents was not available to us. This led us to investigate the use of an alternative large text document collection. In this case we used the document set from the TREC-8 and TREC-9 ad hoc retrieval tasks. This consists of around 500,000 text documents taken from 1994, some 4 years earlier than the SDR data set which is from February to June 1998. There is likely to be considerable vocabulary mismatch between these document collections, e.g. names, places, events, and the aim of this experiment was to find out if a pilot collection of this type could still provide improvement in retrieval performance.

In addition, we again used the two small collections of truly contemporaneous text documents. These sources are taken from New York Times Newswire Service (excluding non-NYT sources) and Associated Press Worldstream Service (English content only), totaling about 20,000 news stories, and are taken from exactly the same period as the spoken document test collection.

4 Experimental Results

This section describes our results for the CLEF 2003 CLSDR task. We report baseline and feedback results for five topic languages: English, French, German, Italian and Spanish. Our results include runs for topic translations using both Sys MT and Pro MT systems. Results for each condition are shown in terms of average precision and the total number of relevant documents retrieved for the complete query set.

In the following tables of results the following labeling conventions are adopted for the selection of topic expansion terms and cfw(i) of the test collection:

TCow(i): topic expansion using only the test collection.
CCow(i): topic expansion using the combined spoken and small text collections.

PCow(i): topic expansion using the TREC document pilot collection.

TCcfw(i): cfw(i) values taken from the test collection in the final retrieval run.

CCcfw(i): cfw(i) values taken from the combined spoken and small text collections in the final retrieval run.

PCcfw(i): cfw(i) values taken from the TREC document pilot collection in the final retrieval run.

Initial results are presented for the following methods:

1. Baseline run without feedback
2. Feedback runs using expanded query from the test collection
3. Feedback runs using queries expanded from the pilot collection and term weight estimated from the test collection. Initial query terms are upweighted by multiply by 1.5
4. Same as 3 but initial query terms are upweighted by 3.5

Results for our CLSDR runs are shown in Tables 1 and 2. It can be seen that as expected the monolingual English result is the best in all cases with respect to both average precision and number of relevant documents retrieved. CLSDR performance is comparable for the French, Italian and Spanish topic statements with lower results for the German topics with Sys MT. This result is a little surprising for Systran French topic translation which has previously been shown to be more effective than other topic translations in our CLEF bilingual text retrieval experiments [6]. PRF using only the test collection is observed to be effective for topic expansion in all cases. Results for query expansion using the merged document collection are more mixed. In the case of Italian and Spanish topics this approach clearly outperforms test collection only query expansion. However, there is little difference between the results for these methods when using French and German topics.

Table 1. Retrieval results for topic translation using Sys MT

Sys MT		English	French	German	Italian	Spanish
1.Baseline	Av.P	0.311	0.227	0.203	0.231	0.250
	Rel-Ret	1587	1424	1369	1531	1548
2. TCow(i), TCcfw(i)	Av.P	0.382	0.281	0.270	0.279	0.292
	% chg.	+22.8%	+23.8%	+33.0%	+20.7%	+16.8%
	Rel-Ret	1795	1558	1498	1638	1641
3. CCow(i), TCcfw(i),1.5	Av.P	0.364	0.283	0.274	0.299	0.304
	% chg.	+17.0%	+24.7%	+34.9%	+29.4%	+21.6%
	Rel-Ret	1824	1618	1541	1684	1720
4. CCow(i), TCcfw(i),3.5	Av.p	0.371	0.276	0.268	0.296	0.307
	% chg.	+19.3%	+21.6%	+32.0%	+28.1%	+22.8%
	Rel-Ret	1789	1577	1524	1653	1707

Table 2. Retrieval results for topic translation using Pro MT

Pro MT		English	French	German	Italian	Spanish
1.Baseline	Av.P	0.311	0.189	0.188	0.234	0.235
	Rel-Ret	1587	1356	1307	1503	1564
2. TCow(i), TCcfw(i)	Av.P	0.382	0.244	0.245	0.288	0.298
	%chg.	+22.8%	+29.1%	+30.3%	+23.1%	+26.8%
	Rel-Ret	1795	1533	1442	1570	1715
3.CCow(i), TCcfw(i),1.5	Av.P	0.364	0.262	0.242	0.301	0.315
	% chg.	+17.0%	+38.6%	+28.7%	+28.6%	+34.0%
	Rel-Ret	1824	1589	1431	1624	1710
4.CCow(i), TCcfw(i),3.5	Av.P	0.371	0.256	0.229	0.293	0.308
	% chg.	+19.3%	+35.4	+21.8%	+25.2%	+31.1%
	Rel-Ret	1789	1574	1420	1602	1682

We carried out further experiments using the TREC-7 and TREC-8 ad hoc document collection as a pilot searching collection. Results are presented for the following methods:

5. Topics are expanded using the TREC document pilot collection and then further expanded using the combined collection from the earlier experiments, final retrieval run with cfw(i) values from the test collection.
6. As 5 with the final retrieval run on the test collection using cfw(i) from the pilot collection.

Table 3. Retrieval results for topic translation with Sys MT and pilot searching

Sys MT		English	French	German	Italian	Spanish
5. PC->Ccow(i), CCcfw(i)	Av.P	0.341	0.257	0.248	0.282	0.260
	% chg.	+9.6%	+13.2%	+22.2%	+22.1%	+4.0%
	Rel-Ret	1667	1564	1436	1635	1529
6. PC->Ccow(i), PCcfw(i)	Av.P	0.338	0.255	0.258	0.284	0.263
	% chg.	+8.7%	+12.3%	+27.1%	+22.9%	+5.2%
	Rel-Ret	1683	1584	1429	1649	1591

Table 4. Retrieval results for topic translation with Pro MT and pilot searching

Pro MT		English	French	German	Italian	Spanish
5. PC->CCow(i), CCcfw(i)	Av.P	0.341	0.252	0.232	0.274	0.259
	% chg.	+9.6%	+33.3%	+23.4%	+17.1%	+10.2%
	Rel-Ret	1667	1520	1393	1609	1621
6. PC->CCow(i), PCcfw(i)	Av.P	0.338	0.258	0.235	0.270	0.258
	% chg.	+8.7%	+36.5%	+25.0%	+15.4%	+9.8%
	Rel-Ret	1683	1531	1378	1621	1629

From the results in Tables 5 and 6 it can be seen that expansion using the TREC document is less effective than using either test collection only expansion or the combination of the test collection with the small text collection from the same time period.

This result is not altogether surprising since the TREC text document sets is taken from a period some 4 years earlier than the TREC SDR documents. This result indicates that while using large text document sets can be useful in CLSDR as illustrated in [5], these documents must have an appropriate match, presumably relating to vocabulary and topic coverage, to the spoken document collection.

5 Conclusions and Further Work

The results for the CLEF 2003 CLSDR task reported in this paper establish baseline performance figures against which our exploration of techniques for CLSDR can be measured. The experiments reported here show that PRF is effective for this task, as would be expected since it is generally a useful technique for text CLIR and SDR. The effectiveness of large additional text collections for parameter estimation for query expansion in CLSDR has been shown to be dependent on the match of the time periods covered in the collections.

References

1. Jones, G.J.F., Federico, M.: CLEF 2002 Cross-Language Spoken Document Retrieval Pilot Track Report. In: Peters, C., Gonzales, J., Braschler, M., Kluck, M. (eds.): Advances in Cross-Language Information Retrieval: Third Workshop of the Cross-Language Evaluation Forum, CLEF 2002, Rome, Italy, September 19 - 20, 2002. Revised Papers. Lecture Notes in Computer Science; Vol. 2785. Springer-Verlag, Berlin Heidelberg New York (2003) 446-457
2. Federico, M.,.Jones, G.J.F: CLEF 2003 Cross-Language Spoken Document Retrieval Pilot Track Report. In: Peters, C. (ed.): Working Notes for the CLEF 2003 Workshop, 21-22 August, Trondheim, Norway. At: http://clef.iei.pi.cnr.it:2002/2003/WN_web/18b.pdf
3. Lam-Adesina, A.M., .Jones, G.J.F: Exeter at CLEF 2003: Experiments with Machine Translation for Monolingual, Bilingual and Multilingual Retrieval. In: Peters, C. (ed.): Working Notes for the CLEF 2003 Workshop, 21-22 August, Trondheim, Norway. At: http://clef.iei.pi.cnr.it:2002/2003/WN_web/50.pdf.
4. Jones, G.J.F, Lam-Adesina, A.M.: Exeter at CLEF 2002: Cross-Language Spoken Document Retrieval Experiments. In: Peters, C., Gonzales, J., Braschler, M., Kluck, M. (eds.): Advances in Cross- Language Information Retrieval: Third Workshop of the Cross-Language Evaluation Forum, CLEF 2002, Rome, Italy, September 19 - 20, 2002. Revised Papers. Lecture Notes in Computer Science; Vol. 2785. Springer-Verlag, Berlin Heidelberg New York (2003) 127-146
5. Bertoldi, N., Federico, M.: Cross-Language Spoken Document Retrieval on the TREC SDR Collection. In: Peters, C., Gonzales, J., Braschler, M., Kluck, M. (eds.): Advances in Cross-Language Information Retrieval: Third Workshop of the Cross-Language Evaluation Forum, CLEF 2002, Rome, Italy, September 19 - 20, 2002. Revised Papers. Lecture Notes in Computer Science; Vol. 2785. Springer-Verlag, Berlin Heidelberg New York (2003) 476-484
6. Jones, G.J.F, Lam-Adesina, A.M.: Exeter at CLEF 2001. In: Peters, C., Braschler, M., Gonzalo, J., Kluck, M. (eds.): Evaluation of Cross-Language Information Retrieval Systems: Second Workshop of the Cross-Language Evaluation Forum, CLEF 2001, Darmstadt, Germany, September 3-4, 2001. Revised Papers. Lecture Notes in Computer Science, Vol. 2406 Springer-Verlag Berlin Heidelberg New York (2002) 59-77

N-grams for Translation and Retrieval in CL-SDR

Paul McNamee and James Mayfield

The Johns Hopkins University, Applied Physics Laboratory,
11100 Johns Hopkins Road,
Laurel, MD 20723-6099, USA
{mcnamee, mayfield}@jhuapl.edu

Abstract. We report on a first attempt to perform cross-language spoken document retrieval. Without prior monolingual speech retrieval experience we applied the same general approach we use for bilingual retrieval that is typified by the use of overlapping character n-grams for tokenization and a statistical language model of retrieval. An innovative approach was adopted for coping with out-of-vocabulary words and misspelled or mistranscribed words: direct translation of individual n-grams was the sole mechanism to translate source language queries into target language terms. Though this approach shows promise, especially for non-speech retrieval, our performance appears to lag that of other teams participating in this novel evaluation.

1 Introduction

In the past we have conducted experiments that investigated the use overlapping character n-grams for tokenization of documents and queries of written text. Heretofore we have not had the opportunity to systematically examine the use of n-grams on transcribed text, though others have performed such monolingual studies. For the CLEF 2003 evaluation a novel task of cross-language spoken document retrieval (CL-SDR) was developed. The CL-SDR task used the TREC-8 and TREC-9 spoken datasets, which are English audio, and provided an English transcription to all teams. Existing relevance judgments were used with translated topic statements. This prevented a need to conduct an expensive evaluation of new topics and judgments. For more detail about the CL-SDR task experimental design see the overview paper by Federico and Jones in this volume.

This was our first time using the TREC-8 and TREC-9 spoken document dataset. Our submissions were created in very short order – in one day. We pre-processed the data so it had similar SGML markup as the *ad hoc* TREC collections and then indexed the English text using only 5-grams. The index took 33 minutes to build. We did not make use of any collection expansion for these runs. Our processing was similar to the work we did for the bilingual track [1], except that we used only 5-grams as translation terms and did not use pre-translation expansion (which was not permitted for 'primary' submissions).

The runs we submitted for the spoken document evaluation are summarized in Table 1.

C. Peters et al. (Eds.): CLEF 2003, LNCS 3237, pp. 658–663, 2004.
© Springer-Verlag Berlin Heidelberg 2004

Table 1. Official submissions for the Cross-Language Spoken Document Evaluation. Mean average precision is shown in the column on the far right

Submission	Lang	Task / Condition	MAP
aplspenena	EN	Monolingual	0.3184
aplspfrena	FR	Primary	0.1904
aplspdeena	DE	Primary	0.2206
aplspnlena	NL	Secondary	0.2269
aplspitena	IT	Secondary	0.2046
aplspesena	ES	Secondary	0.2395

2 Related Work

In monolingual text retrieval the use of words or stemmed words to represent documents is routine, and this is also true for retrieval of transcribed speech. Alternative approaches have been examined, for example, Corinna Ng and colleagues have examined the use of phoneme n-grams to represent language [2]. In their study they found that a combination of phoneme n-grams was more useful then a single choice of n; however this technique was not as successful as the use of words. Kenny Ng examined a variety of approaches for tokenization of spoken documents in his Ph.D. thesis at MIT [3]. He found that phoneme 3-grams worked as well as transcribed text (*i.e.,* words), but only if phonemes were accurately recorded. His thesis did not examine whether the use of character n-grams might perform better than word-based retrieval, though he did identify this as an interesting area to pursue.

3 Approach

Our approach to speech retrieval is to index documents with overlapping character n-grams using the HAIRCUT retrieval engine [4][5]. We have found superior results with $n=4$ or $n=5$ in many European languages (see [5]) and we use a statistical language model of retrieval [6][7][8]. Accordingly we used $n=5$ for our official submissions; however, we performed several post hoc experiments using words, stemmed words, and 4-grams that we analyze below. We ran one monolingual baseline in English and for our bilingual runs we needed a method to translate source language queries from Dutch, French, German, Italian, and Spanish.

In preparation for our cross language work for the 2003 evaluation [1], we performed some training experiments using the CLEF 2002 test suite. We developed a new method for query translation that we believe has promise for combating several important problems in bilingual retrieval articulated by Pirkola *et al.*: vagaries of lemmatization, translation of proper names which are not typically found in translation lexicons, how to handle out-of-vocabulary words, and difficultly translating multiword phrases [9]. Our approach involves tokenizing source language queries into a set of overlapping character n-grams. Given a suitable parallel corpus, a statistical translation lexicon can be developed that matches each source language term (*i.e.,* n-gram) with one or more appropriate target language terms. Typically we map source language 5-grams to target language 5-grams, but heterogeneous mappings are possible. In experiments below we also explore stem-to-stem, and 4-gram-to-4-gram translations. We used the Snowball stemmer created by Porter [10].

Over the last two years we have downloaded over 300 MB of text in each of the eleven official languages of the European Union from the Europa web site [11]. As a result, we were able to produce statistical dictionaries that map Dutch, French, German, Italian, and Spanish terms to English terms. Details about the parallel corpus we have built can be found in [1]. Although the n-gram mappings we obtain are not perfect, they appear to be suitable for retrieval purposes and appear to be reasonably accurate on both common nouns and proper names. An example of translating the common word milk is shown in Table 2 (below); Table 3 presents 5-gram translations for a proper name, Mexico, which appears in topic 85, and a multiword phrase, tobacco industry, from topic 89.

The end-to-end process we described for cross-language spoken retrieval against transcribed English documents is depicted below.

Table 2. Term translations for the word milk from German to Italian and French to Dutch. Four term types are used: words, stems, 4-grams and 5-grams. Here and in this paper underscores are used to denote space characters in n-gram sequences

	German	Italian		French	Dutch
words	milch	latte	words	lait	melk
stems	milch	latt	stems	lait	melk
4-grams	milc	latt	4-grams	lait	melk
	ilch	latt			
5-grams	_milc	_latt	5-grams	_lait	_melk
	milch	_latt		lait_	melk_
	ilch_	latte			

Table 3. 5-gram translations for the name Mexico (Mexique), from French to English, and the phrase 'tobacco industry' (tabakindustrie) from German to English. A potential translation is shown for each 5-gram spanning part of the source language word/phrase

French	English	German	English
_mexi	_mexi	_taba	bacco
mexiq	mexic	tabak	bacco
exiqu	mexic	abaki	bacco
xique	oxic_	bakin	cco_i
ique_	ical_	akind	cco_i
		kindu	ustry
		indus	indus
		ndust	indus
		dustr	indus
		ustri	indus
		strie	indus
		trie_	indus

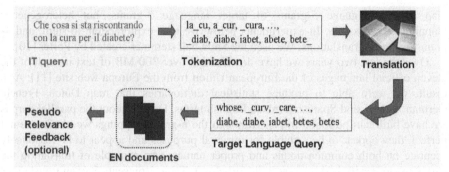

Fig. 1. End-to-end bilingual processing using direct n-gram translation

One further technique can be used to improve performance. We have observed that significant improvements can be obtained in bilingual retrieval when a large source language collection is available for pre-translation query expansion [12]. In post hoc experiments we explored the use of pre-translation query expansion with additional post-translation expansion (*i.e.,* normal blind relevance feedback).

4   Results

In Figure 2 we plot the performance for training (TREC-8) and test (TREC-9) topics.

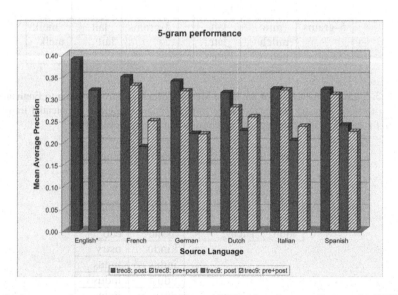

Fig. 2. Performance for monolingual and bilingual SDR using character 5-grams for TREC-8 and TREC-9 topics. Each run uses blind relevance feedback and the lined bars denote the use of pre-translation query expansion

Performance is consistently lower for the TREC-9 topic set, regardless of source language. For the bilingual runs, pre-translation expansion resulted in a tangible improvement in three of the source languages over relevance feedback alone on the TREC-9 topic set; however, this behavior was not observed with the TREC-8 topics where pre-translation expansion degraded performance slightly. This is not in accordance with our previous experience searching textual archives [12] – it may be that the difference in genre affects the efficacy of pre-translation expansion.

In Figure 3 we plot the relative performance of three tokenization methods for both the training data and the test set. Interestingly we observe a difference between monolingual and bilingual performance. With monolingual queries the use of stemmed words results in slightly higher accuracy then the use of character n-grams. But, when bilingual retrieval is performed the trend is strongly in the opposite direction and 5-grams have a decided advantage over stems.

We examined a few individual queries and noted one effect that is unique to cross-language spoken document retrieval. The transcribed text in documents and queries represents abbreviations in an atypical fashion. For example, the abbreviation HIV would appear as H. I. V. in transcribed text (*i.e.,* as three letters separated by full stops). This created a problem for translation because we tokenized this using 5-grams as 'h_i_v', an n-gram sequence unlikely to occur in the parallel text we mined for statistical translations ('_hiv_' would be normal). The problem occurs because our translations were mined from written text, not transcribed speech. Only 3 of 50 topics in the TREC-8 topic set contained such abbreviations; however 14 of 50 topic statements in the TREC-9 topics contained such atypical abbreviations.

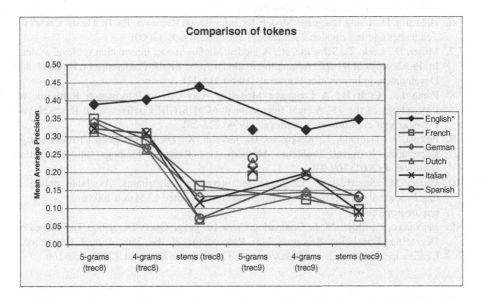

Fig. 3. Comparing tokenization in CL-SDR. The same token type was used for translation, as well as for retrieval

5 Conclusions

We have developed a new method for query translation in cross-language information retrieval that we have applied to spoken documents. Our method involves translation of individual character n-grams – this results in multiple terms being translated for each word in a source language query. This approach appears to work well and bilingual retrieval performance compares favorably to monolingual performance. We have also learned that caution must be exercised when translation resources are derived from written sources and applied to spoken document collections.

References

1. McNamee, P., Mayfield, J.: JHU/APL Experiments in Tokenization and Non-Word Translation. In this volume.
2. Ng, C., Wilkinson, R., Zobel, J.: Experiments in Spoken Document Retrieval Using Phoneme N-grams. In: Speech Communication, 32 (2000) 1-2, 61-77
3. Ng, K.: Subword-based Approaches for Spoken Document Retrieval. Ph.D. Thesis. MIT, (2000)
4. McNamee, P., Mayfield, J.: Scalable Multilingual Information Access. In: Peters, C., Gonzalo, J., Braschler, M., Kluck, M. (eds.): Advances in Cross-Language Information Retrieval: Third Workshop of the Cross-Language Evaluation Forum, CLEF 2002, Rome, Italy, September 19 - 20, 2002 ; revised papers. Lecture Notes in Computer Science; Vol. 2785. Springer-Verlag, Berlin Heidelberg New York (2003) 207-218
5. McNamee, P., Mayfield, J.: Character N-gram Tokenization for European Language Text Retrieval. To appear in Information Retrieval.
6. Hiemstra, D.: Using Language Models for Information Retrieval. Ph. D. Thesis. Center for Telematics and Information Technology, The Netherlands, (2000)
7. Miller, D., Leek, T., Schwartz, R.: A hidden Markov model information retrieval system. In: Proceedings of the 22nd Annual International ACM SIGIR Conference on Research and Development in Information Retrieval. (1999) 214-221
8. Ponte J., Croft B.: A Language Modeling Approach to Information Retrieval. In: Proceedings of the 21st Annual International ACM SIGIR Conference on Research and Development in Information Retrieval. (1998) 275-281
9. Pirkola, A., Hedlund, T., Keskusalo, H., Järvelin, K.: Dictionary-Based Cross-Language Information Retrieval: Problems, Methods, and Research Findings. In: Information Retrieval, 4 (2001) 209-230
10. Porter, M.: Snowball: A Language for Stemming Algorithms. Available online at http://snowball.tartarus.org/texts/introduction.html, (visited 13 March 2003).
11. http://europa.eu.int/
12. McNamee, P., Mayfield, J.: Comparing Cross-Language Query Expansion Techniques by Degrading Translation Resources. In: Proceedings of the 25th Annual International Conference on Research and Development in Information Retrieval. (2002) 159-166

Spoken Document Retrieval Experiments with IR-n System

Fernando Llopis and Patricio Martínez-Barco

Grupo de investigación en Procesamiento del Lenguaje y, Sistemas de Información,
Departamento de Lenguajes y Sistemas Informáticos,
University of Alicante, Spain
{llopis,patricio}@dlsi.ua.es

Abstract. This paper describes the first participation of IR-n system at Spoken Document Retrieval, focusing on the experiments we made before participation and showing the results we obtained. IR-n system is an Information Retrieval system based on passages and the recognition of sentences to define them. So, the main goal of this experiment is to adapt IR-n system to the spoken document structure by means of the utterance splitter and the overlapping passage technique allowing to match utterances and sentences.

1 Introduction

Usually, research work on natural language processing has started from written documents instead of spoken documents due to spoken document processing has a lot of disadvantages induced by its informal disposition among other reasons.

As appointed by Dahlbäck [1]:

"... spoken input is often incomplete, incorrect and contains interruptions and repairs; full sentences occur only very occasionally. Therefore new basic units for the development of dialogue models have to be proposed ..."

Thus, some of the most important problems to solve in spoken document processing are [2]:

- The lack of punctuation marks, that impedes the well understanding of sentences because boundaries are unknown. This understanding must be induced by pause detection. This is the reason why the "sentence" concept is replaced by the "utterance" concept. Utterance is defined, from a pragmatic point of view, as a sequence of words chained by a speaker between two pauses. In the same way, the "paragraph" is replaced by the "turn" that is defined from a pragmatic point of view as the set of utterances that a speaker can express between two speaker changes (when several speakers participate in the dialogue), or the set of utterances that a speaker expresses about the same subject (in monologues or newsreels).
- Moreover, turns may be considered like null or empty when they do not contribute to the discourse, that is, turns having the function of pointing

C. Peters et al. (Eds.): CLEF 2003, LNCS 3237, pp. 664–671, 2004.

out the speaker is *on* the conversation: "ejem...", "yes...", "I know..."; as well as other turns without semantic content such as "good morning", "have a good weekend", and so on.

– Furthermore, turns can be interrupted due to overlaps, or speaker mistakes, causing repetitions and modifications of previous information.

This sort of problems is increased with problems derived from the automatic transcription process which incorporates noise, spelling mistakes, and unrecognizable words due to deficiencies in the original recording or speak recognition fails.

Due to this, the use of spoken documents in information retrieval tasks allows to test the system robustness against document mistakes. Then, the main goal of this paper is to test the robustness of IR-n System and to study some text processing techniques that could improve this robustness in spoken documents.

IR-n is an Information Retrieval system based on passages [3] [4]. Passages are defined using a fixed number of sentences from the original document. It seems obvious that IR-n has been developed to work on written documents with a clear structure based on known sentence boundaries. However, in order to test its robustness, IR-n has been submitted to the CLEF SDR Track.

SDR task is based on processing non-structured documents that proceed from an automatic transcription of radio news. Our main objective is to test if IR-n system can be applied to document collections where sentence boundaries are unknown. This experiment is focused on the estimation of sentence boundaries by means of the pauses recognized along the transcription process. So, the main hypothesis is based on the following ideas:

– longest pauses mean the end of utterances
– IR-n System can accept utterances instead of sentences to define passages.

So, the experiments will focus on determining what is the average length of a pause between utterances to build an utterance splitter that will feed the IR-n system.

However, using this model, passage definitions may be faulty. The terms of a query may be dispersed among several passages, and some relevant documents may be discarded. This problem can be avoided by using passage overlapping, since this technique allows more than one passage sharing the same fragment of document.

2   CL-SDR Track Description

Cross-Language Spoken Document Retrieval (CL-SDR) is a new track proposed for CLEF 2003. The track is mostly based on existing resources, available by NIST, which were used at TREC-8 [5] and TREC-9 [6].

The benchmark track is an extension of evaluation data prepared by NIST for TREC 8-9 SDR tracks. It has a collection of automatic transcripts (557 hours) of American-English news recordings broadcasted by ABC, CNN, Public

Table 1. Technical specifications of the CLEF'2003 CL-SDR Track

- Objective: the track aims at evaluating CLIR systems on noisy automatic transcripts of spoken documents with known story boundaries.
- Development data (from TREC 8 SDR):
    1. Document collection: B1SK Baseline Transcripts, known bounds download from NIST.
    2. Topics: Short topics in English, Dutch, French, German, Italian, and Spanish.
    3. Relevance assessments: Topics-074-123.
    4. Parallel document collections (optional and only available through LDC): Textual resources.
- Evaluation data (from TREC 9 SDR):
    1. Document collection: B1SK Baseline Transcripts, known bounds download from NIST.
    2. Topics: Short topics in English , Dutch, French, German, Italian, and Spanish.
    3. Relevance assessments: Topics-124-173.
    4. Parallel document collections (optional and only available through LDC): Textual resources.
- Primary Conditions (mandatory for all participants):
    1. Monolingual IR without using any parallel collection (contrastive condition).
    2. Bilingual IR from French or German.
- Secondary Condition (optional):
    1. Monolingual IR using any available parallel collections.
    2. Bilingual IR from other languages.
- Submission of runs:
    1. Maximum 12 runs per participant, with the limit of 3 runs for each considered source language.

Radio International, and Voice of America between February and June 1998. Transcripts are provided with known story boundaries (21,754 stories); and a collection of 100 English topics, either in terse or short format. The TREC collection has been extended with translations of the short topics into five European languages: Dutch, Italian, French, German, and Spanish.

Technical specifications of the task are shown in table 1.

3   Passage Definition at IR-n System

Taking advantage of using sentences in IR-n as a basic unit to the passage definition task, the sentence will be used to define the passage overlapping too.

The overlapping degree (G_{sol}) in IR-n system shows the sentence number from which the definition of the next passage starts. The main features of this value are the following:

1. G_{sol} must be lower than the passage size. Having the same value means that no overlapping is used.
2. The lower the value G_{sol} is, the higher the amount of text shared by two consecutive passages will be.
3. As a result, the lower the value G_{sol} is, the more number of passages will be defined in the document.

The use of passage overlapping means to redefine the passage concept to IR-n in the following way:

- Given a document D consisting of N sentences.

$$D = f_1..f_N \tag{1}$$

- Taken into account that n is the number of sentences integrating a passage.
- Given an overlapping degree G_{sol}
- The following passages will be defined from the document D

$$P_i = f_{G_{sol}*(i-1)+1}, ..., f_{\min(G_{sol}*(i-1)+n,N)}, i \in [1..N/G_{sol} - 1] \qquad (2)$$

Given that definition, and supposing a passage size of 15 sentences, an overlapping degree of 10, and a document size of 35 sentences, the passage generation will be performed in the following way:

1. $P_1 = f_1..f_{15}$
2. $P_2 = f_{11}..f_{25}$
3. $P_3 = f_{21}..f_{35}$

The increase of the efficiency in document retrieval is an immediately advantage of passage overlapping. However, the response time increases (to a large extent when the overlapping degree is lower) because the number of passages to be evaluated is greater.

Nevertheless, the use of lower overlapping degrees improves the system results noticeably, and it has not excessive influence on the searching time.

Overlapping does not increase the searching cost so much due to two main reasons:

1. IR-n does not evaluate each one of the document passages, since the similarity measure [7] in some cases may be avoided. The first passage to be evaluated is the one starting in the first sentence of the document in which a query term appears. That is due to passages starting in a previous sentence can not obtain a similarity measure higher than this first passage, by the way in which the similarity measure has been defined in IR-n.

   For this same reason, the last passage to be evaluated is the one finishing in the last sentence of the document in which a query term appears.

   These same conclusions may be extended to passages not located at the limits of the document, that is, internal passages. Given an overlapping degree G_{sol}, if a passage does not contain query terms during its first sentences then its evaluation can be omitted. For example, if G_{sol} is equal to 1, the evaluation of those passages which first sentence does not contain any query term is not needed.

   Because of this, the number of passages to be evaluated is reduced, and, consequently, to use of small overlapping degrees has not the same influence as if each passage of the document is evaluated.

2. Another important aspect is related to the system implementation. IR-n implementation is based on storing all the information about word occurrences in main memory. Thus, the segmentation process is performed during the execution over data structures located at main memory.

   Considering that the most influencing factors to time processing are related to disc access times, this minor increase of time when a greater number of passages is processed, it is not significant to the final time.

For this reason, IR-n uses an overlapping degree ($G_{sol}=1$) being the value that obtains the best performance.

4   Experimental Work

According to the track specification, the test collection used in this experiment was TREC-8. During these experiments several passages sizes (from 1 to 9 sentences) and several pause recognition sizes (0.1, 0.2, and 0.3 seconds) have been valuated. Moreover, the IR-n system with and without query expansion has been tested.

Tables 2, 3 and 4 show the results without query expansion.

Tables 5, 6 and 7 show the results with query expansion.

Table 2. Training results without query expansion using 0.1 seconds to discover pauses

	Recall	\multicolumn{6}{c}{Precision at N documents}
	Recall	5	10	20	30	200	AvgP
IR-n 1 F K3	78.49	0.4980	0.4490	0.3398	0.2837	0.1041	0.3301
IR-n 2 F K3	79.26	0.5347	0.4633	0.3612	0.3102	0.1067	0.3540
IR-n 3 F K3	79.43	0.5429	0.4735	0.3602	0.3095	0.1099	0.3695
IR-n 4 F K3	79.81	0.5592	0.4735	0.3786	0.3204	0.1106	0.3774
IR-n 5 F K3	79.65	0.5469	0.4878	0.3786	0.3224	0.1107	0.3812
IR-n 6 F K3	80.09	0.5633	0.5102	0.3888	0.3293	0.1120	0.3845
IR-n 7 F K3	80.14	0.5796	0.4980	0.3878	0.3279	0.1123	**0.3852**
IR-n 8 F K3	80.20	0.5796	0.4980	0.3888	0.3265	0.1135	0.3850
IR-n 9 F K3	80.31	0.5755	0.5000	0.3888	0.3197	0.1141	0.3817

Table 3. Training results without query expansion using 0.2 seconds to discover pauses

	Recall	\multicolumn{6}{c}{Precision at N documents}
	Recall	5	10	20	30	200	AvgP
IR-n 1 F K3	78.71	0.4898	0.4429	0.3490	0.2884	0.1052	0.3343
IR-n 2 F K3	79.26	0.5306	0.4694	0.3602	0.3095	0.1073	0.3600
IR-n 3 F K3	79.92	0.5633	0.4796	0.3786	0.3122	0.1101	0.3756
IR-n 4 F K3	79.70	0.5755	0.4959	0.3806	0.3204	0.1112	0.3825
IR-n 5 F K3	80.09	0.5755	0.5000	0.3888	0.3231	0.1121	0.3834
IR-n 6 F K3	80.14	0.5714	0.4878	0.3816	0.3245	0.1132	0.3823
IR-n 7 F K3	80.42	0.5714	0.4837	0.3857	0.3136	0.1145	0.3801
IR-n 8 F K3	80.64	0.5837	0.5000	0.3898	0.3177	0.1150	0.3842
IR-n 9 F K3	80.42	0.5796	0.5000	0.3949	0.3184	0.1142	**0.3856**

These tables show that the best result is obtained using the model with query expansion, a passage size of 5 sentences and 0.2 seconds to recognize a pause between two utterances at the utterance splitter.

5   System Evaluation

This system was evaluated with the TREC SDR-9 collection according to the track specification. Moreover, a bilingual test was performed using French queries that were translated into English by Power Translator, Free-translator and Babel Fish.

Table 4. Training results without query expansion using 0.3 seconds to discover pauses

		Precision at N documents					
	Recall	5	10	20	30	200	AvgP
IR-n 1 F K3	78.88	0.4653	0.4347	0.3429	0.3007	0.1063	0.3341
IR-n 2 F K3	79.48	0.5469	0.4796	0.3745	0.3068	0.1088	0.3687
IR-n 3 F K3	79.98	0.5469	0.4776	0.3714	0.3238	0.1110	0.3784
IR-n 4 F K3	80.36	0.5837	0.4816	0.3796	0.3211	0.1128	**0.3805**
IR-n 5 F K3	80.20	0.5837	0.4796	0.3837	0.3136	0.1138	0.3794
IR-n 6 F K3	80.25	0.5878	0.4755	0.3816	0.3082	0.1145	0.3729
IR-n 7 F K3	80.25	0.5837	0.4837	0.3847	0.3095	0.1140	0.3751
IR-n 8 F K3	80.58	0.5714	0.4735	0.3796	0.3156	0.1135	0.3712
IR-n 9 F K3	80.64	0.5796	0.4633	0.3755	0.3156	0.1131	0.3672

Table 5. Training results with query expansion using 0.1 seconds to discover pauses

		Precision at N documents					
	Recall	5	10	20	30	200	AvgP
IR-n 1 F1	83.44	0.5347	0.5082	0.3959	0.3320	0.1119	0.4029
IR-n 2 F1	83.94	0.6000	0.5143	0.4133	0.3422	0.1161	0.4307
IR-n 3 F1	84.98	0.5959	0.5204	0.4112	0.3544	0.1170	0.4373
IR-n 4 F1	85.42	0.6041	0.5388	0.4143	0.3517	0.1176	0.4392
IR-n 5 F1	85.15	0.5959	0.5408	0.4255	0.3612	0.1192	0.4494
IR-n 6 F1	85.20	0.6204	0.5306	0.4378	0.3653	0.1208	**0.4530**
IR-n 7 F1	85.42	0.6000	0.5327	0.4327	0.3680	0.1212	0.4503
IR-n 8 F1	85.31	0.6082	0.5327	0.4367	0.3653	0.1215	0.4528
IR-n 9 F1	85.37	0.6041	0.5388	0.4347	0.3639	0.1218	0.4489

Both monolingual and bilingual tests were performed with and without query expansion. The best results for monolingual and bilingual queries are shown in tables 8 and 9 respectively.

6   Conclusions and Future Work

Although we expected to know more information about other systems at the conference, we are pleased to see these results being above average for SDR track, taking into account that IR-n system was not designed to work on spoken documents.

Nevertheless, more experiments are expected to be done to increase the system performance.

Table 6. Training results with query expansion using 0.2 seconds to discover pauses

		Precision at N documents					
	Recall	5	10	20	30	200	AvgP
IR-n 1 F1	82.51	0.5429	0.5102	0.4020	0.3361	0.1144	0.4160
IR-n 2 F1	84.43	0.5837	0.5469	0.4194	0.3476	0.1167	0.4421
IR-n 3 F1	85.09	0.5837	0.5449	0.4265	0.3497	0.1172	0.4540
IR-n 4 F1	85.37	0.6163	0.5429	0.4306	0.3578	0.1194	0.4606
IR-n 5 F1	85.53	0.6041	0.5469	0.4408	0.3680	0.1206	**0.4620**
IR-n 6 F1	85.64	0.6041	0.5490	0.4398	0.3653	0.1212	0.4619
IR-n 7 F1	85.92	0.6041	0.5367	0.4337	0.3639	0.1219	0.4584
IR-n 8 F1	85.97	0.6000	0.5408	0.4378	0.3633	0.1220	0.4596
IR-n 9 F1	85.86	0.6041	0.5347	0.4398	0.3612	0.1226	0.4594

Table 7. Training results with query expansion using 0.3 seconds to discover pauses

		Precision at N documents					
	Recall	5	10	20	30	200	AvgP
IR-n 1 F1	83.44	0.5551	0.4959	0.4102	0.3435	0.1177	0.4154
IR-n 2 F1	84.76	0.6000	0.5245	0.4224	0.3558	0.1211	0.4385
IR-n 3 F1	85.26	0.6531	0.5286	0.4337	0.3605	0.1238	0.4527
IR-n 4 F1	85.15	0.6286	0.5367	0.4235	0.3680	0.1248	0.4520
IR-n 5 F1	85.15	0.6327	0.5388	0.4265	0.3653	0.1254	0.4540
IR-n 6 F1	85.04	0.6367	0.5306	0.4276	0.3694	0.1257	0.4544
IR-n 7 F1	85.26	0.6367	0.5347	0.4255	0.3639	0.1254	**0.4564**
IR-n 8 F1	85.53	0.6367	0.5327	0.4316	0.3646	0.1251	0.4554
IR-n 9 F1	85.48	0.6367	0.5367	0.4265	0.3565	0.1252	0.4518

Table 8. Monolingual results with query expansion

System	AvgP
ITC-irst	0.3944
Exeter	0,3824
Alicante	**0,3563**
JHU/APL	0,3184

Table 9. Bilingual results with query expansion

System	AvgP
ITC-irst	0.3064
Alicante	**0,2846**
Exeter	0,2825
JHU/APL	0,1904

Acknowledgements

This work has been partially supported by the Spanish Government (CICYT) with grant TIC2000-0664-C02-02 and (PROFIT) with grants FIT-150500-2002-416 and FIT-150500-2002-244.

References

1. Dahlbäck, N.: Towards a dialogue taxonomy. In: Elisabeth Maier, Marion Mast, and Susann LuperFoy, editors, Dialogue Processing in Spoken Language Systems, volume 1236 of Lecture Notes in Artificial Intelligence. Springer Verlag, 1997.
2. Fernández, M.G.: Un modelo para la especificación lingüística y la gestión computacional en diálogos hombre-máquina mediante instrucciones expresadas en lenguaje natural. PhD thesis, Universidad de Sevilla, Departamento de Filología Inglesa. Facultad de Filología, Sevilla, 2000.
3. Llopis, F. and Vicedo, J.L.: IR-n system, a passage retrieval system at CLEF 2001. In: Peters, C., Braschler, M., Gonzalo, J., Kluck, M. (eds.): Evaluation of Cross-Language Information Retrieval Systems: Second Workshop of the Cross-Language Evaluation Forum, CLEF 2001, Darmstadt, Germany, September 3-4, 2001, Revised Papers. Lecture Notes in Computer Science, Vol. 2406 Springer-Verlag Berlin Heidelberg New York (2002) 244-252
4. Llopis, F., Vicedo, J.L. and Ferrández, A.: IR-n system at Clef-2002. In: Peters, C., Gonzales, J., Braschler, M., Kluck, M. (eds.): Advances in Cross- Language Information Retrieval: Third Workshop of the Cross-Language Evaluation Forum, CLEF 2002, Rome, Italy, September 19 - 20, 2002, Revised Papers. Lecture Notes in Computer Science; Vol. 2785. Springer-Verlag, Berlin Heidelberg New York (2003) 291-300
5. Eighth Text REtrieval Conference, volume 500-246 of NIST Special Publication, Gaithersburg, USA, nov 1999. National Institute of Standards and Technology.
6. Ninth Text REtrieval Conference, volume 500-249 of NIST Special Publication, Gaithersburg, USA, nov 2000. National Institute of Standards and Technology.
7. Chen, J., Diekema, A., Taffet, M., McCracken, N., Ozgencil, N., Yilmazel, O. and Liddy, E.: Question Answering: CNLP at the TREC-10 Question Answering Track. In: Tenth Text REtrieval Conference (Notebook), volume 500-250 of NIST Special Publication, Gaithersburg, USA, nov 2001. National Institute of Standards and Technology.

ITC-irst at CLEF 2003:
Cross-Language Spoken Document Retrieval

Nicola Bertoldi and Marcello Federico

ITC-irst - Centro per la Ricerca Scientifica e Tecnologica,
I-38050 Povo, Trento, Italy
{bertoldi,federico}@itc.it

Abstract. This paper summarises the results of ITC-irst in the Cross-Language Spoken Document Retrieval track at the Cross Language Evaluation Forum 2003. The target collection consisted of automatic transcriptions of American Broadcast News manually segmented into stories. Topics consisted of 50 short queries in English, for which human-made translations into several languages are available: Dutch, French, German, Italian, and Spanish. Experiments were carried out by applying a bilingual document retrieval system which has been slightly modified in the query expansion module. Significant performance improvements were achieved by applying query expansion both on the target collection and on a larger corpus of written news.

1   Cross-Language Spoken Document Retrieval Track

This paper reports the results of ITC-irst in the Cross-Language (CL) Spoken Document Retrieval (SDR) track at the Cross Language Evaluation Forum (CLEF) 2003. The track addressed the retrieval of stories within a collection of automatically transcribed American Broadcast News. Topics corresponded to 50 short queries manually translated from English into Dutch, French, German, Italian, and Spanish by native speakers. A mandatory monolingual run, using English topics, was required from all participants to evaluate their retrieval engines. A detailed description of the track can be found in [1].

2   The ITC-irst CLSDR System

Our experiments in the CLSDR track were basically performed using the ITC-irst bilingual retrieval system described in [2] and papers referred therein. No specific work was done to adapt the system to the target collection, which indeed contains transcription errors. Training of the system's parameters required a bilingual dictionary, the target document collection, and a document collection in the source language.

Query Expansion Strategy. The system was slightly modified to enable multiple query expansion exploiting not just the target collection, but also other

C. Peters et al. (Eds.): CLEF 2003, LNCS 3237, pp. 672–675, 2004.

document collections. The basic query expansion algorithm performs the following steps: (i) a first retrieval step is carried out using the original query; (ii) the 15 most *relevant* words in the 5 top ranked documents are added to the original query; (iii) finally, the retrieval phase is performed again.

As the number of stories in the SDR target collection is quite small, an effective query expansion is hard to obtain. In order to overcome this problem, further resources were exploited, consisting of a large collection of written news, which is almost contemporary to documents in the original target collection. The basic idea was also to extract useful content words from this parallel corpus. After considering different options, the following strategy was finally chosen: query expansion is first performed on the additional collection, then again on the target collection.

The additional collection consists of newpaper articles of the North American News Text corpus[1]. In particular, 313K documents from *Los Angeles Times*, *Washington Post*, *New York Times*, and *Associated Press Worldstream*, issued between September 1997 and April 1998. Indeed the available texts do not entirely cover the test period, and it is difficult to predict what impact this gap has on system's performance.

German Word Decompounding. The usual preprocessing was slightly improved in order to better cope with German compound words. As retrieval is substantially based on content words, it is important to catch each basic concept expressed by compounds. Moreover, the presence of compound words dramatically impacts on the coverage given by any bilingual dictionary. Hence, an algorithm based on the dynamic programming paradigm was deviced, which exploits a statistical model of word compounding.

3   Evaluation

ITC-irst submitted 9 official runs to the CLSDR track: one for the mandatory monolingual task, and two for each of the following topic languages: French, German, Italian, and Spanish. Unofficial runs were also performed and are here reported for comparison. In particular, official runs are typed in **bold**.

Monolingual Performance. An English monolingual run was required from participants in order to evaluate the quality of their retrieval system. For this run, query expansion on a parallel corpus was not allowed. On the primary condition, our mAvPr was .3944, the best result reported in the CLSDR track.

Query Expansion Strategy. Four different query expansion strategies were compared: no query expansion at all (**mono**), query expansion using only the target collection (*mono-brf*), using only the parallel collection (*mono-brfpar*), and double query expansion using the parallel corpus first and then the target corpus (*mono-brf-brf*). Results are reported in Table 1.

---

[1] http://www.nist.gov/speech/tests/sdr

Table 1. mAvPr results for different query expansion strategies: no query expansion at all (**mono**), query expansion on the target collection only (*mono-brf*), on the parallel collection only (*mono-brfpar*), and double query expansion, first on the parallel corpus and then on the target corpus (*mono-brf-brf*)

Run	mAvPr
mono	.3176
mono-brf	.3944
mono-brfpar	.3954
mono-brf-brf	.4244

Performance improvements over single expansion strategies are around 24%, with respect to the baseline. The double expansion strategy is even more impressive: an improvement of 33% relative was observed with respect to the baseline, and of 7% with respect to both *mono-brf* and *mono-brfpar*. Similar effectiveness of the double query expansion policy was also observed for bilingual retrieval.

Bilingual Performance. The ITC-irst bilingual retrieval system integrates retrieval scores obtained over a set of N-best probable translations of the input query [3]. Table 2 compares performance achieved by using a different number of translations, namely 1 (**1bst**), 5 (*5bst*), and 10 (*10bst*). Using more than one translation improves the mAvPr for all languages, except German; remarkably, the relative improvement obtained for Spanish is around 14%.

German word decompounding also resulted effective, as shown in Table 2 by comparing runs with (*de-en-doc*) and without (**de-en**) word decompounding.

Moreover, our query translation approach was compared with the Babelfish translation service available on the Internet[2]. As it provides only one translation per query, the 1-best modality has been considered in this experiment. Names of these runs are indicating with **sys**. As shown in Table 2, performance with the commercial translation service resulted better than with our statistical model, more or less over all language pairs. This result is under investigation as previous experiments on different collections provided more comparable performance levels.

4   Conclusion

This paper reported the results of ITC-irst in the Cross-Language Spoken Document Retrieval track at the Cross Language Evaluation Forum 2003. The language pairs considered were French-English, German-English, Italian-English, and Spanish-English. In this track, the bilingual document retrieval system developed at ITC-irst was applied with little changes to the query expansion phase. Effective performance improvement was achieved by also applying query expansion on a large additional corpus of written news of the same period of the

---

[2] http://world.altavista.com

Table 2. mAvPr results for different query translation approaches. **1bst**, *5bst*, and *10bst* runs refer to the ITC-irst N-best approach, with $N = 1, 5, 10$, respectively; **sys** runs are obtained translating queries with the Babelfish translation service, powered by Systran. For German, results are given without (*de-en*) and with (**de-en-dec**) decompounding of compound nouns

Run	Query	mAvPr
fr-en-1bst-brf-bfr	FR	.2281
fr-en-5bst-brf-bfr	FR	.2314
fr-en-10bst-brf-bfr	FR	.2360
fr-en-sys-brf-bfr	FR	.3064
de-en-1bst-brf-bfr	DE	.2523
de-en-dec-1bst-brf-bfr	DE	.2676
de-en-5bst-brf-bfr	DE	.2590
de-en-dec-5bst-brf-bfr	DE	.2660
de-en-10bst-brf-bfr	DE	.2398
de-en-dec-10bst-brf-bfr	DE	.2618
de-en-sys-brf-bfr	DE	.2880
it-en-1bst-brf-bfr	IT	.2347
it-en-5bst-brf-bfr	IT	.2511
it-en-10bst-brf-bfr	IT	.2470
it-en-sys-brf-bfr	IT	.3218
es-en-1bst-brf-bfr	ES	.2746
es-en-5bst-brf-bfr	ES	.2955
es-en-10bst-brf-bfr	ES	.3132
es-en-sys-brf-bfr	ES	.3555

target collection. Consistent performance improvements were also obtained by splitting German compound words.

Acknowledgements

This work was carried out within the project WebFAQ, funded under the FDR-PAT program of the Province of Trento, and under the EU project PF-STAR.

References

1. Federico, M., Jones, G.: The CLEF 2003 Cross-Language Spoken Document Retrieval Track. This volume.
2. Bertoldi, N., Federico, M.: ITC-irst at CLEF 2003: Monolingual, Bilingual, and Multilingual Information Retrieval. This volume.
3. Federico, M., Bertoldi, N.: Statistical cross-language information retrieval using n-best query translations. In: Proc. of the 25th ACM SIGIR Conference on Research and Development in Information Retrieval, Tampere, Finland (2002) 167–174

Appendix – Results for 2003 Campaign

The following pages contain an overview of results for the multilingual, bilingual, monolingual and GIRT tracks. Results for the interactive, question answering, spoken document retrieval and image retrieval tracks are presented elsewhere.

After this introductory text, the next twelve pages give a listing of all runs submitted for these tracks and their respective characteristics:

Institution:	the name of the participant's organization responsible for the run
Country:	origin of participant's organization (ISO 3166 country codes)
Run Tag:	unique identifier for every experiment. Can be used to match individual result pages with this list.
Task:	which track/task the experiment is part of.
Topic language:	language of the topics used to create the experiment (ISO identifiers for language).
Topic fields:	identifies the parts of the topics used for query creation (combination of T=title, D=description and N=narrative).
Run Type:	type of experiment (automatic/manual).
Judged:	specifies if experiment was used for relevance assessment pooling.

The following ten pages compare the top entries for every track/task. The recall/precision curves for at most five groups are shown. These are based on the best entries by the respective groups, with the topic fields fixed to title+description(mandatory experiment for every participant) and only automatic experiments being used. For the multilingual, bilingual to English, bilingual to Russian and GIRT experiments, the top entries regardless of topic language are presented.

The individual result pages for every official run are published electronically, on the CLEF website www.clef-campaign.org, under the heading "CLEF 2003", "Working Notes". In the electronic material on the website, each experiment is presented on one page, and the following details are given:

1. A table providing the following information:
   - Average precision figures for every individual query. This allows comparison of system performance for single queries, which is important since variation of performance across queries is often very high and can be significant.
   - Overall statistics, giving:
     - the total number of documents retrieved by the system
     - the total number of overall relevant documents in the collection, and
     - the total number of relevant documents actually found by the system
     - interpolated precision averages at specific recall levels
     - non-interpolated average precision over all queries
     - precision numbers after inspecting a specific number of documents
     - R-precision: precision after the last relevant document was retrieved.

2. Two graphs consisting of:
   - a recall/precision graph, providing a plot of the precision values for various recall levels. This is the standard statistic and is the one most commonly reported in the literature.
   - a comparison to median performance. For each query, the difference in average precision, when compared to the median performance for the given task, is plotted. This graph gives valuable insight into which type of queries is handled well by different systems.

More information on the interpretation of the standard measures used for scoringexperiments in CLEF (average precision, recall levels, precision/recall graphs, etc.)can be found in the paper "CLEF 2003 Methodology and Metrics" by M. Braschlerand C. Peters in this volume.

Table of Runs. 1 Institution, 2 Country, 3 Run Tag, 4 Task, 5 Topic Language, 6 Topic Fields, 7 Run Type, 8 Judged

1	2	3	4	5	6	7	8
CEA/LIC2M	FR	lic2mde1	Multi-4	DE	TDN	Auto	
CEA/LIC2M	FR	lic2men1	Multi-4	EN	TDN	Auto	Y
CEA/LIC2M	FR	lic2mes1	Multi-4	ES	TDN	Auto	
CEA/LIC2M	FR	lic2mfr1	Multi-4	FR	TDN	Auto	Y
CEA/LIC2M	FR	lic2mfr2	Multi-4	FR	TDN	Auto	Y
Clairvoyance	US	ccmix	Biling_IT	DE	TD	Auto	Y
Clairvoyance	US	ccngm	Biling_IT	DE	TD	Auto	
Clairvoyance	US	ccwrd	Biling_IT	DE	TD	Auto	
CLIPS/IMAG	FR	2003CLIPSFRENG01	Biling_EN	FR	TN	Auto	Y
CLIPS/IMAG	FR	2003CLIPSMONFR01	Monoling	FR	TN	Auto	Y
CMU	US	cmul2Scomb	Biling_ES	IT	TD	Auto	
CMU	US	cmul2Scombfb	Biling_ES	IT	TD	Auto	
CMU	US	cmul2Spara	Biling_ES	IT	TD	Auto	
CMU	US	cmul2Sparafb	Biling_ES	IT	TD	Auto	
CMU	US	cmuG2lcomb	Biling_IT	DE	TD	Auto	
CMU	US	cmuG2lcombfb	Biling_IT	DE	TD	Auto	
CMU	US	cmuG2lpara	Biling_IT	DE	TD	Auto	
CMU	US	cmuG2lparafb	Biling_IT	DE	TD	Auto	Y
CMU	US	cmuM4fb	Multi-4	EN	TD	Auto	Y
CMU	US	cmuM4fbre	Multi-4	EN	TD	Auto	
CMU	US	cmuM4lowfb	Multi-4	EN	TD	Auto	
CMU	US	cmuM4lowfbre	Multi-4	EN	TD	Auto	
Daedalus	ES	spenQTdoc	Biling_EN	ES	TD	Auto	Y
Daedalus	ES	spenQTor1	Biling_EN	ES	TD	Auto	
Daedalus	ES	spenQTor3	Biling_EN	ES	TD	Auto	
Daedalus	ES	spenQTor3full	Biling_EN	ES	TD	Auto	
Daedalus	ES	frenQTdoc	Biling_EN	FR	TD	Auto	Y
Daedalus	ES	frenQTor3full	Biling_EN	FR	TDN	Auto	Y
Daedalus	ES	itspQTdoc	Biling_ES	IT	TD	Auto	
Daedalus	ES	itspQTor1	Biling_ES	IT	TD	Auto	
Daedalus	ES	itspQTor3	Biling_ES	IT	TD	Auto	
Daedalus	ES	itspQTor3full	Biling_ES	IT	TD	Auto	
Daedalus	ES	gegeQdoc	Monoling	DE	TD	Auto	Y
Daedalus	ES	gegeQor	Monoling	DE	TD	Auto	Y
Daedalus	ES	gegeQorand	Monoling	DE	TD	Auto	
Daedalus	ES	gegeQorlem	Monoling	DE	TD	Auto	Y
Daedalus	ES	enenQdoc	Monoling	EN	TD	Auto	

Table of Runs. 1 Institution, 2 Country, 3 Run Tag, 4 Task, 5 Topic Language, 6 Topic Fields, 7 Run Type, 8 Judged

1	2	3	4	5	6	7	8
Daedalus	ES	enenQor	Monoling	EN	TD	Auto	
Daedalus	ES	enenQorlem	Monoling	EN	TD	Auto	
Daedalus	ES	enenQorrf	Monoling	EN	TD	Auto	Y
Daedalus	ES	spspQdoc	Monoling	ES	TD	Auto	
Daedalus	ES	spspQor	Monoling	ES	TD	Auto	
Daedalus	ES	spspQorlem	Monoling	ES	TD	Auto	
Daedalus	ES	spspQorrf	Monoling	ES	TD	Auto	Y
Daedalus	ES	frfrQdoc	Monoling	FR	TD	Auto	Y
Daedalus	ES	frfrQor	Monoling	FR	TD	Auto	
Daedalus	ES	frfrQorand	Monoling	FR	TD	Auto	
Daedalus	ES	frfrQorlem	Monoling	FR	TD	Auto	
Daedalus	ES	spxxQTdoc	Multi-4	ES	TD	Auto	
Daedalus	ES	spxxQTor3	Multi-4	ES	TD	Auto	
Daedalus	ES	spxxQTorall	Multi-4	ES	TD	Auto	
Daedalus	ES	spxxQTorallrr	Multi-4	ES	TD	Auto	
Daedalus	ES	spxxQTordirect	Multi-4	ES	TD	Auto	Y
ENEA/La Sapienza	IT	ENEASAPDTA	GIRT_DE	DE	T	Auto	Y
ENEA/La Sapienza	IT	ENEASAPDTC	GIRT_DE	DE	T	Auto	Y
ENEA/La Sapienza	IT	ENEASAPDTDC	GIRT_DE	DE	TD	Auto	Y
ENEA/La Sapienza	IT	ENEASAPETC	GIRT_EN	EN	T	Auto	Y
ENEA/La Sapienza	IT	ENEASAPETDC	GIRT_EN	EN	TD	Auto	Y
Fernuni Hagen	DE	FUHpD3	GIRT_DE	DE	D	Auto	Y
Fernuni Hagen	DE	FUHpT2	GIRT_DE	DE	T	Auto	Y
Fernuni Hagen	DE	FUHpTD1	GIRT_DE	DE	TD	Auto	Y
Fernuni Hagen	DE	FUHpTD4	GIRT_DE	DE	TD	Auto	Y
Fernuni Hagen	DE	FUHpTD5	GIRT_DE	DE	TD	Auto	Y
Fondazione Ugo Bordoni	IT	fub03es3	Monoling	ES	TD	Auto	
Fondazione Ugo Bordoni	IT	fub03es4	Monoling	ES	TD	Auto	
Fondazione Ugo Bordoni	IT	fub03esAV	Monoling	ES	TD	Auto	
Fondazione Ugo Bordoni	IT	fub03esB	Monoling	ES	TD	Auto	Y
Fondazione Ugo Bordoni	IT	fub03fr3	Monoling	FR	TD	Auto	
Fondazione Ugo Bordoni	IT	fub03fr4	Monoling	FR	TD	Auto	
Fondazione Ugo Bordoni	IT	fub03frAV	Monoling	FR	TD	Auto	Y
Fondazione Ugo Bordoni	IT	fub03frB	Monoling	FR	TD	Auto	Y
Fondazione Ugo Bordoni	IT	fub03it3	Monoling	IT	TD	Auto	
Fondazione Ugo Bordoni	IT	fub03it4	Monoling	IT	TD	Auto	
Fondazione Ugo Bordoni	IT	fub03itAV	Monoling	IT	TD	Auto	

Table of Runs. 1 Institution, 2 Country, 3 Run Tag, 4 Task, 5 Topic Language, 6 Topic Fields, 7 Run Type, 8 Judged

1	2	3	4	5	6	7	8
Fondazione Ugo Bordoni	IT	fub03itB	Monoling	IT	TD	Auto	Y
Hummingbird	CA	humDE03td	Monoling	DE	TD	Auto	Y
Hummingbird	CA	humDE03tde	Monoling	DE	TD	Auto	
Hummingbird	CA	humES03td	Monoling	ES	TD	Auto	
Hummingbird	CA	humES03tde	Monoling	ES	TD	Auto	
Hummingbird	CA	humFI03td	Monoling	FI	TD	Auto	Y
Hummingbird	CA	humFI03tde	Monoling	FI	TD	Auto	Y
Hummingbird	CA	humFR03td	Monoling	FR	TD	Auto	Y
Hummingbird	CA	humFR03tde	Monoling	FR	TD	Auto	
Hummingbird	CA	humIT03td	Monoling	IT	TD	Auto	
Hummingbird	CA	humIT03tde	Monoling	IT	TD	Auto	
Hummingbird	CA	humNL03td	Monoling	NL	TD	Auto	Y
Hummingbird	CA	humNL03tde	Monoling	NL	TD	Auto	
Hummingbird	CA	humRU03t	Monoling	RU	T	Auto	Y
Hummingbird	CA	humRU03te	Monoling	RU	T	Auto	Y
Hummingbird	CA	humRU03tm	Monoling	RU	T	Auto	Y
Hummingbird	CA	humRU03td	Monoling	RU	TD	Auto	Y
Hummingbird	CA	humRU03tde	Monoling	RU	TD	Auto	Y
Hummingbird	CA	humRU03tdm	Monoling	RU	TD	Auto	Y
Hummingbird	CA	humRU03tdn	Monoling	RU	TDN	Auto	Y
Hummingbird	CA	humRU03tdne	Monoling	RU	TDN	Auto	Y
Hummingbird	CA	humRU03tdnm	Monoling	RU	TDN	Auto	Y
Hummingbird	CA	humSV03td	Monoling	SV	TD	Auto	Y
Hummingbird	CA	humSV03tde	Monoling	SV	TD	Auto	Y
IMS/U Padua	IT	IMSBGZ0	Biling_EN	DE	TD	Auto	
IMS/U Padua	IT	IMSBGZ3	Biling_EN	DE	TD	Auto	Y
IMS/U Padua	IT	IMSBSZ0	Biling_EN	ES	TD	Auto	
IMS/U Padua	IT	IMSBSZ3	Biling_EN	ES	TD	Auto	
IMS/U Padua	IT	IMSBFZ0	Biling_EN	FR	TD	Auto	
IMS/U Padua	IT	IMSBFZ3	Biling_EN	FR	TD	Auto	
IMS/U Padua	IT	IMSBIZ0	Biling_EN	IT	TD	Auto	
IMS/U Padua	IT	IMSBIZ3	Biling_EN	IT	TD	Auto	Y
IMS/U Padua	IT	IMSMGPO	Monoling	DE	TD	Auto	
IMS/U Padua	IT	IMSMGSP3	Monoling	DE	TD	Auto	Y
IMS/U Padua	IT	IMSMGST1	Monoling	DE	TD	Auto	Y
IMS/U Padua	IT	IMSMEPO	Monoling	EN	TD	Auto	
IMS/U Padua	IT	IMSMSPO	Monoling	ES	TD	Auto	

Table of Runs. 1 Institution, 2 Country, 3 Run Tag, 4 Task, 5 Topic Language, 6 Topic Fields, 7 Run Type, 8 Judged

1	2	3	4	5	6	7	8
IMS/U Padua	IT	IMSMSSP2	Monoling	ES	TD	Auto	
IMS/U Padua	IT	IMSMSST1	Monoling	ES	TD	Auto	
IMS/U Padua	IT	IMSMFPO	Monoling	FR	TD	Auto	
IMS/U Padua	IT	IMSMFSP1	Monoling	FR	TD	Auto	
IMS/U Padua	IT	IMSMFST1	Monoling	FR	TD	Auto	Y
IMS/U Padua	IT	IMSMIPO	Monoling	IT	TD	Auto	
IMS/U Padua	IT	IMSMISP1	Monoling	IT	TD	Auto	
IMS/U Padua	IT	IMSMIST2	Monoling	IT	TD	Auto	Y
IMS/U Padua	IT	IMSMDPO	Monoling	NL	TD	Auto	
IMS/U Padua	IT	IMSMDSP3	Monoling	NL	TD	Auto	Y
IMS/U Padua	IT	IMSMDST1	Monoling	NL	TD	Auto	Y
IRST	IT	IRSTit2es_1	Biling_ES	IT	TD	Auto	Y
IRST	IT	IRSTit2es_2	Biling_ES	IT	TD	Auto	
IRST	IT	IRSTit2es_3	Biling_ES	IT	TD	Auto	
IRST	IT	IRSTit2es_4	Biling_ES	IT	TD	Auto	
IRST	IT	IRSTde2it_1	Biling_IT	DE	TD	Auto	Y
IRST	IT	IRSTde2it_2	Biling_IT	DE	TD	Auto	
IRST	IT	IRSTde_1	Monoling	DE	TD	Auto	Y
IRST	IT	IRSTes_1	Monoling	ES	TD	Auto	
IRST	IT	IRSTfr_1	Monoling	FR	TD	Auto	Y
IRST	IT	IRSTit_1	Monoling	IT	TD	Auto	Y
IRST	IT	IRSTen2xx_1	Multi-4	EN	TD	Auto	Y
IRST	IT	IRSTen2xx_2	Multi-4	EN	TD	Auto	
IRST	IT	IRSTen2xx_3	Multi-4	EN	TD	Auto	
IRST	IT	IRSTen2xx_4	Multi-4	EN	TD	Auto	
JHU/APL	US	aplbifidea	Biling_DE	FI	TD	Auto	Y
JHU/APL	US	aplbifideb	Biling_DE	FI	TD	Auto	Y
JHU/APL	US	aplbiitesa	Biling_ES	IT	TD	Auto	
JHU/APL	US	aplbiitesb	Biling_ES	IT	TD	Auto	
JHU/APL	US	aplbideita	Biling_IT	DE	TD	Auto	
JHU/APL	US	aplbideitb	Biling_IT	DE	TD	Auto	
JHU/APL	US	aplbifrnla	Biling_NL	FR	TD	Auto	Y
JHU/APL	US	aplbifrnlb	Biling_NL	FR	TD	Auto	Y
JHU/APL	US	aplmodea	Monoling	DE	TD	Auto	Y
JHU/APL	US	aplmodeb	Monoling	DE	TD	Auto	
JHU/APL	US	aplmoena	Monoling	EN			
JHU/APL	US	aplmoenb	Monoling	EN			

Table of Runs. 1 Institution, 2 Country, 3 Run Tag, 4 Task, 5 Topic Language, 6 Topic Fields, 7 Run Type, 8 Judged

1	2	3	4	5	6	7	8
JHU/APL	US	aplmoesa	Monoling	ES	TD	Auto	Y
JHU/APL	US	aplmoesb	Monoling	ES	TD	Auto	
JHU/APL	US	aplmofia	Monoling	FI	TD	Auto	Y
JHU/APL	US	aplmofib	Monoling	FI	TD	Auto	Y
JHU/APL	US	aplmofra	Monoling	FR	TD	Auto	Y
JHU/APL	US	aplmofrb	Monoling	FR	TD	Auto	
JHU/APL	US	aplmoita	Monoling	IT	TD	Auto	Y
JHU/APL	US	aplmoitb	Monoling	IT	TD	Auto	
JHU/APL	US	aplmonla	Monoling	NL	TD	Auto	Y
JHU/APL	US	aplmonlb	Monoling	NL	TD	Auto	
JHU/APL	US	aplmorua	Monoling	RU	TD	Auto	Y
JHU/APL	US	aplmorub	Monoling	RU	TD	Auto	Y
JHU/APL	US	aplmosva	Monoling	SV	TD	Auto	Y
JHU/APL	US	aplmosvb	Monoling	SV	TD	Auto	Y
JHU/APL	US	aplmuen4a	Multi-4	EN	TD	Auto	Y
JHU/APL	US	aplmuen4b	Multi-4	EN	TD	Auto	
JHU/APL	US	aplmuen8a	Multi-8	EN	TD	Auto	Y
JHU/APL	US	aplmuen8b	Multi-8	EN	TD	Auto	
Kermit	FR/UK	xrce_ML4_run2	Multi-4	EN	TDN	Auto	Y
Kermit	FR/UK	kcca300	Multi-4	EN	TDN	Auto	Y
Medialab	NL	Medialab_b	Monoling	NL	TD	Auto	Y
Medialab	NL	Medialab_geo_1	Monoling	NL	TD	Auto	
Medialab	NL	Medialab_geo_2	Monoling	NL	TD	Auto	
Medialab	NL	Medialab_geo_3	Monoling	NL	TD	Auto	
Medialab	NL	Medialab_geo_4	Monoling	NL	TD	Auto	
Medialab	NL	Medialab_geo_5	Monoling	NL	TD	Auto	
Medialab	NL	Medialab_htr_1	Monoling	NL	TD	Auto	Y
Medialab	NL	Medialab_htr_2	Monoling	NL	TD	Auto	Y
Medialab	NL	Medialab_htr_3	Monoling	NL	TD	Auto	
Medialab	NL	Medialab_htr_4	Monoling	NL	TD	Auto	
Medialab	NL	Medialab_htr_5	Monoling	NL	TD	Auto	
NII	JP	NiiDic01	Biling_IT	DE	D	Auto	Y
NII	JP	NiiDic02	Biling_IT	DE	D	Auto	
NII	JP	NiiMt01	Biling_IT	DE	D	Auto	Y
NTU	TW	NTUm4Topn	Multi-4	EN	TD	Auto	
NTU	TW	NTUm4TopnLinear	Multi-4	EN	TD	Auto	
NTU	TW	NTUm4TopnTp	Multi-4	EN	TD	Auto	Y

Table of Runs. 1 Institution, 2 Country, 3 Run Tag, 4 Task, 5 Topic Language, 6 Topic Fields, 7 Run Type, 8 Judged

1	2	3	4	5	6	7	8
NTU	TW	NTUm4TopnTpCw	Multi-4	EN	TD	Auto	
Océ	NL	oce03DEnoXbm	Monoling	DE	TD	Auto	
Océ	NL	oce03DEnoXpr	Monoling	DE	TD	Auto	Y
Océ	NL	oce03ESnoXbm	Monoling	ES	TD	Auto	
Océ	NL	oce03ESnoXpr	Monoling	ES	TD	Auto	Y
Océ	NL	oce03FInoXbm	Monoling	FI	TD	Auto	Y
Océ	NL	oce03FInoXpr	Monoling	FI	TD	Auto	Y
Océ	NL	oce03FRnoXbm	Monoling	FR	TD	Auto	
Océ	NL	oce03FRnoXpr	Monoling	FR	TD	Auto	Y
Océ	NL	oce03ITnoXbm	Monoling	IT	TD	Auto	
Océ	NL	oce03ITnoXpr	Monoling	IT	TD	Auto	Y
Océ	NL	oce03NLnoXbm	Monoling	NL	TD	Auto	Y
Océ	NL	oce03NLnoXpr	Monoling	NL	TD	Auto	Y
Océ	NL	oce03st01	Monoling	NL	TD	Auto	
Océ	NL	oce03st02	Monoling	NL	TD	Auto	
Océ	NL	oce03SEnoXbm	Monoling	SV	TD	Auto	Y
Océ	NL	oce03SEnoXpr	Monoling	SV	TD	Auto	Y
Ricoh/USL	JP	rdetde03	Monoling	DE	TD	Auto	Y
Ricoh/USL	JP	rdetdp03	Monoling	DE	TD	Auto	
Ricoh/USL	JP	restde03	Monoling	ES	TD	Auto	Y
Ricoh/USL	JP	restdp03	Monoling	ES	TD	Auto	
Ricoh/USL	JP	rfrtde03	Monoling	FR	TD	Auto	Y
Ricoh/USL	JP	rfrtdp03	Monoling	FR	TD	Auto	
Ricoh/USL	JP	rittde03	Monoling	IT	TD	Auto	Y
Ricoh/USL	JP	rittdp03	Monoling	IT	TD	Auto	
Ricoh/USL	JP	rnltde03	Monoling	NL	TD	Auto	Y
Ricoh/USL	JP	rnltdp03	Monoling	NL	TD	Auto	
SICS	SE	sicsSVind	Monoling	SV	TD	Auto	Y
SICS	SE	sicsSVtad	Monoling	SV	TD	Auto	Y
SICS	SE	sicsSVtadaRR	Monoling	SV	TD	Auto	Y
SICS	SE	sicsSVtmd	Monoling	SV	TD	Auto	Y
SINAI Group	ES	uja03ShortRR	Multi-4	EN	TD	Auto	
SINAI Group	ES	uja03ShortRRPrf	Multi-4	EN	TD	Auto	
SINAI Group	ES	uja03ShortRSV2	Multi-4	EN	TD	Auto	
SINAI Group	ES	uja03ShortRSV2m	Multi-4	EN	TD	Auto	Y
SINAI Group	ES	uja03LargeRR	Multi-8	EN	TD	Auto	
SINAI Group	ES	uja03LargeRRPrf	Multi-8	EN	TD	Auto	

Table of Runs. 1 Institution, 2 Country, 3 Run Tag, 4 Task, 5 Topic Language, 6 Topic Fields, 7 Run Type, 8 Judged

1	2	3	4	5	6	7	8
SINAI Group	ES	uja03LargeRSV2	Multi-8	EN	TD	Auto	Y
SINAI Group	ES	uja03LargeRSV2m	Multi-8	EN	TD	Auto	
Tagmatica	FR	KWSynonyms	Monoling	FR	TD	Auto	
Tagmatica	FR	KWSynonymsSL	Monoling	FR	TD	Auto	
Tagmatica	FR	basicKeyWords	Monoling	FR	TD	Auto	
Tagmatica	FR	patterns	Monoling	FR	TD	Auto	Y
U Alicante	ES	IRn-ites-exp	Biling_ES	IT	TD	Auto	
U Alicante	ES	IRn-ites-noexp	Biling_ES	IT	TD	Auto	
U Alicante	ES	IRn-al-exp-nsp	Monoling	DE	TD	Auto	Y
U Alicante	ES	IRn-al-exp-sp	Monoling	DE	TD	Auto	Y
U Alicante	ES	IRn-al-nexp-nsp	Monoling	DE	TD	Auto	
U Alicante	ES	IRn-al-nexp-sp	Monoling	DE	TD	Auto	Y
U Alicante	ES	IRn-es-exp	Monoling	ES	TD	Auto	Y
U Alicante	ES	IRn-es-noexp	Monoling	ES	TD	Auto	
U Alicante	ES	IRn-fr-exp	Monoling	FR	TD	Auto	Y
U Alicante	ES	IRn-fr-noexp	Monoling	FR	TD	Auto	
U Alicante	ES	IRn-it-exp	Monoling	IT	TD	Auto	Y
U Alicante	ES	IRn-it-noexp	Monoling	IT	TD	Auto	
U Alicante	ES	IRn-m-exp-nsp	Multi-4	EN	TD	Auto	
U Alicante	ES	IRn-m-exp-sp	Multi-4	EN	TD	Auto	Y
U Alicante	ES	IRn-m-nexp-nsp	Multi-4	EN	TD	Auto	
U Alicante	ES	IRn-m-nexp-sp	Multi-4	EN	TD	Auto	
U Alicante	ES	IRn-mi-exp-sp	Multi-4	EN	TD	Auto	
U Buffalo	US	UBmonoDErf1	Monoling	DE	TD	Auto	
U Buffalo	US	UBmonoDErf2	Monoling	DE	TD	Auto	Y
U Buffalo	US	UBmonoENrf1	Monoling	EN	TD	Auto	
U Buffalo	US	UBmonoENrf2	Monoling	EN	TD	Auto	Y
U Buffalo	US	UBmonoESrf1	Monoling	ES	TD	Auto	
U Buffalo	US	UBmonoESrf2	Monoling	ES	TD	Auto	Y
U Buffalo	US	UBmonoFIrf1	Monoling	FI	TD	Auto	Y
U Buffalo	US	UBmonoFIrf2	Monoling	FI	TD	Auto	Y
U Buffalo	US	UBmonoFRrf1	Monoling	FR	TD	Auto	
U Buffalo	US	UBmonoFRrf2	Monoling	FR	TD	Auto	Y
U Buffalo	US	UBmonoITrf1	Monoling	IT	TD	Auto	
U Buffalo	US	UBmonoITrf2	Monoling	IT	TD	Auto	
U Buffalo	US	UBmonoNLrf1	Monoling	NL	TD	Auto	
U Buffalo	US	UBmonoNLrf2	Monoling	NL	TD	Auto	Y

Table of Runs. 1 Institution, 2 Country, 3 Run Tag, 4 Task, 5 Topic Language, 6 Topic Fields, 7 Run Type, 8 Judged

1	2	3	4	5	6	7	8
U Buffalo	US	UBmonoSVrf1	Monoling	SV	TD	Auto	Y
U Buffalo	US	UBmonoSVrf2	Monoling	SV	TD	Auto	Y
U Buffalo	US	UBENmultishort2	Multi-8	EN	T	Auto	Y
U Buffalo	US	UBENmultishort3	Multi-8	EN	T	Auto	Y
U Buffalo	US	UBENmultirf1	Multi-8	EN	TD	Auto	
U Buffalo	US	UBENmultirf2	Multi-8	EN	TD	Auto	Y
U Buffalo	US	UBENmultirf3	Multi-8	EN	TD	Auto	
U Buffalo	US	UBESmultishort2	Multi-8	ES	T	Auto	Y
U Buffalo	US	UBESmultirf1	Multi-8	ES	TD	Auto	
U Buffalo	US	UBESmultirf2	Multi-8	ES	TD	Auto	Y
U Buffalo	US	UBESmultirf3	Multi-8	ES	TD	Auto	
U Exeter	UK	exeitqdsptcpro	Biling_ES	IT	TD	Auto	
U Exeter	UK	exeitqspdbipro	Biling_ES	IT	TD	Auto	
U Exeter	UK	exeitqydspbipro	Biling_ES	IT	TD	Auto	
U Exeter	UK	exeitqydspbisys	Biling_ES	IT	TD	Auto	
U Exeter	UK	exedeqdittcpro	Biling_IT	DE	TD	Auto	
U Exeter	UK	exedeqitdbipro	Biling_IT	DE	TD	Auto	Y
U Exeter	UK	exedeqyditbipro	Biling_IT	DE	TD	Auto	
U Exeter	UK	exedeqyditbisys	Biling_IT	DE	TD	Auto	
U Exeter	UK	exedemonopro	Monoling	DE	TD	Auto	Y
U Exeter	UK	exedemonosys	Monoling	DE	TD	Auto	Y
U Exeter	UK	exedetcmono	Monoling	DE	TD	Auto	
U Exeter	UK	exespmonopro	Monoling	ES	TD	Auto	
U Exeter	UK	exespmonosys	Monoling	ES	TD	Auto	Y
U Exeter	UK	exesptcmono	Monoling	ES	TD	Auto	
U Exeter	UK	exefrmonopro	Monoling	FR	TD	Auto	
U Exeter	UK	exefrmonosys	Monoling	FR	TD	Auto	Y
U Exeter	UK	exefrtcmono	Monoling	FR	TD	Auto	
U Exeter	UK	exeitmonopro	Monoling	IT	TD	Auto	
U Exeter	UK	exeitmonosys	Monoling	IT	TD	Auto	
U Exeter	UK	exeittcmono	Monoling	IT	TD	Auto	
U Exeter	UK	exemult4d	Multi-4	EN	TD	Auto	
U Exeter	UK	exemult4p	Multi-4	EN	TD	Auto	
U Exeter	UK	exemult4s	Multi-4	EN	TD	Auto	Y
U Exeter	UK	exemult4u	Multi-4	EN	TD	Auto	
U Exeter	UK	exemulttc	Multi-4	EN	TD	Auto	
U Oviedo/AIC	ES	ex25x25	Monoling	ES	TD	Auto	

Table of Runs. 1 Institution, 2 Country, 3 Run Tag, 4 Task, 5 Topic Language, 6 Topic Fields, 7 Run Type, 8 Judged

1	2	3	4	5	6	7	8
U Oviedo/AIC	ES	ex50x50	Monoling	ES	TD	Auto	Y
U Sunderland	UK	sundb	Biling_ES	IT	T	Auto	
U Sunderland	UK	sundrc	Biling_ES	IT	T	Auto	Y
U Tampere	FI	UTAmul1	Multi-8	EN	TD	Auto	Y
U Tampere	FI	UTAmul2	Multi-8	EN	TD	Auto	
U Tampere	FI	UTAmul3	Multi-8	EN	TD	Auto	
U Tampere	FI	UTAmul4	Multi-8	EN	TD	Auto	
U Tampere	FI	UTAmul5	Multi-8	EN	TD	Auto	
U Twente	NL	ut3	Monoling	NL	TD	Auto	Y
UC Berkeley	US	bkbifide1	Biling_DE	FI	TD	Auto	Y
UC Berkeley	US	bkbiites1	Biling_ES	IT	TD	Auto	
UC Berkeley	US	bkbiites2	Biling_ES	IT	TD	Auto	
UC Berkeley	US	bkbideit1	Biling_IT	DE	TD	Auto	
UC Berkeley	US	bkbideit2	Biling_IT	DE	TD	Auto	
UC Berkeley	US	bkbifrnl1	Biling_NL	FR	TD	Auto	Y
UC Berkeley	US	BKRUBLGR2	Biling_RU	DE	TDN	Auto	Y
UC Berkeley	US	BKRUBLER1	Biling_RU	EN	TD	Auto	Y
UC Berkeley	US	BKRUBLGR1	Biling_RU	EN	TD	Auto	Y
UC Berkeley	US	BKRUMLEE1	Biling_RU	EN	TD	Auto	Y
UC Berkeley	US	BKRUBLER2	Biling_RU	EN	TDN	Auto	Y
UC Berkeley	US	BKRUMLEE2	Biling_RU	EN	TDN	Auto	Y
UC Berkeley	US	BKGRMLGG1	GIRT_DE	DE	TD	Auto	Y
UC Berkeley	US	BKGRMLGG2	GIRT_DE	DE	TD	Auto	Y
UC Berkeley	US	BKGRBLEG1	GIRT_DE	EN	TD	Auto	Y
UC Berkeley	US	BKGRBLRG1	GIRT_DE	RU	TD	Auto	Y
UC Berkeley	US	BKGRBLRG2	GIRT_DE	RU	TD	Auto	Y
UC Berkeley	US	BKGRBLGE1	GIRT_EN	DE	TD	Auto	Y
UC Berkeley	US	BKGRMLEE1	GIRT_EN	EN	TD	Auto	Y
UC Berkeley	US	BKGRMLEE2	GIRT_EN	EN	TD	Auto	Y
UC Berkeley	US	BKGRBLRE1	GIRT_EN	RU	TD	Auto	Y
UC Berkeley	US	bkmonode1	Monoling	DE	TD	Auto	Y
UC Berkeley	US	bkmonoes1	Monoling	ES	TD	Auto	
UC Berkeley	US	bkmonofi1	Monoling	FI	TD	Auto	Y
UC Berkeley	US	bkmonofi2	Monoling	FI	TD	Auto	Y
UC Berkeley	US	bkmonofr1	Monoling	FR	TD	Auto	Y
UC Berkeley	US	bkmonoit1	Monoling	IT	TD	Auto	
UC Berkeley	US	bkmononl1	Monoling	NL	TD	Auto	Y

Table of Runs. 1 Institution, 2 Country, 3 Run Tag, 4 Task, 5 Topic Language, 6 Topic Fields, 7 Run Type, 8 Judged

1	2	3	4	5	6	7	8
UC Berkeley	US	BKRUMLRR1	Monoling	RU	TD	Auto	Y
UC Berkeley	US	BKRUMLRR3	Monoling	RU	TD	Auto	Y
UC Berkeley	US	BKRUMLRR2	Monoling	RU	TDN	Auto	Y
UC Berkeley	US	BKRUMLRR4	Monoling	RU	TDN	Auto	Y
UC Berkeley	US	bkmonosv1	Monoling	SV	TD	Auto	Y
UC Berkeley	US	bkmonosv2	Monoling	SV	TD	Auto	Y
UC Berkeley	US	bkmul4en1	Multi-4	EN	TD	Auto	
UC Berkeley	US	bkmul4en2	Multi-4	EN	TD	Auto	
UC Berkeley	US	bkmul4en3	Multi-4	EN	TD	Auto	Y
UC Berkeley	US	bkmul8en1	Multi-8	EN	TD	Auto	
UC Berkeley	US	bkmul8en2	Multi-8	EN	TD	Auto	
UC Berkeley	US	bkmul8en3	Multi-8	EN	TD	Auto	Y
Univ. A Coruna/COLE Group	ES	coleTDlemZP03	Monoling	ES	TD	Auto	
Univ. A Coruna/COLE Group	ES	coleTDNlemSM03	Monoling	ES	TDN	Auto	
Univ. A Coruna/COLE Group	ES	coleTDNlemZP03	Monoling	ES	TDN	Auto	
Univ. A Coruna/COLE Group	ES	coleTDNpdsSM03	Monoling	ES	TDN	Auto	Y
Univ. Amsterdam/LIT	NL	UAmsC03ItSp4GiSb	Biling_ES	IT	TD	Auto	
Univ. Amsterdam/LIT	NL	UAmsC03GeIt4GiSb	Biling_IT	DE	TD	Auto	Y
Univ. Amsterdam/LIT	NL	UAmsC03FrDu4GiSb	Biling_NL	FR	TD	Auto	Y
Univ. Amsterdam/LIT	NL	UAmsC03FrDu4Gr	Biling_NL	FR	TD	Auto	Y
Univ. Amsterdam/LIT	NL	UAmsC03FrDuSblSS	Biling_NL	FR	TD	Auto	Y
Univ. Amsterdam/LIT	NL	UAmsC03EnRu4GiSb	Biling_RU	EN	TD	Auto	Y
Univ. Amsterdam/LIT	NL	UAmsC03EnRu4Gr	Biling_RU	EN	TD	Auto	Y
Univ. Amsterdam/LIT	NL	UAmsC03EnRuSbl	Biling_RU	EN	TD	Auto	Y
Univ. Amsterdam/LIT	NL	UAmsC03GeGi4GriR	GIRT_DE	DE	TD	Auto	Y
Univ. Amsterdam/LIT	NL	UAmsC03GeGiSbliR	GIRT_DE	DE	TD	Auto	Y
Univ. Amsterdam/LIT	NL	UAmsC03GeGiWrd	GIRT_DE	DE	TD	Auto	Y
Univ. Amsterdam/LIT	NL	UAmsC03GeGe4GSbO	Monoling	DE	TD	Auto	
Univ. Amsterdam/LIT	NL	UAmsC03GeGe4GiSb	Monoling	DE	TD	Auto	Y
Univ. Amsterdam/LIT	NL	UAmsC03SpSp4GiSb	Monoling	ES	TD	Auto	Y
Univ. Amsterdam/LIT	NL	UAmsC03SpSpSS3w	Monoling	ES	TD	Auto	
Univ. Amsterdam/LIT	NL	UAmsC03FiFi5GiSb	Monoling	FI	TD	Auto	Y
Univ. Amsterdam/LIT	NL	UAmsC03FrFr4GiSb	Monoling	FR	TD	Auto	Y
Univ. Amsterdam/LIT	NL	UAmsC03ItIt4GiSb	Monoling	IT	TD	Auto	
Univ. Amsterdam/LIT	NL	UAmsC03DuDu4GiSb	Monoling	NL	TD	Auto	Y
Univ. Amsterdam/LIT	NL	UAmsC03DuDuSS3w	Monoling	NL	TD	Auto	
Univ. Amsterdam/LIT	NL	UAmsC03RuRu4GiSb	Monoling	RU	TD	Auto	Y

Table of Runs. 1 Institution, 2 Country, 3 Run Tag, 4 Task, 5 Topic Language, 6 Topic Fields, 7 Run Type, 8 Judged

1	2	3	4	5	6	7	8
Univ. Amsterdam/LIT	NL	UAmsC03RuRu4Gr	Monoling	RU	TD	Auto	Y
Univ. Amsterdam/LIT	NL	UAmsC03RuRuSbl	Monoling	RU	TD	Auto	Y
Univ. Amsterdam/LIT	NL	UAmsC03RuRuWrd	Monoling	RU	TD	Auto	Y
Univ. Amsterdam/LIT	NL	UAmsC03SwSw4GSbO	Monoling	SV	TD	Auto	Y
Univ. Amsterdam/LIT	NL	UAmsC03SwSw4GiSb	Monoling	SV	TD	Auto	Y
Univ. Amsterdam/LIT	NL	UAmsC03EnM44GiSb	Multi-4	EN	TD	Auto	Y
Univ. Amsterdam/LIT	NL	UAmsC03EnM44Gr	Multi-4	EN	TD	Auto	
Univ. Amsterdam/LIT	NL	UAmsC03EnM4SS4G	Multi-4	EN	TD	Auto	
Univ. Amsterdam/LIT	NL	UAmsC03EnM84GiSb	Multi-8	EN	TD	Auto	Y
Univ. Amsterdam/LIT	NL	UAmsC03EnM84Gr	Multi-8	EN	TD	Auto	
Univ. Amsterdam/LIT	NL	UAmsC03EnM84Gr6	Multi-8	EN	TD	Auto	
Univ. Amsterdam/LIT	NL	UAmsC03EnM8SS4G	Multi-8	EN	TD	Auto	
Univ. Amsterdam/LIT	NL	UAmsC03EnM8SS4G6	Multi-8	EN	TD	Auto	
Universität Hildesheim/AIS	DE	UHImnenR1	Monoling	EN	TD	Auto	Y
Universität Hildesheim/AIS	DE	UHImnenR2	Monoling	EN	TD	Auto	
Universität Hildesheim/AIS	DE	UHImlt4R1	Multi-4	EN	TD	Auto	Y
Universität Hildesheim/AIS	DE	UHImlt4R2	Multi-4	EN	TD	Auto	
Université de Neuchâtel	CH	UniNEde	Monoling	DE	TD	Auto	Y
Université de Neuchâtel	CH	UniNEde2	Monoling	DE	TD	Auto	
Université de Neuchâtel	CH	UniNEsp	Monoling	ES	TD	Auto	
Université de Neuchâtel	CH	UniNEsp2	Monoling	ES	TD	Auto	
Université de Neuchâtel	CH	UniNEfi	Monoling	FI	TD	Auto	Y
Université de Neuchâtel	CH	UniNEfi2	Monoling	FI	TD	Auto	Y
Université de Neuchâtel	CH	UniNEfr	Monoling	FR	TD	Auto	Y
Université de Neuchâtel	CH	UniNEfr2	Monoling	FR	TD	Auto	
Université de Neuchâtel	CH	UniNEit	Monoling	IT	TD	Auto	
Université de Neuchâtel	CH	UniNEit2	Monoling	IT	TD	Auto	
Université de Neuchâtel	CH	UniNEnl	Monoling	NL	TD	Auto	Y
Université de Neuchâtel	CH	UniNEnl2	Monoling	NL	TD	Auto	
Université de Neuchâtel	CH	UniNEru1	Monoling	RU	TD	Auto	Y
Université de Neuchâtel	CH	UniNEru2	Monoling	RU	TD	Auto	Y
Université de Neuchâtel	CH	UniNEru	Monoling	RU	TDN	Auto	Y
Université de Neuchâtel	CH	UniNEru3	Monoling	RU	TDN	Auto	Y
Université de Neuchâtel	CH	UniNEsv	Monoling	SV	TD	Auto	Y
Université de Neuchâtel	CH	UniNEsv2	Monoling	SV	TD	Auto	Y
Université de Neuchâtel	CH	UniNEms	Multi-4	EN	TD	Manual	Y
Université de Neuchâtel	CH	UniNEms1	Multi-4	EN	TD	Auto	

Table of Runs. 1 Institution, 2 Country, 3 Run Tag, 4 Task, 5 Topic Language, 6 Topic Fields, 7 Run Type, 8 Judged

1	2	3	4	5	6	7	8
Université de Neuchâtel	CH	UniNEms2	Multi-4	EN	TD	Auto	
Université de Neuchâtel	CH	UniNEms3	Multi-4	EN	TD	Auto	
Université de Neuchâtel	CH	UniNEms4	Multi-4	EN	TD	Auto	
Université de Neuchâtel	CH	UniNEml	Multi-8	EN	TD	Manual	Y
Université de Neuchâtel	CH	UniNEml1	Multi-8	EN	TD	Auto	
Université de Neuchâtel	CH	UniNEml2	Multi-8	EN	TD	Auto	
Université de Neuchâtel	CH	UniNEml3	Multi-8	EN	TD	Auto	
Université de Neuchâtel	CH	UniNEml4	Multi-8	EN	TD	Auto	

Bilingual FI–>DE; Recall–Precision Graph
Top performing experiments by the best five groups; TD topic fields; Automatic

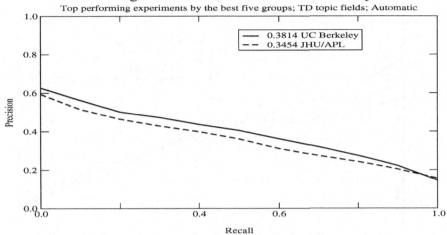

Bilingual X–>EN; Recall–Precision Graph
Top performing experiments by the best five groups; TD topic fields; Automatic

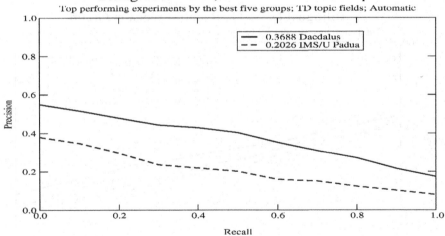

Bilingual IT–>ES; Recall–Precision Graph

Top performing experiments by the best five groups; TD topic fields; Automatic

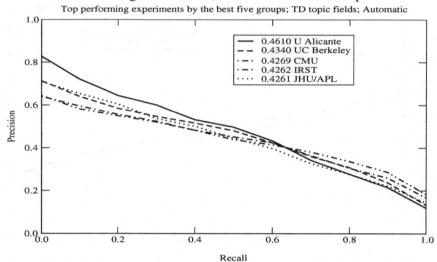

Bilingual DE–>IT; Recall–Precision Graph

Top performing experiments by the best five groups; TD topic fields; Automatic

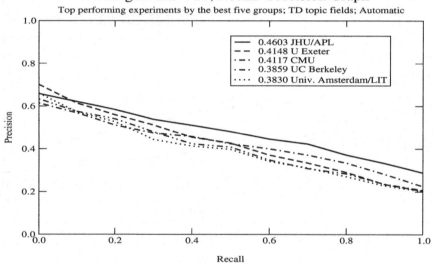

Bilingual FR–>NL; Recall–Precision Graph

Top performing experiments by the best five groups; TD topic fields; Automatic

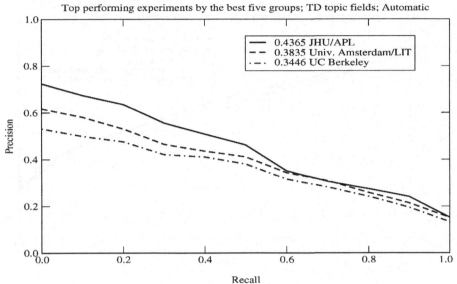

Bilingual X–>RU; Recall–Precision Graph

Top performing experiments by the best five groups; TD topic fields; Automatic

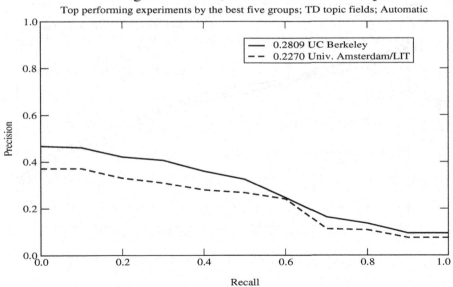

Monolingual DE; Recall–Precision Graph

Top performing experiments by the best five groups; TD topic fields; Automatic

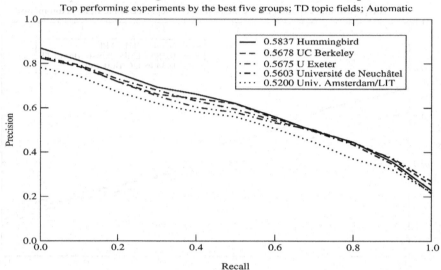

——	0.5837 Hummingbird
– –	0.5678 UC Berkeley
· – ·	0.5675 U Exeter
· – ·	0.5603 Université de Neuchâtel
· · · ·	0.5200 Univ. Amsterdam/LIT

Monolingual ES; Recall–Precision Graph

Top performing experiments by the best five groups; TD topic fields; Automatic

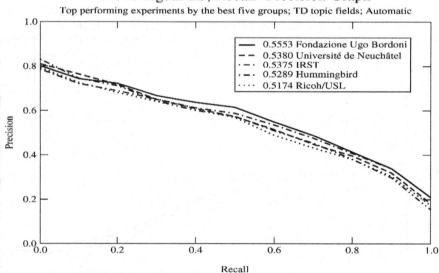

——	0.5553 Fondazione Ugo Bordoni
– –	0.5380 Université de Neuchâtel
· – ·	0.5375 IRST
· – ·	0.5289 Hummingbird
· · · ·	0.5174 Ricoh/USL

Monolingual FI; Recall–Precision Graph

Top performing experiments by the best five groups; TD topic fields; Automatic

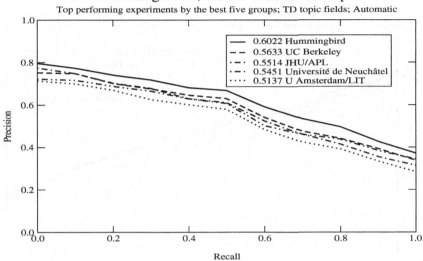

——	0.6022 Hummingbird
– –	0.5633 UC Berkeley
· — ·	0.5514 JHU/APL
· — ·	0.5451 Université de Neuchâtel
· · · ·	0.5137 U Amsterdam/LIT

Monolingual FR; Recall–Precision Graph

Top performing experiments by the best five groups; TD topic fields; Automatic

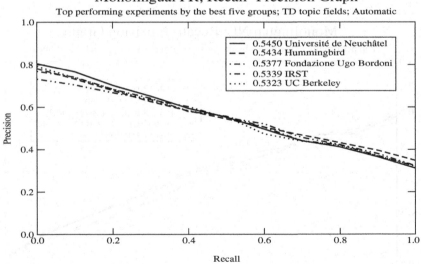

——	0.5450 Université de Neuchâtel
– –	0.5434 Hummingbird
· — ·	0.5377 Fondazione Ugo Bordoni
· — ·	0.5339 IRST
· · · ·	0.5323 UC Berkeley

Monolingual IT; Recall–Precision Graph

Top performing experiments by the best five groups; TD topic fields; Automatic

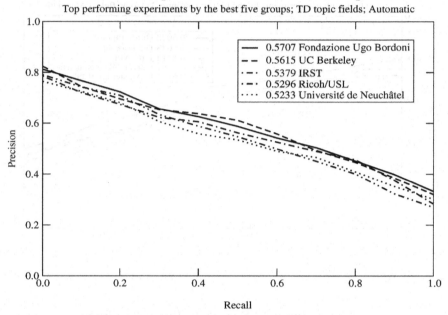

Monolingual NL; Recall–Precision Graph

Top performing experiments by the best five groups; TD topic fields; Automatic

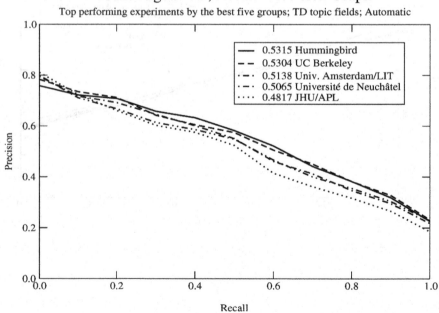

Monolingual RU; Recall–Precision Graph
Top performing experiments by the best five groups; TD topic fields; Automatic

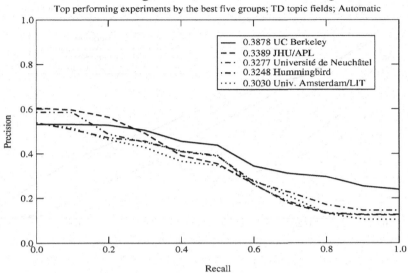

Monolingual SV; Recall–Precision Graph
Top performing experiments by the best five groups; TD topic fields; Automatic

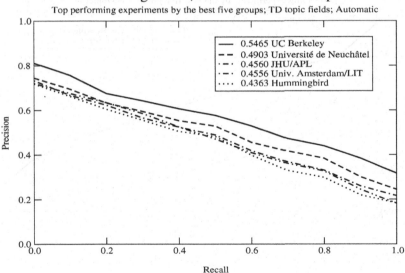

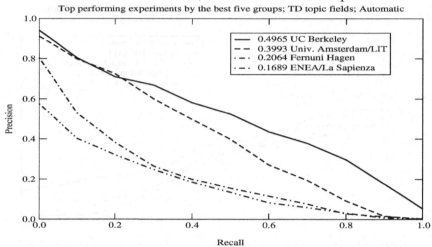

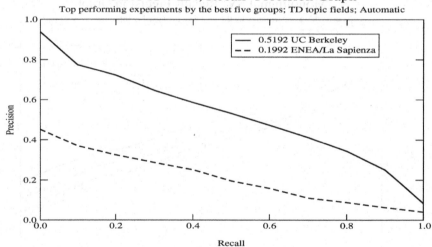

Author Index